THE STORY OF THE
Roman Catholic Dioceses of
HARBOUR GRACE & GRAND FALLS
Newfoundland

The People, the Clergy and Parishes in the Diocese
Move of Harbour Grace Diocese To Grand Falls
Historical genealogical information

James M. Fleming Sr.

"At such a time our thoughts go back instinctively to the hardy pioneers, both priests and people, who amid incredible hardships planted the seed of the faith in the innumerable coves and bays of our far-flung coast line. The great figure of John Dalton, first Bishop of Harbor Grace, looms large on the horizon. With barely six priests to help him in bringing the consolation of religion to the people scattered throughout the many settlements of our east coast from Conception Bay to the far reaches of Labrador, and with the only means of communications being the row boats of the fisherman. Bishop Dalton laid the firm foundations of the new Diocese."

Taken from the message of Bishop J. M. O'Neill in the book "1856 Centenary of the Diocese of Harbor Grace 1956"

THE STORY OF THE

Roman Catholic Dioceses of

HARBOUR GRACE & GRAND FALLS

Newfoundland

Immaculate Conception Church
Harbour Grace

Immaculate Conception Cathedral - Grand Falls

The People, the Clergy and Parishes in the Diocese
Harbour Grace Diocese moves to Grand Falls
Historical genealogical information

James M. Fleming Sr.

10614 NE 149th Street
Bothell, WA 98011 USA

Previous Book Published by James M. Fleming Sr.
"St. Patrick's Roman Catholic Parish and the early People of Carbonear, Newfoundland." 2002

Printed on acid-free paper

Library Number: ISBN 0-9742526-0-3=OA=

1. A History of the Harbour Grace-Grand Falls: Roman Catholic Dioceses.
James M. Fleming Sr.

Published by James M. Fleming Sr.

Printed in Canada by:
Print Atlantic

DEDICATED TO

Bishop Martin Currie for his support and assistance is completing this undertaking.
Bishop of Grand Falls

Late Bobbie Connolly for his influence and our desire to carry on his Work.
Historian of Harbour Grace

Late Msgr. Joseph O'Brien, D.P. for his Spiritual Influence.
Parish Priest, Harbour Grace, 1957-1985

and

Peggy Fahey Whalen for her inspiration, dedication, encouragement, support and many contributions.
Curator of Conception Bay Museum

Dedicated to the many Bishops, Priests, Sisters, Brothers and Parishioners who helped make Harbour Grace and Grand Falls the great Parishes and Dioceses they have been.

"Our past has been witness to a chapter unique in the annals of Christendom.
In the case of Newfoundland, the laity with the faith came first, and called for their clergy to join them.

Robert J. Connolly book,
"1856-Centenary of the Diocese of Harbor Grace-1856"

ACKNOWLEDGEMENTS

This book was prompted by the personal influence of the late R. J. "Bobby" Connolly who was admired for his resolute desire to document the History of the Catholic Church in Newfoundland. He had published two books on the Harbour Grace Parish and the Diocese. He provided many items of research material from my long relationship with him. It would be wrong not to extract from his books since he was the expert on the Parish and no history book would be complete without reprinting some of his articles since his books have long been out-of-print. Behind this book represents information from many people from Newfoundland and particularly Harbour Grace and the Grand Falls Diocese who have provided so much information, without which, this book could not have been written. Extraordinary assistance was provided by Peggy (Fahey) Whalen who through her expertise as the Curator of the Conception Bay Museum, provided many personal articles, official pictures and exhaustive research, which greatly promoted the publication of this book. We thank Bishop Martin Currie of Grand Falls for his approval to have his Archivists and staff give us extra special Diocesan support namely Sister Magdalen O'Brien, Ina Mulroney, Pierce Carey and especially Jonathan Gaye, who worked tirelessly for the last several months to provide a great amount of historical data about the Grand Falls Diocese. Also outstanding help from Larry Dohey, Archivist of the St. John's Archdiocese, Sister Perpetua Kennedy, Archivist of the Presentation Sisters, Sister Paula Penney, Archivist of Mercy Sisters and Brother J.B. Darcy of the Christian Brothers. And special thanks to Bride Maddox for the personal papers of the late Msgr. Joseph O'Brien of Harbour Grace. Also the special contributions from Lilly Ryan who went out of her way to supply a great many items about Harbour Grace. Thanks also to Harbour Grace parishioners: Gerald Brazil, Joyce Skanes from the HG Rector, Ann Coombs, Shirley Reynolds, Sharleen Mutrey, Garry McCarthy, Jerome McCarthy, Ron Martin, Sharon Brake, Annie Doran, Michael F. Fahey, Dorothy and Reginald Coombs, Gordon Pike, William Dobbin, Ray and Eileen Peddle, Gerald Ryan, Julia Edwards and the late Nellie (Ryan) Barron. Thanks to Grand Falls Parishioners: Bishop Currie's Secretary, Mary Edwards; Marriage Tribunial Notaries – Denise Howse, Mrs. Rose Matthews and Louis Barker. We owe a debt of gratitude to the following **priests:** Most Rev. Alphonsus L. Penney; Fr. John Arkorful; Fr. Francis J. Aylward; Fr. James Beresford, Fr. Ramon Bolatets, Fr. Ronald Bromley; Fr. Leo Burke; Fr. Linus Coady, Fr. Brian Colbert; Fr. James A. Davis, CssR, Fr. Clem Flaherty; Fr. Tony

Hageman; Fr. David Heale; Fr. William Hearn, Fr. William Houlahan; Fr. Joseph Moriarty, s.f.m; Fr. Eugene Morris; Fr. Donald J. Murray, M.S.F; Fr. John Adde Nweah and Fr. Frederick Terry. Thanks to all the clergy, staff, parishioners and Parish secretaries who have provided invaluable materiel for this book. **Sisters** who helped out with information: Sr. Amelia Mooney, Sr. M. Gertrude Wall, pbvm; Sr. Elizabeth Whelan, pbvm; Sr. Helena Murphy, pbvm; Sr. Connie Power, pbvm; Sr. Angela Mackenzie, pbvm and Sr. Katherine Bellamy, rsm. **Parish Secretaries:** Badger – Mrs. Jean Mercer; Baie Verte – Mrs. Ellie Gavin; Bay de Verde – Mrs. Gloris Noonan; Brigus – Mrs. Rosalitia Walsh; Carbonear – Mrs. Jeannie Clarke; Colliers – Mrs. Barbara Murphy; Conception Harbour – Mrs. Laura Costello; Gander – Mrs. Joan Kieley; Cathedral Parish – Mrs. Ann Fewer; Harbour Grace – Mrs. Joyce Skanes; Harbour Main – Patricia Dalton; Holyrood – Patricia Doran; King's Cove – Nell Bowen; North River – Mary Rose; Northern Bay; Port Union – Elizabeth Peters; St. Alban's – Darlene Collier; St. Brendan's – Betty O'Reilly; Tilting – Paula McGrath; Whitbourne – Patti Kennedy. **Knights of Columbus:** – Mr. William Dobbins, Grand Knight of Harbour Grace Council. Mr. Ernest Duder – Grand Knight of Grand Falls Council and Mr. Ronald Bouzane – Grand Knight of Little Bay Council. **Archives:** Sr. Perpetua Kennedy, pbvm, Archivist at Presentation Generalate. St. John's.; Sr. Paula Penney, rsm, Archivist at Sisters of Mercy, St. John's.; Sr. Matha Bourne, MM and Brother Kevin Dargan, MM at Maryknoll Mission Archives, NY.; Fr. Jacques Money, S.J., Jesuit Archives of the Upper Canada Province.; Fr. Robert Conolly, SFM at Scarboro Foreign Mission archives.; Ms. M.C. Harvey, Redemporist archives of the Edmonton-Toronto Province. Irish Augustinian Archive, St. Augustine's, Taylor's Lane, Ballyboden, Dublin 16 (Ireland). Ireland; Rev James P. Logan, Chancellor of the Diocese of Baker, Bend, Oregon. Rev Pat Conlan, ofm, Franciscan Fraternity, Adam & Eve's, 4 Merchants Quay, Dublin 8. The late Jennie O'Brien, Mary Carroll, and Bert Parsons of Carbonear, Michael McCarthy of Mt. Pearl, Dr. John Fitzgerald of Memorial University and Brenda Permenter of the St. John's library. Special thanks to my son, Jim Fleming Jr. for his help in setting up our Website www.newfoundlandcatholic.com. He and my daughter Kathy were both born in Stephenville. Thanks to my daughter, Patricia Hickok for proof reading and my wife Mary for putting up with me for spending many long hours in researching and writing this book. We are sorry for anyone we have omitted from this list. The people we have had contact with, have all been so very generous and helpful. Our sincere thanks.

ILLUSTRATIONS

HARBOUR GRACE

in Harbour Grace, 2 pictures; **176.** - Bishop Dalton KC Council; **177.** - First Council and Mr. O'Brien, 1st Grand Knight; **179.** – Msgr. Joseph O'Brien Silver Jubilee Mass; **180.** – Msgr. O'Brien Picture; **181.** – Msgr. Joseph O'Brien donates picture to KC; **182.** – Msgr. Edward O'Brien 100th Birthday, HG KC.; **183.** – Msgr. Joseph O'Brien funeral; **184.** - Official opening of HG KC Council chambers. ©; **185.** - KC Program for Columbus Day; **186.** - Reg Coombs and current Harbour Grace KC Clubhouse. ©; **192.** - Grand Concert programme; **193.** - Barn Dance Committee, RH HG; **194.** - St. Patrick's Day Concert Harbour Grace and First Communion Class.

GRAND FALLS

195. - Diocese of Grand Falls emblem. ©; **196.** - Co-Cathedral Grand Falls; **197.** - Interior of Co-Cathedral; **198.** – Torn Down old and new Cathedral Grand Falls; **203.** - Diocese of Grand Falls. Map. ©; **205.** - Bishop Currie arrives in Grand Falls; **207.** - Bishop John Dalton, 1st Bishop; **208.** - Bishop Henry Carfagnini, 2nd Bishop; **209.** - Bishop Ronald McDonald, 3rd Bishop.; **210.** - Bishop John March, 4th Bishop.; **211.** - Bishop March and Priests & Bishop March and Rev Cullen. **212.** - Bishop John O'Neill, 5th Bishop; **213.** - Bishop O'Neill and Priests & Bishop O'Neill in Rome; **214.** - Littledale Clergy Retreat 1948; **215.** - Clergy gathering at 100th Anniversary of Diocese; **216.** - Bishop Alphonsus Penney, 6th Bishop; **217.** - Bishop O'Neill presents Bishop Penney w/cross & Bishop Penney 1975. ©; **218.** - Bishop J. Faber MacDonald, 7th Bishop; **219.** - Bishop Faber MacDonald and Priests. & Bishop with two priests; **220** – Bishop MacDonald and Parish Staff; **221.** - Bishop Martin Currie, 8th Bishop. ©; **222.** - Bishop Currie and Priests & with Pope John Paul II. ©; **223-245.** PARISHES: Avondale; Badger; Baie Verte; Bay de Verde; Bishop Falls; Bonavista; Brent's Cove/La Scie; Buchan's, Brigus; Carbonear; Clarenville; Collier's; Conception Harbour; Conche; Gambo; Gander; Grand Falls-Windsor Cathedral, Grand Falls-Windsor, St. Joseph's; Harbour Breton; Harbour Grace; Harbour Main; Holyrood; King's Cove; Little Bay/St. Patrick; Norris Arm; North River; Northern Bay; Plate's Cove; Port Union; St. Alban's; St. Brendan's; Tilting, Fogo; Trinity; Whitbourne; Fortune Harbour. **250-254.** - Priests born in Grand Falls: Rev. James A. Davis, Rev. Matthew Blackmore, Rev. Norbert J. Mackenzie, Rev. Vincent Mackenzie, Rev. Patrick A. McCormack, Rev. William J. Houlahan, Rev. Donald J. Murray.; **255-256** – Tribute to Mackenzie Twins; **261.** – Picture of Nuns; **267.** - Notre Dame Academy in Grand Falls; **268.** - Grade 5, Notre Dame 1954, 2 pictures; **269.** - Class Play at Notre Dame, grade 7, 1954 and Hockey Team; **270.** - St. Michael's High school in Grand Falls & Basketball Champions; **271.** - Bishop dedicates St. Catherine's school; **272.** - Combined Fund Canvass 1958 and List of Canvasser's; **273.** - Own Canvass Organization; **274.** - 1981 Annual General Meeting of Catholic Education Council and Nuns; **277.** - Parishioners at Communion; **278.** - Main Grand Falls RC Cemetery & Msgr. Finn tombstone. ©; **280.**-Union Street Cemetery, Rev. Pat McCormack tombstone. ©; **282** - Valley Road Cemetery. **283.** - Grand Falls KC Building; **284.** - First State KC Convention in Grand Falls; **286.** - Ecumenical movement in Knights of Columbus; **287.** - Executives of Notre Dame Council 1969 & 2002 Christmas KC Crib. ©.

TABLE OF CONTENT

When the Harbour Grace Diocese was established in 1856, it was given the responsibility for the people of Labrador. In our appendices we have documented the Diary of Rev. John March and later Bishop and Bishop J. M. O'Neill with an account of their visits to Labrador beginning in 1889.

See appendix B, page 301.

PROLOGUE

This book was prepared to update and consolidate into print much of the history of the Diocese of Harbour Grace as well as the new Diocese of Grand Falls. Harbour Grace has the distinction of being the only other Parish in Newfoundland that was established as a Mission in 1784, the same year as the birth of Catholicism in Newfoundland at St. John's. The Parish is 218 years old and the Harbour Grace Diocese was in place for 109 years until 1965 when the Diocese of Grand Falls was established. While Harbour Grace has a long and proud Catholic history, Grand Falls has a great history to emulate. To honour the 150th Anniversary of the combined Diocese's in 2006, we have added the Grand Falls Parish and Diocese to the original Harbour Grace history which was prepared as a companion book to an earlier book on Carbonear printed in 2002. It was our goal to print an historical book with genealogical information, which provides the reader with a little knowledge of the people who lived and prayed in Harbour Grace and Grand Falls in the early days of their existence. For those who grew up in Harbour Grace and Grand Falls it may provide a little help in researching their ancestors. My interest with Newfoundland comes from my being married at St. Patrick's Church in Carbonear by Rev Leo J. Burke in 1954 to Mary Mackey who was born there and the fact that we have come back to visit from the United States for the last many years to do research and to visit the wonderful people of Harbour Grace, Carbonear and Newfoundland. Harbour Grace and nearby communities have provided 25 known priests to the Catholic community in Newfoundland History. There are many historical Parish and Diocese *First's* and significant historical items represented in this book and since the Bishops, Priests, Sisters and Brothers played such an important part in the Parishes and Diocese history we have listed many of those who were assigned to the Diocese or born in any of the Parishes of the Diocese and who played such an importance role in the guidance of the Catholic Church for the many years of its existence in Newfoundland. We wish to commemorate the late Bobbie J. Connolly, a great friend and wonderful historian of Harbour Grace. May God bless him for the help and assistance he has personally given to me and the great many contributions he has made to the History of the Roman Catholic Church in Newfoundland. During his 91 years, he had been a Teacher, School Inspector, Harbour Grace and Church Historian, writer and long member of the Knights of Columbus. He won the St. Gregory Medal and Canadian Order of Canada.

THE ROMAN CATHOLIC CATHEDRALS

Both in Harbour Grace and Grand Falls

ARE DEDICATED TO THE

IMMACULATE CONCEPTION

Immaculate Conception

The dogma that the Blessed Virgin Mary was free from original sin from the first instant of her existence. Officially taught by Pope Pius IX after consultation with the world's bishops, it was promulgated in the papal bull *Ineffabilis Deus* on December 8, 1854, the day that remains its liturgical feast. This dogma holds that the Blessed Virgin Mary "was, from the first moment of her conception, by the singular grace and privilege of almighty God and in view of the merits of Jesus Christ the Saviour of the human race, preserved free from all stain of original sin."

**"O Mary conceived without sin,
Pray for us who have recourse to thee."**

INTRODUCTION

Harbour Grace has played a special and important role in the History of the Catholic Church in Newfoundland. It enjoys the same position as St. John's by having an actual Mission status at the same time as St. John's. It was elevated to the first Diocese, outside of St. John's, when Catholicism began to expand within the Colony. It was given the oversight of Labrador at the same time as the Diocese was designated. One of the Grandiose Cathedrals in North America was erected in Harbour Grace. Its history has been dynamic and must be recognized as a bulwark ecclesiastical hierarchy in Newfoundland. The Harbour Grace Diocese played a pivotal role as a successful pattern for the even later expansion of the St. George's Diocese. Harbour Grace is distinguished for many important events. The first mission priest at Harbour Grace was the first priest in Newfoundland history to give up his life in the line-of-duty in 1799. The third Parish Priest at Harbour Grace was the first priest in Newfoundland history to celebrate his 50th Golden Jubilee in the Colony. Harbour Grace was so important to the Church in Newfoundland that the Presentation Sisters were sent there as the first Sisters Convent outside St. John's. Harbour Grace has had such a glorious and commendable history; it was a somewhat controversial decision when they decided to move the Diocese to Grand Falls in 1953-1965. Historically, imagine in 1856 erecting a new Catholic hierarchy outside the Capital city in Newfoundland and the requirements to build a new Cathedral and all the administrative tribunals to establish new parishes and to control the expanding parishes and missions over three-fourths of the Island all the way to the West Coast of Newfoundland plus Labrador. All this was accomplished under primitive conditions without roads or transportation, other than by sea or walking and still some lingering animosity of the expanding Catholicism. All this, only 72 years after the initiation of the official Catholic entry into Newfoundland (1784); 60 years after the Consecration of the first Bishop James L. O'Donel (1796); 24 years after Newfoundland receiving Responsible Government and only nine years after St. John's itself became a Diocese (1847). When the Diocese was moved to Grand Falls in 1965, although it did centralize the Diocese into the mid-Newfoundland area, since St. George's had taken over the West Coast, there was a diminishment of the past glorious history of Harbour Grace, which we would like to capture for posterity in this book.

The history of the Roman Catholic Church in Newfoundland is replete with incidents of the tenacity of the poor Irish immigrants in the practice of their Catholic faith under penal conditions. They conquered all these obstacles, maintained their faith and they became the bulwark of the Catholic Church in Newfoundland for going on 300 years.

Prowse says it best: "The Catholic Church in this Colony was founded by poor Irishmen and by Irishmen alone, with no extraneous help; it was begun in an evil time of persecution and penal laws, when the Catholic Priest was hunted like a bandit, when all outward observance of the faith were prohibited under the direst pains and punishments; for years it was only amidst the lonely rocks and under the canopy of heaven that the Holy Sacrifice of the Mass could be offered up by the solely persecuted clergy. To human eyes the Catholic Church in the Colony seemed a very poor institution, despised and rejected by men. Outwardly she might appear feeble and failing, but she was growing strong with a Divine strength resting on the sure foundation of the eternal rock of the faith. the puny seed planted by these poor Catholic Irishmen in Newfoundland, watered by Divine grace, has grown into a great tree, a devoted and noble branch of the Holy Church, under whose beneficent influence piety and charity, pure religion, morality and the blessings of a Christian education have been spread over our land."

A History of Newfoundland, D.W. Prowse, Q.C., 1895.

Chapter 1

EVOLUTION OF THE CATHOLIC CHURCH IN NEWFOUNDLAND

One of the ordinances which Sir Humphrey Gilbert promulgated when he took possession of Newfoundland in 1583 was that religion should be according to the Church of England. Yet history indicates little, if any, evidence of religion on this Island in the 17th century. In speaking of Captain Whitbourne's mission to Newfoundland in 1615, to promote law and order, Governor Murray says, "little or no regard was paid by many to the sanctity of the Sabbath", and he added "that Whitbourne found it easier to point out these mischief's than to devise a remedy." The tendency was towards confusion and anarchy, for the fish merchants from Bristol were influential enough to have Parliament enact cruel and prohibitory laws which worked in their favor. Religion denominations did not become involved until years later when the Church of England and protestant churches began to be built and when the greater numbers of the Irish Catholics began coming to Newfoundland.

Lord Calvert Baltimore established a Catholic Colony at Ferryland in 1627 but this did not last but for a short period. The Catholic French settlement at Placentia was established in 1662 and had Priests until they left in 1713 under the Treaty of Utrecht and the French officially gave up Placentia in 1763 when they lost to the English.

All colonies under the control of Great Britain had penal restrictions which did not permit Papists (Catholics) to practice their religion in areas under English control and these restrictions were in place when the Irish Catholics began arriving in Newfoundland in the seventeenth century. They could not practice their religion under English directives in Newfoundland. Evidence was found that indicate that they did have disguised priests say Masses and prayer services under secret circumstances. Only the Anglicans and dissenting Protestants could practice their religion. When Governor Richard Dorrill came to Newfoundland in 1755 he issued the first direct Proclamation against Catholics. When the Governor heard that a Papist Priest was saying Mass in Harbour Grace, he directed the Magistrate Charles Garland to arrest the priest and bring him to St. John's for penalties. The Magistrate said it was in Harbour Main and they did not find the priest, supposedly named McNamara, who had fled to St. Pierre and Miquelon. People who attended the Services were fined, some had their houses burned and some were sent back to Ireland. He caused the burning of a Harbour Grace house in which Mass had been celebrated and a jail was built of money extracted from Catholics as fines in Harbour Main. In 1764 Governor Hugh Palliser began his rule of unequalled tyranny surpassing even Dorrill in bigoted persecution against Catholics. The following order was in effect:

> ***"For the better preserving the peace, prevent robberies, tumultuous assemblies, and other disorders of wicked and idle people remaining in the country during the winter, Ordered --That no Papist servant, man or women, shall remain at any place where they did not fish or serve during the summer preceding. That no more than two Papist men shall dwell in one house during the winter, except such as have Protestant masters. That no Papist shall keep a Public House, or sell liquor by retail. That all children of Roman Catholics born in this country be baptized according to law. That the masters of Irish servants do pay for their passage home."***

He authorized the direct pull down of all huts or houses put up by Catholics which prevented them from procuring a livelihood. Some say he considered the Irish a foreigner and disorderly element and he feared any riots similar to the rebellion of the colonists in the United States. One riotous assemble was squalled in Harbour Grace in 1764, when mostly Catholics were accused of gathering together to disturb the peace of Our Lord the King. Those in Harbour Grace received three dozen lashes on the bare back with a cat-of-nine-tails and all other offenders (except Mr. Felix McCarthy who was fined 30 pounds) at the same time received one dozen each.

People Married Each Other

While some Catholics may have given into the baptism of their children by English Clergy, most of the Irish Catholics married each other and baptized their own children until they could go back to Ireland and have their marriage and baptisms validated by a Catholic Priest. They refused to pledge allegiance to the Protestant Church or have the Church of England marry them or baptize their children, like the law required. Records from the Register of St. Patrick's Church in Waterford, Ireland from 1752-1770, show 18 baptisms and one marriage from people who came back from (de Terra Nova) Newfoundland. The one marriage in 1762 stated,

> **"Robin Holly and Jane Broders, Marryed about three years ago in Newfoundland according to the custom of the place, renewed and ratified their consent here this day in presence of William Broders and Catherine Broders, Waterford, Nov 29, 1762 - John St. Legere, Priest."**

On 30 Jan 1833, a petition was presented to the Assembly by Bishop Dr. Fleming, Catholic Bishop of St. John's and many other citizens from Harbour Grace, asking that Wesleyan clergymen be permitted to perform the marriage ceremony, and that all marriages celebrating by them to date be confirmed and legalized. No doubt this action by Bishop Fleming resulted in the following changes in the marriage laws in Newfoundland.

NEW MARRIAGE LAWS IN NEWFOUNDLAND

IN 1833, AN ACT TO REPEAL THE LAWS NOW IN FORCE CONCERNING THE CELEBRATION OF MARRIAGES, AND TO REGULATE THE FUTURE CELEBRATION OF MARRIAGES IN THIS ISLAND. Digest of the Laws of Newfoundland, 1847., p.192.

Sec 1. Repeals Imperial act 5 G.4. cap.8, except parts repealed former marriage acts, and rendering valid all marriages had in Newfoundland within a certain period.

Sec 2. All future marriages, except in cases hereinafter mentioned, to be celebrated by persons of Holy Orders, by resident ministers of congregations having a church or chapel; or by teachers or preachers of religion, duly licensed by the Governor, to celebrate marriages.

Sec 3. All marriages under this act to be celebrated in presence of two witnesses, under a penalty of 50 pounds upon the person celebrating the same; but the want of such witnesses not to invalidate any marriage.

Sec 4. Any person authorized or licensed under this act celebrating a marriage between persons either of whom shall be minors, not having published the banns for such marriage upon three successive Sundays in some church or chapel, or where there is no church or chapel, not having placarded public notice for three weeks preceding the day appointed for such marriage in some place of public resort, without the consent of such minors' parents or guardians, to be guilty of high misdeanour, and to suffer a penalty not exceeding 50 pounds.

,Sec 5. All marriages to be registered in a book (to be kept for such purpose by the person celebrating the same), by the entry therein of a certificate of such marriage, signed by the person celebrating, by the persons married, and by two witnesses present. Such register or book to be open to public examination at all convenience times, and an attested copy of any entry therein to be given to any person requiring it upon payment of 2s, 6d. Any person celebrating a marriage, and omitting to register the same, to pay a penalty of 5 pounds.

Sec 6. The entry of any marriage in manner aforesaid in any such book of registry, or an attested certificate of such entry (the handwriting of the attesting minister being proven) shall be sufficient proof of the marriage to which such entry refers.

Sec 7. Any person destroying or defacing any registry of any marriage with intent to avoid, cancel, or annul such marriage guilty of felony.

Sec 8. Magistrates duly licensed by the Governor may celebrate marriages where no person authorized, as before mentioned, shall reside within ten miles of the residence of the woman about to be married, and laymen duly licensed may celebrate marriages where no person authorized as aforesaid, shall reside within fifteen miles of the residence of the woman about to be married.

Sec 9. All persons celebrating marriages where there in no church or chapel, shall, within twelve months after any marriage, cause a certificate thereof to be registered in the office of the Colonial Secretary under a penalty of 5 pounds; and the Colonial Secretary shall, within seven days after receipt thereof, enter the same in a public register; and such register shall be open to public inspection, and every person requiring it shall be entitled to a copy and certificate of any entry of marriage therein, under the hand of the Secretary, upon payment of 2s, 6d.

Sec 10. The entry of any marriage in such public register, or such copy and certificate of such entry (the handwriting of the Secretary being proven) shall be sufficient proof of the marriage to which such entry refers.

Sec 11. All penalties imposed by this act may be recovered in any court of record, and shall be paid half to the informer, and half to the crown, for the use of the Colony. END

Catholics finally received the right to practice their own religion

Some say the War against England by the US Colonists forced the British to take some of their troops out of Ireland and permitted the Penal Laws in Ireland to be relaxed. Thereby resulting in the rescinding of the restrictive secret government directive for Newfoundland in 1783 and Governor Campbell in 1784 permitting some Catholics in St. John's to request Rome to legally send a Catholic priest to Newfoundland for the first time. On 30 May 1784, Pope Pius VI established Newfoundland as a Prefecture Apostolic. Rev. James Louis O'Donel, OSF, a Franciscan from Ireland, came to Newfoundland on 9 June 1784 and was appointed First Prefect Apostolic in Newfoundland. Rev. O'Donel was now subject to Rome and no longer London. He built the first Chapel in St. John's and established a Mission at Harbour Grace, both in 1784. Even with these permissions, many things were still restricted, they could not bury their dead, they were harassed for building Chapels, they were looked upon with contempt by the Protestant Merchants and the policy of forcing Catholics to take an oath of allegiance to the Church of England to get jobs was still prevalent. And to avoid suspicions, even the Clergy had to walk a tight straight line. Because of the Penal Laws restrictions, the Catholic Priests were reluctant to keep records of the marriages and baptisms in the early years in Newfoundland.

British Emancipation Act - 1829

In April 1829, the British Parliament passed the Emancipation Act, which Catholics throughout the British Empire had all restrictions against them removed. The Catholics in Newfoundland rejoiced but the Supreme Court in December said it did not apply to Newfoundland.

Representative Government - 1832

It was not until 26 August 1832, when Representative Government was granted, that all legal restrictions against Newfoundland Roman Catholics were finally lifted. It took a gutsy Priest like Bishop Fleming to flat out refuse to pay for the burials and the marriages of Catholics like they always had to do. The religious friction carried over later when elections were permitted in Newfoundland and even some riots broke out between supporters of Catholic and Protestant candidates. There were religious oriented confrontations all the way up to the Harbour Grave Affray in 1883.

Chapter 2

EARLY HISTORY OF HARBOUR GRACE PARISH LIFE

Harbour Grace was constituted the first Mission of St. John's by Rev. James L. O'Donel ofm, Preface Apostolic in 1784 and Father Patrick Phelan ofm, who accompanied Father O'Donel to Newfoundland, was assigned as first Mission priest at Harbour Grace in the same year. When the people of Harbour Grace heard Father Phelan was coming to Harbour Grace, they rented a stone store and converted it into a Chapel with 10 pews put into it for Father Phelan to say Mass. It was not until 1806 that a free standing Chapel was constructed by Rev. Father Ewer ofm. The Harbour Grace Parish has had a total of one Store-chapel, one wooden-Chapel, one stone-Church and two Cathedrals.

Father Patrick Phelan 1784-1799

First Priest to die in Line-of-duty

Father Phelan was a Franciscan Friar and was known as a zealous worker who annually made two visitations of his Mission-Parish. While no records were found of his marriages and births, there no doubt were many performed by him in his 15 years of service as a Catholic Priest. It was when returning from one of his visitations, in September 1799, that Father Phelan drowned off Grate's Cove. Some accounts say he was returning from Fogo, which, if true was quite a distance from Harbour Grace by boat. It would normally be assumed that his mission comprised the Conception Bay Peninsula, from Holyrood to Bay de Verde and every location in between. Needless to say, the boat in which he was a passenger capsized in a storm and all the passengers and crew died. Father Phelan's body was the only one recovered and he was found upright in the water with his breviary under his arm, a cane in one hand and a small bag containing his vestments in the other. His body was taken to Harbour Grace and his sorrowing people laid him to rest in a new Catholic grave yard, on Bennett's Lane, where they erected over his remains a monument bearing the following Grave Stone:

Inscription: IN ECCELSIS DEO. Here lieth the body of the Rev. Patrick Phelan of the order of St. Francis, Missionary of Harbor Grace, who departed this life the Third day of September 1799. His pastoral zeal in propagating truth, His generous effusions of Liberality towards the distressed, and his vehement thirst after peace and good order, register his friendship with God, and make his memory dear to man. His panegyric borrows no beauty from the daubing of words, but from the impression of past merit. Now terminating his Apostolical career, he craves the prayers of his faithful flock in order to arise into life by resting in peace. This his grateful people devoted to his memory, repeating. REQUIESCAT IN PACE. (Shortis News Article)

Archives

In the Grand Falls Archives we found the following hand written document about Father Patrick Phelan. "In the spring of 1784, Dr O'Donnel, (sic) as Prefect Apostolic, arrived in St. John's from Ireland, accompanied by Father Patrick Phelan and another priest also named Phelan, to assist in publicly organizing the Church in Newfoundland. Father Patrick Phelan was appointed Parish priest of Harbor Grace, which then formed an extensive and most laborious Mission, embracing, as it did, not only the greater part of Conception Bay, but also Trinity and Bonavista Bay. The privations and hardships of this good priest of whom too little in known, in ministering to his scattered flock cannot now be estimated. The veneration in which his name is still held by the residences of those who knew him is the only record existing for his virtues; his boundless charity is well testified by the fact that, at his death, it was found, he was not worth a shilling."

Revelations about Father Phelan and the first Chapel

In 1886, the Parish Priest, Very Rev. Father John Roe, asked Mr. James L. Prendergast, an old Merchant, MHA and an outstanding Catholic born in 1800, for some information on historical questions pertaining to the past Church History. In his four page letter, found in the Archives in Grand Falls, Mr. Prendergast stated the following:

> ***"I enclose you with the information I could gather on the late Father Phelan, as the old people of that time are dead. On Father Phelan arrival here the Catholics hired the Mercantile premises of Walter Roberts who left the country who left Mr. Henderson before one time his Agent for 20 pounds, 7 years. Mr. H. was I believe a Quaker but most liberal and kind man particularly to Irishmen and Catholics. His Stone Store was converted into a Chapel and ten pews were erected in it at forty shillings a year to pay the rent. After Father Phelan's death the Rev. Father Ewer came from Ferryland to this place and the Rev Father Fitzpatrick was sent here who visited him here for some years during his time the Catholics of Conception Bay collected money sufficient and purchased the whole establishment and land appertaining thereto, the bill of sale was made out to the Committee and fearing any of them would get in debt, they made it pass in trust to Father Fitzgerald (sic) for his time and to his successors in office for the use and benefit of the Catholics of Conception Bay. The abstract of the two documents, I cannot send over as the Records were sent to St. John's. Since the death of Mr. Everson, the Register of deeds. If you write to McCarthy your member to apply to the Register office in St. John's he will get a copy of an abstract of them and also of the will of the late Father Ewer which I think would be worth getting."***

This letter interjects a new wrinkle in our history, as to the fact that there was a Chapel in Harbor Grace before the first one built by Father Ewer in 1806. Mr. Prendergast states that this store-made-chapel was rented for Father Phelan's on his arrival in 1784 and later when Father Fitzpatrick took over in 1800, this store-made-chapel and the land thereto was then purchased by the Catholics of Conception Bay. So Harbour Grace has had a Chapel since 1784, the same as St. John's. To find old historical documents is a trill and this one shows that the Irish Catholics in early Harbour Grace were a proud and devoted lot and took things into their own hands to support their first priest with a Chapel that no one else has reported on. We did not find any information of where this store and property was located in Harbour Grace or whether it was the same location where the first 1806 chapel was built. The store was stone and the second chapel was of wooden construction.

Father Ambrose Fitzpatrick second Parish Priest

Following Father Phelan's death, Father Ambrose Fitzpatrick was assigned to Harbour Grace and remained there from 1800 to 1806. During this period, the rented store and land was purchased by the Parishioners for Father Fitzpatrick to say Mass. In 1806, Father Thomas Ewer, Parish Priest of Ferryland came to visit Harbour Grace and was asked to be assigned here and he traded Parishes with Father Fitzpatrick, who was sent to Ferryland, where Father Ewer had been for 18 years from 1788 to 1806.

Father Thomas Ewer, third Parish Priest, builds separate Chapel in Harbour Grace

When Father Ewer took charge of the Harbour Grace Mission in 1806, he built a wooden Chapel, with a tower approximately 100 feet high. By 1830 the Mission of Harbour Grace officially became a Parish. In that year, Bishop Fleming set out for Ireland to recruit Missionaries for Newfoundland. Of the priests who arrived in 1833, one of them was a Rev. Charles Dalton who was assigned to Harbour Grace in 1833 following Father Ewer's death. According to the minutes of the Pew Committee of Harbour Grace (1830-1836), they continually spoke of the deteriorating condition of the wooden chapel and spoke of the need for a new Church. Church birth and marriage records for Harbour Grace and satellite churches began in 1806 and were all recorded in one book at Harbour Grace. Each priest would go out to any local church community and marry or baptize a person or persons and go back to Harbour Grace to record the event into the one book. The individual Parishes later began their own records. Carbonear began in 1850.

ADDRESS ON DEPARTURE OF REV NICHOLAS HERRON

"At a meeting of the Roman Catholics of Harbour Grace, and vicinity, holden in the St. Patrick's Free School, on Sunday the 14th August, 1831, agreeable to public notice given by Mr. Wm Innott, Chairman of the Roman Catholic Committee, pursuant to the Requisition to him directed, and signed by Mr. Thomas Foley, and other respectable persons of that body, for the purposes of appointing a select Committee to draw up an Address to be presented to the Rev. Nicholas Herron, expressive of the veneration and esteem in which he is held by all classes of the community, and their deep regret at his being about to leave our country ---

Mr. John Fitzgerald was unanimously called to the Chair and Mr. James L. Prendergast was requested to act as Secretary.

The following Resolutions were unanimously agreed to: -

That this meeting view with gratitude and satisfaction, the many virtues and amiable qualities which the Rev. Nicholas Herron possesses in so eminent a degree, and which have so justly endeared him to all classes. That Messers. William Innott, J. L. Prendergast, John Fitzgerald, and Justin Dwyer, of Harbour Grace, and Messrs James Redmond, W. Brown, and Richard Walsh, of Carbonear, be nominated a Committee, to draw up an Address in the name of the Roman Catholics of Conception Bay, receive signatures thereto, and present the same to the Rev. Nicholas Herron. That Messrs John Richards and Robert Walsh be deputed to proceed to Brigus, Port-de-Grave and other settlements in that direction, for the accommodation of persons inhabiting that part of the Bay, who may be desirous of subscribing their names to the address.

That the proceedings of this Meeting and the Address be published in the Conception Bay, Mercury and Newfoundlander, newspapers."

On behalf of the Meeting,

JOHN FITZGERALD, **Chairman**

JAMES L PRENDERGAST, **Secretary**

On Wednesday afternoon, four Gentlemen of the Committee, viz. Messrs W. Innott, J.L. Prendergast, J. Fitzgerald, and Justin Dwyer, waited upon the Rev. Mr. Herron, who received them in the Sacristy of the Roman Catholic Chapel, with the following address: --

To the Rev. Nicholas Herron

Reverend Sir: - we, the Roman Catholic inhabitants of Conception Bay, on the prospect of your being about to depart for your native country, beg leave to present you with the following address, in testimony of our veneration and respect. Though your residence among us has been of short duration, the piety and benevolence of your conduct has been such, that we felt truly grateful to a kind Providence for sending one whose life is so bright an example, to instruct us in the maxime and duties of our Holy Religion; and we now are happy to have it in our power to express the high sense which we entertain of the zeal, the fidelity, constancy, and steadiness, with which you have discharged your arduous and important duties; whilst the suavity and urbanity of your manners, harmonized every discordant feeling, and introduced a state of concord into society, which we fervently hoped you were destined long to preserve.

We owe it in justice to you and to your own feelings to acknowledge, that, it is to the excellency of character and disposition, which led you to exercise your parochial duties in compassionate attention to humble misery, -- in unhesitating sacrifice of self – with a guileless simplicity of heart – an overflowing benevolence of temper, and an assiduous watchfulness to fulfill the functions of your sacred charge – these amiable and Christian virtues endeared you to your flock, acquired the love and affection of all classes and denominations, and now cause the prospect of your removal to be deeply, sincerely, and universally deplored. We beg, therefore, that you will accept of our unfeigned acknowledgements of gratitude and esteem, and our good wishes for your welfare and safety; and that your Divine Master, whose glory it is your study to advance, and the spiritual interest of those people you endeavour to promote, may accompany you, by sea and land, with his glorious presence, and wherever your lot may be cast, in the exercise of your pious labours furnish you with the graces of his spirit, and render your exertions eminently and abundantly successful, is the ardent prayer of your Affectionate and obedient Servants

[Signed by 543 persons]

To which the Rev Mr. Herron was pleased to return the following Reply: --

"To the Roman Catholics of Conception Bay

Dear Friends – The very flattering address you have done me the honour to present, I receive with heartfelt gratitude, and shall ever cherish as the most valued testimony of your fond esteem and regard. In the renumeration of the virtues you are kind enough to attribute to me, you have much overrated my merits. In the humble discharge of the functions of my office, I did but do my duty. You cannot possibly feel more sincere regret at our parting than I do. When I received an appointment to this place, I hoped to have had the pleasure of spending many happy years amongst you. The manifestations of public regard in my favour, reconcile me to my present fate, and whatever my future destinies may be, I can never forget your friendship. I now beg of you to accept the assurance of my warmest, most cordial thanks, and that the fervent prayer of my heart shall be your every happiness."

Harbour Grace, August 17, 1831 NICHOLAS HERRON,

Harbour Grace Pewholders Meeting

The minutes of the Harbour Grace Pew Committee for the period 1830 to 1836 indicates the following. In a meeting of Pewholders of the Roman Catholic Chapel held on 7 Oct 1830 in the Vestry Room of the Chapel for the purpose of taking into consideration subjects of importance relative to the peace and tranquility of the Congregation and to adopt such rules and regulations as will secure to them so desirable an object. The Right Rev Doctor Fleming addrefsed the meeting and recommended the adoption of several resolutions.

1. That as we duly appreciate the values of union and happiness among ourselves we therefore approve and adopt the arrangements recommended by the Right Rev Doctor Flemming for the future government of the Pewholders.
2. That we do hereby agree to pay the sum of one Pound annually for each pew on the ground floor and that the same shall be placed in the hands of a Committee for the time being to be applied for the repairs and benefit of the Roman Catholic Chapel as may appear to the Committee necessary from time to time.
3. That the first Sunday in May next being the day on which the Sums just levied on the Pews become due. The Secretary shall send a written notice to have published from the Altar stating that the said Sums will be collected on the Sunday following.
4. That in consideration of the painting and other repairs expended this last summer on the Roman Catholic Chapel by the Very Revd T. Ewer, the Committee will remunerate him as far as their funds enable them on the first Sunday in May next.
5. That a General Committee be forthwith appointed from which thirteen shall be Annually chosen and that seven of them shall form a quorum and whose duty will be for the time being to collect the money due on the Pews and see that the necessary repairs are done to the Chapel.
6. That the Annual Meeting of the General Committee shall be convened to meet in the Roman Catholic Chapel on the Third Sunday of November at which the Secretary shall lay before them the receipts and expenditures of the past year.
7. That books be purchased in which the Secretary shall record all transactions relative to the Chapel.
8. That the Pewholders shall affix their names in writing to the Resolutions certifying their entire abrogation.
9. That a deputation from the Committee do wait on the Very Revd T. Ewer to present him with a Copy of their Resolutions and to express to him their thanks, affection and regard and to assure him that as he relies on the honor and confidence of his flock that no exertion on their part will be wanting in adding to his dues.
10. That the thanks of this meeting are partly due to the Right Revd Doctor Flemming for the kind and very handsome manner in which he has assisted as to form our resolutions.

Parishioners in Harbour Grace Parish in 1830

John Fitzgerald SS	Thomas Candler	Thomas Dunford
David Keefe	Thomas Griffin	Patrick Neagle
Thomas Fitzgerald	Edward Heally	Daniel Donovan
James L. Prendergast	John Shea	Richard Walsh
Daniel Green	Roger Hanrahan Jr	Michl Keefe
James Coughlan	Justin Dwyer	Patrick Butler
Roger Hanrahan	James Cooney	Patrick Kelly
William Talbot	Edward Farrell	Thomas Martin
James Fox	Martin Kelly	Arthur Thomey
John Fitzgerald	James Power	Michl Keefe
James Jones	Arthur Grobert	Patrick Hearn
Nichs Brown	Randal Donovan	Martin Murphy
James Stapleton	Francis Lynch	Phillip Hunt
John Codey	Walter Phelan	Richd Shea
Francis Ronan	Michl Green	John Murphy
Jeremiah Hartry	John Spillane	William Walsh
Richard Lahey	Michl Conners	James Scully
Michl Dooling	Maurice Power	David Power
Doctor Molloy	Edw Keefe	Richard Butt
Peter Browne	Garrett Condon	James Britt
James Bryan	Richard Condon	Thomas Neagle
Peter Fannon	James McDonald	Denis Thomey
Timothy Kenndy	John Kenseloe	Timothy Hearn
Phillip Walsh	Henry Wistman	John Kavanagh
James Walsh	Denis Sullivan	John Richards
Robert Rocket	Richard Power	Thomas Dunn
Lawrence Keefe		

These names were listed in the Harbour Grace Pew Committee minutes (1830)

Harbor Grace, 27 July 1831

Subscriptions entered into at the request of the Very Rev Mr. Ewer for the purchase of musical instruments for the use of the Choir of the Roman Catholic Chapel of Harbor Grace by Daniel Donovan Collector.

Very Revd Mr Ewer	**10-0-0**				
Revd Mr Devereux	**0-10-0**	**Martin Kelly**	**0-2-0**	**Patk Neagle**	**0-5-0**
Revd Mr Mackin	**0-5-0**	**Wm Thorne**	**0-2-6**	**Jas Jones**	**0-5-0**
William Sinnott	**0-15-0**	**Francis Ronan**	**0-5-0**	**Arthur Thomey**	**0-5-0**
Thomas Foley	**0-10-6**	**Jerry Hartery**	**0-5-0**	**Richd Walsh**	**0-5-0**
John Fitzgerald	**0-5-0**	**Maurice Power**	**0-5-0**	**Michl Green**	**0-5-0**
Peter Brown	**0-10-0**	**Thomas Malone**	**0-5-0**	**Walter Dillon**	**0-5-0**
Thomas Marks	**0-10-0**	**Roger HanrahanJr**	**0-2-6**	**Wm Innott Jr**	**0-5-0**
Michl Flynn	**0-10-0**	**Mrs. Dnl Green**	**0-5-0**	**Jhn Fennell**	**0-5-0**
Arthur Grahead??	**0-2-6**	**Jas Gearey**	**0-5-0**	**Jas Prendergast**	**0-2-6**
David Keefe	**0-5-0**	**Randal Donovan**	**0-5-0**	**Thos Martin**	**0-5-0**
Willm Meagher	**0-5-0**	**Francis Lynch**	**0-5-0**	**Patk Devereux**	**0-5-0**
Pierce Hanrahan	**0-5-0**	**Thos Dunford**	**0-5-0**	**John Neilly**	**0-2-6**
Danl Cantolon??	**0-5-0**	**Wm Walsh**	**0-5-0**	**Regan and**	
Edwd Shelly	**0-2-6**	**Justin Dwyer**	**0-2-6**	**Donovan**	**0-10-0**
Richd Condon	**0-5-0**	**Garrett Condon**	**0-5-0**	**Edw St.John**	**0-5-0**
Wm Drysdale	**0-2-6**	**Timy Kennedy**	**0-5-0**		
Richd Lahey	**0-2-6**	**Jas Fitzgerald**	**0-1-0**	**Total 13-12-0**	
Michl Dooling	**0-2-6**	**Garrett Wall**	**0-2-6**		

At the request of Mr. Daniel Donovan I have collected the above list of subscriptions for the purpose as above stated. James L. Prendergast, Secy

This Pewholders Committee met from Oct 1830 under Father Ewer until 1833 and then under Father Charles Dalton till 1836

Through out the years they discussed and voted on the following-type subjects, this is a summary:

1. Dispose by public auction such vacant pews in the Chapel and empowered to grant a bill of sale for them.
2. Pews to be purchased by the highest bidder.
3. Richd Mackey to be Clerk of the Chapel. Floors and pews to be cleanly washed months of June and November and Chapel regularly swept every Saturday during the ensuing year. He is to receive ten pounds currency yearly.
4. Chairman authorized to build a moveable Chair on the ground floor. Agreement with a carpenter. Also iron work, fringe for curtains and locks be purchased to complete the chair in the gallery. Carpet purchased for the altar. Also purchase musical instruments, etc etc., for use of choir, requested by Father Ewer and vestments for the altar.
5. 1831. Erection of a pew on the gallery on the north side of the choir for parishioner to pay five pounds currency.
6. 1831. Thos Foley and Wm Innott to request Wm Keough to inspect Chapel to ascertain the repair necefsary to the done and probable cost of same.
7. 1831. Select Committee met and signed an agreement with Richd Power to repair the roof of the Chapel and find all materials for the sum of twenty-five pounds.
8. 1831. That windows be opened in the Gallery on the sides of the Choir. Place a Gothic window at the south of Mr. Hartery's pew. Rchd Power.
9. 1831. Paint ceiling and molding all around.
10. 1831. Prepare address for departure of Rev Herron from the Island.
11. 1832. Meeting held in the St. Patrick's Free school. A special collection on Easter Monday and New Years Day to aid the funds of the RC Chapel.
12. 1832. Need for subscription for money for a fence for the new grave yard. Revd Ewer request.
13. 1833 Nov 24- Annual Meeting with Revd Charles Dalton.
14. 1833 Dec - Approved to pay two pounds and 17 shillings for repairs to Irish Grave Yard,
15. 1834. Consult with Revd Mr. Dalton about annual pew rent of 20 shillings owing to the contemplating of a new Chapel intended to be built.
16. 1834 May 10 - Cash for amt collections at the Chapel door on this date -7 pounds 11 shillings.
17. 1834 Nov 29 - Held in Chapel after Mass. Secretary to buy a box of candles suitable for the altar. Also that the remainder of Mr. Rich Mackey's salary as clerk for his attendance to the Chapel be discharged forthwith.
18. 1834. EXPENSES: boards, nails, paint and oil. repair steeple window, 6 pane glass, chapel window, two locks, lantern. sweeping brush and candles.
19. 1834. Dec 7 -Meeting in vestry room of Chapel. To deliberate on the dilapidated state of the RC Chapel. Worked for a plan to commence subscription for a new one.(Chapel). To build a new Chapel and no expense of improvements to be made on present Chapel, unless it is absolutely necefsary for the comfort of the congregation. Randal Greene to act as clerk.
20. 1835 Jan 1 - Paid Revd C. Dalton - 50/18/2.
21. 1835 Jan 1 - Annual Meeting of Roman Catholics of Harbor Grace and its vicinity. VRevd C. Dalton n Chair. Chose Committee for new year. VRevd Dalton to be Treasurer. Six new members appointed to committee for raising subscriptions for the erection of a new Chapel.
22. 1836 Jan 3 - Annual Meeting. Election of select committee for the ensuing year. In back of the Committee Book there was this hand drawn picture of a Chapel.

Hand drawn picture of a Chapel.

Found on last page of Pewholders Minutes

This hand drawn picture of a Church was drawn on the last page of the Pewholders book from 1830 to 1836. It follows all the talk about building a new Church. Whether this is what the second Stone Church looked like, we do not know.

Rev Charles Dalton builds Stone Second Church

For years the old wooden church built by Rev Ewer in 1806 was in need of repairs according to the Pew Committee minutes of 1830-1836. The need for a new Chapel continued when Rev Charles Dalton took over as Parish Priest in 1833 and he finally took action. Rev Charles Dalton went to Rome with Bishop Fleming in 1846 for a health visit and to look for stone for his new church. He had the wooden chapel torn down and began excavation in 1848 for a new Stone Church in Harbour Grace.

Concerning the Stone Building about to be erected

The following item appeared in *THE WEEKLY HERALD*, June 5, 1850

"A new Catholic Chapel is to be erected here forthwith. The old tower has been taken down, and large quantities of stone and other materials have been collected on the spot. We understand Mr. Keough of St. John's has been over taking plans and examining the proposed site."

On Monday, May 10 1852, the cornerstone for the new Stone Church was laid by Rt. Rev Dr. Mullock, assisted by several clergymen. On that occasion there was a procession though the Town, and at the end of the ceremonies, the Bishop delivered an address, following which a subscription for the building was opened, and the sum of 550 pounds was contributed on the spot. The new stone Church was consecrated in 1853 by Bishop Mullock.

Foundation Stone for New Church

31 May 1852

"The Foundation stone of the New Catholic Church in Harbour Grace was laid by Rt Rev Dr Mullock on May 31, 1852. At ten in the forenoon a procession was formed on Cochrane Street, which, having perambulated the town for about an hour, arrived on the site of the new building.(east of the Court House Road). After the services were ended, Bishop Mullock proceeded to deliver an address, at the conclusion of which, we are informed, a subscription for defraying the expenses of the building, were opened, and the sum of 550 pounds towards that object was contributed on the spot. "

"The Weekly Herald", June 2, 1852.

A YEAR LATER

1853

"The new Catholic Chapel, commenced here about a twelve-month since, is nearly completed. It is a solid, compact building, with a nice ornamental front facing the sea; upwards of 100 feet long and will accommodate, it is thought, about 1200 persons. It is quite credible to the Congregation."

"THE WEEKLY HERALD", SEPTEMBER 14, 1853

Since it was facing the sea, it must have been on the same site as the present Church. Therefore, this newly built stone church was the basis on which the First Cathedral was built, when it was consecrated in 1868, by Bishop Dalton, one year before he died.

The Official Opening of the New Church In Harbour Grace

29 October 1853

"The Catholics of Harbour Grace, who have enjoyed but very indifferent Church accommodations for many years past, owing to the inferior description of building in which they have been obliged to worship, were highly gratified last Sunday (October 29) by the opening of their present beautiful new Church, which, though somewhat plain and unpretending in its external appearance, is not surpassed in its interior by any similar edifice in the whole island. The Builder, Mr. Power (of St. John's) deserves great credit for the admirable style in which he has put the erection out of hands, and the most unaffected gratitude is due to the VRev Charles Dalton for his judgment, foresight and perseverance through the entire undertaking, which, notwithstanding unsuccessful voyages and short harvests, and many adverse and untoward circumstances sufficient to discourage a less energetic mind, is now completed to the great joy of the congregation resorting thither for divine worship. His Lordship, Bishop Mullock, who officiated at the opening ceremony, is, I understand, much pleased with the building."

"The Weekly Herald", November 30, 1853

LETTER TO THE EDITOR OF THE WEEKLY HERALD NOVEMBER 9, 1853

Sir: Your Catholic readers will be gratified to hear that two collections have been made in the Chapel here within the past few months, at one of which the sum of 75 pounds was raised, and at the other (last Sunday, November 6) no less than 128 pounds. These amounts, I believe, are to be appropriated toward the completion of the new Chapel."

Supporter

Yours, etc...

A SUPPORTER

Dedicated

The second stone Church was dedicated on 29 October 1853 by Bishop Mullock, three years before anyone knew of a new diocese at Harbour Grace. When the New diocese was established in 1856, this Church was planned by Bishop Dalton to be embodied into the First Cathedral which he dedicated in 1868 but it was not completed until 1884. There is no doubt that this stone church was used as the first quasi Cathedral after 1856 when the Diocese was formed until the new official Cathedral was dedicated in 1868. We do not know when the Harbour Grace Chapels or Churches were first called Immaculate Conception, since Pope Pius IX had decreed the Dogma of the "Immaculate Conception" in 1854.

Chapter 3

NEW DIOCESE IN NEWFOUNDLAND

New Second Diocese at Harbour Grace

The Vicariate of St. John's was only raised to the status of a Diocese in 1847 and Bishop Mullock had taken over the new Diocese on the death of Bishop Fleming in 1850. It was the increasing Catholic population into the Outports of Central Newfoundland that prompted Bishop Mullock in 1855 to petition Rome to establish a second Diocese. Church officials in St. John's and Rome struggled during the months between November 1855 and February 1856, to determine diocesan boundaries with a view to providing better spiritual development opportunities for people in the Harbour Grace area. Harbour Grace was canonically erected a Bishopric on 26 Feb 1856, by Pope Pius IX. Catholic population at that time was 57,000. Information has it that Rev. Kyran Walsh was asked and turned down the request for him to be consecrated the first Bishop of Harbour Grace. He had been invited to Newfoundland in 1839 by Bishop Fleming and was ordained in St. John's at age 30 the same year by the Bishop and he was entrusted by the Bishop as his special assistant in overseeing the building of the Cathedral in St. John's. After he turned down the Bishopric, Rev. Kyran Walsh in 1857 on the death of Dean Mackin in Brigus, spent a few months at Brigus until Rev. O'Keefe came and then he was assigned as first Parish Priest of Harbour Main as well as being Vicar General to Bishop Mullock until his own death in 1868 at age 59.

FIRST BISHOP IN NEW HARBOUR GRACE DIOCESE

1856-1869

Most Rev. John Dalton

Most Rev. John Dalton

Right Reverend John Dalton

This picture is on the wall at the, "Dalton Council" of the Knights of Columbus Hall in Harbour Grace. It is believed to be the only known full-length painting on canvas of Bishop Dalton. It is about 22 inches high and 15 inches wide within a glass frame. It must have been taken or painted between 1856 and his death in 1869. There have been reports that one of the early nuns was a artist and she may have painted this portrait. We owe a debt of gratitude to Peggy Whelan for her personal efforts to secure and duplicate this picture. Thanks to Ron Martin for his help. We are pleased to have been able to publish this old picture in our book for all to see. It is indeed one-of-a-kind and a treasured historical masterpiece.

In 1856, when the 2nd Diocese in Newfoundland was constituted at Harbour Grace, Father John Dalton, a Franciscan Priest, Parish Priest at Carbonear was selected to be the first Bishop. He was consecrated by Bishop Mullock on 25 May 1856. Bishop Mullock was assisted by Revs. Charles Dalton, Francis Vereker and Denis Mackin and in the presence of 15 other Priests. He became the first Bishop of the three-month old Bishopric of Harbour Grace. This was the second Consecration to take place in Newfoundland. (The first being in St. John's when Bishop Fleming was Consecrated in 1829). On 1 June 1856, Right Rev. John Dalton was installed in the newly erected See of Harbour Grace. His uncle, Father Charles Dalton, PP, Harbour Grace was living in the palace in Harbour Grace so the new Bishop John Dalton stayed in Carbonear until after his uncle died in 1859, when he moved to Harbour Grace in 1860. The Diocese included all settlements along the Northeastern coast of the Island from Seal Cove, Conception Bay to Cape Norman. Bishop Dalton had the distinction of ordaining Rev. James Brown of Carbonear on 20 December 1856. He was ordained in Carbonear and was the first native born Priest to be ordained in Newfoundland history.

DEATH OF VERY REV. CHARLES DALTON, P.P.,V.G.

"A telegram last Friday, 17 June 1859, brought the melancholy information of the death on that morning of the Very Rev. Charles Dalton, V.G. for a period of more than a quarter of a century, the Parish Priest of Harbour Grace. The Reverend deceased had attained to a very advanced age and throughout his career was remarkable to those virtues of the priestly character, and for a kindness and simplicity of disposition that ever show conspicuously in the intercourse with the world. He was too one of the most hospitable of men, as many amongst us knew and no one ever left him without feeling assured of the sterling qualities of his heart. He will be deeply mourned by all who knew him, but in an especial degree by his Rt. Rev., Nephew, and the bishop of Harbor Grace, to whom he would offer the tribute of one cordial and respectful on a sad sympatric occasion of his bereavement." Newfoundlander, Monday 20 June 1859

Plan Building of Cathedral for Harbour Grace

Bishop John Dalton immediately began to consider a Cathedral for the new Diocese and planned for it to be constructed onto the recently completed stone Church. Part of the stone church was to be incorporated into the new edifice. News accounts by the HG Standard of 7 Sept 1864, "reported the loss of the schooner, "Jamima", belonging to W. Donnelly, Esq., was being used to convey stone from Kelly Island to Harbour Grace for the building of the Cathedral. The ship was wrecked in a heavy storm on 8 August 1864 and Capt Keefe and two of his crewman, Neil and Stapleton, were washed overboard".

In 1865, Bishop Dalton dispensed the fisherman from not fishing on Lady's Day 15th August (the Feast of the Assumption) if they gave all the proceeds they received from the fish they caught on that day to the Church. History indicates Bishop Dalton began construction for the first Cathedral in 1868.

Bishop Dalton's Lady's Day Pastoral Letter

PASTORAL

JOHN, ***by the Grace of* God *and favour of the Apostolic Sea, Bishop of Harbor Grace.***

To the Faithful of said Diocese, engaged in the Fishery at Labrador and elsewhere, Health and Benediction in the Lord.

Dearly Beloved, --

Having, as you know, undertaken to enlarge and remodel the Cathedral of Harbor Grace, which may be considered the Mother Church of every one subject to Our Jurisdiction, and being unable to accomplish that good work without your co-operation, We confidently appeal to you to give us now, willingly, as you have so often done, the assistance which we require.

In order to render compliance with Our request easy, and to avoid trespassing on your private resources, as well as not to interfere with the rights of those who expect a return from you for the supplies with which they have furnished you, We have resolved to allow you to fish for the Cathedral on Lady's Day next, on condition that the proceeds of that days' fishery be exclusively devoted to the purpose for which that permission is granted.

We need hardly remind you that on no other account have We the remotest intention to exonerate you from the obligation of abstaining from servile work on the 15th August; and that no one within the limits of the Diocese of Harbor Grace, whether ordinarily belonging to it or not, who is unwilling to fulfill the condition upon which it is given, can avail himself of the dispensation which we hereby grant, without incurring the guilt of mortal sin. We earnestly hope that your labours, during the present Summer may be crowned with ample success, and that you may have on your return home the consolation to feel that you had done everything that lay in your power to deserve well of the Divine Providence, which will have saved you amidst the perils of the ocean and rendered your industry fruitful. -- The Grace of Our Lord Jesus Christ be with you all. Amen.

J. DALTON, Bishop of Harbor Grace

June 1st 1865.

This was found in the Archives in Grand Falls

No Bishop's in Newfoundland

When Bishop Mullock of St. John's died 29 March 1869, Bishop Dalton went to St. John's for about one month to take care of the administration left by Bishop Mullock and when he came back to Harbour Grace in April 1869, as the only Bishop on the Island, he himself became sick and died unexpectedly on 5 May 1869 at the young age of 49. Since he basically only did the planning for the Cathedral before he died, the actual construction fell to the next Bishop. Newfoundland had no Bishop on the Island from 1869 to 1870. Rev. Edward O'Keefe, PP, Brigus, was Administrator in St. John until Bishop Power arrived in 1870 and Rev. John J. Walsh, PP, Harbour Grace, was Administrator in Harbour Grace until Bishop Carfagnini arrived in 1870.

SECOND BISHOP OF HARBOUR GRACE

1870-1880

Most Rev. Henry Carfagnini

Bishop Henry Carfagnini had been a curate at Harbour Grace earlier under Bishop Dalton and had been responsible for the architecture of the Harbour Grace Cathedral which was modeled after St. Peter's Cathedral in Rome. Rev. Carfagnini had left Harbour Grace and upon Bishop Dalton's death he returned from Rome in 1870 as the new Bishop of Harbour Grace to replace Bishop Dalton. Bishop Carfagnini was an Italian and the Irish parishioners did not seem to get along with him and although he was a great architect and builder and did a great job of building the Cathedral, he caused some disagreements with the parishioners. He instituted a second BIS in Harbour Grace and demanded more control over the Sisters which resulted in a Papal investigation and he was directed to return to Italy and left in 1880 before completing the new Cathedral.

In 1871 Bishop Carfagnini requested an Italian friend and fellow Franciscan, Rev. Diomede Falconio, who was in the United States, to come to Newfoundland as his Administrator, more or less to take care of the daily Church functions and dealings with the parishioners while the Bishop concentrated on the building of the Cathedral. Rev. Falconio became a mainstay in the Diocese and got along well with the people of the Parish. He departed Harbour Grace in 1882 and later became the Papal Delegate to the United States and ultimately a Cardinal.

Reverend Diomede Falconio

+ D. Card. Falconio Paris

Departure of the Very Rev. D. Falconio, O.S.F.

"The event of the past week has been the departure, from Harbor Grace, of the Very Rev. Diomede Falconio. O.S.F., Administrator of the Roman Catholic Cathedral. The Very Rev. Father Falconio was born in Italy in the year 1842, entered the Franciscan Order in 1860, and finished his education in the Roman Province. In 1855 he was chosen by the Superior General of the Order for the American Mission, and was ordained priest January 4th, 1865, in Buffalo, by Bishop Tino, and in July following was elected Professor of Philosophy and Vice-President of the Franciscan College, Allegany, N.Y. In 1867, he was appointed Secretary of the Franciscan Province of the Immaculate Conception and Professor of Dogmatic Theology. In 1868 he was elected President of the Seminary and College of Saint Bonaventure, Allegheny, Catt Co., New York; and at the request of Dr. Carfagnini, he came to Newfoundland in 1871 -- arriving in Harbor Grace 26th December. The number and highly complimentary character of the following addresses presented to the Very Rev. Gentleman on the eve of his departure amply testify to the high regard entertained for him by the people to whose spiritual wants he has ministered since his arrival here. Indeed, the urbane and amiable manners of the Rev. Gentleman have won for him the esteem and good will of all classes in the community, by whom his departure is generally regretted. He will leave here today (accompanied by a deputation of citizens and of all the Catholic societies in town) for St. John's *via* Portugal Cove in the steam-yacht *Lizzie,* kindly and generously placed at his disposal by the House of Messrs. John Munn & Co. The *Lizzie* will call at Carbonear on the way to the Cove for the purpose of taking on board a deputation of citizens of that town who will likewise accompany his Reverence. After a short visit to the United States, where he shall have the pleasure of meeting many old friends, he will precede to Gallipoli, Italy, to reside with his former Bishop, Most Rev. H. Carfagnini." *(For the Harbor Grace Standard.)*

Farewell to Very Rev. D. Falconio. O.S.F.

"At a meeting of the Roman Catholics of Harbor Grace, Carbonear, and Spaniards Bay, held at the Total Abstinence & Benefits Society's Hall on Thursday, the 8th instant, for the purpose of adopting an address to the Very Reverend D. Falconio, O.S.F., on his departure from this colony; it was Resolved, - That the address now read be adopted. *Resolved,* - That a deputation - consisting of Messrs. C.L.Kennedy, Isaac Pumphrey, Thomas Green, John Hennessey, M.J. Flynn, John Strapp, Thomas Geary, J.L. Keefe, John Kenneally, T.R. Collins, M. Brien, William Hennessey, Nicholas Hanrahan, John Mitchell and Nicholas Fitzgerald - be appointed to present the said address on behalf of the Catholic meeting to the said Reverend Gentleman. *Resolved,* -- That a vote of sincere thanks be given to MESSRS. John Munn & Co. for their kindness in offering the steamer *Lizzie* to convey the Very Rev. D. Falconio to Portugal Cove."

Resolved. -- That the proceedings of this meeting be inserted in the STANDARD of Saturday. C.L.Kennedy, Chairman. Isaac Pumphrey, Secretary ***Harbor Grace, June 8, 1882***

New Papal Delegate to the United States

"The dispatch from Rome announcing that the Pope had nominated Archbishop Diomede Falconio, papal delegate to the United States, to succeed Cardinal Satolli, recalls the fact that when Archbishop Falconio's appointment was hinted at a few days ago, a story was published to the effect that American prelates had entered a protest at Rome against the succession of Falconio. The ground for the protest was said to be that the regular clergy objected to the appointment of a secular priest, Falconio being a Franciscan. Father James M. Connolly, secretary to Archbishop Corrigan denied emphatically that there had been any such protest, either uttered or implied." 1897 "No priest or prelate of this country said he "would for a moment think of protesting against any appointment made by the Vatican. A private soldier in the army would not think of criticizing his general. In the church the discipline is just as strict in that respect, and the idea is utterly absurd. Any such action would be an insult to the Vatican, and it is not likely that any American prelate would be guilty of it." The new papal delegate was born in Poscocostanzo, Italy, fifty-five years ago. After completing his early theological education in Europe he came to America in 1865 and completed his studies at the house of his order, St, Bonaventure's College, Allegheny, and Cattaraugus County, N.Y. Upon the completion of his studies there he was ordained a priest in 1866 by the late Bishop Timon, of Buffalo. After being ordained, he became a teacher in St. Bonaventure's College for a time. He next went as a Missionary priest to the diocese of Harbor Grace, Newfoundland. He had been there but a short time when he was made vicar-general of the diocese and during the absence of the bishop on a visit to Rome, he administered the affairs of the diocese, having been made administrator by the Bishop before his departure. Early in 1885 Archbishop Falconio left Newfoundland and came to New York, where for about six months; he was a member of the Franciscan Monastery and engaged in the work of a missionary priest. While engaged in this work he received an offer, from St. Bonaventure's College there, but declined the offer. In the latter part of 1885 he returned to Italy to visit his aged father, who was in ill health. After this visit to his father he took up the work of a Franciscan priest in various parts of Italy. At a meeting of the general chapter of the Order of St. Francis held in Rome in 1889, Father Falconio was elected procurator general of a branch of the order in Italy. The term of his office was for six years, but when he had served about three years he was made Bishop of Lacodosia, Italy. This office he filled until last October, when he was elevated to the Archbishopric, being made Archbishop of the Archdiocese of Acerauza and Materia. In this office he had continued until appointed papal delegate." -- *Halifax Paper* July 11th 1897. **(Cardinal Falconio died in Rome in 1917 at age 75.)**

3rd Bishop at HG
1881-1906
Bishop Ronald McDonald

The new Bishop was Most Rev Ronald McDonald, who came from Nova Scotia in 1881, and worked feverishly with his experience as an architect and finally completed the New Cathedral in 1884. It took the efforts of three Bishops before it was completed. Bishop John Dalton did the planning, Bishop Henry Carfagnini did most of the building and Bishop Ronald McDonald finally finished it. This Cathedral was one of the greatest Cathedrals built in North America and was being built when most the Catholic parishioners were well-to-do and donated much money and many articles for this outstanding Cathedral.

Picture of Proposed Harbour Grace Cathedral

Picture of Cathedral as envisaged by the Architects

The First Harbour Grace Cathedral

"The design of the Cathedral was basically conceived by Bishop Carfagnini, who arranged with a celebrated Italian architect to prepare the plans but he left before it was completed and Bishop McDonald completed the Nave and furnished it and in 1884 he raised the two front towers to 70 feet high and procured bells from the McShane Works in Baltimore. The bell in the West tower, weighing 2,000 pounds, was presented by Captain John Hennessey, while the bell in the East tower was donated by Dennis Shea. History indicates that the building could accommodate 2,500 to 3,000 worshippers. Stone from Kelly's Island, Conception Bay, trimmed with freestone from Scotland was the principal component. The transept, surmounted by a huge Dome, was as large as the Nave.

The interior of the Cathedral, finished in Romanesque style, was said to connoisseurs of architecture to be the most beautiful in all North America. The roof of the Nave was supported by 18 columns of Peter head granite, surmounted by Corinthian capitals of pure Italian marble. They were the gift of Hon. W. J. S. Donnelly, Receiver-General, at a reputed cost of $9,000.00. The ceiling was richly ornamented with elaborate stucco work. In the centre panel was a painting of the Madonna, after Murillo, by a Sister at Harbor Grace. The fourteen side windows of the Nave were of stained glass, representing the Way of the Cross. They were donated by John Strapp, a prominent member of the Congregation. The organ, at a cost of $7,000.00, was presented by Mr. Donnelly, Sr. a leading fish merchant at Harbor Grace. On either side of the Transept were three chapels and altars. The High Altar, directly under the Dome, and covering the intersection of the Transept with the Nave, occupied the entire centre of the Transept, and was supported by eight columns. The Sanctuary rail of massive Ash and Walnut enclosed the High altar and the six side chapels. The Sanctuary was covered with handsome Brussels carpet, relieved with gold, the gold setting off the green. It was procured in England - another gift. This was one of the most beautiful Cathedrals in all of North America; many came to dedicate the new Cathedral. The new Cathedral was an expansion of the Stone Church completed in 1853 (31 years before) and 16 years since it was begun in 1868, but was a truly great edifice and a truly dominating Cathedral."

First Cathedral in Harbour Grace, dedicated in 1884

Prelates visit Harbor Grace – 1884

"On Thursday 17 July 1884, there arrived here from St. John's per steamer "Lady Glover". His Grace, Dr. O'Brien, Archbishop of Halifax, their Lordships, Dr. Faber, Bishop of Montreal and Dr. MacIntyre, Bishop of Charlottetown, attended by their respective chaplains. The Prelates were accompanied by His Lordship, the Bishop of Harbor Grace and by the Rev Fathers Howley and Scott of St. John's and Fathers Morris of Topsail and Phippard of St. George's Bay. The Rev. Fathers Walsh of Carbonear and Tarahan and McCarthy of the Cathedral; together with a large number of citizens, assembled on the steamer's wharf to receive the distinguished visitors. Several of the houses along Water Street were decorated with flags in their honour and the Cathedral also presented a very handsome appearance. Since their arrival here their Lordships have been the guests of Dr. McDonald. On yesterday, we learn, the blessing of two bells lately imported for the Cathedral took place. A very large congregation assembled to witness the interesting ceremony. His Lordship, Bishop. Fabre officiated, attended by Bishops MacIntyre and McDonald and a large number of priests. This morning Dr. McDonald with his visitors left overland for St. John's. We understand their Lordships were much pleased with their visit and spoke in high terms of the beauty and finish of the Cathedral". ***Harbor Grace "Standard" Saturday, July 19, 1884***

The Magnificent interior of the New Cathedral

The 1871 Lovell Directory describes Harbor Grace: "The Town has a pretty appearance from the harbor, but lacks public buildings of any consequence, with the exception of the Roman Catholic cathedral, the dome of which forms a prominent object in entering the port. This building has lately been enlarged and its interior lavishly decorated, surpassing in this respect any church in the colony"

Cathedral Destroyed by Fire

Only five years later on 2 September 1889, the New Harbour Grace Cathedral burned to the ground and the people of the Immaculate Conception Diocese were devastated. They had put all their money into the Cathedral and donated most of the inside furnishings, Mass instruments, church paraphernalia and paintings, which had all gone up in smoke. It was completely paid for but did not carry any insurance. Following its destruction by fire, Fr. John Roe and Fr. Thomas Lynch were sent to America to collect funds for the restoration of a new Harbour Grace Cathedral. After the fire in 1889, the Catholic parishioners, at this time, were not as well off and could not replace all the lavished articles previously donated and lost in the fire. When the Cathedral was destroyed by fire, Church services were at first held in the Academy hall. However, as accommodations there proved to be unsuitable for the large congregation, the T.A. Hall was then used. The cornerstone of the Total Abstinence Hall had been laid by Rt. Rev. D. Falconio OSF, on June 6, 1873.

Pictures of burned out Cathedral - 1889

The Parishioners view the devastating loss of their beautiful Cathedral.

Please note the tombstone in front. This validates the fact that two nuns may have been buried in front of the Church, as rumor has it. But there is no evidence today.

Chapter 4

THE GREAT DISASTER

HARBOR GRACE STANDARD, SEPTEMBER 7, '89

Destroyed by Fire

The Cathedral in Ashes

"The following, so far as we have been able to gather them, are the particulars in connection with the unfortunate disaster which has shorn Harbor Grace of its beautiful Cathedral:

The Particulars of the Fire

The Bishop, it appears was preparing to go to Salmon Cove by the early train that starts at 4 a.m. He arose at a quarter to three, and, having finished his morning devotions he went down to his Study and was all ready to leave, when the Convent bell rang out. His Lordship thought that it was the usual bell which rings at the Convent at 5 o'clock and that he had missed the outgoing train. Wondering that his watch and the Convent bell did not agree, the Bishop ran out of the Palace. At this time there was not a soul on the ground, so the Bishop himself was the first on the scene of the disaster.

The flames which he saw coming from the eastern wing of the sacristy had not up to this time gained much headway; and had ten men with buckets of water been there, they would have arrested the progress of the fire. The Bishop immediately hurried back, and called Father Rowe, they got the key of the western wing of the Church and unlocked the door. The Bishop made an effort, at the evident risk of his life, to reach the Tabernacle on the Altar of the Blessed Sacrament in the eastern transept; but the darkness caused by the smoke was by this time so dense that he mistook the Altar of the Sacred Heart (which was near by) for the Blessed Sacrament Altar. When about to retrace his steps the Bishop fell to the floor partly suffocated; but he managed to clutch the altar-rail, and guided by it to crawl along to the western entrance almost exhausted. Meantime Father Rowe had gone to give the alarm. He had not been absent more than ten minutes when the fire bells of town were heard ringing out and he returned with the first detachment of the fire brigade.

When the hose first began to play upon the fire one would have hoped that the devouring element would be kept under subjection, but this hope soon vanished when the flames were seen ascending between the double walls of the dome. In ten minutes the cupola was ablaze, the fire running with lighting rapidity along the woodwork, the paints and other flammable material aiding the conflagration. The firemen and townsmen, without distinction, worked indefatigable but soon the flames had communicated with the dome, and all hope of saving the noble structure was then abandoned. An hour and a half after the alarm was given the magnificent dome fell with a tremendous crash, driving the sparks in brilliant volume skyward. The brilliantly grand scene was witnessed by hundreds of interested spectators. It was soon evident that the building

(containing the convent and school) just to the eastward of the Cathedral was in great danger. But, fortunately, men with the aid of water and of wet blankets extinguished the burning embers as soon as they fell upon or else quickly swept them off the roof. All further danger was past as soon as the blazing dome went down -- the supports being consumed, it fell upon the marble altars with a terrible crash, heard far and near the sparks being thrown in a brilliant spray high up into the air. The fire, besides being damped by the molten lead off the roof, was fortunately confined by the masonry work of the Cathedral.

The wood-work of the interior, however, was now well ablaze, and the fire quickly extended to the organ-gallery and the towers. To save the fine musical instrument nothing could be done; and it was not long before it shared the fate of the other inside Church furniture. And so the fire fiercely burned! At 6 o'clock the roof of the eastern tower with its fine bell fell to the ground, the sparks ascending in a bright cloud. After a time the smoldering timber within the walls was partly extinguished by a big dash of water. By the exercise of much trouble and daring the western tower, in which the other large bell was hung, was left nearly intact. The firemen gaining an entrance through the windows, copiously played the welcome water upon the rapidly approaching flames, and after a time succeeded in quelling them, and saving the structure, which now stands -- not much injured -- a monument to the indefatigable labors of our trusty firemen and others. The ravages of the fire happily stopped here. But the magnificent Cathedral, with its grand dome, was a charred, blackened wreck; the walls of the former were much injured by the fire and its woodwork was entirely consumed. The stone front of the edifice, with the western tower, stands practically intact, but looking very lone and desolate -- a sad monument of departed grandeur.

The building with all the Church furniture, plate, vestments, etc must have cost not less than $250,000. It is hopeless to think of seeing it replaced in its pristine grandeur, as times are so much changed for the worse since the date of its conception, about thirty years ago. Catholics in Harbor Grace were then more numerous and prosperous. The work began and continued under devoted priests and prelates and the people were generous with their means which at that time were abundant. At present the outlook of the Catholic population is gloomy indeed. However, before the debris had ceased burning, Dr. Macdonald had received many expressions of sympathy from outsiders -- Among them are the names of His Excellency the Governor, Sir Terence O'Brien, Llewellyn, the Lord Bishop of Newfoundland, Rev Father Doutney, of St. Kyran, Father Clancy of Placentia, Rev S. Flynn, Little Bay mines; Hon M. Fenelon, Colonial secretary and P. J. Scott, Esq., M.H.A.

Right Rev. Dr. Power, Bishop of St. John's and Rev. J. Scott of that Diocese, are at present on a visit of condolence to Dr. Macdonald. What form the re-construction of the Cathedral will assume, is not yet determined upon, much, it is said, will depend on the amount of assistance from the outside. There is, we understand, a building fund of the new Episcopal Residence, of some three or four thousand dollars, which will be transferred to the building fun of the new Cathedral. His Lordship has, we

learn, received from one member of the congregation the handsome contribution of $400, and has an offer from another person, whose name we are now not at liberty to mention, of the very munificent donation of $2000. Smaller sums with the above give hope that the re building will commence at an early date. The noble edifice that was destroyed was finished about three years ago, and all its artistic details completed -- such as marble altars, stained-glass windows, carpets, and a magnificent set of stations of the Cross, erected by the Bishop no later than last spring. The Cathedral was entirely free of debt, but not one dollar insurance on it.

The Harbor Grace Cathedral was, as we said above, begun about thirty years ago. It had gained a world-wide reputation for especially its style, beauty and finish; its magnificent dome would have done credit to a far larger, far more pretentious city. It was greatly admired by all that saw it. Very unfortunately there is no insurance whatever either on building or Church furniture and the loss consequently is a very heavy one. The damage inflicted on the town itself is very great; it has in its beautiful Cathedral been despoiled of its great adornment.

Much sincere sympathy is felt for Bishop Macdonald and his people.

Bishop Macdonald and the Catholic people of Harbor Grace wish to convey their heartfelt thanks to the citizens of the town of all denominations, who so zealously assisted in endeavoring to arrest the progress of the flames. They also desire to give public expression of their gratitude to the kind sympathizers whose names are mentioned above, and as well to the unknown donors of such generous contributions.

Mass and all other services of the Church will till further notice be conducted in the Academy Hall.

(Second article)

HARBOR GRACE STANDARD, SEPTEMBER 11, 1889

THE CONTENTS OF THE CATHEDRAL

Subjoined will be found a brief, necessarily imperfect account of the contents of the late Cathedral, all of which were destroyed in the conflagration which early on Monday week robbed Harbor Grace of its most imposing public structure: The Cathedral had seven altars. The grand one was of valuable marble. There were three smaller ones in the little chapels in the eastern transept -- and three others in the western transept -- all fully and expensively furnished with carpets, altar linen, candlesticks, books, vases, flowers, etc,. etc. that were expressly imported for each altar. The little chapels, in which the altars were erected were finished in the best style. The ceilings were frescoed, and the side walls handsomely paneled. Each one was enclosed with a handsome iron or bronze railing. All were enclosed with a heavy, substantial railing of oak and mahogany, which surrounded the whole sanctuary.

The Sanctuary was covered with a very valuable carpet, especially manufactured for the purpose, only a year or two ago. The Cathedral was

supplied with 140 pews of oak and mahogany, which with the altar railings, were only recently imported. There was also a valuable pulpit of oak and a grand set of Station pictures, resting on brass brackets in terra cotta, only erected about four months since. It had its valuable and grand piano. Ten highly polished Aberdeen granite pillars with white Carrara caps supported the ambulatory walls. The dome was also supported by massive pillars.

In statuary there were three of the Blessed Virgin, two of St. Joseph and St. Francis, besides a valuable Dead Christ, adoring angels, etc.

In paintings there was a valuable oil painting of St. Francis, of the Blessed Virgin, of the Sacred Heart, of St. Patrick, of St. Peter, and of Mary Magdalen. In stained windows there were three very fine, full-sized ones in the rear of the High Altar; one of the Immaculate Conception, of St. Patrick and of St. Joseph; also in the little chapels of St. Francis, Blessed Virgin, and Sacred Heart, there were handsome and valuable smaller ones.

Inside and around the Sanctuary there were the much admired and costly Throne, with chairs for the Bishop and seats for the ministers; as well as three marble topped tables of mahogany, one a very large one -- all new.

For use on the high altar on special occasions there were grand candlesticks, and crucifix four feet high. In Chandebels and Dalmatics there were four and five sets of some colours, and double sets of all. There were eight copes of different colors, some of which were new and valuable. A large stock of lace and other albs, surplices, chalices, monstrance, ciborium's, processional crosses, mitres, croziers, cruets, missals, book-stands, etc. etc. The above is but an imperfect summary of the valuable and extensive church furniture, etc., of the old Cathedral. It may perhaps suffice to give some feeble idea of what's gone.

-- ALL PUT OUT -- The smoldering embers of the Cathedral fire were extinguished by water on Monday. The foundation-walls are much disfigured, and, it is believed, much damaged by the heat of the conflagration. None of the vaults have been injured. The interior of the Cathedral is now an unsightly heap of ruin. All the doors have been closed up, with the exception of one in the western transept. No person is allowed inside, fear of falling of any wall or other part. The scene on the grounds appears lone and desolate, the walls presenting a grim and weird aspect. During the week services have been held in the Academy Hall. Being found unsuitable for the accommodation of a large number of persons, the Total Abstinence Hall is now being fitted up, and made suitable for the intended purpose. The people naturally are put to much inconvenience, and will be so until a new Church is built. ----

The Cathedral Rebuilding Fund

Amount already acknowledged	$ 7,335
Very Rev. James Quinan Sydney	10
Mr. John Hogan, Harbor Grace	100
Mr. Thomas Finn, Carbonear	4
Mrs. Teresa A. O'Neil, Bay-de-Verde	40
Mr. Daniel A. Ryan, King's Cove	100
Mr. Edmund J. Ryan, King's Cove	25

A donation taken up by Very Rev. Stephen O'Flynn, Little Bay, for the re-building Fund realized $250.

John Roe, Secretary

--- THE RIGHT SPIRIT -- Our contemporary the *Colonist* of Wednesday, commenting on the recent kindly act referred to below, says: At the evening session of the Diocesan Synod of the Church of England, held last evening, a resolution of sympathy to the Bishop of Harbor Grace and his flock, in his loss, by the burning of their beautiful Cathedral, was proposed by Rev. Rural Dean Harvey, and seconded by Rev. J. M. Noel, Rector of Harbor Grace, and carried unanimously. On proposing the resolution, Rev Mr. Harvey spoke, in touching language, of the great loss which Bishop McDonald and his flock had sustained, and said in such calamities it was the duty of Christians to sympathize, one with another. He dwelt on the labors and personal sacrifices which Bishop Macdonald and his predecessors and their people must have made to erect and complete such a beautiful structure. The remarks of the Venerable Rural Dean, who is the oldest Church of England clergyman in Newfoundland, evidently struck a sympathetic chord in the breast of every one present. Rev. Mr. Noel residing in the same town and having personal knowledge of the Bishop of Harbor Grace gave impressive testimony of the energy and self-sacrificing labors of his fellow-townsman. Bishop Jones, in putting the resolution, signified his hearty approval, and the resolution passed with acclamation. A touch of nature, says the Bard of Avon, makes the whole world kin; this resolution is a public declaration of the fact that, in no part of the world are there more kindly feelings for one another than exists among the intelligent members of different denominations in Newfoundland. This is the right spirit; well deserving of being cultivated. Only the fire-brand, the infidel, or the political demagogue, would have it otherwise. Besides its primary object of helping to alleviate the sorrows of the Bishop of Harbor Grace, the resolution of the Synod will otherwise bear abundant fruit, in promoting charity and good-will even beyond the borders of Newfoundland.

HARBOR GRACE STANDARD, SEPTEMBER 18, 1889
BURNING OF THE H.G. CATHEDRAL

Troubles come and troubles go, but with some, troubles linger. Why, with some, do troubles linger forever? Because of man's ingratitude to man when he allows it to take the place of sympathy. Happily, however, this does not apply to the great majority of Christians, and to none it is less applicable than to Newfoundlanders at home or abroad. Sympathy tends greatly to alleviate trouble, and it is not alone soothes and strengthens the person on whom it is bestowed but it elevates the man who bestowed it. Why? Because the trouble is then divided, each one accepting his share and responsibility as it were. Further, sympathy is the forerunner of help -- an adage, which, I hope, will be fully verified in the instance which prompts me to pen these few lines.

The sad intelligence of the destruction of the magnificent Cathedral at Harbor Grace has doubtless, are this, reached, by wire all Europe and the western hemisphere, and soon will the many Newfoundlanders residing in Canada and the United States have learnt, through the press and by letters from their friends, the sorrowful tidings of the destruction of that beautiful church in which many of them have often attended the Holy Sacrifice of the Mass and the Divine Service, and upon which it need to be their pleasure to gaze in delightful admiration, and in the construction of which they so

freely gave of their means. They will, I am sure, extend that generosity for which Newfoundlanders are ever proverbial and lend a hand to our bereaved Bishop in this, the hour of trial, by contributing towards the erection of a new Cathedral, which His Lordship contemplates starting as soon as funds sufficient to warrant the undertaking on a large scale are raised.

Already the good people of Holyrood have signified their willingness to help on the good work, as was evidenced at a meeting of Roman Catholics of that town, convened by His Lordship on Sunday last, when the handsome sum of one thousand dollars was then and there subscribed. This amount, together with the munificent donations already mentioned through the Standard, must give the good Bishop heart to cheer up against the sad blow and encourage him to despair not. Of course, owing to the poorness of the times, nothing equal to the late magnificent structure can be attempted, nevertheless, we have every reason to hope that we soon shall see built an edifice that will, in some degree, alleviate the great sorrow caused by the heart-rending scene which took place on the morning of the 2nd of Sept 1889, that fatal morning on which our beautiful Cathedral became a mass of ruins, involving a loss of a quarter of a million dollars ($250,000). The great giver of good is merciful and will send aid. Let us, too, help, and success will crown our efforts." -- *Colonist*

End

Chapter 5

BUILDING OF THE SECOND CATHEDRAL

Bishop McDonald began immediately to build a second Cathedral. Looking at the pictures of the shell of the burned out first Cathedral, it seems that the second Cathedral was built around what remained of the first Cathedral. Both pictures of the front of each Cathedral seem to be quite similar.

Riverhead people began the construction of the Second Cathedral

Action to rebuild was at fever pitch, everyone was involved and in The Standard in February 1890 we find this article:

> ***"The first contribution in free labor to rebuilding the Cathedral was made on Thursday last. The people of Riverhead, St. Joseph's Church decided early in the week to make a move in getting all the scaffold poles for the building. The weather favored the project and Thursday afternoon 70 teams moved into line and filed in procession to the Cathedral grounds. The work thus begun will be pushed on vigorously, so that all will be ready for the actual building at an early date. The women kept the home fires burning, while the men thronged the battle line. Thus the good people of Riverhead can always claim credit for their ready response, and really for having been the first to start the work."***

"The slating of the Cathedral was completed on Wednesday, December 17. 1890. The portion of the building under construction during the summer was opened for Divine Service on Christmas morning, when Mass for the first time was celebrated at 6:30 and 10:30 o'clock. The exterior of both transepts was by then almost completed. Records show that when Bishop McDonald finished his tour of Confirmations on Sunday, 7 June 1891, he had confirmed 1,157 children from Holyrood, Harbour Main, Carbonear, Avondale, Conception Harbour and other smaller places including Riverhead, but because of the unfinished state of the Cathedral, he deferred Confirmation at the Cathedral Parish until the next season."

Work Progressing on Second Cathedral

"Work on the Harbor Grace Cathedral is progressing rapidly, and the workmen have taken advantage of the continuance of the fine weather to begin covering part of the roof. A few days since His Lordship, Dr. McDonald made a house to house call on the members of his flock in Harbor Grace realizing thereby the sum of 500 dollars toward the building fund. Altogether the building is farther advanced than could have been hoped by the most sanguine Harbor Grecian. This in a measure is due to kind friends, but mostly to the untiring energy and zeal of Dr. McDonald." "Colonist" November 27, 1891

Harbor Grace Cathedral
Progress Report - 11 October 1892

"Very noticeable progress is now being made with the work on the interior of the Cathedral. The work of plastering will be finished in a short time. The final plastering of the transept is advanced so far, that the altar will be moved into it next week for Divine Service. The Cathedral when finished will undoubtedly be a graceful and ornamental building. The chancel will be ceiled in ornamental wood. The effect of this in contrast, with the light airy arches of the transept and nave, will be very admirable. His Lordship Dr. McDonald exercises constant supervision over the work, and can be seen occasionally on the scaffolding giving some workman a few "points" in Gothic architecture. The planning of arches, the study of the effects of light and shade on the interior, the strict adherence in every point to the principles of Gothic architecture entail an amount of labor and thought which, happily, is lessened by His Lordship's large experience of thirty years in architectural work. A great amount of money is required to carryout the completion of such a large building. The amount paid monthly in wages is quite a large sum. The imposing front which His Lordship intends placing on the Cathedral will cost between $10,000 and $12,000. The funds for this purpose are now low, but it is expected that the Church Fair which will be held next month will bring in a very considerable sum. Judging from the spirit of emulation which pervades the circle of ladies who are now laboring so energetically for the Church Fair, and whose services in such a good cause are deserving of praise, we have no doubt, there will be reason for congratulations on all sides."

Taken from the *HARBOR GRACE STANDARD, Tuesday, October 11, 1892*

The Cathedral Fancy Fair

"The Fair in aid of the Harbor Grace Cathedral Rebuilding Fund, held for the past four evenings in the Academy Hall, is proving in every way up to the expectations of its friends. The receipts up to last night aggregated the handsome total of over $1,300 -sufficient, in all truth, to show how the Fair, notwithstanding the hard times, is being patronized by the townspeople. It is under the management of Rev John March, of the Cathedral, who has left nothing undone to add to its success in every possible way. The management and the appointment of the Hall are everything to be wished for -- all that the deft fingers of the ladies could will make them. Two tables are set on the right hand for the disposal of fancy and useful articles.

Table 1 is presided over by Mrs. John Hogan, Mrs. J. Murphy, Mrs. J. Casey, Mrs. A. T. Drysdale, Mrs. Sergeant Freeman and Miss Keefe, Miss O'Brien, Miss Lynch and Miss Kennedy. Table 2 is in charge of Mrs. John Cody, assisted by Mrs. M. McKenzie, Mrs. D. A. Flynn, Mrs. P. Colbert, Mrs. J.T. Lawton, and Mrs. T. Hanrahan, while Miss Scully, Miss O'Flynn, Miss Maggie McDonald, Miss Thomey, Miss Murphy, Miss Maddie Cody, and Miss Nan O'Mara, have charge of the Toy Table. The left hand side of the Hall is attractively occupied by the Refreshment and Fruit Table, presided over by Mrs. J. Coughlan, ably assisted by Mrs. P Farrell, Mrs. R. Hayden, Mrs. Wm Hennessey, Mrs. Ken Thomey, Miss Goff and Miss Maggie Thomey. With such a coterie of skilled assistants, and such a display of the utile dulce, it were a matter of wonder, indeed, if success large and ample, did not crown the efforts put forth to make the Fair of 1892 what it has proved to be. Mention must not be omitted to be made of the sturdy farmers of Riverhead and Spaniard's Bay, who between them have contributed to the Fair over

200 barrels of first-class potatoes -- which gift, 'twere needless to say is much appreciated, as it deserves to be. The Fair will remain open for a while longer, so that those of the citizens who have not yet had the opportunity of attending it may have the chance to do so. List of prizes and winners will be published next issue."

Taken from the HARBOR GRACE STANDARD, November 25, 1892.

Consecration of the Second Cathedral

This Second Cathedral, the present church, was consecrated in 1892. We are assuming the New Cathedral was dedicated by Bishop McDonald on the Feast of the Immaculate Conception - 8 December 1892.

Second Cathedral Opened in 1892
Immaculate Conception Church

A Beautiful Picture of the 2nd Cathedral

This picture was given to Monsignor Joseph O'Brien as a commemorative on his retirement in 1984 and it was graciously given to us for this book by Bride Maddox, his retired housekeeper. She has also provided many items of information for this book. The lower side door opening leads to the basement under the church where Bishop Dalton and others are buried.

This picture was taken in summer 2002 when they were about to open the church after one year of repairs of the electrical system. Mass was finally resumed and offered on 3 August 2002.

4th Bishop at HG
1906-1940
Bishop John March

When Bishop Ronald McDonald resigned due to ill health on 27 March 1906 at age 71 and retired to Montreal, where we believe he was made Archbishop before he died in 1912 at age 76.

Msgr John March was consecrated Bishop at the Bay Metropolis Cathedral by Archbishop Howley on 4 Nov 1906, assisted by Bishops McNeil and McDonald. The sermon was delivered by his friend Msgr F.D. McCarthy of Carbonear. In 1907 Bishop March inaugurated the Ecclesiastical Student's Fund. The first Knights of Columbus Council in Newfoundland was established in Harbour Grace in 1909 under the patronage of Bishop March. In July 1911, Most Rev Stagni, the Apostolic Delegate visited Harbour Grace.

Apostolic Delegate Visit To Harbour Grace

Left to Right: Most Rev. John March, DD., Most Rev Pellegrino Francesco Stagni, S.M. (Apostolic Delegate) and Rt. Rev. E. F. Walsh, V.C. D.P. *Taken in Harbour Grace.*

Newfoundland Bullet Express

This picture shows, from left to right, Monsignor Stagni, his Chaplain on his left, Bishop March in the doorway and Patrick Lee, the conductor of the Newfoundland Express Railcar.

BISHOP JOHN MARCH CONTINUES HIS MINISTRY OF THE DIOCESE

On 17 June 1911 the Church burned down at Avondale the day following the death of Father Roe. The church was rebuilt and the first Mass was offered on 27 Dec 1912. Also in 1912, the new Immaculate Conception Parish in Grand Falls was created with Rev. William P Finn as first Parish Priest. Bishop Ronald McDonald died in Montreal on 17 Sep 1912 at age 76. In 1913, Bishop March was fired at by an unemployed man while saying Mass in Church. He survived the attack and forgave the man. In 1916 two parishes were formed in the Diocese, Our Lady of Perpetual Help Parish was established at Gambo with Rev. John S. Kavanagh as first Parish Priest and St. Ignatius Parish at St. Alban's was formed with Rev. Stanislaus St. Croix as first Parish Priest. In 1918 a fire destroyed the 2nd Holy Cross Church in Holyrood and Father Finn said the first Mass in the new Church on Christmas Eve in 1919. Also in 1919 the "Notre Dame Council" of the Knights of Columbus was established by Father Finn at Grand Falls. A new concrete block Church replaced the old wooden structure at Grand Falls in 1920. In 1921 the first resident Priest, Rev. James A. Hinchey, was assigned to Bishop Falls, a mission of Grand Falls, In 1921 the Parish Priest at Whitbourne moved his residence to Gambo. In 1924 the Northern Bay Church burned to the ground and Fr. Leslie Fitzgerald was injured during a brave attempt to rescue the Blessed Sacrament.. The origination date of Assumption Parish in Avondale is listed as 1927. Msgr. F.D. McCarthy of Carbonear was appointed first Prothonotary Apostolic in Newfoundland in 1929. In 1930 two new Parishes were formed: Sacred Heart Parish in Bishop Falls became a separate Parish with Rev. James Hinchey as first Parish Priest and St. Therese's Parish in Buchans with Rev. T.D. O'Neill as first Parish Priest. On 4 Nov 1931 Bishop March celebrated his Episcopal Silver Jubilee. In 1933, the Presentation Sisters took over the administration of Notre Dame Academy in Grand Falls. In 1934, the St. Patrick's Church and Rectory in Brigus were destroyed by fire. Msgr. Murphy rebuilt the Church and house. 1934 was the 25th Anniversary of the Dalton Council of the Knights of Columbus in Harbour Grace. In 1938, Rev. Finn and the men of the town built a Chapel in Windsor. Also in 1938, Corpus Christi Parish in Northern Bay celebrated its 100th Anniversary. On 13 March 1939, Bishop March celebrated his 50th Golden Jubilee and on 12 Jan 1940, Bishop March died at Harbour Grace at age 77. He is buried at Harbour Grace and has a Monument at Northern Bay in his honour.

Statue of Blessed Virgin in front of Harbour Grace Immaculate Conception Cathedral Church.

The statue of the Blessed Virgin in front of the church was presented by the Dalton Council of the Knights of Columbus in 1924 to Bishop John March for the Immaculate Conception Cathedral Church. This was the 15th Anniversary year of the Dalton Council.

5th Bishop at HG

1940-1953

Bishop John M. O'Neill

Bishop John M. O'Neill was consecrated Bishop of Harbour Grace in 7 July 1940 by Most Rev Illdebrando Antoniutti, Apostolic Delegate to Canada and Newfoundland. He began at a time when World War II was just beginning and little did he know he would move to Grand Falls in 1953. In September 1943, St. Joseph's Convent opened in Windsor as home to seven Presentation sisters. They had lived in Grand Falls from 1939 to 1943. In 1944 the Holy Name Society was introduced into Harbour Grace be Msgr. Peddle. On 24 June 1944, Msgr. F. D. McCarthy of Carbonear celebrated the first Diamond Jubilee (60) in Newfoundland History. Msgr. F.D. McCarthy died just 6 days later on 30 June 1944. After the fire in Harbour Grace in 1944, Bishop O'Neill appealed for funds for the Harbour Grace fire victims. In September 1945, the first Presentation Sisters arrive in Bishop Falls. Rev. Hogan built the Convent. In July 1946, St. Joseph's Parish in Gander was started in a converted army barracks with Rev. Philip J. McCarthy as first Parish Priest. On 14 September 1946, the Cornerstone of the Holy Cross School was laid in St. Alban's. The new Immaculate Conception Parish in Colliers was consecrated in 1948 with Rev. Thomas D. O'Neill as first Parish Priest. On 1 April 1949, Newfoundland was formally accepted into the Canadian Federation. In 1949 the Whitbourne Parish was taken over be the Redemporists Fathers. They built the St. Alphonsus Monastery and Church. On 1 Nov 1950, Bishop O'Neill was present in Rome at the historical event of the Definition of the Dogma of the Assumption of the Blessed Virgin Mary. In 1952, St. Pius X Parish in Baie Verte was consecrated. In 1953, St. Joseph's Church and Parish in Gander were officially established. On 31 Jan 1953, Msgr. William P. Finn died at Grand Falls after 41 years as first Parish Priest. On 25 March 1953, Bishop O'Neill consecrated the new Marble Altar in the Cathedral at Harbour Grace (also the Bishop's Sacerdotal Silver Jubilee). On 25 May 1953, Bishop O'Neill of Harbour Grace elevated the Church in Grand Falls to the status of Co-Cathedral, officially the title Harbour Grace-Grand Falls Diocese. On 26 August 1953, five Presentation sisters occupied the new Convent at Buchan's.

Co-Cathedral at Harbour Grace and Grand Falls 1953-1965

5th Bishop at HG & GF
1953-1965
Bishop John M. O'Neill

During the Co-Cathedral era, Bishop O'Neill rotated between Harbour Grace and Grand Falls to governor the Joint Diocese and to make preparations for the ultimate transition from Harbour Grace to Grand Falls. In 1953, Our Lady of Mt. Carmel at Norris Arm was consecrated with Rev. Michael Carey, SFM as first Parish Priest. In June 1955, Bishop O'Neill moved into his New Residence at Grand Falls. Also in 1955, a new Marble altar was put in place at Carbonear as a memorial to Msgr. F. D. McCarthy for his 55 years as Parish Priest. In 1955, Bishop O'Neill erected a new Parish at Badger and appointed Rev. Leonard Kelly as first Parish Priest. On Saturday, 28 Sep 1957, he blessed and officially opened the St. Michael's Regional High School in Grand Falls and on 30 Sep 1957, he blessed and officially opened St. Joseph's School and Convent at Gander. On 7 Nov 1957, the Presentation Sisters arrived at Assumption Parish in Avondale and opened the Assumption School. First Principal was Sr. Gertrude Bishop. On 11 Aug 1958, the new Parish of Sacred Heart was established with Rev. Ronald J. Walsh as first Parish Priest. In June 1959, St. John Apostle Parish in Brent's Cove was consecrated with Rev. Linus Coady as first Parish Priest. Also in 1959 Baie Verte was split into two separate parishes: Baie Verte and La Scie. In 1961 the Sisters of Mercy arrived at Baie Verte to establish a Catholic School system. Also in 1961, two High Schools were opened: St. Claire's in Carbonear under the Presentation Sisters and St. Francis High School at Harbour Grace with the Christian Brothers taking over the teaching under Brother Duffy. On 21 June 1964, the first Mass was said in the new Co-Cathedral in Grand Falls by Msgr. W. P. Hogan. On 30 Oct 1964, the Name of the Diocese was changed to Grand Falls by decree of Sacred Consistorial Congregation Decree executed at Harbour Grace. And it was from 1962-1965 that the Vatican Council II was convened by Pope John XXIII as an Ecumenical Council.

On 23 June 1965 the present Cathedral at Grand Falls was blessed by Cardinal Roy of Quebec. Grand Falls was officially declared the Grand Falls Diocese. The Harbour Grace church reverted to a Parish.

Harbour Grace Diocese to Grand Falls
1965

5th Bishop at GF
1965-1972
Bishop John M. O'Neill

The Diocese was officially declared the Grand Falls Diocese and Bishop O'Neill was permanently residenced at Grand Falls and the Immaculate Conception Church at Grand Falls became the Cathedral Parish of the new Diocese and Harbour Grace reverted back to a Parish. Although the Immaculate Conception Church in Harbour Grace is no longer a Cathedral, it was approved as a Historical building in 1990 and is the Roman Catholic Parish Church for Harbour Grace.

See Chapter 25 – GRAND FALLS DIOCESE for activities after 1965 at Grand Falls.

The Transition back to a Parish at Harbour Grace

When Rev. Joseph M. O'Brien was assigned to Harbour Grace in 1957, he inherited the position of the transitional Parish Priest of the Co-Cathedral Parish in Harbour Grace, with the duty to phase down the Co-Cathedral role of his parish. He began to work to have the Christian Brothers come to Harbour Grace and to prepare for a new St. Francis High school in 1961. The same year he was raised to Monsignor Rank as a Domestic Prelate. When the transfer of the Diocese to Grand Falls in 1965, Monsignor Joseph O'Brien became the Parish Priest without a Diocese and he attempted to uphold the reverence of the Harbour Grace parish to the same stature it was as a Diocese. In 1967 he celebrated his Silver Jubilee. He rebuilt the St. Francis High School in 1974, after it had burned down in 1973. He was active in the Knights of Columbus and renovated the St. Joseph's Church in Riverhead in preparation for the 100th anniversary in 1984 and the celebration of the 200th anniversary of the Catholic Church in Newfoundland. Msgr. Joseph M. O'Brien retired in 1984 after a couple heart attacks and his personal home was completely destroyed by fire in 1985 and he died on 12 Nov 1987 at age 70. He is buried in Harbour Grace. He was a priest for 45 years.

200TH ANNIVERSARY
ROMAN CATHOLIC CHURCH IN NEWFOUNDLAND
1784-1984

THE VISIT OF POPE JOHN PAUL II AND THE 200TH ANNIVERSARY OF BOTH THE ROMAN CATHOLIC CHURCH IN NEWFOUNDLAND AND HARBOUR GRACE PARISH

1784-1984

Pope John Paul II

The central symbol of the 200th Anniversary logo is the cross, recalling that our celebrations are centered on Jesus Christ. The cross is gold, a symbol for Christians of its victory. One arm of the cross is extended, as on the coat-of-arms of Pope John Paul II, as a sign that the cross embraces all persons, and is a call to reconciliation. Superimposed on the cross is the design from the "Fisherman's Ring" worn by the popes as a mark of their office.

This Metal Plaque Is Displayed In The Entry Way Of Immaculate Conception Church In Harbour Grace.

HARBOUR GRACE

Harbour Grace shares with St. John's the distinction of being the oldest continuous Catholic Parish on the island. Records of Irish Priests attempting to serve clandestinely the Catholic population of the district extend back to the 1750s but it was not until the arrival of Fr. Patrick Phelan, an Irish Franciscan, in 1784, that permission was granted to build a Chapel in Conception Bay until after the arrival in 1806 of Fr.Thomas Ewer who was responsible for structures in Carbonear, Bay de Verde, Port de Graves, Harbour Main, Brigus, Cupids and Northern Bay.

200th Anniversary
Emblem
1784-1984

Harbour Grace Parish Celebrates 200th Anniversary – 1984

"Since Harbour Grace was established 15 August 1784, one of the earliest Parishes in Newfoundland and the oldest one outside of St. John's, Harbour Grace celebrated their own 200th Anniversary. The communications Chairman of the Organizing Committee set aside 12-16 August 1984 for their activities. Sunday night 520 youths between the ages of 14 and 19 were bussed into Harbour Grace for a huge youth rally at St. Francis High School. The morning had a more serious side of the rally. They presented workshops on 12 different aspects of life that are concerns of young people, such as friendship, loneliness, relating to one's parents, pre-martial sex, and drugs and alcohol. The keynote address for the workshops was given by Bishop J. Faber MacDonald, the Bishop of Grand Falls. A special Mass began at 5 pm followed by a meal and a dance which began at 6:30 pm and ended at 11:00 pm when a candle light prayer service outside St. Francis School rounded out the rally's activities. The young people returned to their homes the next morning." **NEWS**

Harbour Grace Church An Historical Monument

When the Cathedral Church of the Immaculate Conception at Harbour Grace was approved as a National Monument in 1990, with all its glory and history of the Catholic Church, a Plastic sign in the entrance way of the current church is displayed for visitors.

Emblem for the

Heritage Foundation of Newfoundland and Labrador

The Cathedral of the Immaculate Conception 1892

The third church built on this site, this structure replaced the formal Cathedral which was destroyed in the devastating fire of 1889. The Cathedral is a variant on the French Gothic revival style and may have been designed by Bishop Reginald MacDonald.

1892-1992
100th Anniversary

SECOND CATHEDRAL AND PARISH CHURCH 100TH ANNIVERSARY

In 1992 the current Parish Church celebrated the 100th Anniversary of the Cathedral Church and a plaque is displayed in the front hallway leading into the Church. (1892-1992). This Church was the Diocese Cathedral for 73 years from 1892 to 1965 and has been the Harbour Grace parish church since 1965 and still retains its majestic vision when the dual steeples are viewed from the Town, from the sea or as you approach Harbour Grace from the surrounding areas. This Church was designed by Bishops Dalton and Carfagnini and completed by Bishop Ronald McDonald.

Restoration Of Immaculate Conception Church

The restoration of the Parish Church was begun in 1987 by the Knights of Columbus Dalton Council and was expanded in 1991 under Father Beresford when he first took down the two steeples and began restoring the brickwork on both sides of the front side of the church as well as the back of the Church. The Knights of Columbus have been supervising this repair project and it is still underway. The Church was declared a registered heritage structure by the Heritage Foundation of Newfoundland and Labrador in April 1990. In the Millennium year of 2000, sufficient repair had been made to replace the two steeples to make the Church look like its admirable self seen for years from both the water side and in-town for its twin steeples.

The Dalton Council of the Knights of Columbus must be congratulated for the outstanding work they have done with the fund drives and the constant concern and supervision to complete this work to make the Church restored to its past splendor. Donations are still being solicited.

Sign outside the Immaculate Conception Church in Harbour Grace.

Harbour Grace Church Without Steeples

Picture of Harbour Grace Church with steeples taken down.

The Church steeples on the ground while repairs are being made to the Church's brick foundations on which the steeples are mounted.

Millennium Celebrations For Year 2000

Immaculate Conception Parish in Harbour Grace

RENEWAL PRAYER FOR THE NEW MILLENNIUM

Gracious God and Father, we are your people embraced by your love. We thank you for your presence with us throughout all time. As we celebrate the 2000 years since the birth of Jesus, your Son...Create us anew. Liberate us from all that keeps us from you. Send your Holy Spirit, enabling us to recreate our world and restore justice. Heal us from every form of sin and violence. Transform us to live your word more profoundly. Reconcile us so enemies become friends. Awaken us to the Sacred. Nurture our relationships; enliven our parishes, reunite our families. Fill us with joy to celebrate the fullness of life. Empower us to be a community of love growing always in your likeness by the grace of Christ Our Lord. Amen.

The Two Steeples Were Replaced For The Millennium Celebrations In The Year 2000.

Steeple lifted backing in place for Millennium Year

RISING AGAIN – The first of two twin towers was lifted back in place on the Church of the Immaculate Conception on August 17 2000. The steeples had been sitting on the ground in front of the Harbour Grace RC Church since 1991, while the tower wells were being rebuilt and prepared to bear their 90-tonne weight.
Bill Bowman, COMPASS.

Chapter 6

HISTORY OF CHURCHES IN HG

The history of the Chapels and Churches in Harbour Grace from 1784 has been written about in many papers and pamphlets and there seems to be some divergence of opinion especially about dates of events. To summarize:

1784 - 1799 - Catholic services were performed in a rented store with 10 pews which was leased by the people for first PP, Father Phelan to say Mass.
1800 - 1806 - Same rented store was purchased by the people for 2d PP, Father Fitzpatrick to perform Catholic services.
1806 - 1853 - The first separate wooden Chapel was built by 3rd PP, Father Ewer and carried on by the 4th PP, Father C. Dalton.
1852 -The third Chapel was a stone Church which was begun when evacuation was started in 1848 and the foundation was laid by Rt. Rev. Dr. Mullock in 1852.
1853 - This stone Chapel was opened 29 Oct 1853 and officiated by Bishop Mullock. VRev. Charles Dalton praised.
1856 - When the Diocese was established three years later in 1856 and Rev. John Dalton was consecrated the first Bishop in the same year, he immediately thought about building a Cathedral for the Diocese. From all accounts, he decided to add-on to the new stone church completed in 1853.
1868 - Bishop Dalton dedicated the first Cathedral or fourth Church in Harbour Grace in 1868, one year before he died. He was assisted by Rev. Henry Carfagnini who left as President of St. Bon's in St. John's to come to Harbour Grace to serve as an architectural supervisor but returned to Rome soon thereafter.
1869 - Bishop Dalton began to plan the construction of a Cathedral but died suddenly before much was accomplished on the Cathedral.
1870 - Bishop Carfagnini became Bishop in Rome and returned to Harbour Grace and began a concerted effort to complete the new Cathedral. But he was forced to leave in 1880 before the Cathedral was completed.
1883 - St. Joseph's Church in Riverhead was completed.
1884 -The second Cathedral was completed in July 1884, under Bishop McDonald's Tutelage, with many Prelates visiting Harbour Grace.
1886 - St. Joseph's RC Church was officially dedicated by Bishop McDonald in Riverhead, Harbour Grace on 13 Nov 1886.
1889 - The new Cathedral was completely burned down by fire. 2 September.
1889 - 1890 - Fathers Roe & Walsh sent to USA to solicit funds for the new Cathedral.
1890 - Almost immediately Bishop McDonald began to construct the current Church as the second Cathedral in Harbour Grace and it was completed in 1892.
1892 -The Second Cathedral dedicated by Bishop McDonald. 8 December.
1906 - Original Date of All Hallows Parish, North River.
1912 - Original Date of Immaculate Conception Parish in Grand Falls.
1953 - Grand Falls made Co-Cathedral with Harbour Grace, Bishop O'Neill.
1965 - Harbour Grace Diocese itself was transferred to Grand Falls.
1973 - New St. Anne's Church at Spaniard's Bay.
1984 - 100th Anniversary of St. Joseph's Church, Riverhead. (1884-1984)
1984 - 200th Anniversary of the Catholic Church in Newfoundland (1784-1984)
1992 - Parish celebrates the 100th Anniversary of the current Church. (1892-1992)

Chapter 7

IMMACULATE CONCEPTION CHURCH

Current Church built in 1892 and being restored today.

The Immaculate Conception Parish celebrated the 100th anniversary of the Church in 1992. This Church was the second Cathedral built to replace the first Cathedral that burned in 1889. It has had a glorious history. It was the Harbour Grace Diocese Cathedral for 73 years from 1892 to 1965 when Grand Falls became the Diocese Headquarters. Since 1965 the Immaculate Conception Church has remained the Parish Church of Harbour Grace. Some events were:

1892 - Church Consecrated as second Cathedral by Bishop McDonald. 1893 - Bishop McDonald dedicates new Nun's Chapel over St. Joseph's School. 1893 – Rev. James F. Ryan died HG and buried in Harbour Grace, age 27. 1897 - Sister M. Clare Lovelock buried in Convent Cemetery, age 52. 1899 – Rev. Stephen O'Flynn died Little Bay and buried in Harbour Grace, age 49. 1901 - Sister M. Agnes Banuil buried in Convent Cemetery, age 67. 1904 – Rev. John T. Colbert died in Conche and buried in Harbour Grace, age 31. 1905 – Rev. Thomas E. Lynch died in St. John's and buried in Harbour Grace age 46. 1906 - Bishop McDonald resigned due to ill health age 71. 1906 - Consecration of Bishop March, first native born Bishop at Harbour Grace. 1906 – VRev. George A. Thibault ORDAINED here by Bishop March. 1907 – Rev. James W. Donnelly ORDAINED here by Bishop March. 1909 - First Knights of Columbus Council in Newfoundland began Harbour Grace. 1910 - Sister M. Catherine Flynn buried in Convent Cemetery, age 82. 1910 - Sister M. Teresa King buried in Convent Cemetery, age 69. 1913 - Demented person shot at Bishop March in Church. 1914 - Sister M. DePazzi Lovelock buried in Convent Cemetery, age 72. 1914 - Sister M. Francis Flynn buried in Convent Cemetery, age 82. 1914 – Rev. John F. Kirwan ORDAINED here by Bishop March. 1914 – Rev. John W. Enright ORDAINED here by Bishop March. 1915 - Sister M. John Shortall buried in Convent Cemetery, age 51. 1929 - Sister M. Margaret Northcutt buried in Convent Cemetery, age 38. 1934 - Dalton Council of Knights of Columbus celebrates Silver Jubilee. (1909-1934) 1939 - Bishop March celebrates 50th Jubilee in Harbour Grace. (1889-1939) 1940 - Funeral of Bishop March took place here. Buried in Harbour Grace. 1940 - Bishop O'Neill consecrated Bishop of Harbour Grace. 1942 - Celebration of 50th Anniversary of Church. (1892-1942) 1944 - Holy Name Society organized in Harbour Grace by Msgr. Peddle. 1944 – Rev. Edward J. Shea ORDAINED here by Bishop O'Neill. 1945 – Rev. Ronald J. Walsh ORDAINED here by Bishop O'Neill. 1947 – Rev. William J. Hennebury died in St. John's and buried in Harbour Grace. age 33. 1949 - Sister M. Anna Whelan died here and buried in Convent Cemetery, age 66. 1950 - Holy Year by Pope Pius XII. 1950 - Sister M. Patrick O'Keefe died here and buried in Convent Cemetery, age 72. 1951 - Presentation Sisters celebrate 100th Anniversary at Harbour Grace. (1851-1951) 1952 – Rev. Francis R. Terry died at St. Brendan's and buried in Harbour Grace. age 37. 1953 - Grand Falls made Co-Cathedral with Harbour Grace. 1955 - Bishop O'Neill moves from Harbour Grace to Grand Falls. 1956 - Harbour Grace celebrates 100th Anniversary of Diocese. (1856-1956) 1956 - Mr. Bobbie Connolly writes Book "1956 - Centenary of HG Diocese - 1956". 1956 – VRev. Thomas D. O'Neill, dies in Colliers and buried in Harbour Grace, age 64. 1958 – Rev. Walter P. Walsh dies in St. John's and buried in Harbour Grace, age 45. 1961 - Opening of St. Francis High School by Christian Brothers. 1962 – Msgr. William Hogan Casey died in Conception Harbour and buried in Harbour Grace, age 70. 1965 - Harbour Grace Diocese moved to Grand Falls. 1973 - The HG Presentation Convent closed down after 122 years. 1973 - St. Francis High School burned down and rebuilt. 1974 - Bishop J. M. O'Neill died in St. John's and buried in Harbour Grace, age 70. 1974 – The HG Presentation Convent was torn down. 1980 – Rev. Ronald J. Walsh died at St.

Brendan's and buried in Harbour Grace, age 65. 1984 - St. Joseph's Church in Riverhead celebrates 100th Anniversary. (1884-1984) 1984 - Harbour Grace Parish participates in 200th Anniversary of RC Church in Nfld. (1784) 1987 – Msgr. Joseph O'Brien dies and is buried in Harbour Grace, age 70. 1989 - Bishop F. MacDonald opens new St. Columba elementary school. 1990 - Twin steeples taken down for repairs. 1992 - 100th Anniversary of Immaculate Conception Church. (1892-1992) 1995 - Christian Brothers leave St. Francis High School. 1999 – Msgr. William P. Hogan died in St. John's and buried in Harbour Grace. age 83. 2000 - Celebrated Millennium Year 2000 "Pilgrimage Back to our Roots". 2000 - Two steeples put back up for the Millennium Year celebrations. 2001 - Small electrical Fire in back of Church. Closed until 3 August 2002.

Interior of Cathedral – 1940

The old first wooden altar in the second Cathedral.

New Marble Altar

In the 1950's there seemed to have been a movement to replace the older ornate wooden altars with new modern marble altars. So on 1 July 1952, on the occasion of Bishop John M. O'Neill's Sacerdotal Silver Jubilee, a new marble altar was installed in the Immaculate Conception Cathedral here in Harbour Grace. Just three years later in 1955, they replaced the wonderful wooden altar in Carbonear with a new modern marble altar. Little did they know that after the Vatican Council II in 1965 some churches, like the one's in Spaniard's Bay and Riverhead, Harbour Grace, would have their wonderful older wooden altars removed completely and destroyed and replaced by a table and a cross. Hence we have lost some of our most sacred and magnificent symbols for our adoration in our Lord's house of worship – our altars.

The current Marble Altar.

The Marble altar in the Cathedral of the Immaculate Conception at Harbour Grace.

Plaque On Back Of The Marble Altar.

PRESENTED BY THE
PRIESTS AND PEOPLE OF THE DIOCESE
ON THE OCCASION OF THE
SACRADOTAL SILVER JUBILEE
OF
BMOST REV'D. J. M. O'NEILL, DD
BISHOP OF HARBOUR GRACE
JULY 1ST, 1952.

There are three altars in the Church, The left side brown wooden altar of Mary and Joseph, the main center white marble altar above and on the right side a brown wooden altar to Our Lady of Perpetual Help. There are three smaller type portable altars which may have been part of the first Cathedral but we do not know. One is a small white one and one has a grotto with a statue of Mary.

ST. JOSEPH'S ALTAR **OUR LADY OF PERPETUAL HELP**

Bishop Buried under the Church

Records have indicated that Bishop John Dalton was buried under the altar of the second stone Immaculate Conception Church in 1869. This fact was verified by the Church crews who went under the Church in 1988 and found six caskets stored there. One casket alone believed to be that of Bishop Dalton located in the center under the altar and five other caskets, (located behind a brick wall) two large and three smaller ones - believed to be Mr. and Mrs. William Donnelly and possible three of the children of their son, W. J. S. Donnelly, whose first three children died between 1869 and 1874. All of these caskets are encased in a special smooth plastic-like preservative encasement, apparently for safety from water under the Church.

Mr. William Donnelly was a very important church member and businessman in Harbour Grace, who died in 1864. He may have been buried under the Church in 1864. He had contributed large sums of money to build and furnish the new Cathedral.

OBITUARY
William Donnelly, Esq.

> **"On Sunday morning, March 17, 1864 (St. Patrick's Day-added) there passed away at Harbor Grace, after a very short illness, William Donnelly, a prominent merchant here, at the age of 64 years. Mr. Donnelly was a native of Newfoundland, where he resided throughout, first doing business in Spaniard's Bay, and subsequently for 15 years in Harbor Grace. His career was one of strict integrity, and he left a handsome fortune, the result of a life of steady toil and frugality. His passing was keenly felt by the many who were the objects of his unostentatious and extensive charities, while all classes felt that the death of this worthy man left a marked gap in society – "a gap that cannot be filled at least in the days of his contemporaries." His funeral took place on the following Wednesday from the Cathedral here."**

William Donnelly had a famous and prosperous son, Hon. W. J. S. Donnelly and he had about 8 children, of which four had died at an early age: Maggie, 3 months, 1869; Gertrude, 4 months 1871; Isabelle, 6.9 years 1874, and Alfred, 12 months 1884. W. S .J. Donnelly, himself died in 1914 at age 70. What specific members of the Donnelly family are buried under the Church is unknown.

Two Nuns buried in front of Church

While some people say there are two Nuns buried under the Church that does not seem to be the case. Speaking with the Church crews that went under the Church in 1988 to check the drainage and verify the caskets under there, they did not find any known caskets for nuns. There were also rumors that said there were two Nuns buried along the road in front of the Church leading to Water Street. This does not seem to be a rumor because in the 1889 picture of the burned out Church with the people standing around in front of the Church, you can see a leaning headstone in front of the Church, along the area where the current driveway is located. There is none there today. There could be one or two graves along that road but there are no grave stones visible today or any records of who they may have been.

Restoration History

The restoration of the Church began in 1987 and the Church was approved as a Historical Site in 1990. This permitted Provincial money to be spent for the repair and restoration of the outside of the Church only. The inside is the responsibility of the Parish. The twin steeples were taken down in 1991 in order to redue both concrete uprights that support the steeples. It has taken a long time to replace all the bricks piece by piece as well as repair all the windows, the roof, the back wall of the Church and much of the inside. They are getting help from the bricklaying students at the local trades' school. To coincide with the Millennium Year the two steeples were put into place in 2000. Repairs and restoration of the Church continues unto today. The restoration Program is under the oversight of the Knights of Columbus Council - "Dalton Council of Harbour Grace". Private donations are always welcome. It has always been said that this Church with the two prominent twin-steeples so close to the waterfront, was always a good omen for the boats leaving the Harbour and a glowing beacon for the fishing boats returning to Harbour Grace. That God was looking after the fisherman and that they had made it safely back home again.

Memorial Windows

In the 1980s, the church decided to offer the parishioners the chance to donate to have the name of their loved ones or in memory of a family member painted on the windows in the church, Today there are the following names painted on the six windows on the left side of the church as you enter the church.

1. **In memory of *Msgr. Joseph M. O'Brien*, Pastor of Harbour Grace. 1957-1984. Donated by the Thompson Memorial Committee.***
2. **In loving memory of *Walter Hayes and the Lynch Family.* Donated by Alice (Lala) Hayes, 1989**
3. **In memory of *Frank and Margaret Fleming.* Donated by their children, Margaret, Frank and Marie.**
4. **In Memoriam: My parents, *John and Sarah Connolly and Deceased Members of Family,* Donated by Robert J. Connolly, 1989.**
5. **In loving memory of our Son, *William P. Hearn,* Drowned Nov. 11, 1989. Donated by Mother, Father & 7 Brothers.**
6. **In loving memory of *Martin (Mar), Jerome & Pamela Barton Lee.* Donated by Marie, Robert & Diane Fox.**

*** MSGR. JOSEPH OBRIEN'S NAME ON THE FIRST WINDOW WAS DONATED BY THE THOMPSON MEMORIAL FUND.THIS WAS A TRUST FUND ESTABLISHED BY THE THOMPSON ESTATE TO GRANT A SUM OF MONEY EACH YEAR TO EACH OF THE THREE CHURCHES IN HARBOUR GRACE: THE ROMAN CATHOLIC, THE UNITED CHURCH AND THE ANGLICAN CHURCH.**

The other window-names were donated by the individuals indicated.

It is believed that the windows on the right side of the Church may be offered to donors in the future, those who may want to recognize their loved ones or people who have made significant contributions to the Parish. They probably would be available, "first come – first serve" to any one who would make the required contribution.

IMMACULATE CONCEPTION CHURCH 1890s

Horse and Buggy on Side Road to Church

Immaculate Conception Co-Cathedral, Harbour Grace.
Palace on left side and convent on right side. 1954

The Palace at Harbour Grace

The Priest's house at Harbour Grace would have been built in the late 1700's for the first Priest assigned to Harbour Grace. It generally would have been called a Presbytery or rectory as the house of the Priest. Later when Harbour Grace became a Diocese with a bishop, the home of the bishop was called a Palace. The first old wooden Palace as shown below was probably built in the mid 1800's.

This old Palace was located next to the Church.

THIS BRICK STRUCTURE WHICH REPLACED THE OLD PALACE WAS ITSELF TAKEN DOWN IN 1914.

This was the brick Palace at Harbour Grace until 1914 when the following Palace was built as a stately and outstanding Palace which was felt by many to be one of the best Palaces in Newfoundland.

This magnificent Palace was torn down in 1984 for some reason and a small rectory-type building was built to replace it because the Bishop had moved to Grand Falls.

The Last Palace at Harbour Grace

The Palace next to the Immaculate Conception Church with St. Francis High School in the background.

Today the current rectory of the Parish is shown below. As we mentioned earlier, there is a tendency to tear down the more stately buildings and replacing them with smaller simpler buildings which are not as significant.

Today's Rectory at Harbour Grace

Chapter 8

HISTORICAL MISSIONS OF HARBOUR GRACE DIOCESE

Harbour Grace and Labrador

Original Harbour Grace Mission

When Harbour Grace was initially created as a Mission Church in 1784, it covered the whole Peninsula, from Holyrood to Bay de Verde. The Parish Priests administered to all the Catholics in the area. They began early to erect Chapels throughout their area; King's Cove in 1815, Brigus in 1824, Carbonear in 1826, Harbour Main in 1857, etc. All this was done by the original pioneer priests assigned to Harbour Grace. History tells us that most of Conception Bay to Holyrood was covered by Harbour Grace until chapels were built, parishes were established and priests were assigned to specific local communities and they became parishes unto there own.

Parish Historical Information

Brigus was established as St. Patrick's Parish in 1824 when a chapel was built by the first parish Priest, Very Rev. Dean Denis Mackin. History tells us that they had their first school in 1805 and that Church was celebrated in private homes from 1805 to 1824. In 1906, Bishop March established the Parish of All Hallows, North River. It embraced North River, Bay Roberts and several smaller communities which, until then, had formed a part of the historical parish of Brigus.

Northern Bay was established as Corpus Christi Parish in 1838 by the first parish priest, Fr. Bernard Duffy. Today, missions include Holy Rosary at Western Bay and St. Joseph's at Kingston. Bay de Verde was attended to by Northern Bay from 1838-1880, when the Assumption Parish was established at Bay de Verde by the first Parish Priest, Fr. Gregory Battcock.

Holyrood was served by Harbour Grace from the early 1800's to 1857 when it became a Mission of Harbour Main until 1883 when the Holy Cross Parish at Holyrood was established by the first Parish Priest, Fr. Gregory Battcock.

Harbour Main was established as Sts Peter and Paul Parish in 1857 by the first parish priest, Fr. Kyran Walsh.

Conception Harbour was a Mission of Harbour Main from 1857 until 1884, when on January first, Fr. Patrick O'Donnell the first parish priest established St. Anne's Parish. Its original boundaries were from Middle Arm, exclusive, to the western end of Brigus Barrens, inclusive. In 1948, the parish was divided, when Colliers, hitherto a Mission of Conception Harbour, became its own parish with Fr. Thomas D. O'Neill, the first parish priest. Avondale was a Mission of Harbour Main from 1890 to 1909, when the Assumption Parish was established at Avondale by Fr. Richard Shehan as the first parish priest.

Whitbourne was originally established in 1887 by the first parish priest Fr. Pat W. Browne. In 1909 it became a Mission of Gambo until 1949. In 1949 the Redemporists took over Whitbourne under the first Superior Fr. Gerald Murphy, CssR. They built the St. Alphonsus Monastery and assumed charge of Chapel Arm, Placentia Junction, Bellevue, Heart's Desire, Heart's Content, Turk's Cove and Gooseberry Cove. The parish returned to Diocesan control when the Redemporists left in 1971, and the first Diocesan Priest, Fr. Ronald Bromley, was assigned there.

Bishop Fall's was a Mission of Whitbourne from about 1890 to 1912 when Fr. William Finn was appointed first Parish Priest of Grand Fall's. Although there was a resident priest at Bishop Fall's from 1921-1929; it was still a Curacy of Grand Fall's. In 1930, Fr. Hinchey was the first Parish Priest of Bishop Fall's included Badger, Norris Arm and Botwood.

Windsor Parish of St. Joseph's was established in 1940 and Badger was placed under Windsor until 1955 when Fr. Leonard Kelly was appointed first parish priest at Badger. Botwood and Norris Arm were Missions under Bishop Falls. In 1953, Norris Arm became a separate parish and Bishop Fall's included only Botwood.

Grand Falls Parish began in 1912 with Fr. William Finn as first parish priest. Grand Falls Parish became a Co-Cathedral in 1953. The Diocese of Harbour Grace was moved to Grand Fall's in 1965.

Buchans was a Mission of Grand Falls from 1927-1929, when in 1930, Buchans was elevated to the status of a Parish - St. Theresa's, with Fr. T.D. O'Neill as the first parish priest.

Carbonear had a Chapel built there in 1826 by Fr. Thomas Ewer of Harbour Grace. They received their first resident priest, Fr. Gleeson, in 1842, it became independent from Harbour Grace in the south and no doubt was given responsibility for some of the communities to the east and north of them. In 1889, when Msgr. F.D. McCarthy was appointed to Carbonear, the Parish extended to Kingston on the North shore of Conception Bay and included New Perlican, Heart's Desire and Heart's Content in Trinity Bay. Carbonear gave up Kingston to Northern Bay. Turk's Cove and Heart's Content went to Whitbourne from 1949 to 1971, when the Redemporists took over Whitbourne and they were probably returned to Carbonear in 1971.

Connolly's book, "Centenary of the Diocese of Harbor Grace" states that Bay de Verde was a Mission of Carbonear in 1854 until 1880 when Bay de Verde was established and it included Daniel's Cove and Fr. Joseph Donnelly built the Church in Grate's Cove in 1911. Heart's Delight had a RC Church in 1869. The RC

Church in Heart's Desire was built in the 1870s, and the present Church built in 1956. There was no RC Church in Heart's Content.

The origination dates of other Parishes were: St. Brendan's in 1891 (St. Jacques 1956); Gambo in 1916, Buchans in 1932, Baie Verte in 1952, Gander in 1953; Norris arm in 1953; Brent's Cove 1959, Port Union in 1982 (served from Bonavista 1842-1982).Clarenville in 1990, Fortune Harbour, records date back to 1879 but it was closed in 1953 and administered from Norris Arm.

BELIEVED TO BE AT THE BLESSING OF BAY DE VERDE CHURCH IN 1903.

Front Row: Rt. Rev. John March;(later Bishop), Most Rev. Michael F. Howley and Rt. Rev. Edward F. Walsh. Back Row: Rev. Joseph V. Donnelly (later Msgr.); Rev. William Veitch (later Msgr.); Rev. John J. St. John (later Msgr.); Rev. Felix D. McCarthy (later Msgr.). ***Grand Falls Archives.***

Labrador as a Mission of the Diocese

In 1820 the French Diocese of Quebec gave Labrador to Newfoundland for Bishop Scallan to spiritually administer to the people of Labrador. The new Vicar Apostolic of Newfoundland had a difficult time to send his few priests to Labrador but apparently made periodic visits from St. John's. On the division of the Newfoundland Diocese into two parts in 1856, and the new Harbour Grace Diocese was established, Labrador became the responsibility of the new Harbour Grace Diocese.

Newfoundland Missionaries to Labrador

Fr. John O'Connor, Curate at Harbour Grace, (1852-1856) was the first of the Harbour Grace missionary's to Labrador. When he became Parish Priest at Carbonear, (where Bishop Dalton lived at the time) he volunteered to accompany those engaged in the fishery on that coast to attend to their spiritual needs during the fishing season extending from May to October. This he did for three successive years (1856-1859). His journey each season extended through six degrees of latitude and involved 1400 miles by devious routes. It included the Straits of Belle Isle and about 400 miles along the shore of Labrador. In 1860, when Bishop Dalton left Carbonear to live in Harbour Grace, Fr. O'Connor remained as Parish Priest of Carbonear and did not return to Labrador. There is information that Rev. (later Bishop) Carfagnini spent some time in Labrador. When Bishop Ronald McDonald took over in 1881 he also sent priests to Labrador. While Rev. John March was Parish Priest at Harbour Grace he is credited with tours to Labrador in 1889, 1890, 1891, 1894, 1896, and 1899. (*See his diary in Appendix D*). During these early years, Rev. Richard M. Walker went in 1898, Rev. Dr. Stephen Whelan in 1900, Rev. J. Murphy in 1901, Very Rev. John H. Scully in 1903 and 1905, Rev. John Colbert went with Fr. Scully in 1903, and Rev. John Mackey in 1904. Later when Rev. John March became Bishop and took over the Harbour Grace Diocese in 1906, he answered the call to the Indians to send them regular missionaries from Newfoundland. Rev. James Donnelly, a Carbonear native, then a Curate at Harbour Grace after his ordination, spent his first two summers in Labrador in 1907-1908. Rev. William P. Finn from 1906-1908, Rev. John Kavanagh in 1910, Rev. James J. Walker in 1910, 1912, 1916 and 1917. Rev. Edward O'Brien first visited Labrador while a young curate at Fogo in 1912. Rev. Dr Edward Jones in 1913, Rev. John Kirwan in 1915, VRev. Thomas D. O'Neill in 1918, 1928 and 1929, Rev. William H. Casey in 1919, Rev. Michael F. Dinn in 1920 was selected to open the Mission to the Moniaignals Indians on the north West River. Rev. James A. Hinchey in 1922, Rev. Leslie Fitzgerald in 1923, Rev. William McC Murphy 1924, Rev. Jeremiah Howard in 1925, & 1926, Rev. John M. O'Neill (later Bishop) in 1927, 1933 & 1935, Rev. Joseph Hogan in 1930, Rev Joseph Peddle in 1931, Rev J. Ronald Jones in 1932, Rev. Francis P. Meaney in 1934 & 1936, Rev. Michael Kinsella 1937 & 1942, Rev. Walter P. Walsh 1938 & 1939 and Rev. William J. Hennebury in 1940. After Bishop John M. O'Neill took over in 1940 (since he had gone to Labrador in 1927, 1933 and 1935) he continued the sending of priests to Labrador. Rev. Francis R. Terry 1941, Rev. Leo J. Burke 1943, Rev. Joseph M. O'Brien 1944, Rev. Edward Shea in 1945 and Rev. Edward A. Walsh in

1946. History of Harbour Grace priests is replete with stories of those priests who went to Labrador throughout the years. The most memorable were: Rev. Dr. Stephen J. Whelan, D.D., the first Parish Priest of North River who spent 17 summers (1906-1923) in Labrador and died in Labrador in the summer of 1923 at age 46. He was martyr to an illness accentuated by the terrible ice blockade of that summer. The journey up the coast of the land that a recent writer said, "God gave Cain", was a nightmare. North River must tell the sad story of his lifeless homecoming. They buried him in honor on the hill overlooking the parish which he founded at North River, Newfoundland. In the mid 1920s, Following Father Whelan, the greatest and last extended supporter of the Labrador Missions was Father Edward O'Brien, Parish Priest of Northern Bay (1915-1970), who spent 26 summers (1921-1946) administering to the Indians and Eskimos in Labrador. His first two years were with Father Whelan. In 1927 Msgr. O'Brien founded a new Mission to the Indians of Davis Inlet, thus bringing the Harbour Grace flag of faith farthest north in our Diocese. Following this tremendous period of Labrador support, in 1946, Labrador was made a Vicariate and placed under an Oblate Bishop and Msgr. Edward O'Brien handed the keys of the spiritual Kingdom of Labrador to Bishop Scheffer, OMI, and his Oblates. Incidentally Father "Whitehead" as the Eskimos called Father O'Brien, (because of his white hair) was honored by being made an *honorary* Oblate Priest (OMI) in 1946. Father Edward O'Brien went on to become one of the longest and oldest priests in Canadian history, when he died in 1986 at age 101 and was a priest for 76 years.

Heroic Catholic Services To Fisherman In Labrador

As we see from the above accounts of the Missionary work to Labrador, these Priests were heroic men who traveled in peril and luck to get to the fishing sites along the Labrador coast to provide Catholic services to their parishioners during the summer fishing season. Some trips took 3-4 months and covered some thousands of miles. Harbour Grace's responsibility began in 1856 and lasted until 1946, some 90 years. We had the great excitement of finding the Diary of Rev. John March beginning in 1889 on his trips to Labrador and continues on with Bishop O'Neill until 1972 and we have reproduced this diary in **Appendix D.**

The later summers were also taken up by providing Catholic services to the local Labradoreans themselves. Msgr. Edward O'Brien also set up Churches and coordinated educational and personal services during his long 26 years of summer support. (1921-1946) He was the Parish Priest at Northern Bay.

The Oblates Take Over Administration Of Labrador

On 26 March 1946, Rev. Lionel Scheffer, OMI, was notified that Pope Pius XII had named him the first Apostolic Vicar of Labrador. He was consecrated Bishop on 29 April 1946 in Ottawa and Lourdes-de-Blanc-Sablon, Labrador, became the Episcopal See of the new Apostolic Vicariate created by Rome with Bishop Lionel Scheffer, OMI, as First resident Bishop. This was later renamed Schefferville in his honour. He died in October 1966.

The Knights of Columbus "Dr. Whelan Council 5662 was chartered in Labrador in 1945?." This Meeting Hall was named "The O'Brien Hall" in honour of Msgr. Edward O'Brien and the Council was named in honour of Rev. Stephen Whelan. Both of whom gave many years of their lives to the welfare of the people of Labrador.

Monsignor Edward O'Brien and the indigenous people of Labrador where he administered for 26 plus years.

Chapter 9

ST. JOSEPH'S CATHOLIC CHURCH

Riverhead, Harbour Grace

Riverhead, Harbour Grace lies between the Town of Harbour Grace and Harbour Grace South. Settlement probably dates from the early eighteen century as the nearby town began to flourish. Early settlers were the Delaney, Jordan, McCarthy, Mackey, Russell, Ryan and Shanahan families. Since most were of Irish decent, it became primarily a Roman Catholic community. Later they were joined by the Galway's from Upper Island Cove, the Merchant William Guilefoyle and a Collins family in the 1830s. Most of the residents took part in the seal and Labrador fisheries supplied by Harbour Grace merchants.

THE PRESENT CHURCH

St. Joseph's Catholic Church, Riverhead, Harbour Grace

According to some accounts St. Joseph's Church in Riverhead was a new Church in 1883 but was not officially dedicated until 13 Nov 1886, by Bishop Ronald McDonald. This Church became a mission of Immaculate Conception Parish of Harbour Grace. St. Joseph's Church at "the River" featured a bell donated by the family of Riverhead merchant Peter Dwyer in 1886 and it has served the Roman Catholic population of Harbour Grace South, the Thicket, Otterbury and the Gullies as well as Riverhead.

Records were found that indicate there was money being donated for the Riverhead, Harbour Grace Church during the time of Bishop Dalton (1856-1869). Since the First Bishop died intestate, without a will, in the probate of his estate, there were records indicating funds had been collected for a Riverhead church. Other information seems to indicate that there may have been a small Church here before 1883. In the Affray, they mention a new church in 1883.

THE OLD CHURCH AND SCHOOL

St. Joseph's Church and school at Riverhead, Harbour Grace
Picture is courtesy of Shirley Reynolds

This marvelous and attractive Church and companion School of old seemed to have been sacrificed for the newer simpler Church. The school was replaced by a two story building which later was cut down to one story, which is the building that exists today. History seems to have shown that many of the classical historical buildings which had character and dignity were replaced with ordinary simple buildings without as much class. This seems to be the case here in Riverhead.

Even the old altar which was replaced in the 1990's was a very dignified and prominent altar. This picture of the wedding of Reginald Coombs and Dorothy Russell on 7 July 1953, with attendants, Mary Glavine and Richard Coombs, shows the wonderful old church altar.

St. Joseph's altar in Riverhead during wedding in 1953.

The Vatican Council II in the 1970s decreed that the old wonderful altars that the people paid for would be replaced by a Table and a Cross. This is St. Joseph's Church in Riverhead as it looks today. Courtesy of Peggy Whalen.

The transition of St. Joseph's Church in Riverhead.

The Riverhead community first appeared in the Census as separate from Harbour Grace in 1901. During Bishop March's tenure (1906-1940) he enlarged and renovated the Church at Riverhead and he also erected a new Roman Catholic school and a new two story Hall in 1929 at Riverhead. The St. Joseph's Hall was used by the parishioners for card parties, bingos, weddings, dances, and St. Joseph Feast day celebrations. The Parish Committee had the Hall cut down to a single story in 1992. In 1991 the old tower was replaced by a new one and the stained glass windows were replaced by new black windows under Msgr. Joseph O'Brien and the Altar was replaced in St. Joseph's Church. The Church was repainted and a new carpet was installed from the altar down the middle isle. This renovation was done in preparation for the two anniversaries coming up in 1984. In 1984, then Parish Priest Msgr. Joseph O'Brien and Bishop Faber MacDonald celebrated the 100th Anniversary of St. Joseph's Church. The parishioners had a wonderful celebration and reception following Mass. It was celebrated in 1984, even though it was completed in 1883 and dedicated in 1886. But the 1984 date did coincide with the anniversary celebrations throughout Newfoundland commemorating 200 years of the Catholic Church in Newfoundland. (1784-1984) and Pope John Paul II visit to Newfoundland.

On 18 March 1984, on the Feast of St. Joseph, Bishop Faber MacDonald officiated at the 100th Anniversary of the Church of St. Joseph Church at Riverhead of Harbour Grace.

THE PEOPLE OF RIVERHEAD

Centennial Celebrations

of the

Church of St. Joseph
Riverhead

on the

Feast of St. Joseph

March 18th 1984 - 7:30 pm

Presiding:
Most Rev W.C.MacDonald DD
Bishop of Grand Falls
1884-1984

Written Inside

This 100-year old wooden building is our Church.
Although touched by time, elements and constant use,
it is much more than a building.
Our Church is a symbol- even a sacrament -
of a living faith reflected in the
hearts and lives of its people, both past and present.
Today you enrich not only this building with your presence, but
more importantly the lives of each of us here.
You are most truly welcome!

The People of Riverhead
Copy of Anniversary Programme

Ignatius Fahey sitting on horse with baby John Peddle attended by Michael A. Fahey, 1966, behind St. Joseph's Church and Parish Hall.

Bishop J. M. O'Neill talking to Cornelius McCarthy, old School Master on Confirmation Day in 1961 in St. Joseph's Church yard in Riverhead, HG. Lady on far right with shadow in Katie Callahan.

Roman Catholic School In Riverhead in 1846

Roman Catholic School Board records show a school in Riverhead in 1846. The School Master was Mr. Lovat.

> ***Riverhead (RC Board) A large and neat looking School house is built at the head of the deep bay which forms the Harbour of Harbor Grace; though a commodious building, it has no stove, and the Master prefers keeping the School in his own dwelling in the winter. The day in which I visited this school (Feb 9) being very stormy, with a great fall of snow, only half the children were present, the total number being 54 and 25 being assembled. The Master, Mr. Lovat, appears competent to the charge of a School of this humble class.***
>
> **Report on schools by Mr. Bertram Jones 1846**

"In the Riverhead School in 1870, Michael Scully was teacher, with 108 boys and a salary of 50 pounds plus 4 pounds fees. At Feather Point, Michael Kelly was teacher, with 28 boys and girls and a salary of 25 pounds plus 5 shillings in fees."

"In 1884, there were two schools in Riverhead. A boys school registered 57 boys instructed by Hugh Kilfoy and a girls school with 39 students taught by Mrs. Stapleton as teacher." **ENL, V2**

An interview was conducted with Annie Doran

by Peggy Whelan

"Annie Doran attended St. Joseph's School in Riverhead, Harbour Grace years ago.(1940s) She remembers these teachers: Master Cornelius McCarthy, Ms. Angela Hickey, Mrs. Alice (Shannahan) Fahey, Ms. Belle Hearn, Ms. Eileen Kelly, Mrs. Marg (Kelly) Reynolds, Ms. Bridget Flynn, Sister Noel, Sister Perpetua and Sister Sylvia Hickey (her father was Captain on the William Carson, he died aboard the ship of a heart attack.) The school began with three classrooms and later opened up seven classrooms. The school was always painted green and white. There was always a Christmas Tree and people took 4-5 whole days preparing for the event. We made fudge for Christmas on the old stove and put it out in the snow to cool it off and hoped no one stole the fudge. Master McCarthy lived next door to the old school. He taught in Upper Island Cove, the Daltonian Club and at St. Joseph's. Boy was he strict and he was moody. He had two suits. If he wore a gray suit of clothes, we knew we were in for a hard day. If he wore a navy blue suit we knew we were in for a good day. He was very quick with that old pointer. He would crack your knuckles if you didn't know your lesson. He would keep you after school until you learned your lesson. If you didn't learn it, it was your own fault. He wanted you to learn and that was it. I remember the Coca Malt days. Every year we celebrated the Tenniberry. Seven or eight priests always attended. Every day for a full week during lent we left Riverhead at 6:30 am and walked to the Cathedral in Harbour Grace and back again until Easter Sunday. We walked twice on Good Friday. There were no cars then like now, a horse and cart if you were lucky. There was no saying you weren't going, you had to go and that was it. Today we don't go to the length of themselves. Sad." *Peggy Fahey., 10 August 2002.*

Roman Catholic School in Otterbury

There was also a Roman Catholic School in Otterbury, just down on Water Street a few blocks towards Harbour Grace from the Riverhead road. This school was old and the ENL lists this school in 1884 with 45 registered student. It apparently was used until the 1960's when it was closed. It has been taken over and recently remodeled by the Harbour Grace Historical Society under the direction of Gorde Pike.

The old Otterbury School as an Historical relic.

There are three Otterbury's in Conception Bay, one at Harbour Grace, one at Clarke's Beach and one located northeast of Carbonear. This term refers to an abandoned fishing community and all three share some geographic features, being located on steep slopes above shores with little shelter. Seary suggests all three may have been named for Ottery St. Mary's, Dorset or that the name may be a corruption of "otter-burrow".
In the 1871 Lovell Directory the only Otterbury listed is a small fishing settlement, 4 miles from Carbonear with 11 people listed. Mail weekly. Population 75.

Harbour Grace Affray

26 December 1883

It was in Riverhead in 1883 where the Harbour Grace Affray took place. When the word came out that the Protestant Orangemen wanted to march past the new Catholic Church in Riverhead under threats of damaging this new church, the Irish went to Pippy Lane to met the Orangemen and divert their march down to Water Street. This is where a conflagration took place between the two parties. The first to be killed was Jimmy Callahan, an Irishman, who was on a white horse with a green flag. He was shot and killed. Then the riot began and five people were killed and 17 injured. All the Riverhead prisoners were acquitted but this sectarian violence has lingered as a bad chapter in Harbour Grace History. The Orangemen never tried to march down to Riverhead again.

SCENE OF THE HARBOR GRACE TRAGEDY

This was an artist's depiction of the Tragedy, as he called it. This took place on St. Stephen's Day, December 26, 1883. Both conflicting sides are shown separated by the police or military troops along the railroad tracks. The Artist is not known.

HIS MAJESTY'S SHIP TENEDOS

Crew of the HMS Tenedos at Harbour Grace, winter 1883-1884.
To help keep law and order after Affray 1883.

IMMEDIATE DEATHS:

Jimmy Callahan, RC	**South Side**	**Shot through the head.**
William French, LOA	**Courage's Beach**	**Wounds on back of head.**
William Janes, LOA	**Carbonear**	**Shot twice.**

FATALLY WOUNDED:

John Bray, Not in procession.	**Courage's Beach**	**Fracture of scull.**
Thomas Nicholas, LOA	**Otterbury**	**8 shots in back & side.**

17 WOUNDED.

Those accused of the crimes were jailed in St. John's until the trial. Some remained the whole time and others were released in less time. They were all released when the court acquitted all of the accused. Outside the court in St. John's there were members of both sides threatening action if either side lost. It is felt that this intimidation may have had an influence on the acquittals.

THE PEOPLE OF RIVERHEAD, HARBOUR GRACE

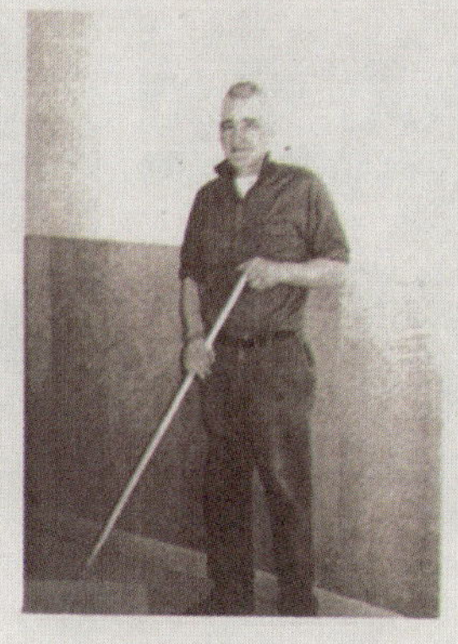

The People of Riverhead

Chapter 10

SPANIARD'S BAY AND UPPER ISLAND COVE

Both Spaniard's Bay and Upper Island Cove are satellite Parishes of Harbour Grace. Spaniard's Bay has had an illustrative history and dates back to the early 1800's. Upper Island Cove has a shorter history and a very small token church in comparison. The Parish Priest at Harbour Grace is responsible for the Masses and Services at both Spaniard's Bay and Upper Island Cove.

Spaniard's Bay

Spaniard's Bay appeared to have been frequented by Basque and Portuguese fishermen (referred to as Spaniard's by English fishermen) in the 1500s and 1600s. In 1610, John Guy noted a path leading from Spaniard's Bay to Trinity Bay, suggesting at least seasonal occupation of the area. Initial settlement of Spaniard's Bay was concentrated at Mint Cove and Northern Cove. By 1805, when the population was estimated to have been about 400, 38 families were occupying 36 registered properties in Spaniard's Bay. Family names included Peddle, Kelly, Neil, Besom, Brown, Foster, Phelan, Seymour, Vokey, Butt, Braggs, Baker and Menchion. Most early settlers were of Dorset origin, while Irish immigration in the area increased after 1798. From 1820 to about 1860, Spaniard's Bay builders supplied vessels for the seal hunt and the Labrador fishery. But after William Donnelly of Mint Cove, a renowned ship builder, moved to Harbour Grace in 1857 shipbuilding went into a decline.

The first School opened in Spaniard's Bay in 1829. In 1839, the first Roman Catholic school was opened in Spaniard's Bay with 44 children in attendance. It was in 1843 that a new Roman Catholic School Board built a Roman Catholic school on Chapel Hill in Mint Cove, Spaniard's Bay with 16 male and 9 female students in attendance. The School served as a place of Roman Catholic worship until the Church was built. The first Roman Catholic Chapel was completed in Mint Cove, on Chapel Hill in Spaniard's Bay in 1844 and accommodating some 30 people. The Chapel and School were financed by William Donnelly, a merchant born in Harbour Grace in 1797 and died March 17, 1846.

OLD ST. ANNE'S CHURCH & SCHOOL - CIRCA 1920's

The old Church on the left and the old small school on the right. Note the small shed on the left side corner of the fence. This was used to house the Priest's horse and buggy or sleigh in the winter time when he came to say Mass. Although there are light poles in the area, the Church did not have electric lights.

This was the first St. Anne's Church in Spaniard's Bay before it was torn down in 1973. Last Mass was said by Msgr Joseph O'Brien on 26 Dec 1973.

LAST MASS IN OLD CHURCH

Msgr Joseph O'Brien saying last Mass at old St. Anne's.

This old Church had an upper balcony on both sides and around the back of the Church. Each of the side balconies were separate for boys or girls and the organ was in the back center portion of the balcony. This Church was torn down after this Mass and the altar and a large picture was taken out (we understand in pieces) and sent to Immaculate Conception Parish in Harbour Grace. Again we have the loss of a beautiful ornate altar being replaced by a table and a cross hanging on a curtain. It seems by desecrating a wonderful altar; we have also lost an important sacred part of our Catholic heritage.

The new current Church was authorized by the Bishop and building began immediately and the Parish committee organized the building by hiring a foreman and a crew of workers. They completed the new Church by the fall of 1974. Msgr Joseph O'Brien oversaw the building. Bishop O'Neill donated $3000.00 and it is estimated the total cost was $200,000. The balance of the money was collected by the parishioners. Bishop Penney gave the official Blessing of the new Church in September 1974. Later, the altar of this church was taken out and destroyed and a table and across hanging from a curtain was substituted as it is today.

Some History On Spaniard's Bay

In the 1871 Lovell Directory for Newfoundland, there are two Spaniards' Bay listed, one at Harbour Grace and one at Trinity. The Harbour Grace Spaniards' Bay was a large fishing settlement on the bay of the same name, north side of Conception Bay in the District of Harbour Grace. Most of the population spend the summer on the Labrador, prosecuting the cod fishery. Spaniards' Bay is almost surrounded by high hills and the view of Conception Bay from some of them is beautiful in the extreme. Point after point is seen stretching out into the waters of the bay, on several of which pretty churches stand out prominently. Altogether, some of the prettiest views of Conception Bay may be had from this neighborhood. It is six miles from Harbour Grace. Mail weekly. Population 1182. In the Encyclopedia Nfld-Labrador, the Spaniards' Bay at Trinity is listed as Spaniard's Cove and is listed as an abandoned fishing community in Trinity Bay. It was Spaniards' Bay up until the 1900s.

THE CURRENT ST. ANNE'S CHURCH IN SPANIARD'S BAY

This current St. Anne's Church (in old Mint Cove) is located on Broad Cove Road South in Spaniard's Bay. A school, on the right in front of the Church, was built in 1942 and was closed in the 1960's when the Catholic Schools (Sr. Columba and St. Francis) were opened in Harbour Grace. There are two cemetery areas within the St. Anne's Parish, one behind and on the right side the Church (East); and the second along the left side the old School house (West). The following names were found in a cemetery survey conducted in 1999.

EAST CEMETERY

BRAZIL, Thomas, died RR 28 Nov 1899, age 24.	MERCER, John W. 1926-1995, age 68.
BRAZIL, James, died 2 Dec 1846, age 50.	MERCER, Susie, wife 1932-----.
BRAZIL, Leo Francis, 1920-1991.	MERCER, Bernard 1906-1996.
BRAZIL, Josephine, wife 1931.	MERCER, Mary Fitzgerald, 1901-1998.
BRAZIL, Walter F. 1924-1992. Wife Margaret.	MERCER, Jeremiah, 1901-1975.
BRAZIL, James, 1919-1986, age 67.	MURPHY, William O. 1935-1980.
BRAZIL, Vincent, 1914-1972.	PEDDLE, Joseph, 1924-1996 and wife Susanna 1914----.
BYRNE, Helen Marie, died, 1968, age 5, 10 months.	PEDDLE, Capt Gregory, died sea, 15 Oct 1989, age 45.
CALLAHAN, Michael E. 1937-1987.	PEDDLE, Bernard, died 21 Jan 1966, age 51.
COOMBS, William J. 1917-1986 and wife Emma 1920-----.	PEDDLE, Kathleen, died 5 Nov 1984, age 57.
COOMBS, John F. 1923-1993 and wife Sadie 1927-----.	ROSE, Martin, died 28 Sept 1984, age 66.
COOMBS, James W. 1915-1988.	RYAN, Paula, 1967-1967.
COOMBS, Richard P. 1887-1967.	SULLIVAN, William J. 1920-1998 and wife Mary 1919-----.
COOMBS, Annie M. 1887-1974.	THOMPSON, James, died 25 Apr 1849, age 58.
DAWSON, Mabel, died 21 March 1856, age 51.	THOMPSON, Catherine, died 15 Feb 1882, age 94.
DELANEY, John M. 1894-1983. Merchant Navy.	WHALEN, Ronald, died 6 Aug 1968, age 55.
DWYER, Patrick, Elizabeth & William.	WHALEN, Thomas J. 1944-1997.
FITZGERALD, Michael Joseph, 1903-1967.	WHALEN, Krista E. 1991-1991.
FITZGERALD, Annie, 1916-1991.	WHALEN, Reginald, 1964-1994.
FITZGERALD, Jack, died 13 May 1995.	WHALEN, Peter, died, 1970, age 64.
GUSHUE, Paul J. `1956-1996.	WHALEN, Veronica, died 1977, age 63.
GUSHUE, James J. 1923-1986.	WHALEN, William L. 1915-1995, age 79.
HUTCHINGS, Catherine C. 1931-1974.	WHELAN, Rodney, 1972-1973.
MERCER, Lavinia, died, 20 Nov 1997, age 86.	YOUNG, P. Thomas, 1903-1992.
MERCER, Lawrence J. 1922-1977.	YOUNG, Mary A. 1914-1991.
MERCER, Mary F. 1922-1991.	

WEST CEMETERY

ADEY, Mary Theresa, d. 1943, age 3 months (With Kent's)
BABB, Joseph, d. 1905, age 48.
BRAZIL, Thomas Joseph, 1880-1953, age 73. and wife:
BRAZIL, Elizabeth .B.1884-1959, age 75.
BRAZIL, William, 1888-1958, age 70, and wife:
BRAZIL, Ellen, 1892-1956, age 64.
BRAZIL, Margaret 1897-1985, age 88 and husband:
BRAZIL, John 1890-1966, age 76.
BRAZIL, Michael, d. 1953, age 69.
BRAZIL, Matt, d. 1958, age 63. RNRegt WWI. DCM
BRAZIL, Joseph F. 1884-1938, age 54, and wife:
BRAZIL, Mary, 1894-1990, age 96.
BRAZIL, John, d. 1922, age 44.
BRAZIL, Mary J. d. 1925, age 43. Wife of Daniel.
BYRNE, William P. 1899-1962, age 63. (wife Amelia b. 1908)
BRYNE, Raymond, 1938-1948, age 10.
BRYNE, Loretta, 1940-1940.
BYRNE, Bernard, d. 1927, age 94.
BYRNE, Mary, d. 1927, age 96. Son Henry.
CAIN, John William, son Thos/Mary, d.1950, Age 27.
CAIN, Thomas J., d. 1954, age 68.
CAIN, Mary, widow late Thomas, 1888-1973.
CAIN, Norma. (Illegible)
CAIN, Joseph, d. 1911, age 58. (son Thomas)
CALLAHAN, James J. 1902-1971, age 69 and wife:
CALLAHAN, Annie, 1909-1997, 89.
CALLAHAN, James J. 1902-1971, same.
CLAVINE, Mary, d. 1907, age 5 months.
CLEARY, Michael John, d. 1906, age 68.
COOMBS, Margaret, 1921-1939, age 18,
COOMBS, Kenneth, 1924-1942, age 18.
COOMBS, Mary, 1918-1982, age 64 all three children of Richard and Annie Coombs.
COOMBS, Henry, 1890-1964, age 74. Hus: Susanna.
COOMBS, Mary, d. 1936, age 20. and
COOMBS, James, d. 1937, age 4 and
COOMBS, Thomas, d. 1948, age 26. Children of: Henry and Susie Coombs.
COOMBS, Ronald F. 1927-1998, age 71.
COOMBS, Mary, child, d. 1907, age 10. Dau; Henry/Emma.
COOMBS, Emma, d. 1934, age 73.
COOMBS, Henry, d. 1938, age 81.
COOMBS, Mona, 1932-1937, age 5, dau: Richard/Annie.
COSTELLO, Matthew, d. 1940, age 85. and wife
COSTELLO, Johanna, d. 1944, age 82.
DELANEY, William 1858-1936, age 78 and
DELANEY, Johanna, 1858-1935, age 77 and
DELANEY, Cornelius, 1897-1966, age 69.
DWYER, Patrick, d. 1910, age 54, hus: Mary Ann Dwyer.
FAHEY, Edward, 1933. Baby.
FINN, Mary, d. 1941, age 39. Wife of Richard.
FINN, Richard, d. 1952, Placentia.
FINN, Elizabeth, d. 1941, age 83.
FINN, Richard, d. 1903, age 40. (sons James & Richard)
FINN, Francis, d. 1907, age 45.
FINN, John, d. 1903, age 38.
FINN, Edward, d. 1937, age 78.
FINN, Sarah, d. 1924, age 62. wife Edward.
FINN, Thomas, 1857-1946.
FITZGERALD, Agnes, 1923-1988; Josephine 1920-1968 and Terry 1957-1958, 2 mos.
FITZGERALD, John 1917-1996, age 79.
FITZGERALD, David d. 1978, age 64. NF Forestry WW2
FITZGERALD, Thomas P. d. 1956, age 54.
FITZGERALD, John Joseph d. 1956, age 58.
FITZGERALD, Jeremiah, d. 1935, age 68 and wife
FITZGERALD, Bridget, d. 1934, age 70.
FLEMING, Mary Ann, 1880-1958, age 78.
FLYNN, William, 1903-1992, age 89. and wife
FLYNN, Alice, 1902-1989, age 87.
GALWAY, John W.son of James/Catherine, d.1948, age 22.
GALWAY, Theresa, dau of James/Catherine, d 1948, age 32.
GODSELL, Edward Jos 1885-1955, age 70 and wife:
GODSELL, Roseann, 1880-1956, age 76.
GODSELL, John, d. 1921, age 34. Also Alice Godsell.
KENT, James, d. 1939, age 74.
KENT, Margaret, d. 1961, age 93. and
KENT, Mark, d. 1906, age 7 months and
MERCER, Madeline, 1924-1982. age 58.
MOORE, Mary A. RIP.
PEDDLE, Regina, d. 1974-, age 20.
PEDDLE, Cecil Ronald, d. 1962- age 24.
PEDDLE, Lawrence, d. 1972, age 59.
PEDDLE, James and Bridget.
PEDDLE, John W. baby, d. 1912, age 6 months.
PEDDLE, Joseph, d. 1948, age 63.
PEDDLE, Elizabeth, d. 1968, age 78. Wife of Joseph.
PEDDLE, Desmond, d. 1975, baby. Son of Desmond/Mary.
PORTER, James, d. 1947, age 18
ROSE, Martin, d. 1955, age 72 and wife:
ROSE, Bridget, d. 1926, age 39.
RYAN, Matthew, d. 1971, age 91.and wife:
RYAN, Annie, d. 1915, age 35.
RYAN, Edward and Ellen and children: Thomas, John and Mary Finn.
RYAN, John, d. 1921, age 22.
RYAN, James, d. 1921, age 71.
RYAN, John and Bridget, RIP.
RYAN, Matthew, d. 1907, age 33. and son:
RYAN, John Thomas, d. 1901, age 10 months.
SN…., Thomas, d. 1985, age 25.
THOMPSON, Catherine, d. 1909, age 77.
WHALEN, John J. 1899-1965, age 66
WHELAN, Elizabeth, 1874-1957, 83.
WHELAN, Bernard Francis, 1969-1972, age 3.
WHELAN, Margaret, d. 1930, age 93.
YOUNG, Frances, d. 1931, age 52. (son Thomas)

SPANIARD'S BAY CEMETERY

Courtesy of Gerald Brazil

Upper Island Cove

Upper Island Cove is a fishing community situated in a rocky bight north of Spaniard's Bay and a sheltered beach south of Bryant's Cove. Known as Upper Island Cove since the mid-nineteenth century. Before 1800 the King, Drover, Pynn, Mercer, Hibbs, Smith, Bishop and Lilly families were in Upper Island Cove, while the Byrne, Dobbin, Lynch, and Sharpe families were living at nearby Spoon Cove, part of Upper Island Cove since 1965. In the 1871 Lovell Directory, there were two Island Cove's; one in Harbour Grace and one in Bay de Verde. To avoid confusion, Island Cove, HG became Upper Island Cove and Island Cove, BDV became Lower Island Cove.

Island Cove at Harbour Grace in 1871 was listed as a large fishing settlement in the District of Harbour grace. Distant from Harbour Grace 9 miles by road. Mail weekly. Population 979.

SACRED HEART CHURCH

Sacred Heart Church in Upper Island Cove.

There is evidence that Catholic Services may have been conducted in St. Peter's Anglican Church in Upper Island Cove before they had a Roman Catholic Church here. The encyclopedia says there was a Roman Catholic School opened up in Upper Island Cove in 1842. We were told that there was a Roman Catholic School here on the beach which was moved to the above current location some time back and it was also used for church services.

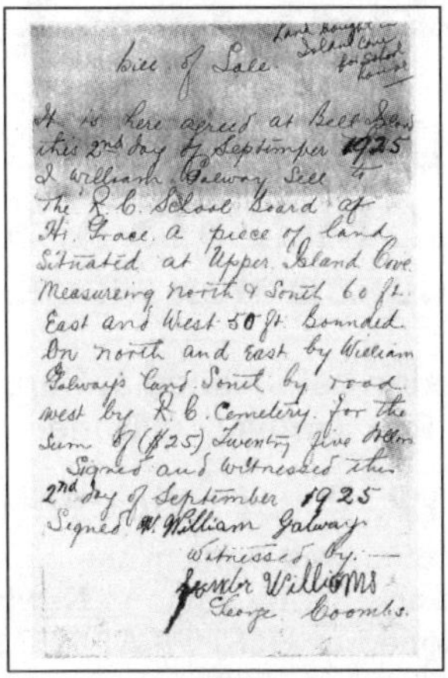

Bill of Sale

It is here agreed at Bell Island
this 2nd day of September 1925
I William Galway sell to
The R.C. School Board of
Hr. Grace a piece of land
Situated at Upper Island Cove
Measuring North & South 60 ft
East and West 50 ft Bounded
On north and east by William
Galway's land South by road
west by R.C. Cemetery for the
sum of ($25) Twenty five dollars
Signed and witnessed this
2nd day of September 1925
Signed W. William Galway
Witnessed by:—
Leander Williams
George Coombs.

Bill of Sale

The above Bill of Sale is for the land which the school (currently the Church) was built and indicates the following:

Bill of Sale

"It is here agreed at Bell Island this 2nd day of September 1925. I, William Galway sell to the R.C. School Board of Hr. Grace. A piece of land Situated at Upper Island Cove. Measuring North and South 60 ft. East and West 50 ft. Bounded on North and East by William Galway's land. South by road. West by R.C. Cemetery for the sum of ($25) Twenty five dollars. Signed and witnessed this 2nd day of September 1925. Signed William Galway. Witnessed by – Leander Williams and George Coombs."

Since Both Spaniard's Bay and Upper Island Cove are Missions of Harbour Grace, in the 1970s, Msgr Joseph O'Brien, Parish Priest in Harbour Grace, closed the small Catholic School and it was used exclusively as a Catholic Chapel. This small Sacred Heart Roman Catholic Church in Upper Island Cove (UIC) was used for Sunday Masses all year around by Msgr. Joseph O'Brien but today, Masses are only said during the summer months. The Catholics in UIC attend St. Anne's in Spaniard's Bay during the other months of the year. There is a small Catholic cemetery in Upper Island Cove next to the small Church and the following names were found in the burial records from 1902 to date: The cemetery is located on the left of the Church behind the fence.

Coombs, Dobbin, Ford/Forde, Galway, Garland, Mahoney, McCarthy, Mercer, Mugford, Murphy, Neil, Young.

Chapter 11

CHRONOLOGICAL
LIST OF ALL PRIESTS ASSIGNED TO
THE IMMACULATE CONCEPTION PARISH, HARBOUR GRACE

1784- First Mission established at Harbour Grace by Rev James L. O'Donel

1784-1799 - 1st PP. Rev. Patrick Phelan, 15 YEARS

Father Patrick Phelan ofm, was born in the 1750s in *Kilkenny,* Ireland and ordained about 1783 at about age 30. He came to Newfoundland with Rev James L. O'Donel in 1784 and was assigned as FIRST PP AT THE HARBOUR GRACE MISSION for 15 years until his untimely death in 1799 at about age 45. When the people heard Fr Phelan was coming, they rented a store and put 10 pews in it for the first Store-Chapel of Harbour Grace. He signed the letter of petition to raise Rev. O'Donel to Bishop in 1794. While on the rounds of his extended mission, he drowned off Grate's Cove in 1799. See further information on *First Priest to Die in Line of Duty in Newfoundland.*

1800-1806 - 2nd PP. Rev. Ambrose Fitzpatrick, 6 YEARS

Father Ambrose Fitzpatrick was born in *Ireland* and came to Newfoundland and was assigned as 2D PP, HARBOUR GRACE in 1800 on the death of Father Phelan in 1799 and remained 6 years until 1806, when he exchanged with Fr. Ewer for Ferryland. The Store-chapel and the land was purchased by the parishioners and used by Fr. Fitzpatrick during his time at Harbour Grace. He remained in Ferryland for 9 years until 1815. He apparently left Newfoundland for PEI and later went onto Boston.

1806-1833 - 3rd PP. Very Rev. Thomas A. Ewer, 27 YEARS

Father Thomas Ewer ofm, was born in Dublin, *Ireland* in 1749 and ordained in Rome on 19 Jun 1776 at age 27. In 1788 he arrived in Newfoundland and assigned as First Parish Priest of Ferryland by VRev. Dr. O'Donel for 18 years from 1788-1806. He celebrated his 25th Jubilee in 1801. In 1806 he was assigned as 3RD PP, HARBOUR GRACE, which he exchanged with Rev. Ambrose Fitzpatrick who went to Ferryland. During his 27 years a in Harbour Grace he built the First wooden Chapel in 1806; he began the First recorded records in the Mission in 1806; he established the BIS in HG in 1814; he was the First Priest to celebrate his 50th Jubilee in Newfoundland in 1826 (1776-1826); he built Chapels in Brigus in 1824 and in Carbonear in 1826. Father Ewer died on 6 Feb 1833 at age 87. He was a Priest for 57 years. He was in Newfoundland for 45 years. He had the distinction of being Vicar General to the first three Vicar Apostolic's – Rev. James O'Donel; Rev. Patrick Lambert and Rev. Thomas Scallan. He had six curates: Rev. Dean Mackin (1818-1824) to Brigus; Rev. Nicholas Devereux (1819-1830); Rev. Marcus Cronin (1818-1822); Rev. William Hearn (1817-1818); Rev. Nicholas Herron (1830-1831) to Ireland and Rev. Michael Berney (1831-1833) to Burin.

1833-1859 - Very Rev. Charles Dalton, 26 YEARS

Father Charles Dalton ofm, was born in *Waterford, Ireland* in 1786 and professed/ordained a Franciscan Priest, about 1815 at age 29. He was a guardian from 1819-1825 and ministered as a friary in Clonmel and superior from 1817-1830. He arrived in Newfoundland in 1831 and was assigned as the 4th PP, HARBOUR GRACE in 1833 on death of Fr. Ewer, for 26 years from 1833 to his death on 17 Jun 1859. At Harbour Grace: he was an original member of the Carbonear BIS in 1835; he bought a house and land from Dr. Stirling in 1839 and later gave this land to the Sisters; he signed the foundation document for St. John's Cathedral in 1841; he went to Europe with Bishop Fleming in 1845 for his health and to buy stones for the new HG Chapel; he began the new stone Church in Harbour Grace in 1852 and its dedication in 1853. He assisted in the consecration of his nephew, Rev. John Dalton as First Bishop of new Diocese of Harbour Grace in 1856.He was Vicar General to his nephew Bishop John Dalton for 3 years from 1856-1859. He died at Harbour Grace on 17 Jun 1859 at age 73. He was a Priest for about 47 years. He was buried in Harbour Grace.

1859-1872 – Rev. John J. Walsh, 13 YEARS

Father John J. Walsh was born in 1829 and ordained in about 1854 at age 25. In 1855 he was assigned as curate at Fogo Island and Harbour Grace until 1859 when he was appointed 5TH PP, HARBOUR GRACE, where he remained for 13 years until 1872. In 1861 he provided calming efforts when violence broke out in Harbour Grace. He was present when Bishop Dalton dedicated the new Cathedral on 8 Dec 1868 the feast of the Immaculate Conception. In 1869-1870 he administered the Harbour Grace Diocese upon the death of Bishop Dalton. He was Parish Priest when Bishop Carfagnini arrived in 1870 and Rev. Diomedes Falconio arrived as Administrator of Diocese in 1871. In 1876 he was assigned PP, St. Bernard's for two years until 1878. He meet Bishop McDonald in 1881. He was assigned as PP, Portugal Cove in 1884 for 15 years until his death on 14 Nov 1899 at age 70. He was a Priest for 45 years. He is buried in Belvedere, St.John's. He had three curates at Harbour Grace: Rev. John T. Vereker (1866); VRev. P.A. Slattery (1871) and Rev. William Veitch (1871-1875).

1872-1881 - Very Rev. Francis E. Walsh, 9 YEARS

Father E. F. Walsh was assigned to Harbour Grace for 9 years from 1872-1881. In 1881 he was on hand to meet Bishop McDonald when he arrived as new Bishop of Harbour Grace. No further information was available. He had two curates: Rev. Stephen Flynn (1877) and Rev. Donald W. McInnis (1877- 1882). Bishop McDonald was at Harbour Grace for 25 years (1881-1906)

1881-1890 - Very Rev. John Roe, 9 Years

Father John Roe was born in *Kilkenny*, Ireland on 19 Oct 1855 and ordained at All Hallows on 24 Jun 1880 at age 25 for Harbour Grace. He was sent to Newfoundland immediately to visit his uncle, Rev Hennebury at Trepassey. His first assignment was curate to Fr. Veitch at King's Cove for 1 year.(1880-1881). He then was PP, Harbour Grace for 8 years 1881-1890. He was at Harbour Grace when the new Cathedral was dedicated in 1884 and also there when the Cathedral was burned to the ground in 1889. He was present when St. Joseph's Church dedicated at Riverhead, HG in 1886. From 1890-1891 he was sent to the USA to solicite funds to rebuild a new Cathedral. On return he was assigned as PP, Northern Bay for 14 years from 1891-1905. In 1906 he was PP at Harbour Main for 5 years until his death on 16 Jun 1911 at age 56. He was a Priest for 31 years. He had three curates at Harbour Grace: Rev. F.D.McCarthy (1884-1886); Rev. Joseph Murphy (1888-1891) and Rev. John March (1889-1891). In 1898 he was deacon at the Memorial Mass for Fr. O'Connor at Carbonear.

1891-1906 – Rev. John March, 15 Years

Father John March was born in *Northern Bay* on 13 July 1863 and after attending college in Montreal and the propaganda College, he was ordained in Rome on 16 Mar 1889 at age 26. His first assignment was to Harbour Grace as curate and PP, for 15 years from 1891-1906. He attended the opening of the new brick Church at Carbonear in 1891. He attended the conferring of Pallium in St John's in 1905. He was consecrated Bishop of Harbour Grace by Archbishop Howley in St. John's on 4 Nov 1906. He was Bishop of Harbour Grace for 34 years until his death on 12 Jan 1940 at age 77. He was a Priest for 51 years. He celebrated his 50th Jubilee in 1939. While at Harbour Grace he was fired at in Church by an unemployed man in 1913 and survived the attack. He was the First native born Bishop of Harbour Grace. He was a proponent for the First Knights of Columbus Council in Harbour Grace in Newfoundland in 1909. He had one curate: Rev. John Patrick Mackey (1904).

1906-1912 – Rt. Rev. William P. Finn, 6 Years

Monsignor William P. Finn was born in *Carbonear* on 14 May 1879 to William Finn and Anne Marshall. He attended the Grand seminary in Quebec for 6 years from 1897-1903. He was ordained at the Seminary in Quebec in 1903 at age 24. His first assignment was to St. Brendan's in 1906 and onto Harbour Grace for 6 years 1906-1912, where he helped to organize the Catholic Cadets Corp (1910) and was Chaplain of the Brigade. He was also an advocate for the First Knights of Columbus Council in Newfoundland at Harbour Grace. Bishop March consecrated the new Church at Bay Roberts in 1909. When Grand Falls became a Parish from a Mission in 1912, Rev Finn became the First Parish Priest and remained for 41 years until his death in 1953. In 1919, he built the concrete church and he instituted the Notre Dame Knights of Columbus Council in Grand Falls. His Silver Jubilee was in 1928. The first chapel of St. Joseph burned at Windsor in 1938 and Rev. Finn built the new church in Windsor and said the first Mass in the new church on 3 September 1940. He was elevated to Monsignor at Grand Falls on 9 December 1945 by Bishop O'Neill. In 1952 he celebrated his 49th Anniversary of the Priesthood. He died in Montreal on 31 January 1953 at age 73 and is buried in Grand Falls. He was 4 months short of his 50th Golden Jubilee. He had three curates: Rev. Stephen J. Whelan (1909); Rev. Edward O'Brien (1910) and Rev. Edward J. Jones (1912).

1912-1918 – Rev. James J. Walker, 6 Years

Father James J. Walker was born in *Brigus* in 1878. He attended the Propaganda College in Rome for 6 years from 1902-1908. He was ordained on 5 June 1908 in Rome at age 30. From 1912-1918 he was assigned as Parish Priest at Immaculate Conception Parish in Harbour Grace. At the time of his death, he was Parish Priest at St. Brendan's. He died suddenly at the altar after celebrating Mass at St. Claire's Hospital in St. John's on 6 September 1927 at age 49. He was priest for 19 years. He was buried in his hometown of Brigus.

1918-1926 – Rt. Rev. Michael F. Dinn, 8 Years

Monsignor Michael F. Dinn was born in *Carbonear* on 26 September 1891 to Richard Dinn and Mary Dooley.(His mother died at his birth). He attended the Carbonear Academy and received his A.A. as a Prefect at St. Bon's from 1907-1910. From 1911-1914 he attended and received his B.A. from the National University of Dublin. He attended All Hallows form 1914-1918 and was ordained by Archbishop Walsh in Dublin on 24 February 1918 at age 27. On returning to Newfoundland, he followed Fr. James Walker as Parish Priest at Harbour Grace and remained there for 8 years from 1918-1926. He was curate to Fr. Finn at Holyrood for one year and from 1927-1928 he was curate to Father Mackey at Bay de Verde. In 1928 he followed Rev. Mark Dwyer at Bonavista and remained there for 6 years until 1934.In 1934 he became the third Parish Priest of North River upon the death of Rev. Thibault. At North River he started the construction of a new brick church. He was there for 21 years until his own death in 1955.On 7 July 1940. Bishop O'Neill selected him as Vicar General of the Diocese with the title of Monsignor and in 1942 was raised to the rank of Domestic Prelate by Pope Pius XII. His stepmother, Bridget Dinn died on 8 April 1940. In 1950 he attended the Requiem Mass for Archbishop Roche. After 37 years a Priest, he died on 17 July 1955 at St. Clare's Mercy Hospital in St. John's at age 64. He is buried in North River. He had three curates: Rev. Henry T. Renouf (1918-1919); Rev. Francis Pumphrey (1919) and Rev. Thomas D. O'Neill (1918-1930).

1926-1934 – Rev. Jeremiah Howard, 8 Years

Father Jeremiah Howard was born in *Daniel's Cove* on 25 November 1893. He was ordained in Harbour Grace in 1925 at age 32 and his first assignment was as Parish Priest of Harbour Grace for 8 years from 1926-1934. He was at Harbour Grace at Bishop March's 25th Episcopal Jubilee on 4 Nov 1931.His next assignment was as Parish Priest at St. Joseph's and St. Patrick's Parish in Bonavista succeeding Rev. Finn and remained there for 19 years from 1934-1953. In 1938 his mother died at Daniel's Cove. In 1950 he celebrated his Silver Jubilee. His final assignment came in 1953 as Parish Priest at Harbour Main following the death of Father Mark Dwyer and he remained there for 16 years until his retirement to Holyrood in 1969 at age 78. In 1975 he celebrated his Golden Jubilee. He died at Holyrood on 11 April 1976 at age 82. He was a Priest for 51 years. He is buried at Holyrood.

1934-1940 – Rev. Francis P. Meaney, 6 Years

Father Francis P. Meaney was born in *Brigus* on 19 Nov 1909 and graduated from St.Bon's, and attended the Grand Seminary in Quebec, when he was ordained on 26 May 1934 at age 25. His first assignment was as Parish Priest at Harbour Grace for 6 years from 1934-1940, where he spent some time in Labrador. He was at Harbour Grace in 1934 when the Parish celebrated its 150th Anniversary (1784-1934). He was at Harbour Grace on Bishop March's 50th Jubilee (1889-1939) and the Bishop's death on 12 Jan 1940, at age 77 In 1940 he was assigned as the First PP, Windsor, where he spent the next 40 years until he retired in 1980 at age 71. He spent 8 years in retirement from 1980 to his death on 11 Sep 1988 at age 79. He celebrated his 50th Jubilee in 1984. He was a Priest for 54 years. He is buried in Corner Brook.

1940-1948 – Rt. Rev. Joseph W. Peddle, 8 Years

Monsignor Joseph W. Peddle was born in Spaniard's Bay on 8 December 1904 to John Peddle and Susan Delaney. He attended St. Bon's from 1922-1925 and receive his A.A. Degree. He spent 6 years at the Laval University in Quebec, where he was ordained on 14 May 1931 at age 27. He visited his parents in Corner Brook in June 1931. His first assignment was as Curate to Father William Finn in Holyrood from 1931-1935. On Father Finn's death in 1935, Father Peddle took over as Parish Priest of Holyrood for the next five years from 1935-1940. He then spent the next eight years as Chancellor to Bishop O'Neill at the Harbour Grace Cathedral. Father Peddle has the distinction of being assigned as Parish Priest at Carbonear on two separate occasions. His first assignment was for five years from 1948-1953. In between he was Parish Priest at Grand Falls and Chancellor at the Cathedral at Grand Falls for 4 years from 1953-1957. He was honoured with his Domestic Prelate in 1954 and in 1955 was made Vicar General to Bishop O'Neill at Grand Falls. In 1957 he returned to Carbonear for the next 17 years until his retirement in 1974 at age 70. In 1966 he became a Charter member and Chaplain to the newly established Msgr. McCarthy Knights of Columbus Council at Carbonear. He returned to St. John's and died there two years later on 16 March 1976 at age 71 and is buried in Carbonear. He was a Priest for 45 years. He had one curate at Harbour Grace: Rev. Francis R. Terry (1940-1944).

1949-1957 – Rt. Rev. William P. Hogan, 8 Years

Monsignor William P. Hogan was born in Harbour Grace on 11 March 1916. He attended St. Peter's Seminary in London, Ontario for five years from 1943c-1948. He was ordained in the Cathedral at Harbour Grace by Bishop O'Neill on 6 June 1948 at age 32. After one year as a curate, his first assignment was as Parish Priest at Harbour Grace for eight years from 1949-1957. In 1950 he attended the Requiem Mass for Archbishop Roche. In 1957 he was Parish Priest of the Cathedral Parish in Grand Falls for 17 years until 1974, when he was assigned as Parish Priest of St. Patrick's Parish in Carbonear for seven years from 1974-1981. In 1961 he was invested as a Domestic Prelate by Pope John XXIII. He celebrated his 25th Silver Jubilee in 1973. In 1974, he was assigned as Parish Priest at Holyrood for 14 years until his retirement in 1988 at age 72. He retired to Leslie Street in St. John's. He died in St. John's in 1999 at age 83.He is buried in Harbour Grace.

1957-1984 – Rt. Rev. Joseph M. O'Brien, 27 Years

Monsignor Joseph M. O'Brien was born in Carbonear on 18 February 1917 to James O'Brien and Margaret Mackey. He attended the Carbonear Academy from about 1923-1933 under his uncle Lawrence Mackey. He attended St Bon's for 2 years from 1933-1935. He went to Rome on the ship, the "USS Newfoundland" in 1937. Father Joseph O'Brien attended the Irish College in Rome for 5 years from 1937-1942 and was ordained on 25 October 1942. Since it was during World War II, Father Joseph O'Brien and Father Loyola Lacey had to travel a long and circuitous route all over Europe to return to Newfoundland. It took them several months. Father Joseph O'Brien was a nephew to Msgr. Edward O'Brien and Rev. John Mackey. His first assignment was as curate to Fr. J. H. Scully at Conception Harbour for 6 years from 1942-1948. He was then assigned as Parish Priest at Tilting, Fogo for 7 years from 1948-1955. His next assignment was to Bishop Fall's for 2 years from 1955-1957. His final assignment was to Harbour Grace where he remained for 27 years from 1957 to his retirement in 1984 at age 67. He received the title of Domestic Prelate in 1961 from Pope John XXIII. St. Francis High school for boys was opened in 1961 under the Christian Brothers. The High school burned to the ground in 1973 and Msgr. O'Brien rebuilt it in 1974. Msgr. O'Brien lived in retirement for three years from 1984-1987. His personal home in Harbour Grace was completely destroyed by fire on 7 August 1985. After 45 years a priest, he died at Harbour Grace on 12 November 1987 at age 70. He is buried in the priests plot in the Harbour Grace cemetery. He had eight curates: Rev. William Shallow (1959-1964); Rev. James Beresford (1964-1966); Rev. Aloysius Antle (1966-1970); Rev. Michael J. Walsh (1970-1975); Rev. A. Wayne Cummings (1975-1978); Rev. Richard Anstey (1978-1979); Rev. Francis Aylward (1979) and Rev. Michael Ryan (1980-1984)

1984 - 1987 – Rev. J. Kevin Barker, 3 Years

Father J. Kevin Barker was born in Open Hall, BB on 22 July 1928. He received his early education in Open Hall and later attended St. Bon's followed by 2 years at St. Louis, Mo, USA. He completed his Philology studies at Laval University, Quebec City and his Theology studies at Holy Heart Seminary, Halifax, N.S. Before his ordination he worked for a number of years at the Ernest Harmon USAF Base and a number of years with Canada Post Office, Gander, NL. He was ordained at Grand Falls by Bishop O'Neill on 29 May 1966. His first assignment was a curate to Fr. Meaney at St. Joseph's Parish, Windsor. On 3 June 1967, he was appointed Parish Priest at Our Lady of Perpetual Help at Gambo for 2 months and then as Parish Priest at St. Patrick's Parish in Fogo for 9 years from 1967-1976. After one year at Bonavista, he returned to Gambo as Parish Priest for 4 years from 1977-1981. Here he attended the 125th Anniversary of the Grand Falls Diocese in 1981. His next assignment was as Parish Priest at Northern Bay for three years from 1981-1984, where he was also administrator of Bay de Verde for one year. On 24 Oct 1984, he was assigned as Parish Priest at Harbour Grace for three years from 1984-1987. It was during his assignment that the large Palace was demolished (1985-1986) and a new Priest's residence was built. It was during Fr. Barker's Pastorate that the renovations of the former Harbour Grace Cathedral were commenced. In June 1987 he was sent to St. Joseph's Parish in Windsor for 3 years from 1987-1990, where he built a new Priest's House. In August 1990 he was assigned to St. Joseph's and St. Patrick's Parish in Port Union in 1990 for six years until 1996, when he was sent to Gander where he spent two years until 1998 when he retired for health problems at age 70. While at Gander was also the civilian Chaplain to the Air Force Base. Currently he is still very active in many parishes throughout our own Diocese and the Archdiocese of St. John's.

1987-1990 – Rev. Michael J. Walsh, 3 Years

Father Michael J. Walsh was born in St. Brendan's on 24 June 1937. He attended All Hallows in Ireland for six years from 1958-1964 and was ordained on 21 June 1964 at age 27. He was assigned to Bay De Verde for 3 years from 1966-1970, then onto Harbour Grace for 5 years from 1970-1975. His next assignment was as Parish Priest at Brent's Cove for 3 years from 1976-1979 and as Administrator at Buchans for two years. In 1983 he was assigned as Parish Priest at Sts Peter and Paul Parish in Harbour Main for four years until 1987. He then returned to Harbour Grace as Parish Priest for three years from 1987-1990. He celebrated his 25th Silver Jubilee in 1989 at Harbour Grace and he opened the new St. Columba Elementary school in 1989. He was on a Sabbatical for one year from 1990-1991. While at Harbour Grace he had one curate: Rev. Andrew Lane (1989). He is currently working in the Archdiocese of Montreal.

1990-1996 – Rev. James A. Beresford, 6 Years

Father James A. Beresford was born in Buchan on 4 October 1940 to James Beresford and Nellie Ryan. He attended St. Bon's for one year from 1957-1958 and then onto All Hallows, Ireland for six years from 1958-1964. He was ordained in Grand Falls by Bishop O'Neill on 21 June 1964. His first assignment was as curate to Msgr. Joseph O'Brien at Harbour Grace for two years from 1964-1966. He then was assigned as Parish Priest at King's Cove for 8 years from 1966-1974.He then went to Ottawa for two years to study Licentiate Law from 1974-1976. On his return he was Chancellor at Grand Falls Cathedral Parish for four years from 1976-1980. From 1979-1980 he was Vicar Capitular in Grand Falls. From 1980 to 1984 he was Parish Priest at Badger for four years. He was then assigned as Parish Priest at Port Union for 5 years from 1984-1989. He celebrated his 25th Silver Jubilee in 1989 at Port Union. After one year on loan to St. Paul's Parish in St. John's, he was assigned as Parish Priest at Harbour Grace for 6 years from 1990-1996. While at Harbour Grace he continued the repairs to the Church and took down the two steeples in 1990. In 1996 he took a sabbatical for one year and returned to St. John's for assignment. He is currently the Parish Priest at Placentia, NF.

1996-2001 – Rev. Ramon Bolatets, SVD, 5 Years

Father Ramon Bolatets was placed on loan to the Grand Falls Diocese in Newfoundland. His first assignment was as Administrator to St. Peter and Paul Parish in Harbour Main. His second assignment was as Parish Priest to Our Lady of Fatima Parish in Clarenville. From 1995-1996 he spent one year as Administrator at Holyrood. In 1996 he was assigned as Parish Priest at Harbour Grace for five years from 1996 to 2001, when he was returned to his mother Diocese. During his time at Harbour Grace, he continued with the Church repairs under the Knights of Columbus supervision and he had the steeples put back up and held the celebration for the Millennium Year of 2000. Currently assigned in Florida. USA.

2001-2002 – Rev. Gregory Eduah, 1 Year

Father Gregory Eduah is on loan from his African Diocese and was Administrator at Harbour Grace for one year, during which Immaculate Conception Church was closed because of a fire in the vestibule and all Services were performed at St. Joseph's Church in Riverhead. Immaculate Conception Church opened for Mass on 3 Aug 2002. He is currently assigned to the Archdiocese of St. John's.

2002-Today – Rev. Francis J. Aylward

Father Francis J. Aylward was born in King's Cove on 25 Nov 1950 the son of Francis and Marie Aylward. He was ordained at King's Cove on 25 April 1976 by Bishop Penney. He was assigned to Bay de Verde for two years from 1979-1981 and then was Co-Pastor at Sacred Heat Parish in Conche (St. Anthony) for two years from 1981-1983. In 1984 he was appointed Parish Priest of Our Lady of Perpetual Help at Gambo for 5 years until 1989 when he was assigned to Port Union for one year and in 1990 he was Parish Priest of St. Patrick's Parish in Tilting, Fogo, where he remained for four years. In 1994 he was appointed Parish Priest at Northern Bay for 8 years where he remained until 2002 when he was assigned to his present assignment of Parish Priest at Immaculate Conception Parish in Harbour Grace.

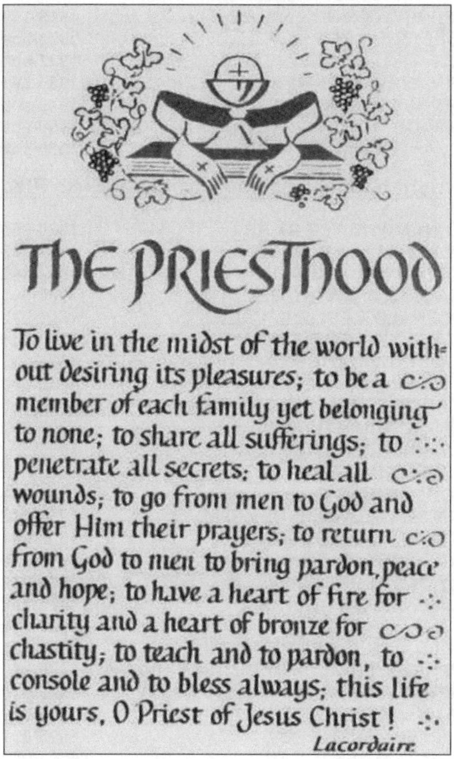

Chapter 12

KNOWN PRIESTS BORN IN

Harbour Grace and Vicinity (25 priests)

Priests by Birth-Death Date & Ordination Place

1. O'FLYNN, STEPHEN REV	1850-1899	HG
2. LYNCH, JOHN J. REV	1858c-1929	HG
3. LYNCH, THOMAS E. REV	1859-1905	HG
4. SCULLY, J.H. VERY REV	1875-1948	Rome
5. BRENNAN, WALTER RT REV Bay Roberts	1880-1965	Dublin
6. PUMPHREY, FRANCIS REV	1890-1937	Quebec
7. CASEY, WILLIAM H. RT REV	1892-1962	Quebec
8. FITZGERALD, LESLIE G. VREV	1898-1966	Halifax
9. FOLEY, JOHN LEO REV MM	1900-1938	Maryknoll, NY
10. O'NEILL, JOHN M. BISHOP	1903-1974	Quebec
11. PEDDLE, JOSEPH RT REV Spaniard's Bay	1904-1976	Quebec
12. JONES, J. RONALD REV	1906-1953	Halifax
13. WALSH, WALTER P. REV	1913-1958	Rome
14. MORIARITY, EDWARD REV SFM	1914-1983	HG
15. MORRISSEY, THOMAS REV North River	1914-1992	Toronto
16. WALSH, RONALD J. REV	1915-1980	HG
17. HOGAN, WILLIAM P. RT REV	1916-1999	HG
18. MORIARITY, JOSEPH REV SFM	1918-retired	St.John's
19. PUMPHREY, GREGORY B. REV	1919-1995	Grand Falls
20. PEDDLE, JOHN REV Tilton, CB	1931-active	HG
21. COADY, LINUS J. REV	1932-active	HG
22. HEARN, EDWARD J. REV	1935-LPH	HG
23. HEARN, WILLIAM REV	1949-active	HG
24. CUMMINGS, A. WAYNE REV North River	1950-active	N. River
25. LANE, ANDREW J. REV AFR SJ/HG	1955-active	HG

Alphabetical Listing–Birth Date-Birth Place

1. BRENNAN, WALTER RT REV	1880-0802	Bay Roberts
2. CASEY, WILLIAM H. RT REV	1892-0826	HG
3. COADY, LINUS J. REV	1932-0421	HG
4. CUMMINGS, A WAYNE REV	1950-0611	North River
5. FITZGERALD, LESLIE G. VREV	1898-0221	HG
6. FOLEY, JOHN LEO REV MM	1900-0714	HG
7. HEARN, EDWARD J. REV	1935-1217	HG
8. HEARN, WILLIAM REV	1949-0703	HG
9. HOGAN, WILLIAM P. RT REV	1916-0311	HG
10. JONES, J. RONALD REV	1906-0922	HG
11. LANE, ANDREW J. REV AFR	1955-1231	SJ/HG
12. LYNCH, JOHN J. REV	1858c 1929	HG
13. LYNCH, THOMAS E. REV	1859-1905	SJ/HG
14. MORIARITY, EDWARD REV SFM	1914-0423	HG
15. MORIARITY, JOSEPH REV SFM	1918-0818	HG
16. MORRIESSEY, THOMAS REV	1914-0225	North River
17. O'FLYNN, STEPHEN REV	1850-0129	HG
18. O'NEILL, JOHN M. BISHOP	1903-1026	HG
19. PEDDLE, JOHN REV	1931-1124	Tilton, CB
20. PEDDLE, JOSEPH RT REV	1904-1208	Spaniards Bay
21. PUMPHREY, FRANCIS REV	1890-0106	HG
22. PUMPHREY, GREGORY B. REV	1919-0714	HG
23. SCULLY, J.H. VERY REV	1875-0708	HG
24. WALSH, RONALD J. REV	1915-0914	HG
25. WALSH, WALTER P. REV	1913-0422	HG

KNOWN PRIESTS ORDAINED BY
Bishops of Harbour Grace or Grand Falls

Date, Location Ordained, Born and Bishop (69)

NAME	DATE ORD	LOC	BORN	BISHOP
Rev. James Brown	1856 Dec 20	Carb	Carbonear	Bishop Dalton
Rt. Rev. Joseph V. Donnelly	1870 Dec 4	HG	St. John's	Bishop Carfagnini
Rt. Rev. William Veitch	1871 Oct 29	HG	Holyrood	Bishop Carfagnini
Rev. Philip A. Carolan	1872 Sep 29	HG	Ireland	Bishop Carfagnini
Rev. Stephen Flynn	1875 Jun	HG	HG	Bishop Carfagnini
Rev. Richard F. Walsh	1875 Autumn	HG	Hrb Main	Bishop Carfagnini
VRev. Gregory J. Battcock	1878	HG	Ferryland	Bishop Carfagnini
Rev. Richard M. Walker	1883 May	HG	Brigus	Bishop McDonald
VRev. Walter M. Tarahan	1883 May 20	HG	Brigus	Bishop McDonald
Rev. Thomas E. Lynch	1883 May 20	HG	SJ-HG	Bishop McDonald
Rev. John J. Lynch	1883 Sep 8	HG	HG	Bishop McDonald
Rt. Rev. Joseph Murphy	1887 Dec 29	Carb	Carbonear	Bishop McDonald
Rev. Dr. Pat W. Browne	1887 Dec 29	Carb	Carbonear	Bishop McDonald
Rev. Lawrence Hayden	1888 Jun 8	HG	Kingston	Bishop McDonald
Rev. Stephen J. Whelan	1900 Aug 1	Carb	Carbonear	Bishop McDonald
VRev. George A. Thibault	1906 Jul 25	HG	Salmon River	Bishop March
Rev. James W. Donnelly	1907 Sep 21	HG	Carbonear	Bishop March
Rt. Rev. John F. Kirwan	1914 Sep 4	HG	Torbay	Bishop March
Rev. John W. Enright	1914 Nov 25	HG	Ireland	Bishop March
*Rev. Leo J. Burke, SFM	1936 Aug 24	HG	Brigus	Bishop March
Rev. Edward T. Moriarity, SFM	1936 Aug 24	HG	HG	Bishop March
Rev. Edward M. Shea	1944 Feb 1	HG	Brigus	Bishop O'Neill
Rev. Ronald J. Walsh	1945 Jun 17	HG	HG	Bishop O'Neill
Rev. Edward A. Walsh	1945 Jun 17	HG	Holyrood	Bishop O'Neill
Rev. Luke J. Woodrow	1947 May 4	HG	Northern Bay	Bishop O'Neill
Rt. Rev. William P. Hogan	1948 Jun 6	HG	HG	Bishop O'Neill
Rev. Gregory Pumphrey	1948 Jun 12	GF	HG	Bishop O'Neill
Rt. Rev. Richard T. Woodford	1949 Jun 29	SJ	St. Mary's	Bishop O'Neill
Rev. Frederick J. Terry	1950 Jun 11	HM	HM	Bishop O'Neill
Rev. Michael R. Hynes	1953 May 5	Bell Is	St. John's	Bishop O'Neill
Rev. Leonard J. Kelly	1955 Jun 5	Windsor	Windsor	Bishop O'Neill
Rev. Patrick McCormack	1955 Jun 12	GF	GF	Bishop O'Neill
Rev. Linus J. Coady	1957 Jun 5	HG	HG	Bishop O'Neill
Rev. Edward F. Hearn	1959 Jun 7	HG	HG	Bishop O'Neill
Rev. J. Richard Hawco	1959 Jun 7	HG	HM	Bishop O'Neill
Rev. William Shallow	1959 Jun 14	GF	GF	Bishop O'Neill
Rev. John Peddle	1961 Jun 11	HG	Tilton	Bishop O'Neill
Rev. Neil McDonald	1961 Jun 25	GF	Badger	Bishop O'Neill
Rev. James A. Beresford	1964 Jun 21	GF	Buchans	Bishop O'Neill
Rev. Joseph Crawford, CssR	1964 Jun 21	GF	Carbonear	Bishop O'Neill
Rev. Michael J. Walsh	1964 Jun 21	GF	St. Brendan's	Bishop O'Neill
Rev. Francis R. O'Brien	1965 Jun 12	GF	St. John's	Bishop O'Neill
Rev. David Aylward	1966 Mar 5	GF	Grand Falls	Bishop O'Neill
Rev. Aloysius Antle	1966 May 29	GF	Fleur de Lys	Bishop O'Neill
Rev. William D. Matthews	1966 May 29	GF	La Scie	Bishop O'Neill
Rev. J. Kevin Barker	1966 May 29	GF	Open Hall	Bishop O'Neill

NAME	DATE ORD	LOC	BORN	BISHOP
Rev. William J. Houlahan	1966 Jun 11	GF	GF	Bishop O'Neill
Rev. John G. Mackey	1966 Jun 11	GF	GF	Bishop O'Neill
Rev. Edward R. Brophy	1967 Jun 25	HG	St. John's	Bishop O'Neill
Rev. John Murphy	1967 Jul 25	HG	Conc. Hrb	Bishop O'Neill
Rev. Matthew Kane	1969 Jun 9	Gander	Gander	Bishop O'Neill
Rev. Bernard O'Neill	1969 Jun 22	Carb	Bell Is	Bishop O'Neill
Rev. Aidan B. Beresford	1970 Jun 7	GF	Buchans	Bishop O'Neill
Rev. Martin Parsons	1970 Jun 7	GF	Baie Verte	Bishop O'Neill
Rev. David W. Heale	1970 Jun 14	HG	St. John's	Bishop O'Neill
Rev. Roy A. Walsh	1972 Jun 25	Windsor	Windsor	Bishop O'Neill
Rev. A. Wayne Cummings	1975 May 16	No. River	No. River	Bishop Penney
Rev. William E. Hearn	1975 Jun 17	HG	HG	Bishop Penney
Rev. Francis J. Aylward	1976 Apr 26	KC	Kings Cove	Bishop Penney
Rev. Richard Anstey	1978 Jul 12	GF	GF	Bishop Penney
Rev. Lawrence George	1978 Dec 6	Carb	Carbonear	Bishop Penney
Rev. Michael A. Ryan	1978 Dec 15	Gander	Gander	Bishop Penney
Rev. Dr. Brian J. Dunn	1980 Aug 28	HG	St. John's	Bishop MacDonald
Rev. Andrew J. Lane, AFR	1985 Aug 9	Gander	SJ-HG	Bishop MacDonald
Rev. Brian G. Colbert	1985 Dec 29	Gander	Bauline	Bishop MacDonald
Rev. David Ostler	1987 May 16	Cornwell	Cornwell	Bishop MacDonald
Rev. Anthony Hageman	1988 Jun 5	Colbourne	GF	Bishop MacDonald
Rev. Michael Barker	1989 Jun 23	GF	Buchans	Bishop MacDonald
Rev. David E. Joy	2002 May 30	Gander	St. John's	Bishop Currie

69

This list may not be complete because many of the older priests were ordained in Newfoundland without any specific location or Diocese noted.

- Ordained for a religious Order but was incarnated into the Diocese of Harbour Grace.

Coat of Arms of Bishop of Harbor Grace.

Chapter 13

LIFE SUMMARIES

PRIESTS KNOWN TO BE BORN IN HARBOUR GRACE & VICINITY (25)

1850-1899	FLYNN, STEPHEN REV *(24)* Age 49
1858c-1929	LYNCH, JOHN J. REV *(45c)* Age 71
1859-1905	LYNCH, THOMAS E. REV *(22)* Age 46 (St. John's-Harbour Grace)
1875-1948	SCULLY, J.H. VERY REV *(48)* Age 73
1887-1965	BRENNAN, WALTER RT REV (*47*) Age 78 (Bay Roberts)
1890-1937	PUMPHREY, FRANCIS REV *(18)* Age 47
1892-1962	CASEY, WILLIAM H. RT REV *(43)* Age 70
1898-1966	FITZGERALD, LESLIE G. VREV *(43)* Age 68
1899-1938	FOLEY, JOHN LEO REV MM (6) Age 39 (d. China)
1903-1974	O'NEILL, JOHN M. BISHOP (34) Age 70.
1904-1976	PEDDLE, JOSEPH MSGR (45) Age 71 (Spaniard's Bay)
1906-1953	JONES, J. RONALD REV (23) Age 47.
1913-1958	WALSH, WALTER P. REV (21) Age 45
1914-1983	MORIARTY, EDWARD REV SFM (47) Age 69
1914-1992	MORRISSEY, THOMAS REV (55) Age 78 (North River)
1915-1980	WALSH, RONALD J. REV *(35)* Age 65
1916-1999	HOGAN, WILLIAM P. RT REV (63) Age 83
1917-Retired	MORIARTY, JOSEPH REV SFM Retired Stephenville
1919-1995	PUMPHREY, GREGORY B.REV *(47)* Age 76
1931-Active	PEDDLE, JOHN REV Assigned Pasadena (Tilton, CB)
1932-Active	COADY, LINUS J. REV Assigned Bishop Falls
1935-Inactive	HEARN, EDWARD J. REV Left Priesthood (LPH)
1949-Active	HEARN, WILLIAM REV Assigned Kings Cove
1950-Active	CUMMINGS, A. WAYNE REV Assigned GF-Windsor (North River)
1955-Active	LANE, ANDREW J. REV AFR, Assigned Toronto (St. John's-Harbour Grace)

Number in parenthesis (12) indicates the number of years being a priest

RT. REV. WALTER BRENNAN, D.P.

Monsignor Walter Brennan was born in Bay Roberts in 1887. He was ordained in Dublin, Ireland in Feb 1918. His first assignment was to Bonne Bay for 7 years from 1918 to 1925. After one year at Petries he was assigned the first Parish Priest at Holy Redeemer Parish in Corner Brook where he remained for 5 years from 1926-1931. In 1927 he attended the opening and blessing of the Sacred Heart Convent in Corner Brook. In 1931 he was assigned as Parish Priest at St. Theresa's Parish in St. George's Diocese for 5 years. In 1938 he was assigned Parish Priest at St. Stephen's Church in Stephenville vice Msgr. Adams and remained there for 13 years until 1951. In 1941 he attended the Requiem Mass for Bishop Renouf. In 1943 he celebrated his Silver Jubilee in Stephenville. In 1944 he attended the burial of Msgr. Andrew Sears and later in the year was invested as Vicar General for Bishop O'Reilly vice Msgr. Adams. In 1946 he received his Domestic Prelate and in 1947 attended the Golden Jubilee of Archbishop Roche and in 1950 attended the Requiem Mass of Archbishop Roche. In 1952 he blessed the Immaculate Conception Church in Deer Lake. He died in Deer Lake in 1965 at age 78. He was priest for 47 years.

RT. REV. WILLIAM H. CASEY, D.P

Monsignor William Hogan Casey was born in Harbour Grace on 26 August 1892 to Judge John Casey and Margaret Hogan. He was baptized on the same date by Rev. John March. His sponsor's were John Murphy and Catherine Lynch. He attended the Laval Seminary in Quebec City, Quebec for 7 years from 1912-1919. He was ordained in Quebec on 25 May 1919 at age 27. His first assignment was as Curate to Rev. Dr. Whelan in North River, CB for 3 years from 1919-1922. In 1922 he was appointed Parish Priest at Fortune Harbour, N.D.B. following Father John Nolan, and remained there for 18 years until 1940. At this time he assumed the pastoral charge of Assumption Parish in Bay de Verde in 1940 on the retirement of Father Mackey and remained there for 8 years until 1948. He celebrated his Silver Jubilee at Bay de Verde on 21 May 1944. From Bay de Verde, he was appointed Parish Priest at St. Anne's Parish, Conception Harbour in 1948 on the death of Father Scully and remained for the next 14 years until his retirement in 1961. On 13 Jan 1959, he was invested by Pope John XXIII as a Domestic Prelate and Monsignor. He died at St. Clare's Hospital, St. John's on 3 February 1962 at age 70. He was a Priest for 43 years. He is buried in the priests' plot in the Harbour Grace Cemetery.

REV. LINUS J. COADY

Father Linus J. Coady was born on 21 April 1932 at Harbour Grace. He was baptized, confirmed and ordained at Harbour Grace by Rev. John M. O'Neill (later Bishop O'Neill). He attended Laval University in Quebec City for six years from 1951-1957. He was ordained at the Cathedral in Harbour Grace by Bishop O'Neill on 5 June 1957. His first two years was spent as Curate at Grand Falls from 1957-1958. He then was assigned as an assistant to Rev. Pumphrey in Baie Verte for a year. He was assigned as the first Parish Priest at La Scie for six years from 1959-1965. After he left, Rev. Ronald Bromley moved the center of the Parish to Brent's Cove. In 1965 he was assigned as Parish Priest of Our Lady of Mt Carmel Parish in Norris Arm for 4 years until 1969. In 1969 he was assigned as Parish Priest at Sts Peter and Paul Parish in Harbour Main for 11 years until 1980. In 1980 he returned to Brent's Cove after 21 years for five year until 1985. Father Coady wrote the "History of Parish of Brent's Cove". He celebrated his Silver Jubilee (25) in June 1982. His next assignment was as Parish Priest at St. Patrick's Parish in Brigus for 4 years from 1985-1989. In 1989 he was on Sabbatical for one year to Quebec. On his return he returned to Brigus until 1993. In 1991 he celebrated his 34th Anniversary at Brigus. In 1993 he was assigned to Sacred Heart Parish in Bishop Falls where he currently resides.

REV. A. WAYNE CUMMINGS

Father A. Wayne Cummings was born in North River on 11 Jun 1950 to Daniel and Bride Cummings. He was ordained in North River by Bishop Alphonsus Penney on 16 May 1975. He was assigned to Harbour Grace for 3 years as curate to Msgr. Joseph O'Brien from 1975-1978. In 1978 he was appointed Parish Priest of Buchans for 1 year from 1978-1979. He was appointed Parish Priest of Whitbourne for 2 years from 1979-1981. His next assignment was as Parish Priest of Assumption Parish in Bay de Verde for 2 years from 1982-1984. In 1986 he was assigned to Tilting, Fogo for 4 years from 1986-1990. He closed the Marian Year ceremony in Fogo in 1988. In 1990 he was the first Parish Priest of the new Our Lady of Fatima Parish for Clarenville for 3 years until 1993. From 1993-1994 he was on a Sabbatical for one year of study. From 1994-1995 he was administrator at St. Patrick's Parish in Brigus. He was Parish Priest in Harbour Main and Holyrood from 1996-1999. He was on sick leave from 1999-2002 and currently Parish Priest at St. Joseph's Parish in Grand Falls-Windsor.

VERY REV. LESLIE G. FITZGERALD, Ph.D.

Very Rev Nicholas (Leslie) G. Fitzgerald was born in Harbour Grace on 21 February 1898 to Patrick Fitzgerald and Margaret Fleming. He was baptized on the same day by Rev. John March; his sponsor's were Timothy Connors and Margaret Hennessey. He attended the Harbour Grace Academy until 1914 when he went to St. Bon's until 1917 when he proceeded to Holy Heart Seminary at Halifax for 6 years from 1917-1923. He was ordained in Halifax on 24 June 1923 at age 25. His first assignment was at North River, then to Northern Bay as a curate to Father Edward O'Brien for 2 years. While serving at Northern Bay he was injured during a brave attempt to rescue the Blessed Sacrament during the fire at the Church. He also did missionary work in Labrador for three years during his curacy at North River and Northern Bay. In 1925, Bishop March sent him to King's Cove as a curate to Father John Scully until 1930. He received a fellowship, and wrote a thesis on "Civilization in the North"; in the same year, he received his Doctorate in psychology. He then became parish priest of Coachman's Cove from 1930-1934, when he was transferred to Bonavista until 1937. On the death of Rev. F. J. Pumphrey, Fr. Fitzgerald was appointed to St. Brendan's, where he labored until 1944. In 1944 he was appointed 3rd Parish Priest at Buchans following Father Thomas O'Neill and Father Fitzgerald remained there for 21 years until 1965 when he went to Texas USA for medical treatment. On 24 June 1948 he celebrated his Silver Jubilee in Buchan's. In 1949 he published a book of poems entitled, "Lone Eagles of God." He was blind in one eye in the 1950s. He died on Long Island, New York on 6 May 1966 at age 68. He was a Priest for 43 years. He is buried in New York.

REV STEPHEN FLYNN

(No picture)

Father Stephen Flynn (O'Flynn) was born on 25 January 1850 in Harbour Grace to Michael Flynn and Catherine Fleming. He was at the All Hallows seminary for 6 years from 1868-1874. He was ordained a sub-deacon on 8 December 1874 at Immaculate Conception, Harbour Grace. He was ordained by Bishop Carfagnini in Harbour Grace in June 1875 at age 25. His first assignment was as Parish Priest at St. Patrick's Parish in Carbonear for 3 years from 1876-1879. In 1878 he was Chaplain to the new second BIS in Harbour Grace. His sister Ellen died in Carbonear at age 24 in October 1879. In 1879 he was appointed as first Parish Priest at Fortune Harbour for 6 years until 1885. On 4 July 1883 he visited the MicMac Indians with Bishop McDonald. He was then assigned to Little Bay in 1885 and remained there for 14 years until his death in 1899. His mother Catherine, wife of Michael J. Flynn, died on Ascension Day in May 1885 at age 74. His father, Michael J. Flynn died at Harbour Grace on 11 March 1886 at age 77. Father Flynn died while in a carriage ride over the bridge in St. John's on 14 August 1899 at age 49. He was a priest for 24 years. He is buried in the Priests' Plot in Harbour Grace Cemetery. He is listed as Rev. Stephen O'Flynn.

REV. JOHN LEO FOLEY, MM

Father John Leo Foley was born in Harbour Grace on 14 July 1899 to Postmaster and Mrs. J. Foley. He was baptized on the same day by Rev. John March; his sponsor's were John Casey and Mary Kennedy. He attended the Harbour Grace Academy for 11 years from 1905-1916 and on to St. Bon's for one year in 1917-1918. His father died in 1918 and he left St. Bon's. He joined the Newfoundland Regiment in World War I for one year and returned to St. Bon's in 1919 until 1920, when his mother moved the family to Boston, USA. He worked for the Edison Company in the USA for 5 years from 1920-1925. He then entered the Maryknoll College in New York where he spent seven years. He was ordained a Sub-deacon on 14 June 1931 at the Maryknoll Seminary in USA and was ordained on 5 June 1932 at age 32, at Maryknoll HQ in New York. His first Mass was in Malden, Mass, in 1932 and in August 1932 he was sent to China where he contracted Typhoid Fever and died on 17 October 1938 at age 38. He was a Priest for only 6 years.

REV. EDWARD HEARN

Father Edward Hearn was born on 17 Dec 1935 at Riverhead, Harbour Grace, son of William Hearn and Ellen Moriarity. He was educated at Laval University (Grand Seminaire), Quebec City. Fr Hearn was ordained at Harbour Grace, 7 June 1959, at age 24. He was assigned to Grand Falls until 1961. He was appointed administrator at Badger for two years from 1961-1963 and Parish Priest at Conche for seven years from 1963-1970. He was Parish Priest at Corpus Christi Parish at Northern Bay for three years from 1970-1973. He left the priesthood and was laicized in 1977 in Montreal. He is a brother to Rev. William Hearn. He presently resides in Montreal.

REV. WILLIAM E. HEARN

Father William Edward Hearn was born in Harbour Grace on 3 July 1949 to William Hearn and Ellen Moriarty. He was ordained on 17 June 1975, at age 26 at Harbour Grace by Bishop Alphonsus Penney. He was the first ex-pupil from St. Francis High School, at Harbour Grace to be ordained. He was assigned as Parish Priest at St. Patrick's Parish in Fogo for three years from 1976-1979. He then was assigned as Parish Priest at Conche for two years from 1979-1981. In 1981 he was assigned as Parish Priest at St. Gabriel's Parish in St. Brendan's for three years until 1984. In 1984 he was Parish Priest at Baie Verte and Brent's Cove for 7 years until 1991. Then to Our Lady of Perpetual Help at Gambo (and St. Brendan's) for two year from 1992-1994, when he was placed on loan to St. George's Diocese in 1994 as Parish Priest of St. Ignatius Parish in St. Alban's Parish until 1999. He was on sabbatical from 1999-2000. He was assigned to St. Patrick's Parish in Carbonear for one year from 2001-2002. He currently is assigned as Parish Priest at King's Cove, Plate Cove and Port Union.

RT. REV. WILLIAM P. HOGAN, D.P.

Monsignor William P. Hogan was born in Harbour Grace on 11 March 1916 to Timothy Hogan and Josephine Kennedy. After graduating from school, he entered the teaching profession in 1936 and taught in the parish of Cape St. George until 1939. He worked at Argentia Naval Base until 1942 when he entered St. Peter's Seminary in London, Ontario. He was ordained in Harbour Grace by Bishop J. M. O'Neill on 6 June 1946. His first appointment was to the Cathedral at Harbour Grace until 1957, when Bishop O'Neill appointed him to Grand Falls to transform the Parish into an Episcopal Sea and Cathedral Parish of the Diocese. He was appointed by Pope John XXIII as Domestic Prelate on August 28th, 1961 and Rector of the Cathedral by Bishop O'Neill. He went to Rome with Bishop O'Neill for several months each year from 1961-1964 to attend the Vatican Council II. In 1966 he was appointed as Administrator of the Diocese at Grand Falls. After Vatican Council II, the Holy See established the position of Episcopal Vicar and Msgr. Hogan was appointed E.V. in 1966. In November 1972 he was elected to Vicar Capitular and Administrator of Diocese after Bishop O'Neill resigned from Bishop of Grand Falls. On 6 June 1973 he celebrated his Silver Jubilee at Grand Falls. In 1974 he was assigned as Parish Priest at St. Patrick's Parish in Carbonear, where he remained for 7 years, from 1974-1981. His final assignment was as Parish Priest at Holyrood for seven years from 1981-1988. He retired to Leslie Street, St. John's in 1988 at age 72. He died on 30 August 1999 at age 83. He was a priest for 53 years. He is buried in the Priest's Plot, Roman Catholic Cemetery at Harbour Grace.

REV. J. RONALD JONES

Father James Ronald Jones was born in Harbour Grace on 22 Sep 1906 to James Jones and Catherine Jordan. He was baptized on 25 September 1906 by Rev. John March; his sponsor's were Gulielmas J. Lynch and Margaret Lynch. He attended Holy Heart Seminary in Halifax and was ordained there on 24 June 1930 at age 23 years 9 months. He is listed in the Catholic Clergy Fund minutes in 1932. That summer, he is listed in the Harbour Grace baptismal book as doing missionary work on Labrador. He was assigned as a curate at Grand Falls from 1936-1938. He attended the 25th Anniversary of Bishop O'Reilly as Parish Priest at Lourdes on 17 June 1942. He died at Lourdes on 18 November 1953 at age 47. He was buried at Lourdes. He was a priest for 23 years.

REV ANDREW J.LANE M. Afr.

Father Andrew J. Lane was born in St. John's on 31 December 1955 to Cornelius Lane and Agnes Murphy who were living in Flatrock. In 1961 they moved to Harbour Grace and Rev Lane entered the Priesthood as a native of Harbour Grace. From 1961-1967 he attended the Presentation Convent School in Harbour Grace and attended St. Francis Central High School in Harbour Grace from 1967-1972. After completing a B.A. at Memorial University in 1975, he entered the First Cycle of the Missionaries of Africa (White Fathers) in Ottawa and spent the next three years in Algeria as part of his Pastoral Training Period. During the first year he studied spoken and written Arabic and for the remaining two years he taught Mathematics in a secondary school at Laghouat in southern Algeria. In 1982 he moved to Toulouse, France and was ordained a deacon on 13 October 1984 in Toulouse and was ordained a Priest on 9 August 1985 at age 30 at Immaculate Conception Church in Harbour Grace by Bishop J. Faber MacDonald. After ordination, he returned to Algeria for one year and in 1986 left for Rome where he started a Licentiate in Arabic and Islamic Studies at the Pontifical Institute of Arabic and Islamic Studies (PISAI). Upon completion of the Licentiate in early 1990, he left for Egypt where he divided his time between teaching in Cairo and pastoral work in Assouan, In 1992 he returned to Rome to take up a position as a lecturer in Arabic and Islamic Studies at the PISAI. He taught in Rome until 1997 when he moved to Toronto to begin his Ph.D Programme in Islamic Studies at the University of Toronto. In 2002 he finished his doctoral Programme with a dissertation on the medieval Quran commentator Mahmud ibn Umar al-Zamakhshari (d.1144). He is currently residing in Toronto, Ontario. He is the nephew of Sr. Helena of Plate Cove.

REV. JOHN J. LYNCH

Father John J. Lynch was born in Harbour Grace to Captain Thomas Lynch and Catherine Keough in about 1858. He was ordained in Harbour Grace on 8 September 1883 by Bishop McDonald. In 1885 he followed Father Thomas Lynch as Parish Priest of Sacred Heart Parish at Conche and stayed there for 13 years until 1898. In 1906 he was assigned as Parish Priest at Corpus Christi Parish at Northern Bay, following Father John Roe, and remained there for 9 years until 1915. He went to the USA in about 1915 and was attached to the Diocese of South Dakota, where he served his priestly duties for 14 years until his death in 1929. He died at the hospital in Central City, South Dakota, USA on about 1 March 1929 at age 71. He was a priest for about 45 years. His sister Catherine was the mother of Bishop J. M. O'Neill.

REV. THOMAS E. LYNCH

Father Thomas E. Lynch was born in St. John's in 1859 and moved to Harbour Grace at age 6. He attended St. Bon's for 4 years from 1878-1878 and went onto the Cambray Seminary in France as a native of Harbour Grace in 1878 for 5 years until his ordination in Harbour Grace in 1883 by Bishop McDonald. He was assigned to Conche for one year from 1883-1884. In 1884 he was a curate at Carbonear for one year and then was appointed Parish Priest at Carbonear in 1885 for 4 years. In 1888 he entertained the visitors to Carbonear at the laying of the cornerstone of the new Brick Church. After the fire at the Harbour Grace Cathedral in 1889, he was sent to USA to solicite funds for the new Cathedral. On his return in 1890 he was assigned to Bonavista and in 1891 was appointed Parish Priest at King's Cove for 14 years until 1905. He died at the General Hospital in St. John's on 1 Nov 1905 at age 46. He was priest for 22 years. He is buried in Harbour Grace.

REV. EDWARD T.MORIARITY, SFM

Father Edward Thomas Moriarity was born on 23 April 1914 in Harbour Grace to Edward and Lillian Moriarity. He attended Academy School in Harbour Grace and attended St. Francis Xavier Seminary in Scarboro from 1931-1936. He was ordained for the Scarboro Missions on 24 August 1936 at Harbour Grace by Bishop March. He sailed for China in 1938 to attend the language school in Lishui, China. He was Pastor of the Chinese Missions at Toronto and Vancouver from 1940-1944. In 1946 he returned to China as Mission Procurator and Pastor and was arrested by the Communists and remained under house arrest for three years from 1949-1952. In 1952 he returned to Canada and was sent to British Guiana in 1953 to set up a new Mission there. His next assignments were in New Amsterdam, Georgetown and St. Vincent where he was Vicar General until 1962. In 1962 he was reassigned as Chaplain at Scarboro General Hospital. He took a leave of absence in 1965 and 1966 reappointed to St. Vincent, NF but returned to Canada on sick leave. From 1967 to 1973 he spent time at Scarboro motherhouse and he worked in the St. John's Diocese on loan for one year. In 1976 he celebrated his 40th Jubilee in the Bahamas. In 1977 he returned to the Scarboro HQ as Chaplain at the Hospital and in 1983 he was admitted to hospital for a brain tumor and he passed away quietly on 11 July 1983 at age 69 and is buried in St. Augustine Priest's cemetery in Ontario. He was priest one month short of 47 years. He is a first cousin to Rev J. Jos Moriarity, SFM.

REV. J. JOSEPH MORIARITY, SFM

Father John Joseph Moriarity was born in 18 August 1917 at Harbour Grace to Joseph and Anastasia Moriarity. The family moved to St. John's when he was a baby and he attended Holy Cross School for 9 years from 1924-1933 and St. Bon's from 1933-1936. It was at St. Bon's when he realized "that his future lay in the missions" after he heard a talk from Fr. Alphonsus Chafe, s.f.m. and Fr. Craig Strang s.f.m. He studied at Memorial U in 1937. He entered the Scarboro Foreign Missions Society in 1938 and was ordained a Foreign Missions priest at St. John the Baptist Cathedral (now Basilica) on 19 June 1945 at age 27 by Most Rev. Thomas Flynn. He was posted that same summer in Santa Domingo to study Spanish. His first assignment was at Yamasa, R.D. as assistant from 1945-1947. From there he went to San Jose de Ocoa, D.R. as an assistant until Nov 1949, when he became Pastor in Boya. He left the parish in Nov 1952 and was reassigned in July 1953 to Wainwright, A.B. for a year as assistant pastor. From Sept 1954-July 1957, he was pastor in Port Mourant, British Guyana. In 1957 he was reassigned to Uamasa, D.R. He was Pastor in Monte Plata in 1959. From Sept 1965 until Sept 1967 he was Parish Priest at St. Theresa's Parish in Buchan's, NF. After his time in Buchan's he was appointed to the Bahama Missions and in Oct 1967 he became Parish Priest at Rock Sound, Bahamas. From 1970 until his retirement in 1983, he was on loan to St. George's Diocese, NF. He was Administrator at St. Anne's Parish in Searston, Codroy Valley and Our Lady of Fatima Parish in Piccadilly, Port au Port. He retired from active parish duties in 1983 at age 66. He celebrated his Silver Jubilee in 1970 and his Golden Jubilee in 1995. He spent most of his 25 years in the Caribbean expect for one year as a military Chaplain from 1953-1954 at the Wainwright Combat Camp during the Korean conflict. He is currently in retirement in Stephenville at age 85

REV. THOMAS M MORRISSEY, SFM

Father Thomas M. Morrissey was born in North River, C.B., Newfoundland on 25 Feb 1914 to William and Ellen Morrissey. He received his early education there at all Hallows School and went onto St. Bon's in St. John's. He later entered St. Francis Xavier Seminary in Toronto for 6 years from 1931-1937. He was ordained by Archbishop McGuigan in Toronto on 3 December 1937 at age 23 for the Scarboro Missions. His first Mass was in Charlestown, Mass, USA on 5 December 1937. He first went to Lishui, China to study Chinese for 2 years. In 1941 he was curate at Tangchi. When the Sino-Japanese war broke out, he joined the exodus and an arduous journey of 1500 miles to Yuanling, China. From the Chafe Report, Father Morrissey became ill and without food during a Japanese attack. In 1944 was in Lishui District in China and left to return to Newfoundland and assigned to Harbour Main. In 1946 he returned to the China Missions after World War II. He was Pastor at Tungyang and spent 13 years in China until 1951 when the Communist take over forced suspension of foreign missionary activity. He went directly to Japan to study Japanese and remained about 32 years in Japan between 1951 and his retirement in 1990. He spent some time in between in Canada and had an extended leave in 1983. No other Newfoundland native spent as much time living among the Japanese as Father Morrissey. He wrote a book, "From North River to the Land of Cherry Blossoms" in 1983. He retired from Japan in 1990 and returned to Canada to live at Scarboro Missions central house but in 1991 he moved to Providence Villa because of his frail health. He died at the Providence Villa, Scarborough, Ontario on 26 July 1992 at age 78. He was a priest for 55 years.

BISHOP JOHN M.O'NEILL DD

Bishop John M. O'Neill was born in Harbour Grace on 26 October 1903 to Michael O'Neill and Catherine Lynch. He received his early education at Bay de Verde and then he attended St. Bon's for 5 years from 1916-1921 and graduated with an honors diploma in Senior Matriculation. He proceeded to Laval University in Quebec in 1921 for 6 years until 1927. He was ordained in Quebec on 24 April 1927 at age 23 ½ and two months later he received his Doctor of Divinity "Summa Cum Laude". His first assignments on return to Newfoundland were to Little Bay and Grand Falls and in 1931 he was appointed the first resident Parish Priest at Buchans for two years until 1932. Bishop March died on 12 January 1940 and Father John O'Neill was announced Bishop on 21 May 1940 and he was appointed to Harbour Grace on 12 June 1940 at age 36. He was Consecrated Bishop by Apostolic Delegate Antoniutti on 7 July 1940 as 5th Bishop of Harbour Grace (1940-1953) on the death of Bishop March and remained there for 13 years until 1953. In 1941 he delivered the panegyric at the Requiem Mass for Bishop Renouf. On 14 May 1944 he organized the Holy Name Society at Harbour Grace. In 1952 he celebrated his Silver Jubilee at Harbour Grace. In 1955 he attended the Centenary Ceremonies in St. John's. In 1953 Grand Falls was made a Co-Cathedral with Harbour Grace and he moved there in 1955. Grand Falls became the Diocese in 1965. Bishop O'Neill was there for 19 total years until 1972, when he retired for ill health. On 19 January 1957 his father died in St. John's at age 81. He retired as a Bishop on 18 November 1972 at age 69 due to ill health. He died in St. John's on 2 March 1974 at age 70. He was buried in the priests' plot in Harbour Grace. He was a priest for 46 years and a Bishop for 32 years.

REV. JOHN PEDDLE

Father John Peddle was born in Tilton, Conception Bay on 24 Nov 1931 to Lawrence Peddle and Ellen Mary Fitzgerald, the oldest of fourteen children. He attended the one room school in Tilton. After graduation he worked six years as a telegraph operator with the Canadian National Railway. From 1955-1957 he attended St. Jerome's College in Kitchener, Ontario. He then proceeded to St. Augustine's Seminary in Toronto, Ontario until 1961 and was ordained 11 June 1961, at age 29 at Harbour Grace by Bishop J. M. O'Neill. He was assistant at St. George's for 4 years from 1965-1969. He was appointed Parish Priest at Harbour Breton for 4 years from 1969-1973. In 1976 he was assigned to St. George's Diocese Priest senate vice Rev Gale. He was Parish Priest at Deer Lake for 4 years from 1976-1980. In 1980 he was appointed Parish Priest at St. Bernard's for 4 years until 1984. He was Parish Priest at Fortune Bay until 1989. In 1986 he celebrated his Silver Jubilee at Fortune Bay. In 1989 he was PP at Port au Port for 5 years from 1989-1994. In 1992 he was also PP at Our Lady of Fatima at Piccadilly. From 1994-1995 he was PP, at Port au Choix. His present assignment is Parish Priest at Pasadena.

RT. REV. JOSEPH W. PEDDLE D.P.

Monsignor Joseph W. Peddle was born in Spaniards Bay on 8 December 1904 to John Peddle and Susan Delaney. He was baptized on 11 December 1904 by Rev. John March; his sponsor's were Brendan Delaney and Bridget Delaney. He attended St. Bon's from 1922-1925 and received his AA Degree. He spent 6 years at the Laval University in Quebec, where he was ordained on 14 May 1931. He visited his parents in Corner Brook in June 1931, at age 26+. His first assignment was as Curate to Father William Finn in

Holyrood from 1931-1935. On Father Finn's death in 1935, Monsignor Peddle took over as Parish Priest at Holyrood for the next five years from 1935-1940. He then spent the next eight years as Chancellor to Bishop O'Neill at the Harbour Grace Cathedral. Monsignor Peddle has the distinction of being assigned as Parish Priest at Carbonear on two separate occasions. His first assignment was for five years from 1948-1953. In between he was Parish Priest, Grand Falls and Chancellor at the Cathedral at Grand Falls for 4 years from 1953-1957. He was honored with his Domestic Prelate in 1954 and in 1955 was made Vicar General to Bishop O'Neill at Grand Falls. In 1957 he returned to Carbonear for the next 17 years until his retirement in 1974 at age 70. In 1966 he became a Charter member and Chaplain to the newly established Monsignor McCarthy Knights of Columbus Council at Carbonear. He retired to St. John's and died two years later on 16 March 1976 at age 71 and is buried at Carbonear. He was 45 years a priest.

REV. FRANCIS PUMPHREY

Father Francis Pumphrey was born in Harbour Grace on 6 January 1890. He attended St. Bon's for 3 years from 1905-1908 to obtain his A.A. Degree. He taught at Norris Arm for 4 years from 1908-1912 and at the Harbour Grace Academy for one year from 1912-1913. In 1913 he proceeded to the Laval Seminary at Quebec and studied there for 6 years from 1913-1919. He was ordained by Cardinal Begin at Quebec on 25 May 1919 at age 29. After one year assignment at Harbour Grace, he was appointed Parish Priest at Little Bay for 8 years from 1919-1927. He then was assigned at Parish Priest at St. Gabriel Parish in St. Brendan's for 10 years from 1927 where he remained until he resigned due to ill health in 1937. Following his resignation, he had an operation at St. Mary's Hospital in Montreal and he died there on 12 August 1937 at age 47. His body was transported back to Corner Brook where he was buried on 19 August 1937. He was a Priest for 18 years. He is the uncle of Father Gregory B. Pumphrey.

REV. GREGORY B. PUMPHREY

Father Gregory Bonaventure Pumphrey was born in Harbour Grace on 14 July 1919 to Joseph Pumphrey and Agnes Martin. He attended St. Bon's for 2 years from 1941-1942. He proceeded to St. Peter's Seminary at London Ontario for 6 years from 1942-1948. He was ordained by Bishop O'Neill in Grand Falls on 12 June 1948. He was first Priest to be ordained in Grand Falls. His first assignment was curate to Father Hynes in Grand Falls for 8 years from 1948-1956. He then was appointed Parish Priest at St. Patrick's Parish in Fogo, following Rev. Joseph O'Brien, and he remained there for 9 years from 1956-1964. In 1964, following the retirement of Father Edward Jones, Rev. Pumphrey was appointed Parish Priest at St. Patrick's Parish in Brigus and remained for 6 years until 1970. The next two years was Parish Priest at St. Pius X Parish in Baie Verte. **(1970-1972).** In 1973 he was appointed

Parish Priest at Corpus Christi Parish in Northern Bay, following Father Edward Hearn, for 5 years from 1973-1978. It was here that he celebrated his Silver Jubilee in 1973. His next posting was as Parish Priest at King's Cove for 3 years from 1978-1981. In 1981 he was assigned as Parish Priest at Immaculate Conception Parish in Colliers for 3 years until his retirement on 24 October 1984 at age 65. In 1990 his residence was on Veterans Road in St. John's. From his retirement in 1984 until his death in 1995 he was a regular relieving Priest at many parishes particularly Carbonear, where he was loved by all. He died in St. John's on 29 July 1995 at age 76. He was waked at St. Teresa's Church in St. John's and his funeral Mass was in Carbonear on 1 August 1995. He is interned in the priests' plot of the Cemetery in his home town of Harbour Grace. He was a Priest for 47 years.

VERY REV. JOHN H. SCULLY

Very Rev. J. H. Scully and his Sister

Very Rev. John Henry Scully was born in Harbour Grace on 8 July 1875 to John and Alice Scully. He was baptized the same day by Very Rev. D. Falconio; his sponsor's were James Wall and Sarah Neil. He was a student at the Harbour Grace Academy for one year in 1881. He proceeded to the Propaganda College in Rome for 9 years from 1891-1900. He was ordained in the Eternal City on 20 May 1900 at age 25. His first assignment was as curate at Fortune Harbour and Brigus for 4 years from 1900-1904. In 1905, upon the death of Father Thomas Lynch at King's Cove, Father Scully was appointed Parish Priest to King's Cove and remained there for 25 years until 1930. In 1925 he celebrated his Silver Jubilee at King's Cove. In 1930, upon the death of Father Joseph Donnelly, Father Scully was selected to replace him as Parish Priest at St. Anne's Parish at Conception Harbour and he remained there 18 years until his own death in 1948. The depression of practically ten years duration was felt very keenly by his parishioners and by himself. On January 24, 1948, whilst returning from celebrating Mass, Fr Scully fell on the ice and had to be conveyed to St. Clare's Hospital. Although no bones were broken, this accident had influenced his condition. He died at St. Clare's Mercy Home in St. John's on 30 January 1948 at age 73. He was a Priest for 48 years. His cousin was Monsignor Ronald McD Murphy who celebrated his Requiem Mass.

REV. RONALD J.WALSH

Father Ronald Joseph Walsh was born in Harbour Grace on 14 September 1915 to Ronald and Isabel Walsh. He was baptized that same day by Rev. J. J. Walker; his sponsor's were Thomas O'Neill and Lucy Rose. His brother was Father Walter Walsh **(1913-1958).** Having spent two years at the Redemptorist Novitiate at Brockville, Ontario, Fr. Ron was accepted as an ecclesiastical student for the Diocese of Harbour Grace. He attended the Petit and Grand Seminaries of Laval University and was ordained at Harbour Grace on 17 June 1945 at age 30. His first assignment was as curate to Monsignor William Finn at Grand Falls for two years from 1945-1947. In 1947 he was appointed

Parish Priest at Coachman's Cove, following his brother Father Walter Walsh, and remained there for 6 years until 1953. In 1953 the center of the parish was moved to Baie Verte from Coachman's Cove and Father Ronald Walsh became first Parish Priest to St. Pius X Church in Baie Verte for 5 years until 1958. On 9 September 1958 his brother, Father Walter Walsh, died at St. John's at age 45 and is buried at Harbour Grace. On the transfer of Father Leonard Kelly from Badger in 1958, Father Walsh was appointed Parish Priest at Sacred Heart Parish in Badger and remained there for 3 years until 1961. He was transferred to St. Anne's parish in Conception Harbour. He celebrated his Silver Jubilee in 1970. He was Parish Priest of St. Gabriel's Parish at St. Brendan's from 1977 to his death in 1980. He died in St. Brendan's on 25 October 1980 at age 65. He was Priest for 35 years. He is buried in the priests' plot in the Harbour Grace Cemetery

REV. WALTER P. WALSH

Father Walter Patrick Walsh was born in Harbour Grace on 22 April 1913, the third son of Ronald and Isabel Walsh. He was baptized on 23 April 1913 by Rev. John March, his sponsor's were James and Maria Dunn. He was a brother to Father Ronald Walsh. **(1915-1980).** He attended the Harbour Grace Academy for 10 years from 1919-1929 and St. Bon's and Memorial University for two years from 1929-1931. He was accepted for the priesthood by Bishop March for the Diocese of Harbour Grace. He proceeded to the Irish College in Rome for 6 years from 1931-1937. He was ordained by Cardinal Sebaggiana at the Irish College in Rome on Holy Saturday, 27 March 1937 at age 24. He celebrated his first Mass on the following Easter Sunday. When he returned to Newfoundland, his first assignment was as curate to Father Mackey at Assumption Parish in Bay de Verde for one year from 1938-1939. In 1939 he was assigned as assistant to Monsignor McCarthy at St. Patrick's Parish in Carbonear for one year until 1940. During these two assignments, he spent two summers as a missionary in Labrador. He preceded his brother, Father Ronald Walsh, as Parish Priest of Coachman's Cove for 7 years from 1940-1947. In September 1950 he attended the Requiem Mass for Archbishop Roche. He was Parish Priest at Our Lady of Perpetual Help Parish in Gambo for 8 years from 1950 until his own death in 1958. He died on 9 September 1958 at St. Clare's Mercy Home in St. John's at age 45. He was a priest for 21 years. He is buried in the priests' plot in Harbour Grace Cemetery.

THE BEAUTIFUL HANDS OF A PRIEST

We need them in Life's early morning,
We need them again at its close,
We feel their warm clasp of friendship,
We seek them when tasting life's woes.

When we come to the world we are sinful,
The greatest as well as the least.
And the hands that make us pure as Angels
Are the beautiful hands of a priest.

At the altar each day we behold them,
And the hands of a king on his throne,
Are not equal to them in greatness,
Their dignity stands all alone.

For there in the stillness of morning,
Ere the sun has emerged from the East,
There, God rests between the pure fingers,
Of the beautiful hands of a priest.

And when we are taking life's partner,
Other hands may prepare us the feast,
But the hands that will bless and unite us,
Are the beautiful hands of a priest.

When the death dews on our eyelids are failing,
May our courage and strength be increased,
By seeing raised o'er us in blessing,
The beautiful hands of a priest,

God bless them and keep them all holy,
For the Host they daily caress,
What can a poor sinner do better,
Than ask Him, Who chose them to bless?

Chapter 14

ROMAN CATHOLIC CEMETERIES

HARBOUR GRACE

Catholic Church Property

As history shows us the Channel Islands, off England, had early connections with Newfoundland. It is believed that Sir Walter Raleigh, who was Governor of the Jersey, encouraged his people to become involved in the Newfoundland fishery and they first established a fishing station at Ferryland. They dominated Harbour Grace from the early 1600s up to the year 1765. Historical writer's state that it is most likely that St. John's received its name from a Jerseymen who named it after the parish of St. John's in Jersey. The History of Harbour Grace also indicates that much of its area was settled by Jersey men from Jersey, the largest of the British Channels Islands, long before the English themselves arrived. Reference was made to the Jersey era, as in the case of the land that the Roman Catholic Church now occupies before the dawn of the Harbour Grace Diocese in 1856. From O'Keefe's Grove in the East to Riverhead in the West, including Mosquito and the South Side of Harbour Grace, stores, stages, flakes, wharves and gardens were Jersey property. A Jersey firm named Juer had the land between Cochrane and LeMarchant Streets, what is known as Bennett's Lane, where the old Catholic graveyard was located, and it was given to the Church by the Thistles, another Jersey family. Fr Phelan was buried in 1799 in this special Roman Catholic Cemetery on Bennett's Lane. Land deed records in Grand Falls Diocese Archives indicates that 23 acres of land was transferred from Amy Thistle to Dr. Sterling in 1811 and Dr. Sterling sold it as a Memorial to Rev. Charles Dalton in 1839, which was later willed to the Nuns in 1858.

Catholic Cemetery Policies

It is interesting to note that in Newfoundland as a whole, Catholics were not permitted to bury there dead until August 1811, when Governor Duckworth, writing to Vicar General Rev. Father Ewer, granted the Roman Catholic Congregations "the indulgence…of being permitted to bury their own dead." The practice of charging burial fees as early as 1836 when an "infamous tax…imposed upon Catholics…the payment of twelve shillings for every Catholic that was buried." These fees were abolished during the administration of Bishop Fleming, who refused to permit his congregations to pay them.

Bennett's Lane Cemetery

While in Harbour Grace we apparently had a different relationship concerning Catholic burials, which seems to defy the St. John's orders not to permit Catholic burials. This involves the cemetery on Bennett's Lane, which was donated to the Catholic Church by the Thistle's. This Roman Catholic cemetery in Harbour Grace dates back to 1799, when Rev. Patrick Phelan was the first Priest to died in the service of his Church and was probably the first to be buried in this small burial site given to the fledgling Church by their Channels Island friends. This cemetery was used by Catholics from 1799 to 1861. The grave stones were recorded by Edward Chafe in 1987 and published in the NLGS Ancestor in 1988. They were also later recorded by Peggy Fahey and her daughter Sharlene in 1992, when they used talcum powder and stone brushing to read the old pitted stones. Many stones are unreadable. In 1996 a group from the Historical Society under Gorde Pike also recorded the information and attempted to reconstruct the tombstones for posterity.

Some of the Catholic burials in the Cemetery on Bennett's Lane.

C1754-1799 - Phelan, Patrick Rev. PP, Harbour Grace, drowned 3 Sep 1799, age 45+.
1755-1811 - Prendergast, Anastasia, wife of James, died 27 Sep 1811, age 56.
1740-1802 - Power, Peter, died 16 Nov 1802, age 62.
1768-1830 - Coughlan, Mary, died 1 Jan 1830, age 62.
1794-1803 - Coughlan, William Jr., died 9 June 1803, age 9 yrs.
1813-1815 - McGee, Anne, died 29 June 1915, age 2.
1760-1808 - Kelly, Richard, died 9 June 1808, age 48 and also his 6 children who died young.
1790-1837 - Molloy, William, MD, died Oct 1837, age 47. Also daughter and son.
1777-1842 - Condon, Frances, died 20 Feb 1842, age 65. and son, Richard, died 21 Oct 1870, age 63.
1786-1820 - Fox, ___-wife of James, died 7 Sept 1820, age 34. Mother of 5.
1792-1829 - Fox, Alice, wife of James, died 7 April 1829, age 37.
1786-1852 - Fox, James, died at St.John's, 19 Oct 1852, age 66.
1784-1852 - Keefe, Michael, died 21 May 1852, age 68.
1791-1861 - Keefe, Johanna, wife of Michael, died 2 Oct 1861, age 70.
1760-1820 - McGraill, John, died 6 Feb 1820, age 60.
1771-1831 - Dunford, Thomas, died 11 June 1831, age 60.
1759-1821 - Lombard, Thomas, MD, died 13 Nov 1821, age 62.
1764-1828 - Lombard, Mary, wife MD, died 22 Feb 1828, age 64. Also GDau.
1758-1810 - Mullowney, David, died 10 May 1810, age 52.
Mullowney,____, died 1803, age ____.
1795-1830 - Phelan, Elizabeth, died 17 Dec 1830, age 35.
------- 1849 - Mitchell, William, died 6 Aug 1849.
1816-1856 - Sullivan, Anne, died 10 Aug 1856, age 40. Sister. Died 1859.
1787-1852 - Green, Daniel, died 29 May 1852, age 65. HG Businessman.
1806-1830 - Green, Elizabeth, died 9 Aug 1830, age 24.
1803-1830 - McCarthy, Bridget, died 29 Aug 1830, age 27. Green's sister.
1819-1852 - Green, Elizabeth, wife of John, died 7 March 1852, age 33.
1763-1839 - Foley, Thomas, died 11 June 1839, age 76.
1766-1810 - Foley, Judith, wife of Thomas, died 6 July 1810, age 44.
-------1811 - Murphy, Johanna, wife of Edward, died 10 Sept 1811.
1813-1845 - Green, Catherine, wife of Daniel, died July 1845, age 32.
1733-1801 – Ferrers, MD (MD 37 years-Carbonear & HG)

The oldest Catholic Cemetery in Harbour Grace
on Bennett's Lane

SIGN: Heritage Site – Earliest Grave 1802
The oldest known grave is Fr. Phelan in 1799.

Main Roman Catholic Cemetery

It was in 1840's that the Catholic Church purchased the land where the present large Roman Catholic Cemetery stands. In May, 1888, a stone wall was begun around the new RC Cemetery, the work being done mostly by free labor. The wall was surrounded with wooden palings, and was completed by the end of the year. Three substantial pillars of brick and freestone were constructed for the entrance, ornamental iron gates were installed, and a road made through the cemetery. In 1991, the Newfoundland Genealogical Society, with permission from the Parish, made a survey of all the tombstones and recorded and published a Harbour Grace Cemetery booklet of all the known grave sites and tombstones available as of that date.

This cemetery has a special Priests Plot or section where Priests are buried.

PRIESTS BURIED IN HARBOUR GRACE

PRIESTS BY DATE OF DEATH

Priests Buried in Bennett's Lane & Main Roman Catholic Cemetery (19)

NAME	DIED	WHERE	BURIED
***PHELAN, Patrick Rev.**	**1799 Sep 3**	**Grates Cove.**	**Bennett's Lane.**
EWER, Thomas VRev.	**1833 Feb 6**	**Harbour Grace.**	**HG. NR**
DALTON, Charles VRev.	**1859 Jun 17**	**Harbour Grace.**	**HG. NR**
DALTON, John Most Rev.	**1869 May 5**	**HG,**	**Under HG Church.**
RYAN, James F. Rev.	**1893 Apr 17**	**Harbour Grace.**	**HG.**
FLYNN, Stephen Rev.	**1899 Aug 14**	**Little Bay.**	**HG.**
COLBERT, John T. Rev.	**1904 May 9**	**Conche.**	**HG.**
LYNCH, Thomas E. Rev.	**1905 Nov 1**	**GHosp. SJ.**	**HG.**
MARCH, John Most Rev.	**1940 Jan 12**	**Harbour Grace.**	**HG.**
HENNEBURY, William J. Rev.	**1947 Sep 8**	**SCMH, SJ.**	**HG.**
TERRY, Francis R. Rev.	**1952 Sep 3**	**St. Brendan's**	**HG.**
O'NEILL, Thomas Rev.	**1956 Apr 7**	**Colliers.**	**HG,**
WALSH, Walter Rev.	**1958 Sep 9**	**SCMH, SJ.**	**HG.**
CASEY, William H. Rt. Rev.	**1962 Feb 3**	**SCMH, SJ.**	**HG.**
O'NEILL, J.M. Most Rev.	**1974 Mar 2**	**St. John's.**	**HG.**
WALSH, Ronald J.Rev.	**1980 Oct 25**	**St. Brendan's.**	**HG.**
O'BRIEN, Joseph, Rt. Rev.	**1987 Nov 13**	**Harbour Grace.**	**HG.**
PUMPHREY, Gregory Rev	**1995 Jul 29**	**St. John's**	**HG.**
HOGAN, Wm P. Rt. Rev.	**1999 Aug 30**	**St. John's**	**HG.**

Reference: Harbour Grace RC Cemetery Listing. NLGS Project 1991, plus later information.

NR – No Record, believed buried at HG. Should be buried in Bennett's Lane.
*** Known Priest buried in Bennett's Lane Cemetery**

The oldest-born citizen burials in HG Main Cemetery

This list is not all inclusive. Some burials are listed only with a death date. Some have no year.

HUSBAND	WIFE
Roger Hanrahan, born 1766, died 1847, age 81.	
Michael Greene, born 1773, died 1842, age 69.	Mary Greene,(wife) born 1781, died 1850, age 69.
Matthew Dooling, born 1778, died 1865, age 87.	
William Walsh, born 1778, died 1862, age 84.	
Denis Shughrue, born 1779, died 1866, age 87.	Ellen Shughrue, (wife) born 1792, died 1870, age 78.
Thomas Fitzgerald, born 1781, died 1872, age 91.	Anne Fitzgerald, (wife) born 1784, died 1870, age 86.
John Murphy, born `1782, died 1860, age 78.	Ellen Murphy, (wife) born 1800,, died 1864, age 64.
	Honora Strapp, born 1843, died 1864. age 28.
	(Daughter of Ellen & John Murphy)
John Sheridan, born 1782, died 1870, age 88.	Ann Sheridan, (wife) born 1800, died 1867, age 67.
Joseph Ryan J.P. born 1784, died 1863, age 79.	
Richard Shea, born 1784, died 1846, age 62.	Mary Shea, (wife) born 1795c, died 1863, age 68c.
	(Richard Shea, Son, born 1816, died 1838, age 22.
	(Daniel Shea, son, born 1823, died 1871, age 48.)
	(James Shea, son, 1833, died 1871, age 38.)
Arthur Grubert, born 1786, died 1857, age 71.	Elizabeth Grubert, (wife) born 1792, died 1863, age 71.
	(Mary Grubert, born 1821, died 1849, age 28.)
	(Daughter of Arthur & Elizabeth)
James Keefe, born 1786, died 1839, age 53.	Mary Keefe, (wife) born 1785, died 1837, age 52.
John McLean, born 1786, died 1867, age 81.	Charlotte McLean, (wife) born 1791, died 1851, age 60.
John Fitzgerald, born 1786, died 1858, age 72.	
Thomas Burke, born 1787, died 1832, age 45.	Bridget Burke, (wife) born 1790, died 1865, age 75.
Daniel Green, born 1787, died 1852, age 65.	Rachel Gushue Greene, (wife) born 1795, died 1876, age 81.
Arthur Thomey, born 1788, died 1870, age 82.	
John Shea, born 1790, died 1859, age 69.	Ellen Shea, (wife) born 1798, died 1860, age 62.
Laurence Deigan, born 1790, died 1848, age 58.	(Erected by wife Catherine)
Michael Keating, born 1791, died 1866, age 75.	
Andrew Drysdale, born 1791, died 1869, age 78.	Mary Drysdale, (wife) born 1795, died 1873, age 78.
Edward O'Dwyer, born 1791, died 1857, age 66.	Mary O'Dwyer, (wife) born 1801, died 1855, age 54.
	Timothy O'Dwyer, born 1824, died 1850, age 26.
	(Son of Ed & Mary),
John Hennessy, born 1791, died 1848, age 57.	Ann Hennessy (wife) born 1800, died 1884, age 84.
Michael Murphy, born 1791, died 1868, age 77.	
Patrick Rohan, born 1793, died 1871, age 78.	
(Husband William Mitchell)	Mary Mitchell, (widow) born 1795, died 1862, age 67.
John Dawley, born 1794, died 1827, age 33.	
Maurice Walsh, born 1794, died 1870, age 76.	(Daughter: Mary Kelly, born 1824, died 1895, age 71.)
John Dunn, born 1784, died 1862, age 68.	Margaret Dunn (wife) born 1812, died 1878, age 66.
Garrett Wall born 1795, died 1875, age 80.	
David Keefe, born 1796, died 1840, age 44.	Catherine Keefe, (wife) born 1778, died 1868, age 90.
Michael Dooling, born 1796, died 1840, age 44.	Catherine Dooling, (widow) born 1809, died 1874, age 65.
Thomas Griffen, born 1797, died 1870, age 73.	Mary Griffen,(wife) born 1795, died 1849, age 54.
Edward Shanahan, born 1797, died 1871, age 74.	(Erected by son: Nicholas Shanahan)
Margaret O'Toole, born 1798, died 1873, age 75.	(Son Patrick O'Toole)
William Dixon, born 1801. died 1839, age 38.	Alice Dixon, (wife) born 1797, died 1863, age 66.
Daniel Walsh, born 1801, died 1871, age 70.	Catherine Walsh, (wife) born 1805, died 1926, age 75.
John Kelly, born 1801, died 1861, age 60.	
(Husband Wm Molloy, MD)	Joanne Morris, (wife) born 1798, died 1868, age 70.
	Elizabeth Butler, born 1801, died 1864, age 63.
William Innott, born 1802, died 1865, age 63.	
Edmund Foley, born 1802, died 1858, age 56.	
(Husband John Hays)	Anastasia Hays, born 1802, died 1876, age 74.
Edmond Keefe, born 1804, died 1849, age 45.	Bridget Keefe, (wife) born 1812, died 1877, age 65.
Patrick Hart, born 1804, died 1874, age 70.	Alice Hart, (wife) died Unk year, age 75.
Michael Hennesy, born 1805, died 1853, age 48	(Erected by wife, Barbara Hennesy)
Maurice O'Connell, born 1806, died 1874, age 68.	Catherine O'Connell (wife) born 1824, died 1889, age 65.
Maurice Power, born 1806, died 1844, age 38.	

David Goff, born 1807, died 1879, age 72.
Catherine Goff, (wife) born 1823, died 1883, age 60.
James Walsh, born 1807, died 1887, age 80.
Bridget McCarthy, born 1809, died 1906, age 96.
Joseph Graham, born 1809, died 1881, age 72.
Catherine Graham, (wife) born 1820, died 1879, age 59.
Matthew Harper, born 1811, died 1875, age 64.
Ann Harper,(wife) died 1880.
Patrick Devereaux, born 1812, died 1889, age 77.
William Howlet, born 1812, died 1864, age 52.
James Fleming, born 1813, died 1887, age 76.
Norah Fleming, (wife) born 1819, died 1870, age 51.
John Fitzgerald, born 1814, died 1892, age 78.
Ellen Fitzgerald, (wife) born 1822, died 1884, age 62.
(Husband Stephen Shea)
Ann Shea, born 1814, died 1875, age 61.
William Cody, born 1815, died 1854, age 39.
Michael Stapleton, born 1816, died 1895, age 79.
Catherine Stapleton, (wife) born 1819, died 1889, age 70.
Bartholomew Shughrue, born 1816, died 1890, age 74.
Ellen Shughrue, (wife) born 1820, died 1884, age 64.
Mary Greene, born 1816, died 1879, age 63.
John Callahan, born 1818, died 1871, age 53.
Catherine Callahan, (wife) born 1816, died 1886, age 70.
(Husband John Tobin)
Anastasia Tobin, born 1818, died 1983, age 45.
Michael Fitzgerald, born 1819, died 1887, age 68.
John Pumphrey, born 1819, died 1877. age 56.
(Erected by Mary Pumphrey, wife)
John Scully, born 1819, died 1889, age 70.
Alice, Scully, (wife) born 1837, died, 1897, age 60.
John Maney, born 1819, died 1853, age 34.
(Son of Philip and Margaret Maney)
Dennis Shea, born 1819, died 1911. age 92.
Mary Shea, born 1825, died, 1896, age 71.
Mary Shea, born 1833, died 1887, age 54, Boston
(Sister of Dennis),
Mary Dwyer, born 1820, died 1892, age 72.
John C. Mitchell, born 1820, died 1882, age 62.
(Erected by his wife Elizabeth Mitchell)
Thomas Strapp, born 1820, died 1896, age 76.
James Callahan, born 1820, died 1892. age 72.
Johannah Doyle, born 1820, died 1885, age 65.
Capt Henry Thomey, born 1821 – died 1911, ago 90
Lawrence Keefe, born 1821, died 1855, age 34.
Michael Quinn, born 1821, died 1864, age 43.
Thomas Lynch, born 1822, died 1903, age 81.
Michael Mulcahy, born 1823, died 1896, age 73.
Catherine Mulcahy, (wife) born 1832, died 1908, age 76.
John Sheridan, born 1824, died 1912, age 88.
Ellen Sheridan, (wife) born 1829, died 1921, age 92.
Michael Shortis, born 1824, died 1877, age 53.
Frances Green, born 1825, died 1908, age 83.
Peter Dwyer, RH, born 1825, died 1893, age 68.
Michael J. Jones born 1825, died 1912, age 87.
Ellen Jones (wife) born 1834, died 1892, age 58.
Michael O'Brien, born 1825, died 1900, age 75.
Eliza O'Brien (wife) born 1840, died 1888, age 48.
Charles Layton, born 1826, died 1887, age 61.
(Wife Mary Layton).
John Murphy, born 1826, died 1858, age 32.
Patrick Connors, born 1827, died 1898, age 71.
Mary Connors, (wife) born 1827, died 1877, age 50.
Roger Scully, born 1828, died 1899, age 71.
Elizabeth Scully, (wife) born 1841, died 1903, age 62.
Patrick Lynch, born 1828, died 1863, age 35.
Ann Lynch, (wife) born 1831, died 1889, age 58.
James Rohan, born 1828, died 1852, age 24.
William Dunn, born 1829, died 1905, age 76.
Joseph Innott, born 1829, died 1902, age 73.
Caroline Innott, (wife) born 1830, died 1902, age 72.
Michael Mackey, born 1829, died 1897, age 68.
Thomas Cody, born 1830, died 1894, age 64.
Ellen Cody,(wife) born 1840, died 1905, age 65.
Husband Capt Green)
Agnes Mary Green, (wife Capt) born 1831. died 1868, age 37.
Mary O'Neill, born 1831, died 1919. age 88.
John Keefe, born 1830, died 1864, age 34.
(Erected by wife Mary Keefe.)
Michael Scully, born 1831, died 1892, age 61.
James Clance, born 1832, died 1916, age 84.
Bridget Clance, (wife) died 1886.
James Gould, born 1832, died 1912, age 80.
Anastasia Gould, (wife) born 1843, died 1898, age 55.
Michael Mulcahy, born 1832, died 1926, age 94.
Mary Mulcahy (wife) born 1842, died 1927, age 85.
Nicholas Shannahan, born 1832, died, 1917, age 85.
Mary (Fitzpatrick) Shannahan, born 1844,died 1919,age75.
Cornelius McCarthy, born 1832, died 1914, age 82.
Bridget McCarthy (wife) born 1839, died 1924, age 85.
Margaret McCarthy (sister) born 1838, died 1805, age 67.
Thomas Power, born 1832, died 1864, age 32.
Patrick Brien, born 1835, died 1891, age 56.
Anne Brien, (wife) born 1833, died 1861, age 28.
John Martin, born 1835, died 1918, age 83.

Margaret Thomey, born 1835, died 1904, age 69.

James L. Keefe, born 1835, died 1890, age 55.
Lawrence Hayes, born 1835, died 1905, age 70. **Theresa Hayes, (wife) born 1843, died 1915. age 72.**
John Hogan, born 1835, died 1902, age 67.
(Erected by husband Andrew Hartrey) **Ellen Hartrey, born 1836, died 1870, age 34.**
Charles Louis Kennedy, born 1836, died 1916, age 80, Baltimore
Nicholas Fitzgerald, (by wife) born 1838, died 1906, age 63.
William Miller, born 1839, died 1914, age 75. **(Erected by his wife Mary Hart.)**
Edward Guilfoyle, born 1840, died 1918, age 78.
Andrew Power, born 1840, died 1885, age 45.
Charles McCarthy, born 1840, died 1885, age 45. **(Erected by son Michael McCarthy & Mother)**
Thomas Gregory Green, born 1842, died 1864, age 22.
(Husband Richard Hickey) **Mary Hickey, born 1842, died 1873, age 31.**
(Husband John Strapp) **Frances Mary Strapp, born 1842, died 1874, age 32.**
Jeremiah Shea, born 1843, died 1913, age 70. **Mary Shea, (wife) born 1848,died 1902, age 54.**
Patrick Moriarty, born 1843, died 1908, age 69. **(Erected by wife Mrs. Moriarty)**
James Fitzgerald, born 1844, died, 1882, age 38.

Margaret Browne, born 1844, died 1864, age 20.
William Tobin, born 1844, died 1923, age 79. **Bridget Tobin, (wife) born 1843, died 1915, age 72.**
William O'Neill, born 1845, died 1881, age 36.

Mary Kennedy, born 1846, died 1916, age 70.
Patrick Doyle, born 1845, died 1932, age 87. **Susannah Doyle, (wife) born 1848, died 1938, age 90.**
William Kearney, born 1848, died 1936, age 88.
(Husband Jeremiah Shea) **Mary Shea, born 1848, died 1902, age 54.**
Michael Guilfoyle, born 1849, died 1933, age 84.

Above Information taken from the NLGS Project Recording of the HG Cemetery 1991 by Edward Chafe

Main Roman Catholic Cemetery in Harbour Grace

LIST OF NAMES IN HARBOUR GRACE ROMAN CATHOLIC CEMETERY – 2002

ABBOTT
ALLEN
ANDREOLI
ANONSEN
ASH
AYLWARD
AYRE
BARNES
BARRINGTON
BARRON
BARTLETT
BARTON
BATEMAN
BEAUCAGE
BOYLETT
BRADBURY
BRAZIL
BREEN
BRIEN
BRIFFETT
BROWNE
BURKE
BURSEY
BUTLER
BUTT
BYRNE
CAHILL
CAIN
CALLAHAN
CALLANAN
CAMPBELL
CARBERY
CARROLL
CASEY
CLANCE
CLARE
CLARKE
CLATTENBURG
CLEARY
COADY
COLBERT
COLLINS
CONNOLLY
CONNORS
COOKE
COOMBS
COONEY
CRANE
CROKE
CURNEW
DALTON
DAVIS
DAWLEY
DAWSON
DEADY
DEIGAN
DEVEREAUX
DIXON
DODD
DOOLEY
DOOLING
DORAN
DOYLE
DRISCOLL
DRYSDALE
DUFF
DUFFY
DUGGAN
DUNN
DWYER
EDWARDS
EMBERSON
EMERSON
ETHRIDGE
FAHEY
FALLON
FARRELL
FEWER
FINN
FITZGERALD
FITZPATRICK
FLEMING
FOLEY
FORWARD
FOSTER
FOWLOW
FREEMAN
FUREY
GALWAY
GARLAND
GLAVINE
GOFF
GORMAN
GOULD
GRAHAM
GRANVILLE
GREEN
GRIFFIN
GRUBERT
GUILFOYLE
GUSHUE
HAIRE
HAMILTON
HANRAHAN
HANRATTY
HARPER
HART
HARTERY
HARTIGAN
HAYDEN
HAYES
HEALEY
HEARN
HENNEBURY
HENNESSEY
HIBBS
HICKEY
HOGAN
HOLLOWAY
HOWLET
HUNT
HURDLE
HYNES
INNOTT
JOHNSON
JONES
JORDAN
JOY
KANE
KEARNEY
KEATING
KEEFE
KEHOE
KELLY
KENNEDY
KENT
KEOUGH
LAHEY
LANE
LAYTON
LeBLANC
LEE
LEWIS
LILLY
LITTLEJOHN
LYNCH
MacISSAC
McCARTHY
McCORMACK
McGRATH
McKAY
McLEAN
McNAMARA
MACKEY
MADDIGAN
MAHER
MALONEY
MANEY
MANNING
MARCH
MARSHALL
MARTIN
MEADUS
MERCER
MILLER
MISCH
MITCHELL
MOLLOY
MORIARTY
MORRISSEY
MULCAHY
MURPHY
MURRAY
NICHOLL
NORRIS
NORTHCOTT
O'BRIEN
O'CONNELL
O'CONNOR
O'DWYER
O'FLYNN
O'GRADY
O'KEEFE
O'LEARY
O'NEILL
O'RIELLY
O'SHEA
O'TOOLE
OLDFORD
OLIVE
PARSONS
PAYNE
PEARCE
PEDDLE
PENNEY
PIKE
POWER
PUMPHREY
PURCELL
QUIGLEY
QUINN
REDDICK
REDDY
REYNOLDS
ROHAN
ROSE
RUSSELL
RYAN
SCULLY
SEAMAN
SHANAHAN
SHEA
SHEEHAN
SHEPPARD
SHERIDAN
SHORT
SHORTIS
SHUGARUE
SINNOTT
SINYARD
SLOAN
SMALLCOMBE
SMART
SMITH
SMOKEHAM
SPARKES
STEFIE
ST. JOHN
STAPLETON
STOODLEY
STRAPP
SULLIVAN
TAYLOR
TERRY
THISTLE
THOMEY
TOBIN
TRAVERSE
WALBOURNE
WALL
WALSH
WHALEN
WHELAN
WHITE
WHITTLE
YETMAN

NFLD, LABRADOR GENEALOGICAL SOCIETY PROJECT 1991

HARBOUR GRACE ROMAN CATHOLIC CEMETERY RECORDS 2002

Presentation Sisters buried in Harbour Grace

The Presentation Sisters are buried in a special cemetery on the old Convent land which they owned and sanctified as their own burial site. The Nuns cemetery was blessed in 1881.

SISTERS

1. Sr. M. Rose Barter, died, 8 Sept 1860, age 27 years.
2. Sr. M. DeSales Lovelock, died, 11 Oct 1868, age 22 years.
3. Sr. M. Xaverius Lynch, died, 25 Nov. 1882, age 69 years.
4. Sr. M. DeSales Lovelock, died, 8 May 1885, age 72 years.
5. Sr. M. Josephine French, died, 17 March 1886, age 90 years.
6. Sr. M. Veronica Power, died, 6 April 1887, age 61 years.
7. Sr. M. Clare Lovelock, died, 26 Aug 1897, age 52 years.
8. Sr. M. Agnes Banuil, died, 27 Aug 1901, age 67 years.
9. Sr. M. Catherine Flynn, died, 9 Dec 1910, age 82 years.
10. Sr. M. Teresa King, died, 17 Dec 1910, age 69 years.
11. Sr. M. DePazzi Lovelock, died, 17 Jan 1914, age 72 years.
12. Sr. M. Francis Flynn, died, 27 Jan 1914, age 82 years.
13. Sr. M. John Shortall, died, 20 May 1915, age 51 years.
14. Sr. M. Margaret Northcott, died, 19 Oct 1929, age 38 years.
15. Sr. M. Anna Whelan, died, 10 May 1949, age 66 years.
16. Sr. M. Patrick O'Keefe, died, 11 Oct 1950, age 72 years.

ALL BURIED IN THE HARBOUR GRACE CONVENT CEMETERY.
NEAR ST. COLUMBA PRIMARY SCHOOL.
(Now Harbour Grace Elementary School)

The grave sites are a mute and forlorn reminder of those noble women of God who joyfully give up all things for Christ. The three who came to Harbor Grace in 1851 (Xaverius Lynch, Josephine French & DeSales Lovelock) are all buried in Harbour Grace plus 13 more, three of whom were nieces of Sister M. DeSales Lovelock.

In 2002 the Presentation Sisters from St. John's had the grave stones replaced onto a new concrete slab and greatly improved the burial area.

Chapter 15

FIRSTS AND SPECIAL TRIBUTES

To parishes of Harbour Grace & Grand Falls.

1. First Mission, *Outside of St. John's,* was at Harbour Grace in 1784.

2. Harbour Grace shares with St. John's the distinction of being the *oldest continuous Catholic Church* in Newfoundland. Both in 1784.

3. The only Harbour Grace Parish Priest who *signed the letter of petition* to raise Rev. James L. O'Donel to Bishop in 1796: Rev. Patrick Phelan.

4. First Priest to Die in Newfoundland in the *Line of Duty*: First Mission Priest at Harbour Grace, Rev. Patrick Phelan in 1799.

5. Harbour Grace Priest who established *the second BIS* in Newfoundland at Harbour Grace in 1814: Rev. Thomas Ewer.

6. *First Priest to celebrate a Golden Jubilee in Newfoundland* History: Harbour Grace assigned priest Rev. Thomas Ewer in 1826. (1776-1826).

7. Only Priest to have distinction of being *Vicar General to first three Vicar Apostolic's in Newfoundland:* Rev. Thomas Ewer (1806-1833) to Rev. James O'Donel, Rev. Patrick Lambert and Rev. Thomas Scallan.

8. Only Harbour Grace Priest *to buy house and 23 acres of land for the Presentation Sisters* in Harbour Grace. 1839: Rev. Charles Dalton.

9. First Presentation Sisters *outside St. John's,* introduced to Harbour Grace in 1851. Rev. Charles Dalton and Bishop Mullock.

10. *First Bishop* at Harbour Grace Diocese: Bishop John Dalton (1856-1869).

11. Only uncle who was *Vicar General to his nephew* Bishop in Newfoundland history: Uncle VRev. Charles Dalton to nephew Bishop John Dalton. Harbour Grace. 1856-1859.

12. First Parish where Presentation Sisters *owned their own land* and Convent. Harbour Grace, willed directly to them by Rev. Charles Dalton in 1858.

13. The First Harbour Grace Parish Priest to *Administer* the Harbour Grace Diocese during the absence of a Bishop: Rev. John J. Walsh, 1869-1870.

14. Only Diocese in Newfoundland to have an *Italian born Bishop*: Bishop Henry Carfagnini, 1870-1880.

15. Historical religious event: the *"Harbour Grace Affray"* took place at Harbour Grace - 1883.

16. Only Diocese in Newfoundland history to have the *Cathedral burn* to the ground at Harbour Grace: 1st Immaculate Conception Cathedral in 1889.

17. Two Priests from Harbour Grace were sent to the *USA to solicite funds* for the new Cathedral: VRev. John Roe and Rev. Thomas Lynch. (1890-1891).

18. First Bishop to be *consecrated in Harbour Grace*: Bishop March - 1906.

19. *First Native Born* Bishop of Harbour Grace: Bishop March – 1906.

20. The only Bishop in Nfld that was a proponent for the first Knights of Columbus in Nfld at Harbour Grace in 1909: Bishop John March.

21. *First Knights of Columbus* Council in Newfoundland: Dalton Council # 1448 – 1909. First Chancellor was Rev. Dr. S. J. Whelan.

22. *First Chaplain* to first KC Council in Newfoundland history: Parish Priest at Harbour Grace, Rev. William P. Finn.

23. The Priest who helped organize the *Catholic Cadet Corps* (1910) and the Chaplain of the Brigade at Harbour Grace: Msgr. William F. Finn.

24. *First Parish Priest* at new Grand Falls Parish: Rev. William Finn in 1912.

25. Only known Bishop in Newfoundland history, to be *shot at in Church*: Bishop John March in 1913, in Harbour Grace Cathedral.

26. *Bishops to die in office* at Harbour Grace: Bishop Dalton in 1869 and Bishop March in 1940.

27. The only Nfld Diocese to have *two Vicar Generals at same time.*
A. Msgr. Dinn, VG to Bishop O'Neill - 1940-1944 and
B. Msgr. F. D. McCarthy *Honorary* VG to Bishop O'Neill 1940-1944.

28. Only Diocese in Newfoundland history to *lose its Diocese status*: Harbour Grace to Grand Falls. 1965.

29. Second Diocese in Newfoundland history to *move its Diocese location*: Harbour Grace to Grand Falls. 1965. (St. George's moved to Corner Brook in 1946).

30. The First Grand Falls Parish Priest to *Administer to Grand Falls* Diocese during the absence of a Bishop: Rev. E. T. Bromley, 1999-2001.

31. HG-GF Diocesan Priests who were appointed *Vicar Generals*:
Rev. John J. Walsh – 1860-1869.
Rev. John J. Walsh – 1870-1872.
Rt. Rev. M. F. Dinn – 1940-1955.
Rt. Rev. Joseph W. Peddle – 1955-1965.

32. Harbour Grace-Grand Falls Dioceses sent at least 34 known *Priests to Labrador*: (See Chapter 8)

33. Diocesan Priests who were *First Parish Priests:*
1st PP, Fortune Harbour, 1879. Rev. Stephen Flynn.
1st PP, Coachmans Cove, 1880. Rev. Richard Shean.
1st PP, Whitbourne, 1887. Rev. Pat W. Browne.
1st Res. PP, Avondale, 1909. Rev. Richard Shean.
1st PP, Grand Falls, 1912. Rev. William P. Finn.
1st PP, Gambo, 1916. Rev. John S. Kavanagh.
1st PP, St. Alban's, 1916. Rev. Stanislaus St. Croix.
1st PP, Corner Brook, 1926. Msgr. Walter Brennan.
1st PP, Bishops Falls, 1930. Rev. James A. Hinchey.
1st Res PP, Buchans, 1931. Rev. John M. O'Neill.
1st PP, Gander, 1946. Rev. Philip J. McCarthy.
1st PP, Colliers, 1948. Rev. Thomas D. O'Neill.
1st PP, Norris Arm, 1953. Rev. Michael Carey.
1st PP, Baie Verte, 1953, Rev. Ronald J. Walsh.
1st PP, Badger, 1955. Rev. Leonard Kelly.
1st PP, Brent Cove, 1959. Rev. Linus J. Coady.
1st PP, La Scie, 1959. Rev. Linus J. Coady.
1st PP, Clarenville, 1990. Rev. A. Wayne Cummings.

34. Harbour Grace born Priests who were *Monsignors:* Rt. Rev. William H. Casey, Rt. Rev. William Hogan, and Rt. Rev. Joseph Peddle of Spaniards Bay.

35. Harbour Grace born Priest who wrote a book of Poems: "*Lone Eagles of God*": Very Rev. Leslie G. Fitzgerald.

36. *First Priest to be ordained* in Grand Falls: Harbour Grace born, Rev. Gregory B. Pumphrey, 1948.

37. There are *Three Bishop's buried in Harbour Grace Cemetery*: Bishop Dalton (1869), Bishop March (1940) and Bishop O'Neill (1974).

38. Harbour Grace Priest who wrote the *"History of Brent's Cove"*. Rev. Linus Coady.

39. Harbour Grace Priest who was *burned trying to rescue the Blessed Sacrament* during a Church fire at Northern Bay. Very Rev. Leslie G. Fitzgerald.

40. Harbour Grace Priest who *visited the MicMac Indians* with Bishop McDonald in 1883. Rev. Stephen Flynn.

41. The following priests from the Diocese were *members of Orders:*

Rev. M. Blackmore, CssR	Rev. N.J. Mackenzie, S.J.
Rev. P.J. Burke, SFM (LPH)	Rev. V.J. Mackenzie, S.J.
Rev. M.P. Carey, SFM	Rev. E. Moriarity, SFM
Rev. Joe Crawford, CssR	Rev. J. Moriarity, SFM
Rev. J. Davis, CssR	Rev. T.M. Morrissey, SFM
Rev. John Leo Foley, MM	Rev. Adrian Murphy, CssR
Rev. J. Glavine, CssR	Rev. Gerald Murphy, CssR
Rev. Andrew Lane, AFR	VRev. T. Ryan, S.J.
Rev. Anthony Martin, SFM	Msgr. F.J. Ryan, S.J.
	Rev. L.M. Wall, SFM

42. Three known Diocese priests who were *assigned to China*:

- Rev. John Leo Foley, MM.
- Rev. Edward Moriarity, SFM.
- Rev. Thomas M. Morrissey, SFM. *(and Japan)*

43. Harbour Grace Priest who accompanied Bishop O'Neill to Rome for the *Vatican Council II* for several months each year from 1961-1965. Msgr. William P Hogan.

44. Harbour Grace Priests who were *assigned outside Newfoundland and died there:*

- Rev. John Leo Foley in China.
- Rev. John J. Lynch in USA.
- Rev. Thomas M. Morrissey in Ontario.

45. Harbour Grace Priest who was placed under *house arrest in China* for three years. Rev. Edward Moriarity, SFM.

46. Harbour Grace Priest who spent one year in the Newfoundland Regiment in *World War I.* Rev. John L. Foley, MM.

47. Harbour Grace Priest who spent 25 years at *Santa Domingo* from 1945-1970 and later went back to visit and see Pope John Paul II in 1979. Rev. Joseph Moriarity, SFM.

48. Harbour Grace Priest who wrote the book, *"From North River to the Land of Cherry Blossoms"*, about his *assignment to Japan*. Rev. Thomas M. Morrissey, SFM. Spent more time in Japan than any other priest.

49. Spaniard's Bay born priest who served *two separate assignments at Carbonear,* 1948-1953 and 1957-1974 for a total of 22 years: Msgr. Joseph W. Peddle.

50. Diocesan Priests who were *related*:

- Rev. William Hearn brother to Rev. Edward Hearn.
- Rev. Leo Burke brother to Rev. Pat Burke.
- Rev. Norbert Mackenzie twin brother to Rev. Vincent Mackenzie
- Rev. Walter Walsh brother to Rev. Ronald Walsh.
- Very Rev. Charles Dalton was uncle to Bishop Dalton.
- Bishop John March uncle to Very Rev. Thomas O'Neill.
- Msgr. Edward O'Brien uncle to Msgr. Joseph O'Brien.
- Rev. John Mackey uncle to Msgr. Joseph O'Brien.
- Rev. Francis Pumphrey uncle to Rev. Gregory Pumphrey.
- Rev. J. J. Lynch uncle to Bishop O'Neill.
- Rev. Bernard Duffy uncle to Msgr. E. F. Walsh.
- Rev. J. Kevin Barker uncle to Rev. Michael Barker.
- Bishop O'Neill cousin to Very Rev. Thomas O'Neill.
- Rev. Edward Moriarity cousin to Rev. Joseph Moriarity.
- Rev. J. H. Scully cousin to Msgr. Ronald McD Murphy.
- Three brothers: Rev. William McC Murphy, Rev. Aidan Murphy, CssR and Rev. Gerald Murphy, CssR.

51. Harbour Grace Priest who was appointed *Superior for the Chinese Missions* at the Scarboro Headquarters in Vancouver, B.C. Rev. Edward Moriarity, SFM.

52. *Summary of Service*: Deceased Bishops of Diocese.

Bishop, 12 years, Priest, 23 years:	1- Bishop John Dalton, age 49.
Bishop, 31 years, Priest, 53 years:	3- Bishop Ronald McDonald, age 76.
Bishop, 32 years, Priest, 46 years:	5- Bishop John M. O'Neill, age 70.
Bishop, 33 years, Priest, 51 years:	4- Bishop John March, age 76.
Bishop, 34 years, Priest, 58 years:	2- Bishop Henry Carfagnini, age 81. (Only 10 years in Newfoundland)

53. Harbour Grace Priest who was *baptised, confirmed* and *ordained* by Rev. John M. O'Neill (Later Bishop): Rev. Linus J. Coady.

54. *Summary of Service*: Harbour Grace deceased Priests:

Priest, 6 years, age 38 – Rev. John Leo Foley, MM. d. China.
Priest, 18 years, age 47 – Rev. Francis Pumphrey. d. Montreal.
Priest, 21 years, age 45 – Rev. Walter P. Walsh. d. St. John's.
Priest, 22 years, age 46 – Rev. Thomas E. Lynch, d. St. John's
Priest, 23 years, age 47 – Rev. J. Ronald Jones. d. Lourdes.
Priest, 24 years, age 49 – Rev. Stephen Flynn. d. Little Bay.
Priest, 35 years, age 65 – Rev. Ronald J. Walsh. d. St. Brendan's.
Priest, 43 years, age 70 – Msgr. William H. Casey. d. St. John's.
Priest, 43 years, age 68 – Very Rev. Leslie Fitzgerald. d. New York.
Priest, 45 years, age 71 – Msgr. Joseph Peddle. d. St. John's.
Priest, 45c years, age 71 – Rev. John J. Lynch. d. S. Dakota, USA.
Priest, 46 years, age 70 – Bishop John M. O'Neill, d. St. John's.
Priest, 47 years, age 78 – Msgr. Walter Brennan, d. Deer Lake.
Priest, 47 years, age 69 – Rev. Edward Moriarity, SFM. d. Ontario.
Priest, 47 years, age 76 – Rev. Gregory B. Pumphrey. d. St. John's.
Priest, 48 years, age 73 – Very Rev. J. H. Scully. d. St. John's.
Priest, 51 years, age 83 – Msgr. William P. Hogan. d. St. John's.
Priest, 55 years, age 78 – Rev. Thomas Morrissey, SFM. d. Ontario.

55. Only Diocese in Newfoundland to have *Co-Cathedrals*: Harbour Grace and Grand Falls from 1953-1965.

56. Two Priests *buried in Grand Falls* Cathedral cemetery:
Msgr. W. P. Finn (1953) and Rev. Pat A. McCormack (1965).

57. *Origination Dates* of Parishes in Diocese:

Harbour Grace 1784, King's Cove 1815, Brigus 1824, Carbonear 1826, Northern Bay 1838, Tilting Fogo 1840, Harbour Main 1857, Harbour Breton 1860, Baie Verte 1880, Bay de Verde 1880, Holyrood 1883, Conception Harbour 1884, Whitbourne 1887, St. Brendan's 1891, Conche 1906, North River 1906, Grand Falls 1912, Gambo 1916, St. Alban's 1916, Avondale 1927, Buchan's 1929, Bishop Falls 1938, Windsor 1940, Gander 1946, Colliers 1948, Norris Arm 1953, Badger 1955, Brent's Cove, 1959, Plate Cove 1966, Port Union 1982, Clarenville 1990.

58. Diocesan Priests that received *Doctorates* (8):

Bishop O'Neill, DD; Msgr. Joseph Murphy, L.L.D.; Msgr. Edward O'Brien, Hon. L.L.D.; Very Rev. Edward Jones, DD; Very Rev. Leslie Fitzgerald, Ph.D; Rev. Stephen Whelan, DD; Rev. Pat Browne, DD, Std, Ph.D and Rev. Brian Dunn, DD.

59. Knights of Columbus *Councils named after Diocesan Priests* of Harbour Grace or Grand Falls: (16)

Harbour Grace – Dalton Council. # 1448 on 29 Nov 1909.
Grand Falls – Notre Dame Council, # 2053 on 19 Nov 1919.
Buchans – Bishop March Council. # 3315 on 20 May 1950.
Labrador City – Wabush – Rev. Dr. Whelan Council. # 5662 on 19 Apr 1965
Gander – Rev. Patrick McCormack Council. # 5769 on 26 Nov 1965.
Carbonear – Msgr. McCarthy Council. # 5902 on 6 Nov 1966.
Bishop Falls – Msgr. Finn Council. # 5904 on 11 Nov 1966.
Harbour Breton – Fr. Michael Haynes Council. # 7127 on 4 Jun 1978.
Brigus – Rev. Dr. E. J. Jones Council. # 7146 on 25 Jun 1979.
Harbour Main – Bishop O'Neill Council. # 7207 on 26 Nov 1978.
Gambo – Cullen-Walsh Council. # 7285 on 25 Mar 1979 (merged w/5769 in 1994)
King's Cove – Msgr. Williams Council. #8640 in 19 Feb 1984.
Norris Arm – Rev. Carey Council. # 8643 on 19 Feb 1984.
Baie Verte – Rev. T.P. Sheen Council. # 9289 on 1 April 1986.
Fogo – Msgr. J.M O'Brien Council. # 9654 on 8 Nov 1987.
Whitbourne – Rev. Browne Council. # 9661 on 1 Nov 1978.
Little Bay – Rev. Pumphrey Council. # 11577 on 23 April 1995.

60. Other Knights of Columbus Councils in the Diocese:

Avondale – Cabot Council # 6001 on 7 Oct 1967.
Melrose –Port Union – St. Patrick's Council # 8317 on 1 March 1983.
Plate Cove – Tracey Murphy Council # 8737 on 1 June 1983.
Badger – Joseph Coleman Council # 8686 on 1 April 1984.
Windsor – P. J. Connors Council # 8700 on 1 April 1984.

61. Two *twin brothers* from Grand Falls who became Jesuit Priests: Revs. Vincent and Norbert Mackenzie. Born 6 July 1918.

62. Priests from the Diocese who are *buried under a Church*:

VRev. Kyran Walsh buried at Harbour Main, 1868.
Bishop Dalton buried at Harbour Grace Cathedral, 1869.
Rev. Matthew Scanlan buried at Bonavista, 1871.
Rev. James Cummins buried at Northern Bay, 1875.
VRev. James Brown buried at Harbour Main, 1887.
VRev. Jeremiah O'Donnell buried at Harbour Main, 1891.
Rev. Patrick O'Donnell buried at Harbour Main, 1906.
Rev. Gregory Battcock buried at Holyrood, 1910.
VRev. John Roe buried at Harbour Main, 1911.

63. Priests known for being *healers.*

VRev. Dr. Edward J. Jones, VRev. Michael J. Kinsella, Rev. James A. Hinchey and Rev. John Patrick Mackey.

Chapter 16

CATHOLIC EDUCATION IN HARBOUR GRACE

In the early days of Irish Catholic settlements in Newfoundland, records seem to indicate that tutors or educated adults taught the Catholic students in private homes. Accounts of history have borne out the fact that some prosperous Irish families even brought tutors with them from Ireland to teach their children. According to Sister Dinn's pamphlet printed in 1975, it is worthy to note that the inhabitants of Harbour Grace were the first to petition for aid to education, when they requested the Government for aid to their Free School founded in 1826. A committee was set up to study the matter with the results that several schools benefited from this request.

Along with money for the Protestant Schools, the sum of one hundred pounds per annum were allocated to aid St. Patrick's Free School in Harbour Grace and the sum of one hundred pounds per annum in aid of the Presentation Convent School at St. John's and that the said several sums be granted for the period of five years. This was the first time government aid was received by the Roman Catholic schools. Up to this time, the Presentation Convent School had been maintained solely by Bishop Fleming.

When Newfoundland received Representative Government from England in 1832, the House of Assembly began to pass laws for the operations of the government, police departments, and passed the Educational Acts of 1836 – 1839. Newfoundland began to become a civilized Colony. In 1838, an amendment to the 1836 Act added 150 pounds for textbooks, to be divided and distributed by "His Excellency the Governor among the several Boards of Education who may approve the same".

Church authorities built on the already established Church-tutor-School educational systems throughout the Island and permitted the establishment of a Denominational System of Education, which began in 1843.

The Roman Catholic School Boards were established at Harbour Grace and Carbonear in 1843. These Board's under Rev. Charles Dalton, PP, Harbour Grace and Rev. James P. Gleeson, PP, Carbonear.

IN THE *"DIGEST OF THE LAWS OF NEWFOUNDLAND"* PRINTED IN 1847, BY E. M. ARCHIBALD, ESQ. P. 176. WE COPY THE FOLLOWING:

6 Vict. Cap. 6 -- An Act for the encouragement of Education in this colony. -[22d May, 1843.]
See. 1. - 5,100 pounds annually granted for the support of education, of which one-half to be appropriated to support of Protestant, and one-half to support of Roman Catholic schools.
2. Distributes the above sum amongst the districts of St. John's, Brigus, Harbour Grace, Carbonear, Trinity Bay North, Trinity Bay West, Trinity Bay South, Bonavista Bay South, Bonavista Bay North, Fogo, Twillingate, Bay Bulls, Ferryland, St. Mary's, Placentia, Burin and Fortune Bay.
3. Defines the boundaries of the foregoing districts.
4. The Governor to appoint, in said districts, Protestant Boards of Education, to consist of seven persons, of whom the senior clergyman of the district shall be one: provided that where the amount appropriated to the Protestant part of any district shall be less than 25 pounds, such sum shall be appropriated by the adjoining Protestant Board.
5. The Governor to appoint a Catholic Board of Education in each district in manner prescribed in preceding section. 6........11
12. Certain other schoolhouses in the districts of St. John's and Conception Bay and the schoolhouses in all other districts where the majority of the population are Roman Catholics, to be held by the Roman Catholic boards. 13........15
16. Catholic boards of St. John's and Harbour Grace to appropriate portions of the money granted to them to the support of certain Catholic schools.

The same year when Protestants received legislative sanction to authorize the use of the bible in their schools, they were separated from Roman Catholic schools and there developed a bi-denominational school system within Newfoundland.

St. Patrick Free School

In 1843 the Roman Catholic School board was established in Harbour Grace and the first Catholic free school was St. Patrick's for the poor Catholic children. This school was located a short distance from the first wooden Chapel, across from the bay.

Report on St. Patrick's School by the School Inspector, Mr. Bertram Jones
22 January 1846

This school, formerly known as St. Patrick's Free School, lies under the very great disadvantages of having a mean and most inconvenient school room. The Teacher, Mr. Fennell, is a person fully competent to conduct it, and the children are here much better supplied with books than in most of their schools. The number present at the inspection was 75; their progress in arithmetic and writing was satisfactory, and their reading moderately good.

In 1864-65 Eugene Hamilton was Teacher at St. Patrick's Free School, HG.

The public Harbour Grade Academy was also established in 1843 but for the children who could pay for their education and was a non-denominational school under a separate Board of Directors. John I. Roddick was chosen Master, with a yearly salary of 50 pounds.

Roman Catholic School Board in Harbour Grace - 1848

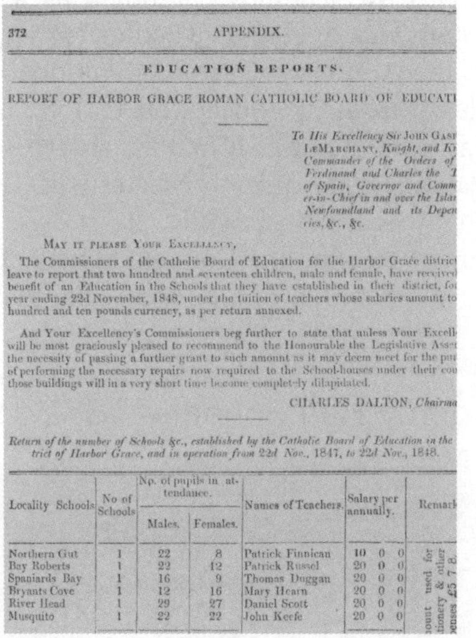

372 APPENDIX.

EDUCATION REPORTS.

REPORT OF HARBOR GRACE ROMAN CATHOLIC BOARD OF EDUCATI

To His Excellency Sir JOHN GASP LEMARCHANT, *Knight, and K Commander of the Orders of Ferdinand and Charles the T of Spain, Governor and Comm er-in-Chief in and over the Islan Newfoundland and its Depen cies, &c., &c.*

MAY IT PLEASE YOUR EXCELLENCY,

The Commissioners of the Catholic Board of Education for the Harbor Grace district leave to report that two hundred and seventeen children, male and female, have received benefit of an Education in the Schools that they have established in their district, fo year ending 22d November, 1848, under the tuition of teachers whose salaries amount to hundred and ten pounds currency, as per return annexed.

And Your Excellency's Commissioners beg further to state that unless Your Excell will be most graciously pleased to recommend to the Honourable the Legislative Asse the necessity of passing a further grant to such amount as it may deem meet for the pu of performing the necessary repairs now required to the School-houses under their co those buildings will in a very short time become completely dilapidated.

CHARLES DALTON, *Chairma*

Return of the number of Schools &c., established by the Catholic Board of Education in the trict of Harbor Grace, and in operation from 22d Nov., 1847, to 22d Nov., 1848.

Locality Schools	No of Schools	No. of pupils in attendance.		Names of Teachers.	Salary per annually.	Remark
		Males.	Females.			
Northern Gut	1	22	8	Patrick Finnican	10 0 0	ount used for tionery & other penses £5 7 8.
Bay Roberts	1	22	12	Patrick Russel	20 0 0	
Spaniards Bay	1	16	9	Thomas Duggan	20 0 0	
Bryants Cove	1	12	16	Mary Hearn	20 0 0	
River Head	1	29	27	Daniel Scott	20 0 0	
Musquito	1	22	22	John Keefe	20 0 0	

Presentation Sisters Arrive

With the coming of the Presentation Sisters in Harbour Grace in 1851 two schools were built that year, both for girls, one being named "St. Mary's" and the other "St. Joseph's". The old school, known as St. Patrick's, was then pulled south across the road, to the bank overlooking the sea, yet still only a short distance from the wooden Chapel north of the road.

For the next three decades this building served as a rugged elementary school for boys. Though it boasted a large enrollment, St. Patrick's was staffed with only one teacher. For example, the Inspector's Report for the year 1870, indicated that Eugene Hamilton as teacher with an enrollment of 118 boys. However, the average daily attendance that year was only 48. Of the enrollment, 57 boys were over 12, while 61 were under 12. His annual salary was 100 pounds, plus 8 2/3 pounds for fees.

ROMAN CATHOLIC HARBOUR GRACE ACADEMY

On his appointment to Harbour Grace in 1880, Bishop McDonald immediately saw the pressing need for a boys school befitting the Capital of the Diocese, and in 1882, he opened the Roman Catholic Harbour Grace Academy. It was a fine building with a bell in the tower to summons the boys to school. They had three classrooms on the ground floor separated by glass partitions. There were three teachers: Preparatory room was in charge of Mr. Michael Scully who had been the last teacher at St. Patrick's school. Next room was Mr. Thomas Hanrahan as teacher. In the Third room Mr. J. J. Wickham was in charge. Total of 147 students. St. Patrick's School closed when the Academy became operational. Thomas Hanrahan taught at the Academy from its conception in 1882 until he died in the autumn of 1916 at an early age of 54. In 1887 and the 1890 Directory lists the Principal as Patrick Devine, Second Master was Thomas J. Hanrahan, and Assistant Master was Michael Scully. Its classrooms were closed in 1944 and the boys then attended the Convent School. Today the Academy building is used by the Knights of Columbus as their Council-Meetings building on Harvey Street.

Academy Hall School – 1882-1944

Town Parade on Harvey Street, Harbour Grace
As it passes the Academy Hall—1890s

Academy Hall from 1882 to 1944.

Concert at Academy Hall

Concert

17 December 1889
8 pm o'clock

ACADEMY HALL
Harbour, Grace

PRESENT:
His Lordship Bishop McDonald
Rev. Frs. Donnelly and March
and
Rev. Messrs Noel and Smart

Manager - Master William Kennedy
Opening. Instrumental Solo - Master Wm Kennedy
"Moonlight on the Lake" - Miss Rose Hogan
"May Delights" - Master Henry Strapp
"Maiden's Prayer" - Miss Alice Brien

Company Singers:
Annie Fitzgerald, May Glendon, Maggie Fitzgerald, Fanny Kennedy, Alice Brien, Mary Hennessey, Aggie Thomey, Maddie Cody, Master Henry Strapp, Lizzie Winslow, Belle Kennedy, John Hennessey, and T. Hogan.

"Whispering Hope" - Duet - Miss Aggie Thomey & Miss Mary Hennessey
"Poor Old Joe" - Master Ronald Kennedy (5 years old)*
"Give My Love to All At Home" - Miss Alice Brien

Chairman of the Evening - Mr. Isaac Pumphrey

Sister Columba Elementary School

An Roman Catholic Elementary School was built in 1960 by the Presentation sisters and Sister Columba became the Principal and on her Golden Jubilee in 1966, the school was known as the St. Columba School, in recognition of Sr. Mary Columba Peddle. Sr Columba retired in 1972 at age 80, after 49 years of teaching business education in Harbour Grace. In 1989 a new St. Columba elementary school was opened in Harbour Grace and was blessed and officially opened on November 20, 1989 by Bishop Faber MacDonald of Grand Falls. Also on hand was the Education Minister, Dr Phil Warren and Sister Regina Quigley, General Superior of the Presentation sisters, who cut the ribbon to mark the official opening of the $2.4 million educational facility. The Principal was Sister Bride Power.

> **Sister Power described the opening as, "a milestone in the history of education in our community, recalling with pride, the dedicated men and women who have set high standards of excellence in academic pursuit. A history dating back to Bishop Howley who begun the first Presentation school in Harbour Grace in 1851. She noted that Msgr O'Brien, 30 years ago, decided to change the name of the Presentation School to St. Columba School." In remembrance of Sister Columba and with respect for Msgr. O'Brien, she continued, "Inspired by the example of those gone before us, may we continue to develop a true center of learning where youth are encouraged to develop their potential, each persons contribution is seen as important, a Christian community which fosters love of God and one another."**

Also present were Bill Finn, the board chairman, Gerry Fallon, Catholic Education Council, executive director, Rev. Michael Walsh, Parish Priest, and the committee chairman for the blessing ceremonies, Pat Collins, and Language Arts Coordinator with the RC School Board for Conception Bay North.

St. Columba School – Harbour Grace Elementary School

St. Columba's Elementary Kindergarten Class 1979-1980

When the old St. Francis High school was destroyed by fire in the spring of 1973, the building, then under construction, which was to have housed the new St. Columba, had to be converted into a high school, causing a lengthy delay in the construction, of the new St. Columba.

When the people of Newfoundland voted against continuing the religious denominational school system in 1997, Sister Columba School was renamed the Harbour Grace Elementary School and the Christian Brothers at St. Francis High school left Harbour Grace. Both of these schools became public schools with no longer any religious affiliation.

No more Denominational Schools

When the people of Newfoundland voted to discontinue the denominational system of Education in 1997 all the schools became secular/public schools. In 1998, all students in the area, grades 8-12 were sent to St. Francis in Harbour Grace and grades one to seven were sent to St. Columba in Harbour Grace. In 1999, all grades 10-12 were sent to Carbonear Collegiate and St. Francis became a community school for grades 5-9. Presently Collegiate covers 10-12 grades for students from Perry's Cove, Salmon Cove, Victoria, Freshwater, Carbonear, Harbour Grace, Riverhead, HG and Harbour Grace South. The government stripped all Catholic crucifixes, statues and other items from the walls and halls and renamed many of the schools with secular names.

The current trend for the future seems to be that all schools on Catholic property or have Catholic names will be closed. There will ultimately be no vestige of Catholicism in any government school in any town in Newfoundland.

Chapter 17

CATHOLIC VETERANS AND SHIP CAPTAINS

FROM HARBOUR GRACE

Veterans

Each town in Newfoundland is proud of the men who went off to war when their country called them. Harbour Grace and nearby communities were no exceptions. We have tried to enumerate many of the names of those deceased Harbour Grace Catholic citizens who joined the Military services in both the First World War and the Second World War as well others who joined to give their service in other times of peace or war. Most of these names were taken from the Harbour Grace Roman Catholic cemetery. Of the total 35 names of deceased Catholic veterans, there were 14 who participated in the WWI and 6 died in that war. There were 21 who participated in WWII and two died in that war. There were two who were in both WWI and WWII. There are four who were members of the famed Royal Newfoundland Regiment, there were 10 in the Army and 12 in Navy, 4 in the OS Forestry Unit and 2 in the Merchant Navy. Two were unknown. A special documentation is included for Cpl Matthew Brazil for his heroism in World War I. He was awarded the French Croix de Guerre but did not receive it. He died in 1958 in St. John's and his son accepted his medal on behalf of the Brazil family in 1983, 25 years after his death. We regret any Catholic veteran we have overlooked.

Ship Captains

Every coastal town in Newfoundland had its share of ship Captains who went off to the foreign countries with supplies to and from Newfoundland. These men sailed the seas and some lost their lives doing it. It takes some heroes to take a ship all over the world knowing what problems they will encounter or whether they will ever come back or not. We can be proud of all those who made it back safely and we must honour and never forget those who were not so lucky. Harbour Grace indeed can be proud of the many Catholic ship Captains and Master Mariners who graced the far seas and Labrador seal hunts. We have identified some 60 names and we regret if we have inadvertently omitted any other names which were not discovered in our research.

Deceased Catholic Veterans from Harbour Grace

Catholics in Harbour Grace and Vicinity who gave there service to Newfoundland during World War I and II. We have listed those who are deceased. These names were taken from the records of the Harbour Grace Catholic Cemetery and Maryknoll Missionary records for Father Foley. We are sorry for any names that were left off.

Brazil, Matthew	**Died, 1958, age 63**	**Corp, Royal Nfld Regt, WWI**
Butler, James	**Died, 1962, age 61**	**NF, Overseas Forestry Unit WWI**
Casey, Francis	**Died, 1961, age 61.**	**IRT. WWI**
Crane, John C.	**Died, 1984, age 67**	**Seaman, Royal Navy WWII**
Edwards, Peter J.	**Died, 1968, age 44**	**GNR, Royal Artillery WWII**
Fahey, Timothy A,	**Died, 1991, age 77**	**NF, Overseas Forestry Unit II**
Fahey, William T.	**Died, 1975, age 63**	**Seaman, Royal Navy WWII**
Fitzgerald, Isaac, Pte	**Died, 1988, age 65**	**Canadian Army, WWII**
Foley, John Leo, Rev.	**Died, 1938, age 38**	**Nfld Regt, WWI, died China.**
Furey, Francis	**Died, 1980, age 66**	**NF, Overseas Forestry Unit II**
Galway, Leo Joseph	**Died, 1994, age 72**	**Royal Navy WWII**
Guilfoyle, Peter	**Died, 1918, age 26**	***KilledS.S. Florizel Disaster. WWI**
Jordan, William	**Died, 1969, age 55**	**Seaman, Royal Navy, WWII**
Kennedy, John T.	**Died, 1918, age NL**	***Corp, Killed WWI**
Kehoe, William J.	**Died, 1915, age 26**	***Died Battle Ship-McNaughton, WI**
Lynch, Francis J.	**Died, 1978, age 70**	**Seaman, Merchant Navy, WWII**
McCarthy, Justin	**Died, 1982, age 94**	**Private 185th BN, WWI=II**
McCarthy, T.J.	**Died, 1973, age 53**	**MWO, RN, RCN WWII**
McGrath, Ronald	**Soldier in WWI**	**Grandson, John Thomey WWI**
McGrath, Thomas	**Soldier in WWI**	**Grandson, John Thomey WWI**
Moriarity, Patrick	**Died, 1990, age 81**	**Engr, Merchant Navy, WWII**
Moriarty, James J.	**Died, 1955, age 36**	**Royal Navy, Seaman. WWII**
Morrissey, Michael	**Died, 1963, age 80**	**Royal Nfld Regiment, WWI**
Morrissey, Patrick	**Died, 1926, age 37**	**PTE, died, Montreal.**
Morrissey, Thomas J.	**Died, 1944, age 26**	***Royal Navy, Killed WWII**
Murphy, Walter J.	**Died, 1915, age 19**	***#407,RNFRegt,DiedMudies WI**
O'Neill, George	**Died, 1962, age 53**	**NF, Overseas Forestry Unit II**
O'Neill, Michael	**Died, 1962, age 59**	**1st Ofc, Cdn Merchant Marine II**
O'Neill, Patrick J.	**Died, 1958, age 51**	**59 Nfld Hvy Regt, R.A. WWII**
Power, James	**Died, 1918, age 23**	***PTE, Killed WWI**
Reddy, Patrick R.	**Died, 1941, age 26**	***HM Royal Navy, Killed WWII**
Reynolds, Francis	**Died, 1971, age 59**	**Royal Artillery, Army, WWII**
Sheehan, James P.	**Died, 1983, age 70**	**Seaman, Merchant Navy WWII**
Strickland, Eprain	**Died, 1955, age 61**	**Vet WW I & II**
Walsh, Frank P.	**Died, 1917, age 22**	***KIA France, WWI**
Whelan, Richard Pte	**Died, 1928,age 31**	**World War I.**

Total 35

Underlined and * indicates killed in war.

LANCE CORPORAL MATTHEW BRAZIL

Matthew Brazil was born in Spaniard's Bay on 25 August 1894, the son of Thomas and Mary (Peddle) Brazil and baptised in Church of Immaculate Conception in Harbour Grace by Rev. J. Murphy on 2nd Sept 1894. He was a miner on Bell Island where he worked for 42 years. When the first Great War began he saw a need for his services and joined the Royal Newfoundland Regiment (Regiment # 1368) in 1915 at age 20. He served for four years taking part in many of the more notable campaigns. During his military service he performed honorable service qualifying for the Distinguished Conduct Medal, the Military Medal and the Croix De Guerre, and was wounded three times. He was also decorated with the various service medals.

> Lance Corporal Matthew Brazil was awarded the military Medal (MM) in 1918. This award was given for the conspicuous bravery under heavy machine gun fire in full view of the enemy. At the time he was in charge of a Lewis Gun team and when his gun was running short of ammunition, he collected what ammunition he could from the dead and wounded to refill his magazines. In 1918, Corporal Brazil was awarded the Distinguished Conduct Medal (DCM) for conspicuous bravery and devotion to duty during the attack from Ledgehem towards the Lys. On October 14, 1918, during this attack, all the platoon except himself and one other man had become casualties. They then attached themselves to the platoon on the left. When the attack was temporality held up by four field guns firing at close range, this NCO went forward with the platoon which was attempting to outflank the guns. When the platoon could advance no farther on account of fire from the guns and machine guns, L/Cpl. Brazil and another man voluntarily doubled forward with a Lewis Gun by short rushes under intense fire from one gun and four machine guns, until they reached a position well on the right flank. On arriving there, while the other man opened fire with his Lewis Gun, L/Cpl Brazil opened fire with his rifle. Under this coverage fire the platoon was able to advance and finally captured the four field guns and four machine guns. It was entirely due to L/Cpl Brazil's dash and bravery that the platoon was able to advance, capture the hostile guns and enable the advance to press forward. Cpl Brazil was Section commander at Ledgehem when he won the DCM. Accounts show that Brazil played a crucial part in the action which saw Thomas Ricketts being awarded the Victoria Cross (VC) for his (Ricketts) bravery at the Battle at Ledgehem. Ricketts was eighteen years old at the time. It is little noted that Brazil may have been the Section Commander with Ricketts and Pte. Richard Powers at the time Ricketts was awarded the VC. Captain Frost praised the splendid conduct of all three of these men. It must have been difficult in determining which one of these men should be awarded the Victoria Cross. He was discharged on March 31, 1919.

Shortly after he arrived home in 1919, he married Agnes Delaney. They were blessed with three sons (Gerald, Matthew and Michael) and six daughters (Cecilia, Margaret, Mary, Claire, Joan and Eileen). It was seventy years after he served in the First World War and 25 years after his death, that he was honoured with the French Croix de Guerre that he earned during the First World War but never received. On 6 Oct 1983, his son Michael accepted the medal on behalf of the Brazil family. During the war he received several injuries. In Gallipoli he was severely frostbitten. He was gassed at the Battle of Ypres and at Boulogne he was severely gassed on several occasions. At Beaumont Hamel he received wounds to his left leg and face. He later was seriously scalded in his right hand and took a bullet in his right wrist in a bombing attack. Despite all this he remained in action until the end of the war, when he returned to Bell Island.

He died at the DVA Ward of St. John's General Hospital on 6 February 1958 at age 63. *Printed from the Daily News, St. John's Tuesday, February 16, 1958.*

LANCE CORPORAL MATTHEW BRAZIL
D.C.M., M.M., C. de C.

"The toil of the day is over,
And the heat of the noon-day sun
Gives place to the shade that God has made
When the race of the strong is run."

The royal Canadian Legion in Spaniard's Bay, the Cpl Matthew Brazil Branch is named in his Honour.

In Honour of Lance Corporal Matthew Brazil

Lance Corporal Matthew Brazil, D.C.M., M.M., C. de G.
1894-1958

OPENING OF VETERANS MEMORIAL HIGHWAY

RIBBON OF HIGHWAY

Leo Moriarty, 87, a world War 2 veteran from Harbour Grace cut the ribbon to mark the official opening of the latest section of the Veterans Memorial Highway to be completed. The ribbon was held by two other veterans, Ed Sampson and Ted Norman, members of Branch 23, Royal Canadian Legion, Carbonear. Transportation Minister Percy Barrett; MHAs George Sweeney and Roland Butler and Harbour Grace Mayor Don Coombs were also on hand for the Dec. 6, 2002 ribbon cutting. *Bill Bowman, The Compass – Dec. 10-16, 2002.*

Installation Officers Hr. Grace Canadian Legion - 1962

Julia Edwards, President of HG Legion Club. 2003

CATHOLIC SHIP CAPTAINS FROM HARBOUR GRACE

THESE NAMES WERE TAKEN FROM DIRECTORIES, BOOK OF NFLD AND OTHER DOCUMENTS AND WERE LISTED AS CAPTAIN OR MASTER MARINER AS WELL AS INFO FROM ROMAN CATHOLIC CEMETERY LISTINGS.

1. **BAILEY, HENRY, CAPTAIN – Brought "Fleetwing" safely to HG wharf. 1872. Donate SVDP – 1877. Victoria 1871.**
2. **BARRY, JOHN CAPTAIN – Donate SVDP – 1877. LeMarchant Rd – 1885.**
3. **BRIEN, MICHAEL CAPTAIN – Donated to SVDP - 1877**
4. **COLBERT, B. CAPTAIN – Caledonian House - 1870**
5. **COSTELLO, THOMAS CAPTAIN - See Capt Charles Fitzgerald.**
6. **DELANEY, MARK CAPTAIN – SS "Vanguard" Brought Herring To Montreal - 1886**
7. **DOYLE, CAPTAIN – From Waterford in 1844.**
8. **DRYSDALE, ANDREW T. CAPTAIN – (1790-1869) Age 79. Postmaster. Wife: May Died 1873, Age 78.**
9. **DUNN, JOHN CAPTAIN – Donated to SVDP – 1877.**
10. **FITZGERALD, CHARLES CAPTAIN – Wed: 1885. Margaret Costello, Eldau of Capt. Thomas Costello, SJ.**
11. **FITZGERALD, DANIEL CAPTAIN – Water Street – 1885-1904. Master Mariner 1885-1890-1904.**
12. **FITZGERALD, MICHAEL CAPTAIN –Dau: Wed Constable McDonald 1880.**
13. **FITZGERALD, NICHOLAS CAPTAIN – Victoria – 1894. Master Mariner, His Dau Wed: John Phippard, 1880. He Died 1906, Age 68. Wife give SVDP.1877.**
14. **FITZGERALD, WILLIAM CAPTAIN – 1819-1887, Died Labrador, Age 68.**
15. **FRANCIS, A. CAPTAIN – Wed: 1880. Mary Jos McGrath, RH HG.**
16. **GORDON, SAMUEL CAPTAIN - (1813-1877) Ship Owner 1871.Donate SVDP, 1877.**
17. **GREEN, DANIEL CAPTAIN – (1817-1882), Age 65. Wed: 1856. Alice Grace, SJ., Merchant, HG. Capt D. Greene, famous seal-killer of HG, Died 9 June 1882.**
18. **GREEN, JOHN CAPTAIN – Wed: 1856, Ellen Molloy. Bennett's Lane – 1885. Captain Brig "Saxon"**
19. **GREEN, THOMAS CAPTAIN – (1827-1889), Age 62. Wed: 1ST 1853, Agnes Dooling, (1831-1868), Age 37, Buried HG & Wed: 2ND 1868, Lucy Drysdale. Brazil Lane 1871.**
20. **HANRAHAN, NICHOLAS CAPTAIN – (1818-1898), Age 80. Water Street 1864-1885, Wed: 1859, Julia McCarthy, Carbonear. Captain Brig "Iona", HG. 1861, 11,000 seals.**
21. **HAYDEN, TIMOTHY, CAPTAIN – Donate SVDP, 1877.**
22. **HAYES, GEORGE, CAPTAIN – Born 1878, Died, 15 Nov 1924, age 46. Buried HG Cemetery. Brother of James.**
23. **HAYES, MICHAEL, MASTER 1829, News – Shipment of goods from St. John's.**

24. HAYES, WILLIAM CAPTAIN – 1854 Wed Mary Green, Dau: Daniel Green.

25. HEALE, RICHARD CAPTAIN – 1890 Wed Elfreda Morris, HG. Master Of Sch: "Island Maid".

26. HENNESSEY, JOHN CAPTAIN – Born 1840. Donate SVDP, 1877. Donated Bell for RC Cathedral, West Tower, 1884.

27. HENNESSEY, WILLIAM CAPTAIN – Master Mariner 1871. 207 Water, St. Donate SVDP, 1877.

28. HOGAN, DANIEL CAPTAIN – 1885-86 Master Mariner.

29. HOULIHAN, JOSEPH CAPTAIN – Master of Brigantine "William Donnelly" Launched at Harbour Grace 1865. Master for one year.

30. JONES, HENRY CAPTAIN – Born 1879, Died 24 Mar 1959, age 80. Buried in HG RC Cemetery. Wife: Isabella.

31. KEARNEY, DENIS CAPTAIN – Wed 1889, Mary Murphy, Otterbury. 1890-Master Mariner.

32. KEEFE, JAMES L. CAPTAIN – (1835-1890). Age 55. Donate SVDP, 1877.

33. KEEFE, JOHN CAPTAIN – (1836-1880). Donate SVDP, 1877. Wife Mary Keefe Died 6 Jan 1880, Age 41. He Died 27 Nov 1880, Age 44.

34. KEEFE, LAWRENCE CAPTAIN – Born 1801. Died 29 July 1855, Age 54. Buried in HG RC Cemetery. Wife Rebecca died 1863, age 58.

35. KEEFE, MICHAEL L. CAPTAIN –Donate SVDP, 1877. Wed: 1878, Agnes Pumphrey. 1885-86 Master Mariner.

36. KEHOE, JOHN CAPTAIN –

37. KEHOE, M.T. CAPTAIN – 1908-1915 Master Mariner.

38. KEHOE, THOMAS CAPTAIN – 1894-97-1898- Master Mariner, 1904 Master Mariner and 1935-36 Captain.

39. KEHOE, WILLIAM CAPTAIN –

40. LAYTON, CHARLES, CAPTAIN – Born Norfolk, England, 4 Nov 1826, Died HG, 9 Sep 1887, Age 61. Buried HG RC Cemetery. Commanded the "Charles" and made 72 trips across the Atlantic in nine years, averaging four complete voyages a year.

41. LYNCH, THOMAS CAPTAIN –Born 1822. Donate SVDP, 1877. Died 4 Mar 1903, Age 81, Buried in HG RC Cemetery. Punton & Munn built "James" for Capt Lynch. Father of Rev. John J. Lynch who was born c1858 and ordained in HG on 8 Sept 1883.

42. MCCARTHY, JUSTIN CAPTAIN – (1808-1853) Age 45. Wife: Margaret. (1809-1880) age 71. His son Justin Jr was Born 1848, Died 1927, age 79. Buried HG RC Cemetery.

43. MURPHY, JAMES CAPTAIN – 1866, He brought in 17,450 Pelt and 2nd Trip brought in 5,950 Pelts.

44. MURPHY, JOHN CAPTAIN – In 1832 he lost his house in a Fire. And he died in 1858, Catalina. Master of Brig, "Adament". Dau Wed Capt. D. Pumphrey 1879.

45. O'NEILL, DENNIS CAPTAIN – 1871, Master Mariner, Victoria. 1877, SVDP.

46. O'NEILL, RICHARD CAPTAIN –

47. POWER, DAVID CAPTAIN – (1823-1872) Age 49. Captain of Brig, "Breadalbane".

48. POWER, JOHN CAPTAIN – 1890-1894-97-1898 Master Mariner.

49. POWER, RICHARD CAPTAIN – (1819-1884) Age 65, Native HG.

50. PUMPHREY, DANIEL CAPTAIN – Born 1853. Donate SVDP, 1877. Wed Dau of Captain John Murphy, Ellen Mary 1879. Died 1910, Age 57.

51. PUMPHREY, JOHN *LATE* CAPTAIN – Listed on SVDP, 1877.

52. PUMPHREY, WILLIAM CAPTAIN – Wed 1870, Jane F. Prendergast, SJ. Donate SVDP, 1877.

53. SMART, EDMUND CAPTAIN – Born 8 Oct 1843. Master Mariner. 1864-65. Wife Ellen died 1869, age 24. Lost at sea, 20 Dec 1872, Age 29. Tombstone in HG cemetery. His sister Ellen born 6 Jan 1845-died 22 Dec 1869, age 24. Parents: Martin & Catherine Smart.

54. SMART, JAMES CAPTAIN – 1864-65 Mariner.

55. SMART, MARTIN CAPTAIN – Born HG 1809. 1864-65 Master Mariner. 1st wife: Margaret, died 1868, age 38. 1871, Master Mariner, Victoria. He died 1884, age 75. His 2nd wife, Catherine, died 1887, age 46. Donate SVDP, 1877.

56. STRAPP, JOHN CAPTAIN – Wed Frances M. Keefe, Dau of Capt. Lawrence Keefe 1865. Donate SVDP, 1877.

57. THOMEY, ARTHUR CAPTAIN –Born 1788, Died 6 Jan 1870, age 82. Died at Early Harbour, Labrador. Buried HG RC Cemetery. (Wife) Donate SVDP, 1877.

58. THOMEY, HENRY W. CAPTAIN –Born 1821, Mosquito. 1839, 1st Voyage as Master. Wed: Leonora Forward 1848. Master of "Isabel Ridley" for 28 years (1839-1867). Took Rev. Carfagnini to Labrador in 1864. Ship Owner 1871. (Wife) Donate SVDP, 1877. He Died 6 January 1911, Age 90. Buried in HG RC Cemetery.

59. WALSH, PATRICK CAPTAIN – Wed Mary Ann Graham, 1889, HG. He is from Riverhead.

60. WHELAN, JOHN CAPTAIN – Dau Wed A. Dawe in Bay Roberts in 1882.

Note: SVDP is St. Vincent de Paul

The Barque "Fleetwing" commanded by Captain Henry Bailey. (Book Nfld)

Chapter 18

HISTORY OF

ST. FRANCIS HIGH SCHOOL

Harbour Grace

1961 – Official Opening by Christian Brothers.

1963 – Second Grade XI Class Graduation.

1967 – First Year-Book – Concepts.
Distribution of Prizes, Scholarships & awards.

1968 – Graduation Concepts.

1973 – Fire destroyed St. Francis High School.

1974 – St. Francis HS rebuilt by Msgr. Joseph O'Brien.

1975 – First ex-pupil ordained at Harbour Grace.
Rev. William Hearn.

1983 – Diana and Charles visit St. Francis High School.

1985 – Knights of Columbus present a Flag Pole to
St. Francis High School.

1986 – Concepts published.

1994 – Male Athlete of Year – Mike Fahey.

1995 – Christian Brothers leave St. Francis HS.

1999 – Presenting Concepts – '99 - Final Edition of Concepts.

Opening of St. Francis High School

On 5 September 1961, St Francis Catholic High School opened for Catholic boys in Harbour Grace with the Christian Brothers taking over the teaching under Rev. Brother C.P. Duffy as its first Principal. This was the same year that St. Claire's Catholic High School opened in Carbonear for the Catholic girls. The first concert was presented on Dec. 8, 1961 and a prominent part was taken by the Glee Club at the official blessing and opening of the school on May 2, 1962. On this occasion the school was honoured by the presence of His Excellency Bishop O'Neill, Very Rev. Bro. W. C. Penney, Provincial of the Christian Brothers, Premier J.R. Smallwood, Hon. Max Lane, acting Minister of Education, Magistrate W. E. Mercer and many other dignitaries of Church and State.

HARBOUR GRACE – Premier J. R. Smallwood speaking at the official opening of St. Francis High School on May 2, 1962. The platform: His Excellency, J.M. O'Neill, D.D. Bishop of Harbour Grace-Grand Falls, Rev. Bro. W.C. Penney, Brother Provincial, Hon. C. M. Lane, acting minister of Education, Bro. C. P. Duffy, Principal.

St. Francis High School, Harbour Grace

THE SECOND GRADE XI CLASS GRADUATED 1963

STAFF AND FACULTY OF ST. FRANCIS HIGH SCHOOL

TOP ROW: Bro Donald Murphy, James Mahoney, Ronald Connolly, Bro. J. M. McHugh, Shannon Ryan, Con W. Lane, Bro. William Murphy. FRONT ROW: Bro. Charles Duffy, Msgr. Joseph O'Brien, and Rev. William Shallow. Year Courtesy of Lillian Ryan, RH, HG.

St. Francis High School Baseball Team

ST. FRANCIS HOCKEY CHAMPS 1963-1964

FIRST ROW (L-R) Mike Whelan, Billy Hearn, Tom Dunphy, Joe Hunt, Danny Power, Joe George, Tom Coady, Ron Sullivan, Greg Power, Frank McCarthy, Steve Hearn, Cyril Shugarue, Brian Dunphy, Kevin Coady and Dan Dunphy. BACK ROW (L-R): Joe Shugarue, Bro. Murphy, Andy Moriarty, Francis Sullivan.

Come Home Year 1966

Dedicated Supporters of St.Francis

THE FIRST YEAR BOOK, CONCEPT WAS PUBLISHED 1967
PRIZE PRESENTATIONS 1967

Under the distinguished patronage of
His Excellency, Most Rev. John M. O'Neill, S.D.T.

SIXTH ANNUAL

DISTRIBUTION OF PRIZES

OF

ST. FRANCIS CENTRAL HIGH SCHOOL

HARBOUR GRACE

December 9TH, 1967

PROGRAMME

The Rt. Rev. Joseph W. Peddle, D.P., V.G. Presiding

SCHOLARSHIPS AND AWARDS

SCHOLARSHIP FOR FIRST PLACE IN RELIGION
IN GRADE XI
(Donated by His Excellency, the Bishop)
Michael Fortune

SCHOLARSHIP FOR GENERAL EXCELLENCE IN GRADE XI
(Donated by Rt. Rev. Joseph M. O'Brien, D.P.)
Thomas Carpenter

ELECTORAL SCHOLARSHIP FOR HARBOUR GRACE DIST.
Thomas Carpenter

THE JOHN FITZGERALD KENNEDY MEMORIAL AWARD
FOR LEADERSHIP
Jerome Delaney and William Hearn

THE ATHLETIC OF THE YEAR AWARD
William Hearn

SCHOLARSHIP FOR GENERAL EXCELLENCE IN GRADE X
(Donated by Rt. Rev. Joseph W. Peddle, D. P.)
John Butt

AWARD FOR FIRST PLACE IN RELIGION IN GRADE X
(Donated by Mr.. and Mrs. Edward Freeman)
Terrence Hearn

GRADE X CONFEDERATION SCHOLARSHIPS
(Presented by the Government of Newfoundland and Labrador)
John Butt   Terrence Hearn
Edward Gallant   John Slade

SCHOLARSHIP FOR GENERAL EXCELLENCE IN GRADE IX
(Donated by Rev. Fr. A. Antle)
David Northcott

AWARD FOR FIRST PLACE IN RELIGION IN GRADE IX
(Donated by Mr. and Mrs. Wilbur Furey)
David Northcott

KNIGHTS OF COLUMBUS SCHOLARSHIP FOR GRADE IX
(Donated by the Dalton Council, Knights of Columbus)
David Northcott

PRICE (NFLD) COMPANY SCHOLARSHIP
Andrew Murray

AWARD FOR SECOND PLACE IN GRADE IX
(Donated by the Golden Eagle Refining co, of Canada, Ltd)
Alexander Harris

AWARD FOR THIRD PLACE IN GRADE IX
(Donated by Quinn's Supermarket)
Wayne O'Grady

THE R.J. CONNOLLY SCHOLARSHIP FOR ENGLISH LITERATURE

Grade XI……………………………………William Hearn
Grade X…………………………………………John Slade
Grade IX…………………………………David Northcott

THE REV. BR. P.V. STRAPP MEMORIAL SCHOLARSHIP FOR SCIENCE
(Donated by the late Miss Magdalen Morrissey)

Grade XI…………………………………….Kevin O'Grady
Grade X………………………………………….John Butt
Grade IX……………………………………David Northcott

THE GREGORY SHORT MEMORIAL SCHOLARSHIP FOR ENGLISH LANGUAGE
(Donated by the McCarthy Council, Knights Of Columbus)

Grade XI………………………………….Jerome Delaney
Grade X………………………………………..John Slade
Grade IX……………………………………….John Healey

THE CLARENCE O'GRADY MEMORIAL SCHOLARSHIP FOR MATHEMATICS
(Donated By The Dalton Council, Knights Of Columbus)

Grade XI………………Kevin O'Grady, Leo Griffin
Grade X……………………………Edward Gallant
Grade IX……………………………David Northcott

THE AWARDS FOR FIRST PLACE IN LATIN
(Donated By Mr. And Mrs. John Finn)

Grade XI…………………………..Jerome Delaney
Grade X…………………………………….John Butt
Grade IX………..Wayne McCarthy, Kevin Peddle

THE AWARDS FOR FIRST PLACE IN FRENCH
(Donated by the North Eastern Fish Industries, Ltd)

Grade XI……Jerome Delaney, Thomas Carpenter
Grade X………………………………..John Butt
Grade IX…………………………David Northcott

THE AWARDS FOR FIRST PLACE IN HISTORY

(Donated by Mr. John Furey)

Grade XI........................Thomas Carpenter
Grade X................John Butt, George Hogan
Grade IX..........................David Northcott

GRADE XI AWARDS

THOMAS CARPENTER – First Place in Class. Winner of the Scholarship for General excellence in Grade eleven. Winner of the electoral Scholarship for HG Dist. Winner of Award for History. Tied for award for French. Honors Diplomas.
JEROME DELANEY –Second Place in Class. Tied for John Fitzgerald Kennedy Memorial award for Leadership. Winner of Gregory Short Memorial Scholarship for English Language. Winner of the Award for Latin. Tied for award in French. Honors Diploma.
KEVIN O'GRADY – Third Place in Class. Winner of the Rev. Br. PV Strapp Memorial Scholarship for Science. Tied for the Clarence O'Grady Memorial Scholarship for Mathematics. Honors Diploma.
MICHAEL FORTUNE – Winner Of The Scholarship For First Place In Religion. Honors Diploma.
WILLIAM HEARN – Tied for the John Fitzgerald Kennedy award for leadership. Winner of RJ Connolly Scholarship for English Literature. Winner of the Student's Council's Athletic of the Year. Award. Honors Diploma.

HONORS DIPLOMAS

Thomas Carpenter
Jerome Delaney
Michael Fortune
Leo Griffin
William Hearn
Edward Kane
Kevin O'Grady
Clarence Peddle
Harold Sheppard

MATRICULATION DIPLOMAS

Stephen Cooney
Kevin Dobbin
Dennis Galway
James Garland
John Kavanaugh
Paul Moriarity
Dan Power

PASS DIPLOMAS

Edward George
Brian O'Grady
Desmond Peddle
Donald Purcell

GRADE X AWARDS

John Butt – First Place in class.
John Slade – Second Place in Class
Edward Gallant – Third Place in Class.
Terrence Hearn – Fourth Place in Class.

GRADE X DIPLOMAS

John Butt
Kevin Coady
Clarence Coombs
Hayward Dobbin
William Fahey
William Finn
Gerald Fitzgerald
Noel Fitzgerald
Edward Gallant
Loyola George
Terrence Gregory
Terrence Hearn
George Hogan
Thomas Hurdle
Thomas Kane
Brian Manning
Terrence Merrigan
Joseph Murray
Gregory Penney
Thomas Rogers
James Ryan
Stan Short
John Slade
Joseph St. John
John Thistle
Raymond Whalen
Gregory White
Thomas Young

GRADE IX AWARDS

David Northcott – First Place in Class
Alexander Harris – Second Place in Class
Wayne O'Grady – Third Place in Class

GRADE IX DIPLOMAS

Brian Ash
William Barry
Gerard Butt
James Cooper
Gary Crawford
Ronald Crawford
Eric Davis
John Dunphy
Philip Dwyer
Paul Finn
John Goff
Alex Harris
John Healey
Bernard Hunt
Wayne Jordan
Thomas Lynch
Fred McCarthy
James McCarthy
Wayne McCarthy
Ignatius Miller
Andrew Murray
David Northcott
Wayne O'Grady
Paul Oliver
Eric Peddle
Kevin Peddle
Gerald Reynolds
John Rose
Bernard Ryan
Joseph White
Douglas Young
Terrence Young

GRAMMAR SCHOOL SECTION

All awards in the Grammar School are donated through the kindness of
SAUNDERS, HOWELL and CO., Ltd.

GRADE VIII AWARDS

Emmanuel Hudson – First place in Class.
Anthony Keough – Second Place in Class.
Anthony Finn – Third Place in Class.
Edward Shannahan & David White – First Place in Religion (Tie)

GRADE VIII DIPLOMAS

Robert Barrett
Paul Butt
Paul Coady
Patrick Collins
James Connors
Nicholas Coombs
Thomas Dunphy
Anthony Finn
Ronald Fitzgerald
Ronald Gallant
Linus Garland
Patrick Gear
Stephen Gear
Nicholas George
Donald Hogan
Emmanuel Hudson
Stephen Kennedy
Anthony Keough
Dennis King
John Littlejohn
Gerald McCarthy
Wayne McCarthy
Francis Merrigan
John Merrigan
Donald Morrissey
Terrence Neil
Alvin Rose
Edward Shannahan
Reginald Shannahan
Phillip Short
Gerard Thomey
Morris Walbourne
Alphonsus White
David White
Frederick White
Martin White

GRADE VII AWARDS

Ronald Lane – First Place in Class
Francis Littlejohn – Second Place in Class
Patrick Merrigan – Third Place in Class

Taken From the Programme 1967

GRADE.NINE

(First Row L-R) – Doug Young, Jack Dwyer, Bernie Ryan, Gerald Reynolds, Ronnie Crawford, (Second Row) Mr. Hogan, Terry Young, Wayne O'Grady, Jack Fitzgerald, Mike Fahey, Eric Peddle, Jack Cooper, Wayne McCarthy, Bro Duffy. (Third Row) Fred McCarthy, John Goff, Eric Davis, Raymond Fitzgerald, David Northcott, Paul Finn, Ignatius Miller and Tom Lynch.

(First Row L-R) Alexander Harris, Andrew Murry, Kevin Peddle, John Rose, Brian Ash, (Second Row) Gerard Butt, Cyril Moriarity, Paul Oliver, Joe White, Jim Peddle, Wayne Peddle, John Healy, Mr. Delaney. (Third Row) John Dunphy, Wayne Jordan, Bill Barry, Gary Crawford, Larry Sheehan.

1968 GRADUATION CONCEPT

The aim of St. Francis Central High School is to help mould Christian gentlemen and scholars. The fact that in so many areas our school is successful in this aim is indicative of the excellence of our teachers and their Christian example. Yet, above all, the success of our school has been most dependent on those who first helped us and continue to do so --- our parents. To you, our parents, we say sincerely, "thank you". And it is with gratitude and pride we dedicate these pages to you.

THE CONCEPT FOR 1968
ST. FRANCIS CENTRAL HS

Faculty and Teachers - 1968

1968 - Faculty: Principal - Brother R. E. Hall;
Vice Principal - Mr. C. Lane.

1968 - Teachers:

Bro. G. Blackmore (Math XI, Econ XI, French XI Eng XI, Student Council and Glee Club).
Mr. C. Lane (VP, Grade 8 Purple, Bookstore)
Mr. W. Kennedy (Grade 8 Gold, Christmas Drive)
Bro. E. Farrell (Eng XI French VII, VIII and X)
Mr. W. Carroll (Math X, History IX & X, Geography IX)
Mr. M. O'Brien (Eng IX, Math IX, Latin VIII & IX, Reading II, Science IX, Library and Film Club)
Mr. J. Hogan (Biology X & XI, Math IX, Eng IX, History IX, Geography IX, Discussion Club and Intramurals)
Mr. J. Hunt (Grade 7 Gold and Hockey)
Bro. J. Gale (Grade 7 Purple and Yearbook)

The Graduates of 1968 were:

William Bowman, John Butt, Kevin Coady, Hayward Dobbin, Clarence Coombs, William Fahey, William Finn, Gerald Fitzgerald, Noel Fitzpatrick, Edward Gallant, Loyola George, Terrence Gregory, Kenneth Haïre, Terrence Hearn, George Hogan, Thomas Hurdle, Brian Manning, Terrence Merrigan, Joseph Murray, Gregory Penney, Thomas Rogers, James Ryan, Stanislaus Short, John Slade, Joe St. John, John Thistle, Raymond Whalen, Gregory White, and Thomas Young.

Grade 10 students – 1968

Eric Davis, Brian Ash, Kevin Coombs, Ron Crawford, Jim McCarthy, Hugh Rafferty, Bill Barry, Ged Butt, Jim Cooper, Gary Crawford, Mike Fahey, Alex Harris, Tom Lynch, Phil Dwyer, Pat Ford, John Dunphy, John Goff, Paul Finn, John Healy, Bernard Hunt, Larry Sheehan, Bernard Ryan, Bill Saltman, Alex Slade, Terry Young, Gerald Reynolds, Jack Rose, Mike Power, John White, Fred McCarthy, Andrew Murray, Wayne O'Grady, Bernard Murphy, Wayne Peddle, Kevin Peddle, Wayne McCarthy, Dave Northcott, Eric Peddle.

Grade 9 students – 1968

Ron Gallant, Pat Collins, Fred White, Linus Garland, Tom Dunphy, Steve Gear, Paul Coady, Pat Gear, Ron Fitzgerald, Frank Merrigan, Rickie Fitzgerald, Nick Coombs, Don Morrissey, Bob Barrett, Denis King, Alvin Rose, Maurice Walborne, Tony Finn, Emanuel Hudson, Dan Hogan, Phonse White, Steve Kennedy, Nick George, Reg Shanahan, Dave White, Gerald Thoomey, Aidan Moriarity, Jack Coombs, E. Shanahan, Gerald McCarthy, Wayne McCarthy, John Littlejohn, Tony Keough, John Merrigan, Phil Short, Cyril Moriarity.

Grade 8 students – 1968

Greg Haire, Clarence Merrigan, Phil Edwards, Mike Donnelly, Aidan Collins, Wade Abbott, Tony Clark, Kevin Edwards, Pat O'Grady, Keith Abbot, Pat O'Keefe, Bill Reardon, Bill Thoomey, Jerome Jordan, Don Emerson, Gerry Wrice, Frank George, Melvin Drover, Ed Slade, Martin White, Pat Merrigan, Jerome George, Jerome McCarthy, Gerard Gregory, Ken Green, Pat Thomas, Terry Dwyer, Reg Coombs, Ed Finn, Michael Foley, Ron McCarthy, Terry Reynolds, Ronnie Lane, Ron MacDonald, David Ash, Bill Martin, Dave Penney, Jack Harrington, Walter Moriarity, Clarence Butt, Joe Oliver, Gus McCann, Bobby Haire.

Grade 7 students – 1968

Bill George, Gregory Peddle, Phonse O'Keefe, Moses Slade, Tim Dwyer, Phonse Fitzgerald, Bren Reynolds, Gerald Coombs, Maurice Slade, Kevin Reynolds, David Moriarity, Junior Power, Gerald Sullivan, Vince Hunt, Paul McCarthy, Jim Reynolds, Gus Short, John Hogan, Dan Rafferty, David Swain, David Reynolds, John Lynch, Larry O'Grady, Laurie Merrigan, Jimmy Brien, Chris Hearn, Maurice Sullivan, Leslie Kearney, Terry Callendar, Jack George, George Kearney, Donald Coombs, Lloyd McCarthy, Harry Kavanaugh, Kevin Casey, Peter Foley, Jim Gushue, Andrew Lane, Loyola Keough, John Ryan, Brian McNamara, Lloyd Hobbs, Arthur Hurdle, Reg McCarthy, Kevin Lynch, Paul O'Grady, Jim Broomfield, Peter Moriarity, Brendan Coombs, Kevin Casey.

Activities – 1968

Student Council, Discussion Club, Film Club, Library Staff, Concert, Track, Hockey, Soccer, Senior Glee Club, Junior Glee Club.

HOCKEY TEAM 1969 Front Row – John Goff, Paul Coady, Paul Finn, Jack Rose, David Northcott, Gordon Jordan, Wayne McCarthy, John Dunphy. Back Row: Jerome Jordan, Reg Shannahan, Wayne Peddle, Bro. Farrell, Tom Lynch, Terry Quinn, Joe St. John, Wayne Martin, Carl Chipman, Jack Harrington and Bob Noseworthy.

St. Francis High School Fire

On 3 April 1973 St. Francis High School in Harbour Grace was completely destroyed by fire with all its contents. However the fire could not destroy the spirit that has been built up over the past twelve years, as was evident when the hockey team won the Conception Bay North School championship a few days later.

The Team that wasn't suppose to win, but did. (1973)

Monsignor Joseph O'Brien and the Brothers at St. Francis High School were dedicated to the boys that attended the school. This was an outing to Godden's Cabins near Lady Lake for rest and recreation from the grind of daily study. Early 1970's.

Fire at St. Francis High School

Fire at St. Francis—'a living nightmare'

Article by Bill Bowman, rewritten with permission of "The Compass"

Twisted steel, broken bricks and cinders are all that remain of the building that for twelve years had been the home of St. Francis High School.

The story of the fire itself need not be recalled here. It is one of which we're all too painfully aware.

All we know is that when dawn broke over Harbour Grace on April 4, the memories of that place on the hill, memories of the sounds that had echoed through its halls for a decade and more were all that was left.

It was our second home. We did everything there except sleep. We learned, played, sang, danced, ate and sometimes when the teachers weren't looking, fought. We became a part of it and it a part of us. That is why now, the broken bricks are not really all that is left. The people who were and are St. Francis, are still very much alive and the school spirit is still very much alive in them.

This fact was very much in evidence during and in the wake of the terrible fire. On that night, scores of lads stood around and wept openly as they watched their school turn into a raging inferno.

Early Wednesday morning several students came up to see what remained and silence overtook them.

Priceless memoranda that had been collected over the twelve year period of the building's existence had all been lost. The building itself was no work of art. It was a brick faced L-shaped box that stood out on the hill. It was too small and had certainly outgrown itself since it was opened in 1961. The boys are lucky in a way to be getting a new building. They are lucky also in that they have the future in which to build the new St. Francis.

In the wake of the fire—and that is what is was like 'a wake'—curious events took place. People were shaking hands with the Christian Brothers and offering their condolences as if someone or something belonging to them had passed away. The truth of the matter is, it has!

We are in difficulties on all sides, but never cornered; we see no answer to our problems, but never despair; we have been persecuted but never deserted; knocked down, but never killed; always, wherever we may be, we carry with us in our body the death of Jesus, so that the life of Jesus, too, may always be seen in our body.
2 Corinthians 4:8-10

Taken from 1973 Souvenir Booklet

ST. FRANCIS HIGH SCHOOL SOUVENIR BOOKLET

1973

Peace Prayer of St. Francis

Lord, make me an instrument of your peace.
Where there is hatred, let me sow love.
Where there is injury, pardon.
Where there is doubt, faith.
Where there is despair, hope.
Where there is darkness, light.
Where there is sadness, joy.

O Divine Master, grant that I may not
so much seek to be consoled as to console.
To be understood as to understand.
To be loved as to love.
For it is in giving that we receive.
It is in pardoning that we are pardoned.
and in dying that we are born to eternal life.

St. Francis Graduating Class 1973

The Spiritual Guides were Msgr. Joseph M. O'Brien and Father M. Walsh.

Even with the fire in April, there was a 1973 graduation: The graduates were: Steve Abbott, Dan Aleven, Greg Archibald, Dave Archibald, Randel Babb, Leo Brien, Wayne Butt, Terry Callender, Barry Crain, Brian Doran, Leo Dunphy, Paul Dwyer, Gerry Earle, Mike Farrell, Frank Galway, Joe Gregory, Jim Harris, Chris Hearn, Clayton Hunt, Kevin Hurley, Tom Murphy, Kevin Murray, Greg O'Grady, Dennis O'Leary, Terry Peddle, John Purcell, Bren Reynolds, Mike Rogers, Mike Sheehan, Ambrose Slade, Maurice Slade, Wayne Thistle, Lloyd Wagner and Tom Wiseman. In 1973 the Staff included: Principal - Br. G.C. Blackmore; Vice Principal - Mr. C.W. Lane; Secretary- Miss M. Fleming. Teachers- Mr. E. Duggan, Bro. E. Follett, Bro R. Hall, Mr. M. Hynes, Mr. W. Kennedy, Mr. A. Murphy, Mr. S Norris, Mr. R. Sullivan, and Bro. W. White.

Rebuilt St. Francis

Msgr. Joseph O'Brien rebuilt a new St. Francis High School following the fire in 1973. The official reopening of the school was on May 3, 1974.

You are cordially invited to attend the

Blessing by Most Reverend A.L. Penney, D.D.
Bishop of Grand Falls

and the official opening of

St. Francis High School, Harbour Grace

to be held on

Friday, May 3, 1974 at 8:15 p.m.

in the

Auditorium of St. Francis

and

To the Reception following in the School

17 JUNE 1975

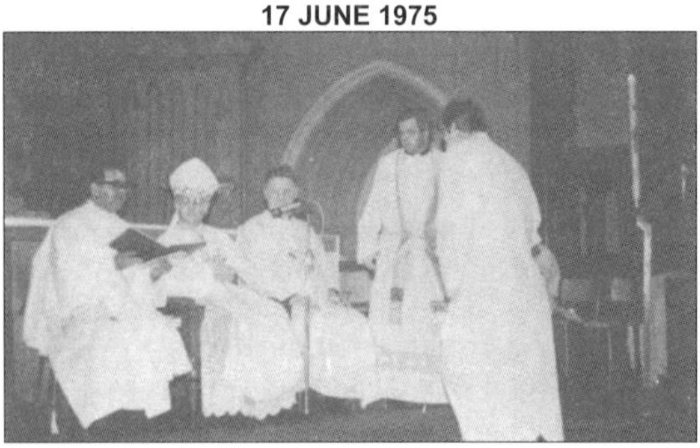

REV. WILLIAM HEARN BECAME THE FIRST EX-PUPIL TO BE ORDAINED.

Princess Diana and Prince Charles visits St. Francis High School – 1983

Princess Diana & Charles mingle with people of Harbour Grace
Courtesy of Harbour Grace Tourism Office.

The Royal Yacht "Britannia" moored in Harbour Grace bay after bringing Prince Charles and Princess Diana to Harbour Grace.

The Dalton Council of Knights of Columbus presented a flag pole at St. Francis Central High School on 1 June 1985.

CONCEPT '86

Senior Basketball "A"

BACK ROW (L to R): S. O'Neill, B. Guilfoyle, S. Lee, K. Harrington, J. Hosel, L. Mackey, S. Cleary, Mr. Simmons. FRONT ROW: B. White, K. Wrice, D. Martin, P. Sheppard, D. White, S. Laird.

St. Francis Central High School Senior Basketball Team

ST. FRANCIS CATHOLIC HIGH SCHOOL
MALE
ATHLETE OF THE YEAR

Michael Fahey

June 24, 1994

THE CHRISTIAN BROTHERS LEAVE ST. FRANCIS HIGH SCHOOL HARBOUR GRACE 1995

"O Divine Master, grant that I may not so much seek to be consoled as to console, to be understood as to understand, to be loved as to love." (from the Peace Prayer of St. Francis)

PRESENTING CONCEPT '99

The students and staff of St. Francis High School proudly end the millennium with this lasting tribute to our school

This, the final edition of *Concept,* is dedicated to Mr. Jack Rose, student, teacher, Assistant Principal and Principal of St. Francis High School.

Faculty

Mr. Sean Cashin, Ms. Ann Coombs, Mr. Lewis Dawe, Ms. Arlene Delaney, Ms. Judy Dwyer, Ms. Carmen Jarvis, Mr. Ed Jarvis, Mr. Don King, Ms. Lori King, Ms. Josie LeShane, Mr. Norm Littlejohn, Ms. Tracey, Mr. Garry McCarthy, Mr. Jerome McCarthy, Mr. Tony McCarthy, Ms. Marian Penney, Mr. Robert Pike, Ms. Christine Rose, Ms. Laura Lee Scott, Mr. Cy Simmons, Ms. Kim Welsh, Ms. Ann Doran-White, Mr. Dave White.

Support Staff

Mrs. W. O'Driscol, Mrs. S. Rose, Mrs. A. Mackenzie, Mr. D. Murphy, Mrs. C.A. Broomfield.

Senior Graduates

Karen Barrett, Aiden Brazil, Kelly Bowman, Matthew Chafe, Scott Conway, Tracy Cumby, John Dunne, Paul Fahey, Chris Farrell, Jonathon Fong, Ellen Fortune, Sheldon Gallant, Terri-Lynn Galway, Krista Garland, Sherry Lynn Grant, Chris Hearn, Angela Hunt, Ian Hutchings, Anne Hynes, Lionel Janes, Chris Kennedy, Chris King, Katherine King, Jennifer Laing, Donna Lambert, Amanda Lewis, John Littlejohn, Michael Martin, Charles McCarthy, Melanie McCarthy, Scott McCarthy, Stephanie McCarthy, John Mesh, Laura Moriarty, Adrienne Murray, Jodie Lynn O'Leary, Melissa O'Neil, Chris Oates, Andrea Oliver, Robin Oliver, Roger Osmond, Crystal Parsons, Glenda Parsons, Ryan Parsons, Jeff Peddle, Kelly Piercey, Robyn Pike, Stephen Pike, Trina Pike, Tammy Power, Brian Reynolds, Mark Reynolds, Stephanie Reynolds, Cherie-Lynn Rogers, William Rogers, Allan Rose, Leslie Rose, Kandice Rowe, Kevin Seward, Maxine Short, Christa Skinner, Jennifer Slade, Renee Smith, Matthew Stacey, Gerald Sullivan, Leo Sullivan, Kristen Swain, Mark Sweeney, Patrick Thomey, Corbett Thoms, Lisa Vaters, Cathy Whelan, Sheila White, Steven White and Jamie Williams.

St. Francis Crusader of the year Awards

Stephanie McCarthy, Sheila White & Paul Fahey

Courtesy of Jerome McCarthy

Chapter 19

THE PRESENTATION NUNS IN HARBOUR GRACE

Bishop Michael A. Fleming, OSF was successful in recruiting the first Presentation sisters outside of Ireland to come to St. John's in 1833. They founded a House of the Order of St. John's and on 1 July 1851, founded the first Convent outside St. John's in Harbour Grace. During those early years there have been many ups and downs but the sisters have never failed in their dedication. They became an integral part of the town and it is difficult to imagine being without them. Bishop Flemings' successor, Bishop Mullock appointed, one of the first Nuns who came to St. John's in 1833, to Harbour Grace in 1851. She was Sister M. Xaverius Lynch to found a House of the Order in Harbour Grace.

The parish Priest at Harbour Grace, VRev. Charles Dalton was most desirous to have a Convent established and had in 1839 purchased a house and land for the new Community. Bishop Mullock was also anxious for the Foundation and on 30 June 1851, he appointed Sister M. Xaverius Lynch, Sister M. DeSales Lovelock and Mother M. Josephine French to start the Harbour Grace Convent. He also sent Miss Mary Flynn, a postulant from Galway, with them to be a member of the new Institute. She had left Galway for the Newfoundland Mission, with Mothers Josephine and de Sales and had been teaching in St. John's since her arrival in 1846, though reserved for the Convent at Harbour Grace.

On July 1, 1851, Bishop Mullock accompanied by Mother Magdalen, then Superioress of the St. John's Convent, conducted the Sisters to Harbour Grace. They arrived in the evening by boat from Portugal Cove and were cordially welcomed by VRev. Charles Dalton. Present also to greet them were Rev. Father J. Dalton and Father E. Condon and the Irish Society. In addressing the Irish Society the Bishop requested its members to be attentive to the Community he had just brought for the benefit of their children and future generations.

Sister M. Xaverius was appointed Superioress by Bishop Mullock and on the following Monday, July 1, school was opened, of which even girls of 21 years and over, joyfully availed. There was also Sunday school and instructions for adults. All the women of the town assembled on Sundays - mistresses and servants. These instructions were given by

Mother M. Xaverius and Mother M. Josephine, alternately, a hundred or more generally attended. Mother de Sales and Sister Mary Flynn taught catechism to the young, also alternately on Sundays. In addition, girls who could not attend school on week days were taught reading and writing. As the house Father Dalton had purchased for a Convent was still occupied, the Sisters resided in Father Dalton's Parish house until the following 16 July 1852, when they moved into their own convent. On January 31, 1852, Bishop Mullock arrived from St. John's to receive Sister Mary Flynn to the Holy Habit, as Sister M. Catherine Joseph. The ceremony took place on the Feast of the Purification. His Lordship being assisted by the VRev. Charles Dalton. Rev. Fathers J. Dalton, cc and E. Condon, cc were also present. This was the first time outside of St. John's that a Sister had received the religious habit. Bishop Mullock preached an eloquent and instructive sermon. As this was the first time outside of St. John's that a Sister had received the Holy Habit, crowds had assembled to witness the ceremony, some coming several miles. The old wooden Chapel not being large enough to accommodate such numbers, some climbing up to the windows on the outside to see something of what was going on. Heavy snow storms that February 1852, detained Bishop Mullock in Harbour Grace for two weeks. On July 16, 1852 when the Sisters moved in to their Convent, a room was set apart for a Chapel in which the Blessed Sacrament was deposited. On the same day, Sarah Barter, who had accompanied the sisters from St. John's to be a lay Sister, began her postulant-ship. On November 13, 1854, Bishop Mullock received Sister Sarah Barter to the Holy Habit and in religion she became known as Sister M. Rose. On July 30, 1858, VRev. Charles Dalton bequeathed to the Sisters the house and land he has purchased from Dr. William Stirling, covering an area of 23 acres. Some of this land was used for farming by the Bishops and they paid yearly rent to the Convent. In 1887 the Nuns received through Bishop McDonald, 11 pounds, 16 shillings for 3 acres, 3 roads and 30 rods of land taken the year before for the enlargement of the second road to Carbonear and later - on January 13, 1898 - the Convent received two hundred dollars from the Railway for that part of their property through which the railroad tracks ran. In 1884, as the Convent was very old and required too frequent repairs, Bishop McDonald thought it wise to build a new Convent. The Reverend Mother was of like opinion and the new residence was built, on the feast of St. Mary Magdalen, just a few feet south of the former residence, part of which was left standing for occupation whilst the Convent was being built. The Sisters moved in on November 8, 1884.

This new convent was located several feet south of the former building, acquired from Dr. Stirling. To acquire funds for the erection of this convent, a Christmas tree sale was held on St. Stephen's Day. The total expense of erecting the second convent was 889 pounds. The convent was used for 90 years and it held a prominent place in the life of Harbour Grace.

In 1893, a Nun's Chapel was built over the St. Joseph's school. Attended by Father Roe, Bishop McDonald dedicated this on Christmas Eve to the Holy Family. The cost was 240 pounds, 11 shillings and 3 pence, including 122 pounds for labor.

Closing of Convent

On 30 June 1973 the Presentation Convent in Harbour Grace was closed after 122 years. (1851) and was dismantled and torn down in 1974. The Harbour Grace Sisters would commute from the Carbonear Convent. Although the consulting engineers found the building unsuitable for future occupancy, many of the residents showed great concern over the decision. Many wrote a petition and expressed their deep regret to save the building. This was not only a loss of an historical Catholic church building of Harbour Grace but was a loss of a distinguished segment of our Parish and the Community, that had molded the minds and hearts of our children for over a century both in education and spirituality. Their spirit will live on forever in the lives of all of our parishioners.

Rev Frederick Terry and the Sisters from Harbour Main,

PRESENTATION SISTERS WHO SERVED IN HARBOUR GRACE (1851-1973)

BANVIL, S.M. Agnes
BARTER, S.M. Rose
BERESFORD, S. Sarah (Damien)

CAREY, S. Rosalie
COLLINS, S. Eileen (Andrea)
COSTELLO, S. Marilyn
COUSINS, S.M. Dominic
CROKE, S.M. Loretto
CURRAN, S.M. Patrick

DELAHUNTY. S. Paula (DeSales)
DEVINE, S. Margaret
DOWNEY, S.M. Andrina
DOYLE. S.M. De Pazzi
DOYLE, S. Monica
DUGGAN, S.M. Alphonsus

EVANS, S.M. Concepta

FARDY, S.M. Xaveria
FINN, S.M. Carmela
FLEMING, S.M. Scholastica
FLYNN, S. Mary Catherine
FRENCH, S.M. Josephine
FUREY, S.M. Flavian

GARDINER, S.M. Zita
GOFF, S.M. De Sales
GREENE, S.M. Callista

HANNON, S.M. Columba
HAYES, S.M. Eileen
HEANEY, S. Miriam
HEPDITCH, S.M. Columba
HICKEY, S. Ronalda
HOGAN, S.M. Brendan
HYNES, S.M. Anna
HYNES, S. Sarah (Consolata)

JORDAN, S.M. Cecilia

KING, S. Frances (Seraphina)
KING, S.M. De Lourdes
KING, S.M. Theresa

LOVELOCK, S.M. Clare
LOVELOCK, S.M. De Pazzi
LOVELOCK, S.M. De Sales
LUNDRIGAN, S.M. Mildred
LYNCH, S.M. Xaverius

MAHER, S.M. Berchmans
MARCHE, S. Inez (Stephen)
MCCARTHY, S.M. Bonaventure
MCCARTHY, S. Sheila (Presentation)
MOLLOY, S. Frances (Noelle)
MOLLOY, S. Mary (Olivia)
MOORE, S. S.M. Anastasia
MORRISSEY, S. Rosalie (Fidelis)
MURPHY, S. Marie (Rosalie)

NOONAN, S.M. Joseph
NORTHCOTT, S.M. Rose

O'BRIEN, S. Marie (Euphrasia)
O'KEEFFE, S.M. Agnes
O'KEEFFE, S.M. Patrick
O'KEEFE, S.M. Regis

PEDDLE, S.M. Columba
PHILPOTT, S.M. Cecilia
PITTMAN, S. Laurane (Anne Marie)
POWER, S. Consolata (Anselma)

REDDY, S.M. Kostka
ROCHE, S. Marie
RYAN, S. Jean (Soubirous)

ST.GEORGE, S.M. Vincent
SESK, S. Agnes (Olivette)
SHORTALL, S.M. John
SNOW, S. Dorothy (Pacelli)
STAPLES, S. Sylvia
STAPLETON, S. Betty (Reginald)
STUCKLESS, S. Margaret (Fintan)
SULLIVAN, S. Catherine (Cornelia)
SULLIVAN, S. Maureen (Miriam Joseph)
SUTTON, S. Frances

WADDLETON, S. Mary (Florence)
WALSH, S. Kathleen (Fidelma)
WALSH, S.M. Stephanie
WHELAN, S.M. Anna
WHELAN, S. Elizabeth (Josef)
WHITE, S. Genevieve (Pierre)
WHITTY, S. Ellen (Scholastica)

Sr. Kennedy, Archivist Pres Convent 2001

Chapter 20

CATHOLIC ORGANIZATIONS IN HARBOUR GRACE

Society for Propagation of the Faith

Established March 1862

	L s p		L s p
The Rt. Rev. Dr Dalton	- 3 -	Mrs. Mary Connors R.H	- 1 4
Mr. John Ryan	- 2 8	" Ellen Martin Town	- 1 3
" John Humphrey	- 2 8	" Catherine Leary	- 1 3
" Michael Fitzgerald	- 2 8	Miss Mary Ann Condon	- 2 8
" John Scully	- 2 8	Mrs. Foster	- 2 8
" Nicholas Doyle	- 2 8	" Maher	- 2 8
" Michael Stapleton	- 2 8	" Goff	- 2 8
" James Callahan	- 2 8	" Jones	- 2 8
" Denis O'Neil	- 2 8	" Discon	- 2 8
" James L. Prendergast	- 2 8	Mr. Michl Flinnon	- 2 8
" Owen Hamilton	- 2 8	Mrs. Anne Dunn	- 2 8
" Maurice Connell	- 2 8	" Anne Hennessey R-H	- 2 8
Mrs. Michl Fitzgerald	- 2 8	" Mary Parsons	- 2 8
" Daniel Fitzgerald	- 2 8	Mr. Thos Green Lmr	- 2 8
" John Hogan	- 2 8	Miss Mary Hart	- 2 8
" John Callahan	- 3 -	Mrs. Mary Wall	- 2 8
Mrs. John Callahan	- 2 8	" Bridget Cashan	- 2 8
Mrs. Dooling	- 2 8	" Martha Coady	- 1 4
" David Flinn	- 1 4	Mrs. Richd Fleming R-H	- 2 8
" John Flinn	- 1 4	" Catherine Power R-H	- 2 8
" Michael Keefe	- 1 4	Mrs. Leyton	- 2 8
" Joseph Fitzgerald	- 1 4	" Catherine Pumphrey	- 2 8
" John Hart	- 1 4	Mrs. M. Coady	- 1 4
" Michael Dwyer	- 1 4	" Michl Keefe	- 1 4
" Stanislaus Fitzgerald	- 1 4	" John Hart	- 1 4
Mrs. Mary Anne Penney	- 1 4		

The above information was taken from a hand written old bound note-taking book found in the Mackey family attic on Patrick Street, Carbonear. Other notes in the book were found about mathe and contracts. Rt. Rev. J. Dalton was Parish Priest at Carbonear from 1849-1856 when he became the first Bishop of the newly created Diocese of Harbour Grace from 1856 to his death in 1869. In 1862, Most Rev. J. Dalton was the Bishop of Harbour Grace. The names appear to be mostly Harbour Grace Catholics, with some R-H from Riverhead, HG. A few may be from Carbonear. ***Lawrence Mackey (1830-1912) note book, Carbonear.***

Society of the Immaculate Conception

"This society was established by Bishop Carfagnini in the 1870s. The Bishop explained what the objects of the Society are: they are two-fold in view: "The beauty of the Temple of God and more so, that of His spiritual temple which who are, my Beloved Sisters. It was indeed my object that you might adorn and beatify by your exertions and contributions this house of God and in so doing, you are entitled to my thanks, as well as those of all the faithful of this community: besides the eternal reward which you may expect from God who dwells in it. But the principle object was that you might obtain from God, through the intercession of His Immaculate Mother, your Patroness, the grace to enable you to adorn and beautify your souls with virtues. In erecting your Society, I placed its members in a special manner under the protection of the Mother of God and gave Her to them as an example for their imitation."

When Bishop Carfagnini was leaving in May 1880, Janet M. Drysdale, President and Maggie Greene, Secretary of the Immaculate Society gave a farewell address to the Bishop from the women of the Parish. As well as all the Catholic Societies of Harbour Grace, including by the following:"

P. Devereaux, PRESIDENT and D.A. Flynn, SECRATARY of BIS.
Andrew T. Drysdale, PRESIDENT of the T.A. & B Society.
James Graham, SECRETERY of TAB.
M.J. Flynn, acting PRESIDENT of the St. Vincent de Paul Society.
John Cody, SECRETARY of StVdP.

Christian Doctrine Literary Association

In 1891 a Reading Room in connection with the Christian Doctrine Literary Association (C. D. & L.) was opened. English and American periodicals were carried. The Room was located in the Academy Hall. On July 4, 1891, The Association presented Father John Roe, on his departure from Harbour Grace after 12 year, for his new assignment as PP, Northern Bay, an address and present and their sincere congratulations on his well-merited promotion and their deep regret at his departing from them. The officers at this time were: President – Rev. John Roe; Vice- President - Mr. John J. Murphy; Asst VP - Mr. William J. Lynch; Treasurer – Mr. A. T. Drysdale; Secretary - Mr. John P. Kennedy; and Members of the Council: Messrs. Patrick Farrell, D.A. Flynn, John Casey, Thomas Hanrahan, Patrick Walsh and Edward Callahan.

The annual meeting was held on 6 November 1891 when several new members were admitted as well as the following officers elected for the ensuing year.

Rev. J. March, cc - PRESIDENT
Mr. J. J. Murphy - VICE PRESIDENT (re-elected)
Mr. Patrick Walsh - ASSISTANT VP & Librarian
Mr. A. T. Drysdale - TREASURER (re-elected)
Mr. John Casey - SECRETARY
COUNCIL: Messrs. P. Farrell, D.A. Flynn, E. Callahan, T. Hanrahan, J.T. Lawton and W. Sharp.

The Catholic Cadet Corps

The Catholic Cadet Corps or C.C.C. was organized at Harbour Grace in 1910. On Sunday, 24 September 1911, the C.C.C. of Harbour Grace marched to St. Joseph's Church, Riverhead to attend Mass. Their band accompanied them. Mass was celebrated by Father Finn, Chaplain of the Brigade. After Mass they returned to their Armory on LeMarchant Street.

They had a Promotion Meeting on 27 September 1911 and the "Harbor Grace Standard" carried the account, which is summarized here.

> **" The Cadets to a number of about 100 members, occupied centre of the large hall, where they were drawn up in a long column, fully uniformed, carrying their rifles. The Bandsmen with their bright instruments occupied seats in front, on the right side. His Lordship Bishop March, Patron of the Corps, ever ready to advance the interest of the boys, was present to confer the distinctions, and with Father Finn, the Corps Chaplain and Chairman of the meeting, was seated on the platform, from which Lt. Colonel W.H. Kennedy and Major William Grouchy, Drill Instructor, directed their part of the proceedings. The Chairman opened the meeting. The Corps had only been one year in existence, with difficulties and organization, was today a Corps of over 100 strong, well drilled and well-disciplined and with the prospect of a long and increasingly successful career. Promotions and Honours were handed out. They received the Episcopal Blessing and received their Commissions. At the close, His Lordship addressed them and congratulated them on their fine work. The Band which had played throughout the evening, ended the proceedings with God Save the King." News**

CADETS AT PARADE – HARBOUR GRACE 1911

Holy Name Society

On Sunday, May 4, 1944, a meeting was called of all the Catholic men of the Parish of Harbour Grace. Its purpose was to organize here the Holy Name Society. Bishop O'Neill attended the meeting and the Rector of the Cathedral, Father J. W. Peddle, was also present. The Bishop pointed out the prime purpose of the Society is the promotion of exemplary Catholic living in the practice of reverence at all times for the Holy Name. He also spoke of the importance of frequent Holy Communion in building and sustaining in the individual an essential Christian life, in accordance with the mind of the Church. The Bishop names Father Peddle the Spiritual Director.

They elected the following officers for Holy Name Society; 1944

PRESIDENT - M. P. Stapleton
FIRST VICE PRESIDENT - E. D. Freeman
SECOND VICE PRESIDENT - D. P. Thomas
SECRETARY - W. B. Kennedy
TREASURER - Joseph Dunn
MARSHALL - Richard Carroll

Children of Mary

Girls of the St. Columba School participated in religious activities in the name of Mary. The Children of Mary were believed to have been started in the 1950's and operated by the Presentation Sisters assigned to the Parish. Its mission was to offer membership in a youth group for the school girls of all ages in the Catholic Church and provide them an opportunity to participate in the Church functions: religious, spiritual and social. They dressed in white dresses and went to church as a group and participated in the Sacraments and prayer sessions. They practice their religion as a unified group of Catholic girls, giving their life to Our Lady of Perpetual Help.

St.Vincent De Paul

St. Vincent De Paul was originally established in Harbour Grace and Carbonear in 1875 by Bishop Carfagnini. The names of the members in 1877 Minutes. See Chapter 23 for more information on the older St.Vincent de Paul Society.

CATHOLIC PARADE IN HARBOUR GRACE

Parade down Water Street, Harbour Grace. Dalton Council Flag # 1448. Behind KC flag are Children of Mary dressed in blue and white carrying Children of Mary flag. A parade from Presentation Convent, up Cathedral Street, up Harvey Street, down Lee's Lane to Water Street.

First, Shamrock of St. Patrick's of Carbonear, 1826 is date of first Chapel. Frank Neil (overcoat over arm), NS, HG, Galway (cigarette in hand), RH HG, Mr. Whalen (Cap on by car) RH,HG, Moss Hunt Next to Whalen) no cap, SS, HG, Jack Emberson (outside behind Galway), HG, Frank Reynolds (inside Emberson), RH, HG, Mr. Hogan, (Light jacket holding sign) Carbonear, Sea Cadets walking in front of Northern Bay sign, Men wearing rectangle signs are members of the Holy Name Society.

Chapter 21

Harbour Grace

BENEVOLENT IRISH SOCIETY

OF CONCEPTION BAY

There has been three Benevolent Irish Society's (BIS) established in Newfoundland. The first in St. John's in 1806, the second in Harbour Grace in 1814 and the third in Carbonear in 1835. The BIS of Conception Bay was established by Father Thomas Ewer and Dr. William Stirling of the Royal Navy in Harbour Grace in 1814. They drew up the constitution and had it sanctioned by the then Governor, Sir Richard G. Keates, giving it the title of the *Benevolent Irish Society of Conception Bay*. The BIS is an Irish Organization dedicated to the welfare of Irish people that need help or Irish children who need education. They were begun to include all men of Irish decent, regardless of religion, but generally became totally Catholic and later even included Irish women. The Harbour Grace BIS met on a regular basis, always attended Mass on St. Patrick's Day and marched in full regalia throughout Harbour Grace. They also attended and marched at every funeral of a member, a prominent Catholic person or member of the Clergy. They received donations and held activities to make money to help the poor by providing food and articles when needed. They generally had a Committee of Charity and a Committee of Review and Correspondence. In St. John's the BIS built schools and had a large Club House for their members for meetings, parties or fund raising events. Harbour Grace experienced a very unhappy incident during the Bishopric of Bishop Carfagnini. The Italian Bishop had difficulty with the English language and was a very demanding person. It seemed that some of the Irish members of the Parish and especially the BIS members did not so eye-to-eye with the Bishop. They did not want to relinquish their control of the BIS to the Bishop and when he was not make the Patron of the Society, Bishop Carfagnini established a second BIS and renounced the first BIS. The Bishop also desired to exercise more control over the Presentation Sisters and their finances and they refused. The dual BIS' in Harbour Grace caused a division between members of the families and the clergy. Letters were written to Rome concerning Bishop Carfagnini and he was called to Rome to explain the situation and returned to Harbour Grace but things did not improve. More letters and finally a Bishop Conroy came to Newfoundland as the Pope's representative to investigate. Bishop Conroy spent a couple weeks here and finally made his report but became ill and died in St. John's in 1878. His report caused Bishop Carfagnini to return to Rome in 1880. Rome also directed the second BIS to be disbanded. While we did not find any book of minutes of the Harbour Grace BIS, we did find the minutes of one of their meetings held on there 15th Anniversary on 19 Feb 1829 as printed in a local newspaper. Most of there meetings were published for public information.

The Weekly Journal, Harbor Grace,
Thursday February 19, 1829
BENEVOLENT

IRISH SOCIETY

OF CONCEPTION BAY

"This being the Fifteenth Anniversary of the *Benevolent Irish Society of Conception Bay*, the Meeting took place at the Waterford Arms Hotel, which was numerously and respectably attended.

The President, Mr. J. R. Innott, opened the proceedings and briefly explained the nature and objects of the Institution, and congratulated the Society on the prosperous state of funds.

The following Gentlemen were then unanimously admitted as Members."

Martin Kelly, proposed by the President		
Joseph Shea	""""	by the First Assistant
Walter Dillon	" ""	by Rev. D. Mackin
Richard Mackey	" " "	ditto
John Ryan	" " "	ditto
David Keefe	" " "	ditto
James Cooney	" " "	by President
Garrett Condon	" " "	by Vice-President
Richard Power	" " "	by 2d Assistant
Michael Connors	" " "	by Mr. W. Walsh, Chair of R&C
Francis Ronan	" " "	by Mr. W. Walsh, Chair of R&C
Arthur Grubert	" " "	ditto
Patrick Kelly	" " "	ditto
Michael Keefe	" " "	ditto

"The Treasurer's accounts were presented and approved of: balance in his hands, 365 Pds, 2s, 2d including the collection of the evening, which was 36 Pds, 16s."

"The Committee of Charity's book was presented by their Chairman, which was read and approved by the Meeting. It appeared that the sum of 70 Pds, 16s has been distributed to the poor for the last year."

The following Resolutions were proposed by the President and seconded by the Vice-President.

Resolved unanimously

"That the most cordial and respectful thanks of the Society are due and hereby given to the Very Revd Mr. Ewer, for his great countenance and support, and zealous attachment to its interests and welfare."

Resolved unanimously

"That the thanks of the Benevolent Irish Society of Conception Bay, are due and hereby given to the Revd Nicholas Devereux and the Revd Dennis Mackin, for the assiduity and zeal they have evinced in promoting the interests of the Society."

Resolved unanimously

"That the warmest thanks of thanks of the Benevolent Irish Society of Conception Bay are due and hereby given to the Revd John Burt, for the countenance and support he has uniformly given the Society, and for his liberal donation of Two Guineas."

Resolved unanimously

"That the grateful thanks of the Benevolent Irish Society of Conception Bay, are due and hereby given to Mr. Geo. P. Jillard, for his generous donation of One Pound."

Resolved unanimously

"That the thanks of the Benevolent Irish Society of Conception Bay, are due and hereby given to the Committee of Charity, for their judicious disposal of the funds committed to their Management, and the zeal they have uniformly evinced, in promoting the comforts of the distressed."

***Proposed* by William Stirling, Esq., and seconded by the Second Assistant.**

Resolved unanimously

"That this Society in reviewing its proceedings for the period of its existence, have with humility and gratitude to ascribe its prosperity and respectability to the agency of that power, which is "wonderful in council and excellent in working" - and while they unite in imploring the countenance of the blessings which have hitherto characterized their exertions in favour of those who are ready to perish; they have amply testimony to support them in the belief that the means of Charity have not flowed in vain, in the enjoyment they deserve from so pure and delightful source, it is natural for this body to take a retrospective view of the character and conduct of one of its earliest friends, and most liberal benefactor's. Mullowney, Esq., who, in the discharge of the duties devolving on him as its Treasurer, from 1814 to his demise in February 1828, exhibited to the public and to this Society the dignified exertion of talent and liberality, in favour of the suffering children of adversity, which have uniformly been the characteristics of the wise and virtuous in all ages; in adverting to this subject, the Society have to deplore the event that deprives his family, and this Institution of his impertard services, and while they lament the loss suffering humanity has sustained in his person, they console themselves with the solemn and affecting assurance, that his bright example will in future excite the most generous exertion and sympathies in support of the inheritance of the widow and orphan, and that the rays of the benevolence will continue to shed a pure and hallowed light on this society, though emanating from the sepulchre."

The Chairman of the Committee of Charity handed a letter to the President which was read as follows: -

Sir,

"I beg leave through you, in the name and in behalf of the Committee of Charity, to return a vote of thanks to our Secretary, Mr. John Prendergast, including the Gentlemen who assisted in forwarding the object of the Society, - Charity to all mankind; and the zeal manifested by them for its true interest; also for the compliment paid to the Committee of Charity in heading and framing a book for their accommodation, - filled with a sense of the blessings which must naturally flow to the Society from the unanimity and zeal of its members."

I beg leave to subscribe myself for the Committee of Charity.

Your most obedient
Humble Servant,
DANIEL DONOVAN, C.C.C.

To

Joseph R. Innott, Esq.
President of the Benevolent
Irish Society of Conception Bay

Proposed by the Second assistant, and seconded by Mr. Daniel Candler.

Resolved unanimously

"That a Committee be appointed to carry into effect a former Resolution of this Society, - that a House be built for the uses and benefit of the Benevolent Irish Society of Conception Bay, and that the Committee shall have full power to transact all matters and business relative thereto."

The following gentlemen were nominated --

WILLIAM STIRLING, Esq.
Mr. THOMAS FOLEY
"" JOSEPH R. INNOTT
"" JAMES L. PRENDERGAST
"" DANIEL DONOVAN
"" RICHARD POWER
Doctor MOLLOY.

Proposed by Mr. William Innott, and seconded by William Stirling, Esq.

Resolved unanimously

"That the sum of Fifty Pounds from the funds shall be at the disposal of the Committee, to carry into effect the foregoing resolution. Proposed by the Rev. Dennis Mackin, and seconded by William Stirling, Esq."

Resolved unanimously

"That the sum of Thirty Pounds be placed at the disposal of the Committee of Charity, to meet the claims of the necessitous of the ensuing quarter."

"The President having left the Chair, the Revd D. Mackin was called thereto, and after an appropriate address to the Meeting, proposed that they would proceed to the election of a President for the ensuing year."

"Mr. Joseph R. Innott, was then unanimously re-elected. The President resumed his seat, and proceeded to the election of Officers for the ensuing year, when the following gentlemen were unanimously chosen."

Mr. John Fitzgerald	re-elected	Vice-President
" Thomas Foley	"	First Assistant
" James L. Prendergast	"	Second Assistant
" William Mullowney	"	Treasurer
" John Prendergast	"	Secretary
" Daniel Donovan, Chair	"	Committee of Charity
" Michael Greene	"	Committee of Charity
" William Walsh	"	Committee of Charity
" Daniel Candler	"	Committee of Charity
" Randal Donovan	"	Committee of Charity
" Justin Dwyer, Chair	"	Comm. of Review & Corr.
" Joseph Shea	"	" " " "
" Martin Kelly	"	" " " "

Published in the Weekly Journal 19 February 1829

53rd Anniversary Meeting – 1867.

"The 53rd anniversary of the Conception Bay Benevolent Irish society was held in their Rooms on Sunday last, the 17th instant, at 3 o'clock. The president, John Fitzgerald, Esq., on taking the chair, congratulated the Society on arriving at its 53rd Anniversary and also its general improvement and respectability. The Treasurer handed his A/C, which, when audited, was unanimously passed, showing a balance in favor of the Society of 73 pounds, 2 shillings, and 9 pence currency."

Among the donations read, were:

Pd 5 – Rev. J. Dalton;	Pd 5 – W. J.S.S Donnelly
3 guineas - John Munn;	Pd 2 – Rutherford Bros.
Pd 1 – Rev. John Walsh;	Pd 1 – H.W. Trapnell
Pd 1 – Capt. D. Green;	Pd 1 – W. Squarey
Pd 1 – N & J Jillard	

The day's collection amounted to 55 pounds.

The Standard

Chapter 22

KNIGHTS OF COLUMBUS IN HARBOUR GRACE

In 1909 representatives from the USA Knights of Columbus came to Newfoundland to see if the Catholic Men were interested in starting up a Knights of Columbus Council here. And after much discussions, Bishop Power in St. John's was not in favor of it but Bishop March of Harbour Grace was for it. On 10 June 1909 a meeting was held at the Academy Hall to propose the adoption of the first KC council in Newfoundland and on 20 Nov 1909 the Council was formed and was named in honour of our First Bishop – Bishop Dalton. The first Council in Newfoundland was established in Harbour Grace and was called the "Bishop Dalton Council" on 29 November 1909 and the second Council was established in the St. John's area and was called "Terra Nova Council" on 30 November 1909. In the year 2000, Newfoundland had 50 Councils with about 6500 members.

The Bishop Dalton Council of Harbour Grace has been very active throughout the years and is proud of being the "First" or "Mother Council" in Newfoundland and the leader to all other Councils.

The First Officers of DALTON COUNCIL, # 1448, Knights of Columbus:

Grand Knight:	*M.A. O'Brien*
Deputy Grand Knight:	*William S. Madigan*
Chancellor:	*Rev Dr S.J. Whelan*
Recorder:	*C.L.Kennedy*
Financial Secretary:	*M.T. Jones*
Treasurer:	*John Foley*
Lecturer:	*Thomas Hanrahan*
Advocate:	*John Casey*
Warden:	*W.H. Kennedy*
Inside Guard:	*Thomas S. Hanrahan*
Outside Guard:	*William Dooley*
Trustees:	*Thomas Hanrahan*
	John Casey
	R. O'Brien
Chaplain:	*Rev. William P. Finn*

The original members of the First Dalton Council officers in 1909. Mr. M.A. O'Brien was the first Grand Knight. Courtesy of Dalton Council in Harbour Grace.

First Grand Knight – Mr. M.A. O'Brien – 1909

GRAND KNIGHTS SINCE 1909 WERE:

Michael O'Brien-1909-1911; Walter Strapp-1911-1912; Rev Dr Stephen Whelan-1912-1913; John Casey-1913-1914; Thomas Hanrahan-1914-1915; Wm H. Kennedy-1915-1919; Rev M. Dinn -1919-1922; Albert J. Walsh-1922-1924; Wm S. Madigan-1924-1926; D.F. Meaney-1926-1928; Wm S. Madigan-1928-1929; Michael P. Stapleton-1929-1933; Francis J. Sullivan-1933-1934; Michael P. Stapleton-1934-1935; P.G.Roach-1935-1937; Rev John M. O'Neill-1937-1938; Dr G.A. Strapp-1938-1940; Brendan P. Walsh-1940-1944; R.J.Connolly-1944-1946; Wm B. Kennedy-1946-1951; R.J.Connolly-1951-1953; Dr E.O'Brien Freeman-1953-1956; Kevin J.Lawlor-1956-1958; Walter P. Walsh Sr-1958-1960; Kevin J. Lawlor-1960-1965-John A. Finn-1965-1966; Bernard F.Foley-1966-1967; Edward L. Kelly-1967-1968; Bernard F. Foley-1968-1970; Thomas F. Duggan-1970-1972; Gerald Peddle-1972-1973; Reginald B. Coombs-1973-1975; John L. McNamara-1975-1976; Gerald Peddle-1976-1977; Francis P. Sullivan-1977-1979; Wm J. Whelan-1979-1980; Gerald Peddle-1980-1981; Cyril White-1981-1982; Thomas F.Duggan-1982-1983; Sean P. O'Brien-1983-1985; Gerald Peddle-1985-1987; Gerald F. Ryan-1987-1990; Michael J. Reynolds-1990-1994; Gerald Brazil-1994-1995; Ronald J. Martin-1995-1997; John Kent-1997-2000; Grant Keohler-2000-2002; and William Dobbin-2002-2003.

HIGHLIGHTS OF HG KC COUNCIL #1448

1909 – First Knights of Columbus Council in Newfoundland here at Harbour Grace. Dalton Council Nr. 1448. Named after Bishop John Dalton, first Bishop of Harbour Grace. (Nov 29)

1924 – Dalton Council presented the Statue of the Blessed Virgin to Bishop March for the front of the Immaculate Conception Cathedral. 15th Anniversary of the Council. (1909-1924).

1934 – 25th Anniversary. (1909-1934).

1959 – 50th Anniversary. (1909-1959).

1966 – 48th Newfoundland State Convention held at Harbour Grace. May 21-23

1967 – Reception for Msgr. Joseph O'Brien on his Silver Jubilee. (Oct 25)

1968 – Grand Knight Bernard Foley attends official opening of new home of McCormick Council at Gander.

1972 – First Knights of Columbus Convention held in Labrador. May 18-22.

1974 – New General Assembly established for Fourth Degree Assembly in Harbour Grace area. (April 7)

1976 - Chaplain for Knights of Columbus in Newfoundland for 42 years was Msgr. Edward O'Brien. (1934-1976)

1983 – Visit to the Academy Hall on 400th Anniversary. (1583-1983).

1984 – 75th Anniversary. (1909-1984)

1984 – 100th Birthday of Msgr. Edward O'Brien held at Harbour Grace. Nov 13.

1987 – Msgr. Joseph O'Brien dies at age 70. (Nov 13)

1991 – Dalton Council of Harbour Grace won the Star Council Award. This was made to HG Grand Knight Mike Reynolds by District Deputy Gerald Ryan at annual Columbus Day celebrations in October.

1991 – 82nd Anniversary celebration included the dedication of a flagpole outside the Academy Hall dedicated to the memory of Msgr. J.M. O'Brien by Bishop Thomas Daily, Supreme Chaplain of KC assisted by Father James Beresford. (Nov 29) He also laid a wreath at the grave of Rev. Stephen Whelan in North River.

1992 – 500th Anniversary of Columbus discovery of America. (Oct 12)

1992 – Walter Whelan selected as Knight of the Year for the Columbian Year 1991-1992. Presented by Grand Knight Mike Reynolds. (May 8)

1993 – Official Opening of renovated New Council Chambers. (Aug 14)

1999 – 90th Anniversary. (1909-1999)

25th Anniversary of HG Council KC
(1909-1934)

1934 marked the Silver Anniversary of the inception of the Dalton Council in Harbour Grace and the Terra Nova Council in St. John's. Father Edward O'Brien succeeded Father William Finn as State Chaplain in this Jubilee Year. Father O'Brien served a total of 42 years as State Chaplain. A special meeting of the Council took place in Harbour Grace. (1934-1976)

1959 - 50th Anniversary of HG Council KC
(1909-1959)

KC EMBLEM

The Grand Knight and the Executive of
Dalton Council, No. 1448,

Knights of Columbus

Cordially invite you to attend

A Reception

in honour of the Silver Jubilee of

The Right Reverend Monsignor J. M. O'Brien

Wednesday, October 25th, 1967, 5:30 p.m. to 6:30 p.m.

at the Daltonian Club, Harbour Grace

Silver Jubilee of Msgr. Joseph O'Brien, Chaplain KC Council

Msgr Joseph O'Brien's Silver Jubilee Mass.

Knights of Columbus
Msgr. O'Brien Council 9654
Fogo Island, Newfoundland
Chartered Nov 8, 1987

Msgr. Joseph O'Brien was honoured when they chartered a New Council at Fogo on 8 Nov 1987 and named it the "Msgr. O'Brien Council 9654.

48th Newfoundland State Knights of Columbus Convention.

48th
Newfoundland
State Convention

Knights of Columbus,

Harbour Grace, Nfld.

May 21 - 23, 1966.

PRAYER FOR THE POPE .. Mon. E. J. O'Brien

Let us pray for our Pontiff Paul VI. The Lord preserve him and give him life and make him blessed upon the earth, and deliver him not up to the will of his enemies.

Convention Chairman .... J. L. McNamara

Toast to The Queen

Introductions .... J. L. McNamara

Convention Welcome . J. A. Finn, Grand Knight

Toast to the Clergy . C. J. Fleming, Grand Knight
Rev. Dr. Whelan Council

Response .... Mon. J. W. Peddle, V.G.

Toast to Order ...... F. Flynn, State Secretary

Response .... K. J. Lawlor, State Deputy

Introduction of Guest Speaker .
J. A. Finn, Grand Knight

Guest Speaker . Mr. Justice James G. Higgins, Q.C.

Vote of Thanks .... John Hodge, Lecturer

God Save The Queen

Held at Harbour Grace, May 21-23 1966.

1972
State Convention of the Knights of Columbus Held for first time in Labrador.

"The State convention of the Knights of Columbus of Newfoundland took place at Labrador City on May 18th to May 22nd. A chartered EPA jet took off from Torbay on Thursday, May 18th and, after stops at Gander and Deer Lake, proceeded to Labrador City with one hundred and nine K of C members from all over Newfoundland. Members of Dalton Council, Harbour Grace, were: Msgr. E. J. O'Brien, State Chaplain, Msgr J.M. O'Brien, Thos Duggan, Walter P. Walsh, Gerald Peddle, Thos. Walsh, Reg Coombs and Bernard Fitzpatrick. This was the first time a convention of this kind was held in Labrador and the K of C there are to be congratulated on making it such an outstanding success." NEWS

Dalton Council Honoured for Restoration of Churches

Dalton Council had a busy Columbian year in 1978/79 and was honoured by the Supreme office for its work with donations and the restoration of the Immaculate Conception Church in Harbour Grace and St. Joseph's Church in Riverhead.

Donate Msgr. Edward O'Brien Picture To Knights Of Columbus

Msgr. Joseph O'Brien donates a picture of Msgr. Edward O'Brien with natives of Labrador to Dalton Council of Harbour Grace Knights of Columbus.

Monsignor Edward O'Brien Celebrated his 100th Birthday

1884-1984

On 13 November 1984, Msgr. Edward O'Brien, retired after 55 years as Parish Priest of Northern Bay and 42 Years as State Chaplain of the Knights of Columbus, held his 100th Birthday at the "Dalton Council" in Harbour Grace. He holds the distinction of being a priest for 76 years and living exactly one-half or 100 years of the 200 years of the Newfoundland Catholic Church. (1784-1984)

MSGR. EDWARD O'BRIEN'S 100TH BIRTHDAY

1884-1984

Left to right: Msgr. W. Hogan, Bishop Alphonsus Penney, Dave Murphy (Carbonear), Bill O'Keefe (Carbonear), Msgr. Edward O'Brien of Northern Bay (100), Marian Murphy (Carbonear), and Msgr. Joseph O'Brien at Knights of Columbus in Harbour Grace, Fourth Degree. **(Courtesy of Lillian Ryan, RH, HG)**

1984 - 75th Anniversary of HG Council KC
(1909-1984)

The Newfoundland Knights of Columbus Councils celebrated the 75th Anniversary of the original Council's in 1909. They have 45 branches and about 6000 members. The Government and St. John's Municipal Council appreciated the outstanding services of the Order and renamed the Cross-town-Arterial in the Capital City to "Columbus Drive" on this occasion.

This Year coincides with the 200th Anniversary of the Catholic Church in Newfoundland. 1784-1984 and Pope John Paul II visit to Newfoundland.

Msgr. Joseph M. O'Brien dies – 13 Nov 1987

6 — The Compass, Newfoundland, November 18, 1987

Honour Guard

Members of the Fourth Degree of Dalton Assembly, Knights of Columbus formed an honour guard on Monday during the Funeral Mass for Msgr. J.M. O'Brien. The Knights were followed by members of the Royal Canadian Legion who were also present for the solemn ceremony. (Compass photo)

1988
Harbour Grace Knights of Columbus

The election of Officers of Dalton Council, KC was held on Sunday 6 June 1988 and resulted in the following executive for the 1988/1989 Columbian Year:

CHANCELLOR - Gerald Peddle
GRAND KNIGHT - Gerald Ryan (Re-elected)
DEPUTY GRAND KNIGHT - Art Hurdle Jr
FINANCIAL SECRETARY - Harold Cashin
TREASURER - Reg O'Neill
RECORDER - John M. Ethridge
CHAPLAIN – Rev. Michael Walsh
TRUSTEE - Tom Duggan
OUTSIDE GUARDS - Michael Louvelle & Ray Peddle
INSIDE GUARD - Tom Delaney

Dalton Council celebrates 80th Anniversary

"On Nov 29, 1989, the "Mother Council" of the Knights of Columbus in Newfoundland – "Dalton Council" celebrated the 80th Anniversary of its founding. Just 27 years after the founding of the Knights of Columbus in America (1882). Columbianism took roots in Newfoundland with the forming of Dalton Council # 1448. After receiving the approval of Bishop John March, the Council was chartered and Mr. M.R. O'Brien was elected first Grand Knight and Rev. William P. Finn was appointed the first Chaplain. At the ceremonies held on Nov 28, 1989, greetings were brought by the M.H.A. for Harbour Grace by Major Paul Moriarity; and from Supreme Director of the K of C, Gerry Glavine. All of the above praised the work of the Knights of Columbus and referred specifically to the good community work it is doing and also the work it is doing with the restoration of St. Joseph's and Immaculate Conception Church. Grand Knight Gerald Ryan brought greetings from Dalton Council and Father Michael Walsh from the Parish. A good turnout enjoyed the evening's festivities. There were representatives from various other Councils including Brigus, Terra Nova and Carbonear." *Monitor Feb 1990*

Souvenir of Official Opening

NEW COUNCIL CHAMBERS - DALTON COUNCIL, NO. 1448

KINGHTS OF COLUMBUS

Harbour Grace, August 14th, 1993

Executive 1993-1994
Dalton Council, No. 1448

Grand Knight……………………….Michael Reynolds
Deputy Grand Knight…………………Ronald Martin
Chancellor………………………………Arthur Hurdle
Recorder…………………………………Gerald Brazil
Financial Secretary…………………………Reg O'Neill
Treasurer…………………………………..John Ethridge
Lecturer……………………………….Francis Littlejohn
Advocate………………………………..Francis Sullivan
Warden………………………………….Walter Whelan
Inside Guard……………………………..Randy Wrice
Outside Guards……………….Ray Peddle & John Kent
Trust………Patrick Haire, John Hearn, Sean O'Brien
Chaplain…………………Rev. Father James Beresford

COLUMBUS DAY and
92ND ANNIVERSARY CELEBRATIONS
Saturday, November 10, 2001
Harbour Grace, NF

Executive 2001-2002

Grand Knight.........................Grant J. Koehler
Deputy Grand Knight.............Jack Kent, P.G.K.
Chancellor...................Francis Sullivan, P.G.K.
Financial secretary.................William Dobbin
Recorder................................Reginald O'Neill
Advocate.....................................Denis O'Neill
Warden........................... Sean O'Brien, P.G.K.
Inside Guard........................Thomas McCarthy
Outside Guards...Henry Mercer & Jerry Reynolds
Trustees............William Doran, Ernest Purcell
& Walter Whelan.

2002-2003 - GRAND KNIGHT IS BILL DOBBIN

2003 – Special Recognition to Reginald Coombs to celebrate his 65th Year as a Knight and the first elected Faithful Navigator to the Harbour Grace Council. Born 80 years ago in 1923, he joined the HG Knights of Columbus in July 1938 and was a founding member of the Fourth Degree. He was Grand Knight from 1973-1975. Our thanks for his many years of Service.

REGINALD COOMBS

HG KC COUNCIL PROGRAMS AND PROJECTS

Rosaries for deceased parishioners. - Pallbearers at Funerals.
Columbus Day Celebrations. - Christmas Hampers. - Parish Council.
Church collections.- Restoration of the Church.
Keep Christ in Christmas. - Support Elizabeth House in SJ.
St. Clare's and Janeway Hospital support. - Community Service.
Summer games in Harbour Grace-Carbonear 1992.
Sponsorship of programs that serve: families, Church, youth and community.

Current Dalton Council Clubhouse, Knight's of Columbus, on Harvey Street in Harbour Grace. Old Academy Hall.

Chapter 23

ST. VINCENT DE PAUL SOCIETY

HARBOUR GRACE

We understand the St. Vincent de Paul Society was started in Harbour Grace in 1875, during the Bishopric of Bishop Carfagnini, and his Patronage that he started the SVDP in Carbonear in 1874. The spiritual director was Rev William Veitch and the President Felix J. McCarthy, Esq.

Annual Report of St. Vincent de Paul - 1877

President: A. T. Drysdale
Secretary: John Cody
Treasurer: Thomas Strapp

The report includes the following information. That 74 families, representing 310 persons, were visited during the past year, and the amount distributed, including work done in the Net Factory, reached the sum of 110 pounds, 19 shillings and 10 pence.

November 25, 1877

The following is a partial list of subscriptions (arranged alphabetically) which illustrates how well the brotherhood exemplified in 1877.

Apsey, John F,	0-10- 0	Fitzgerald, Henry J.	0- 7- 6
Allan, Celby G.	0-10- 0	Fitzgerald, Mrs. Capt N.	0- 5- 0
Allan, Dr William M.	0- 5- 0	Flynn, Michael J.	0- 5- 0
Bennett, Thomas R (Judge)	1- 0- 0	Fleming, Richard	0- 5- 0
Bemister, John (Sheriff)	1- 0- 0	Ford, William M.	0- 5- 0
Bailey, Captain Henry	0-10- 0	Godden, Rev. John	0-12- 6
Brien, Capt. Michael	0-10- 0	Godden, Joseph M.H.A.	0-10- 0
Brown, Capt. James	0- 5- 0	Gordon, Late Capt. Sam	0-10- 0
Barry, Capt. John	0- 5- 0	Graham, Joseph (Cooper)	1- 0- 0
Carfagnini, Most Rev. Dr.	3-12- 0	Green, Capt. Thomas	1- 0- 0
Cody, John (Water St)	0- 5- 0	Hayden, Capt. Timothy	0-10- 0
Connell, Mrs. Maurice	1- 0- 0	Hayden, Mrs. Capt. Tim.	0-10- 0
Devereaux, Patrick	0-10- 0	Hanrahan, Capt. Nicholas	0- 5- 0
Devereaux, Mrs. Pat.	0-10- 0	Hennessey, Capt. William	1- 0- 0
Dove, Rev James	0- 5- 0	Hennessey, Capt. John	1- 0- 0
Drysdale, A.T.	0-10- 0	Hogan, John	0- 5- 0
Drysdale, Mrs. A.T.	0- 5- 0	Hogan, Mrs. John	0- 5- 0
Drysdale, Miss Anastasia	0- 5- 0	Innott, Joseph	0- 5- 0
Drysdale, Miss Janet	0- 5- 0	Jillard Brothers	1-10- 0
Dunn, Capt. John	0-10- 0	Jarvis, James	0- 7- 6
Dwyer, Peter (Riverhead)	1- 0- 0	Jones, Michael	0- 5- 0
Emerson, Lewis W.	1- 0- 0	Keefe, Late Mrs. Bridget	0- 5- 0
Emerson, George H.	0-10- 0	Keefe, Capt. James L.	1- 0- 0

Falconio, Very Rev. D.	**1- 0- 0**	**Keefe, Capt. John**	**0- 5- 0**
Keefe, Capt. Michael L.	**0-10- 0**	**Roach, Jeremiah**	**0- 2- 6**
Kennedy, Charles L.	**0-10- 0**	**Rogers, David**	**0- 5- 0**
Kennedy, Mrs. Charles L.	**0- 5- 0**	**Ross, Rev Alexander**	**0- 5- 0**
Lahey, Robert	**0- 5 -0**	**Ross, C.W. & Co**	**1- 5- 0**
Lynch, Capt. Thomas	**1- 0- 0**	**Rutherford, C.C. & Co**	**0-10- 0**
Lynch, John (M.W.W.)	**0- 7- 6**	**Rutherford, Richard**	**0- 5- 0**
Lynch, Mrs. John (M.W.W.)	**0- 5- 0**	**Ryan, Edward (Cooper)**	**0- 2- 6**
Lynch, Mrs. Capt. Thomas	**0- 5- 0**	**Scully, Michael**	**0- 5- 0**
Munn, John & Co	**5- 5- 0**	**Smart, Capt. Martin**	**1- 0- 0**
Munn, J.F.	**0-10- 0**	**Smith, William**	**0- 5- 0**
Munn, James	**0- 7- 6**	**Squarey, Mrs. Robert T.**	**0- 5- 0**
McInnes, Rev. D.	**0-10- 0**	**Squires, John**	**0- 5- 0**
McKinnon, Murdock	**0-12- 6**	**Stephenson, John (Ship Hd)**	**0- 5- 0**
McRae, Roderick	**0- 5- 0**	**Stephenson, John**	**0- 5- 0**
Mackinson, Mrs. George	**0- 5- 0**	**Strapp, Capt. John**	**2- 0- 0**
Martin, George	**0- 5- 0**	**Strapp, Thomas**	**1- 0- 0**
Murphy, Mrs. John	**0- 5- 6**	**Strathie, John**	**0- 5- 0**
Mitchell, Mrs. John	**0- 5- 0**	**Tapp, William**	**0-10- 0**
McCarthy, Simon	**0- 5- 0**	**Taylor, E.W.**	**0- 7- 6**
Moore, Mrs. Henry	**0- 5- 0**	**Taylor, Peter**	**0- 6- 0**
Morris, John S.	**0- 5- 0**	**Thompson, William**	**0- 5- 0**
Nicholas, William (Barber)	**0- 2- 6**	**Thompson, W.H.**	**0-10- 0**
Noel, Rev. J. M.	**0- 5- 0**	**Tobin, Late Peter J. (Teacher)**	**0- 3- 0**
Oke, Mrs. Austin	**0- 5- 0**	**Tobin, William**	**0- 5- 0**
Oke, Mrs. Edward	**0- 1- 6**	**Thomey, Mrs. Capt. Henry**	**0- 5- 0**
O'Neil, Mrs. Capt. Denis	**0- 5- 5**	**Thomey, Mrs. Capt. Henry W.**	**0- 5- 0**
Parsons, James & B. Co	**1- 0- 0**	**Walsh, Mark**	**0- 2- 6**
Parsons, Josiah	**0- 5- 0**	**Walsh, William (Cooper)**	**0- 2- 6**
Parsons, Mrs. Ebenezer	**0- 7- 6**	**Walsh, Walter (Cooper)**	**0- 2- 6**
Paterson & Foster	**1- 5- 0**	**Ward, William M.**	**0- 2- 6**
Payne, Charles	**0- 5- 0**	**Warren, William**	**0- 2- 6**
Pike, Albert	**0- 5- 0**	**Watts, Claudius**	**0- 8- 0**
Pike, Capt. George	**0- 5- 0**	**Webber, Valentine**	**0- 2- 6**
Pike, Capt. Joshua	**0- 5-0**	**Webber, Charles**	**0- 2- 6**
Prendergast, James L.	**0-10- 0**	**Whelan, late James (Cooper)**	**0- 5- 0**
Pumphrey, Capt. Daniel	**0- 5- 0**	**Whelan, Miss Ann**	**0- 2- 6**
Pumphrey, Capt. Jeremiah	**0- 2- 6**	**Williams, Mrs. Edward**	**0- 1- 5**
Pumphrey, Mrs. Capt. John	**0- 5- 0**	**Williams, William**	**0- 2- 6**
Pumphrey, late Capt. John	**0-10- 0**	**Whiteway, Edward**	**0- 5- 0**
Pumphrey, Capt. William	**0- 5- 0**	**Woods, Sidney**	**0- 5- 0**
Quintin, Edward W. & Son	**0-10- 0**	**Youdall, Hugh & Co**	**0-10- 0**
Richards, John (Cooper)	**1- 0- 0**		

Total Amount Collected...........................	119-19- 0
Government Grant................................	30- 0- 0
Amount received for manufactured goods.....	91-14- 9

GRAND TOTEL: 241-13- 9

Thomas Strapp, Treasurer

Annual Report of St. Vincent de Paul – 1879

"During the year 150 poor families were visited at their homes, representing 658 persons. It will be seen by the Treasurer's account that the total receipts for 1879 amounted to 335 pounds, 9 shillings and 9 pence. General collections 138 pounds, 5 shillings, and 8 pence; Legislative grant 30 pounds; amount received from manufactured goods, 167 pounds, 4 shillings and 1 pence. And expenditures, 336 pounds, 10 shillings and 8 pence.

During the past winter, over 40 poor boys were employed in the Net Factory, being thus enabled to earn an independent support, as well as learn a useful and necessary handicraft to those employed in the fisheries. The Society having learned that many deserving poor families were without seed potatoes, last May distributed half a barrel each to 64 families.

We have much pleasure in acknowledging the liberality displayed by the Trade, in purchasing material manufactured in the Factory.

On behalf of the Society, A.T. Drysdale, President and John Cody, Secretary."

STATEMENT OF ST. VINCENT DE PAUL'S ACCOUNT WITH THE TREASURER FOR 1879.

To balance from 1878........................	**2- 18 - 8**
To amt. paid in outdoor relief, Labor done in factory, picking Oakum and seed potatoes................	**197-17- 0**
To amt. paid for twine & rope.............	**99- 9-11**
To amt. paid for coal for Factory...........	**3- 5 -0**
To amt. paid for printing, etc...............	**5-14-11**
To Superintendent's Salary................	**12- 5 -0**
To rent of Factory & conf. room...........	**15- 0 -0**
	336-10 -8
February. By general collection	**138- 5 -8**
July. By Government Grant	**30- 0 -0**
November. By amt rec'd for Manufactured Goods	**167- 4 -1**
	335- 9 -9
Balance due Treasurer:	**1- 0 -11**

Harbor Grace,
November, 23rd, 1879 Thomas Strapp, Treasurer.

Chapter 24

EVENTS IN THE PARISH

Early English laws in Newfoundland required that any man coming to Newfoundland for the spring and summer fishing season had to return home in the fall because habitation in Newfoundland was ostensibly forbidden. The early few that stayed had to live out in the back country or forbidden harbors to keep from getting found out and deported. When the Catholics finally got permission to practice their religion out-in-the-open they tended to consolidate in one Town or a particular section of any Town. Many Towns have sections called "Riverhead", after a similar place in Ireland and they became little Catholic communities. They were generally located away from the local Town at the head-of-the bay or river, probably for fishing and as an outlet for trade. In Newfoundland there are basically three Riverhead locations; St. John's, Harbour Grace and St. Mary's.

People were bound together around their Church and Roman Catholic values were guided by the Priest or religious teachers, if the Town was lucky enough to have any. The Catholic family always had the loyalty, involvement and concern of their Church and their Parish Priest. The Priests played a leading role in almost all aspects of the Parish and the Catholic community, especially education. He hired the teachers, built the schools and keeps them in good working order.

Marriages occurred in the non-fishing seasons, when most of the men were back home and could partake in the ceremonies. Catholic marriages were big events in the Parish and almost everyone in the Parish attended them and enjoyed the receptions. After the wedding the Priest would came and bless the newly weds new home.

Babies were born at home, usually delivered by midwives and were baptized usual the same day or the next day by the Priest. Since there were no undertakers in the early years, a local Catholic woman would go to the home of one who had just died and prepare the body for waking and burial. This was usually after the Priest had given the dying person Extreme Unction or the Last Rites. The local Knights of Columbus or Altar Sodality would say a Rosary at the wake, which was usually held in the living room or parlor at the person's home.

During the economic hard times many the families received packages from friends or family members who left Newfoundland to get a job in mainland Canada or the United States.

The parishioners of the Parish would put on plays or concerts on St. Patrick's or St. Joseph's Day and during the Christmas or Easter seasons, or when every they felt the need. The Bishop came every four years for Confirmation for all the children who were close enough to be confirmed before the next 4 years. Ages 6-12-15. Most houses had a Holy water fountain to bless their children when they were sick or to bless those on their birthday or other special occasions. They blessed all new babies. Many families said the Rosary every day or weekly as a family. Prayer was very important within the family as well as in Church and the Stations of the Cross were religiously said by many of the parishioners in Church before or after the Mass. The Churches had Community Rosary services on Sunday night and Benediction once a month and Stations of the Cross and 40 hours devotions were regularly scheduled. Once a year there was a Mission in the Parish and everyone was encouraged to attend. They were usually conducted by a far away Priest or visiting Missionary Priest. Men were all members of the Holy Name Society and women took part in the Altar Sodality and girls became members of the Children of Mary. Good Friday was a day to be in Church especially between 12 noon and 3 PM, in commemoration of Jesus' crucifixion and death on the cross. Our candles were blessed on Candle man's Day in February and we received our ashes on Ash Wednesday. Children went to Church every morning in the Catholic Schools and participated in school plays and concerts usually at graduations or on special occasions during or at the end of the school year. Jannying was an ancient custom of house-visiting by adult neighbors when Mummers would dress up in funny clothes with their heads covered and they would come around on boxing day, the day after Christmas, and they would be welcomed into your home and they would dance around in your kitchen and stage a happy time for their friends. They maybe would have a little snort and go onto the next neighbor. You were suppose to guess who they were.

Parish Entertaining

The Parishioners at the Immaculate Conception Church in Harbour Grace or St. Joseph's Church in Riverhead would initiate and participate in various entertainment activities throughout the year. Historically the BIS, St. Vincent de Paul and other Catholic organizations in the Parish were all supported by the parishioners of the Parish. When St. Patrick's Hall was completed in 1882, it became the centre of stage activities and gala events put on by the Parish. The Parishioners would put on Fairs, like the one held in 1892 to collect money to rebuild the new Cathedral. They put on their plays and concerts and all the players were members of the Parish and they practiced their events and used their own furniture for props. Special events were scheduled to distribute prizes and diplomas at graduations and Church sponsored Christmas bazaars every year. Harbour Grace and Riverhead, like most other Catholic communities, made the Parish the social centre as well as the spiritual centre. The Parishioners put on concert, plays, dances, played bingo, and celebrated their marriages in the Church Hall or school.

A GRAND CONCERT WAS HELD IN RIVERHEAD HALL

Under the Distinguished Patronage of
His Excellency, Bishop O'Neill.

A GRAND CONCERT

in

St. Joseph's Hall, Riverhead

on

FRIDAY, DEC. 10th

by the Pupils and Ex-pupils of the Superior School.

PROGRAMME:

1. Opening Chorus: "The Flag of Newfoundland."
2. Monologue: "When I'm a Woman...... Miss Margaret Walsh.
3. Flower Drill................................ Junior Girls.
4. War Savers' Flag Drill................................ Junior Boys.
5. Dialogue: "The Goodman is always right" Miss Mary Hunt, Masters A. Northcott, J. Reynolds, W Guilfoyle.
6. Song and Dance: "Daises"................................ Junior Girls.
7. Dialogue: "A busy morning"................ Miss Julia Callahan, Masters T. Walsh, G. Reynolds, A Northcott, J. Callahan and J. Sullivan.
8. Chorus: "Christmas is Coming."
9. Vocal Solo: "To the End of the World with You" Mrs. J. St. John.
10. Dialogue: "Christmas Letters"........ Misses Mary Kearney, Annie Doran, Bridgie Kearney, Christina Russell, Mary Sullivan, Masters P. McCarthy, J. Sullivan.
11. Recitation: "Don't Quit"........................ Miss Julia Callahan
12. Operetta: "LET US GO TRAVELLING."

GOD SAVE THE KING.

(Munn & Oke, Pr

St. Patrick's Day in Harbor Grace – 1879

St. Patrick's Day was as usual observed by our towns people here (Harbor Grace) in a general Holiday. The Two Benevolent Irish Societies (BISs) honoured their patron Saint in the customary way.
Harbor Grace Standard, 22 March 1879

Confirmation at Carbonear and Bryants Cove - 1879

The Lord Mayor of Newfoundland on his return on Wednesday last (May 28) from Carbonear where he administered the ordinance of Confirmation. Crossed over to the South Side of this Harbor and received a very lively welcome from the good people and on the following forenoon, the pretty little Church at Bryant's Cove was consecrated and in the evening some 40-50 received the rite of Confirmation. Harbor Grace Standard, May 31, 1879

(We were not able to find where this church was in Bryant's Cove)

Barn Dance Committee, Riverhead, Harbour Grace

From LEFT TO RIGHT: Richard Doran, Andrew Short, Frankie Reynolds, Gerald Burke, Ron Callahan, Kevin Reynolds and Father Ed Shea.

VARIETY CONCERT - 1955

St. Patrick's Day Concert

This was a St. Patrick's Day concert put on in Harbour Grace.
Madeline Kennedy was in charge.

First Communion Class

Rev James Beresford and one of the Sisters at a First Communion Class at St. Joseph's Church at Riverhead, Harbour Grace.

GRAND FALLS DIOCESE

COMING

COMMEMORATIVE EVENT

150th Anniversary

1856-2006

Chapter 25

GRAND FALLS DIOCESE
Immaculate Conception Parish

When the A.N.D. Company began operations in Grand Falls in 1905, the employees began to move into the Town and there was a need for a Catholic Church and a visiting Priest was dispatched to Grand Falls in 1905, the same year as the first Chapel was built. The first resident Priest was assigned in 1912 when Rev. William P. Finn was assigned to Grand Falls. It was a Parish under the Harbour Grace Diocese. The Diocese was in Harbour Grace for 109 years, from 1856 to 1965.

GRAND FALLS CONCRETE CHURCH

In 1918 the original church was destroyed by fire and a new Romanesque concrete church was completed by Father Finn in 1920. It was graced with a Carrara marble altar from Italy and stained glass windows, donated by the parishioners, depicting the mysteries of the Rosary, one in honour of our Lady, the veterans for two wars, the Holy Family, three saints and one to the Bishop. The Stations of the Cross are also of marble construction. This building was in the shape of a cross with the altar at the head of the cross. This Immaculate Conception church became the co-cathedral.

Immaculate Conception Co-Cathedral

THE INTERIOR AND ALTAR OF THE OLD CHURCH

The Interior of the old Co-Cathedral Immaculate Conception Church was a very impressive Church with a majestic and ornate Altar.

CO-CATHEDRAL HARBOUR GRACE AND GRAND FALLS

When the Parishes in the Diocese began to expand into the central part of Newfoundland and parishes were exchanged between Diocese's for more equitable supervision; it was decided to move the Harbour Grace Diocese to Grand Falls. The transition was gradual and Grand Falls was declared a Co-Cathedral with Harbour Grace in 1953 while a new Cathedral was being built in Grand Falls. Bishop O'Neill moved from Harbour Grace to Grand Falls in 1955. For the period 1953-1965 the Co-Cathedral Parish in Grand Falls was this Immaculate Conception Church.

THE REMAINS OF THE OLD CO-CATHEDRAL

The new Cathedral was built next to the Co-Cathedral and the old Co-Cathedral was torn down.

The new Cathedral was built to the right of the old co-cathedral and incorporated the beautiful marble altar, altar rail, stained glass windows and the stations of the cross of the former Co-Cathedral church and was completed in 1965. The Diocese designation was officially transferred from Harbour Grace to Grand Falls. The Immaculate Conception Parish in Grand Falls became the Cathedral Parish and the Immaculate Conception Church in Harbour Grace reverted back to a Parish status under the new Grand Falls Diocese. Later when repairs were required, a liturgical architect was engaged to bring the functioning of the building in line with the Second Vatican Council. This required the downsizing of the main altar and the erection of an Altar of Repose with sliding doors to close during Mass. Opened after Mass for adoration of the Blessed Sacrament.

The New Immaculate Conception Cathedral Church in Grand Falls.
Updated picture taken by Jonathan Gaye in 2002

Vatican Council II Changes

The first year as a Diocese was a memorable year because it was the final year of the Vatican Council (1962-1965) and major changes were forthcoming which would change many of the old traditions and procedures of ordinary Catholic life. The emphasis changed from the negative (Fear of God) to a more positive approach (love of the forgiving Father). Bishop O'Neill had been in Grand Falls for 10 years and was well qualified to begin to implement these changes. To summarize some of these changes and when they were made are describes below.

Almost immediately actions were taken to say the Masses in English and no longer in Latin and the altars were turned around and the priest faced the people. Girls were permitted to serve the Mass and women were permitted to give out communion. Parish Councils were formed to help the Priest in administering the Parish.

Changes in the Roman Catholic Church and In Newfoundland

1966 – Catholics were permitted to eat meat on Fridays.

1969 – First folk Mass for teenagers was celebrated at St. Georges.

1969 – Vatican dropped some Saints from Roman calendar, namely St. Christopher.

1969 – Dioceses set up Diocesan Consultors and a Senate to assist the Bishop.

1969 – The majority of Presentation sisters reverted to their Baptismal names.

1970 – The Knights and Masons held a joint meeting in Corner Brook.

1970 – All American Bishops were given permission to have Saturday Masses to fulfill Sunday Mass requirements

1970 – Pope Paul VI issued, "Vatican Decree on Mixes Marriages." Giving Bishops authority to interpret laws on mixed marriage rather than the Vatican. Local priests given dispensation of marrying non-Catholics rather than the Bishops.

1970 - Christian Brothers in Corner Brook were the first to be given the extraordinary power of distributing Holy Communion.

1971 – Pope Paul VI decreed that Cardinals at ago 80 lose their right to vote in papal elections.

1982 – Special RCMP Mass in Corner Brook.

1983 – Pope John Paul II signs a new Code of Canon Law. Protecting Latin texts and insuring modern language translations are accurate.

1984 – First Rites of Christian Initiation of Adults (RCIA) initiated in Grand Falls.

1984 – Grand Falls implement Presbyterium in Diocese.

1985 – The Extraordinary Synod of Bishops at the Vatican included a lay auditor. The Supreme Grand Knight of the Knights of Columbus. USA.

1985 – First World Youth Day established by Pope John Paul II.

1986 – The first Altar Girl at St. Joseph's Parish, Gander. Joanne Bowen.

1987 –1988 - Pope John Paul II announces Marian Year to Blessed Virgin Mary.

1987- Atlantic Liturgical Congress met in St. John's.

1990 – Synod of Bishops in Rome. Pope John Paul II defends celibacy for Latin-Rite priests.

1992 – Pope John Paul II releases the new Catholic Catechism.
1992 – The "Helping Hand" an interchurch Goodwill Centre opened at Bay Roberts: Catholic, Anglican and United Church.
1994 – The English language edition of the Catechism approved. First in 450 years.
1994 – Pope John Paul II issues document entitled, "The Roman Liturgy and Inculturation." No radical experimentation in liturgy without Vatican approval.
1994 – Pope John Paul II approved two modifications in church law to make it easier for Bishops to impose penalties, including laicization, on clerics found guilty of sexual abuse of a minor.
1994 – First Vatican Ambassador to Israel to represent the Holy See.
1994 – Pope John Paul II hosted a world Family Gathering in Rome for one family from each Catholic Diocese in the world.
1995 – Pope John Paul II, "Encyclical on Human Life" made public.

1965-1972 – BISHOP JOHN M. O'NEILL

The new Diocese at Grand Falls began immediately to expand the Diocese area with additional Parishes to provide services to the Catholic people under their jurisdiction. Sisters were send to new locations to provide educational services for the children and events began to explode throughout the Diocese. On 13 June 1966, Bishop O'Neill blessed two new schools at Brigus. In July 1966, a new St. Patrick's Parish was consecrated at Plate Cove, with Rev. Michael Hynes as first Parish Priest. Also in 1966, Presentation Sisters were sent to La Scie for two and half years and in 1968 they were moved to Brent's Cove. On 6 June 1968, the Bishop ordained Rev. Matthew Kane at Gander; this was the first ordination at Gander. On 21 Dec 1969, he blessed and opened a High School at Baie Verte. In 1971, the Parish of Whitbourne was returned to Diocese control from the Redemporists. On 18 Nov 1972, Bishop John M. O'Neill, after 32 years as Bishop, retired as Bishop of Grand Falls and Msgr. Alphonsus Penney was appointed Bishop of Grand Falls.

1972-1979 - BISHOP ALPHONSUS PENNEY

In 1973 the Presentation Sisters Convent was closed in Harbour Grace and the Nuns commuted from the Carbonear Convent. In Sept 1973 he introduced the Sisters of Service to the Diocese and also convened the first Diocesan Pastoral Meeting GF. In June 1974, a new St. Patrick's Church was opened at Tilting, Fogo by Rev. J. Kevin Barker. He was elected Co-Chairman of the Episcopal Commission for Religious Education CCCB in Dec 1975. In 1978, the new "Rev. Ed. J. Jones" Knights of Columbus Council was established at Brigus. In 1979 Archbishop Skinner retired in St. John's and Bishop Alphonsus Penney was appointed as his replacement in St. John's after only seven years in Grand Falls.

1980-1999 – BISHOP J. FABER MACDONALD

On 25 March 1980, Bishop J. Faber MacDonald was installed as Bishop of Grand Falls. His Bishopric was one of celebration of anniversaries of the Parishes. In 1981, the Conception Bay Renewal Centre was established at Conception Harbour and in 1982, a new Parish of St. Joseph and St. Patrick was consecrated at Port Union. On 7 Nov 1982, the Presentation sisters celebrated their 25th Anniversary at Assumption Parish in Avondale, with Bishop MacDonald present. Later on 21 to 27 Nov 1982, Sts Peter and Paul Parish at Harbour Main celebrated the 125th Anniversary of their founding as a Parish. On 9 Oct 1983, Holy Cross Parish in Holyrood celebrated its 100th Anniversary and on 26 Oct 1983, Bishop MacDonald celebrated the 150th Anniversary of Presentation sisters in Newfoundland at the Grand Falls Cathedral. On 1 Jan 1984, St. Ann's Parish in Conception Harbour celebrated their 100th Anniversary. On 26 Feb 1984, a Gymnatorium was opened at St. Joseph's elementary school at Harbour Main. In 1985, Rev. William Ryan and St. Joseph's Parish in Harbour Breton celebrated their 135th Anniversary. In Aug 1985, St. Patrick's Parish in Fogo, Tilting celebrated their 150th Anniversary using 1835 as the Origination date. Two sad events happened at Plate Cove; in April 1986, the Presbytery was destroyed by fire at Plate Cove, Rev. Lawrence George and on 14 Nov 1985, St. Patrick's Church and Parish Centre were also destroyed by fire at Plate Cove. On 21 Feb 1986, the oldest priest in Canada, Msgr. Edward O'Brien died in retirement at Carbonear at age 101. He was priest for 76 years. In May 1986, Rev. Brian Dunn blessed the fishing boats at St. Brendan's in Bonavista Bay and on 5 Dec 1986, the Student Council was elected at Holy Cross Central High School at St. Alban's. Grand Falls Diocese commemorates the Marian Years. – 1997-1998. Also in 1988, Corpus Christi Parish in Northern Bay celebrated its 150th Anniversary. On 20 Nov 1989, a new St. Columba Elementary School was opened at Harbour Grace by Bishop MacDonald and on 29 Nov 1989, the Dalton Knights of Columbus Council at Harbour Grace, first in Newfoundland, celebrates its 80th Anniversary as the "Mother Council" in Newfoundland. On 24 June 1990, Bishop J. F. MacDonald blessed the new office of the Newfoundland Service Committee, established for Charismatic Renewal in Newfoundland. It is located at Markland on the isthmus of the Avalon. In 1991, St. Ignatius Parish in St. Alban's celebrated its 75th Anniversary and the same year, Carbonear celebrated the 100th Anniversary of its St. Patrick's Brick Church and also celebrated the 150th Anniversary of its Parish. On 22 Sep 1991, St.

Joseph's Parish Centre at Gander was dedicated by Bishop MacDonald, in honour of Rev. Philip McCarthy, Parish Priest - 1946-1974. The sad news was received of the death of Sister Bernadette Aucoin on 21 June 1992 in an auto accident near Brent's Cove in her 64th year. She was Administrator of Brent's Cove Parish. On 16 April 1993, Rev. Tony Hageman opened a new Church at Badger with Bishop MacDonald officiating. On 3 June 1995, the Christian Brothers left St. Francis Catholic High School at Harbour Grace and the Christian Brothers left Grand Falls in 1989. In 1999, a new steeple was put up on St. Patrick's Church in Carbonear by Rev. William Matthews. After 18 years a Bishop, Bishop MacDonald returned to New Brunswick and Rev. E. T. Bromley became Administrator of the Diocese for over two years until a new Bishop was appointed.

2001 – TODAY – BISHOP MARTIN W. CURRIE

On 31 January 2001, Our new Bishop, Bishop-elect Martin William Currie from Nova Scotia was ordained as Bishop of Grand Falls vice Bishop J. Faber MacDonald who was transferred back to New Brunswick. In the summer of 2001, the Msgr. Finn building in Grand Falls was dismantled. Bishop Currie established a commission to study the future of the Diocese's in Newfoundland. He entertained African Bishops and discussed the future of permitting the loaning of African Priests for the Diocese. Rev. David E. Joy was ordained in Gander on 30 May 2002. Bishop Currie met Pope John Paul II at the Youth Day in Toronto in 2002.

GRAND FALLS DIOCESE TODAY

Today the Diocese of Grand Falls covers 19,200 square miles, which is nearly half of the geographic territory of the island of Newfoundland, which covers 43,000 square miles. The Grand Falls Diocese consists of thirty active Parishes. Twenty-four parishes are along the extensive and rugged sea coastline, while six are inland parishes.

Our Diocese was originally known as:

Diocese of Harbour Grace: 1856-1953
Co-Dioceses of Harbour Grace-Grand Falls: 1953-1965
Diocese of Grand Falls: 1965 – today

In 2003, the Diocese of Grand Falls was served by twenty (20) active priests. Of these, seven are on loan from other dioceses, two from Canada, one from St. George's Diocese and four from African Dioceses. Religious sisters and pastors of neighboring parishes minister to parishes which no longer have resident priests. Two Diocese priests are working outside the Diocese.

The Diocese of Grand Falls is a vibrant and dynamic diocese, serving the Catholic People in central and eastern Newfoundland with joy and enthusiasm.

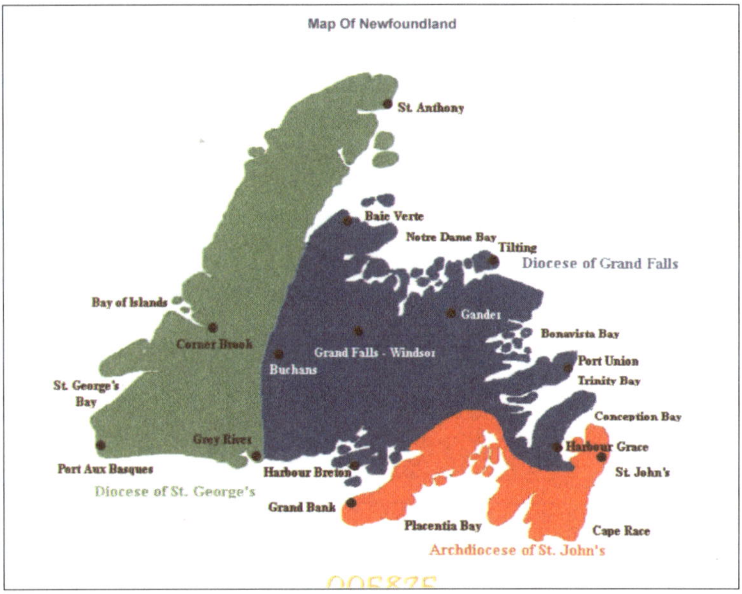

Diocese of Grand Falls (blue color) in center-northeast coast of Newfoundland.

CATECHETICAL PROGRAMS FOR DIOCESE

The move away from the denominational system of education by the voters of Newfoundland in 1997, and the loss of Catholic Schools, offered the Catholic community of the Diocese of Grand Falls both a challenge and an opportunity. The challenge was to find ways to build and nurture the relationship between families and the parish community so that together we help the young people to grow in faith and knowledge, wisdom and grace. To this end, the Diocese of Grand Falls desires to assist parents in their role as the "first and best teachers of their children in the easy of faith", as the prayer in the Rite of Baptism reads. The Diocese offers support and encouragement to parents through the presence of Pastors and Pastoral Leaders volunteer Catechetical Coordinators in each parish, the Director of Catechetics on the diocesan level. All of these people are available to work with parents and to meet their needs through whatever means are found necessary in their role as the primary educators of their children in the ways of faith. There will be gatherings of parents, meetings, prayers and celebrations, as well as sessions at which parents will have the opportunity to deepen their own knowledge and faith. Volunteer Catechetical Coordinators will also receive training and formation. As a resource for families, the Diocese offers the Home Program of the *Born of the Spirit* catechetical series, published by the Canadian Conference of Catholic Bishops. This is an excellent resource, easy to use and attractively designed.

COMBINED HISTORY OF HARBOUR GRACE AND GRAND FALLS DIOCESE'S

1784 - 1830 - Harbour Grace Mission
1784 - 1799 – 1st PP, Rev. Patrick Phelan, 15 years
1784 - 1799 - Mass Said In Leased-Owned Store-Chapel
1800 - 1806 - 2nd PP, Rev. Ambrose Fitzpatrick, 8 years
1800 - 1806 - Mass Said In Purchased Store-Chapel
1806 - 1833 - 3rd PP, Very Rev. Thomas Ewer, 27 years
1806 - 1852 - First Separate Chapel, Fr Ewer
1830 - 1856 - Harbour Grace Immaculate Conception Parish
1833 - 1859 - 4th PP, Very Rev. Charles Dalton, 26 years
1848 - Laid Foundation For 2nd Church, Stone. Fr. C. Dalton.
1852 - Stone Church Completed, Fr. C. Dalton

1856 - 2ND DIOCESE ESTABLISHED AT HARBOUR GRACE

1856 – 1965 - Immaculate Conception Diocesan Parish
1856 - 1869 - 1ST BISHOP, HG, Bishop John Dalton, 13 Years
1856 - 1860 - Bishop John Dalton lived in Carbonear.
1860 - 1869 - Bishop John Dalton lived in Palace in HG.
1868 - Bishop John Dalton Dedicates 1st HG Cathedral.
1869 - Bishop John Dalton, Died, Age 49. (Buried under Church)
1869 - 1870 - Admin of Diocese, Rev. John J. Walsh
1870 - 1880 - 2ND BISHOP, HG, Bishop Henry Carfagnini, 10 Years
1880 - Bishop Henry Carfagnini returned to Rome.
1881 - 1906 - 3RD BISHOP, HG, Bishop Ron McDonald, 25 Years
1884 - Original First Cathedral Finally Completed.
1884 - 1889 - Regular Services in New Cathedral.
1886 - St. Joseph's Church Dedicated In Riverhead, HG.
1889 - New HG Cathedral Burned To The Ground.
1889 - 1892 - Church Held In St. Patrick's Hall.
1892 – 1208 - 2ND HG Cathedral, Current Church Opened.
1906 - **50th** Anniversary of Diocese **(1856-1906)**
1906 - 0327 - Bishop Ronald McDonald, retired, ill, age 71.
1906 - 1940 - 4TH BISHOP, HG, Bishop John March, 36 Years
1912 - Grand Falls Parish Established.
1913 - Bishop John March fired at by man in Church.
1940 - 0112 - Bishop John March, died, age 77.
1940 - 1953 - 5TH BISHOP, HG, Bishop John O'Neill, 13 Years

1953 - GRAND FALLS CO-CATHEDRAL WITH HARBOUR GRACE

1953 - 1965 - 5TH BISHOP, CO-HG-GF, Bishop John H, O'Neill, 12 Years.
1955 - Bishop John O'Neill moves from HG to GF.
1956 - **100th** Anniversary of Diocese **(1856-1956)**

1965 - GRAND FALLS BECAME DIOCESE VICE HARBOUR GRACE

1965 - 1972 - 5TH BISHOP, GF, Bishop John H, O'Neill, 7 Years.
1965 - HG Immaculate Conception Church Reverts to Parish Church
1972 - 1118 - Bishop John O'Neill, Retired, Age 69

1972 - 1979 - 6TH BISHOP, GF, Bishop Alphonsus Penney, 7 Years.
1974 – Bishop O'Neill died in retirement at age 70.
1979 – Bishop Penney became Archbishop of St. John's.
1980 - 1999 - 7TH BISHOP, GF, Bishop J. Faber Macdonald, 19 Years.
1981 - 125th Anniversary of Diocese **(1856-1981)**
1992 – 100TH Anniversary of HG Church. **(1892-1992).**
1999 – Bishop Faber MacDonald returned home to Nova Scotia.
1990 - Immaculate Conception Church, HG, declared a Historical Site.
1999 - 2001 - Admin of Diocese, Rev. Edward Bromley
2001 - Today - 8TH BISHOP, GF, Bishop Martin W. Currie

GRAND FALLS DIOCESE GETS NEW BISHOP

Bishop Martin Currie was ordained and installed as the 8th Bishop of Grand Falls in 31 January 2001. He immediately visited all the Parishes in the Diocese.

BISHOPS AND VICAR GENERALS OF THE DIOCESE

BISHOPS OF HARBOUR GRACE/GRAND FALLS

1856 --------- Harbour Grace Diocese established.
1856-1869 - 1 - Bishop John Dalton, HG, 13 years.
1869-1870 ---- Rev. John J. Walsh, PP - Administrator of Diocese
1870-1880 - 2 - Bishop Henry Carfagnini, HG, 10 years.
1881-1906 - 3 - Bishop Ronald McDonald, HG, 25 years.
1906-1940 - 4 - Bishop John March, HG, 34 years.
1940-1953 - 5 - Bishop John M. O'Neill, HG, 13 years
1953 ---------- Grand Falls declared a Co-Cathedral with HG.
1965 ---------- Diocese Moves from Harbour Grace to Grand Fall's.
1953-1972 - 5 - Bishop John M. O'Neill, GF, 19 years.
1972-1979 - 6 - Bishop Alphonsus Penney, GF, 7 years.
1979-1980 ---- Rev. James A. Beresford, Administrator of Diocese
1980-1999 - 7 - Bishop Jos Faber MacDonald, GF, 19 years.
1999 -2001 ---- Rev. E.T. Bromley - Administrator of Diocese
2001-Today - 8 - Bishop Martin W. Currie, GF

VICAR GENERALS OF HARBOUR GRACE/GRAND FALLS

1856 -------- Harbour Grace Diocese established.
1856-1859 - Very Rev. Charles Dalton - Bish Dalton
1860-1869 – Rev. John J. Walsh - Bish Dalton
1869-1870 - No Bishop Harbour Grace
1869-1870 – Rev. John J. Walsh - Diocesan Administrator
1870-1872 – Rev. John J. Walsh - Bish Carfagnini
1872-1880 - Very Rev. Jeremiah O'Donnell - Bish Carfagnini
1880-1884 - Very Rev. Jeremiah O'Donnell - Bish McDonald
1884-1906 – Msgr. E.F. Walsh - Bish McDonald
1906-1912 – Msgr. E.F. Walsh - Bish March
1912-1940 – Msgr. F. D. McCarthy - Bish March
1940-1944 – Msgr. McCarthy - *Honorary Vicar General* *
1940-1955 – Msgr. M. F. Dinn - Bish O'Neill
1955-1965 – Msgr. J.W. Peddle - Bish O'Neill
1953 --------- Grand Falls declared a Co-Cathedral with HG.
1965 --------- Diocese Moves from Harbour Grace to Grand Fall's.
1965-1972 – Msgr. J.W. Peddle - Bish O'Neill
1972-1979 – Msgr. R.T. Woodford - Bish Penney
1979-1980 - Rev. James A. Beresford, Diocesan Administrator
1980-1988 – Msgr. R. T. Woodford – Bish Faber MacDonald
1988-1999 – Msgr. E. T.Bromley - Bish Faber MacDonald
1999 - 2001 - No Bishop Grand Falls
1999 - 2001 - Rev. E.T. Bromley, Diocesan Administrator
2001 - Today – Msgr. E.T. Bromley - Bish Martin Currie.

* Msgr. F. D. McCarthy was Vicar General for 28 years from 1912 to 1940, until Bishop O'Neill was consecrated Bishop. At Msgr. McCarthy's funeral in 1944, Bishop O'Neill explained that he had asked Msgr. McCarthy to remain on as "Honorary Vicar General" for period 1940-1944, while a younger Priest was selected as Vicar General. (Msgr. Dinn). Msgr. McCarthy was very gracious and readily accepted this proposal.

Chapter 26

BISHOPS OF HARBOUR GRACE AND GRAND FALLS

MOST REV. JOHN DALTON, OSF
1820-1869

Born: 1820 - Ireland
Ordained: 1846 - Ireland
Bishop: 1856-1869 - 13 Years, Harbour Grace
Died: 5 May 1869, Age 49 - Harbour Grace

FIRST BISHOP

Most Reverend John Dalton, OSF

Bishop John Dalton was born in 1820 in Thurles, Ireland and came to Newfoundland in 1839. The following year he began his studies to become a Franciscan and in 1846 at age 26 he was ordained a Priest at St. Isidore's College in Rome. He returned to Newfoundland in 1849 to take over as 2d Parish Priest at Carbonear on the death of Father Gleeson. He was Parish Priest at Carbonear for 7 years from 1849-1856. He was a nephew to Fr. Charles Dalton, Parish Priest of Harbour Grace (1833-1859). He attended the Consecration of the New Cathedral in St. John's in 1855. On 20 Jan 1856 he was announced to be the first Bishop of the newly established Diocese of Harbour Grace, by Pius IX. (The second Diocese in Newfoundland) He was consecrated Bishop by Bishop Mullock on 25 May 1856 at age 36 and took over the new Harbour Grace See on 1 June 1856. Since his uncle Father Charles Dalton was residing in the Palace in Harbour Grace at the time, Bishop John Dalton remained in Carbonear for three years until his uncle died in 1859 and Bishop Dalton moved to Harbour Grace in 1860. He celebrated the Requiem Mass for his uncle on 17 Jun 1859. Bishop Dalton has the distinction of ordaining the first native-born Newfoundland Priest that of Rev. James Brown of Carbonear, ordained on 20 December 1856 in Carbonear just 7 month after Bishop Dalton became Bishop. He dedicated the New Cathedral for Harbour Grace on 8 December 1868. He attended the Requiem Mass for Bishop Mullock in St. John's who died on 29 March 1869 and on return to Harbor Grace in April, he received an apoplectic stroke and he himself died on 5 May 1869. Both Bishops in Newfoundland were dead at the same time. Rev. Edward O'Keefe of Brigus administered St. John's Diocese in 1869 and Rev. John J. Walsh was appointed to administer the Harbour Grace Diocese. Bishop Dalton died on 5 May 1869, just five months after he dedicated the new Cathedral. Bishop Dalton was only 49 years old and was a priest for 23 years and had only been a Bishop for12 years. He was buried on 8 May 1869 under the main altar of Immaculate Conception Cathedral in Harbour Grace.

MOST REV. HENRY CARFAGNINI, OSF
1823-1904

Born: 23 Mar 1823 - Scanno, Italy
Ordained: 19 Nov 1846 - Rome
Bishop: 1870 - 1904, 34 Years
Died: 12 February 1904, Age 81 – Rome
SECOND BISHOP

Most Reverend Henry Carfagnini

Bishop Henry Carfagnini was born on 23 Mar 1823 in Scanno, Italy. He was ordained in Rome on 19 Nov 1846 at age 23 by Cardinal Cullen of Dublin. He came to Newfoundland in 1856 as first President of St. Bon's where he remained for 7 years from 1856-1863. In 1856 he was MC at the Consecration of Bishop John Dalton in Harbour Grace. On 21 June 1864 he took the vessel, "Isabelle Ridley" to Labrador. He spent a short time at Harbour Grace helping with the construction of the new Cathedral during the period 1864-1868 when he returned to Rome. When Bishop Dalton died in 1869 at Harbour Grace, Bishop Carfagnini was Consecrated Bishop in Rome on 22 May 1870 as the 2d Bishop of Harbor Grace. He reached Newfoundland in October 1870 and spent 10 years as Bishop of Harbor Grace from 1870-1880. He celebrated his Silver Jubilee in 1871. In 1871 he requested Father Falconio to come to Harbour Grace from Rome as his assistant. Bishop Carfagnini was discontented with the operation of the BIS in Harbour Grace and he authorized Second BIS in Harbour Grace with him as Patron in 1877. There were now two BIS's and this action split the Parish and the families in it. Priests took sides in this action and pressure increased for Bishop Carfagnini to leave Harbour Grace. Bishop Conroy was dispatched from Rome to investigate the people concerned and discontentment. Bishop Conroy unexpectedly became sick and died during his two-day visit to Nfld. In 1879 Bishop Carfagnini traveled to the North of the Diocese on his Yacht the "Lizzie". After the investigation of his practices by the Apostolic Delegate in 1878, Bishop Carfagnini was forced to leave Harbour Grace on 27 May 1880 under a cloud. He celebrated his 50th Golden Jubilee in Rome in 1896. Bishop Carfagnini died in Rome on 12 February 1904 at age 81. He was an Archbishop and was a Priest for 58.

MOST REV. RONALD MCDONALD
1836-1912

Born: 2 June 1835 - Nova Scotia
Ordained: 2 October 1859 - Nova Scotia
Consecrated Bishop: 21 August 1881 - NS (31 years)
Died: 16 September 1912, Age 76 – Montreal

THIRD BISHOP

Most Reverend Ronald McDonald

Bishop Ronald McDonald was born in Maryvale, Nova Scotia to Hugh and Flora McDonald on 2 June 1835. He attended the Arichat Seminary for two years from 1853 to 1855 and St. Francis Xavier for 4 years from 1855-1859. He was ordained by Archbishop McKinnon in the St. Ninian Cathedral in Antigonish on 2 October 1859 at age 24. On ordination he was a Professor at Antigonish for three years from 1859-1862. He was then assigned as Parish Priest at Pictou, Nova Scotia for nineteen years from 1862 to 1881. He was consecrated a Bishop on 21 August 1881 and appointed the third Bishop of Harbour Grace in 1881 and remained for twenty-five years until he resigned for ill health in 1906 at age 71. He was an advocate for education throughout the Diocese and he built the academically demanding Harbour Grace Academy in 1882. In 1883 he dedicated the Nun's chapel over St. Joseph's school in Harbour Grace and on 4 July 1883 he visited the MicMac Indians aboard the steamer, "Hiram Perry". He was Bishop of Harbour Grace during the Harbour Grace affray in 1883. He celebrated his Silver Jubilee in 1884 and was appointed to the Board of Trustees at St. Bon's the same year. He was an advocate for agricultural development. In 1888 he laid the cornerstone for the new brick church in Carbonear. He also presided at the Memorial Mass for the late Fr. O'Connor in Carbonear. He retired for ill health on 27 March 1906 to Montreal. He returned as Pastor of Pictou Parish in Nova Scotia and later be became titular Archbishop of Gortyna. He celebrated his 50th Golden Jubilee in 1909. He died in Montreal on 16 September 1912 at age 76. He was priest for 53 years and a Bishop for 31 years. He is buried in Maryvale, Nova Scotia.

MOST REV. JOHN MARCH
1863–1940

Born: 16 July 1863 - Northern bay
Ordained: 16 March 1889 - Rome
Bishop: 1906-1940 - 33 years
Died: 12 January 1940, Age 77 - Harbour Grace

FOURTH BISHOP

Most Reverend John March

Bishop John March was born in Northern Bay on 16 July 1863 to Simeon March and Cecily Hogan. He attended local schools until he was instructed by the Christian Brothers at St. Bon's from 3 years from 1876-1879. He attended the L'Assumption College in Montreal for 2 years from 1879-1881 and proceeded to College St. Sulpice in Montreal for one year until he departed for the Propaganda College in Rome for 7 years from 1882-1889. He was ordained in Rome on 16 March 1889 at age 26 and returned to Harbour Grace. He was Curate and Parish Priest at Cathedral Parish in Harbour Grace for 17 years from 1889-1906. He spent several summers doing Missionary work in Labrador. In 1891 he was President of the Christian Doctrine Literary Association in HG. In 1891 he also attended the opening of the new brick Church in Carbonear. He was present when the second Cathedral was opened in 1892. In 1898 he attended the Memorial Mass for Father O'Connor in Carbonear. In 1902 he attended the Silver Jubilee of Archdeacon O'Neill in St. John's. He attended the Conferring of Pallium, SJ on the RC Cathedral in St. John's. He was consecrated Bishop in St. John's by Bishop Howley on 4 November 1906. He was the first native-born Newfoundlander to be Bishop at Harbour Grace and remained for 34 plus years from 1906-1940. He was a proponent for the first Knights of Columbus Council at Harbour Grace in 1909. On 11 November 1909 he consecrated the new RC Church in Bay Roberts. In 1910 he moved into the Munn residence on Harvey Street, HG. On 27 September 1911 he became Patron of the CCC Corps at Harbour Grace. In 1913 he was fired at by an unemployed man in Church and he survived the attack. He celebrated his Silver Jubilee in 1914 and celebrated his Episcopal Silver Jubilee on 4 November 1931. He celebrated his 50th Golden Jubilee on 16 March 1939. He died at Harbour Grace on 12 January 1940 at age 76. He was Priest for 51 years and a Bishop for over 33 years. He is buried in the priests' plot in Harbour Grace Cemetery. There is a monument in honour of Bishop March in Northern Bay, his birth place.

BISHOP JOHN MARCH AND HIS PRIESTS

Bishop John March and Priests on Msgr. McCarthy's 50th Golden Jubilee in 1934.

BACK ROW: Msgr. W. P. Finn, Rev. Ronald Jones, Msgr. M. F. Dinn, Rev. W. Cullen, Msgr. E. O'Brien, Rev. John D. O'Neill, Very Rev. John Scully, Rev. J. P. Mackey, Rev. Dr. Ed J. Jones, Rev. J. Howard and Rev. John Kavanagh. **FRONT ROW:** Msgr. J. Murphy, Msgr. F.D.McCarthy, Bishop John March, and Very Rev. W. P. Finn. Not in Picture: Rev. W. Williams.

Bishop John March and Rev. William Cullen

MOST REV. JOHN M. O'NEILL DD
1903-1974

Born: 26 October 1903 – Harbour Grace
Ordained: 24 April 1927 – Quebec
Bishop: 1940 -1972 - 32 years
Died: 2 March 1974, age 70 - St. John's

FIFTH BISHOP

Most Reverend John M. O'Neill

Bishop John M. O'Neill was born in Harbour Grace on 26 October 1903 to Michael O'Neill and Catherine Lynch. He received his early education at Bay de Verde and then he attended St. Bon's for 5 years from 1916-1921 and graduated with an honors diploma in Senior Matriculation. He proceeded to Laval University in Quebec in 1921 for 6 years until 1927. He was ordained in Quebec on 24 April 1927 at age 23 and two months later he received his Doctor of Divinity "Summa Cum Laude". His first assignments on return to Newfoundland was to Little Bay (1927-1929), Grand Falls in 1930 and then to Harbour Grace as Sub Deacon for 10 years from 1930-1940. Bishop March died on 12 January 1940 and Father John O'Neill was announced Bishop on 21 May 1940 and he was appointed to Harbour Grace on 12 June 1940. He was Consecrated Bishop by Apostolic Delegate Antoniutti on 7 July 1940 as 5th Bishop of Harbour Grace (1940-1953) on the death of Bishop March and remained there for 13 years until 1953. In 1941 he delivered the panegyric at the Requiem Mass for Bishop Renouf. On 14 May 1944 he organized the holy name Society at Harbour Grace. In 1952 he celebrated his Silver Jubilee at Harbour Grace. Grand Falls was made a Co-Cathedral with Harbour Grace in 1953. In 1955 he attended the Centenary Ceremonies in St. John's. In 1955 he moved to Grand Falls and remained for 19 more years until 1972, when he retired for ill health. On 19 January 1957 his father died in St. John's at age 81. He retired as a Bishop on 18 November 1972 at age 69 due to ill health. He died in St. John's on 2 March 1974 at age 70. He was buried in the priests' plot in Harbour Grace. He was a priest for 46 years and a Bishop for 32 years.

BISHOP JOHN M. O'NEILL AND HIS PRIESTS

Bishop John O'Neill and Priests

Front Row L-R: Rev. Gregory Pumphrey, Rev. Brendan McCarthy, Rev. Leo J. Burke, Rev. Ronald Bromley, Msgr. William Hogan, Bishop John M. O'Neill, Bishop W. Power (Antigonish), Msgr. Joseph O'Brien, Rev. Edward Shea, Rev. Edward Hearn,. Middle Row L-R: Rev. Aloysius Antle, Rev. Edward Brophy, Rev. John Murphy, Rev. Michael Hynes, Rev. Francis Meaney, Rev. Matthew Kane, Rev. Linus Coady, Rev. Francis O'Brien, Msgr. Richard Woodford, Back Row L-R: Rev. John Mackey, Rev. Michael Walsh, Rev. William Matthews, Rev. James Beresford, Rev. William Houlahan, Rev. Raymond Hawco, Rev. Leonard Kelly, Rev. Ronald Walsh, Rev. Philip McCarthy & Rev. Frederick Terry.

Bishop John M. O'Neill in Rome.

TAKEN AT LITTLEDALE ON RETREAT FOR THREE DIOCESES IN 1948.

ont Row: Rt. Rev. Walter P. Brennan, V. G.; Rt. Rev. William P. Finn; Rt. Rev. Michael F. Dinn; v. Andrew L. Bouwhuis, S.J.; Most Rev. John O'Neill, D.D.; Most Rev. Thomas Flynn, Coadjutor; st Rev. Michael J. O'Reilly, D.D.; Rt. Rev. John Rawlins, V.G.; Very Rev. Dean Charles McCarthy; v. Charles Cacciola. **2nd Row:** Rt. Rev. Edward P. Maher; Rt. Rev. Dermot L. O'Keefe; Rt. Rev. orge Bartlett; Rev. James Dunne; Rt. Rev. John J. Murray, D.P.; Rt. Rev. Eric Lawlor; Rev. Francis kman; Rev. Robert J. Greene; Rt. Rev. Ronald McD. Murphy. **3rd Row:** Rev. John Cotter; Rev. Dermott Penney; Rev. John B. Kent; Rev. Francis Bradshaw; Rev. John Enright. **4th Row:** Rev. ward M. Shea; Very Rev. William P. Collins; Very Rev. Dr. Nicholas G. Fitzgerald; Most Rev. hard T. McGrath, D.D.; Rev. William Sullivan; Rt. Rev. Randel Greene; Rt. Rev. William H. Casey. **Row:** Rev. Francis Ryan; Rev. Francis J. Mullowney; Rev. Walter P. Walsh; Rt. Rev Mark P. yer; Rev. Albert Slattery; Rev. Michael Connolly; Rt. Rev. Joseph M. O'Brien; Rev. M.J. Kennedy; v. Thomas Gough. **6th Row:** Rev. Francis Ryan; Rev. James Greene; Rt. Rev James Miller; Rev. gustine Thorne; Rt. Rev. Edward J. O'Brien; Rev. Loyola Lacey; Rt. Rev. Joseph W. Peddle; Rev. lliam McC. Murphy; Rev. Dr. Edward J. Jones, D.D. **7th Row:** Rev. Andrew Nolan; Rev. Cyril gan; Unknown; Rev. William Ryan; Rt. Rev. Harold Summers. **Last Row:** Very Rev. Michael nsella; Rev. John Fleming; Rev. James O'Dwyer; Rt. Rev. William P. Hogan; Rev. James Coady; Rt. v. James Fennessey; Rev. Luke Woodrow; Rt. Rev. Patrick Kennedy; Rev. John Kavanagh; Rev. orge Battcock; Rt. Rev. Anthony Fyme; Rev. Adrian Dee; Rt. Rev. John O'Mara; Rev. Alfred own; Rev. Robert St. John and Rev. Francis Terry. (Identification of Revs. Courtesy of Archbishop A. Penney)
TE: Archbishop Roche, St. John's (not present); Bishop Thomas Flynn, coadjutor, St. John's; Bishop John M. eill, HG-GF (1940-1972); Bishop Michael J. O'Reilly, SG (1941-1970); Later- Bishop McGrath, SG (1970-1985).

BISHOP JOHN M. O'NEILL AT 100TH ANNIVERSARY OF DIOCESE

CLERGY GATHERED FOR THE 100TH ANNIVERSARY OF THE HG-GF DIOCESE – 15 JULY 1956.

1 – Rev. D. L. O'Keefe, 2 – Msgr. E. J. O'Brien, 3 - Bish P. J. Skinner, 4 - Bish J. M. O'Neill, 5 Rev. Ron Walsh, 6 – Rev. Greg Pumphrey, 7 – Rev. Wm A. Hogan, 8 – Msgr. George Bartlett, 9 Msgr. John Rawlins, 10 – Msgr. Harold A. Summers, 11 – Msgr. Edward P. Maher, 12 – Msg Wm Williams, 13 – Msgr. Ronald Mc D Murphy, 14 – Rev. A. L. Penney, 15 – Rev. James O'Dwyer, 16 – Rev. Loyola Lacey, 17 – Rev. Wm K. Lawton, 18 – Rev. Joseph Hogan, 19 – Re Leo Burke, 20 – Rev. James Doody, 21 – Rev. John B. Kent, 22 – Rev. Jeremiah Howard, 23 Rev. Cyril S. Eagen, 24 – Rev. W.H. Casey, 25 – Rev. Kevin Ryan, 26 – Rev. Luke Woodrow, 2 – Rev. John Hunt, 28 – Rev. Francis Jackman, 29 – Rev. Charles Conroy, 30 – Rev. Doctor Jone 31 – Rev. John J. Murray, 32 – Rev. Charles Greene, 33 – Rev. Joseph James, CssR, 34 – Re John Maddigan, CssR, 35 – Rev. Paul Doucette, CssR, 36 – Rev. William Murphy, 37 – Rev. Er Lawlor, 38 – Rev. James Miller, 39 – Rev. Andrew Nolan, 40 – Rev. Wm J. Ryan, 41 – Re Philip Lewis, 42 – Rev. Walter Walsh, 43 – Rev. M. Kinsella, 44 – Rev. Edward A. Walsh, 45 Unknown, 46 – Rev. John Fleming. (Thanks to Archbishop Penney for the names above).

1856-1956

MOST REV. BISHOP ALPHONSUS PENNEY

1924-Today

Born: 29 June 1924 – St. John's
Ordained: 29 June 1949 – St. John's
Monsignor: 27 July 1971- St. John's
Bishop: 1972-1991 - 19 years

SIXTH BISHOP

Most Reverend Alphonsus Penney

Bishop Alphonsus Penney was born in St. John's on 29 June 1924 to Alphonsus and Catherine Penney. He was ordained in St. John's with Rev. Dan Murphy and Rev. Richard Woodford by Bishop O'Neill on 29 June 1949. His first assignment was as assistant at St. Joseph's Parish in St. John's for three years from 1949-1952, when he became Parish Priest for the next 4 years. In 1956 he was assigned as Parish Priest at St. Patrick's Parish in St. John's for one year. In 1957 he became Parish Priest at Sacred Heart Parish in Marystown for 12 years until 1969. In 1960 he was appointer Vicar Forane for the Burin Peninsula. In 1969 he was assigned as Parish Priest of the Basilica Parish in St. John's for three years until 1972. On 27 July 1971 he was honoured with a Prelate of Honour as a Monsignor and in 1972 appointed Vicar General of St. John's. In this same year he was appointed Bishop of Grand Falls and remained there for seven years until 1979. In 1974 he celebrated his Silver Jubilee in Grand Falls. In 1979 he was appointed Archbishop of St. John's where he remained for 11 years until his resignation in 1990. He resigned over the scandal of clergy sexual abuse and his resignation was accepted by Pope John Paul II on 2 February 1991. He has been performing his priestly duties around the St. John's area.

Presented with Cross

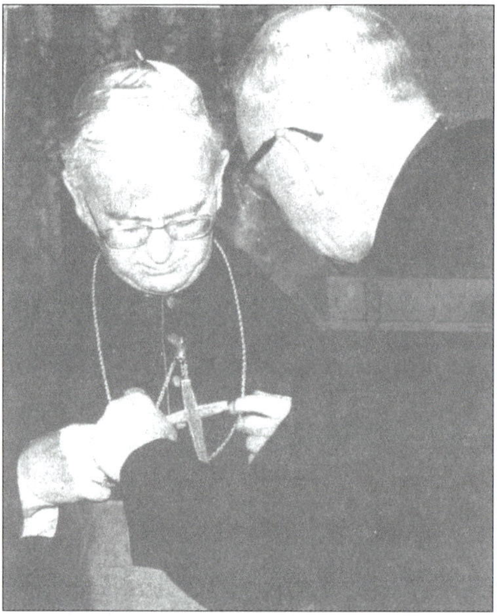

Retired Bishop J. M. O'Neill presents newly ordained Bishop A. L. Penney with a pectoral cross which belonged to late Bishop John March of Harbour Grace. The presentation took place during a dinner at K of C clubrooms, Grand Falls, Jan. 18, 1973.

Bishop Penney in 1975 with his Pastors at Clarenville.

MOST REV. J. FABER MACDONALD
1932-Today

Born: 20 January 1932 – PEI
Ordained: 9 March 1963 – PEI
Bishop: 1980-1999 - 19 years.

SEVENTH BISHOP

Most Reverend J. Faber MacDonald

Most Rev J. Faber MacDonald was born on 20 January 1932 in PEI. He was ordained in Charlottetown on 9 March 1963 at age 31. He was appointed as Vice Chancellor at Charlottetown for four years from 1964-1968. In 1967 he was a Pastoral Liturgical Instructor in Belgium for one year and returned as Chancellor of Charlottetown for seven years from 1968-1975. In January 1980 he was appointed Bishop of Grand Falls by Pope John Paul II and was Consecrated Bishop on 19 March 1980. In 1981 he celebrated the 125th Anniversary of the Grand Falls Diocese. In 1988 he celebrated the Silver Jubilee of his priestly ministry. In 1989 he visited Waterford, Ireland with Archbishop Penney. In 1991 he celebrated the 100th Anniversary of St. Patrick's Parish in Carbonear. When he left the Grand Falls Diocese in 1999, after 19 years as Bishop, he was transferred to Canada.

BISHOP J. FABER MACDONALD AND HIS PRIESTS

Bottom Row (L-R) Rev. William J. Houlahan, Rev. Linus J. Coady, Most Rev. J. Faber MacDonald, Rev. Lawrence George and Rev. Leo J. Burke. **Second Row** (L-R) Rev. Michael A. Ryan, Rev. Edward A. Walsh, Rev. David W. Heale, Rev. Michael R. Hynes, Rev. Brendan J. McCarthy, Unknown, Rev. James A. Beresford, Rt. Rev. Richard T. Woodford, Rev. Gregory B. Pumphrey, Rev. Aloysius Antle, Rev. A. Wayne Cummings, Rt. Rev. William P. Hogan, Rev. Michael J. Walsh, **Third Row** (L-R) Rev. Edward T. Bromley, Rev. Brian J. Dunn, Rev. William D. Matthews, Rev. Frederick J. Terry, Rev. William Hearn, Rev. Ronald M. Bromley, Rev. Philip J. McCarthy, **Back Row** (L-R) Rev. Leonard J. Kelly, Rev. Francis J. Aylward, Rev. J. Kevin Barker.

Bishop Faber MacDonald with his oldest Priest, Rev. Philip J. McCarthy and his youngest Priest, Rev. Dr. Brian Dunn.

Diocesan Council of Religious

Front Row: Sr. Ruth O'Reilly, pbvm; Sr. Elizabeth Lawlor, pbvm; Unknown: Sr. Mary Purcell, pbvm; Sr. Agnes Hutchings, pbvm; Sr. Mary Dower, pbvm; Most Rev. J. Faber MacDonald, D.D.; Sr. Mary Power, pbvm; Sr. Zeta Gardiner, pbvm; Sr. Carmel Kelly, pbvm; Sr. Angela Fowler, pbvm; Bro. Leo P. Taylor, CFC. **2nd Row:** Unknown; Sr. Sarah Beresford, pbvm; Sr. Mary Farrell, pbvm; Sr. Amelia Mooney, pbvm; Sr. Marie Theresa Doyle, pbvm; Sr. Betty Quinlan, pbvm, Sr. Tarcisia Fewer, pbvm; Sr. Francis King, pbvm; Sr. Claudine Horan, pbvm; Sr. Eugenee, pbvm; Sr. Judy Barry, pbvm; Sr. Monica Hickey, pbvm; Sr. Nellie Pomroy, rsm; Unknown. **3rd Row:** Sr. Koska Reddy, pbvm; Sr. Margaret McLaughlan, pbvm; Sr. Frances Molley, pbvm; Unknown; Sr. Geraldine Mason, rsm; Sr. Elizabeth Whelan, pbvm; Sr. Rita Johnson, pbvm; Sr. Paula Delahunty, pbvm; Unknown; Sr. Philomena Christopher, pbvm; ?? Mason, rsm; Bro. Leonard Dalton, CFC; Sr. Cyprian Bouzane, pbvm. **Back Row:** Sr. Agnes O'Mara, rsm; Unknown; Sr. Rose Kennedy, pbvm; Sr. Mary Taylor, pbvm; Sr. Angela Mackenzie, pbvm; Sr. Fabrin Dunne, pbvm; Sr. Marie Furey, pbvm; Sr. Madeline Bouzane, pbvm; Sr. Bride Power, pbvm; Sr. Denise Costello, rsm; Unknown; Unknown; Sr. Eleanor Caul, rsm, Sr. Magdalen O'Brien, pbvm and Bro. Follett, CFC.

MOST REV MARTIN CURRIE
1943–Today

Born: –11 Dec 1943, Sheet Harbour, NS
Ordained: – 12 May 1968, Sheet Harbour, NS
Msgr: – 1992
Bishop: 2001-Today

Most Reverend Martin W. Currie

Most Rev Martin W. Currie was born in Sheet Harbour, Nova Scotia on 11 Dec 1943, the third of nine children of Everett and Mabel (Walsh) Currie. Upon graduation from Sheet Harbour HS, he studied at St. Francis Xavier, earning a BA degree in 1964. In the same year he entered Holy Heart seminary, Halifax for 4 years and was ordained at St. Peter's Church in Sheet Harbour on 12 May 1968 at age 24 by Bishop James Hayes, Archbishop of Halifax. For the nest seven years he was assistant in St. Patrick's Parish, Halifax and St. Charles Parish in Amherst. From 1975-1980, he served in the Archdiocesan Mission Parish in San Jose, Peru. Upon his return he served as Pastor in several parishes, including St. Joseph's Parish Bridgewater, St. Norbert's Parish, Lunenburg, and St. Vincent's Parish in Dartmouth. In 1992 he was appointed Vicar General of the Archdiocese of Halifax. After a brief period of study in Israel, he was appointed Chancellor of the Archdiocese in 1994. As a Monsignor he was appointed Rector of St. Mary's Basilica in Halifax. He was Administrator of the Archdiocese for a year pending the appointment of the new Archbishop Terrence Prendergast, S.J. In 1999, Msgr Currie became Pastor of Immaculate Conception Parish in Truro. He was ordained Bishop of the Diocese of Grand Falls on 31 January 2001 by Archbishop Paulo Romeo, Apostolic Nuncio to Canada. He became the 8th Bishop of Grand Falls.

BISHOP MARTIN CURRIE AND HIS PRIESTS

FRONT ROW L-R: Rev. D.E. Joy, Msgr. E. T. Bromley, VG; Most Rev. M.W. Currie, DD; Rev. B. J. McCarthy and Rev. L. J. Coady. **BACK ROW L-R:** Rev. Dr. B. J. Dunn, DD; Rev. A. W. Cummings; Rev. W. D. Matthews; Rev. E. Morris; Rev. M. Obosu; Rev. A. Hageman; Rev. L. T. Kelly; Rev. W. J. Houlahan; Rev. J. Donkor; Rev. F. J. Aylward; Rev. M.J. Barker; Rev. G. Eduah; Rev. Ramon Bolatets and Rev. D. W. Heale.

Bishop Martin Currie meets with Pope John Paul II during World Youth Day, 2002 in Toronto. Ontario.

Most Rev Martin Currie, Most Rev Jacques Berthalet and Pope John Paul II.

Chapter 27

PARISHES IN GRAND FALLS DIOCESE

Avondale	Our Lady of Assumption	Rev. Gregory Eduah
Badger	Sacred Heart	Rev. Eugene Morris
Baie Verte	St. Pius X	Rev. Thomas Duffenais
	Pastoral Assistant	Sr. Elsie Lahey, rsm
Bay de Verde	Assumption of BVM	Rev. William Houlahan
Bishop's Falls	Sacred Heart	Rev. Linus Coady
Bonavista	Sts Joseph & Patrick Parish	Served by Port Union
Brent's Cove/La Scie	St. John the Apostle	Rev. Tom Duffenais
	Administrator	Sr. Paula Delahunty, pbvm
Brigus	St. Patrick	Rev. Brian Colbert
Buchans	St. Theresa	Rev. Eugene Morris
Carbonear	St. Patrick	Msgr. E.T. Bromley VG,
	Pastoral Assistant	Eleanor Ash
Clarenville	Our Lady of Fatima	Rev. Tony Hageman
Colliers	Immaculate Conception	Rev. Gregory Eduah
Conception Harbour	St. Anne	Rev. Gregory Eduah
	Pastoral Assistant	Sr. Bride Power, pbvm
Conche	Sacred Heart Parish.	Rev. Edward J. Terry
Fortune Harbour	St. Anne's Parish	Served by Bishop's Falls.
Gambo	Our Lady of Perpetual Help	Rev. Emmanuel Mochiah
Gander	St. Joseph	Rev. David W. Heale
Grand Falls-Windsor	Immaculate Conception Cathedral	Bishop Martin Currie
	Administrator	Rev. Gordon McLean
	Asst Pastor	Rev. David Joy, cc Cathedral
	Diocesan Youth Apostolate	Sr. Amelia Mooney, pbvm
Grand Falls-Windsor	St. Joseph	Rev. Wayne Cummings
Harbour Breton	St. Joseph	Rev. Edward Brophy
Harbour Grace	Immaculate Conception	Rev. Francis J. Aylward
	Pastoral Assistant	Sr. Teresa Doyle, pbvm
Harbour Main	Sts Peter and Paul	Rev. Clem Flaherty
Holyrood	Holy Cross	Rev. Clem Flaherty
King's Cove	Sts Peter and Paul	Rev. William Hearn
Little Bay-St. Patrick	St. Mary's- Sacred Heart Parish	Served by Badger.
Norris Arm	Our Lady of Mt Carmel	Rev. Moses Odumad, Admin
Northern Bay	Corpus Christi	Rev. William Houlahan
North River	All Hallows	Rev. Brian Colbert
Plate Cove	St. Patrick	Rev. William Hearn
	Pastoral Assistant	Sr. Elizabeth Whelan, pbvm
Port Union	St. Joseph and St.Patrick	Rev. William Hearn
St. Alban's	St. Ignatius	Rev. John Arkorful
St. Brendan's	St. Gabriel	Rev. Emmanuel Mochiah
Tilting, Fogo	St. Patrick	Rev. John Adde-Nweah
Trinity	Most Holy Trinity	Served by Port Union.
Whitbourne	St. Alphonsus	Rev. Tony Hageman

AVONDALE
Assumption Parish

Church of the Assumption

1886 - The First Church Began.
1890-1909 – Mission of Harbour Main.
1906 – VRev John Roe, PP, from Harbour Main.
1909 – Origination date of Parish.
1909-1921 – 1st PP, Very Rev Richard Shean, 12 yrs.
1911 Jun 17 Rev John Roe, died, age 56 at HM.
1911 Jun 17 – Church burned to ground.
1912 Dec 2 – Church Built. 1st Mass, Rev Shean.
1914 – Rev Richard F. Walsh died, Buried Avondale.
1920 – Rev W. T. Cullen, cc, Shean.
1921-1955 – Rev John S. Kavanagh, PP, 34 years.
1927 – Parish named Our Lady of Assumption.
1935 Jun 21- Rev Kavanagh, Silver Jubilee.
1955 Sep 19 –Rev John S. Kavanagh, ill, age 72.
1955-1985 – Rev Edward A. Walsh, PP, 30 years.
1957 -Assumption Presentation Convent open.
1967 Oct 7 - Knights of Columbus Council "Cabot # 6001" chartered.
1970 Jun 17-Rev Walsh celebrates 25th Jubilee.
1982 Nov 7 – Silver Jubilee of Presentation Sisters.
1985 Dec – First-ever Ordination in Parish: Rev Clem Flaherty by Bishop James Doyle from Ontario.
1985-1988 – Msgr. Richard Woodford, PP, 3 years.
1988 Nov 14 – Msgr. Richard Woodford died, age 68.
1989-1998 – Rev David W. Heale, PP, 9 years.
1991 – Priest shared with Colliers &Conception Hr.
1998-2000 – Rev Michael Ryan, PP, 2 years.
2000-2002 - Rev Michael Barker, PP, 2 years.
2002-Today – Rev Gregory Eduah.

BADGER
Sacred Heart Parish

Missions: Little Bay, Springdale, Pilley's Island

Sacred Heart Church

1905 – 1909 – Mission of Whitbourne. A.N.D. Company, RR Workers.
1905-1909 - Visit by Rev Battcock, Whitbourne.
1909-1912 - Attended by Grand Falls.
1909-1912 - Visited by Rev Dwyer & Finn, GF.
1912-1930 – Mission of Grand Falls.
1930-1940 – Mission of Bishop Falls, Rev Hinchey.
1940-1953 – Mission of Windsor, Rev Meaney.
1940 Sep 3 – First Mass in new School-Chapel.
1949-1952 - Pres Sisters from Windsor at Badger.
1952 – Open OLPH Convent, 4 Nuns Fr. Meaney
1953-1955 – Rev G.B. Pumphrey, Res Priest.
1955-1958 – Rev Leonard J. Kelly, Res Priest.
1958 Aug 11 – Origination date of Parish.
1958-1961 – 1st PP, Rev Ronald J. Walsh, 3 years.
1958 – Little Bay Mission under Badger.
1961-1963 – PP, Rev Edward J. Hearn, 2 years.
1963-1968 – PP, Rev Edward T. Bromley, 5 years.
1965 – Sacred Heart Primary School opened.
1968-1973 – Rev Francis O'Brien, PP, 5 years
1969 - Rev Francis O'Brien, 25th Silver Jubilee.
1973-1974 – Rev D. L. Aylward, PP, 1 year.
1974-1975 – Rev Aidan B. Beresford, 1 year.
1974 – The Convent closed.
1975-1976 – Rev John Murphy, PP, 1 year.
1975-1976 – Rev Murphy reside in Grand Falls.
1976-1984 – Rev James A. Beresford, 8 years.
1976 – Convent re-opened. Rev Beresford.
1984-1988 – Rev Edward Brophy, PP, 4 years.
1984-1988 –Sr Rita Johnson, Pastoral Assistant.
1985 – Parish Center re-opened, Rev Brophy.
1988 – Convent Closed again.
1988-1994 Rev Anthony Hageman, PP, 6 years.
1991-Mar 22 - New School "Avoca" at Badger.
1993-Apr 16 –New Church opened, Bish MacDonald.
1993 – Given Supervision over Buchans.
1994-1997 – Rev Brian G. Colbert, PP.3 years.
1997-Today – Rev Eugene Morris, PP.

BAIE VERTE

St. Pius X Parish

Missions: Coachman's Cove and Fleur de Lys

St. Pius X Church

1840-1880 – Mission of Fogo and Bonavista.
1880-1959 – Mission of Coachman's Cove. (CC).
1880-1908 – Rev Richard M. Shean, PP, CC, 28 yrs.
1908-1912 – Rev Richard M. Walker, PP, 4 years.
1912-1915 – Rev John S. Kavanagh, PP, cc, 3 years.
1915-1930 - Rev Patrick J. Hearne, PP,cc, 15 years.
1930-1934 – Rev Leslie G. Fitzgerald, PP, cc, 4 yrs.
1934-1940 – Rev Joseph Hogan, PP, cc, 6 years.
1937 April –Church burns down at Coachman Cove.
1940-1947 – Rev Walter Walsh, PP, cc, 7 years.
1947-1953 – Rev Ronald J. Walsh, PP,cc, 6 years.
1953 – Parish moved to Baie Verte from CC.
1953 – Rev Ronald Walsh moved From C Cove.
1953-1958 – 1st PP, Rev Ronald J. Walsh, 5 years.
1958-1970 – Rev Leonard J. Kelly, PP, 12 years.
1959 – Coachman Cove Split Baie Verte & La Scie.
1959 – New Church built "St. Pius X", Fr Kelly.
1961 – Mercy Sisters arrived Catholic Schools.
1970-1972 – Rev Greg B. Pumphrey, PP, 2 yrs.
1970-1971 – Rev Matthew Kane, cc, Pumphrey.
1971-1972 – Rev Vincent Romo, cc, Pumphrey.
1971-1972 – Rev Ronald Cashin, cc Pumphrey.
1972-1977 – Rev Matthew Kane, PP, 5 years.
1977-1984 – Rev William Matthews, PP, 7 years.
1979-1980 – Rev Richard Anstey, cc. Matthews
1984-1991 – Rev William Hearn, 7 years.
1991-1994 – Rev Michael J. Barker, PP, 3 years.
1994-1996 – Rev Vincent Gulikers, PP, 2 years.
1996-2002 – Rev Edward Brophy, PP, 6 years.
1997-1998 – Rev Joseph Tebsis, cc, visiting.
1998-1998 – Rev Pius Male, cc, summer.
2002-Today – Rev Thomas Duffenais, PP

BAY DE VERDE

Assumption Parish

Missions: Old Perlican, Caplin Cove, Low Point, Grate's Cove, Red Head Cove

Assumption church

1838-1880 – Attended from Northern Bay.
1843 – First Roman Catholic School.
1878-1883 – VRev Gregory J. Battcock, PP,5 years.
1880 June 11 – Became Parish. School-Chapel.
1883-1918 - 1ST PP, Rev Joseph V. Donnelly, 35 yrs.
1903 – Feb - First Church Blessed.
1905 – Rev Donnelly, at Conferring of Pallium, SJ.
1918-1940 – Rev John P Mackey, PP, 22 years.
1927-1928 – Rev Dinn, cc, Murphy.
1938-1939 – Rev Walter Walsh, cc, Mackey.
1939-1940 – Rev Michael J. Kinsella, cc, Mackey
1940-1948 – Msgr. Wm H. Casey, PP, 8 years.
1944 May 25 –Msgr Wm H. Casey, 25th Jubilee.
1948-1959 – Rev Michael J. Kinsella, PP, 11 years.
1959-1965 – Rev Edward J. Shea, PP, 6 years.
1965-1966 – Rev Michael R. Hynes, PP, 1 year.
1966-1970 – Rev Michael J. Walsh, PP, 4 years.
1970-1977 – Rev William Matthews, PP, 7 years.
1977-1979 – Msgr. Richard Woodford, PP, 2years
1979-1981 – Rev Francis J. Aylward, PP, 2 years.
1982-1986 – Rev Wayne Cummings, PP, 4 years.
1986-1986 – Rev Lawrence George, 1 year.
1986-1989 – Rev David Heale, PP, 4 years.
1990 – Rev David Heale, 20 Anniversary.
1989-1993 – Rev Edward J. Brophy, PP, 3 years.
1992 Jun 25 – Rev Edward J. Brophy, 25th Jubilee.
1993-1994 – Rev Vincent Gulikers, Admin, 1 yr.
1994-1999 – Rev Francis J. Aylward, PP, 5 years.
1999-2000 – Admin. From Avondale, Rev M. Ryan
2000-2000 – Admin. From HG, Rev R. Bolatets.
2000-2000 – Rev Joseph Donkor, Admin
2000-Today – Rev Wm Houlahan, PP.

BISHOP FALL'S
Sacred Heart Parish
Missions: Botwood, Fortune Harbour, Leading Tickles.

Sacred Heart Church

1890-1909 - Attended by Whitbourne.
1903-1906 - Rev Gregory Battcock, Whitbourne.
1906 – School-Chapel.
1909-1921 – Mission of Grand Falls.
1912-1921 - Administered by Rev Wm P. Finn.
1914 – First School-Chapel opened.
1914-1925 – Chapel-School in operation.
1921-1930-Rev James A. Hinchey, GF cc, 9 Years.
1925 – First Church Erected.
1930 – Origination Date of Parish
1930-1940 -1st PP, Rev James A. Hinchey, 10 years.
1940-1955 – Rev Joseph P. Hogan, PP, 15 years.
1945 – Church enlarged and Presbytery rebuilt.
1945 Sep - First Presentation Sisters Arrive.
1948 Aug 23 – Convent opened.
1954 – Rev Joseph P. Hogan, 25th Silver Jubilee.
1955-1957 – Rev Joseph M. O'Brien, PP, 2 years.
1957-1988 – Rev Leo J. Burke, PP, 31 years.
1961 Aug 24 – New Sacred Heart Church on same. day Rev Leo J. Burke, 25th Silver Jubilee.
1966 Nov 11 – KC Council KC, "Msgr Finn Council # 5904 chartered.
1970 Sept – "Leo Burke Academy" Opened.
1986 Aug 24 – Rev Leo J. Burke, 50th Jubilee.
1986-Aug 30 – Present. Convent closed 41 yrs.
1988 Oct 4 – Rev Leo J. Burke, retired, age 75. Resides in Bishop Falls.
1988-1992 –Msgr. Ronald M. Bromley, PP, 4 years (Badger and Buchans)
1993-Today – Rev Coady, Linus, PP.
1996 Aug 24 – Rev Leo J. Burke, 60th Jubilee. Rtd
2001 Aug 24 – Rev Leo J. Burke, 65th Jubilee, Rtd. Retired in Bishop Falls.

BONAVISTA
Sts Joseph & Patrick Parish

Sts Joseph and Patrick Church

1815-1842 – Administered by King's Cove.
1842- Origination Date of Parish
1842- Catholic Church Built and Opened.
1842-1871 – 1st PP, Rev Matthew Scanlan, 29 years.
1855-1857 – Rev James Walsh, cc, 2 years.
1857-1865 – Rev James Brown, cc, 8 years.
1871 Dec 14 Rev Matthew Scanlan, died, age 68.
1871-1873 - Rev William Veitch, PP, 2 years.
1873-1890 – Rev P.A. Carolan, PP, 17 years.
1887-1896 – Rev Walter M. Tarahan, cc, 9 years
1890-1892 – Rev Thomas Lynch, PP, 2 years.
1892-1897 – Rev Richard Walker, PP, 5 years.
1897-1900 – Rev Walter M. Tarahan, PP, 3 years.
1900-1905 – Rev Pat W. Browne, PP, 5 years.
1905-1907 – VRev George Thibault, PP, 2 years.
1907-1912 – Rev Joseph Murphy, PP, 5 years.
1912-1927 – Msgr Mark P. Dwyer, PP, 15 years.
1927-1934 – Rev Michael F, Dinn, PP, 7 years.
1934-1953 – Rev Jeremiah Howard, PP, 19 years.
1953-1964 – Rev Richard Woodford, PP, 11 years.
1964-1970 – Rev J. R. Hawco, PP, 6 years.
1970-1975 – Rev Edward J. Brophy, PP, 5 years.
1975-1976 – Rev Linus J. Coady, 1 year.
1976-1977 - Rev J. Kevin Barker, PP, 1 year.
1977-1978 – Rev David Heale, Admin. Kings Cove.
1978-1980 – Rev Patrick Power, CssR, Admin.
1980-1984 – Rev Edward T. Bromley, PP, 4 years.
1982 – Center of Parish moved to Port Union.
1984-1989 - Rev James Beresford, PP, 5 years.
1989-1990 - Rev Francis Aylward, PP, 1 year.
1990-1996 – Rev J. Kevin Barker, PP, 6 years.
1996-2002 - Rev Brendan McCarthy, PP, 6 years,
2002-Today – Rev William Hearn, PP.

BRENT'S COVE/LA SCIE

St. John the Apostle Parish

Missions: Harbour Round and La Scie

St. John the Apostle Church in La Scie

1880-1959 –Served from Fogo or Coachman's Cove.
1959 – Origination Date of Parish at La Scie.
1959-1965 – 1ST PP, Rev Linus J. Coady, 6 years.
1959-1965 – Rev Coady built, Church-Rectory at La Scie, Harbour Round and Brent's Cove.
1965-1970 – Rev Ronald M. Bromley, PP, 5 years.
1966 – Presentation Sisters arrived La Scie.
1968 – Rev Bromley moves Parish to Brent's Cove.
1968 Dec 14 - Sisters moved to Brent's Cove.
1970-1974 – Rev William J. Houlihan, PP, 4 years.
1974-1975 – Rev Roy A. Walsh, Admin. 1 year.
1976-1979 – Rev Michael J. Walsh, PP, 3 years.
1979–1980 – Brent's Cove attached to Baie Verte.
1979-1980-Rev William Matthews, Admin. 1 year.
1980-1985 – Rev Linus J. Coady, PP, 5 years.
1984-Rev Coady wrote "History of Brent's Cove".
1985-1988-Sr Elizabeth Whelan, Past.Asst, 3 years.
1988-1992-Sr Bernadette Aucoin, Past.Asst, 4 years
1985-1991 – Rev William Hearn, PP, 6 years.
1992 – Sr Bernadette Aucoin, killed auto accident.
1992-1997 - Sr Elizabeth Whelan, Past.Asst, 5 years.
1991-1994 – Rev Michael Barker, PP, 3 year.
1994-1996 – Rev Vince Gulikers, Admin, 1 year.
1996-2002 – Rev Edward Brophy, PP, 6 years.
1997 –Today – Sr Paula Delahunty, Past. Asst.
1998 – Presentation Convent Closed.
2002-Today – Rev Thomas Duffenais, PP

St John the Apostle church in Brent's Cove

BUCHAN'S

St. Theresa's Parish

Buchan's Junction

St. Theresa's Church

1927-1929 – Mission of Grand Falls.
1927- First Mass, Rev Finn from Grand Falls.
1929-1930 – Rev John M. O'Neill, cc, 2 years.
1930-1932 – Rev Thomas D. O'Neill, Res Priest.
1932 July 3 – Origination Date of Parish.
1932-1944 – 1st PP, Rev Thomas D. O'Neill, 12 yrs.
1939-1940 – Rev Patrick Burke, cc, O'Neill.
1941 Jun 24 – VRev Thomas D. O'Neill, 25^{th}Jubilee.
1944-1965 – VRev Leslie G. Fitzgerald, PP, 21 yrs.
1948 June 24 – VRev Leslie G. Fitzgerald, 25th Jubilee.
1950 May 10 – KC Council "Bishop March" # 3315 chartered.
1953 Sep 3 – St. Margaret Pres Nuns Convent open
1960 Jan - St. Theresa's School opened.
1965-1966 – Rev Joseph Moriarity, SFM, Admin.
1966-1970 – Msgr Richard Woodford, PP, 4 years.
1966 – St. Theresa's Altar Society established.
1968 Oct – Church opened, Msgr Woodford.
1970-1976 – Rev J. R. Hawco, PP, 6 years.
1970 – Set up Parish Council, Rev Hawco.
1976-1979 – Rev James Beresford, Adm. 3, Badger.
1979-1980 – Rev A. Wayne Cummings, Adm, 1 year
1980-1982 – Rev Michael J. Walsh, Admin, 2 years.
1982-1984 – Sr M. Bouzane, Admin 2 years.
1984-1988 – Rev Edward J. Brophy, PP, 4 years.
1988 Aug 21 –New Log Church, Buchan's Junction
1988-1992 – Rev Ronald M. Bromley, PP, 4 years.
1992 – St. Margaret's Convent closed.
1993 – Under Supervision of Badger.
1993-1994 – Rev Anthony Hageman, PP, 1 year.
1994-1997 – Rev Brian Colbert, PP, 3 years.
1997-Today – Rev Eugene Morris, PP

BRIGUS

St. Patrick's Parish

Missions: Marysvale, Roaches Line, Cupids

St. Patrick's Church

1696 – Fishing Settlement.
1805 – First School opened.
1805-1824 – Church in Private Homes. Served S.J.
1819-1872 – 1st Roman Catholic Cemetery.
1824 – Origination Date of Parish.
1824 – First Chapel Built. (Land of James Hearn)
1824-1857 – 1st PP, VRev Dean Mackin, 33 years.
1857 Mar 10 - VRev Dean Mackin died age c 65.
1857-1857 – VRev Kyran Walsh, Admin, 1 year.
1857-1868 – Rev Edward O'Keefe, PP, 11 years.
1861 Sep 11-St. Joseph's Convent, Sisters of Mercy,
1868-1869 – VRev Bernard Duffy, 1 year.
1869-1912 – Msgr. Edward F. Walsh, PP, 43 years.
1869-1870 – Rev Edward O'Keefe, Admin, Diocese St. John's, on Bishop Mullock's death.
1870 – Brigus now part of Harbour Grace Diocese.
1871 Feb 28 – Rev Edward O'Keefe, died, age c 56.
1873 Dec 25 –VRev Bernard Duffy, died, Xmas Day.
1876 – New Priest House built by Msgr Walsh.
1880 – Msgr. Walsh spoke on departure of Bishop Carfagnini.
1885 – Msgr Walsh erected new 2nd Church on Mt Dorset Land, Consecrated by Bish Ron McDonald.
1891-1891- Rev Joseph Murphy, cc, Walsh,
1900-1904- Rev J. H. Scully, cc, Walsh,
1903-1904 - Old school down, build St. Pat's hall.
1904 – St. Patrick's Hall completed.
1912 – Msgr. Edward F. Walsh, died, age 70.
1912-1944 – Msgr. Joseph Murphy, PP, 32 years.
1912 Dec 29 – Msgr. Joseph Murphy, 25th Jubilee.
1926 – Sacred Heart Statue front of Church erected.
1927 Feb 15 – VRev Richard Shean, died, age 73.
1927 Sep 26 – Rev James J. Walker, died, age 49.
1934 Aug 18 – Church-Presbytery burned, Murphy.
1935 – 3rd Church & Presbytery built,MsgrMurphy.
1937 Dec 29 – Msgr. Joseph Murphy, 50th Jubilee.
1943 Dec – Msgr Murphy in hospital St. Claire's,SJ.
1944 Jun 20 – Msgr Joseph Murphy, died, SCH, SJ, age 82. Buried Brigus.
1944-1944 – Rev Leo J. Burke, Admin 1 year.
1944-1964 – VRev Edward Jos Jones, PP, 20 years.
1961 Sep 16 – 100th Anniversary of St. Jos Convent.
1964-1970 – Rev Gregory B. Pumphrey, PP, 6 yrs.
1966-1967 – Rev Wm Matthews, cc Pumphrey
1967-1968 - Rev John Murphy, cc, Pumphrey,
1964 – St. Patrick's Hall taken down.
1966 – Two St. Edward's Schools built.
1969 – Bishop O'Neill Collegiate built.
1970-1977 – Msgr. Richard T. Woodford, PP, 7 yrs.
1977-1985 – Rev Brendan McCarthy, PP, 8 years.
1978 – KC Council, "Dr E.J. Jones -# 7146" chartered.
1983 – School built, Rev McCarthy.
1985-1992 – Rev Linus J. Coady, PP, 7 years.
1985 – Shrine of Our Lady of Fatima on west wall.
1990 – Rev Joseph Crawford, CssR, Admin, 1 year.
1992-1997 – Rev Ronald Bromley, PP, 5 years.
1994-1995 - Rev A. Wayne Cummings, Admin, 1 yr.
1997-2000 – Rev William J. Houlihan, PP, 3 years.
2000-2001 – Rev Gregory Eduah, Admin, 1 year.
2001-2002 – Rev Gordan MacLean, Admin, 1 year.
2002-Today – Rev Brian Colbert, PP.

Our Lady of the Snow church in Marysvale

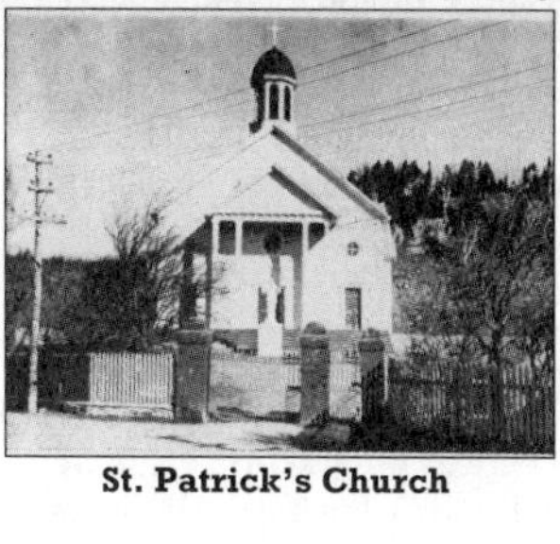

St. Patrick's Church

CARBONEAR

St. Patrick's Parish

Missions: Heart's Desire, Turk's Cove, Heart's Content

St. Patrick's Church

1784-1842 – Mission Of Harbour Grace.
1826 – First Chapel in Carbonear, Fr Ewer, HG.
1835 – Second Chapel, Revs Berney and Dalton, HG
1835 - BIS Established In Carbonear.
1842 – Origination Date of Parish.
1842-1849 – 1st Res PP, Rev James P. Gleeson, 7 yrs.
1843 – RC School Board Established.
1849- Jan 6 – Rev Gleeson, died, age 34.
1849-1856 – 2nd PP, Rev John Dalton, 7 Years.
1852 May 2 First Presentation Convent Carbonear.
1856 - New Diocese Established In Harbour Grace.
1856 – First Bishop of HG, Rev John Dalton.
1856-1874 – Rev John O'Connor, PP, 18 years.
1856-1857 – Rev J. Walsh, cc, O'Connor.
1857-1857 – Rev James Brown, cc, O'Connor.
1857-1858 – Rev M. Scanlan, cc, O'Connor.
1858-1860 – Rev Bernard Duffy, cc, O'Connor.
1873-1873 - Rev James Cummins, cc. O'Connor.
1874-1875 – Rev William Veitch, PP, 1 year.
1874-1876 – Rev Joseph V. Donnelly, cc, Veitch.
1876-1879 – Rev Stephen O'Flynn, PP, 3 years.
1877-1878 – Rev D. McInnis, cc, Flynn.
1879-1884 – Rev Richard F. Walsh, PP, 5 years.
1883-1884 – Rev Thomas E. Lynch, cc, Walsh.
1884-1888 – Rev Thomas E. Lynch, PP, 4 years.
1886 – Rev F.D. McCarthy, cc, Lynch.
1889-1944 – Msgr. Felix D. McCarthy, PP, 55 years.
1891 - Consecration of Brick Church.
1909 Jun 24 - Rev McCarthy Silver Jubilee.
1914-1944 – Msgr. McCarthy, Vicar General.
1914 – Rev Edward Jones, cc. McCarthy.
1929 – Msgr. McCarthy appointed first P.A.in Nfld.
1934 Jun 24 – Msgr. McCarthy 50th Jubilee.
1934 – Rev Joseph Hogan, cc. McCarthy.
1936 – Rev Leo Drake, cc, McCarthy.
1936-1937 – Rev Michael J. Kinsella, cc, McCarthy.
1939-1940 – Rev Walter P. Walsh, cc. McCarthy.
1940-1941 – Rev Patrick Burke, cc. McCarthy.
1941-1944 – Rev Leo J. Burke, cc. McCarthy.
1944 – Rev Edward Shea, cc, McCarthy.
1944 Jun 24 – Msgr. McCarthy Diamond Jubilee (First Diamond Jubilee in Newfoundland History.)
1944 Jun 30 – Msgr. F.D. McCarthy, died, age 83.
1944-1948 – Rev Thomas D. O'Neill, PP, 4 years.
1946 - St. Patrick's Hall Academy Closed.
1948-1953 – Rev J.W. Peddle, PP, 5 years.
1952-May 2 - 100th Anniversary of Pres Sisters in Carbonear.
1953-1957 – Rev Leo J. Burke, Admin, 4 years.
1955 – New Marble Altar honour of Msgr McCarthy, Rev Leo J. Burke.
1957-1974 – Msgr. J. W. Peddle, PP, 17 years.
1950s – Built New Presbytery.
1950s – New St. Joseph's Elementary School.
1961 – Erected St. Clare's School for Girls.
1966 Nov 6 – KC Council "Msgr McCarthy # 5902 chartered..
1973-1974 – Rev David W. Heale, cc, Peddle.
1974-Aug – Msgr. Peddle retired due to ill health.
1974-1980 – Msgr. W. P. Hogan, PP, 6 years.
1967-1970 – Rev Edward Brophy, cc. Peddle.
1970-1973 – Rev Aidan B. Beresford, cc. Peddle
1976-Mar – Msgr. Peddle died in St. J. buried Carb.
1980-1985 – Rev David Heale, PP, 5 years.
1985-1991 – Rev Brendan McCarthy, PP, 6 years.
1990-1991 – Renovated Church in and out.
1991- 100th Anniversary of Brick Church. (1891)
1992-2001 – Rev William Matthews, PP, 9 years.
1997-1998 – St. Clare's School Closed.
1999 – New Replacement Steeple for Church.
2000 –St. Clare's School torn down.
2001-2002 – Rev William Hearne, PP, 1 year.
2002-Today – Msgr. Edward T.Bromley PP.

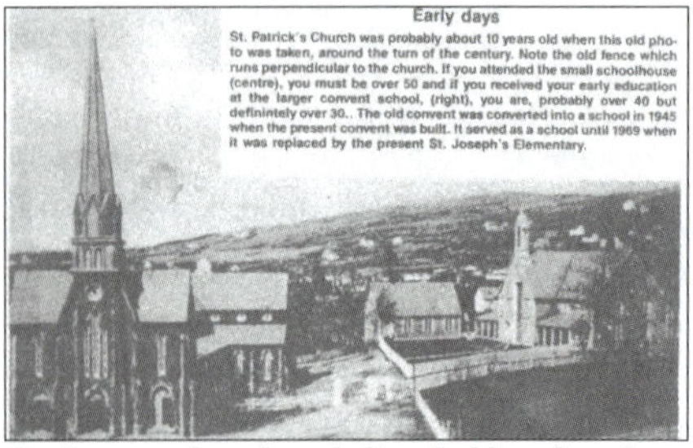

Early days

St. Patrick's Church was probably about 10 years old when this old photo was taken, around the turn of the century. Note the old fence which runs perpendicular to the church. If you attended the small schoolhouse (centre), you must be over 50 and if you received your early education at the larger convent school, (right), you are, probably over 40 but definintely over 30.. The old convent was converted into a school in 1945 when the present convent was built. It served as a school until 1969 when it was replaced by the present St. Joseph's Elementary.

Carbonear church on left and older church on right. (Became the Convent). c1905.

CLARENVILLE

Our Lady of Fatima Parish

Missions: Gooseberry Cove, Little Heart's Base, Southern Bay, Sweet Bay

Our Lady of Fatima Church

1946 – 1ST Mass celebrate in Theater, Rev Wm. Cullen of Gambo.
1949-1950 – Under Whitbourne Parish.
1950-1967 – Under Gambo Parish.
1950-1958 – Rev WalterWalsh, Mass every 2-3 mos.
1958-1965 – Rev Mike Hynes, Mass once a month.
1959 – The first Lady of Fatima Church was built by a few devoted Roman Catholic pioneers of Clarenville.
1967-1974 – Under Plate Cove.
1974-1980 - Under Gambo.
1980-1990 – Under King's Cove. (KC).
1981 31 May – New Roman Catholic Church of Our Lady of Fatima, replacing the former building was officially opened by Bishop J.F. MacDonald.
1980-1990 - Rev Titus Campbell, CssR from KC.
1990 - New Parish Est. By Bishop MacDonald.
1990-1993 – 1st PP, Rev A. Wayne Cummings, 3 yrs.
1993-1993 – Rev Ramon Bolatets, SVD, PP, 1 year.
1993-2002 – Unknown.
2002-Today – Rev Tony Hageman, PP.

Old Church torn down.

COLLIERS

Immaculate Conception Parish

Immaculate Conception Church

1839- First School.
1884-1948 – Mission of Conception Harbour
1948-Aug 4 – Origination Date of Parish
1948-1956 – 1st PP, Rev Thomas D. O'Neill, 8 years.
1948 – Built new school.
1954-Sep 12 –New Church, First Mass, Rev O'Neill.
1956-Apr 7 – VRev Thomas D. O'Neill, died, age 64.
1956-1959 – Rev Leo Walsh, Benedictine Monk, Admin, 3 years.
1959-1964 - VRev Stanislaus St. Croix, PP, 5 years.
1960-1960 - Rev J. R. Hawco, cc, St. Croix.
1964-1966 – Rev Richard T. Woodford, PP, 2 years.
1968-Mar 7–VRev Stanislaus St. Croix, died, age 86.
1966-1974 – Rev Frederick J. Terry, PP, 8 yrs.
1974-1979 – Rev Philip J. McCarthy, PP, 5 years.
1979-1982 – Rev Gregory B. Pumphrey, PP, 3 years.
1982-1983 – Rev Pumphrey on 1 year sabbatical.
1982-1983 – Rev John Punnakunnel, Admin 1 year.
1983-1984 – Rev Gregory B. Pumphrey, PP, 1 year.
1984-Oct 24–Rev Gregory B.Pumphrey, retired.
1984-1991 –Rev Frederick J. Terry, PP, 7 years.
1995-Jul 29 – Rev Greg Pumphrey, died, SJ, age 76.
1991 – Colliers share priest with Conception Hrb.
1991-1998 –Rev David Heale, PP, 7 years.
1998-2000 –Rev Michael A. Ryan, PP, 2 years.
2000 Aug – Rev Ryan leaves Diocese to become Trappist Mink in Ireland.
2000-2002 – Rev Michael Barker, PP
2002-Today – Rev Gregory Eduah, PP

CONCEPTION HARBOUR

St. Anne's Parish

St. Anne's Church

1857-1884 – Mission of Harbour Main.
1857-1861-First Roman Catholic Church Dedicated.
1868-1884 – Rev Jeremiah O'Donnell, HM.
1869 May 24 - Immaculate Conception Mercy Convent.
1884- Jan 1 – Origination Date of Parish.
1884-1891 –1st PP, VRev Jeremiah O'Donnell, 7 yrs.
1888 – Rev Patrick O'Donnell, 25th Silver Jubilee.
1891 Feb 27-VRev Jeremiah O'Donnell,died, age 77.
1891-1917 – 2nd PP, Rev William Veitch, 26 years.
1896 – Rev William Veitch, 25th Silver Jubilee.
1904 – Rev Veitch Built A New Church.
1907 Jun 2 - New Church dedicated, Bishop March.
1909 – Rev Veitch was elevated to Monsignor.
1916-1918 – Rev Thomas D. O'Neill, cc, Veitch.
1917 Jun 25 – Msgr William Veitch, died, age 71.
1918-1929 – Rt. Rev Joseph Donnelly, PP, 11 years.
1919-1926 – Rev W. McC Murphy, cc, Donnelly.
1920 Dec 4 – Msgr Joseph Donnelly, 50th Jubilee.
1929 Aug 21 – Msgr Joseph Donnelly, died, age 84.
1930-1948 – VRev J. H. Scully, PP, 18 years.
1942-1948 – Rev Joseph O'Brien, cc, Scully.
1948-1954 – Rev William H. Casey, PP, 6 years. Ill.
1948 – Mission Colliers forms a new Parish.
1954-1955 – Rev Richard G. Tompkins, admin,1 yr
1955-1962 – Rev Wm H. Casey, PP, 7 years.
1958 – Rev William H. Casey elevated to Msgr.
1960-1962 – Rev Edward Hearn, cc, Casey
1962 May 3 – Msgr William H. Casey, died, age 70.
1962-1977 – Rev Ronald Walsh, PP, 15 years
1977-1980 - Rev C.S. Costello, Rev Michael Ryan and Rev L. George, Rev Edward A. Walsh, Admin.
1980-1981 – Rev Patrick Power,CssR, Admin 1 year
1981-1983 – Rev Paul Doucette, CssR, Admin, 2 yrs.
1984-1988 – Rev William J. Houlahan, PP, 4 years.
1989 – Parish joined with Avondale Parish.
1989-1998 - Rev David Heale, PP. 9 years.
1998-2000 – Rev Michael Ryan. 1 year.
2000-2002 – Rev Michael Barker, PP
2002-Today – Rev Gregory Eduah, PP

CONCHE

Sacred Heart Parish

Missions: St. Anthony and Roddickton

Sacred Heart Church and Cemetery

1840s – French Priests and Chaplains
1859-1865 – Pere Peter M. Richard, PP, 6 years.
1873-1883 – Pere Father Gour/Gore, PP, 10 years.
1878 – Pere Gour/Gore built Church.
1883 – Beginning of Diocesan Priests to Parish.
1883-1884 – Rev Thomas E. Lynch, PP, 1 year.
1884-1886 – Rev Walter Tarahan, PP, 2 years.
1886-1898 – Rev John J. Lynch, PP, 12 years.
(Rev John Lynch built Church and house)
1899-1904 – Rev John T. Colbert, PP, 5 years.
1904 May 9 – Rev Colbert, died, age 31. Buried HG.
1904-1906 – Rev John P. Mackey, PP, 2 years.
1907 – Origination Date of Parish.
1907-1923 –1st PP, VRev George A. Thibault, 16 yrs.
1923-1941 – Rev Willie J. Williams, PP, 18 years.
1926 – Church burned down and rebuilt.
1937-1941 – Rev Patrick Bromley, cc, Williams.
1941-1947 – Rev William J. Hennebury, PP, 6 years.
1947-1955 – Rev Edward A. Walsh, PP, 8 years.
1950 – New Parish House was built.
1955-1963 – Rev Patrick McCormack, PP, 8 years.
1963-1970 – Rev Howard J. Hearn, PP, 7 years.
1970-1974 – Rev John Murphy, PP, 4 years.
1972 – The Church Burned Down and Rebuilt.
1974-1977 – Rev R. J. Cashin, PP, 3 years.
1977-1979 – Rev Matthew Kane, PP, 2 years.
1979-1984 – Rev William J. Houlahan, Co-PP, 5 yrs.
1981-1983 – Rev Francis J. Aylward, Co-PP, 2 yrs.
1984 – Conche transferred to St. George's Diocese.
1984-1990 – Rev Hilary Mahar, PP, 6 years.
1990-1991 – Rev Gerald Fitzgerald, CssR, Admin.
1991-1992 – Rev David Daws, Admin.
1992-1994 – Rev Aidan Devine, PP, 2 years.
1994-1999 – Rev Edward J. Terry, PP, 5 years.
1999-2000 – Rev Ambrose Hynes, St. Anthony.
1999-2001 – Srs Ellen Sullivan & Rona O'Gorman, rsm, Pastorial Administrators.
2000-2001 – Rev Jam Gal, Admin, St. Anthony.
2001-Today – Rev James Robertson, PP,

GAMBO

Our Lady of Perpetual Help

Missions: Dover, Cull's Harbour, Wesleyville, St. Vincent's

Our Lady of Perpetual Help Church

1815-1896 – Mission of King's Cove.
1897-1916 – Mission of Whitbourne.
1900-1903 – Rev Stephan J. Whalen, Visit Priest.
1900-1903 – Rev Whalen started New Church.
1905-1909 – Rev Gregory Battcock, Visit Priest.
1909-1914 – Visiting Priests from Whitbourne.
1914-1916 –Rev John F. Kirwan, from Whitbourne.
1914-1916 RevKirwan built Parish House & School.
1916 – Origination Date of Parish.
1916-1921 – 1st Res PP, Rev John Kavanagh, 5 yrs.
1921-1948 – 2nd PP, VRev W. P. Cullen, 27 years.
1921 – PP, Whitbourne moved Residence to Gambo.
1926 – Rev Cullen moved Church new foundation.
1948-1958 – PP, Rev Walter P. Walsh, PP, 10 yrs.
1958 Sep 9 – Rev Walter P. Walsh, died, age 45.
1950s – Rev Neil McDonald, cc, Walsh.
1958-1959 – Served from Whitbourne, CssR.
1959-1965 – Rev Michael Hynes, PP, 6 years.
1959 – Rev Hynes renovated interior of Church.
1965-1967 – Rev Neil McDonald, PP, 2 years.
1967-1977 – Rev Brendan J. McCarthy, 10 years.
1967-1977 – Rev J. Kevin Barker, cc, McCarthy.
1977-1981 – Rev J. Kevin Barker, PP, 3 years.
1979 Mar 25 – KC council charted and merged with Gander KC Council in 1994.
1979-1981 – Rev Lawrence George, cc, Barker.
1981-1984 – Rev Lawrence George, PP, 3 years.
1984-1989 – Rev Francis J. Aylward, PP, 5 years.
1989-1992 – Rev David Ostler, PP, 3 years.
1992-1994 – Rev William Hearn, PP 2 years.
1994-2002 - Rev Michael J. Barker, PP, 8 years.
2002-Today – Rev Emmanuel Mochiah, PP.
(St. Brendan's)

GANDER

St. Joseph's Parish

Missions: Glenwood, Gander Bay, Benton

St Joseph's Church

1936-1946 – Construction and Armed Forces
1936 – Rev William P. Cullen Gambo. Visit Priest.
1941 – School-Chapel on Base.
1942-1942 – Rev G. J. Fitzgerald
1942-1943 – Rev G.A. Marchand, F/L
1943-1944 – Rev C.A. Matayer
1944-1945 – Revs V. Villeneuo & Rev Genest, S.J.
1945-1946 – Capt Morin & Rev C. Kramer, F/L
1944 –Chapel built by RCMP for RC & all Services.
1946- Temporary Church established.
1946-1974 - 1st Res PP, Rev Philip J. McCarthy, 28 years.
1953 – Origination Date of Parish.
1961 – Rev Philip J. McCarthy, 25th Silver Jubilee.
1963-1965 - Rev Patrick A. McCormack, cc.
1965 Mar 29-Rev Patrick A. McCormack, died, age 35. Buried Gander.
1965 Nov 24 -KC Council "McCormack" chartered.
1974-1977 – Rev Frederick J. Terry, PP, 3 years.
1975 – Rev Frederick J. Terry, 25th Silver Jubilee.
1976-1977 – Rev Aidan B. Beresford, cc, Terry.
1977-1984 – Rev Leonard J. Kelly, PP, 7 years.
1980 – Rev Leonard J. Kelly, 25th Silver Jubilee.
1984-1991 - Rev Edward T. Bromley, PP, 7 yrs.
1987 – Rev Edward T. Bromley, 25th Silver Jubilee.
1987-1989 – Rev David Ostler, cc, Bromley.
1991-1996 – Rev Michael Ryan, PP, 5 years.
1991 Sep 23 -New Parish Center dedicated to Rev Philip McCarthy. (1946-1974)
1994 Apr 8 – Gambo KC merge with Gander.
1989-1991 – Rev Michael J. Barker, cc, Ryan
1996-1998 – Rev J. Kevin Barker, PP, 2 years.
1998-1999 – Rev Brian Colbert, PP, 1 year.
1999-Today – Rev David Heale, PP

GRAND FALLS-WINDSOR
Immaculate Conception Cathedral Parish

Immaculate Conception Cathedral

1905 - A.N.D. Company Inc.
1905-1910 - PP, Rev Gregory Battcock, visit priest.
1905 - Rev Battcock built first Chapel.
1910-1912-1st Res. Adm. Rev Mark P. Dwyer, 2 yrs.
1911 - Rev Mark P. Dwyer built larger church.
1912 June – Mission raised to status of Parish.
1912-1953 – 1st PP, Rev William P. Finn, 41 years.
1919 - Grand Falls Church burned down.
1919 –KC"Notre Dame Council" # 2053 instituted.
1920- Father Finn builds Roman Brick Church.
1921-1930 – Rev James A. Hinchey, cc, Finn.
1928 - Rev William P. Finn, Silver Jubilee.
1929 – Laid cornerstone of Notre Dame Academy.
1929-1930 – Rev John M. O'Neill appointed Administrator for Fr Finn who made a tour of Europe and the holy Lands.
1933 Apr 9 - Presentation Sisters took over direction of Notre Dame Academy.
1934-1936 – Rev Joseph Hogan, cc, Finn.
1936-1938 – Rev J. Ronald Jones, cc, Finn
1937 June – Parish celebrates its Silver Jubilee.
1938-1946 – Rev Philip J. McCarthy, cc, Finn
1945 Dec 9 - Rev William P. Finn elevated to Msgr.
1948 Jun 12-Ordained Rev Gregory Pumphrey GF.
1948-1953 – Rev Gregory B. Pumphrey, cc Finn.
1952 - Rt. Rev William P. Finn, 49th Anniversary.
1953 Jan 31 - Rt. Rev William P. Finn died, age 73. in Montreal. Buried; Grand Falls.
1953-Grand Falls Co-Cathedral w/ Harbour Grace.
1953 Dec 8 – GF Parish to status of Co-Cathedral.
1953-1972-5th Bishop John M. O'Neill, 19 yrs
1953-1957 – Rector, Rev Joseph Peddle, 4 years.
1955-1957 – Rev Michael Hynes, cc, Peddle.
1955 Jun – Bishop moved to new residence at GF.
1957-1974-Rector Rev William P. Hogan, 17 years.
1957-1959 – Rev Linus J. Coady, cc, Hogan.
1959-1960 – Rev Edward Hearn, cc, Hogan.
1961 Aug 28 – Rev William P. Hogan elevate Msgr.
1961-1965 – Rev Neil MacDonald, cc, Hogan
1961-1964 – Rev Brendan J. McCarthy, cc. Hogan.
1962-1963 – Rev Edward T. Bromley, cc, Hogan
1963-1965 – Rev Ronald M. Bromley, cc, Hogan.
1964 – Rev Michael J. Walsh, cc, Hogan.
1965 Jun 29 -New Cathedral Blessed in Grand Falls
1965 OCT 30 – DIOCESE MOVES from HG to GF.
1966-1968 – Rev Francis O'Brien, cc, Hogan.
1966-1972 – Rev John G. Mackey, cc, Hogan.
1968-1969 – Rev John Murphy, cc, Hogan
1969 - Rev Ronald Cashin, cc. Hogan.
1970-1973 –Rev David W. Heale, cc, Hogan
1975 – Rev Aidan Beresford, cc, Hogan.
1973-1979-6th Bishop Alphonsus Penney,7yrs
1973 June 6 -Msgr William P. Hogan, 25th Jubilee.
1974 Mar 02 - Bishop John M. O'Neill died SJ, 70.
1974-1979 – PP, Rev William J. Houlihan, 5 years.
1975-1976 – Rev William Hearn, cc, Houlahan.
1976-1979 – Rev Francis J. Aylward, cc, Houlahan.
1979-1983 – PP, Msgr Richard T. Woodford, 4 yrs.
1980-1998-7th Bishop J.Faber MacDonald, 18 yrs
1980 – Rev Philip McCarthy retires to Grand Falls.
1980-1985 - Rev Brian Dunn, cc, Woodford.
1983 - Rev Francis P. Meaney, cc Woodford.
1983-1988 – Rev Ronald M. Bromley, PP, 5 years.
1986-1987 – Rev Brian Colbert, cc, Bromley.
1988 June 13 - Rev Ronald M. Bromley,25thJubilee.
1988-1991 - Rev Michael Ryan, PP, 3 years.
1989 Sep 10 Cathedral Choir sang St. Peter's,Rome.
1991-1996 – PP, Rev Brian Dunn, 5 yea
1996-1998 – PP, Msgr Edward T. Bromley, 2 years.
1998-2000-Diocese Admin. Rev Ed Bromley, 2 yrs.
2000-Dec12-Today-8th Bishop Martin Currie.
2001 Jun 21-Rev Edward T.Bromley elevated Msgr.
2002 Aug 28 -Today - Rev Gordon McLean, Rector Administrator of Cathedral Parish.
2002 - Today – Rev David Joy, cc, McLean.

Dome of the Marble Altar of the old Co-Cathedral Preserved on the grounds of the current Cathedral.

GRAND FALLS-WINDSOR

St. Joseph's Parish

No Missions

St. Joseph's Church

1905-1940 – Attended by Grand Falls.
1923 – 1st RC School-Chapel in Tinsmith Shop. Windsor.
1938 – Chapel Burned. Fr Finn, from Grand Falls.
1939-1943 – 3 Presentation Sisters from GrandFalls.
1940 – Origination Date of Parish.
1940 – March – Chapel burned to the ground.
1940-1980 – 1st PP, Rev Francis P. Meaney, 40 yrs.
1940 - 0903-Church Rebuilt, First Mass.
1943 – Presentation Convent built in Windsor.
1959-0526 – Rev Francis P. Meaney, 25th Jubilee.
1980 – Rev Francis P. Meaney retires age 70.
1980-1986 – 2nd PP, Rev Michael R. Hynes, 6 years.
1984-1987 – Rev Leonard Kelly, PP, 3 years.
1986-1987 – Rev Michael R. Hynes, Sabbatical, 1 yr.
1987-1988 – Rev Edward Brophy, PP, 1 year.
1988-1990 – Rev J. Kevin Barker, PP, 2 years.
1990 – 50th Anniversary of St. Joseph's Parish.
1990-1995 – Rev Eugene Morris, PP, 5 years.
1995-2000 – Rev Anthony Hageman, PP, 5 years.
2000-Today – Rev A. Wayne Cummings, PP.

HARBOUR BRETON

St. Joseph's Parish

Missions: Gaultois, Rencontre East, St. Jacques

St. Joseph's Church

1860 – Origination Date of Parish.
1862-1871 – 1st PP, Rev Robert Brennan, 9 years.
1871-1887 – Unknown
1887-1891 – Rev W. J. Brown, PP, 4 years.
1891-1906 – Unknown.
1906-1911- Rev Michael F. Power, PP, 5 years
1911-1920 – Unknown.
1920-1933 – Rt. Rev John F. Kirwan, PP, 13 years.
1933-1938 – Rev Michael F. Hayes, PP, 5 years.
1938-1957 – Unknown.
1957-1965 – Rev John M. Molloy, PP, 8 years.
1965-1969 – Rev Gordon F. Grace, PP, 4 years.
1969-1973 – Rev John W. Peddle, PP, 4 years.
1974-1980 – Rev Edwin J. Gale, PP, 6 years.
1981-1983 – Rev Aidan Devine, PP, 2 years.
1983-1989 – Rev J. Ambrose Hynes, Admin 6 years.
1984-1990 – Rev William J. Ryan, PP, 6 years.
1990-1992 – Rev Robert Choquet, Admin, 2 years.
1993-1996 – Rev Michael R. Hynes, PP, 3 years.
1996-1999 – Rev Brian Dunn, PP, 3 years.
1999-2002 – Rev Frank Aylward, PP, 3 years.
2002- Today – Rev Edward Brophy, PP.

HARBOUR GRACE
Immaculate Conception Parish

Missions: Riverhead, Spaniard's Bay, Upper Island Cove

Immaculate Conception Cathedral

1784-1830 - Mission of St. John's
1784-1799 – 1st Res PP, Rev Patrick Phelan, 15 yrs.
1784-1799 – First Chapel in rented Store-Chapel.
1800-1806 – 2nd PP, Rev Ambrose Fitzpatrick, 6 yrs
1800-1806 – Chapel in Store is purchased by Priest.
1806 – First Wooden stand alone Church.
1806-1830 – Res PP, VRev Thomas A. Ewer, 24 yrs.
1817-1818 – Rev William Hearn, cc Ewer.
1818-1824 – Rev Dean Mackin, cc. Ewer.
1818-1822 – Rev Marcus Cronin, cc. Ewer.
1819-1830 – Rev Nicholas Devereux, cc. Ewer.
1826 – VRev Thomas Ewer, first in Nfld 50thJubilee.
1830 – Origination Date of Parish.
1830-1833 – 1st PP, VRev Thomas A. Ewer, 3 years.
1830-1831 – Rev Nicholas Herron, cc. Ewer.
1831-1833 – Rev Michael Berney, cc. Ewer.
1833 Feb 6 – VRev Thomas A. Ewer died, age 87.
1833-1859 – 2nd PP, VRev Charles Dalton, 26 years.
1836 – Confirmation by Bishop Fleming, S.J.
1851 Jul 1 – Presentation Convent opened at HG.
1852 – Foundation of Second Stone Church
1853 – Dedication of Second Stone Church.
1856 – HG raised to 2nd Diocese in Newfoundland.
1856 – Rev John Dalton consecrated 1st HG.Bishop.
1956-1869 – 1st Bishop John Dalton, 13 yrs.
1859 Jun 17 – VRev Charles Dalton died, age 73.
1859-1872 – Rev John J. Walsh, PP, 13 years.
1866 - Rev John T. Vereker, cc. J. Walsh.
1869- Bishop John Dalton, died, age 49. Buried under church in Harbour Grace.
1869-1870 – Rev John Walsh, Admin of Diocese.
1870-1880 – 2d Bishop Henry Carfagnini, 10 years.
1871- Rev P.A. Slattery, cc. J. Walsh.
1871-1875 – Rev William Veitch, cc. J. Walsh.
1872-1881 – VRev Francis E. Walsh, PP, 9 yrs.
1877 – Rev Stephen Flynn, cc. F. Walsh.
1877-1882 – Rev Donald W. McInnis, cc. Walsh.
1881-1906 – 3rd Bishop Ronald McDonald, 15 years.
1881-1891- VRev John Roe, PP, 10 years.
1884-1886 - Rev F.D. McCarthy, cc. Roe.
1884-1108 – Pres. Chapel in St. Joseph's School.
1888-1891 – Rev Joseph Murphy, cc, Roe.
1889-1891 – Rev John March, cc Roe.
1891-1906 – Rev John March, PP, 15 years.
1906-1940 – 4th Bishop John March, 34 years.
1904 – Rev John Pat Mackey, cc. March.
1906-1912 – Msgr William P. Finn, PP, 6 years.
1909 – Rev Stephen Whelan, cc. Finn.
1910 – Rev Edward O'Brien, cc. Finn.
1912 – Rev Edward J. Jones, cc. Finn.
1912-1918 - Rev James J. Walker, PP, 6 years
1918-1926 - Msgr Michael F. Dinn, PP, 8 years.
1918-1919 – Rev Henry T. Renouf, cc. Dinn.
1918-1930 – Rev Thomas D. O'Neill, cc. Dinn.
1919-1919 - Rev Francis Pumphrey, cc. Dinn.
1926-1934 – Rev Jeremiah Howard, PP, 8 years.
1934-1940 – Rev Francis P. Meaney, PP, 6 years.
1940-1953 – 5th Bishop O'Neill, 13 years.
1940-1948 – Rev Joseph W. Peddle, PP, 8 years.
1940-1944 - Rev Francis Terry, cc. Peddle.
1949-1957 – Rev William P. Hogan, PP, 8 years.
1953 – Grand Falls becomes Co-Cathedral w/HG.
1957-1984 – Msgr Joseph M. O'Brien, PP, 27 years.
1959-1964 - Rev William Shallow, cc. O'Brien.
1964-1966 – Rev James Beresford, cc. O'Brien.
1965 – GRAND FALLS BECOME DIOCESE VICE HG.
1965 – HG Church becomes Parish Church.
1966-1970 – Rev Aloysius Antle, cc. O'Brien.
1970-1975 – Rev Michael J. Walsh, cc. O'Brien.
1975-1978 – Rev Wayne Cummins, cc. O'Brien.
1978-1979 – Rev Richard Anstey, cc. O'Brien.
1979-1979 - Rev Francis Aylward, cc. O'Brien.
1980-1984 – Rev Michael Ryan, cc. O'Brien.
1984 – Msgr. Joseph O'Brien, ill, retired, age 67.
1984-1987 – Rev J. Kevin Barker, PP, 3 years.
1987 Nov 13 –Msgr. Joseph O'Brien, died, age 70.
1987-1990 – Rev Michael J. Walsh, PP, 3 years.
1989 – Rev Andrew Lane, cc. Walsh.
1990-1996 – Rev James A. Beresford, PP, 6 years.
1996-2001 – Rev Ramon Bolatets, PP, 5 years.
2001-2002 – Rev Gregory Eduah, Admin, 1 year.
2002-Today – Rev Francis Aylward, PP.

HARBOUR MAIN

Sts Peter and Paul Parish

Sts Peter and Paul church

1811-1833 – Mission of Harbour Grace.
1811, RC First Chapel by Rev Thomas Ewer of HG.
1834-1857 – Mission of Brigus.
1834-1840 – Rev Patrick Ward, PP, 6 years fr Fogo.
1839 - First Roman Catholic School.
1849-1856 - Rev Edward O'Keefe, 1st Res PP, 7 yrs.
1853 Jul 10 - Presentation Sisters Open Convent,
1857 - Origination date of Parish,
Under St. John's Diocese.
1857-1868 - 1st PP, VRev Kyran Walsh, 11 years.
1861-1862 - Rev William Walsh, cc, Walsh.
1863-1868 - Rev Patrick O'Donnell, cc, Walsh
1864, VRev Kyran Walsh, 25th Silver Jubilee.
1868, VRev Kyran Walsh, died, age 59.
1868-1882 - VRev Jeremiah O'Donnell, PP, 14 yrs.
1870 – Harbour Main under Harbour Grace Diocese.
1872-1872 - Rev Patrick J. Delaney, cc, O'Donnell.
1872-1872 - Rev Dan Lynch, cc, O'Donnell.
1872-1872 - Rev W, Veitch, cc, O'Donnell.
1877-1885 - Rev Jos V. Donnelly, cc, O'Donnell.
1884-1886 - Rev John Roe, cc, O'Donnell.
1885-1887 - Rev James Brown, PP, 2 years.
1887 - Rev James Brown, died, age 62.
1887-1891 - Rev Pat W. Browne, PP, 4 years.
1891-1906 - Rev Patrick O'Donnell, PP, 15 years.
1906 Jan 16 - Rev Patrick O'Donnell, died, age 68.
1906-1911 - VRev John Roe, PP, 5 years.
1907, 50th Anniversary of Parish. (1857-1907)
1911 Jun 16 - VRev John Roe, died, age 56.
1911-1927 - VRev Richard M. Shean, PP, 16 years.
1917 - VRev Shean built new Church.
1927 Feb 15 - VRev Richard M. Shean, died, age 73.
1927-1953 - Rev Mark P. Dwyer, PP, 26 years.
1933 - Rev Dwyer enlarged Church in and out.
1934 - Rev Mark P. Dwyer, 25th Silver Jubilee.
1940 - Patron Saints of Parish erected in Sanctuary.
1950s - Electric lights in Church and Presbytery.
Rev Dwyer:
1953 Mar 9 - Rt Rev Mark P. Dwyer, died, age 68.
1953 Jul 10 – 100th Anniversary of Presentation Sisters.
1953-1969 - Rev Jeremiah Howard, PP, 16 years.
1957 - 100th Anniversary of Parish. (1857-1957).
1969-1980 - Rev Linus J. Coady, PP, 11 years.
1980-1983 - Rev James Glavine, CssR, PP, 3 years.
1982 Nov 27 - 125th Anniversary of Founding.
1983-1987 - Rev Michael J. Walsh, PP, 4 years.
1987-1990 - Rev William Houlahan, PP 3 years.
1990-1994 - Rev Edward T. Bromley, PP, 4 years.
1991-1993 - Rev Ramon Bolatets, cc, 2 years.
1995-1997 - Rev A. Wayne Cummings, PP, 2 years.
1996-2002 - Rev Brian Dunn, PP, 6 years.
2002-Today - Rev Clem Flaherty, PP,

Older Sts Peter and Paul Church

HOLYROOD
Holy Cross Parish

Holy Cross Church

1784-1857 - Served by Harbour Grace.
1857-1883 - Mission of Harbour Main.
1881-1891-1st PP, VRev Gregory J. Battcock, 10 yrs.
1882-1884-RevJeremiahO'Donnell, cc.Battcock, rtd.
1883 – Origination Date of Parish.
1891-1898 – 2nd PP, Rev Michael Hanley, 7 years.
1898 – Rev Michael Hanley new larger Church.
1898 – Rev Michael Hanley, ill health to Ireland.
1899 Nov 30 - Larger Church Replaced 1st Church
1900-1904 – Rev Joseph Murphy, Admin, 4 years.
1902 – Star of the Sea Association established.
1904-1908 – Rev John Patrick Mackey, PP, 4 years.
1908-1910 – VRev Gregory J. Battcock, PP, 2 years.
1910 Sep 12-VRev Gregory J. Battcock, died, age 64.
1910-1935 – VRev William P. Finn, PP, 25 years.
1917 – VRev William P. Finn, 25th Silver Jubilee.
1918 – Church Destroyed By Fire, Fr Finn.
1919 – New Holy Cross Church, Fr. Finn.
1919 Dec 24 – 1st Mass on Christmas Eve, Fr Finn.
1926-1927 – Rev Michael F. Dinn, cc, Finn.
1931-1935 – Rev Joseph W. Peddle, cc, Finn.
1935 Aug 3 – VRev William P. Finn, died, age 67.
1935-1940 – Rev Joseph W. Peddle, PP, 5 years.
1940-1959 – Rev Wm. McC Murphy, PP, 19 years.
1944 Jun 22 – Rev Wm. McC Murphy, 25th Jubilee.
1959-1965 – Rev Michael J. Kinsella, PP, 6 years.
1964 May 26 – Rev W. McC Murphy, died, age 68.
1965 Apr 12 – Rev Michael J. Kinsella, died, age 60.
1965-1979– Rev Edward Shea, PP, 14 years.
1981 – Rev Edward Shea retired to Holyrood.
1979-1980 - Rev Linus Coady of Harbour Main looked after Holyrood for 1 ½ years
1969- Rev Jeremiah Howard retired to Holyrood, age 76.
1975 – Rev Jeremiah Howard, 50th Golden Jubilee
1976 Apr 11 - Rev Jeremiah Howard, died, age 82.
1980-1981 – Rev Raymond Lahey, Admin, 1 year.
1981-1988 – Msgr. William P. Hogan, PP, 7 years.
1982 Apr 19 - Parish Council organized.
1979–2001 – Rev Edward J. Shea was retired and living at Holyrood, died, age 86.
1983 Oct 9 – 100th Anniversary of Parish. (1883-1983)
1988-1990 – Msgr. William P. Hogan, PP, 2 years.
1991-1996 – Msgr. Edward T, Bromley, PP, 5 years.
1996-1996 – Rev Ramon Bolatets, Admin 1 year.
1996-1998 – Rev A. Wayne Cummings, PP, 2 years.
1999-2002 - Brian Dunn, PP, 3 years.
2002- Today – Rev Clem Flaherty, PP.

Holy Cross Church

KING'S COVE

Sts Peter and Paul

Mission: Open Hall

Sts. Peter and Paul

1815 – Origination Date of Parish.
1815-1831 – 1st PP, Rev James Sinnott, 16 years
1815-1825 – Mass in Store-Chapel. 1825-1st Chapel.
1826-1831 – Rev Nicholas Devereaux, cc. Sinnott.
1831-1845 – 2nd PP, Rev Nicholas Devereaux, 14 yrs.
1845 Apr 25, Rev Nicholas Devereaux, died, age 67.
1845-1854 – Rev Thomas J. Waldren, PP, 9 yrs.
1848-1850 – Rev William B. Forristal, cc, Waldren
1854 Nov – Rev Thomas J. Waldren, died, age 46.
1854-1871 – Rev Matthew Scanlan, PP, 17 years
1865–1871 - Rev James Cummins, cc & PP, 6 years.
1872-1873 – Rev William Veitch, Admin. 1 year.
1873-1875 – Rev Michael Hanley, PP, 2 years
1873 May 20 - Bishop Carfagnini, 500 confirmed.
1875-1891 – Msgr. William Veitch, PP, 16 years.
1884 Oct 9 – Bishop McDonald bless new Church.
1891-1905 – Rev Thomas E. Lynch, PP, 14 years.
1905–Nov - Rev Thomas Lynch, died, SJ, age 46.
1905-1926 – VRev J. H. Scully, PP, 21 years.
1908 Jun 4 - Laid cornerstone Church at Open Hall.
1913-The 1896 school, just renovated, burned down.
1925 – VRev J. H. Scully, 25th Silver Jubilee.
1926-1940 – Rev W. McC Murphy, PP, 14 years.
1940-1941- Rev William J. Hennebury, Admin, 1 yr.
1941-1956 –Rev Wm J. Williams, PP, 15 years.
1948 – Rev Wm Williams Made Monsignor.
1955-1955 – Rev Patrick McCormack, cc, Williams
1956-1966 – Rev Fredrick J. Terry, PP, 10 years.
1966-1975 – Rev James A. Beresford, PP, 8 years.
1975-1975 – Vacant. Governed by Parish Council.
1975-1978 – Rev David Heale, PP, 3 years.
1979-1981 – Rev Lawrence George, PP, 2 years.
1982-1987 – Rev Michael Walsh, PP, 5 years.
1987-1993 – Rev Michael R. Hynes, PP, 6 years.
1993-1997 – Rev William J. Houlahan, PP, 4 years.
1998-2002 – Rev Brian Colbert, PP, 4 years.
2002-Today – Rev William Hearn, PP.

LITTLE BAY moved to ST. PATRICK

Sacred Heart Parish

Sacred Heart Parish in St. Patrick

1880-1885 – Served by Fortune Harbour.
1885-1899 – 1st PP, Rev Stephen O'Flynn, 14 years.
1889-1905 – Rev Richard F. Walsh, FH, 6 years.
1905-1907 – Rev John Lynch of FH, 2 years.
1908 – Rev John J. Nolan of Fortune Harbour.
1908-1910 – Rev J.J. Nugent, 2nd PP. 2 years.
1910-1912 – Rev John S. Kavanagh, cc.
1912-1914 – Rev Dr Edward J. Jones, cc.
1914-1919 – Rev John J. Nolan of FH, 5 years.
1919-1927 – Rev Francis J. Pumphrey, cc.
1928-1929 – Rev Dr John M. O'Neill, cc.
1930-1934 – Rev Joseph P. Hogan, cc.
1935-1940 – Rev William H. Casey of FH, 5 years.
1940-1958 – Placed under Windsor Parish.
1940-1954 – Rev Francis P. Meaney, PP, 14 years.
1954-1955 – Rev Gregory B. Pumphrey, cc at Badger.
1955-1958 – Rev Leonard J. Kelly, cc at Badger.
1958 – Erection of Badger Parish.
1958 - Little Bay placed under Badger Parish.
1958-1961 – Rev Ronald J. Walsh, PP, 3 years.
1961-1963 – Rev Edward F. Hearn, PP, 2 years.
1963-1968 – Rev Edward T. Bromley, PP, 5 years.
1969-1973 – Rev Francis R. O'Brien, PP, 4 years.
1973-1974 – Rev David L. Aylward, Admin.
1974-1975 – Rev Aidan Beresford, Admin.
1975-1976 – Rev John Murphy, Admin.
1976-1984 – Rev James A. Beresford, PP, 8 years.
1984-1988 – Rev Edward R. Brophy, PP, 4 years.
1988-1994 – Rev Anthony Hageman, PP, 6 years.
1994-1997 – Rev Brian Colbert, PP, 3 years.
1997-Today – Rev Eugene Morris, Admin.

NORRIS ARM

Our Lady of Mt Carmel Parish

Missions: Lewisporte, Boyd's Cove, Twillingate

Our Lady of Mount Carmel Church

1876 – 1st Settlement
1902-1909-Attended by Whitbourne, Rev. Battcock.
1909-1930 – Attended by Grand Falls.
1909-1912 – Rev Mark P. Dwyer, cc
1912-1930 – Rev William P. Finn, Grand Falls.
1912 –Rev William P. Finn, built school & chapel.
1930-1953 – Attended by Bishop Falls.
1930-1940 – Rev James A. Hinchey, BF, 10 years.
1940-1953 – Rev Joseph P. Hogan, BF, 13 years.
1940 - Rev Joseph Hogan, BF, built new Church.
1953 – Origination Date of Parish.
1953-1965 – 1st PP, Rev Michael Carey, SFM, 12 yrs
1965-1969 – Rev Linus J. Coady, 2nd PP, 4 years.
1969-1971 – Rev William Matthews, PP, 2 years.
1971-1979 – Rev Aloysius Antle, PP, 8 years.
1979-1984 – Rev Ronald M. Bromley, Admin. 5 yrs.
1985-1988 – Rev Michael Ryan, PP, 3 years.
1985 Nov 3 – Holt Family church in Lewisporte blessed.
1988-1991 – Rev Willie Klooster, Admin. , 3 yrs
1991-1996 – Rev Brendan J. McCarthy, PP. 5 years.
1996-2002 – Rev Michael Hynes, PP, 6 years.
2002-Today – Rev Moses Odumad, Admin

NORTH RIVER

All Hallows Parish

Missions: Bay Roberts and Butlerville

All Hallows Church

1824-1906 – Mission of Brigus.
1840 – There was an RC Church in North River.
1874 – All Hallows Church built under Brigus.
1906 Oct 2 - Origination date of Parish.
1907-1923 – 1st PP, Rev Stephen J. Whelan, 16 yrs.
1907-Church, Presbytery and School at North River
1907 Dec 1 – First Mass at Church at North River.
1909 - Church at Bay Roberts, Holy Redeemer.
1919-1923 – Rev William H., Casey, cc, 4 years.
1923 Aug 8 – Rev Stephen J. Whelan, died, age 46 at North West River, Labrador.
1923-1934 – VRev George A. Thibault, PP, 11 years.
1931- VRev George A. Thibault, Silver Jubilee.
1934- VRev George A. Thibault, died, age 60.
1934-1955 – Msgr Michael F. Dinn, PP, 21 years.
1940 – Msgr. Dinn given D.P. and Vicar General.
1943 Feb 24 – Msgr. Michael F. Dinn's 25th Jubilee.
1946 – Rev Thomas N., Morrissey, cc 1 year.
1955 Jul 17 – Msgr Michael F. Dinn, died, age 64.
1955-1971 – Rev Joseph P. Hogan, PP, 16 years.
1957c – Rev Hogan builds a new Church.
1971 Apr 15 - Rev Joseph Hogan, died, age 60.
1971-1977 – Rev Leonard J. Kelly, PP, 6 years.
1977-1984 – Rev Frederick J. Terry, PP, 7 years.
1984-1985 – Msgr. Richard T. Woodford, PP, 1 year
1985-1997 – Rev Edward A. Walsh, PP, 12 years.
1997 Sep 1 – Brigus & North River shared PP.
1997-2000 – Rev William Houlahan, PP, 3 years.
2001-2002 - Rev Gordan MacLean, Admin.
2002-2002 – Rev J. Kevin Barker, admin
2002-Today – Rev Brian Colbert, PP

NORTHERN BAY

Corpus Christi Parish

Missions: Kingston, Western Bay, Gull Island, Lower Island Cove

Corpus Christi Church

1838 - Origination Date of Parish.
1838-1871 – 1st PP, VRev Bernard Duffy, 33 years.
1840 – Rev Bernard Duffy built Church and school.
1841 Feb 2 – Confirmation by Bishop Fleming.
1863-1865 – Rev James Cummins, cc, Duffy.
1868-1871 – Rev Ed F. Walsh, nephew, cc, Duffy.
1871-1874 – PP, Rt Rev Joseph V. Donnelly, 3 yrs.
1874-1875 – PP, Rev James Cummins, 1 year.
1875 Aug 30 – Rev James Cummins, died, age 35.
1875-1891 – PP, Rev Michael Hanley, 16 years.
1875 – Holy Rosary Church, Western Bay
1875-1875 – Rev Wm Veitch, cc, Hanley.
1878-1878 – Rev Tierney, cc, Hanley.
1883 May 22–Confirmation, Bishop Ron McDonald.
1891-1906 – PP, VRev John Roe, 15 years.
1906-1915 – Rev John J. Lynch, PP, 9 years.
1906- Rev John J. Nolan, cc, Lynch.
1915-1970 – Rt Rev Edward J. O'Brien, PP, 55 yrs.
1922-1923 – Rev W. J. Williams, cc, O'Brien.
1923-1925 – Rev Leslie Fitzgerald, cc. O'Brien.
1924 Oct 07 – Church burned to ground.
1935 Jun 24 – Rt Rev Edward O'Brien, 25th Jubilee.
1935 Jun 26 – Laid cornerstone for New Church.
1938 Jun 16 – New Church opened. Fr O'Brien.
1960 Jun 24 – Rt Rev Edward O'Brien, 50th Jubilee.
1966-1967 – Rev William Matthews, cc, O'Brien.
1967-1968 – Rev John Murphy, cc, O'Brien.
1970 Jun 24 – Rt Rev Edward O'Brien, 60th Jubilee.
1970 Sep 6 – Rt Rev Edward O'Brien, age 86. Retd.
1970-1973 – Rev Edward J. Hearn, PP, 3 years.
1973-1978 – Rev Gregory B. Pumphrey, PP, 5 years.
1973 – Rev Gregory B. Pumphrey, 25th Jubilee.
1978-1981 – Rev David Heale, PP, 3 years.
1981-1984 – Rev J. Kevin Barker, PP, 3 years.
1984-1991 – Rev William Matthews, PP, 7 years.
1991 May 31 – Rev William Matthews, 25th Jubilee.
1991-1994 – Rev Brian G. Colbert, PP, 3 years.
1994-1999 – Rev Francis J. Aylward, PP, 5 years.
1999-2000 – Vacant.
1999-2000 – Rev M. Ryan, admin from Avondale.
1999-2000 – Rev R. Bolatets, Admin from HG.
2000-2000 – Rev Joseph Donkor, Admin.
2000-Today – Rev William Houlahan, PP.

Holy Rosary Church, Western Bay

St. Joseph's Church, Kingston

Corpus Christi Church

Church pictures at Western Bay and Kingston are courtesy of Edward Chafe Book, History of Corpus Christi Parish, Northern Bay.

PLATE COVE

St. Patrick's Parish

Mission: Summerville

St. Patrick's Church

1857 – First RC Church King's Cove & Plate Cove.
1966 – Origination date of Parish.
1966-1980 – 1st PP, Rev Michael R. Hynes, 14 Yrs.
1980-1983 – Rev Aloysius Antle, PP, 3 years.
1983-1984 – Rev Gregory B. Pumphrey, PP, 1 year.
1984-1989 – Rev Lawrence George, PP, 5 years.
1984 Nov 14 –Presbytery destroyed by fire. Fr Geo.
1990 – Under King's Cove.
1990-1990 – Sr Alice Dower, Admin, 1 year.
1990-1992 - Rev Michael R. Hynes, PP, KC, 2 years.
1993-1997 – Rev William Houlahan, PP, KC, 4 yrs.
1993-1997 – Srs. Sarah Moore, Amelia Mooney & Elizabeth Whelan, Administrators at Plate Cove.
1997-1998 – Rev Sebastian Fernando. On Loan.
1998-1999 - Rev Brian Colbert & Rev Sebastian.
1990-2002 - Rev Brian Colbert, PP, King's Cove, 2 yrs.
2002-Today – Rev William Hearn, PP, King's Cove.

PORT UNION

St. Joseph and St. Patrick Parish

Missions: Trinity, Bonavista and Catalina

Sts. Joseph & St. Patrick Church

1842-1982 – Serviced from Bonavista.
(See Bonavista)
1982 – Origination date of Parish.
1982-1983 - 1st PP, Rev Edward T. Bromley, 1 year.
1984-1989 – Rev James A. Beresford, PP, 5 years.
1989-1990 – Rev Brian Colbert, PP, 1 year.
1990-1990 – Rev Francis J. Aylward, PP, 1 year.
1990-1996 – Rev J. Kevin Barker, PP, 6 year.
1991 – Rev J. Kevin Barker, 25th Silver Jubilee.
1992-1993 – Rev William Houlahan, PP, 1 year.
1996-2002 - Rev Brendan McCarthy, PP, 6 years.
2002 – Rev Brendan McCarthy retired.
2002-Today – Rev William Hearn, PP.

ST.ALBAN'S
St. Ignatius Parish

St. Ignatius Church

1859 – Four Families Settle In Ship Cove, (St. Alban's).
1860-1916 – Visiting Priests from Harbour Breton.
1860-1885 – Mass held in private homes.
1885-1916 – School used as Chapel.
1916– Origination date of Parish (Under St. George's Diocese)
1916-1943 – 1st PP, VRev Stanislaus St. Croix, 27 years.
(Rev Croix built Church, Rectory and School.)
1943-1965 – Rev Michael J. Hayes, PP, 22 years.
1946 – Built Holy Cross School, Rev Hayes.
1955-1965 – Worked on new Church, Rev Hayes.
1965-1969 – Rev Kevin M. Ryan, 4 years.
1965 – New Church officially opened.
1966 – Presentation Sisters arrive, Build Convent.
1969-1979 – Rev Gordon F. Grace, PP, 10 years.
1979-1984 – Rev Bernard F. Buckle, PP, 5 years.
1984-1989 - Unknown
1989-1994 – Rev Joseph A. Gash, PP, 5 years.
1991 – 75TH Anniversary of Parish, Bishops MacDonald & Lahey.
1994 – Became part of Grand Falls Diocese.
1994-1999 – Rev William Hearn, PP, 5 years.
2000-2001 - Rev Michael Obosu, Admin, 1 year.
2001-Today – Rev John Arkorful, Admin.

St. Anne's in Conne River (Mission)

ST. BRENDAN'S
St. Gabriel Parish

St. Gabriel's Church

1815-1891 – Attended by King's Cove.
1860s – School-Chapel for all locations.
1881 – A new Church was constructed.
1891 – Origination date of Parish.
1891-1903- 1st PP,VRev Gregory J. Battcock, 12 yrs.
1891-Initial Church & Rectory.
1896-(Harbour Breton).
1903 – VRev Gregory J. Battcock, 25th Jubilee.
1904-1906 – Rev William P. Finn, 2 years.
1906-1918- Rev John Patrick Mackey, PP, 12 years.
1918-1927 – Rev James J. Walker, PP, 9 years.
1920S – Rev Walker built current Church.
1927-1937 – Rev Francis Pumphrey, PP, 10 years.
1937-1944 – Rev Leslie G. Fitzgerald, PP, 7 years.
1944-1952 – Rev Francis R. Terry, PP, 8 years.
1952 Sep 3 - Rev Francis R. Terry, died, age 37.
1952-1956 – Rev Edward M. Shea, PP, 4 years.
1956 – St. Jacques to St. Brendan's.
1956-1959 – Rev Edward M. Shea, PP, 3 years.
1959-1964 – Rev J. Raymond Hawco, PP, 5 years.
1964-1972 – Rev William Shallow, PP, 8 years.
1969 – Rev Edward Shea, 25th Silver Jubilee.
1970 – Rev Ronald J. Walsh, 25th Silver Jubilee.
1972 – Rev Martin Parsons, Admin.
1980 Oct 25 – Rev Ronald J. Walsh, died, age 65.
1980-1981 –Admin Rev J. Davis, CssR, M. Brehl, CssR, St. Theresa's, SJ, and Rev J. Kevin Barker, Gambo.
1981 – Rev Edward J. Shea retired. age 66.
1981-1984 – Rev William Hearn, PP, 3 years.
1985-1988 – Rev Brian Dunn, PP, 3 years.
1988-1991 – Rev Aloysius Antle, PP, 3 years.
1991 – 100TH Anniversary of Parish.
1991 May 29 – Rev Aloysius Antle, 25th Jubilee.
1991-1994 – Rev William Hearn, PP, 3 year.
1994-2000 – Rev Michael Barker, PP, 6 years.
2000-2002 – Rev J. Donkor, PP, 2 years.
2002 –Today – Rev Emmanuel Mochiah, Admin.

TILTING,FOGO
St. Patrick's Parish
Missions: Island Hrb, Fogo and Joe Batt's Arm

St. Patrick's Church

1700 – Originally Settled. 1738 – 215 Inhabitants.
1786-1840 – Served by French Ship Chaplains.
1787 - Rev Thomas Lonergan refuge in Fogo fr SJ.
1787 Oct 25 – Rev Thomas Lonergan, died, age 38.
1834-1841 – Rev Martin Bergan, 1st Res PP, 7 years.
1838-1st Chapel replaced Chapel-in-Store. FrBergan
1840 – Origination date of St. Patrick's Parish.
1840-1865 – 1st PP, Rev Patrick Ward, 25 years.
1841 May 20 Rev Ward sign Foundation Doc. SJ.
1841 Sep 28 – Rev Martin Bergan, died, age 32.
1855-Rev Patrick Ward at consec SJ, Cathedral.
1855- Rev John J. Walsh, cc, Ward.
1865 Jun 29 - Rev Patrick Ward, died age 57.
1865-1885 – 2nd PP, Rev James Brown, 20 years.
1874- Rev Brown visited Fleur de Lys.
1881 – Rev James Brown, 25th Silver Jubilee.
1886-1892 – Rev Richard M. Walker, PP, 6 years.
1892-1910 – Rev William P. Finn, PP, 18 years.
1909 – Rev Finn built present St. Patrick's Church.
1910-1914 – Rev Edward O'Brien, PP, 4 years.
1914-1944 – Rev Edward J. Jones DD, PP, 30 yrs.
1937 May 26 – Rev Edward J. Jones, 25th Jubilee.
1944-1948 – Rev Michael J. Kinsella, PP, 4 years.
1948-1955 – Rev Joseph M. O'Brien, PP, 7 years.
1955-1964 – Rev Gregory B. Pumphrey, PP, 9 years.
1964-1967 – Rev Brendan J. McCarthy, PP, 3 years.
1967-1977 – Rev J. Kevin Barker, PP, 10 years.
1974 June – New St. Patrick's Church.
1977-1979 – Rev William Hearn, PP, 2 years.
1979-1984 – Rev Edward J. Brophy, PP, 5 years.
1984-1996 – Rev Michael Hynes, 2 years.
1986-1990 – Rev A. Wayne Cummings, PP, 4 years.
1990-1994 – Rev Francis J. Aylward, PP, 4 years.
1994-1997 – Rev Anthony Hageman, PP, 3 years.
1997-1998 – Rev Michael Ryan, PP, 1 year.
1998-2000 – Rev Thomas Duffenais, PP, 2 years
2000-Today – Rev John Adde-Nweah, PP.

TRINITY
Most Holy Trinity

Holy Trinity church

1815-1890 – Mission of King's Cove.
1815-1931 – Rev James Sinnott of KC.
1831-1845 – Rev Nicholas Devereaux of KC.
1833 – Present Church built on land donated by Garland Family.
1845-1854 – Rev Thomas Waldren of KC.
1854-1856 – Rev W. Forrestal & Rev P. Cleary.
1857-1865 – Rev Matthew Scanlan of KC.
1865-1871 – Rev James Cummins of KC.
1871-1873 – Rev William Veitch of KC.
1873-1875 – Rev Michael Hanley of KC.
1875-1890 – Rev William Veitch of KC.
1890 – Origination date of Parish.
1890-1895 – 1st PP, Rev Philip A. Carolan, 5 years.
1895 – Rev Carolan died, age 50, buried in Trinity.
1895-1896 - Rev Joseph Murphy, Administrator.
1896-1938 - VRev Walter M. Tarahan, PP, 42 years.
1938 March 17 – Rev Walter Tarahan died, age 85, buried Trinity. (St. Patrick's Day)
1938-1944 - Rev Michael J. Kinsella, PP, 6 years.
1944-1953 - Rev Leo J. Burke, 4th & last PP, 9 years.
1953 – Parish closed down due to population drop.
1953-1982 – Served from Bonavista (See Bonavista)
1982-Today-Served from Port Union. (See P. Union)

Main Altar in Holy Trinity Church

WHITBOURNE

St. Alphonsus Parish

Missions: Bellevue and Chapel arm

St. Alphonsus Church

1887 – Origination date of Parish.
1887 – Rev John Roe, first Mass at Whitbourne.
1887-1900 – 1st PP, Rev Pat W. Browne Dr, 13 yrs.
1901-1906 – Rev Stephen J. Whelan Dr, PP, 5 yrs.
1905 – Rev Whelan at Conferring of Pallium, S.J.
1906-1909 – Rev Gregory J. Battcock, PP, 3 years.
1909-1949 – Mission of Gambo.
1910-1913 – Rev William P. Finn, PP, 3 years.
1911- Rev William P. Finn built School.
1913-1914 - Rev James W. Donnelly, PP, 1 year.
1914-1915 - Rev John F. Kirwan, PP, 1 year.
1915-1920 – Rev John S. Kavanagh, PP 5 years.
1921 – Fr Cullen moved residence to Gambo.
1921-1945 – VRev W. P. Cullen, PP, 24 years.
1943-1967 – Rev O'Deady, preached Missions.
1946- Rev Cullen retired and hospitalized.
1946-1949 – Unknown.
+1949–1971 - Redemporists take over Whitbourne.
1950-Redemporists build St. Alphonsus Monastery.
1949-1956 – Rev Gerald M. Murphy, CssR, Superior Monastery, 7 years.
1952-1954 - Rev John Lambert, CssR, Assistant.
1953 Jun 24-Rev Gerald Murphy, CssR, 25 Jubilee.
1956-1959 – Rev Madigan, CssR, rector 3 years.
1959-1961 – Rev John W. O'Deady, CssR, 2 years.
1959-1962 – Rev W. Lucian Howard, CssR, 3 years.
1962-1965 – Rev A. MacLellan, CssR, 3 years.
1964-1967 – Rev Wm McGuigan, CssR, , 3 years.
1967-1969 – Rev Walter Mann, CssR, 2 years.
1969-1971 – Rev Albert Stoeckel, CssR, 2 years.
+1971 – Parish returned to Diocese Priests.
1971 – Hearts Content placed under Carbonear.
1971-1979 – Rev Ronald M. Bromley, PP, 8 years.
1979-1981 – Rev A. Wayne Cummings, PP, 2 yrs.
1982-1987 – Rev Aloysius Antle, PP, 5 years.
1987-1991 – Rev Brian G. Colbert, PP, 4 years.
1991-1993 – Rev Vincent Gulikers, PP, 2 years.
1993-1996 – Rev Edward J. Brophy, PP, 3 years.
1996–2001 – Rev John Adde-Nweah, PP, 5 years.
2002-Today – Rev Tony Hageman, PP.

REDEMPTORISTS WHO SERVED AT WHITBOURNE

Rev Patrick Brady – 1956-1958, Dispensed
Rev John Corbett – 1967
Rev Ronald Delaney – 1951-1953, d. 28 Dec 2000.
Rev Paul Doucet –1954-1956,1964-1967,1969,1971.
Rev Edward Gillen – 1953-1956, d. 31 Jan 1980.
Rev James Glavine – 1950-1954, d. 21 Feb 1990.
Rev W. Lucian Howard*–1959-1962,d.7 Oct 1963.
Rev Joseph James – 1956-1960, d. 14 Sep 1999.
Rev Clair Johnson – 1960-1969, d. 15 Feb 1986.
Rev John Lambert, - 1952-1954, d. 7 Jun 1977.
Rev John Madigan* – 1956-1959, d. 7 Feb 2001.
Rev Walter Mann* – 1964-1969, rector 1967-1969.
Rev James Mason – 1966.
Rev Gerald Murphy* – 1949-1956, d. 11 Feb 1957.
Rev A. MacLellan – 1962-1965, d. 17 Jul 1981.
Rev Howard McMahon – 1961-1964, dispensed.
Rev Wm McGuigan* – 1964-1967, d. 5 Apr 1991.
Rev J. O'Deady – 1959-1961, d 18 Sep 1994 as a diocesan priest.
Rev R. O'Donnell – 1968-1969, d. 8 Oct 1982.
Rev Peter O'Hare – 1951-1953, d. 15 May 1959.
Rev Albert Stoeckel*–1954-1959, 1967, 1969-1971.
Rev Erwin Williams – 1958-1960, dispensed.

*** Served as Rector.**

Information received from the Provincial Archives of the Edmonton-Toronto Redemporists. Toronto, Ontario. 2002

THE MISSIONS OF BISHOP'S FALL SACRED HEART PARISH ARE:

St. John the Baptist Church in Botwood (which was never a parish).

Leading Tickles (no church, Fr Coady goes to Barbara Cooke's home to say Mass).
St. Anne's Church in Fortune Harbour (Parish Records date back to 1876-1953) Closed Served from Norris Arm.

FORTUNE HARBOUR

St. Anne's Parish

Missions: Leading Tickles, Robert's Arm, Little Bay, Black Island, Pilley's Island, St. Patrick's and Springdale

St. Anne's Church in Fortune Harbour

1800's – Settled by Irish and English Families.
1815-1844 – Mission of King's Cove parish.
1815-1844 – Revs J. Sinnott & N. Devereaux of KC.
1834 – Episcopal visit of Rt Rev Michael Fleming.
1844-1880 – Mission of Tilting Parish, Fogo
1844-1880 – Rev P. Ward & Rev J. Brown of Fogo.
1880 – Origination date of Parish.
1880-1885 – 1st PP, Rev Stephen O'Flynn, 5 years.
1885-1904 – Rev Richard F. Walsh, PP, 19 yrs.
1887 – Rev Felix D. McCarthy, cc.
1888 – Rev Joseph Murphy, cc.
1889 – Rev Walter M. Tarahan, c
1897 – Rev John Colbert, cc.
1900 – Rev John H. Scully, cc.
1904-1907 – Rev John J. Lynch, PP, 3 years.
1908-1923 – Rev John Nolan, PP, 15 years.
1923-1940 – Rev William Casey, PP, 17 years.
1940-1949 – Rev James A. Hinchey, PP, 9 years.
1949-1952 – Rev Richard Woodford, Admin. 3 yrs
1952-1953 – Rev Frederick J. Terry, Admin. 1 yr.
1953 – Becomes a mission of Norris Arm Parish.
1967 – Placed under jurisdiction of Grand Falls.
1988 – Place under jurisdiction of Bishop's Falls.
1992-Today – Rev Linus J. Coady, PP. BF.

Main Altar in St. Anne's Church

PRIESTS AND RELIGIOUS FROM DIOCESAN PARISHES

AVONDALE

PRIEST FROM AVONDALE (1)

Rev. Clem Flaherty

RELIGIOUS FROM AVONDALE (7)

Rev. Brother Desmond Fewer, OFM. Cap., Sr. M. Dominica Flynn rsm, Sr. M. Kevin Kennedy rsm, Sr. M. Emmanuel Nugent rsm, Sr. Agnes Conway rsm, Sr. Anastasia Moors pbvm, & Sr. Marilyn Costello pbvm.

BADGER

PRIEST FROM BADGER (2)

Rev. Neil MacDonald (LPH) & Rev. Lorri Locke. (Springdale).

RELIGIOUS FROM PARISH (2)

Sr. Celtine Bouzane pbvm & Sr. M. Eileen Bouzane rsm.

BAY DE VERDE

PRIESTS FROM PARISH (2)

Rev. Jeremiah Howard & Rev. William J. Kelly (both Daniel's Cove).

RELIGIOUS FROM BAY DE VERDE (10)

Rev. Bro. W. Howard CFC and Rev. Bro. Gabriel Noonan CFC, Sr. Josephine Ricer rsm, Sr. M. DeSales Ahearn, rsm, Sr. M. Alphonsus Noonan, rsm, Sr. Zita Hyne, rsm, Sr. M. Alphonsus McNamara, rsm, Sr. Theresa Keyes pbvm, Sr. Monica Woodrow pbvm & Sr. Electa Rice sc.

BAIE VERTE

PRIESTS FROM BAIE VERTE (2)

Rev. Aloysius Antle and Mr. Martin Parsons, (LPH)

BISHOP'S FALLS

PRIESTS FROM BISHOP FALLS (3)

Rev. Anthony Martin, SFM (1926-1995) (LPH),Rev. Michael Carey SFM (Fortune Hrb) & Rev. James Glavine CssR (Fortune Hrb).

RELIGIOUS FROM BISHOP FALLS (7)

Sr. Patricia Tobin, pbvm, Sr. Sarah Moore pbvm, Sr. Ruth O'Reilly pbvm, Sr. Elizabeth Daniels pbvm, Sr. Bride Budgell (Fortune Hrb), Sr. Agnes Quirk SCIC (Fortune Hrb) & Sr. St. John of God aps.

BONAVISTA

PRIEST FROM BONAVISTA (1)

Rev. William J. Hennebury (1914-1947).

RELIGIOUS FROM BONAVISTA (1)

Sr. M. Fabian Hennebury, rsm.

BRENT'S COVE/LA SCIE

PRIESTS FROM PARISH (2)

Rev. William Matthews (La Scie) and Rev. Gregory Sullivan. (LPH)

RELIGIOUS FROM BRENTS COVE (4)

Sr. Clotilda Conway, pbvm, Sr. Alice Sullivan, rsm, Sr. Julia O'Connell, rsm & Sr. M. Placide Conway, rsm.

BRIGUS

PRIESTS FROM BRIGUS (11)

VRev. Walter M. Tarahan (1853-1938); VRev. Richard Shean (1854c-1927); Rev. Richard Walker (1859-1941); Rev. Thomas A. Fleming (1865-1930c); Rev. John Kavanagh.(1883-1961); Rev. George Wm Battcock (1892-1984); Rev. Francis P. Meaney (1909-1988); Rev. Leo F. St. John omi, in Texas; Rev. Leo J. Burke (1913--); Rev. Pat Burke (1914c-Unk)(LPH); & Rev. Edward M. Shea (1915-2000).

RELIGIOUS FROM BRIGUS (15)

Bro. P. V. Shea CFC, Sr. Gerard Walker; Sr. Jerome Walker, Sr. Damien Morrissey; Sr. M. Geraldine Morrissey, rsm; Sr. Rita Morrissey, rsm, Sr. M. Helen Shea rsm; Sr. Columba Peddle; Sr. M. Pius Shea rsm; Sr. Valeria Carroll, Sr. Mark Fardy; Sr. Angela Fowler, rsm; Sr. Philomena Walker, rsm, Sr. Raymond. Burke, rsm, & Sr. M. Lucina Cowley, rsm.

BUCHAN'S

PRIESTS FROM BUCHANS (3)

Rev. Aidan Beresford (LPH) (1936); Rev. James A. Beresford (1940--);& Rev. Michael J. Barker (1953)

RELIGIOUS FROM BUCHANS (7)

Sr. Amelia Mooney, pbvm, Sr. Madeline Veitch, pbvm, Sr. Marie Beresford, rsm, Sr. Gen Beresford, rsm, Sr. Ruth Beresford rsm, Sr. Madeline Byrne rsm & Sr. Sheila Martin, sc.

CARBONEAR

PRIESTS FROM CARBONEAR (24)

Rev. James Brown (1825), Rev. Edmund Ryan (1837), Msgr. Edward F. Walsh (1842), Rev. Francis Ryan (1845), Msgr. Felix D. McCarthy (1861), Msgr. Joseph Murphy (1862), Rev. Dr Patrick W. Browne (1864), Rev. James Ryan (1866), VRev. William F. Finn (1868), Rev. Dr. Stephen J. Whelan (1877), Rev. John P. Mackey (1878), Msgr. William P. Finn (1879), Rev. James Donnelly (1883), Msgr. Edward J. O'Brien (1885), VRev. Dr. Edward J. Jones (1887), VRev. William T. Cullen (1893), Msgr. Michael F. Dinn (1891), Msgr. Francis J. Ryan (1892), Msgr. Willie J. Williams (1893), Rev. Joseph Hogan (1903), Rev. Leo Drake (1907), Msgr. Joseph M. O'Brien (1917), Rev. Joseph Crawford CssR (1938) & Rev. Lawrence George (1954).

SISTERS FROM CARBONEAR (21)

Sr. Casmir Crawford, pbvm, Sr. Rose Crawford, pbvm, Sr. Regina Carmel Cullen, SCH, Sr. Xaveria Fardy, pbvm, Sr. M. Gertrude Finn, pbvm, Sr. M. Carmella Finn, pbvm, Sr. Lucia Fitzpatrick, SGM, Sr. Bernadette Hearn, SCH, Sr. Blanche Hogan, pbvm, Sr. Mother Brenda Hogan, pbvm, Sr. Catherine Keneally, pbvm, Sr. Anna Vincent Kiley, SCH, Sr. Margaret Luther, SSH, Sr. Mother Clare Mackey, pbvm, Sr. Felix McCarthy, pbvm, Sr. Marie McCarthy, SCH, Sr. M. Francis McCarthy, Sr. Presentation McCarthy, pbvm, Sr. Theresa McCarthy, pbvm, Sr. Margaret Gregory Murphy, SCH, & Sr. Philip Neri Short, pbvm.

COLLIERS

PRIESTS FROM COLLIERS (2)

Rev. Patrick J. Hearn (1888-1931) & Rev. Francis R. O'Brien (LPH)

RELIGIOUS FROM COLLIERS (3)

Sr. M. Camillus Joseph Cole, rsm, Sr. Mary Theresa Doyle pbvm & Sr. Gladys Whelan pbvm.

CONCEPTION HARBOUR

PRIESTS FROM CONCEPTION HARBOUR (3)

Rev. John Costello, Rev. Patrick Kennedy & Mr. John Murphy (LPH)

RELIGIOUS FROM CONCEPTION HARBOUR (11)

Rev. Bro. Leonard Dalton, CFC, Sr. M. Gertrude Kennedy, rsm, Sr. M. Madeline Trehey, rsm, Sr. M. Liguori Wade, rsm, Sr. M. Scholastica Flynn, rsm, Sr. M. Finbar Buck, rsm, Sr. M. Anthony Wade, rsm, Sr. N. Barbara Wade, rsm, Sr. N. Ignatius Costello, rsm, Sr. Catherine Kenny, rsm & Sr. M. Denise Costello, rsm.

CONCHE

PRIESTS FROM CONCHE (3)

Msgr. Patrick J. Bromley (1902-1981), Msgr. Edward T. Bromley (1935--), & Rev. Ronald Bromley (1936--)

RELIGIOUS FROM PARISH. (2)

Sr. St. John of God, CPS (Elizabeth Carey) & Sr. Agnes Quirk, SCR.

GANDER

PRIESTS BORN IN GANDER (3)

Rev. Michael Ryan (1952-), Rev. Matthew Kane (LPH), & Rev. David Joy.

GRANDFALLS-WINDSORCATHEDRAL

PRIESTS BORN IN GRAND FALLS (11)

Rev. Matthew Blackmore, CssR (1918); Rev. James Davis, CssR (1926); Rev. William Houlahan (1943--); Rev. Norbert Mackenzie, S.J. (1918-1992); Rev. Vincent Mackenzie, S.J. (1918-d); Rev. Patrick McCormack, (1929-1965); Rev. John Mackey (LPH); Rev. William Shallow (LPH); Rev. David L. Alyward (LPH); Rev. Donald J. Murry, MGJ (1924) & Rev. Richard A. Anstey, (LPH)

RELIGIOUS BORN IN GRAND FALLS (17)xxxx

Rev. Bro. Richard Anstey, O.Carm, Rev. Bro. William Flood CFC,; Sr. Mary McHugh, SCIC; Sr. Gertrude Wall, pbvm; Sr. Margaret McLaughlin, pbvm; Sr. Gertrude Mary O'Flynn, Sr. Angela Mackenzie, pbvm, Sr. Kathleen Ryan, pbvm, Sr. Cyprian Ryan, pbvm, Sr. Regina Davis, pbvm, Sr. Joan Whelan, GSIC, Sr. Madeline Cook, GSIC, Sr. Margaret Molloy, SC, Sr. Margaret Harvey, rsm; Sr. M. Noel Croke, rsm, Sr. M. Ita Hennessey, rsm, Sr. Gertrude Hamilton, rsm, & Sr. Michella Browne,csm.

GRAND FALLS-WINDSOR-ST.JOSEPH

PRIESTS BORN IN ST. JOS PARISH (2)

Rev. Roy Walsh (LPH) and Rev. Leonard Kelly.

SISTERS BORN IN PARISH (7)

Sr. Pauline Barry, pbvm (1920-1999); Sr. Genevieve Barry, pbvm (1925-1999), Sr. Brendan Lynch pbvm, Sr. Catherine Lidstone pbvm, Sr. Alice Walsh pbvm, Sr. Sarah Beresford, pbvm & Sr. Margaret Cooke.

HARBOUR BRETON

PRIESTS FROM HARBOUR BRETON (3)

Rev. Joseph Burke (1902), Msgr. Gerald Hull (1921-1984) & Rev. Charles Burke.

RELIGIOUS FROM PARISH

Sr. Joseph Byrne rsm & Sr. M. Carmelita Hartigan rsm.

HARBOUR GRACE

PRIESTS BORN IN HARBOUR GRACE: (17)

Rev. Stephen Flynn (1850-1899), Rev. John J. Lynch (1858c-1929), VRev. John H. Scully (1875-1948), Rev. Frances Pumphrey (1890-1937), Msgr. William Casey (1892-1962), VRev. Leslie Fitzgerald (1898-1966), Rev. John L. Foley (1900-1938), Rev. J. Ronald Jones (1907-1953), Rev. Walter P. Walsh (1913-1958), Rev. Edward Moriarity, SFM (1914-1983), Rev. Ronald J. Walsh (1915-1980), Msgr. William Hogan (1916-1999), Rev. John Jos Moriarity, SFM (1917-Ret), Rev. Gregory Pumphrey (1919-1995), Rev. Linus Coady (1932--), Rev. Edward J. Hearn (1932-LPH),& Rev. William Hearn (1949--)

PRIESTS BORN IN PARISH: (3)

Spaniards Bay: Msgr. Joseph Peddle (1904-1976). Bay Roberts: Msgr. Walter Brennan (1880-) Tilton: & Rev. John W. Peddle (1932--)

HARBOUR MAIN

PRIEST FROM HARBOUR MAIN (6)

Rev. Richard F. Walsh (1842-1914?); VRev. Dean Matthew O'Rourke (1852c-1920c); Rev. James M. Joy (1870-1933); Rev. Francis R. Terry (1915-1952); Rev. Frederick J. Terry (1924--); & Rev. Linus Wall, SFM.

RELIGIOUS FROM HARBOUR MAIN (15)

Rev. Bro. P.V. Strapp, CFC; Rev. Bro. DePaul Costello. Sr. Nano Parsley, pbvm; Sr. Tarcisia Power, pbvm; Sr. Innoventa Donnelly, SFP; Sr. Mary Parsley; Sr. Gregory Gorman; Sr. Dolorosa Hannon; Sr. Patrice Kennedy; Sr. Egbert Myers; Sr. M. Lawrence; Sr. Angela March, pbvm; (Bishop March niece) Sr. Margaret Cashin, pbvm; Sr. Henry Woodford, pbvm; & Sr. Angeline Kennedy, pbvm.

HOLYROOD

PRIESTS BORN IN HOLYROOD (6)

Msgr. William Veitch (1846-1917); Msgr. Mark P. Dwyer (1885-1953); Rev. Leo A. Walsh, OSB; Rev. Edward A. Walsh (1919--); VRev. Dean Matthew O'Rourke & Rev. Philip J. Lewis (1933--).

SISTERS BORN IN HOLYROOD (18)

Sr. Margaret Barron, csm; Sr. Annette Hawco, rsm; Sr. Cecilia Joy, rsm; Sr. Laurenti Timmons, pbvm; Sr. Celine Veitch, rsm; Sr. Mary Rosario, St. Aquinas Hicks, Sr. Mary Kelly, rsm; Sr. M. Assumpta Veitch, rsm; Sr. Isabelle Woodford pbvm; Sr. John Bernadette Carroll, sc; Sr. Lucius Joy, cnd; Sr. Genevieve Mullowney, pbvm; St. Sarah Hynes, pbvm; Sr. Elizabeth Veitch, sc; Mother Mary Xavier Mullowney, pbvm; Mother Margaret Mary Mullowney, pbvm; & Sr. Ariadne Mullowney, sc, Holy Cross (in Montana).

KINGS COVE

PRIESTS FROM PARISH (2)

Rev. Francis J. Aylward (1950--) & Rev. J. Kevin Barker (Open Hall).

RELIGIOUS FROM PARISH (3)

Sr. Monica Matthews rsm, Sr. M. Jerome Walker rsm & Sr. M. Benignus Mullowney rsm.

NORTHERN BAY

PRIESTS FROM NORTHERN BAY PARISH (11)

Rev. Laurence Hayden, CssR, (Kingston) (1859-1909); Bishop John March (1863-1940); Rev. John Fitzgerald, (Western Bay) (1874-1940); Rev. Edward Molloy, CssR, (Gussets Cove) (1881-1953); Rev. James A. Hinchey (1891-1951); VRev. Thomas D. O'Neill (1892-1956); Rev. Edward Molloy, (Gussets Cove), (1901-); VRev. Michael J. Kinsella, (Jobs Cove) (1904-1965); Rev. Morgan Johnson (1907-1978), (Jobs Cove); Rev. Luke Woodrow (1921-1999) (LPH); & Rev. Gregory Hogan, (Western Bay).

NORTH RIVER

PRIESTS FROM NORTH RIVER (3)

Msgr. Walter Brennan, (Bay Roberts) (1887-1965); Rev. Thomas M. Morrissey, SFM, (1914-1992); & Rev. A. Wayne Cummings (1950--).

RELIGIOUS FROM NORTH RIVER ( )

Sr. M. Emeria Cormack, rsm; Sr. Katherine Bellamy, rsm; Sr. Irene Neville, rsm; Sr. Brigid Morrissey, rsm; Sr. Phyllis Corbett, rsm; & Sr. Rosalie Morrissey, pbvm.

PLATE COVE

SISTERS BORN IN PLATE COVE (13)

Sr. Annette Keough, rsm; Sr. Helena Murphy, pbvm; Sr. Cecelia Philpott, pbvm; Sr. Mary Keough; Sr. Susan Keough, csm; Sr. Mary Keough, csm; Sr. Mary Walsh, csm; Sr. Elizabeth Murphy, pbvm; Sr. Rosarii Philpott, pbvm; Sr. Miriam Heaney, pbvm; Sr. Benignus Maloney, rsm; Sr. Agnes Brennan, rsm & Sr. Theresa Ryan, rsm.

PORT UNION

PRIESTS FROM PARISH (4)

Rev. Aidan Murphy CssR; Rev. Gerald Murphy CssR; Rev. William McC Murphy & Rev. Andrew Nolan, CssR (All from Catalina).

RELIGIOUS FROM PARISH (3)

Sr. M. Mark Hennebury, rsm; Sr. M. Carmel Peters, rsm;& Sr. Marie Aidan Murphy, rsm (Catalina).

ST. ALBAN'S

PRIEST BORN IN ST. ALBAN'S (1)

Rev. Gary Hoskins

SISTERS BORN IN ST. ALBAN'S (2)

Sr. Jane Marie Collier; rsm & Sr. Maria Stella Willcott, rsm.

ST.BRENDAN'S

PRIESTS FROM ST. BRENDANS (2)

Rev. Michael R. Hynes (1929--),& Rev. Michael J. Walsh (1937--).

RELIGIOUS FROM ST. BRENDANS (6)

Sr. Anna V.Turner, gsic, Sr. Mary L. Whelan, rsm, Sr. M. Loyola Hynes, rsm, Sr. M. Bridgeman, MM. Sr. M. Digna Beresford, & Sr. Anne Mackey.

WHITBOURNE

PRIEST FROM WHITBOURNE (2)

Msgr. Ronald McD Murphy (1900-1985) & Rev. Robert Delaney, CssR.

RELIGIOUS BURIED IN PARISHES

AVONDALE

PRIEST BURIED IN AVONDALE (1)

Rev. Richard F. Walsh (1842-1914)

BONAVISTA

PRIEST BURIED IN BONAVISTA (1)

Rev. Matthew Scanlan (1803-1871), under Church.

BRIGUS

PRIESTS BURIED IN BRIGUS (8)

Rev. Dean Mackin (1857); Rev. Edward O'Keefe (1871); Rev. Bernard Duffy (1873); Rev. Edward Walsh (1912); Rev. Richard Shean (1927); Rev. James Walker (1927); Msgr. Joseph Murphy (1944); & Rev. Richard M. Walker (1859-1941).

SISTERS BURIED IN PARISH (4)

Sr. M. of the Angel Banks, rsm, Sr. M. Gonzaga Coady, rsm, Sr. M. Ultan Mullowney, & Sr. M. Veronica Crawley.

CARBONEAR

PRISTS BURIED IN CARBONEAR (9)

Rev. James Gleeson (1849), Rev. James W. Donnelly (1926), Msgr. Felix D. McCarthy (1944), Rev. William T. Cullen (1948), Rev. John P. Mackey (1952), Rev. Dr. Edward J. Jones (1964), Msgr. Joseph W. Peddle (1976), Msgr. Edward O'Brien (1986); & Rev. Lawrence George (1992).

SISTER BURIED IN PARISH (18)

Sr. Antonio Shanley (1889), Sr. Agatha Walsh (1897), Sr. Ignatius Phelan (1899), Sr. Claver Kenny (1900), Sr. Joseph Gould (1903), Sr. Aloysius Eagan (1905), Sr. Veronica Collins (1907), Sr. Michael Luther (1907), Sr. Germaine O'Reilly (1909), Sr. Francis McCarthy (1910), Sr. Magdalen Brown (1915), Sr. Patrick Gould (1917), Sr. Gertrude Finn (1923), Sr. Genevieve Mullowney (1939), Sr. Teresa McCarthy (1943), Sr. Carmela Finn (1956), Sr. Clare Mackey (1961) & Sr. Evarista Waddleton (1970)

COLLIERS

PRISTS BURIED IN COLLIERS (1)

Rev. Thomas D. O'Neill (1892-1956)

CONCEPTION HARBOUR

PRISTS BURIED IN CONCEPTION HARBOUR (2)

Msgr. Wm Veitch (1917). Rev. Patrick Hearn. (1938)

GRANDSFALLSWINDSORCATHEDRL

PRIESTS BURIED IN GRAND FALLS (2)

Msgr. W. P. Finn & Rev. Patrick McCormack.

SISTERS BURIED IN GRAND FALLS (1)

Sr. Francesca Green, pbvm

HARBOUR GRACE

PRIESTS BURIED IN HARBOUR GRACE:(18)

Rev. Patrick Phelan (1799), VRev. Thomas Ewer (1833), VRev. Charles Dalton (1859),; Bishop John Dalton (1869) Buried under Church, Rev. James F. Ryan (1893), Rev. Stephen Flynn (1899), Rev. John T. Colbert (1904), Rev. Thomas E. Lynch (1905),; Bishop John March (1940), Rev. William J. Hennebury (1947), Rev. Francis R. Terry (1952); Rev. Thomas O'Neill (1956), Rev. Walter Walsh (1958), Msgr. William H. Casey (1962), Bishop John M. O'Neill (1974), Rev. Ronald J. Walsh (1980), Msgr. Joseph M. O'Brien (1987); & Msgr. William P. Hogan. (1999).

SISTERS BURIED IN HARBOUR GRACE: (16)

Sr. Rose Barter (1860), Sr. DeSales Lovelock (1868), Sr. Xaverius Lynch (1882), Sr. DeSales Lovelock (1885), Sr. Josephine French (1886), Sr. Veronica Power (1887), Sr. Clare Lovelock (1897), Sr. Agnes Banuil (1901), Sr. Catherine Flynn (1910), Sr. Teresa King (1910), Sr. De Pazzi Lovelock (1914), Sr. Francis Flynn (1914), Sr. John Shortall (1915), Sr. Margaret Northcott (1929), Sr. Anna Whelan (1949), & Sr. Patrick O'Keefe (1950).

HARBOUR MAIN

PRISTS BURIED IN HARBOUR MAIN (6)

VRev. Jeremiah O'Donnell, buried under church; Rev. Patrick O'Donnell, buried under church, VRev. Kyran Walsh, buried under church, VRev. James Brown, buried under church, VRev. John Roe, buried under church. Msgr. Mark Dwyer buried in regular cemetery.

HOLYROOD

PRISTS BURIED IN HOLYROOD (8)

Rev. Gregory Battcock, (1854-1910), buried under Church. VRev. William P. Finn (1868-1935); Rev. Jeremiah J. Howard, (1893-1976); Rev. William McC Murphy (1896-1964); Rev. Michael J. Kinsella, (1904-1965); Msgr. R.T. Woodford (1920-1988); Rev. James Kinsella & Rev. Edward M. Shea. (1915-2001).

KING'S COVE

PRISTS BURIED IN KING'S COVE (2)

Rev. Thomas J. Waldren (1808-1854) & Rev. Nicholas Devereux (1845).

NORTHERN BAY

PRISTS BURIED IN NORTHERN BAY (1)

Rev. James Cummins, buried under Church (1875)

NORTH RIVER

PRISTS BURIED IN NORTH RIVER (4)

Rev. G.A. Thibault (1874-1934); Rev. S.J. Whalen (1923); Msgr. M. F. Dinn (1955); & Rev. J. P. Hogan. (1971).

TRINITY

PRISTS BURIED IN TRINITY (2)

Rev. Philip A. Carolan & VRev. Walter M. Tarahan.

Chapter 28

LIFE SUMMARIES

PRIESTS BORN IN GRAND FALLS

1926- Active	REV. JAMES A. DAVIS, CssR. Ordained: 18 June 1950 – Ontario Currently: Serving in New Brunswick
1918-1994	REV. MATTHEW BLACKMORE, CssR, Age 75. Ordained: 20 June 1943 - Ontario Died: Alberta Buried: Edmonton
1918-1990	REV. NORBERT MACKENZIE, S.J., Age 71. Ordained: 27 June 1948 - Toronto Died: Canada Buried: Ontario
1918-1993	REV. VINCENT MACKENZIE, S.J., Age 75. Ordained: 27 June 1948 - Toronto Died: Canada Buried: Ontario
1929-1965	REV. PATRICK A. MCCORMACK, Age 35. Ordained: 12 June 1955 – Grand Falls Died: Gander Buried: Grand Falls.
1943- Active	REV. WILLIAM J. HOULAHAN. Ordained: 11 June 1967 – Grand Falls Currently: PP, Northern Bay
1924- Retired	REV. DONALD J. MURRAY, MSF. Ordained: 28 May 1955 – St. Louis Currently: Retired, San Antonio, TX

REV. JAMES A. DAVIS, CssR

Rev. James Aloysius Davis, CssR was born in Grand Falls on 14 Oct 1926, the 11th child of 16 children of John Davis and Gertrude Hatch. He was baptized the same day by Rev. James A. Hinchey, who he is named after. He attended Notre Dame Academy under Presentation Sisters. After grade XI, he went to St. Clement's Redemporist Centre for students in Toronto. He attended St. Michael's College High School under the Basilian Fathers in 1943. He began his novitiate at St. Peter's Parish in St. John, New Brunswick and finished at St. Mary's College of Brockville making his profession of vows there on 15 Aug 1944. He then proceeded to St. Alphonsus Redemporist Seminary in Woodstock, Ontario for the next 6 years **(1944-1950).** He was ordained in the Seminary Chapel on 18 June 1950, at age 23+ by Bishop John C. Cody, He celebrated his first Solemn High Mass at Immaculate Conception Church in Grand Falls, with Rt. Rev. William P. Finn acting as Deacon. The sermon was preached by Rev. Gerald Murphy, CssR of Whitbourne. His first assignment was assistant to the Novice Master at Marianella Novitiate L'Abord a Plouffe, Quebec from 1950-1953. He did his curacy at St. Anne's Parish in Montreal from 1953-1955. In 1955, he studied at Assumption University in Windsor, Ontario where he obtained his B.A. In 1956, he was assigned as a Professor of French at the Junior Seminary (St. Mary's College) for two years. In 1964, he obtained his M.A. from Laval University, Quebec City, Quebec. In 1968 he volunteered for Pastoral Work in the Redemporist Missions in the Diocese of Joazeiro, Brazil. In 1973 he returned to his native shores to St. Teresa's Parish in St. John's to preach missions and help in parish work. In 1981, with the death of Rev. Ronald Walsh, PP, of St. Brendan's, Fr. Jim performed the weekend liturgy there for a couple months. In 1988, he transferred back to St. Peter's Parish in St. John, NB. Then back to St. Teresa's Parish in St. John's for 3 ½ years. In Jan 1994, he was back at St. Peter's Parish. He celebrated his 50th Anniversary of profession on 15 Aug 1994 and celebrated his Golden Jubilee on 18 June 2000 at St. Peter's. He is known in the Redemporist Community for his dedication to the league of Mary and the Charismatic Prayer Movement; Fr. Davis is still working at St. Peter's Parish in St. John, NB.

REV. MATTHEW BLACKMORE, CssR

Rev. Matthew Blackmore, CssR was born in Grand Falls on 28 October 1918 to James Blackmore and Josephine Ellen Hamilton. He attended Notre Dame Academy in Grand Falls from 1924-1935. The last two, was under the direction of the Presentation Sisters of the Blessed Virgin Mary. Upon graduation at N.D.A., he proceeded to the St. Mary's College (Redemptorist minor seminary) in Brockville, Ontario. On August 2nd, 1938, he was professed under novice master Arthur Conlogue in Saint John, New Brunswick. From 1938-1944, he attended St. Alphonsus Seminary in Woodstock, Ontario. He made his final profession on 2 September 1941 at the Seminary. Rev. Blackmore was ordained a Redemptorist priest on 20 June 1943 at the Seminary chapel by Bishop Martin Johnson of Nelson, B.C. In September of 1944, he began his six months second novitiate under Anthony McBriarty in Woodstock. In 1945 he was stationed to St. Mary's parish in Saskatoon until 1948. He was in charge of the out mission of

St. Gabriel's Athabasco in 1947. He became parish priest at Our Lady of Perpetual Help parish, Dawson's Creek from 1948-1951. He was then stationed at St. Alphonsus Parish, East Kildonan Winnipeg from 1951-1956. From 1956-1961, he was at Yorkton, Saskatchewan, and Winnipeg. In 1975, he was named hospital chaplain at St. Paul's Hospital in St. Joseph's Parish, Moose Jaw, Saskatchewan. In 1982, the Edmonton Province elected him one of their representatives at the Peter Donders beautification ceremonies in Rome. In 1986, he was transferred to Our Lady of Perpetual Help Parish in Calgary, Alberta. He remained there until 1989, when he was transferred to Saskatoon in semi-retirement. He died on 23 June 1994, age 75 in St. Anthony's Home in Moose Jaw, Alberta. Fr. Blackmore is buried in Edmonton.

REV. NORBERT J. MACKENZIE, S.J.

Rev. Norbert J. Mackenzie was born in Grand Falls on 6 July 1918 son of John Mackenzie and Gertrude French. He had a twin brother, Vincent. He was a student at Notre Dame Academy in Grand Falls for 9 years. He entered the Society of Jesus with his twin brother Vincent, on 31 October 1935. He was ordained a Jesuit Priest on 27 June 1948 at the Jesuit Seminary Chapel in Toronto, with his twin brother Vincent. He spent most of his Priestly Ministry in Canada and the USA. He celebrated his 50th Golden Jubilee as a member of the Jesuit Order on 31 October 1985. Fr. Norbert Mackenzie died on 6 Feb 1990, age71. He was a Jesuit for 55 years and a Jesuit Priest for 42 years.

REV. VINCENT MACKENZIE, S.J.

Rev. Vincent Mackenzie, S.J. was born in Grand Falls on 6 July 1918 son of John Mackenzie and Gertrude French. He had a twin brother, Norbert. He was a student at Notre Dame Academy in Grand Falls for 9 years. He entered the Society of Jesus with his twin brother Vincent, on 31 October 1935. He studied Philosophy and Theology at the Jesuit Seminary and Bellarmine College, West Baden, Indiana. He was ordained a Jesuit Priest on 27 June 1948 by Cardinal James MacGuigan. Before and after his Ordination he taught at Kingston's Regiopolis College, pursuing studies in library science at the Catholic University of America in Washington, D.C. In 1953 he assumed responsibility for the Regis College Library and in 1961 oversaw its transfer twice and finally to a location near the University of Toronto. He served in administrative capacities and from 1976-1987 he was Vice-Superior of the Jesuit faculty residence. He celebrated his 50th Golden Jubilee as a member of the Jesuit Order on 31 October 1985. During his vacation periods, he assisted with pastoral ministry among the Native communities. Fr. Vincent Mackenzie entered into Eternal Life on 15 September 1993, age 75. He was a Jesuits for 58 years and a Jesuit Priest for 45 years.

REV. PATRICK A. MCCORMACK

Rev. Patrick Andrew McCormack was born in Grand Falls on 26 Apr 1929 to John McCormack and Francis. From 1935-1947 he attended Notre Dame Academy in Grand Falls under the direction of the Presentation Sisters of the Blessed Virgin Mary. He attended St. Bon's from 1947-1950 and St. Peter's Seminary for 5 years from 1950-1955. He was ordained at the Co-Cathedral of the Immaculate Conception in Grand Falls by Bishop O'Neill at Grand Falls on 12 June 1955, age 26. His first assignment as curate at King's Cove for a few months and then assigned as Parish Priest Sacred Heart Parish in Conche for 8 years from 1955-1963. While at Conche, he was instrumental at getting the Airstrip there. From 1963 until his death, he was assistant at St. Joseph's Parish in Gander. He died in Gander on 29 Mar 1965 at age 36. Solemn Pontifical Mass for the young priest was celebrated on Wednesday, 31 March by His Excellency Most Rev. John M. O'Neill with Rev. E.T. Bromley (a former parishioner) as Deacon and Rev. William Ryan (a classmate) as Sub-deacon. The Master of Ceremonies was Rt. Rev. William Hogan, Rector of the Cathedral. The Funeral Eulogy was given by Rev. Francis P Meaney of Windsor. He was priest for almost 10 years. There is a room in the Hospital in St. Anthony named in his honor and on 26 November 1965, the newly formed Knights of Columbus council in Gander was named "Fr. Patrick McCormack Council" in his honor.

REV. WILLIAM J. HOULAHAN

Rev. William Joseph Houlahan was born in Grand Falls on 6 December 1943 to William Houlahan and Rita Sullivan. He attended Notre Dame Academy under the direction of the Presentation Sisters of the Blessed Virgin Mary from 1949-1958. In 1958-1961, he attended St. Michael's High School under the Irish Christian Brothers. Upon graduation, he proceeded to St. Paul's Seminary in Ottawa, Ontario until 1967. He was ordained at the Cathedral of the Immaculate Conception in Grand Falls by His Excellency Most Rev. John M. O'Neill, on 11 June 1967. From 1967-1970, he was a curate under Rev. F.P. Meaney at St. Joseph's Parish in Windsor. He then proceeded to St. John the Apostle Parish in Brent's Cove, White Bay as Parish Priest. He was appointed Parish Priest of his home parish in Grand Falls in 1974. In 1979, he became Co-pastor of Conche and St. Anthony with Rev. William Hearn. Rev. Hearn was reappointed in 1981 and was succeeded by Rev. Francis J. Aylward. It is note worthy to say that Rev. Houlahan and Rev. Aylward were the last Grand Falls Diocesan priests to serve in Conche and St. Anthony. The northern peninsula was given over to the Diocese of St. George's in 1984. In 1984, he became to twelfth parish priest of Sts. Peter and Paul Parish in Harbour Main. Along with his parish work in Harbour Main, he was given Administration duties of St. Anne's Parish in Conception Harbour. In 1988, Conception Harbour was attached to Assumption parish in

Avondale. With the retirement of Rev. Houlahan's former Parish Priest, Rt. Rev. William Hogan, and the lack of Diocesan priests, Holy Cross Parish in Holyrood was joined with Sts Peter and Paul Parish in Harbour Main. It is note worthy to say that Holyrood was originally a mission of Harbour Main until 1883. In 1991, Rev. Bill went on a sabbatical year. He celebrated his Silver Jubilee on 11 June 1992. Upon his return to active ministry in the Diocese, he was appointed to St. Patrick's Parish in Plate Cove and Sts Peter and Paul Parish in King's Cove. In 1997, he was appointed to St. Patrick's Parish in Brigus and All Hallows Parish in North River. He was appointed to Corpus Christi Parish in Northern Bay and Assumption Parish in Bay de Verde in the Great Jubilee of 2000. Fr. Houlahan is currently assigned to Northern Bay.

REV. DONALD J MURRAY, M.S.F

Rev. Donald Joseph Murray was born in Grand Falls on 3 Oct 1924 to Henry Murray and Ellen Power. He received his early education at Notre Dame Academy In Grand Falls. He attended The Keinok Seminary in St. Louis, Missouri, USA. He was ordained a Missionary of the Holy Family priest on 28 May 1955 at age 30 in St. Louis. That following September he was assigned to work in Mexican American parishes in South central and South Texas. He was an associate Pastor for five years at Our Lady of Guadalupe Parish in Seguin and Sacred Heart Mission in Gonzales. He was then a Pastor for thirty-one years in the following Parishes: Our Lady of Guadalupe in Cuero; Sacred Heart of the Assumption in the Kio Grande Valley and the Holy Family in New Brianfels about 25 miles North of San Antonio. He celebrated his Silver Jubilee on 28 May 1980. Through the many years of and with the outstanding assistance of the parishioners, he was able to remodel two churches, build three religious Education centres, build three parish halls and build one Rectory. Each project was paid for before moving to the next assignment. Fr. Murray, M.S.F. is currently living in retirement in Texas, USA at age 78.

A Special Tribute to the Mackenzie Twins

Grand Falls has a special pride in having the only known twin brothers in Newfoundland history that were priests. These twin brothers were born in Grand Falls on 6 July 1918 and they both entered the Society of Jesuit on 31 October 1935. They were both ordained on 27 June 1948 as Jesuit Priests at the Jesuit Seminary Chapel in Toronto.

Revs. Norbert and Vincent Mackenzie, S.J. taken shortly after their ordination.

Revs. Vincent and Norbert Mackenzie, S.J. taken in Grand Falls, NL during their Golden Jubilee of Profession in 1985.

The Mackenzie Twin Brothers

The Mackenzie Brother Priests saying Mass at a side altar in the Cathedral in honour of their parents.

Mrs. Paula Bradbury viewing the headstones of her brothers, Revs. Vincent and Norbert Mackenzie, S.J., in Pickering, Ontario.

Chapter 29

PRESENTATION SISTERS

That served in Grand Falls Parish Convents

AVONDALE

Assumption Convent
1957-not closed
Superior: S. Gertrude Bishop

Sr. Dorothy Baird; Sr. Joan Baldwin; Sr. St. Jude Barry, Sr. Christine Davis; Sr. Gertrude Bishop; Sr. Madeline Bouzane; Sr. Chrysostom Brennan; Sr. Catherine Burke; Sr. Benedicta Burt; Sr. Sandy Butler; Sr. Matthew Byrne; Sr. Rita Cardoulis; Sr. Rosalie Carey; Sr. Marilyn Costello; Sr. Basil Curtis; Sr. Regina Davis; Sr. Paula Delahunty; Sr. Alice Dower; Sr. Liguori Downey; Sr. Mary Theresa Doyle; Sr. Elizabeth Duff; Sr. Fabian Dunne; Sr. Philippa Ezekiel; Sr. Mary Farrell; Sr. Tarcisia Fewer; Sr. Elizabeth Ann Gosse; Sr. Shirley Hogan; Sr. Agnes Hutchings; Sr. Anna Hynes; Sr. Catherine Hynes; Sr. Madonna Hynes; Sr. Mary Johnson; Sr. M. Gabriella Kelly; St. Patricia King; Sr. Margaret Lannon; Sr. Elizabeth Rae Lee; Sr. M. Seana Lee; Sr. Inez Marche; Sr. Frances Molloy; Sr. Mary Molloy; Sr. Honora Marie Moore; Sr. Marie Murphy; Sr. M. Dominica McCarthy; Sr. Angela McGrath; Sr. Philip Marie McHugh; Sr. Julia O'Connell; Sr. M. Baptista O'Keefe; Sr. Barbara O'Keefe; Sr. Margaret O'Keefe; Sr. Nano Parsley; Sr. Bride Power; Sr. Emmanuel Power, Sr. Judith Power; Sr. Regina Quigley; Sr. Kathleen Rex; Sr. Marie Roche; Sr. Emma Rooney; Sr. Marie Theresa Ryan; Sr. Kieran Seaward; Sr. Margaret Smith; Sr. Carol Anne Staples; Sr. Sylvia Staples; Sr. Olivera Stapleton; Sr. Anna St. Croix; Sr. Mary Taylor; Sr. Patricia Tobin; Sr. Mary Waddleton; Sr. Annette Walsh; Sr. Doris Walsh; Sr. Fidelma Walsh; Sr. Theresa Marie Walsh; Sr. Elizabeth Whelan; Sr. Gladys Whelan; Sr. Jean Whelan; Sr. Josephine Whelan; Sr. Genevieve White;and Sr. Isabel Woodford.

BADGER

Our Lady Perpetual Help
1953-1988
Superior: S. Pancratia Ennis

Sr. S. Constance Barker; Sr. S. M. Dorothea Barnable; Sr. S. M. Christine Bavis; Sr. S. Helen Bonia; Sr. S. Philomena Christopher; Sr. S. M. Dominic Cousins; Sr. S. Margaret Devine; Sr. S. Teresa Devine; Sr. S. M. Fabian Dunne; Sr. S. Joan Dunphy; Sr. S. M. Pancratia Ennis; Sr. S.M. Alban Gough; Sr. S. Rita Johnston; Sr. S. M. Colette Kavanagh; Sr. S. Carmel Kelly; Sr. S. Rosemary Kennedy; Sr. S. M. Consilio King; Sr. S. M. Evangelista King; Sr. S. Margaret McCarthy; Sr. S. Margaret McLoughlin; St. S. Magdalen O'Brien; Sr. S. M. Julia O'Connell; Sr. S. M. Alexandra Pinsent; Sr. S. Laurane Pittman; Sr. S. Anselma Power; Sr. S. Bride Power; Sr. S. M. Winifred Power; Sr. S. Margaret Ryan; Sr. S. M. Augusta Thorne; Sr. S. Mary Taylor; Sr. S. Monica Woodrow; Sr. S. Maureen Whelan and Sr. S. M. Timothy Yeo.

BRENTS COVE

Regina Coeli Convent
1968-1997
Superior: S. Theresa Devine

Sr. Bernadette Aucoin; Sr. Joan Baldwin; Sr. Genevieve Bouzane; Sr. Rita Cardoulis; Sr. Marilyn Costello; Sr. Paula Delahunty; Sr. Madeline Devine; Sr. Marilyn Doyle; Sr. M. Theresa Doyle; Sr. Barbara Felix; Sr. Marie Furey; Sr. Bernadette Marie Hynes; Sr. Rosemary Kennedy; Sr. Agnes Kenny; Sr. Theresa Keyes; Sr. Margaret Lannon; Sr. Brendan Lynch; Sr. Margaret McLoughlin; Sr. Rita McNeil; Sr. Doris O'Keefe; Sr. Laurane Pittman; Sr. Consolata Power; Sr. Elizabeth Quinlan; Sr. Kostka Reddy; Sr. Jean Ryan; Sr. Kathleen Ryan; Sr. Mary Ryan; Sr. Lillian Wakeham; Sr. Doris Walsh; Sr. Elizabeth Whelan; Sr. Maureen Whelan; Sr. Joan White and Sr. Monica Woodrow.

BUCHANS

St. Margaret's Convent
1953-1992
Superior: S. Francesca Green

Sr. S. Teresa Antle; Sr. S. Bernadette Aucoin; Sr. S. M. Theresa Aylward; Sr. S.M. Louise Barker; Sr. S. M. St. Jude Barry; Sr. S. Sarah Beresford; Sr. S. Madeline Bouzane; Sr. S. Mary Brophy; Sr. S. Rita Cardoulis; Sr. S. Philomena Christopher; Sr. S. Patrick Curran; Sr. S. M. Basil Curtis; Sr. S. M. Xavier Dalton; Sr. S. Betty Daniels; Sr. S. M. Regina Davis; Sr. S. Liguori Downey; Sr. Alice Mary Duggan; Sr. S. M. Alphonsus Duggan; Sr. S. Mary Ennis; Sr. S. Mary Farrell; Sr. S. Marie Furey; Sr. S. M. Remigius Gearin; Sr. S. M. Callista Green; Sr. Mother Francesca Greene; Sr. S. Lois Marie Greene; Sr. S. Eulalie Harding; Sr. S. Anne Hickey; Sr. S. Shirley Hogan; Sr. S. M. Colette Kavanagh; Sr. S. M. Ricarda Kelly; Sr. S. Rosemary Kennedy; Sr. S. Dorothy Kenny; Sr. S. Patricia King; Sr. S. M. Evangelista King; Sr. S. Margaret Lannon; Sr. S. Raphael Lawlor; Sr. S. Thomas Marie Lee; Sr. S. Clotilde Martin; Sr. S. Margaret McGrath; Sr. Carmelita McNeil; Sr. S. Clotilde Meaney; Sr. S. Cabrini Miles; Sr. S. Amelia Mooney; Sr. S. Magdalen O'Brien; Sr. S. Catherine O'Neill; Sr. S. Mary Purcell; Sr. S. Laurane Pittman; Sr. S. Consolata Power; Sr. S. Kostka Reddy; Sr. S. Myra Rumsey; Sr. S. Helen Ryan; Sr. S. Rosaria Shea; Sr. S. Eugenie Tapper; Sr. S. Mary Taylor; Sr. S. Patricia Tracey; Sr. S. M. Anita Wall; Sr. S. Fidelma Walsh; Sr. S. Gertrude Wall; Sr. S. Hilary Walsh; Sr. S. Maureen Whelan; Sr. S. Genevieve White; Sr. S. Joan White;and Sr. S. Patricia Whittle.

CARBONEAR

St. Joseph's Convent
1852-not closed
Superior: S. Ignatius Phelan

Sr. M. Gabriel Antle; Sr. M. Anne Aylward; Sr. Dorothy Baird; Sr. M. Pauline Barry; Sr. M. Gertrude Bishop; Sr. Helen Bonia; Sr. M. Cyprian Bouzane; Sr. M. Patrice Bourgeois; Sr. Bride Budgell; Sr. Catherine Burke; Sr. M. Matthew Byrne; Sr. Magdalen Brown; Sr. M. Rosalie Carey; Sr. M. Bernardine Clinton; Sr. M. Sebastian Coffey; Sr. M. Veronica Collins: Sr. Dorothy Corrigan; Sr. Helen Corrigan; Sr. M. Patrick Curran; Sr. M. Basil Curtis; Sr. Angela Curtis; Sr. Lucilla Daley; Sr. M. Paula Delahunty; Sr. Margaret Devine; Sr. M. Madeline Devine; Sr. M. Fabian Dunne; Sr. M. Wilma Dunphy; Sr. Aloysius Eagan; Sr. M. Xaveria Fardy; Sr. Mary Farrell; Sr. Tarcisia Fewer; Sr. M. Carmella Finn; Sr. M. Gertrude Finn; Sr. M. Zita Gardiner; Sr. M. Joseph Gould; Sr. M. Patrick Gould; Sr. M. Anthony Greene; Sr. M. Martha Greene; Sr. M. Columba Hannon; Sr. M. Beatrice Healey; Sr. M. Columba Hepditch; Sr. Agnes Hutchings; Sr. M. Madonna Hynes; Sr. Sarah Hynes; Sr. Mother M. Edward Jackman; Sr. M. Colette Kavanagh; Sr. Carmel Kelly; Sr. Gabriella Kelly; Sr. Elizabeth Kennedy; Sr. M. Joachim Kennedy; Sr. Josephine Kennedy; Sr. M. Perpetua Kennedy; Sr. M. Claver Kenny; Sr. Theresa Keyes; Sr. M. DeLourdes King; Sr. M. Evangelista King; Sr. Frances King; Sr. M. Stanislaus Lawlor; Sr. M. Raphael Lawlor; Sr. Mother M. Clare Mackey; Sr. M. Berchmans Maher; Sr. M. St. Stephen Marche; Sr. Frances Molloy; Sr. Mary Molloy; Sr. Anastasia Moore; Sr. Rosalie Morrissey; Sr. M. Genevieve Mullowney; Sr. Mother Margaret Mary Mullowney; Sr. M. Charles Murphy; Sr. Helen Murphy; Sr. M. Bonaventure McCarthy; Sr. Frances McCarthy; Sr. Rita McCarthy; Sr. M. Teresa McCarthy; Sr. M. Ignatius McGettigan; Sr. M. Josephine McIntosh; Sr. Angela McKenzie; Sr. Carmel Nolan; Sr. Paulette Nugent; Sr. M. Calasanctius O'Brien; Sr. Magdalen O'Brien; Sr. Marie O'Brien; Sr. M. Julia O'Connell; Sr. Germaine O'Reilly; Sr. M. Ignatius Phelan; Sr. M. Cecilia Philpott; Sr. M. Rosarii Philpott; Sr. Laurane Pittman; Sr. Bride Power; Sr. M. Consolata Power; Sr. Mary Purcell; Sr. Regina Quigley; Sr. Cornelius Quinlan; Sr. M. Kostka Reddy; Sr. Kathleen Rex; Sr. M. Agatha Roche; Sr. Marie Roche; Sr. Margaret Ryan; Sr. M. J. Frances Ryan; Sr. Mary Ryan; Sr. M. Antonia Shanley; Sr. M. Dorothy Snow; Sr. Catherine Sullivan; Sr. M. Patrice Sullivan; Sr. Frances Sutton; Sr. Mary Taylor; Sr. M. Laurenti Timmons; Sr. Assumpta Thorne; Sr. Barbara Tobin; Sr. Patricia Tobin; Sr. M. Evarista Waddleton; Sr. Mary Waddleton; Sr. Lillian Wakeham; Sr. Agatha Walsh; Sr. Annette Walsh; Sr. Elizabeth Whelan; Sr. Jean Whelan; Sr. Isabella White; Sr. Ellen Whitty and Sr. Isabella Woodford.

CONCEPTION HARBOUR

Immaculate Conception Convent
1869 - Mercy Nuns

GANDER

Presentation Convent
1957-not closed
Superior: Frances O'Toole
(Not Available)

GRAND FALLS-WINDSOR

Nagle Hall & St. Catherine Center
1967-not closed
Superior: S. Margaret Smith

Sr. S. M. Margaret Barker; Sr. S. M. Christine Bavis; Sr. S. Helen Bonia; Sr. S. M. Celestine Bouzane; Sr. S. Madeline Bouzane; Sr. S. M. Chrysostom Byrne; Sr. S. M. Bride Budgell; Sr. S. Anita Cardoulis; Sr. S. Margaret Carter; Sr. S. M. Philomena Christopher; Sr. S. Rose Coady; Sr. S. M. Basil Curtis; Sr. S. M. Sebastian Coffey; Sr. S. Elizabeth Daniels; Sr. S. Paula Delahunty; Sr. S. Mary Dillon; Sr. S. Alice Dower; Sr. S. Mary Dower; Sr. S. Theresa Doyle; Sr. S. M. Fabian Dunne; Sr. S. Eileen Emberley; Sr. S. M. Concepta Evans; Sr.. S. M. Philippa Ezekiel; Sr. S. Marie Furey; Sr. S. Mary Gibbons; Sr. S. Yvonne Marie Grace; Sr. S. Dolores Hall; Sr. S. M. Eileen Hayes; Sr. S. Miriam Heaney; Sr. S. Shirley Hogan; Sr. S. M. Angelique Hollett; Sr. S. Helen Hoskins; Sr. S. Lorraine Hoskins; Sr. S. Agnes Hutchings; Sr. S. Bertrand Hynes; Sr. S. Rita Johnston; Sr. S. M. Colette Kavanagh; Sr. S. Josephine Kennedy; Sr. S. M. John Regis Kennedy; Sr. S. M. Mark Kennedy; Sr. S. Mary Kennedy; Sr. S. Agnes Kenny; Sr. S. M. Evangelista King; Sr. S. Frances King; Sr. S. Patricia King; Sr. S. M. DeLourdes King; Sr. S. Elizabeth Lee; Sr. S. M. Theresa Lee; Sr. S. Georgina Long; Sr. S. M. Inez Marche; Sr. S. Miriam Martin; Sr. S. Catherine Meaney; Sr. S. Amelia Mooney; Sr. S. Anastasia Moore; Sr. S. Rosalie Morrissey; Sr. S. M. Charles Murphy; Sr. S. M. Thaddeus McCann; Sr. S. Margaret McCarthy; Sr. S. Sheila McCarthy; Sr. S. Angela McGrath; Sr. S. Carmel Nolan; Sr. S. M. Julia O'Connell; Sr. S. Catherine O'Neill; Sr. S. Frances Pennell; Sr. S. Laurane Pittman; Sr. S. Mary Purcell; Sr. S. Marion Power; Sr. S. Mary Power; Sr. S. Regina Quigley Sr. S. Hilda Reardon; Sr. S. M. Kostka Reddy; Sr. S. Emma Rooney; Sr. S. Myra Rumsey; Sr. S. Margaret Smith; Sr. S. Anna St. Croix; Sr. S. Margaret Stuckless; Sr. S. Augusta Thorne; Sr. S. Patricia Tracey; Sr. S. Madeline Veitch; Sr. S. Lillian Wakeham; Sr. S. M. Annette Walsh. Sr. S. M. Aquin Walsh; Sr. S. Mabel Whelan; Sr. S. Maureen Whelan, Sr. S. Patricia Whittle; Sr. S. Ellen Whitty and Sr. S. Corona Wyse.

GRAND FALLS-WINDSOR

Immaculate Conception Convent
1933-1979
Superior: M. Xavier Mullowney
(SEE PAGE 264)

GRAND FALLS-WINDSOR

St. Joseph's Convent
1943-not closed
Superior: M. Joseph Noonan

Sr. S. M. Dorothea Barnable; Sr. S. Marie Patrice Bourgeois; Sr. S. M. Celestine Bouzane; Sr. S. M. Cyprian Bouzane; Sr. S. M. Teresita Bradbury; Sr. S. M. Chrysostom Brennan; Sr. S. Anne Carew; Sr. S. M. Sebastian Coffey; Sr. S. Patrick Curran; Sr. S. Philomena Christopher; Sr. S. M. Regina Davis; Sr. S. Teresa Devine; Sr. S. M. Andrina Downey; Sr. S. M. Liguori Downey; Sr. S. Teresa Doyle; Sr. S. Eileen Emberley; Sr S. M. Pancratia Ennis; Sr. S. M. Concepta Evans; Sr. S. M. Philippa Ezekiel; Sr. S. Monica Fagan; Sr. S. Sharon Fagan; Sr. S. M. Tarcisia Fewer; Sr. S. M. Gonzaga Furey; Sr. S. Miriam Heaney; Sr. S. Shirley Hogan; Sr. S. Agnes Hutchings; Sr. S. Rita Johnston; Sr. S. M. Colette Kavanagh; Sr. S. Carmel Kelly; Sr. S. M. Gabriella Kelly; Sr. S. Elizabeth Kennedy; Sr. S. Rosemary Kennedy; Sr. S. Mary Kennedy; Sr. S. M. De Lourdes King; Sr. S. M. Evangelista King; Sr. S. Elizabeth Lawlor; Sr. S. Elizabeth Lee; Sr. S. Sheila Leonard; Sr. S. Joan Marche; Sr. S. Inez March; Sr. S. Catherine Meaney; Sr. S. M. Clotilde Meaney; Sr. S. Bridget Molloy; Sr. S. Amelia Mooney; Sr. S. Anastasia Moore; Sr. S. Sarah Moore; Sr. S. Carmelita McNeil; Sr. S. Felix McCarthy; Sr. S. Michael McCarthy; Sr. S. Sheila McCarthy; Sr. S. Margaret McLoughlin; Sr. S. Carmel Nolan; Sr. S. Joseph Noonan; Sr. S. Magdalen O'Brien; Sr. S. Julia O'Connell; Sr. S. Catherine O'Neill; Sr. S. Luke Parsley; Sr. S. Barbara Phelan; Sr. S. Laurane Pittman; Sr. S. Anselma Power; Sr. S. Marion Power; Sr. S. Mary Power; Sr. S. Elizabeth Quinlan; Sr. S. Bernadette Ryan; Sr. S. M. Norberta Ryan; Sr. S. Margaret Smith; Sr. S. M. Faustina Smith; Sr. S. Anna St. Croix;

Sr. S. Christine St. Croix; Sr. S. Margaret Stuckless; Sr. S. Catherine Sullivan; Sr. S. Patricia Tobin; Sr. S. Patricia Tracey; Sr. S. Lillian Wakeham; Sr. S. M. Anita Wall; Sr. S. Doris Walsh, Sr. S. Genevieve White; Sr. S. Patricia Whittle and Sr. S. M. Monica Woodrow.

HARBOUR BRETON

St. Bernard's Convent
1872-1894
(MOVED TO ST. JACQUES)
Superior: M. Bernard Green

Sr. S. M. Patrick Fleury; Sr. S. M. Agatha Foley; Sr. S. M. Xavier Gray; Sr. S. M. Aloysius Green; Sr. S. M. Bernard Green; Sr. S. M. Evangelist Keane; Sr. S. M. Magdalen McCormack; Sr. S. M. Alphonsus O'Driscoll; Sr. S. M. Aquin O'Driscoll and Sr. S. M. Joseph.

ST. JACQUES

St. Bernard's Convent
1894-1943

Sr. S. Helen Bonia; Sr. S. M. Camilla Coady; Sr. S. M. Sebastian Coffey; Sr. S. M. Fabian Dunne; Sr. S. M. Patrick Fleury; Sr. S. M. DeSales Goff; Sr. S. M. Bernard Greene; Sr. S. M. Gabriella Kelly; Sr. S. M. Angeline Kennedy; Sr. S. M. Vianney Lawlor; Sr. S. M. Berchmans Maher; Sr. S. M. Alphonsus O'Driscoll; Sr. S. M. Joseph O'Driscoll; Sr. S. M. Regis O'Keefe and Sr. S. M. Xavier Mullowney.

HARBOUR BRETON

Stella Maris Convent
1970-1996

Sr. Louise Barker; Sr. M. Cyprian Bouzane, Sr. Bride Budgell; Sr. Anne Butler; Sr. Rose Crawford; Sr. Alice Dower; Sr. Marilyn Doyle; Sr. Teresa Doyle; Sr. Sharon Fagan; Sr. Mary Johnson; Sr. Elizabeth Kennedy; Sr. Brendan Lynch; Sr. Carmelita McNeil; Sr. Rita McNeil; Sr. Margaret McLoughlin; Sr. M. Cabrini Miles; Sr. Marie O'Brien; Sr. Jean O'Neill; Sr. Martina O'Reilly; Sr. Barbara Phelan; Sr. Laurane Pittman; Sr. Denise Ryan; Sr. Bride Short; Sr. Augusta Thorne; Sr. Patricia Tobin; Sr. M. Gertrude Wall, Sr. Alice Walsh and Sr. Jean Whelan.

HARBOUR GRACE

Visitation Holy Family
1851-1973
Superior: S. Xaverius Lynch
(SEE PAGE 166)

HARBOUR MAIN

Holy Family Convent
1853-1973
Superior: S. Xavier Maloney
(Not Available)

Courtesy of: Sister Mary Perpetua Kennedy
Presentation Congregation Archives, St. John's.

**PRESENTATION SISTERS AT CONFERENCE IN CANON LAW FOR SUPERIORS AT MISERICORDIA COLLEGE IN DALLAS, PA. 1967. **

1ST ROW: Sr. Andrina Downey, Sr. Regina Davis, St. Matthew Byrne, Fr. Joseph Gallen, S.J. and Fr. Thomas Clark, S.J. **2ND ROW:** Sr. Mary Johnson, Sr. Anastasia Moore, Sr. Tarcisia Fewer, Sr. Magdalen O'Brien. **3RD ROW:** Sr. Dorothea Barnable, Sr. Aloysius Penny, Sr. Patricia King, Sr. Liguori Downey, Sr. Madeline Veitch. **BACK ROW**: Sr. Patricia Tobin, and Sr. Christine Davis. All the Nuns are Presentation Sisters of the Blessed Virgin Mary. PBVM, From Newfoundland. *Picture from Jonathan Gaye, GF and Conference info from Sr. Perpetua.*

Chapter 30

CHANGES IN PAST PARISHES

Through the years Parishes were established when the number of people in one location or Town was sufficient to warrant one and other smaller Towns where a Chapel was built and it became a Mission under the larger Parish. But when populations declined, priests were not available or general reorganization of parishes in a given region or area was thought to be advantageous, some parishes were placed under others as missions, with the most populated locations declared the main Parish. Periodically there were changes in Diocese boundaries, when one Diocese took over the supervision of some other parishes or visa versa. Some parishes in question were Bonavista, Brent's Cove, Coachman's Cove, Conche, Fortune Harbour, St. Anthony and Trinity.

BONAVISTA – The Sts Joseph and Patrick Parish of Bonavista began as a Parish in 1842 with Rev. Matthew Scanlan as 1st Parish Priest and it was a separate parish every year until 1982, when it became a Mission under Port Union.

BRENT'S COVE – St. John the Apostle Parish at Brent's Cove began in 1959 when it and Baie Verte was split off as a separate Parish from Coachman's Cove. The first Parish Priest at Brent's Cove was Rev. Linus Coady from 1959-1965 and he returned as Parish Priest from 1980-1985. Today it is one of the 30 Parishes under Grand Falls Diocese.

COACHMAN COVE – Our Lady of Mt Carmel Parish at Coachman's Cove was originally established as a Parish in 1880 with its first Priest as Rev. Richard M. Shean from 1880-1908 and remained a separate Parish until 1953 when Baie Verte was split off as a separate parish and in 1959 when Coachman's Cove became a mission under Baie Verte.

CONCHE – The Sacred Heart Parish in Conche was initially served by French Navy Chaplains such as Pere Peter Richard (1859-1865) and Pere Father Gore/Gour who served from (1873-1883). The first Diocesan Priest was Rev. Thomas E. Lynch in 1883-1884 with Rev. John J. Lynch taking over from 1886-1898. The Origination Date of the Parish was in 1907, when VRev. George A. Thibault was the first Parish Priest from 1907-1923 under the Diocese of Harbour Grace. In 1984, when the Diocese borders were changed, Conche was given over to the St. George's Diocese by the Grand Falls Diocese.

FORTUNE HARBOUR – Records from St. Anne's Parish in Fortune Harbour date back to 1880. The first Parish Priest was Rev. Stephen Flynn from 1880-1885 and the last Parish Priest was Rev. Frederick T. Terry 1952-1953. Priests were assigned until 1953 when Fortune Harbour was closed and served by Norris Arm.

ST. ANTHONY – Priests were initially assigned to St. Francis Xavier Parish in St. Anthony in 1979 under the Grand Falls Diocese, when Rev. Francis J. Aylward was assigned there. In 1984 along with Conche, St. Anthony was also given over to the St. George's Diocese by the Grand Falls Diocese.

TRINITY – The earliest Priest at the Most Holy Trinity Parish in Trinity was Rev. Reginald Bullock who was serving the Parish from 1825-1830. The next Priest at Trinity was listed as Rev. P.A. Carolan from 1890-1895 and Rev. Walter M. Tarahan from 1896-1938. The last Parish Priest was Rev. Leo J. Burke from 1944-1953. In 1953 Trinity became a mission of Port Union.

Many missions of larger Parishes have no priest assigned except for the Primary Parish priest serving these mission churches on Sundays or for special services such as marriages, births and confirmations, when the numbers warrant it. Locations which do not have a church or school to say Mass in, but they have a significant group of Catholics to warrant it, the priest may still say Mass, like they did in the real old days, in a private home. Today, Rev. Linus Coady from Bishop Falls, regularly celebrates Mass in Mrs. Cook's private home in Leading Tickle for the Catholics of that Town.

Other Diocese's in Newfoundland

In addition to the Grand Falls Diocese in Newfoundland, the **ARCHDIOCESE IN ST. JOHN'S** has these parishes: Argentia, Bay Bulls, Bell Island, Burin, Cape Broyle, Fermeuse, Ferryland, Fox Harbour, Freshwater, Gould's, Kelligrews, Kilbride, Lamaline, Long Harbour, Little Placentia, Marystown, Mount Pearl: Mary Queen World, Mount Pearl: St. Peters, Mt Carmel, Outer Cove, Placentia, Portugal Cove, Pouch Cove, Renews, Rushoon, Samonier, in St. John's (SJ): St John the Baptist, (Cathedral), SJ: Corpus Christi, SJ: John Bosco, SJ: Mary Queen Peace, SJ: St. Joseph, SJ: St. Matthew, SJ: St. Patrick, SJ: St. Paul's, SJ: St. Pius X, SJ: St. Teresa's, St. Brides, St. Lawrence, St. Mary's, St. Vincent's, Torbay, Tors Cove, Trepassey, and Witless Bay.

The **DIOCESE IN ST. GEORGE'S** has these parishes: Benoit's Cove, Bird Cove, Cape St. George, CB: - All Hallows, CB:- Curling, CB:- Holy Redeemer (Cathedral), Deer Lake, Lourdes, Paradise, Pasadena, Petty Harbour, Piccadilly, Port Au Choix, Port au Port, Port Saunders, Searston, SG:- Sandy Point, SG: – St. George, SG: – St. Joseph, St. Fintan's, St. Kyran's, Stephenville, and Stephenville Crossing.

The **DIOCESE IN SCHEFFERVILLE, LABRADOR**, has these parishes:

1. Sainte Anne at Kangirsujuaq (1936)
2. Good Shepherd at Black Tickle. (1946)
3. Notre Dame de Lourdes at Lourdes de Blanc Sablon (1946)
4. Notre Dame de la Merci at Pakua Shipi (1946)
5. Saint Augustine at Saint Augustine (1946)
6. Saint Joseph at La Tabatiere (1946)
7. Sacred Heart at Middle Bay (1947)
8. Saint Paul's River at Saint Paul's River (1947)
9. Saint Theresa at Blanc-Sablon (1948) Mission
10. Notre Dame de Fatima at Kuujjuaq (1948)
11. Marie Reine des Coeurs at Puvimituk (1948)
12. Sainte Anne at Tete-a-la-Baleine (1948)
13. Our Lady of Labrador at West Saint Modeste (1948)
14. Our Lady of Assumption at Davis Inlet (1949) Mission
15. Our Lady of the Snows at Sheshatshui (1949)
16. Saint Andre at Kuujjuarapik (1955)
17. Notre Dame de Indiens at Matimekosh (1955)
18. Marie Reine des Indiens at La Romaine ((1956)
19. Our Lady Queen of Peace at Happy Valley/Goose Bay (1958)
20. Our Lady of Perpetual Help at Labrador City (1960)
21. Our Lady of the Assumption at Wabush (1963)
22. Saint Peter at Churchill Falls (1967) Mission
23. Notre Dame de la Visitation at Inukjuak (1986) Mission

Abbreviations: SJ – St. John's, MP – Mount Pearl, CB - Corner Brook, SG – St. George's.

Chapter 31

EDUCATION IN GRAND FALLS

According to the Encyclopedia of Newfoundland and Labrador, the first Catholic School was opened in 1909. After the Immaculate Conception Parish was established in 1912 by Msgr. William P. Finn, the Church burned down and almost all the school. From 1919 to 1929, the Catholic students held classes in the Knights of Columbus Hall as a temporary school, until the 1930s when the Catholic Notre Dame Academy was opened. In 1956-1957 the Christian Brothers established a Foundation and opened St. Michael's High school and a decade later St. Catherine's Girl's School and Convent was in operation. In 1997 when Newfoundland voted to close all denominational schools, all Catholic schools were either closed or converted to secular schools. Since that time the only Catholic Schools in Newfoundland, are St. Bonaventure's which was opened in St. John's in 1999 and is administered under the Jesuits and the following year another school in Corner Brook has opened as a private Catholic school.

Presentation Sisters to Grand Falls

Sisters Take Charge of Notre Dame Academy

"On 18 August 1933, a group of thirteen Sisters accompanied by Rev. Mother de Sales – Superior General of the Presentation Order in Newfoundland, and Mother M. Columba – Local Superior, St. John's, arrived in Grand Falls. They were met at the Station by the revered and zealous Pastor, Rev. William Finn, and driven to a Convent, complete in every detail, equipped with every modern convenience – a veritable Religious Home – provided by the fatherly solicitude of the Pastor and the kind and appreciative thought of the Catholic people of Grand Falls. The cornerstone of the virtues which the Sisters will instill into the minds of the children under their care and bears the legend –

"SALVE SANCTA PARENS."

above which are two shamrocks, as a delicate tribute to the Sisters, who a century ago, came to the Land of the Shamrock to dedicate their lives and work to the Christian education of the youth of Newfoundland. Under this inscription are two lilies with the dates 1833 and 1933 on either side. The Convent is dedicated to the Immaculate Conception of Our Lady, the Spotless Virgin Queen. When on that auspicious morning, Friday, August 18, 1933, the Sisters reached their destination, they repaired to the Parish Church where they assisted at the Holy Sacrifice celebrated by His Excellency, Rt. Rev. Bishop March. On Saturday, the Convent was blessed by His Excellency the Bishop assisted by the energetic Pastor – Rev. Fr. Finn. Then the Blessed Sacrament was brought from the Church and placed in the Tabernacle of the Oratory. Our Sacramental God came to take possession of a new throne, to dwell among His chosen Spouses, to remain with them day and night, guarding, blessing and encouraging them in their labours for Him and welcoming them when each day's labours is ended, to His Divine presence, to whisper to each soul words of loving solicitude and divine comfort. On Sunday the first Mass was celebrated in the new Convent by His

Excellency Bishop March, after which there was Exposition of the Blessed Sacrament until 4 p.m., when Benediction was imparted by Rev. Fr. Finn, assisted by Rev. Fr. Hinchey. In the Parish Church a Missa Cantata was sung by Rev. Fr. Finn at the conclusion of which an eloquent and touching sermon, suitable to the occasion, was preached by Bishop March; and then an Address of welcome, couched in choice and feeling words, was read by D. A. O'Flynn, Esq., on behalf of the Catholic congregation of Grand Falls. His Excellency responded for the Sisters and thanked the people for the whole-hearted welcome which they had extended to the Nuns. On Sunday evening His Excellency returned to Harbour Grace. On Monday morning, September 4th, the Mass of the Holy Ghost was celebrated in the Parish Church by the Reverend Pastor; all the school children were present at the Holy Sacrifice and received Holy Communion. At 9:30 the pupils assembled on the school grounds where they were met by Father Finn and according to grade marched in their respective class rooms where each group was received by the Sister in charge. When everything was in readiness the business of the day commenced and so the first session of school under the direction of the Presentation Nuns in Grand Falls opened." Taken from the Newfoundland Quarterly Magazine

LIST OF PRESENTATION SISTERS WHO SERVED IN GRAND FALLS, NF – IMMACULATE CONCEPTION CONVENT 1933-1979

Barker, S. Margaret	Johnston, S. Rita (Henrietta)	O'Keefe, S.M. Baptista
Barnable, S.M. Dorothea	Kavanagh, S.M. Colette	Parsley, S.M. Luke
Bavis, S. M. Christina	Kennedy, S. M. John Regis	Parsley, S.M. Nano
Bourgeois, S. Marie Patrice	Keyes, S.M. Bertille	Russell, S.M. Roberta
Bradbury, S.M. Teresina	King, S. M. Consilio	Pennell, S. Frances
Brennan, S.M. Chrysostom	King, S. Frances (Seraphina)	Philpott, S. Rosarii
Burke, S. Catherine (Jacinta)	Lawlor, S. M. Mechtilde	Power, S.M. Winifred
Carew, S. Anne (Nolasco)	Lawlor, S. M. Vianney	Reardon, S. Hilda
Carroll, S.M. Paschal	Lee, S.M. Leo	Reddy, S.M. Kostka
Coady, S. Eileen	Maher, S.M. Annunciata	Redmond, S.M. Perpetua
Coffey, S.M. Sabastian	Martin, S.M. Teresita	Ryan, S.M. Helen John
Curtin, S. M. Patricia	Mansfield, S.M. Pius	Smith, S.M. Edwardine
Curtis, S. M. Theophane	Meaney, S. M. Clotilde	Smith, S.M. Faustina
Doyle, S. Leonard Marie	Mooney, S. Amelia (Marietta)	St. Croix, S. Christine
Dunphy, S. Joan (Wilma)	Moore, S. Anastasia	Sullivan, S. Miriam Joseph
Ennis, S. M. Pancratia	Morrissey, S. Rosalie	Sullivan, S. M. Patrice
Fagan, S. M. Catherine Sienna	Mullowney, S.M. Xavier	Timmons, S.M. Laurenti
Fewer, S. M. Tarcisia	Murphy, S. M. Charles	Tobin, S.M. Barbara
Furey, S.M. Gonzaga	McGrath, S. Angela (Marg)	Tobin, S.M. Teresa Francis
Gough, S. M. Alban	McCarthy, S.M. Bonaventure	Tracey, S. Patricia
Greene, S. M. Callista	McCarthy, S. Margaret (Felix)	Waddleton, S.M. Evarista
Harding, S. M. Eulalie	McGettigan, S.M. Ignatius	Waddleton, S. Mary (Florence)
Hayes, S. M. Genevieve	McNeil, S.M. Carmelita	Walsh, S.M.Aquin
Healey, S.M. Beatrice	Nolan, S. Carmel (Alicia)	Walsh, S.M.Austin
Hickey, S. Anne (Albert)	O'Brien, S.M. Calasanctius	Walsh, S.M.Florence (Joseph)
Hogan, S.M. Brendan	O'Brien, S. Marie (Euphrasia)	Whelan, S.M. Domitilla
Howlett, S. Rita (Thomas)	O'Brien, S.M. Redempta	Woodrow, S. Monica
Johnson, S. Mary (Ephrem)	O'Connell, S.M. Julia	Wyse, S.M. Corona
	Presentation Sisters Archives, St. John's	

Notre Dame Academy

The cornerstone for the Notre Dame Academy's was laid in 1929 and it opened in the early 1930s and all the Catholic students went to this school. In 1933 the Presentation sisters took over the direction of the Notre Dame Academy. When St. Michael's High School opened in 1957 the Notre Dame Academy was used for the lower grade from Kindergarten to grade VIII. In 1979 the Presentation Sisters left all schools in the Province because of lack of Vocations.

Notre Dame Academy in Grand Falls

In 1982 it stopped being a school and the name was changed to the Msgr. W.P. Finn Building in honor of Monsignor Finn, Parish Priest – 1912-1953. The students from the Academy moved over to St. Catherine's. The Msgr. W. P. Finn Building was used as an LPN Training School, the parish Youth Center, the Gym and the YMCA. The downstairs was used as a YMCA Day Care. The building was torn down in the summer of 2001.

GRADE 5 NOTRE DAME SCHOOL IN 1954

BACK ROW: Ed Blackmore, Ernest Kelly, Bill Maher, Bill O'Brien, William Flood, Allan Power, Terry Moss, Barbra Aylward, Betty Matthews, Peg Hennessey, ? Connors, Barbra Jesseau, Cheryl MacDonald, Nikki Smith, ? Arnold, Don Lannon, Rose Mary Mollowney. 2nd ROW: Bob Bryn, Bill Collins, Mark Andrews, ? Kelly, Bob Barker, Bill LeDrew, Fred Healy. 3rd ROW: Tom Healy, Mike Fleming, Tom Hanlon, Dave Sullivan, Unk, Unk, Fr Bill Houlahan, 4th ROW: John Southcott, Unk, Jim Dormity, Ron Dunphy, Unk, Bill wall, Unk, 5th ROW: Unk, Unk, Maureen Power, Unk, Unk, Maureen Gunn, Sheila White, Unk, Helen Foley.

GRADE 7, NOTRE DAME SCHOOL IN 1954-1955

FRONT ROW: Mary Hartley, Marie McDonald, Hilda Gale, Barbra Gunn, Shirley Wall, Regina McDonald, Betty Jackman. 2ND ROW: Maureen Hennessy, Madeline Dwyer, Betty Delaney, Patricia Roberts, Joan Flood, Sheila Dwyer, Anne Sullivan, Madonna Moss, Caroline Kelly. BACK ROW: Mary Corbin, Bride Melvin, Judy Blackmore, Madeline Byrne, Janet LeDrew, Mary Hatt, Paula Melvin.

CLASS PLAY AT NOTRE DAME SCHOOL – GRADE 7 IN 1954.

FRONT ROW: Anita Roberts, Cyril Tremblett, Allan Roberts, Mary Mollowney, Art Healey, Curil Anstey. BACK ROW: Sheila Matthews, Jed Blackmore, Margaret Hanlon, Peg Hennessey, Helen Hartly, Joan Power, Rose Mary Gill, John Mackey, David Aylward, George Lewis, Jim Martin, Leo Murphy, Sharon Hanlon.

NOTRE DAME HOCKEY TEAM

FRONT ROW: Unk, George Winslow, Peter Cashin, Charlie Shallow, Ronnie Jackman, Unk. 2ND ROW: Jerome Mullowney, Tom Dunphy, Bill Lannon, Wilfred Griffin, Michael Murphy, Unk.

St. Michael's High School

St. Michael's Regional High school

St. Michael's High school was started in 1956 but the actual building was not opened until early 1957, while Msgr. Joseph Peddle was Chancellor. The High school was under the direction of the Christian Brothers, until they were withdrawn in 1988. The High school was for grades IX to XII. In 1997 when the Province voted to do away with Catholic schools, St. Michael's became a secular High School, which it is today and renamed the "Exploit Valley High School, Greenwood Division."

ST. MICHAEL'S HIGH SCHOOL BASKETBALL CHAMPIONS FROM GRAND FALLS.

Kneeling: Gary Byrne; Colin Kelly; Ross Flood and Mike Shallow. **Back Row:** Bro. J.S. Dawson; CFC; Eric Healey; Jim Burke; Tony Shallow; Rod Goulding, Terry French and Tom Cooke.

St. Catherine's Girls School

St. Catherine's Girls school began in 1962 with the Presentation sisters in charge. It remained active until the Sisters left in 1979, when it was closed and the girls went over to St. Michael's High School. The Notre Dame Academy students moved into St. Catherine's School. When the Newfoundland Voters decided to stop denominational schools and St. Catherine's became a secular school, it was renamed "Mill Crest Academy".

Bishop O'Neill and Msgr. Hogan dedicate St. Catherine's High School – 1962.

THE TEACHER MUSES

Year after year they come to me
These children, with questioning looks,
Year after year they leave me
As they leave their outgrown books;
And I wonder sometimes if I've taught them
Just some of the worthwhile things,
Just some of the things they'll need in life
By they peasants or poets or kings.

Have I taught them the joy of clean living?
That Honor is better than Fame?
That good friends are the greatest of treasures?
Wealth, less than an untarnished name?

Have I taught them respect for the aged?
Protection to those that are weak?
That silence always in golden
When gossip bids them speak?

Have I taught then that Fear is a coward
Who is beaten when they say, "I can"?
That Courtesy ranks with Courage.
In the heart of the real gentleman?
Have I taught them these things and the others
That will help make them brave, king and true?
If I have, then I care not if they tell me
That Irkutsk is a town in Peru.

Adelphian Magazine, St. Bon's, St. John's. 1953

The Combined Funds Canvass – 1958

The St. Michael's Regional High school students

Kevin Dormody
John Hamilton
Michael Blackmore
Frank Edwards
Allan Edwards
Bill Stein
Reginald Stapleton
Anthony Blackmore
Gregg Hatt
Garry Janes
Pat Beson
John Sullivan
Bill Sullivan
Paul Hennessey
Angela Blackmore
Gertrude Kelly
Lorraine Flood
Mary Gardner
Judy Blackmore
Shirley Power
Betty Delaney
Geraldine Quigley
Madeline Byrne
Caroline Kelly
Mary Hartley
Margaret Creaser
Madelyn Dwyer

Frank O'Brien
Bill Foley
John Tremblett
Vincent Jackman
John Stapleton
John Mackey
Cyril Anstey
Leo Murphy
Sylvester Dormody
Gerald O'Brien
James Alyward
Jerry Jesseau
Ronald O'Keefe
Allan Roberts
Joan Flood
Anne Sullivan
Sheila Ryan
Bride Melvin
Paula Melvin
Margaret McLaughlan
Marie McDonald
Mary Corbin
Sheila Matthews
Peg Hennessey
Helen Hartley
Betty Hanlon
Anne Hanlon

Gerard Blackmore
William Tobin
David Alyward
James Grouchy
William Alyward
Arthur Healey
James Comeau
George Lewis
Allan Hennessey
Cyril Tremblett
John Murray
Robert Barker
Bill Maher
Bill Houlahan
Anita Roberts
Mary Maloney
Anne Way
Mary Hatt
Anne Blackmore
Joan Power
Shirley Sweeney
Patricia Smith
Helen Foley
Joan Creaser
Ann Ennis
Betty Matthews
Roseann Molloy

John Kelly
Bill Flood
Mike Fleming
Bill Wall
Bill Collins
John Southcott
Leo Brophy
Pete Tobin
Berks Brown
Dennis Healey
Mark Andrews
Ray Dunphy
Bob Byrne
Charles Pitcher
Dawn Lannon
Betty Connors
Betty Maloney
Barbara Jesseau
Barbara Phair
Lorraine Russell
Patricia Arnold
Shirley Cooke
Marilyn Melvin
Donalda Martin

Co-Cathedral Parish
Combined Funds Canvass
1958

Our Canvass Organization

Most Reverend J. M. O'Neill, S.T.D., D.D., Pastor

Rev. W. P. Hogan, Rector

Rev. L. J. Coady, Assistant Priest

GENERAL CHAIRMAN

Mr. Walter Blackmore

CANVASS COMMITTEE CO-CHAIRMEN

Mr. J. P. Molloy
Mr. M.chael Blackmore

INITIAL GIFTS CHAIRMAN

Mr. Garland Morrissey

SPECIAL GIFTS CO-CHAIRMEN

Mr. Michael Dormody Sr.
Mr. Joseph Blackmore

TEAMS CO-CHAIRMEN

Mr. Kevin Anstey
Mr. Adrian Leger

E. G. R. CO-CHAIRMEN

Mr. Gerard Brown
Mr. Ronald Smith
Mr. Ronald Melvin

ARRANGEMENTS CO-CHAIRMEN

Mr. Valentine Stapleton
Mr. Thomas Conway

SPECIAL GIFTS COMMITTEE

Mr. Wm. Dunphy
Mr. Leo Ryan
Dr. E. Sharpe
Mr. Kevin Griffin
Mr. James Delaney
Mr. Wm. Tobin
Dr. J. F. Comeau
Mr. C. I. Power
Mr. Charles Edwards

DIVISION LEADERS

Mr. T. J. Healey
Mr. M. Brennan
Mr. Leo Hennessey Sr.
Mr. Dermot Griffin

TEAM CAPTAINS

Mr. Gerald Whalen
Mr. J. Power
Mr. Ben Stapleton
Mr. J. Fleming
Mr. Cecil Stein Sr.
Mr. Wm. Lannon
Mr. J. French
Mr. L. F. Kelly
Mr. J. Flood
Mr. K. Anstey
Mr. Wm. Shallow
Mr. J. Hatt
Mr. Cornelius Pitcher
Mr. J. Corbin
Mr. Wm. Griffin
Mr. Harold Farr

SOME OF OUR CANVASSERS

P. Smith
P. Blackmore
J. Tremblett
M. Browne
A. Flood
J. Quigley
G. Cooke
R. Healey
A. Davis
J. Ennis
T. Medzwiecki
J. Delaney
W. Finn
P. Power
K. Harvey
R. Kelly
J. Griffin
J. Hann
A. Barker
S. Healey
J. Molloy
Wm. Tremblett
M. Murphy
R. Griffin
J. Byrne
J. O'Brien
B. Anstey
C. Dwyer Sr.
P. Kearney
T. McLellan
Matt Hamilton
M. Russell
L. Maddox
F. Walsh
H. Reelis
H. Barker
G. Wall
C. McCormick
R. Murray
O. Browne
N. Alyward
P. Colford
Austin Griffin
J. Stapleton
J. Maloney
D. Murphy
M. Skinner
Wm. Browne
T. Griffin
R. Davis
J. White
H. Murray
S. Griffin
W. Dillon
Joe Molloy
L. Hartley
J. McCormick
Wm. Houlahan
Art Griffin
R. McLoughlin
J. Crawley
B. Kelly
M. Dormody Jr.
Bill Bradbury
M. Philpott
J. Murray
Bern Cantwell
Peter Sullivan Jr.
K. Barnes
R. Maloney
Louis Barker
John White
Cyril O'Keefe
R. Murray
C. Stein Jr.
Leo Hennessey Jr.
Walter Fewer
John Paddick
Anthony McDonald
Jerry Rose
B. White

HOSTESS COMMITTEE VICE-CHAIRMEN

Mrs. M. Blackmore
Mrs. John Delaney
Mrs. Leo Hartley
Mrs. Thomas J. Healey
Mrs. J. P. Molloy
Mrs. Val Stapleton

HOSTESS COMMITTEE

Mrs. C. Anstey
Mrs. M. Blackmore
Mrs. W. Blackmore
Mrs. J. Blackmore
Miss A. Brophy
Mrs. G. Brown
Mrs. O. Brown
Mrs. Dr. J. F. Brown
Mrs. A. Byrd
Miss I. Byrd
Miss Rita Bryan
Mrs. Dr. Ball
Mrs. Wm. Bradbury
Mrs. J. Carpenter
Mrs. T. Conway
Miss P. Crawley
Mrs. J. Delaney
Mrs. M. Dormody
Mrs. H. DeLong
Mrs. R. Davis
Mrs. Wm. Dunphy
Mrs. R. Fewer
Mrs. L. Foley
Mrs. J. Fleming
Mrs. R. Griffin
Mrs. K. Griffin
Mrs. M. Grace
Mrs. T. McCarthy
Mrs. L. Hartley
Mrs. T. J. Healey
Mrs. M. Hogan
Mrs. M. Hamilton
Mrs. L. Hennessey
Mrs. A. Leger
Mrs. J. P. Molloy
Mrs. P. Maloney
Mrs. G. Matthews
Mrs. T. Medzwiecki
Miss Colleen Murphy
Mrs. Leo Maddox
Mrs. C. McCormick
Mrs. J. Grace
Mrs. J. O'Brien
Mrs. M. V. Power
Mrs. L. Rose Sr.
Mrs. P. J. Ryan
Mrs. V. Stapleton
Mrs. B. Stapleton
Mrs. C. Stein
Miss Rita Whalen
Miss T. Wall
Mrs. G. Whalen
Miss Margaret Walsh
Mrs. G. Wall

THOSE ATTENDING THE 1984 ANNUAL GENERAL MEETING OF THE CATHOLIC EDUCATION COUNCIL
(Back Row) L to R. Mr. J. Simmonds, Rev. W. J. Kelly, Mr. J. Conway, Rev. J. Doody, Dr. J. Scott, Mr. Wm O'Driscoll, The Most Rev. J. F. MacDonald, The Most Rev. P.A. Sutton, Mr. J. Cochrane, The Most Rev. R.T. McGrath, Mr. P. Furlong, Rev. R. Bromley, Rev. J. McGettigan, Mr. F. J. Kearsey, Mr. D. Galway, Rev. J. K. McKenna, S. J. (Front Row) L to R. Rt. Rev. R. T. White, Mrs. M. Patton, Mr. C.F. Furey, The Most Rev. A. L. Penney, Mrs. D. McCrate, Sister Dolores Hall and Mr. N. Hurley.

The Nobility of the Teaching Profession

If we work upon marble, it will perish.
If we work upon brass, time will efface it.
It we rear temples, they will crumple to dust.
But if we work upon men's immortal minds,
If we imbue them with high principles,
With the just fear of God and love of their fellow man,
We engrave on those tablets something
Which no time can efface,
And which will brighten and brighten to all eternity.

Daniel Webster
(Adelphian Magazine 1953)

Chapter 32

THE 2000 PARISHIONERS LIST FOR GRAND FALLS-WINDSOR PARISH

Adey, Keith & Mary Lou	Bragg, Robert-Lorraine	Cooper,Dennis-Brenda	Etheridge,Marie
Alavardy, Peter & Eliza	Broderick, Joan	Cooper,Allan-Rita	Etheridge,Myrtle
Allan, Bruce & Ruth	Brophy, Hannah	Corbin,Isabelle	Evans,Sandra
Alyward, Edith	Brophy, William-Ursula	Corbin,John	Eveleign,OswaldGenevieve
Alyward, Hazel	Brown, Forbes and Carmel	Corbin,Martin-Stella	Feener,Edwin-Bernadette
Alyward,Ray-Josephine	Brown, Mary	Corbin,Mary	Feore,D.
Andrews, Don – Joan	Browne,Casimir-Deborah	Courtney,James	Fewer,Ada
Andrews, Bruce Madonna	Browne,Dorotrhy	Courtney,Thomas-Yvonne	Fewer,Ann
Anstey, McLennon M..	Browne,Marie	Courtney,WilliamChristina	Flood,Edward-Helen
Anstey, Peter Sr	Browne,Paula	Crawley,Isabel	Flood,Raymond-Joan
Anthony, Derrick - Stella	Browne,William Sr-Clara	Crawley,Kevin-Theresa	Foley,Austin-Catherine
Antle, Keith & Maria	Budgell,RichardAnneMarie	Crawley,W.	Foley,Gerald-Shirley
Armstrong, Don - Deborah	Burke,Gerald-Anne	Croke,Margaret	Fewer,Dennis-Dorothy
Arnold, Kathleen	Burke,John-Ruth	Culletin,Dermot-Verna	Fewer,Kevin-Ellen
Aucoin, Brenden-Mary	Burke,Tom-Maegaret	Curran,Peter-Carol Ann	Finn,William
Baird, Mary	Butler,Annie	Dalton,Maurice	Finn,William-Barbara
Ball, Caroline	Butler,Lisa	Dancey,David-Mary	Fitzgerald,Sophie
Ballard, Barbara	Butler,Mary	Davis,A. Wayne	Fleming,Margaret
Barker, Alphonsus-Shirley	Butler,William Jr	Dawe,Leroy-Marie	Flood,Daniel-Janice
Barker, Andrew-Dianne	Butt,Sheila	Dawe,Ted-Colleen	Flood,Edward-Joyce
Barker, Caroline	Byrd,Zita	Day,Ann	Foley,Pierce-Margaret
Barker, Catherine	Byrne,John-Iris	Daye,Arthur-Barbara	Folkes,Cyril-Lorraine
Barker, Dave	Byrne,Kevin-Angela	Decker,Edward-Anastasia	French,Sadie
Barker, Harold-Bridget	Byrne,Louise	Delaney,Marion	Froude,Patricia
Barker, Isabelle	Byrne,May	Delaney,Patricia	Furey,William-Cynthia
Barker, Louis-Eileen	Byrne,Peter-Allison	Devilla,Jesse Mr Mrs	Furlong,David
Barnes, Douglas-Anita	Byrne,Roy-Debbie	Devine,Mary	Gallagher,Dorreen
Barnes, Kathlene	Carberry,Steve Mr-Mrs	Dooley,Lewis-Peggy	Galuteria,Justo-Isabel
Barry, Fred-Anita	Carey,Lawrence-June	Domrody,Edward-Marina	Gulutira,Maryann
Barry, Thomas	Carey,William-Mary	Downey, Allan	Gambin,Felix-Bridget
Bartle, David-Marie	Carpenter,James-Sheila	Downton,Gordon-Louise	Gardner,Judy
Bartlett, Eileen	Carrigan,David-Joyce	Downton,Hedley	Gaye,Daniel-Cavelle
Becket, Ernest-Dolores	Cashin,Peter-Selina	Downton,Chris-Joanne	Gill,Victor R.
Bennett, Charles-Linda	Cashin,Peter	Ducey,Adrian-Bride	Gillespie,Allan
Benoit, Andrew-Rose	Cater,Terry-Lorraine	Duder,Ernest-Janice	Goodyear,RaymondTeresa
Beresford, Jackie	Chisholm,Jean	Dunn,Raymond	Goulding,Cecil-Frances
Beresford, Sarah	Cluney,Raymond-Linda	Dwyer,Bill-Sheila	Griffin,Anne
Beson, Andre-Melissa	Cluney,Ronald-Loretta	Dwyer,Evelyn	Griffin,Arthur-Margaret
Beson, David-Pansy	Coady,Jim-Marjorie	Dwyer,Patrick-Sheila	Griffin,Dermot-Doris
Beson, Dennis-Stella	Colbourne,Geraldine	Dwyer,Roger	Griffin,Gerard-Viola
Beson, Harvey-Geraldine	Collett,Mark-Kimberly	Earle,Eileen	Griffin,Heather L.
Blackmore,AnthonyRosalie	Collett,Stanley-Agnes	Edwards,Allan-Maxine	Griffin,Joanne
Blackmore, Bryan-Vera	Collins,Bertha	Edwards,Arnold-Freda	Griffin,Lori
Blackmore, Joseph-Joan	Connolly,Edmund	Edwards,Gerard	Griffin,Michael-Dianne
Bonia,James-Monica	Connors,Albert	Edwards,Glen-Patricia	Griffin,William-Geraldine
Bongan, Luz	Connors,John	Edwards,John	Groves,Terrence-Imelda
Boone, Denys-Madonna	Connors,Michael-Debbie	Edwards,Mary	Guillermo,Carmelita
Bouzane, James-Vera	Conway,Richard-Betty	Edwards,Reginald-Mary	Gunn,Angus
Bouzane, Joe-Vera	Cooke,Anthony-Diane	Elliott,Bertram	Halpin,C.
Bouzane, Sheila	Curran,David	Ennis,Ronald-Delores	Hamilton,John-Madeline
Bradbury, Jennifer	Cooke,Mary	Etheridge,Cecilia	Hamilton,Rita
Bradbury, Williamaulin	Coombs,Desmond-Sandra	Etheridge,Jack	Hanlon,John-Bernade

Hanlon,Patrick-Margaret	Kelly,Anita	McHugh,Eric	Power,James-Catherine
Hansford,Roger-Angela	Kelly,Catherine	McKelvie,Bernadette	Power,John-Elizabeth
Hart,Bernadette	Kelly,Geofrey-Gail	McLoughlan,William	Power,John-Dorothy
Hart,Calvin-Catherine	Kelly,Helen	McSween,John-Cheryl	Power,Leo-Anne
Harvey,Neil-Lois	Kelly,Margaret	Melvin,Marilyn	Power,Marie
Hatt,John-Michelle	Kelly,Mary	Melvin,Patrick-Shirley	Power,Patricia
Hatt,Katherine	Kelly,Muriel	Mercer,Jerry-Donna	Power,Philip-Sheil
Hatt,William	Kelly,Sean-Catherine	Mercer,David-Rosemary	Power,Ronald-Margaret
Head,Harvey-Imelda	Kelly,Tom-Margaret	Mercier,Regina	Power,Russell-Ellen
Healey,Allan-Pamela	Kenny,Josephine	Milley,David-Donna	Power,Ruth
Healey,Ann	Keough,Mary	Morgan,Lorraine	Power,William
Healey,Dennis-Kathleen	King, Dr Jim-Anne	Morris,Stanley	Pretty,Glenn-Patricia
Healey,Edward	Lacour,Kevin-Margaret	Morrissey,Margaret	Price,Dennis-Jean
Healey,Eric-Phyllis	Lahey,William	Murphy,Colleen	Price,John-Barbara
Healey,Mary	Lambe,Anthony-Joanne	Murphy,Donald-Clare	Price,Pauline
Healey,Patrick	Lane,Mary	Murphy,Leo	Pumphrey,Gus-Anne
Healey,Sandra	Lannon,Madeline	Murphy,Michael-Phyllis	Quigley,Claude-Alice
Healey,Terrence-Linda	Lefresne,David-Crystal	Murphy,Sean-Sandra	Quigley,Donald-Mae
Healey,Thomas	Lewis,Anthony-Jackie	Newell,Darlene	Race,Michael-Laura
Hearn, Robert-Lorraine	Lewis,Gertrude	Noah,Sean-Carol Ann	Reardon,Kay
Heneghan,Paul	Lewis,John-Pauline	Norman,Wallace-Joyce	Reckling,Jean
Hennebury,Brian-Christine	Lewis,Marjorie	Noseworthy,Esperanza	Reid,Bride
Hennessey,EdwardDelorosa	Lewis,Norman-Alice Mary	Noseworthy,Madonna	Reid,Edward-Mary
Hennessey,Gary-Elizabeth	Lewis,Raymond-Betty	O'Brien,Denise	Reid,Randy-Rosalind
Hennessey,Joseph-Bertha	Lewis,Robert-Sandra	O'Brien,Gerald-Florence	Reid,William-Caroline
Hennessey,Paul-Elizabeth	Lewis,Sean-Cynthia	O'Driscoll,Mary	Reinsborough,John
Hennessey,Sheila	Lindahl,Carl-Jean	O'Driscoll,Robert-Pauline	Ricketts,Mark
Hickey,James-Cecila	Lindahl,Keith-Dorothy	O'Keefe,Mary	Rideout,Keith-Darlene
Higgins,Lawrence	Lindahl,Mary	O'Keefe,Rita	Rideout,Kimberly
Higgins,Peter-Margaret	Lindahl,Theresa	O'Reilly,Albert-Cecilia	Roberts,Darren-Lorna
Hillier,Robert-Lorraine	Linehan,Barry-Barbara	O'eilly,Harry-Carmel	Roberts,Elizabeth
Hiscock,Glenn-Donna	Lingard,Christine	O'Reilly,James-Janice	Roberts,Ron-Maureen
Hiscock,David-Margaret	Locke,John-Corrie	O'Reilly,James-Margaret	Roberts,Neil-Elizabeth
Hogan,Madeline	Loveridge,Alison	O'Reilly,John-Mary	Roberts,William
Holloway,Alice	Lynch,Wayne-Cynthia	O'Reilly,Neil	Rodgers,Anthony-Joan
Hoppel,Albert	MacDonald,MikeBernadette	O'Reilly,Shirley	Rogers,Paula
Houlahan,Rita	MacDonald,Viola	Paddick,John-Carol	Rose,Raymond-Simone
Houlahan, William-Betty	Mackenzie,Linda	Paddick,Sidney-Lorraine	Rose,Rita
House,Gordon	Mackey,John-Marie	Paddock,James-Mary	Rose,Carmel-Ronald
Howard,Frank-Selma	Mackey,Michael-Anne	Parsons,Gary-Chris	Rowsell,Anne
Howse,Denise	Madden,Ignatia	Parsons,Marion	Rowsell,Fred-Gertrude
Howse,Edward-Angela	Maddox,Mary	Pasco,Minda	Rowsell,Raymond
Howse,Wilfred-Eileen	Maher,Bill-Lydia	Peaty,Roy-Madeline	Russell,Lorraine
Humber,Kathleen	Maher,Terri-Llynn	Pelly,Maureen	Ryan,David-Gertrude
Hynes,Derek-Patricia	Maloney,Anne	Penton,Rosalind	Ryan,Duncan-Dianne
Hynes,Harold-Carolanne	Maloney,Roderick	Phair,Frank-Eileen	Sampson,James-Monica
Inder,Brenda	March,William-Madonna	Phair,Ray-Ann	Sanders,George-Mary
Jackman,Arthur-Ruby	Marks,Tom-Allison	Philpott,Gerald-Elizabeth	Sansome,Harold-Yvonne
Jackman,Kevin	Matthews,Gerald-Mary	Piercey,Ralph-Doreen	Saunders,Clayton-Judy
Jackman,Dorothy	McCarthy,Frank-Bonita	Pike,Roger-Brenda	Saunders,William-Lorraine
Jackman,Patricia	McCarthy,Jim	Pitcher,Lorraine	Shallow,Marie
James,David-Signe	McCarthy,Margaret	Pittman,Donald-Elizabeth	Sharpe,Joan
Janes,Eleanor	McCarthy,Noreen	Pittman,Joanne	Shea,Mary
Janes,Fred-Sheila	McCormick,Mary	Poole,Thomas-Mary	Sheppard,Ivan-Peggy
Janes,William-Olive	McCue,Elaine	Power,Alphonsus-Una	Sheppard,Mary
Jerrett,Gerald-Stella	McCullogh,Gail	Power,Augustus-Geraldine	Simms,Douglas
Jesseau,Terry-Paula	McDermott,Kay	Power,Colin-Frances	Simon,Tony-Gladys
Johnson,Annie	McDonald,Bruce-Madeline	Power,Denise	Smith,Ronald-Patricia
Joy,William	McDonald,Alastair-Helen	Power,Dennis-Bernadette	Southcott,Ronald-Rita
Judge,William-Vera	McGettigan,Bill-Lucy	Power,Edwina	Stroud,Christina
Keats,Frank-Mary	McGrath,Patrick	Power,Emily	Sullivan,Jeremiah-Marina

Sullivan,Susan	Thorne,Gerald-Joan	Wall,Gary	Walsh,Sean-Iris
Sullivan,Joe-Darlene	Tobin,Alice	Wall,Gordon	Warford,Carmel-Harry
Sullivan,Reginald-Dinah	Tobin,Gordon-Yvonne	Wall,James-Rosemary	Way,Mary
Sullivan,Ronald	Tobin,Joan	Wall,John	Whelan,Rita
Sullivan,William-Marge	Tremblett,Joe	Wall,John-Donna	Whalen,Veronica
Sullivan,William-Louise	Tremblett,John-Jean	Wall,Joseph-Ursula	Wheeler,George-Leila
Sweeney,David-Joanne	Tremblett, Joseph	Wall,Margaret	Whalen, John-Hickey,Sue
Sweeney,Frank-Louise	Tulk,Harry-Linda	Wall,Patrick-Sheila	White,Catherine
Sweeney,Jack-Joan	Tulk,Patricia	Wall,William-Shirley	White,Kathleen
Sweeney,Leona	Tulk,Sean-Mrs Pauline	Walsh,Austin	White,Stephen-Cathy
Sweetland,Randy-Barbara	Turpin,Alonzo-Irene	Walsh,Catherine	White,Warren-Elizabeth
Tait,Margie	Umeh,J.Faber	Walsh,Joe	White,William-Catherine
Taylor,Brian-Imelda	Veitch,Kevin-Judy	Walsh,Julia	Wicks,Paul-Bernadette
Temple,Dorothy	Verge,Maria	Walsh,Marion	Wicks,Terrence-Catherine
Temple,Jim-Mary	Wakeham,Tony-Patricia	Walsh,Michael-Frances	Wilson,Monica
Thompson,AllanBernadine	Wall,Colin-Nellie	Walsh,Ronald-Stella	Winslow,Harold-Ellen
			Winslow,Robert-Helene

Parishioners receiving Communion at Mass on Sunday

Father Brian Dunn at the altar. Bishop J. Faber MacDonald and Msgr. Richard Woodford giving out Communion at the Cathedral in Grand Falls.

Chapter 33

ROMAN CATHOLIC CEMETERY'S IN GRAND FALLS

The older cemetery in the Grand Falls area is an Interfaith Cemetery on Valley Road along the Trans-Canada Highway. It includes Catholic, Anglican, United Church, Presbyterian, Salvation Army, Pentecostal and others. There are Catholic persons buried there from 1907 to about 1926, except for Margaret Moore who is listed as buried on 25 March 1903, age 38 and Edward Small buried on July 19, 1904, age 11 months. There are thirty-one buried after 1926 apparently buried with their spouse or in their family plot.

In about 1926 the current Main Roman Catholic Parish cemetery near the Cathedral was opened on Union Street and has been used since that time. The lists of names buried in this Main cemetery are listed below. This cemetery also has the two Priests, Msgr W. P. Finn (1953) and Rev Pat A. McCormack (1965) and one Nun, Sister Francesca Green.

Main Catholic Cemetery on Union Street. Showing altar for Masses and Tombstone with crucifix of Msgr. William Finn, the first Parish Priest.

Names in Main Roman Catholic Cemetery

Alaverdy	Cook	Gill	Keegan
Alyward	Cooke	Gillis	Kelly
Anstey	Connors	Glavine	Kennedy
Andrews	Colford	Grace	Kenny
Armstrong	Corbin	Granter	Keough
Arnold	Collett	Green	Knight
Allan	Cooper	Green, Francesca, Sr	Kyritsis
Ballard	Conway	Grace	Labrecque
Barker	Corbin	Griffin	Lane
Ball	Crawley	Griffiths	Lannon
Basha	Croke	Gunn	Lee
Boulos	Cantwell	Gushue	LeDrew
Bargery	Dawe	Grouchy	LeFresne
Barnes	Davis	Gosse	LeMee
Barker	Decker	Hamilton	Lewis
Barrow	Delaney	Hanlon	Lindahl
Barry	Devine	Hannaford	Locke
Beresford	Dillon	Hann	Lynch
Beson	Dormody	Hartigan	Lush
Bennett	Doiron	Hartley	Mackey
Blackmore	Dower	Hatt	Maddox
Bouzane	Down-Burke	Harvey	MacNeill
Bishop	Downey	Hayward	Maloney
Brown	Drake	Hawco	Maher
Browne	Dunphy	Hayes	MacKensie
Breen	Ducey	Healey	Molloy
Broderick	Dunn	Hearn	Martin
Boyle	Duggan	Hennebury	Matthews
Brennan	Duke	Hennessey	Melvin
Broaders	Dwyer	Hillier	Mercer
Brenton	Edwards	Higgins	Morgan
Brophy	Ennis	Hickey	Melvin
Bromley	Eisenhauer	Hogan	Moffatt
Butler	Etheridge	Hollett	Miller
Burt	Fewer	Hoey	Morris
Burke	Finn	Houlahan	McDonald
Byrd	Finn, Wm P. Msgr	Howse	McCarthy
Byrne	Fisher	Humber	McDermott
Bragg	Flemming	Hynes	McCormick
Baird	Flood	Henderson	McCormack, Pat Fr.
Burchell	Foley	Halvorsen	McGrath
Carey	Fogwell	Inder	McHugh
Carroll	Folkes	Jackman	McCue
Canning	Flynn	Janes	McNamara
Carpenter	French	Jesseau	Melvin
Cashin	Fowler	John	McLoughlin
Christopher	Froude	Judge	Mullowney
Clatney	Furlong	Johnson	Morris
Collett	Finlay	Kane	Murray
Collins	Gardner	Kean	Murphy

Mulrooney	Poole	Kearney	Trask
Newhook	Power	Shapleigh	Tremblett
Nichols	Price	Sharpe	Tucker
Nolan	Quigley	Sinnott	Tulk
Nugent	Quinlan	Shea	Thorne
O'Brien	Quirk	Smith	Wakelin
O'Driscoll	Ralph	Skanes	Walker
O'Keefe	Renouf	Southcott	Wall
O'Reilly	Roberts	Stapleton	Walsh
Owens	Rose	Stuewe	Way
Paddick	Russell	Sullivan	Whalen
Parsons	Ryan	Stein	Wheeler
Peddle	Rock46	Stone	Whelan
Penny	Sampson	Stroud	Whiffin
Penton	Saunders	Sweeney	White
Philpott	Scott	Swinton	Wicks
Pincott	Shallow	Snelgrove	Wilson
Pitcher	Seddon	Southcott	Winslow
		Tobin	

Union Street Roman Catholic Cemetery

Union Street Roman Catholic Cemetery at Grand Falls
Darker Tombstone (foreground) is that of Rev. Patrick McCormack - 1965

VALLEY ROAD CEMETERY

Alyward,Rosanna,d. 10-03-19,(26)	Eastman, Eliza J. d. 1-28-20 (16)	Jesseau, Arthur d. 12-23-23- (74)
Arklie, Douglas, d. 11-30-18	Eastman, Gordon d. 9-1-13 (5mo)	Johnson, Ethel d. 1-13-26 (14)
Arnold, Eugene, d. 06-17-20, (18)	Eastman, Thomas d. 9-12-19 (1+)	Kelly, George – d. Aug 11-1916
Ash, Wm James, d, 04-12-23 (27)	Ericson, Oscar d. 9-22-25 Infant	Kelly, Thomas d. 11-28-19 (13mo)
Baird, Anne Boyd, d, Infant	Fewer, Margaret d. 2-18-21 (8mo)	Kelly, Dorothy d. 11-17-18 (10)
Batstone, ClariceJ.d,12-24-23 (1+)	Fewer, Genevieve d. 10-27-24 (2)	Kennedy, Mary e. d. 2-2-18 (48)
Bowin, Leon d. 09-02-10 (6 mon)	Foley, Patrick d. 12-24-24 (8)	Kennedy, Thomas d. 4-15-18 (19)
Boulos, Joseph, d. 10-15-20 (6)	Foley, Austin d. 7-11-20 (1)	Kennedy, Richard d. 4-16-24 (29)
Boulos, Paul E. – 1911-1920 (9)	Foley, Elizabeth d. 12-15-43 (46)	Kennedy, Catherine d. 6-11-34 (69)
Bradshaw, Francis, d. 3-5-48 (74)	Foran, Patrick d. 10-28-18 (65)	King, Albert d. 2-22-19 (11)
Bradshaw, Jessie d. 3-18-24 (44)	Foran, Martha d. 8-1-14 (60)	Knight, Gusele d. 9-6-14 (36)
Bradbury, Mary d. 7-25-12 (30)	Foran, John d. 12-17-13 (35)	Lane, Mary d. 1-24-23 (8)
Brown, John, Ed d. 8-14-28 (29)	Foran, Rose d. 3-26-24 (61)	LeDrew, Edith d. 9-24-23 (27)
Brown, Arthur . – 1905-1915 (10)	Foran, Mary d. 12-29-16 (13+)	LeMoine, Evelyn d. 2-17-22 (14)
Brown,Effie.M.d.10-27-10 (infant)	Foran, William d. 1-17-15 (26)	Lake, Dorothy d. 8-7-10 (11mo)
Brown, Sarah B. – 1913-1918 (5)	Follett, Ruby G. d. 1-22-24 (4+)	Lind, Henry d. – age 74 years.
Brown, Harry F. – 1911-1920 (9)	Frampton, Jessie d. 12-9-16 (13+)	Lane, James d. 2-25-25 (56)
Brown, Eric d. 8-13-23 (15)	Fudge, Elfreda d. 2-18-23 (24)	LeDrew, Graham, d. 8-25-19 (17)
Brown, Gerald d. 1-19-25 (13)	Fever, George d. 3-29-16 (3mo)	LeMoine, Ernest d. 4-2-23 (46)
Brown, McKenzie d. 8-14-22 (3)	Fever, William d. 9-11-17 (6mo)	Martin, Susan d. 9-25-28 (86)
Breen, Elizabeth d. 8-26-15 (15)	Fever, Mary d. 3-17-26 (23)	MacDonald,Matthew d. 4-2-14 (20)
Bronson,Wilfred.d.11-416(Infant)	Fever, John d. 7-7-14 (50)	Maidment, Ezra d. 11-6-20 (51)
Boulos, Louis E. 1918-1920 (1 ½)	Fever, Robert d. 9-19-25 (35)	Mercer, George d. 6-9-27 (31) NFrg
Boulos, SolomonE.d. 3-3-11 (11m)	Frew, F. MacIntosh d. 4-14-17 (19)	Mercer, Austin d. 6-4-42- (79)
Budgell, Havard d. 9-12-27 (24)	KIA WWI	Mercer, Ann E. d. 11-10-50 (82)
Burry,Edward B. d. 11-18-19 (55)	Frew, Kitty d. 12-10-09 (13)	Mercer, Abijah d. 1-9-15 (14)
Bishop, Martha d. 10-19-07 (46)	Gardner, Martin d. 5-1-20 (29)	Mercer, John d. 11-17-24 (11)
Bishop,Emma A. – 1869-1910 (49)	Gardner, Jane F. d. 9-24-07 (16)	Mercer, Eleanor d. 12-3-39 (70)
Bishop, Lillian B. – 1911-1912 (1)	Gardner, Mary E. – 1857-1941 (84)	Mercer, Leslie d. 10-8-43 (37)
Bishop, Charles - 1898-1913 (15)	Gowlay, Janet d. 11-5-20 (54)	Murphy, John d. Jan 16-1925
Butt, Jacob d. 11-16-17 (32)	Gardner, Martin d. 3-23-14 (57)	McCormack,Maria d. 12-30-24 (10)
Butler,Alfreda.M.d. 10-22-21 (2+)	Gardner, Thomas d. 11-25-12 (21)	McVane, Annie d. 6-23-15 (5mo)
Blackmore, Daniel d.11-25-20 (73)	Ginn, Abigaile d. 10-22-24 (37)	Moore, James Sgt d. 2-6-17 (21)
Canning,George – 1826-1915. (89)	Ginn, John P. d.10-23-23 (73)	Moore, Margaret d. 5-1-25 (2)
Canning, Ernest – 1883-1946 (63)	Ginn, Lucy G. d. 10-31-18 (38)	Moore, Margaret d. 3-25-03 (38)
Canning,Lucinda –1881-1924 (43)	Granter, Cecilia d. 9-11-24 (42)	Moss, Robert d. 11-27-21 (73)
Carbery, Mary d. 10-1-15 (42)	Granter, Thomas – 1919-1933 (14)	Moss, Susanna d. 3-4-41 (84)
Campbell, Sadie d. 1-30-11 (7)	Granter, Darius – 1921-1925 (4)	Morrissey, H.A. d 11-14-39 (74)
Cantwell, Teresa d. 9-18-36 (71)	Green, Edgar, - age 55 years	Morrissey, Mary d. 12-6-29 (59)
Cantwell, Pierce d. 10-23-17 (16)	Green, Randolph, - age 20 years.	Osmond, Edgar d. 8-22-43 (69)
Cantwell, William d. 9-17-39 (77)	Green, David d. 10-17-31 (88)	Osmond, Edith d. 11-16-18 (40)
Clayson, Eliza d. 8-1-16 (70)	Green, Susan d. 9-11-25 (89)	Oldford, Mary J. d. 7-29-18 (53)
Chancey, Lloyd d. 12-2-22 (3+)	Green, Hubert d. 12-22-24 (5)	Osmond, George d. 8-4-17 (17)
Chamberlain HB MD d. 9-5-17	Haggett, Selina d. 9-13-23 (84)	Pearce, Abraham – 1842-1924 (82)
Colbourne,Gerald.d.12-27-22 (13)	Hayden, Robert d. 12-25-21 (79)	Philip, Elore, d. 3-3-21 (33)
Collins,Robert G. d. 12-19-25 (23)	Hann, Elia May d. 11-30-18 (30)	Pretty, Hayward d. 1-18-25 (24)
Cranville, Eliza d. 12-6-12 (36)	Hann, Vera C. d. 5-10-17 (15mo)	Pinksen, Rachel d. 3-3-14 (41)
Crocker,Allison d. 10-29-21 (7mo)	Hann, John S. d. 10-31-19 (1)	Pinksen,.Joshua..d.1-7-28(7)
Crocker, Doris d. 10-29-21 (7mo)	Healey, James F. 1918-1919 (1)	Drowned
Currie, Maggie d. 1-26-18 (66)	Hicks, Eva V. d. 6-26-23 (14)	Pitcher, Cornelius d. 1-7-28 (55)
Curtis, Pierce d. 12-5-18 (16)	Hebert, Drevest d. 12-24-15 (2mo)	Pitcher, Bridget d. 2-8-09 (34)
Dart, Wesley d. 8-13-09 (23)	Herbert, Horace – 1848-1919 (71)	Peaty, Mary A. d. 1-22-18 (68)
Doggett, Effie d. 9-14-15 (3mo)	Hollahan, Josie d. 5-6-18 (15)	Pelley, Arthur d. 11-9-16 (11)
Dormody,Anastasia.d.11-1-21(16)	Hopson, Herbert d. 4-20-19 (6 wk)	Pinsent, Elizabeth d. 1-29-20 (21)
Duval, Ida R. d. 10-2-10 (25)	House, James P. d. 9-25-24 (66)	Pinsent, Francis d. 7-10-25 (47)
Dwyer, Emma d. 10-5-48 (71)	Humphreys, Annie d. Mar 9,1929	Pardy, Jessie d. 1-8-26 (29)
Dwyer, John d. 11-29-50 (69)	Huntriss, John d. 6-19-12 (32)	Ralph, Doris d. 10-7-20 (4)
Eastman,Howley.d.10-12-24(8mo)	Ireland, Wm T. d. 12-14-15 (22)	Ryan, Dermott d. 2-23-25 (17)
	Janes, Julia A. d. 10-23-18 (28)	Rowsell, Elsie d. 9-20-23 (6mo)

Rowsell,Raymond.d.6-20-20(1mo)	**Smith, Mary d. 3-5-12 (1 day)**	**Stanford, William d. Apr 24,1919**
Rowsell, Simeon d. 12-2-22 (59)	**Skinner, Thomas d. 5-3-15 (26)**	**Sheppard, Margaret d. 6-14-25 (47)**
Rowsell, Worde, d. 7-14-21 (29)	**Silk, Bessie d. 9-10-27 (29)**	**Soper, Jonas – 1850-1924 (74)**
Rideout, Eliza d. 8-20-15 (44)	**Squires, James d. 12-23-08 (15)**	**Soper, Maria – 1853-1928 (75)**
Rowsell,Gordon.Pte.d,4-14-17(21)	**Shallow, Eleanor d. 5-12-11 (10mo)**	**Soper, Donald – 1914-1921 (7)**
Rideout, Susan d. 5-6-20 (34)	**Shallow, Annie d. 11-16-11 (28)**	**Simpson, William d. 5-11-11 (46)**
Rowe, Dorothy d. 12-4-24 (12)	**Shallow, Harry d. 10-23-11 (2mo)**	**Simpson, George d. 4-11-24 (24)**
Rae, Margaret d. 10-29-23 (16mo)	**Sullivan, Mary d. 2-14-15 (52)**	**Simpson, Robert d. 1-6-24 (21)**
Ryan, Louisa d. Nov-18-1930	**Sullivan, Michael d. 5-9-19 (55)**	**Died at sea,**
Ryan,Margaret d. 1-23-22 (10mo)	**Sanders, George d. June 13, 1957**	**Stroud, Catherine d. 11-21-23 (31)**
Ray, David d. 3-3-27 (79)	**Sanders, Ernest d. July 8, 1916**	**Thomas, Myrtle d. 7-28-16 (2mo)**
Ray, Maria d. 10-21-18 (48)	**Small, Edward d. 7-29-04 (11mo)**	**Taylor, Cecil d. 6-16-15 (2mo)**
Rowsell, Edward d. Oct-4-1924	**Small, Ed d. 12-6-09 (1+)**	**Way, William d. 1-21-23 (11)**
Smith, Gladys d. Aug-18-1911	**Stratton, Stephen d. Mar 8, 1922.**	**Way, Harold d. 1917-1918 (1)**

Valley Road Inter Faith Cemetery

When we analyze the information from the Valley Cemetery, of the 215 burials, we find the following: THE DEATHS BY AGE: 47 died from Infant to age 5; 49 died from age 6 to 21; 26 died from age 22-30; 16 died from ages 31-40; 32 died from ages 41-65; and 34 died from age 66 on up. Eleven have no age listed. The oldest burial was one in 1903 and one in 1904. The remaining burials were 1907 (2); 1908 (1); 1909 (4); 1910 (5); 1911 (7); 1912 (6); 1913 (3); 1914 (6); 1915 (14); 1916 (9); 1917 (9); 1918 (17); 1919 (12); 1920 (15); 1921 (10); 1922 (7); 1923 (15); 1924 (20); 1925 (13) and 1926 (3). There were 31 buried in later years after 1926 and eleven had no year listed. The oldest was age 88 and the youngest was one day old. The two Crocker sisters both died on Oct 29, 1921, both 7 months old (maybe twins). One Medical Doctor was H.B. Chamberlain. One was drowned, Joshua Pinksen, age 7 on Jan 7, 1928. One died-at-sea, Robert Simpson on April 6, 1924 at age 21. Two were "Killed in action" in WWI; F. MacIntosh Frew April 14, 1917, age 19 and on the same day, Pte Gordon Rowsell, April 14. 1917 age 21. According to Volume Four, Book of Newfoundland, page 533, it showed that Newfoundlanders fought in the Battle of Monchy-le-Preux on 14 April 1917. These Grand Falls soldiers were undoubtedly killed in this battle. Three Boulos children died in 1920: Joseph (6) died Oct 15, Paul (9) died Oct 18 and Louis (1 ½) died Oct 27. Three members of the Shallow family died in 1911: Eleanor (10mos) died May 12; Harry (2mos) died Oct 23 and Annie (28) died on Nov 16.

Valley Road Inter Faith Cemetery

Chapter 34

KNIGHTS OF COLUMBUS "NOTRE DAME" COUNCIL OF GRAND FALLS, # 2053

The Notre Dame Council of the Knights of Columbus # 2053 was chartered in the early days of the Grand Falls Parish. It was officially chartered on 19 November 1919 by Rev William P. Finn. It was the fourth Council in Newfoundland after Harbour Grace, St. John's and Bell Island. The first "guys" who started the council went to Harbour Grace, took their degrees and as members of the Dalton Council returned to Grand Falls to begin the Notre Dame council. Some of the original members were Tom Griffin, Jim Murphy, Bill Delaney, Danny Maher and Arthur Jackman. Initial degrees were conferred "in the old town hall". The first Grand Knight was an American, named William Shannahan, with the Anglo-Newfoundland Development Company. In the first executive, the other members were, A.G."Phonse" Duggan, as deputy; Mike Nugent, Chancellor; Bill Delaney, Recorder; Dan Clatney, Financial secretary; Arthur Jackman, treasurer; Jim Murphy, warden; Pat Griffin, lecturer; Jack Kelly, inside guard, Jack David and Walter Fewer, outside guards; and trustees were Bill Gosse, Gregg Kelly and Tom Pumphrey. On 25 July 1932, the old wooden K C Hall that housed the operations of the Notre Dame burned to the ground, along with all the records. On 25 Jan 1933, the present concrete building replaced the ruins of building number one.

Notre Dame Council, Knights of Columbus Building in Grand Falls, situated on Church Road immediately opposite the Cathedral of the Immaculate Conception and official seat of government in the diocese of Grand Falls. This building replaces the old Knights of Columbus Hall which burned down on July 25th, 1932. The above building was opened on January 25th, 1933.

GRAND KNIGHTS SINCE 1919 WERE:

William Shannahan 1919-1920; A.G. Duggan 1920-1923; M.F. Nugent 1923-1924; P.J. Griffin 1924-1926; S.J. Hannaford 1926-1927; J.P. Molloy 1927-1930; C. I. "Cecil" Power 1930-1931; J.P. Molloy 1931-1934; J.L. Hannaford 1934-1936; L. Rose 1936-1937; T.J. Healey 1937-1938; J. P. Molloy 1938-1943; P.A. Mollowney 1943-1945; J. P. Molloy 1945-1947; T.F. Conway 1947-1948; Valentine F. Stapleton 1948-1952; A. G. Duggan 1952-1954; J.B. Cantwell 1954-1955; Benedict J. Stapleton 1955-1956; V.F. Stapleton 1956-1959; G.J. Whelan 1959-1961; Kevin M. Harvey 1961-1965; L.F. Kelly 1965-1966; J. F. Byrd 1966-1967; Donald J. Russell 1967-1971; M.N. Croke 1971-1973; G.J. Burke 1973-1974; M.N. Croke 1974-1976; J. Bouzane 1976-1978; C. Healey 1978-1980; C. Lindahl 1980-1982; D.J. Russell 1982-1984; P. F. Power 1984-1986; J.F. O'Reilly 1986-1988; J.R. Kelly 1988-1990; S. Paddick 1990-1992; P. F. Power 1992-1995; J. F. O'Reilly 1995-1996; E. Mason 1996-1998; W. E. Aylward 1998-2000; J. Tremblett 2000-2001; E. Mason 2001-2002 ;and E. Dudter 2002-Present.

Highlights of the Notre Dame Council

1919, Nov 19 – Notre Dame Council formed in Grand Falls, First Chaplain, Rev William Finn.

1922 – First state convention held in Grand Falls and draws up 1st by-laws for Newfoundland.

FIRST STATE CONVENTION IN GRAND FALLS

THE FIRST STATE CONVENTION WAS IN 1922
FRONT ROW L-R: Judge Casey, Judge Cyril J. Fox, Cyril Cahill, Charles Ellis, William Maddigan, A. G. "Phonse" Duggan, 1st Deputy Grand Knight and second Grand Knight, SECOND ROW: W. Jackman, D.A. O'Flynn, Msgr Finn, Joe Greene, Fr Dean McGrath, D. Jackman, Father Casey. BACK ROW: W. A. Shannahan, First Grand Knight, Joseph Fitzgibbon and Magistrate Murphy.

1923 – Initial KC Building built and occupied in 1926.

1933, Jan 25 – Old Knights of Columbus Building burned to the ground.

1937 – Newfoundland Federation of Labor formed in KC building in Grand Falls.

1944 – 25th Anniversary of KC Council. (1919-1944).

1950, May 20 – Bishop March Council # 3315 was inaugurated at Buchan's by Notre Dame Council. First Grand Knight was E. J. Collins.

1952 – Initial Youth Club conceived by Msgr. Wm Finn and later started by Rev. Michael Hynes in Immaculate Conception Parish.

1961, Apr 30 – The First Fourth Degree was instigated at Notre Dame Council in Grand Falls. Those from Grand Falls.

INCLUDED IN FIRST FOURTH DEGREE CLASS (1961)

Msgr. W. P. Hogan; Rev. F. P. Meaney; Rev. L. F. Burke; Rev. Dr. L. R. Fitzgerald; Rev. L. J. Coady; Rev. R. J. Walsh; Rev. M. F. Hynes; William S. Shallow; K. P. Griffin; Leo L. Hennessey Sr; P. F. Kearney; U.N. Jesseau; J.P. Molloy; J. G. Delaney; M.V. Power; V.F. Stapleton; B.J. Stapleton; Joseph J. Stapleton; F.W. Delaney; L.F. Kelly; G.A. Morrissey; K.M. Harvey; James T. Delaney; S.L. Keough; T.V. Maloney; Leo Ryan; M.A. Davis; H.S. Murray; and A. V. Byrd.

1962, June 3 – The Second Fourth Degree took place at Notre Dame Council in Grand Falls.

INCLUDED IN SECOND FOURTH DEGREE CLASS (1962)

J. R. Power; Don Broderick; Thomas F. Conway; A. Griffin; Leo Fewer; E. J. Connolly; James Cunningham; A. G. Duggan; Mike Croke; Leo Hennessey Jr; D.J. Russell; G.J. Whelan and Phillip Beresford.

1965, Apr 19 – Rev. Dr. Whelan Council # 5662 was inaugurated at Labrador City. Helped launched by Grand Knight of Notre Dame Council. First Grand Knight was Cyril J. Fleming.

1965, Jul 21 – The Twix Teen Youth Club was organized under the sponsorship of the Notre Dame Council Knights of Columbus for the Catholic Youth of the Parish of Grand Falls.

1965, Nov 26 – McCormack Council # 5768 was inaugurated at Gander by Notre Dame Council. First Grand Knight was J. G. Finn.

1966, Oct 12 – Annual Columbus Day celebrations at Grand Falls became an Ecumenical Movement personified, when for the first time all Fraternal Organizations in Grand Falls were in attendance. They included: Oddfellows, Masonic Lodge, Elks Club, and Loyal Orange Lodge who attended the Knights of Columbus Meeting.

EUCUMENTICAL MOVEMENT

ANNUAL COLUMBUS DAY CELEBRATIONS 1966
SEATED L-R: Gideon Samms, Independent Order of Oddfellows; Wilbur Osmond, Masonic Lodge GF; Leonard Ryan, exalted ruler of Elk's Club and William Moores, Loyal Orange Lodge. STANDING: L-R: Lewis F. Kelly, Grand Knight, Notre Dame Council; Terrence V. Maloney, District Deputy; Kevin J. Lawlor, State deputy of KC in Nfld and Robert C. Brockie, Grand Knight of Bishop March Council in Buchans.

1966, Nov 11 – Monsignor Finn Council # 5904 was inaugurated at Bishop's Falls by Notre Dame Council. First Grand Knight was William Pumphrey.

1967, May 28 – The Third Fourth Degree took place at Notre Dame Council in Grand Falls. From Grand Falls Council.

INCLUDED IN THIRD FOURTH DEGREE CLASS (1967)

Dr. M. J. McGuire; P.J. Cashin; L.F. Hanlon; J.F. Gushue; A. J. Walsh; J.F. Byrd; W.P. Beson; K.F. Dutton; S.W. Paddick; D. J. Ryan; James B. Byrne Sr; Dermott J. Russell and Kevin Dormody.

1968, Grand Knight D. J. Russell attended Four Atlantic Provinces meeting at Sydney, Nova Scotia with Supreme Knight, Dr. McDevitt.

1969, May 23-25 – State Convention was held at Grand Falls. Notre Dame Council receives Youth Activities Award.

1969, Nov 19 – 50th Anniversary of Notre Dame Council in Grand Falls.

1994, - 75th Anniversary of the Notre Dame Council in Grand Falls.

1999, - 80th Anniversary of the Notre Dame Council in Grand Falls.

EXECUTIVE OF NOTRE DAME COUNCIL 1969

FRONT ROW L-R: Ernest Becker, treasurer; Kevin Dutton, Chancellor; Msgr W. P. Hogan, chaplain; Grand Knight, Donald J. Russell; deputy Grand Knight, R.M. "Dick" O'Neill; recorder, Mike Croke; and trustee, Tom Burke. BACK ROW L-R: Tony Brophy, trustee; Advocate, K.P. Griffin; warden, Frank Delaney; trustee, Jack Gushue; outside guard, Austin Foley; inside guard, Phil McCarthy. INSERT: T. V. Maloney, financial secretary and state deputy Nfld. Missing: outside guard, James Byrne.

1994, Nov 19 – 75th anniversary of Notre Dame Council in Grand Falls.

BLESSING OF OUTSIDE CHRISTMAS CRIB 2002

December 2002 – Rev David E. Joy Blessing the Knights of Columbus Crib.

Chapter 35

CATHOLIC VETERANS FROM THE GRAND FALLS AREA

Military Veterans

Each town in Newfoundland is proud of the men who went off to war when their country called them. Grand Falls and nearby communities were no exception. We have tried to enumerate all the names of those Grand Falls citizens who joined the Military services in both the First World War and the Second World War as well others who joined to give their service in other times of peace or war. Many were individually recruited and others went into Service as Members of the Catholic Cadet Corps. The Members of the Catholic Cadet Corps who served in World War II, were broken down as follows: Fifty (50) in RA; thirty-six (36) in RN; twenty-two (22) in RAF; six (6) in RCAF; six (6) in Canadian Army; three (3) in British Army; three (3) in US Army; two (2) in Merchant Navy; two (2) in RCN and one (1) in RCE. Roman Catholic Cemetery and Knights of Columbus Records that indicate those Service members who are deceased from all wars are broken down as follows: twenty-one (21) served in World War I; nine (9) served in World War II and one (1) served in Korean War. Three died in WWI and one died in WWII. We are indebted to Louis Barker for the information on the Catholic Cadets and we regret any veteran we have overlooked.

OUR BOYS

Our Newfoundland boys have answered the call,
The players of hockey, of bowling and ball
Have gladly relinquished the dear things in life,
To fight for their king in the midst of the strife.

There are tears in our eyes as we see our boys go,
But God in His Heaven is watching, we know,
And whether in cloudland, on land or on sea
Our boys in His keeping will ever safe be.

Written by Ruth Jackman, 1940
Inter Nos Magazine, Academy of Our Lady of Mercy, St. John's.

Members of the Catholic Cadet Corps who served in WWII.

Alyward, Patrick, RA
Anstey, Bertram, R.A.
Anstey, James, R.N.
Byrd, Arthur, R.A.
Byrd, John, R.C.A.F.
Breen, Edward, R.N.
Burke, Cyril, R.N.
Burke, John, R.N.
Burke, William, R.N.
Browne, Gordon, R.N.
Browne, Michael, R.C.A.F.
Barry, Andrew, R.A.
Barry, Maurice, R.N.
Bouzanne, Bertram, R.A.F.
Beson, Harold,British Army
Beson, Walter, R.N.
Cashin, Peter, R.C.N.
Clatney, John, R.A.
Connors, Cornelius, R.N.
Conway, Frederick, R.A.
Conway, Henry, R.A.F.
Conway, John C. R.A.
Cooke, Donald, R.A.
Cooke, Thomas V. R.A.F.
Cooke, Vincent, R.A.
Dunphy, Thomas, R.C.E.
Davis, Bernard, R.N.
Davis, Brendan, R.A.F.
Davis, Reginald, R.A.
Delaney, Francis, R.A.
Dower, Thomas, R.N.
Duke, James P. RAF
Dunne, Raymond, R.N.
Edwards, Augustus, R.A.
Edwards, Charles, R.A.F.
Edwards, George, U.S.A.
Edwards, Leo, Can Army
Ethridge, John, R.C.N.
French, Desmond, R.C.A.F.
Fewer, Ronald, R.A.F.
Fewer, William, R.A.
Foley, Charles, R.A.
Foley, Clement, R.A.
Foley, Francis, R.N.
Fisher, William, R.A.
Flood, Alphonsus, R.A.
Griffin, Dermott, R.A.
Griffin, Wilfred, R.A.F.
Gouldie, John,British Army
Goudie, George, R.N.
Goodyear, Patrick, R.N.
Hanlon, John R.A.
Healey, John, R.A.
Healey, Patrick, R.N.
Hennessey, Arthur, R.N.
Hennessey, John R.A.F.
Hennessey, William, R.A.F.
Hickey, Thomas, M.N.
Jackman, Arthur, R.A.
Jackman, Cecil, R.N.
Jackman, Harold, R.N.
Jackman, Ronald, R.A.F.
Janes, Wallace, R.A.
Jesseau, Cecil, R.A.
Jesseau, Pius, R.A.
Kelly, A.A. R.C.A.F.
Kelly, Bryan, R.A.
Kelly, Lewis, F., R.A.
Kelly, Michael, R.A.F.
Kelly, Peter, Can Army
Kelly, Richard J. R.A.
Kelly, Samuel M.N.
Kelly, William, R.A.
Lannon, Bernard, R.A.
Lannon, William, R.A.F.
Lewis, Harold, R.N.
Lewis, Kevin, R.N.
Lewis, Patrick, R.A.
Louis, John, R.N.
Matthews, Robert, R.A.F.
Molley, James F. Can Army
Moloney, Jerome, R.C.A.F.
Mullowney, John, R.A.
Mullowney, William, R.A.
Mulrooney, Frank, R.A.
McCarthy, Cecil, R.A.
McDonald, Charles, R.A.
McDonald,Pearce,BritArmy
McDonald, Raymond, R.A.
McDonald, Vincent, R.A.
Morris, Aiden, R.C.A.F.
Morris, James, R.N.
Morris, Ralph, R.A.F.
Morris, William, R.N.
Murphy, James, U.S.A.
Murphy, James, R.N.
Murphy, Michael, R.A.
Murphy, Roy, R.A.F.
Murray, Allan D. R.A.F.
Nugent, James, Can Army
Power, Clifton, R.A.
Power, Cyril, R.N.
Power, Joseph, R.N.
Power, Maurice, R.A.
Power, Raymond, R.A.
Power, Thomas, R.A.F.
Power, William, R.A.
Penton, Leo, R.A.
Quinlan, Donald, R.A.F.
Quigley, Claude, Can Army
Roberts, Gordon, R.A.
Shallow, Augustus, R.A.F.
Shallow, Alonzo, U.S.A.
Shallow, Charles, R.A.F.
Shallow, Douglas R.A.F.
Sullivan, Peter, R.A.
Sullivan, Ronald, R.N
Tobin, James, R.N.
Tobin, Marin, R.A.
Turpin, Alonzo, R.N.
Wall, Gregory, R.A.
Wall, John, R.N.
Wall, Nicholas, Can Arm.
Walsh, Anthony, R.N.
Walsh, Bartholomew, R.N.
Walsh, Joseph, R.N.
Walsh, Lawrence, R.N.
Winslow, George P., R.A.
Whiffin, Leonard, R.A.
Whiffin, Marin, R.A.
White, Cyril, R.N.

Deceased Catholic Veterans from Grand Falls

Catholics in Grand Falls and Vicinity gave there Military service to Newfoundland during World War I, World War II and the Korean War. We have listed those who are deceased. These names were taken from the records of the Grand Falls Grace Cemetery lists and Knights of Columbus 50th Jubilee Book. We are sorry for any names that were left off.

Beson, Patrick Sgt	1914-1918 WWI
Burke, William Stoker 1c	1937-1945 KC died in WWII.
Connors, Maurice Pvt	1914-1918 WWI
Conway, Charles Sgt	1937-1945 WWII
Conway, Fred Pvt	1950-1953 – Korean War
Coulan, Patrick Sgt	1914-1918 WWI
Dunphy, Thomas Corp	1914-1918 WWI
Dunphy, Thomas Sgt	1937-1945 WWII
Edwards, Alphonsus Pvt	1914-1918 WWI
Edwards, John Pvt	1914-1918 WWI
Etheridge, Richard Pvt	1914-1918 WWI
Evoy, Andrew Pvt	1914-1918 WWI
Fewer, Lawrence Pvt	1914-1918 WWI
Frew, MacIntosh F.	WWI, KIA 14 Apr 1917*, age 19. Buried in Valley Rd Cemetery, Grand Falls.
Grace, Martin Sgt	1914-1918 WWI
Grace, Michael Corp	1914-1918 WWI
Hannon, Francis Sgt	1914-1918 WWI
Kelly, Peter Pvt	1937-1945 WWII
Kent, Martin Corp	1914-1918 WWI
Lannon, Bernard Bombardier	1937-1945 KC died in WWII.
Matthews, Robert Sgt	1937-1945 WWII
Mooney, James Pvt	1914-1918 WWI
Moore, James Sgt	1914-1918 WWI. Died 2 Feb 1917, age 21. Buried in Valley Rd Cemetery, Grand Falls.
Morris, Ralph Flt Sgt	1937-1945 WWII
O'Flynn, Michael Pvt	1914-1918 WWI
O'Reilly, William Pvt	1914-1918 WWI
Power, Nicholas Pvt	1914-1918 WWI
Rowsell, Gordon, Pte	WWI, KIA 14 Apr 1917*, age 21. Buried in Valley Rd Cemetery, Grand Falls.
Sargent, John Pvt	1914-1918 WWI
Shallow, Augustus Sgt	1937-1945 WWII
White, Cyril Able Seaman	1937-1945 WWII

Notes: * Book of Newfoundland says Newfoundlanders fought in Battle of Monchy-le-Preux on 14 April 1917. Page 533. KC – Knights of Columbus.
KIA – Killed in action.

Chapter 35

EPILOGUE

After researching information about the Irish, the Catholic Church and Newfoundland in general for over 20 years, we felt that this information should be documented for everyone to appreciate the great trials and tribulations the Irish had to endure in their early days in Newfoundland. Although I am somewhat of an adopted Newfoundlander, it was an honour for me to be permitted to publish this book. This was truly a labor of Love. As we celebrated the Millennium Year 2000, we were celebrating the two thousand years that the Catholic Church has been in existence since Jesus appointed Peter as the first Pope and unto today with Pope John Paul II as the 262nd Pope. The early Catholics endured many persecutions, heresies and loss of rights which produced many martyrs among our early Catholics, Popes, and Clergy. This history provided a role model for the early Irish Catholics in Ireland and Newfoundland. Ireland was converted to Catholicism by St. Patrick in the 5th century (c 421 A.D.) and the Irish through the years have experienced a great many deprivations, like the early Catholic Church itself, and the people have proudly held onto their faith. From the arrival of the Normans to the English control under Henry VIII and the penal laws which deprived the Irish of their rights to practice their religion, the expropriation of their lands, the deportation of their priests and the Mass being prescribed for them. It was not until the beginning of the 18th century that the persecution of the Catholics was eased. When the Irish came to Newfoundland to free themselves from the penal restrictions at home, they disappeared to out-of-way Harbours to set up their homes as exiles and they became the bulwark of the Irish Church in Newfoundland. This book is a tribute to these same poor Irish fisherman who came to Newfoundland for freedom and hide in the woods to be free and had not been able to acknowledge their faith and were persecuted by the authorities in early Newfoundland but exhibited their inherent pride, solemn devotion and dedication to their faith. It has been said that Newfoundland is second only to Ireland itself to have established a truly historical and a profoundly Irish Catholic Church. It was founded by Irish Bishops, built by predominantly Irish architects and manned by mostly Irish Priests, Sisters and Brothers. The Irish Presentation Sisters and Christian Brothers came to Newfoundland as the first to any overseas location outside Ireland. The majority of the names of the Catholic parishioners in this Diocese seem to have theirs origins primarily of Irish decent.

We hope this book provides the people who have interest in such a history and those whose ancestors, parents and family members were a part of this history may enjoy in print what the wonderful people of this Diocese experienced in person. During the penal period in Ireland, when the Irish Catholics were not allowed to practice their religion openly, i.e., Priests were prohibited, it was a crime to attend any Catholic ceremony and was a crime to possess any religious semblance. The Irish people developed practices to show their allegiance to their Church in various ways. The most sought after semblance at the time, because of the Catholics devotion to Mary, was the Penal Rosary. The Irish made a metal bead ring with 10 bumps on it and a little cross. This was used to say the rosary indiscreetly and the English may not be aware what it represented. Those Irish that jumped over to the English side so they could get special privileges were called "jumpers". This stigma stuck to the family-name and were sometimes shunned by the loyal Catholics, who kept their religion, years after the penal period. Another way the Catholics would subversively practice their religion during the penal period was through a carol as a catechism song for young Catholics. It had two levels of meaning; the surface meaning plus a hidden meaning known only to members of the Catholic Church. Each element of the carol had a code word for a religious reality which the children could remember. We all know this carol, as the "12 Days of Christmas".

The partridge in a pear tree was Jesus Christ.
Two turtle doves were the Old and New Testaments.
Three French hens stood for Faith, Hope and Charity.
The four calling birds were the four gospels of Matthew, Mark, Luke and John.
The five golden rings recalled the Torah or Law, the first five books of the Old Testament.
The six geese a-laying stood for the six days of creation.
Seven swans a-swimming represented the sevenfold gifts of Holy Spirit:
Prophesy, Serving, Teaching, Exhortation, Contribution, Leadership and Mercy.
The eight maids a-milking were the eight beatitudes.
Nine ladies dancing were the nine fruits of the Holy Spirit: Love, Joy, Peace,
Patience, Kindness, Goodness, Faithfulness, Gentleness and Self-Control.
The ten lords a-leaping were the Ten Commandments.
The eleven pipers piping stood for the eleven faithful Apostles.
The twelve drummers drumming symbolized the twelve points of belief
in the Apostle's Creed.

Under cover priests in Ireland who risked their lives saying Mass in the woods and mountains at locations known as the Mass Rock. This name even became known at locations in Newfoundland where priests said Mass under the stars, prior to 1784.

HISTORY

OF

ROMAN CATHOLIC CHURCH

IN NEWFOUNDLAND &

HARBOUR GRACE
and
GRAND FALLS

APPENDIX A

RC CHURCH IN NFLD & HARBOUR GRACE HISTORY

RC CHURCH IN HG & GF, NFLD HISTORY (1)

(Selected Events)

387-461 AD. – St. Patrick Bishop of Ireland.
500 AD. – St. Brendan to Greenland?
1000 – Leif Ericson introduces Catholic Faith into Greenland.
1000 – Ericson lands at L-Anse Meadows, Newfoundland.
1215 – Magna Charta.
1497 - Discovery of Newfoundland by John Cabot.
1501 - Portuguese Explorer Gaspar de Corte real in Newfoundland.
1534-35 - French explorer Jacques Cartier arrived in NFLD.
1550 - Carbonear visited by Fishing Admirals.
1576-78 – Frobisher's voyages to Labrador.
1583 - Sir Humphrey Gilbert annexed Newfoundland to England.
1600 - Princess Sheila Na Geira brought to Carbonear.
1604 – 1ST permanent settlement at St. Pierre Miquelon.
1608 – Champlain founded Quebec.
1610 - John Guy 1st settlement Cupids, Newfoundland.
1613 - 1st child born of European Parents in Cupids, NFLD.
1614 - Carbonear First History of Pirate Raids.
1616 - Vaughn Colony at Trepassey (Avalon Peninsula)
1623 - Lord Baltimore founded Colony at Ferryland.
1627 - 1st Rep of RC Church w/Lord Baltimore.
1630 - Arrival of 1st Irish settlers in NFLD.
1641 - Montreal founded by French Jesuit Priests.
1653 - 1st Governor of Newfoundland - Treworgie.
1655 - 1713 - French Governors established Capitol at Placentia.
1675 - 1728 - Age of English Commodores in Newfoundland.
1689- 1713 – The French period at Placentia.
1713 - Treaty of Utrecht. (England full rights over NFLD)
1729 - 1816 - Non-Resident Naval Governors.
1729 - Carbonear one of 6 Judicial Districts.
1729 - Capt Henry Osborne 1st Governor of Newfoundland.
1750 – Increased in immigration from Ireland.
1755 - Catholic convicted of practicing their religion. Carb & HG.
1762 - Carbonear Island captured by French 1st & last time.
1763 - Treaty of Paris. (French out of Newfoundland)
1764-67 - Captain James Cook surveys Newfoundland coast.
1764 – Felix McCarthy fined for alleged riots in Harbour Grace.
1775 - Terrific hurricane & tidal wave, much loss life/property.
- Declaration of American Independence.
1776 - 1783 - American Colonies rebel against England.
1783 - Treaty of Versailles.
1784 - Roman Catholics given religious freedom in Newfoundland.

RC CHURCH IN HG & GF, NFLD HISTORY (2)

1784 - Rev O'Donel appointed as Prefect Apostolic in NFLD
1784 – Harbour Grace – Origination Date.
1784-99 – Rev Patrick Phelan mission Priest at Harbour Grace.
1784-99 – Rev Phelan said Mass in rented store-chapel with 10 pews.
1789 - French Revolution & George Washington, 1st Pres USA.
1793 - Supreme Court est. in NFLD - Chief Justice Reeves.
1796 - Rev Louis O'Donel consecrated Bishop of NFLD in Quebec.
1800-1806 – Rev Fitzpatrick, 2d Mission Priest in Harbour Grace.
1801 - Anne Garland, age 117, dies in Harbour Grace
1804 - Governor Gower encouraged settlement in Newfoundland.
1805 - Post Office Established in St. John's.
1806 - First Newspaper printed
1806 - BIS founded in St. John's
1806 – 1833 - Rev Thomas Ewer takes over Mission in Harbour Grace.
1806 –Rev Ewer builds first church in Harbour Grace.
1806 - Bishop O'Donel returns to Ireland after 22 years.
1807 - Bishop Lambert appointed 2n Vicar Apostolic of St. John's.
1808 - Court House erected in Harbour Grace.
1810 - Governor Sir Duckworth visits Harbour Grace & Carbonear.
1811 - Bishop O'Donel dies in Waterford, Ireland, age 74.
1812 - War of 1812. USA versus England.
1814 - Treaty at Ghent ends War of 1812.
1814 - BIS founded in Harbour Grace. Fr. Ewer.
1815 - Battle of Waterloo
1815 – King's Cove – Origination Date.
1816 - 1st Resident Governor - Admiral Pickmore.
1816 – Church of England at Harbour Grace Burned.
1817 - Bishop Scallan appointed 3rd Vicar Apostolic of St. John's.
1820 – Bishop John Dalton born in Ireland. (HG)
1823 – Bishop Henry Carfagnini born in Italy. (HG)
1824 – Brigus – Origination Date.
1824 - Brigus RC Church built by Rev Dean Mackin.
1825 – Nfld School society established at Harbour Grace
1825 - 1832 - Civilian role - Cochrane 1st Civil Governor.
1825 - First road constructed - Portugal Cove Road.
1825 - Rev James Brown born in Carbonear. 1st native born priest.
1826 - First Roman Catholic Chapel in Carbonear.
1827 – Harbour Grace Boys Academy established.
1830 - Bishop Fleming Appointed Bishop of St. John's.
1832 - Representative Government granted for Newfoundland.
1832 - 1855 - Representative Government.
1832 - Harbour Grace destroyed by fire - 96 buildings burned.

RC CHURCH IN HG & GF, NFLD HISTORY (3)

1833 - First Presentation Nuns to Newfoundland.
1833 - First Convent school by Nuns in St. John's.
1833 - Rev Thomas Ewer dies in Harbour Grace, age 84.
1833 – 1859 – Rev Charles Dalton, PP Harbour Grace.
1833 - Carbonear own newspaper "Star".
1833 - Slavery abolished in England.
1835 - BIS founded in Carbonear.
1835 - Second Roman Catholic Chapel built in Carbonear.
1838 – Northern Bay – Origination Date.
1840 - Election riots Carbonear - Constitution suspended 1841-43.
1840 – Tilting Fogo –Origination Date.
1841 - Foundation stone for RC Cathedral St. John's laid.
1842 – Carbonear – Origination Date.
2 - Carbonear first resident RC Priest - Rev J. Gleeson.
1842 – Mercy Sisters arrive in St. John's.
1843 - RC School Board established at Harbour Grace and Carbonear.
– Harbour Grace Grammar School started – Mr Roddick, Princ.
1844 - Large fire in Harbour Grace.
1844 – Dr William Hanrahan dies in snow in Carbonear.
1845 - Gas introduced at St. John's.
1846 - Meeting to dismiss Sheriff Gaden, Harbour Grace.
1846 – Bishop Henry Carfagnini ordained in Rome, (HG)
1847 - John Brien died Carbonear, Age 102, and Vet Bunker Hill.
1849 – Bishop John Dalton ordained in Rome, (HG)
1850 - Bishop Mullock appointed Bishop St. John's. (SJ)
1850 - 1st Mass in RC Cathedral, St. John's. Bishop Fleming.
1850 – Rev Stephen Flynn born in Harbour Grace.
1852 – Bishop Mullock laid cornerstone HG Stone Church.
1852 – Gas first introduced into Harbour Grace.
1853 – 1st Roman Catholic Stone Church consecrated in HG.
1855 - Newfoundland granted Responsible Government.
1855 - 1934 - Responsible Government.
1855 - Consecration of Roman Catholic Cathedral, St. John's.
1855 - 1864 - Severe depression and pauperism in NFLD.
1855 - Edmond Hanrahan 1st elected Resp. Government.
1856 – 1869. - First Bishop new HG Diocese - Most Rev John Dalton.
1856 - Fr James Brown - 1st Native Born Priest, from Carbonear.
1856 - St. Bon's College opened.
1857 - First Newfoundland Stamp.
1857 – Harbour Main – Origination Date.
1858c – Rev John J. Lynch born in Harbour Grace.
1858 - Harbour Grace nearly destroyed by fire.

RC CHURCH IN HG & GF, NFLD HISTORY (4)

1860 - Carbonear destroyed by Fire - Main Street
1860 – Harbour Breton – Origination Date.
1862 - Riots XMAS day, McNeil shot. Carbonear,
1864 - Alexander O'Donovan, Carbonear Grammar School, dies, age 51.
1866 – 1st Atlantic cable – Ireland to Hearts Content.
1868 – First Cathedral of Harbour Grace dedicated, Bishop Dalton.
1869 – Bishop John Dalton dies at Harbour Grace, age 48.
1869-1870 – Administrator of HG Diocese, Msgr Murphy.
1870 – 1880 - 2nd Bishop of Harbour Grace - Bishop Carfagnini.
1871 – Big fire in Harbour Grace.
1875 – Very Rev J. H. Scully born in Harbour Grace.
1876 - Christian Brothers 1st arrival in St. John's *(SS Moravian)*
1878 - Visit and Death of Bishop Conroy in Nfld. Papal Delegate.
1880 - Bishop Carfagnini leaves Harbour Grace.
1880 – Baie Verte – Origination Date.
1880 – Bay de Verde – Origination Date.
1881 – 1906 – 3RD Bishop of Harbour Grace – Bishop Ron MacDonald
1883 - Carbonear Star & Conception Bay Journal started.
1883 – "Harbour Grace Affray" - Orange men attacked at HG.
1883 – Holyrood – Origination Date.
1884 – First RC Cathedral opened in Harbour Grace.
1884 – Conception Harbour – Origination Date.
1884 - 1st 86 miles of RR completed from St. John's to Harbour Grace.
1885 - Violent storm in June, wrecking many vessels.
1885 - Hurricane and Tidal wave on Labrador coast.
1886 – St. Joseph's RC Church consecrated RH, HG.
1887 – Rev James Brown died in Harbour Main.
1887 – Whitbourne – Origination Date.
1888 – Cornerstone of new RC Church laid in Carbonear.
1889 – New RC Cathedral in Harbour Grace destroyed by fire.
1891 – New RC Church Consecrated in Carbonear.
1891 - St. Brendan's – Origination Date.
1892 – Large fire in St. John's destroyed half the city.
1895 – Bishop Power dies in St. John's, very large funeral.
1898 – Mount Cashel Orphanage formally opened.
1899 – First car, "St. John's" arrived for street railway.
1904 – Bishop Carfagnini dies in Rome.
1904 – "Old Home Week", brought 600 Newfoundlanders from USA.
1906 - 1940 – 4th Bishop of Harbour Grace – Bishop John March.
1906 – Conche – Origination Date.
1906 – North River – Origination Date.
1909 – First Knights of Columbus Council in Nfld at Harbour Grace.

RC CHURCH IN HG & GF, NFLD HISTORY (5)

1912 – Grand Falls – Origination Date.
1914-1918 - World conflict I.
1915 – Railroad opened from Carbonear to Bay de Verde.
1916 – Gambo – Origination Date.
1916 – St. Alban's – Origination Date.
1918 – World Wide Flu kills millions.
1920- Express Train: St. John's to Port Aux Basque, 25 days.
1921 – St. John's incorporated as a City.
1922 – St. Claire's Hospital opened in St, John's.
1923 – Rev Stephen Whelan dies in Labrador, age 46.
1925 – Newfoundland passes women sufferage bill.
1926 – Newfoundland Hotel opened for business.
1927 –Avondale – Origination Date.
1928 - Amelia Earhart - Trepassey to Wales.
1929 - Severe Earthquake and tidal waves all over NFLD.
1929 - 1935 - Depression in Newfoundland.
1929 – Buchan's – Origination Date.
1930 - Cave in at Bell Island Mine.
1931 - 1st winter airmail trip completed.
1931 – Wiley Post record from Harbour Grace to England.
1932 – Rev Linus J. Coady born in Harbour Grace.
1932 - Amelia Earhart flies from Harbour Grace to Ireland.
1933 - *"Spirit of NFLD"*, yacht at Chicago for World's Fair.
1933 – Old Warship "Lobelia" sunk at Harbour Grace.
1934 - Opening of Memorial University.
1935 – Rev Edward J, Hearn born in Harbour Grace.
1935 - Commission Government.
1935 - Very Rev William P. Finn dies in Holyrood, age 67.
1936 - Gander Airport begun.
1936 - Hindenburg passes over St. John's from NY to Germany.
1936 - Worst storm on record at Port aux Croix & Port Sanders.
1938 - Grand Falls station renamed Windsor.
1938 – Bishop Falls – Origination Date.
1939 - FDR fishing trip to Bay of Islands.
1939 - King George VI & Queen Elizabeth land at Holyrood.
1939 - 1945 - World War II.
1940 – Windsor – Origination Date.
1940 - Bishop March dies at Harbour Grace.
1940 – 1953 – 5th Bishop of Harbour Grace – Bishop O'Neill at HG.
1941 - Atlantic Charter signed at Placentia Bay.
1941 - POW camp at Pleasantville closed, German POWs to Canada.

RC CHURCH IN HG & GF, NFLD HISTORY (6)

1941 - US Forces at Pepperell, Argentia and Stephenville.
1942 - 100 Soldiers/Civilians die at KC Hostel fire in St. John's.
1942 - 1st TCA Flight from NFLD to Mainland.
– Mrs. Ellen Carroll dies at North River, age 115.
1942 - US Truxton & Pollux run ashore at St. Lawrence.
1944 - Msgr Joseph Murphy dies in Brigus, age 82.
1944 - Msgr Felix McCarthy, Carbonear, celebrates 60th Jubilee - 1st in NFLD.
1944 - Msgr Felix McCarthy dies in Carbonear, age 83.
1944 - Holy Name Society organized in Harbour Grace.
- $2 Million Dollar Fire in HG Business district.
1945 - HG Fire destroys majority of Business firms.
1945 - US Forces leave Newfoundland.
1946 - 166 war brides arrive in St. John's.
1946 - 1st Telephone service - Gander to Grand Falls.
1946 - Canadian Forces withdraw from Newfoundland.
1946 – Gander – Origination Date.
1947 - 1st Oil burning locomotive make trial run in Nfld.
1947 - New Cabot Hwy opened (450 Cabot Anniversary)
1948 – Colliers – Origination Date.
1949 – Rev William Hearn born in Harbour Grace.
1949 - Telephone open between St. John's & Port aux Basque.
1949 - Newfoundland Confederation with Canada. Census-340,000
1950 - Bell Island Mine ceased work.
1951 - 22,000 Newfoundlanders working on US bases.
1951 - Population of Newfoundland - 356,762
1951 - Elizabeth & Phillip arrive at St.John's.
1952 - Joe Smallwood audience with Pope.
1953 - Grand Falls Parish elevated to Co-Cathedral with Harbour Grace.
1953 - Msgr William P. Finn dies in Grand Falls, age 74.
1953 – Norris Arm – Origination Date.
1953 – 1972 – 5th Bishop of HG-GF, at Grand Falls.
1954 - Jim Fleming wed Mary Mackey in Carbonear.
1954 - Rail-Auto Ferry begins, Gander to Clarenville.
1955 - Centennial or 100th Anniversary of St. John's Cathedral.
1955 – Badger – Origination Date.
1956 - Cardinal Spellman visits EHAFB Stephenville.
1957 – HG Gold Sail Leather plant destroyed by fire.
1958 - Mrs. George Rumson, Carbonear, 100 years old.
1958 - 31,000 NFLD girl's married to Americans since 1941.
1958 – Harbour Grace destroyed by fire.
1959 - Cardinal Spellman ends 4 day Argentia visit.
1959 – Brent's Cove – Origination Date.

RC CHURCH IN HG & GF, NFLD HISTORY (7)

1960 – Harbour Grace gets dial phone system.
1960 - US Forces leave Pepperell.
1961 - Forest fires all over Newfoundland.
1962 - 53 employees laid off at Argentia.
1965 - 1975 - Vietnam War.
1965 – Diocese moved from Harbour Grace to Grand Falls.
1966 – Carbonear est. Knights of Columbus "M*sgr McCarthy*'s" Council.
1966 - John Rorke, 81, dies, Carbonear.
1966 - Catholics in NFLD permitted to eat meat on Friday.
1966 - Newfoundland - "Come-Home-Year".
1966 - ER Harmon USAF Base closed - 850 jobless.
1966 – Plate Cove – Origination Date.
1969 – Presentation Sisters permitted to use baptismal names.
1971 - Msgr Joseph P. Hogan dies in North River, age 68.
1972 – 1979 – 6TH Bishop of Grand Falls, Bishop Penney.
1973 – St. Francis High School burned down in Harbour Grace.
1975 – Pope Paul VI proclaims 1975 Holy Year.
1976 - Carbonear General Hospital opened.
1978 – Pope John Paul II elected Pope. 1st non-Italian in 455 yrs.
1980 – 1999 – 7th Bishop of Grand Falls, Bishop F. MacDonald.
1980 - Newfoundland adopts new Province flag.
1981 - Carbonear Island declared National Historical Site.
1983 - Prince Charles & Diana visit to NFLD.
1984 - Pope John II visits NFLD - 200th Anniversary (1784-1984).
1986 - Msgr Edward O'Brien dies Carbonear, age 101.
1987 - Msgr Joseph O'Brien dies Harbour Grace, age 70.
1988 - 150th Anniversary, Corpus Christi Church, Northern Bay
1990 – Clarenville – Origination date of new Parish.
1990 – Harbour Grace Church declared National Historical Site.
1991 - 100th Anniversary of RC Brick Church, Carbonear.
1991 - 150th Anniversary St. Patrick's Parish, Carbonear.
1994 – New English language RC Catechism approved.
1995 – Education Reform vote, no more denominational schools.
1997 – Government closes all Catholic Schools in Newfoundland.
1997 – Mother Teresa of Calcutta dies at age 87.
1999 - New steeple on St. Patrick's Church, Carbonear.
1999 - Opened new K-10 Catholic School St, Bon's, SJ.
1999 - 2001 – Administrator at Grand Falls: Rev E.T.Bromley.
2000 - Pope John Paul II, 22nd year of Papacy. Age 80.
2000 – Two steeples put back on Immaculate Conception Church, HG
2001 – New Archbishop, St. John's, Bishop Brendan O'Brien.
2001 – 8th Bishop of Grand Falls, Bishop Martin Currie.
2002 – Pope John Paul II, 24th year of Papacy, age 82.

BISHOP MARCH'S DIARY

AND

BISHOP O'NEILL NOTES

1ST SECTION OF THE BOOK
Rev John March – 1889-1899
Trips to Labrador

2ND SECTION OF THE BOOK
Bishop John March – 1906-1939
Running of Diocese, trips, confirmations and appointments.

3RD SECTION OF THE BOOK
Bishop J. M. O'Neill 1940-1972
Running of Diocese, confirmations, appointments, ordinations and assignments.

LAST SECTION OF THE BOOK
List of Clergy that served the Diocese in the times of Bishop March and Bishop O'Neill.

APPENDIX B

BISHOP MARCH'S DIARY AND BISHOP O'NEILL NOTES

1st Section of the Book:
Rev. John March's Missionary work on the Straits of Belle Isle and the Coast of Labrador

Labrador: August and September 1889

Left **Harbour Grace** *Aug. 1st* by SS. Conscript. Had a most enjoyable time doing North. Visited all the priests on my way down. Arrived in **Battle Harbour** on the *7th* at 8:00am. There I met Fr. Le Morrie on his return from Labrador. Left Battle Harbour 2:00pm. Arrived in **Grady** next evening and was kindly received by Mr. MacRoe.

Grady
August 9th: Very wet and disagreeable. Took a glance around the island and posted.

Aug. 10th: Fine day. All fishing. Visited all the Catholics who number in this place, 70 souls-men, women, & children.

Aug. 11th: Sunday. Arouse at 5 o'clock. Prepared my Altar in Mr. MacRoe's store. Heard 20 Confessions and gave as many Communion at Mass. Said Mass at 10:00am and after made a collection. Took dinner with Mr. MacRoe and at 2:00pm started in a skiff for Long Island. Was kindly received by Mr. Dwyer and recovered from the cold in the boat.

Long Island
Aug. 12th: Said Mass in Mr. Dwyer's house. All the Catholics attended. One Confession and Communion. Took a look about the place. Very little fish. Fine weather. People good.

Aug. 13th: Left in Boat after Mass for **Independent.** Reached that place at 4 o'clock and found but two Catholic families in the place all the others down the shore. Left **"Ind".** Two hours later and arrived after dark in **Pack's Harbour**. Stayed at Mr. Dawson's. Most of Catholics down the shore.

Aug. 14th: Arose at 6 o'clock, heard ten Confessions and said Mass for all the Catholics in the place. People good and kind by no fish. Left that place on boat at 11:00 am for **Long Island** and arrived there at 4:00 pm.

Aug. 15th: Said Mass this morning for the shore people. Saw all the fishermen out. Fish scarce.

Aug. 16th: Said Mass at usual hour. Left in Steamer at 1:00pm. Arrived in Grady at 2:00 pm. Saw Mr. MacRoe, very little fish taken here on Lady Day*. Had not time to get the exact amount. Arrived in Indian Tickle at 6:00pm. Next ashore at Mr. Winsor's. Only two Catholic families there. Fitzgerald's and Kavanagh's. Did not remain there but went on in Steamer to Griffin's Harbour. Next ashore to Mr. Power's where I stayed all night.

Griffin's Harbour
Aug. 17th: Said Mass at 9 o'clock this morning in Mr. Power's house. All the Catholics came. All the people here are good Catholics from St. John's and deal with Mr. Testier. One Confession and Communion. No fish for Lady Day as people are from St. John's. Left Griffin's Harbour in boat at 11:00am and arrived in Domino at 3:00pm. Landed at Mr. Costigen's who received me kingly.

Domino
Aug. 18th: Said Mass this morning, Sunday, at Mr. Costigen's. Very few (two families) in this place. Made a collection after Mass. No Lady day fish. All from St. John's. Left Domino in the afternoon and walked to **Black Tickle** where I stayed with Mr. Kelly.

Aug. 19th: Heard 20 Confessions before and had as many Communions. Said Mass in Mr. Harlan's house. Great many Catholics here all from Brigus. After Mass had three baptisms and made a collection, which left in charge of Mr. Burke. Left Black Tickle in the afternoon and arrived in Batteau two hours later.

Batteau
Aug. 19th: Was received here very kindly by Mrs. Bean from Cupids. Rested well and prepared for next day.

Aug. 20th: Heard 10 Confessions and said Mass for all the Catholics here. Fish scarce. Some down the Shore. Most people there are from Brigus. A few from St. John's. Weather to disagreeable to go further on so I had to remain all day.

Aug. 21st: Said Mass this morning, one Confession and Communion. Left Batteau at 1:00 pm arrived in Punch Bowl an hour later. Was kindly received by Mr. O'Brien.

Punch Bowl
Aug. 22nd: Said Mass this morning for crew. No fish worth speaking of. Collection rather small. All from the shipped men. Gave list to Mr. O'Brien. Passed a dull day. In the evening passed in boat with Mr. O'Brien and men to **Corbert's Harbour** where his brother Jeremiah fishes.

Corbert's Harbour
Aug. 23rd: Said Mass this morning in Jeremiah O'Brien's house. Himself and wife very kind. Little or no fish; consequently a small collection.. I did not give list to Mr. M. O'Brien from whom I am to receive payment. Left Corbert's Harbour this evening and arrived in American Harbour at 4:00pm. Only two families here. Did fair with fish.

American Harbour
Aug. 24th: Said Mass this morning at 9 o'clock. All the people in **Hiskott's Island** came except the Walkers who are down shore. Weather unsettled and I not feeling very well I decided to remain here a day and rest myself. Collection small only two men did well here.

Aug. 25th: Said Mass this morning and after breakfast started in boat for **Bolster's Rock**. On arriving I found only two Catholic families -the Glavine's and Hamilton's. These took me over to Primum the same evening where I stayed that night at Mr. Whelan's.

Primum
Aug, 26th: Said Mass this morning. Had a good congregation; but very small collection. Shortly after Mass, I left for **Stylses** in boat where I arrived before dinner time. Stayed here with Mr. Joy from Carbonear. Spent the evening going around visiting the people. Fishing fair here.

Aug. 27th: Said Mass this morning for all the Catholics. There are only Catholics here. The collection was small. One Confession and Communion. Left Primum this evening and arrived in **Vensin Tickles** before dark. Stayed here with Mr. Murphy. People very kind. Catholics few.

Aug. 28th: Said Mass this morning for all the Catholics here and in the neighborhood. All very good- collection zero. Lady Day catch small. Some boats down the Shore. One Confession & Communion. Left Vensin Tickles after breakfast. Capt. Donnelly and Mr. Murphy came with me. Stayed here with Mr. Fleming from Harbour Grace. All Catholics here-fishery not good; people kind. Mr. Hawker very kindly lent us his boat to come to this place. Mr. Hawker's ___on Mr. Rourke's room.

Green Cove
Aug. 29th: Said Mass this morning at Mr. Fleming nearly all the people came from the different places about here. Collection very small. Lady Day catch equally so. No fish going just now. Mr. Fleming more then kind.

Aug. 30th: Passed the day as well as I could. This was the warmest day I've had so far. Left at 4:00pm for Snug Harbour where I was received by Mr. Coady from Harbour Grace.

Snug Harbour
Aug. 31st: Said Mass this morning at Mr. Coady's. All the people came. They are all Catholics here. Fishery not so bad. Collections rather small in proportion to catch. Mr. Coady very kind.

Sept. 1st: Said Mass today, Sunday, and people came from Green Cove and Lord's Arm. A great Congregation. Spent the day in visiting. Money to begot from Mr. Coady at Harbour Grace.

Dead Island
Sept. 3rd: Came from Snug Harbour yesterday and was kingly received by Mr. Brown. Said Mass for them this morning. Only five families living here. All at Mass. One Communion and Confession. Fish scarce. Collection small. Warmest day this summer.

Sept. 4th: waited till 12 o'clock, took dinner at Mr. Brown's and started for Nolan's Harbour where we arrived after half an hour-fair run. Here I was received by Mr. P. J. Fitzgerald who was most kind to me all the time of my stay. Only few people here- about four and five families. Did little with fish but pretty well with the herring. All well. One baptism this evening.

Nolan's Harbour
Sept. 5th: Said Mass this morning for all the Catholics here. Eight Confessions and as many Communions. People good and kind. Not very smooth today-therefore will not leave before tomorrow.

Sept. 6th: Weather rough. No go.

Sept. 7th: Left this morning for **Francis Harbour Bright.** Rough time coming. Arrived all right. Kindly received by Mr. Walsh of Carbonear. Fishery bad here.

Sept. 8th: Said Mass for all this morning. Collection small. One Confession and Communion. Only five Catholic families here. All well.

Sept. 9th: Left today for Murry's Harbour. Roughest time yet. Five hours out.

Murry's Harbour
Sept. 10th: Said Mass this morning in Mr. Clark's house where I stayed. Great many Catholics here. Did not do very well. Collection fair. People principally from Carbonear. All well and came to Mass.

Sept. 11th: Weather rough. Could not start. Found today that it would be useless to go to Petty Harbour as there are only two Catholic families they would not find men enough to row me to Battle Harbour. There are not winter people there.

Sept. 12th: Left this morning after Mass for Battle Harbour where, I arrived after three hours drive of heavy wind. Found Mrs. Kane prepared for me. Learnt here that Fr. McCarthy had made the collection and said Mass for them all.

Battle Harbour
Sept. 13th: Went around today to visit the Catholic families residing in Battle Harbour. Went to see Mrs. Coady's son who has been sick all the summer. He was getting better.

Sept. 14th: Got up early this morning and went to **Sigh's Harbour** a distance of 4 miles and said Mass. There is one residing here all the winter. There were seven Confessions and Communions. Came back to Battle Harbour after Mass. Saw Mr. Murphy there-Fr. Murphy's Brother.

Labrador: August 1890

Left **Harbour Grace** Aug. 4th. Visited all the priests passing with the exceptions of Fathers Walker, Murphy, & Tarahan whom I could not see. Arrived in **Battle Harbour** on the 10th. There I took SS Lady Glover and proceeded north as far as **Windsor's Harbour** where I awaited the return of the Steamer from **Nain.** During my stay there I got a sick call fifteen miles farther north to one MacDonald whom I prepared. Came south as far as Pack's Harbour. Talking on my way Father LeMorrie who was then returning from his mission.

Pack's Harbour
Aug. 22nd: Reached Pack's Harbour today. Fishery very good here. People mostly from Bay Roberts except Ned Ryan.

Aug. 23rd: Said Mass this morning at 9 o'clock. Four Confessions and Communions. Made a fair Collection here. The Lady Day catch did not amount to much. Here as well as Independent it will be turned into Mr. Walsh. After Breakfast I took boat for Long Island calling at **Independent**. Fishery good and collection fair. Arrived at Long Island about 4:00pm

Long Island
Aug. 24th: Said Mass this morning. Sunday-one Confession and Communion. Collection fair. Left Long Island at 2:00 pm. Contrary wind. Reached Grady at 7:00pm. Kindly received by Mr. MacRoe. Prepared for Mass next morning.

Grady
Aug. 25th: Mass this morning at 5 o'clock. A large congregation. Collection fair. Very wet and disagreeable. Expecting passage south in a boat.

Aug. 27th: After two days delay here, I started this morning at 5:30 in a crafter from Green Bay. The crew was composed of six men all Protestants. It was rather rough on board of this craft, but the Capt. and crew were kind. There was a slight breeze in our favour when we started but it did not last long. So we did not reach Indian Tickle before 10 o'clock at night. There is only one Catholic crew here and one family of winter people from the Island near by. I stayed at Kavanagh's & Fitzgerald's who formed one crew. They were in bed when we arrived but they tried to make me as comfortable as possible.

Indian Tickle
Aug. 28th: Said Mass here this morning. There were six Confessions and Communions amongst whom were the Labrador People. The collection was good considering the small number of people. After breakfast we started in a skiff for **Griffin's Harbour**. The wind was against us and we did not reach our destination before 6:00 pm. Between the wind and rain, it was most disagreeable. There to my great surprise, I met Fr. McCarthy who has just arrived there from **Domino.** We stayed here at Mr. Power's from St. John's this night.

Griffin's Harbour
Aug. 29th: Said Mass here this morning and made a fair collection. In the evening we went to tea with Mr. Maurice Fitzgerald. To night I stayed with them all night. The weather very wet and unpleasant.

Aug. 30th: Fr. McCarthy said Mass for them this morning. Somewhat finer today. Left this place at 11 o'clock and reached **Domino** a few hours after. Here I stayed at Mr. Costigan's and Fr. McCarthy went to **Black Tickle** with Mr. Kelly.

Domino
Aug 31st: Said Mass here this morning-Sunday. A great many people to Mass. Fr. McCarthy celebrated on **Dark Tickle** for the people of that place.

Labrador: July, Aug & Sept 1891

Left **Harbour Grace** July 21st by the SS Conscript. Fr. Murphy accompanied one as far as Bonavista of which parish he took charge. I saw all the priests as I came north with the exception of Fr.'s Walsh and Tarahan in Fortune at which place the Steamer did not call. I met Fr. Brown at **Blanc Sablon,** in good health and the best of spirits. Reached **Battle Harbour** on the 29th and took SS Curlew same day arriving at Windsor's Harbour Aug. 1st after a very pleasant passage of 11 days.

Windsor's Harbour
Aug 2nd: Said Mass here this morning for Capt. Hennessy's dealers and took up fair collection. Fishery very good here so far. All well.

Tournwick East
Aug. 5th: Arrived here yesterday morning by SS Curlew. Spent the day, which was very cold as well as I could. All well here except Mr. Kelly of Brigus whom I prepared this morning. Fishery very good. Said mass this morning-the feast of St. Mary Major. All came. Collection good. A few Confessions and Communions.

Tournwick West
Aug. 6th: Reached this place yesterday. Am staying at Silv. Kehoe* of Brigus. Almost all the Catholics here are from Brigus parish. Traps did well here . Prospects bright. Said Mass this morning at 4:00am. Took collection and there paid a visit to Capt. Blanford, who kindly promised me a trip to Ilaac in his little steamer. Saw latest papers just arrived by SS Panthor from which I learnt of the Bishop's absence to Nova Scotia. Took dinner today with Capt. Blanford who was kindness itself.

Ilaac
Aug. 7th: Came here yesterday at noon by Capt. Blanford's steamer. All well here. Hook & line poor. Prospect still good. Said Mass this morning and took collection. Would have enjoyed myself were it not for the flies. Will leave this evening.

Macovick
Aug. 8th: Arrived here yesterday evening after a quick but rather disagreeable passage. Was kindly received by Capt. Dunn. Fishery good. Felt very tired and weary from want of sleep during the proceeding week. Went to bed and had a good sleep. Said Mass this mourning at 4 o'clock and took the usual collection. People here almost equally divided between Protestants and Catholics.

Iron Bound Island
Aug. 9th: Left Macovick yesterday in a small boat, high winds and sea mountains high. Escaped well with a good wetting. Stayed here with Pat Walsh in a store, which is an excuse for a house, full of smoke and dirt. Said Mass at 9 o'clock at which all the Catholics in port attended it being Sunday morning. Took collection as usual which however turned out to be a poor one. After Mass and Ham and Eggs breakfast, I got a crew of five hands in a trap skiff and started with a hard wind for **Rage's Harbour,** a distance of 14 miles. On arriving we were informed that no Catholics had come there this season. So we had to direct our course for the Ragged Islands where we arrived at 11:30pm in an almost exhausted condition, having rowed that day upwards of 30 miles. So after taking a cup of tea with Isaac, I retired to rest. Today the 10th of August, I am taking a badly need repose.

Ragged Islands
Aug. 11th: Said Mass this morning at 4 o'clock. Almost all the people came. The collection did not amount of anything, but they all promised to do what they could on Lady Day. I have been delayed here a few days during which time Isaac with his usual kindness did all in his power to make me happy, I started in a bait skiff for **Jugger Tickle.** On arriving here I was informed there were only two families and being in a great hurry I passed on to Cape Harrison. There is no Catholic family in **Cape Harrison** this year; so I traveled across the hills to Sloop Cove amidst the heat and flies, a distance of 3 ½ miles.

Sloop Cove
Aug. 14th: On arriving here last night, I was kingly received by Capt. Kennedy at whose house I stayed last night. I was preparing today's Mass this morning when I was informed that a crafter going south was about to leave and the Capt. would land in any place going along. Fearing to lose so good a chance, I started leaving orders to fish on Lady Day which they promised to do. It was 3:00am, my intention was to land at Hollen, but the Capt, not being acquainted with the locality and fearing for the safety of his craft, I was obliged to pass that place and continue onto Brig Harbour-reaching this place at 3:00pm. There I found very comfortable quarters with Mr. Strapp.

Brig Harbour
Aug. 14th: Said Mass this morning-took no collection. Thought better not-the next day being Lady Day. After Mass passed over to Emily and stayed at Jim Ryan's. Every thing very comfortable and pleasant.

Emily
Aug. 15th: Said Mass here this morning and sent all fishing. Mr. Ryan's boat had already arrived with 7 pounds. Expect good collection here if the Thoreey's behave themselves. After breakfast I went back to Mr. Strapp's where I took dinner. When I started in a skiff for White Bears. Here I arrived at 8:00pm. Put up with Stapleton.

White Bears
Aug. 16th: Said Mass this morning, Sunday and the shore was crowed. Took up collection which I considered pretty good. All were fishing yesterday after Mass and breakfast I passed over to the other Island.

Aug. 19th: Came over from John Hayden's last night. After arriving I married a young man & a young woman, which event was announced by two shots being fire in rapid succession and which was followed by several volleys from different parts of the Harbour. These collets were answered with shaking vehemence by the "Labrador Band". In this performance by the "Labrador Band" which lasted well nigh midnight; Capt. Nicks took a prominent part. Took steamer this morning for **Rigolette** where we arrived having called at **Smokey** & **Indian Harbour**, at 7 o'clock. Here I met Fr. LeMorrie who remained on board all night and went home on the steamer next day. I was with him as far as Pack's Harbour.

Pack's Harbour
Aug. 21st: reached this place from **Independent** yesterday evening. Said Mass this morning. Fishery good here with the traps, poor with hooks. After Mass, I left for Long Island and met with poor weather, hard wind, heavy sea and rain, every thing in fact to make the trip unpleasant. At last we reached Long Island, just at dark and well we did for the sea in this place ran mountains high. I was soon myself again at Mr. Dwyer's.

Long Island
Aug. 22nd: Said Mass here this morning and took collection. Fishery good with traps and bad with the hook & line. Weather better today but still too rough to leave for Grady. Today Aug. 23rd being Sunday morning, I said Mass at which all the Catholics assisted. There were a few Confessions and Communions. After breakfast I started for Grady where I was kindly received by Mr. MacRoe.

Grady
Aug. 24th: Said Mass here this morning and took collection which did not seem to be as good at it ought to be. After breakfast at Mr. MacRoe's, I secured a passage in a small boat going to Indian Tickle. I was not over particular as the wind was fair. We arrived at 4:00pm.

Indian Tickle
Aug. 25th: On arriving here, I went to Mr. Kavanagh's where I stayed last year. He was then the only Catholic family here, but this year Mr. Ed Moore from Bay de Verde is also in the place. Mr. Moore was prepared for me to stay with him, but having stayed with Mr. Kavanagh last year I decided on not changing. This morning I said Mass at the same house and took a good collection considering the small number of people. After Mass I left for Griffin's Harbour.

Griffin's Harbour
Aug. 26th: Am staying here with Mr. Power-who, with Mrs. Power is very kind to one. I said Mass this morning in Maurice Fitzgerald's house. The largest in the Harbour, which has been bought by Mr. Testier. The collection turned out better then I expected. After breakfast, although it was wet and disagreeable, I left for Domino, where I arrived early in the evening.

Domino
Aug. 27th: I am staying here with Mr. Costigan from St. John's. He is as kind as usual. I said Mass this morning. As the numbers of Catholics in the place is very small, it is only natural to suppose that the collection would be small also. All however gave a little. I will leave this evening for Black tickle.

Black Tickle
Aug. 29th: Said Mass this Morning. A great many present. Mr. Ed Ryan here now. All the people well and doing well. Collection not so good. Most of the people from St. John's.

Punch Bowl
Aug. 30th: This morning is Sunday. I said Mass at Mr. O'Brien's. Mr. Jerry came over so I did not go to **Corbert's Harbour.** No Lady Day fish here. Collection small.

Hiscock's Island
Sept. 1st: Reached here in a boat yesterday. All Brigus people in this place. Saw Mr. & Mrs. Walker who last their two sons this summer. Said Mass this morning for them. The people came here from American Harbour. So I did not go there at all. Left here this evening for Bolster's Rock with Fr. Walker's brothers.

Bolster's Rock
Sept. 2nd: Stayed here with Mr. Callahan of River Heard. They made me very comfortable. Said Mass here this morning. Mr. & Mrs. Hamilton, who have been living here many winters, came to Confession and Communion. Their son and daughter did the same, the former for the first time. No Lady Day fish here. Collection good for small number of people.

Primum
Sept. 3rd: Am staying with Mr. Peter Hamilton father of Mrs. John Murphy. Very comfortable and did well. Fishery poor here except with traps. Collection fair. People kind.

Stylses
Sept. 4th: Am staying today with Mr. Donnelly, Mr. Joy is down the shore this year. Fishery poor. People too late here for salmon. Mr. John Couhalan of Brien's Cove died here about a month ago with Lagrippe. Said Mass this morning. Collection fair. People scarce about this place.

V. Tickle
Sept. 5th: Very few here now. The Dooly's with the exception of Mr., are down the shore yet. They are expected daily. Fishery bad here. Said Mass this morning. Collection a few dollars and started for Snug Harbour. Did not go to Green Cove as Maurice Fleming is down the shore.

Snug Harbour
Sept. 6th: Arrived here yesterday Saturday. Mrs. Coady and Maddie are here and have everything very comfortable. Alice and Jennie went up on the Curlew yesterday. This morning-Sunday-I said Mass in Mrs. Coady's store. A very large congregation present. As they did not do much this year with the herring, the collection was only fair. Intent staying a few days here to rest.

Dead Island
Sept. 11th: Came here yesterday after a longer stay in Snug Harbour than I had intended owning to advance winds. Said Mass here this morning. Very small congregation. The people are fast leaving the place. Mr. Brown and Mary are very kind. Wind very high today cannot leave for Nolan's Harbour.

Nolan's Harbour
Sept. 13th: Wind high today. First said Mass now, but intend starting for the Bight. Fishery bad here. Collection nil. Pat Joe down the shore yet. All well. No fish, no herring.

Francis Harbour Bight
Sept. 15th: Arrived here yesterday in a gale of wind. Said Mass this morning at Walsh's. Collection small. Fish scarce. Herring a failure.

Murry's Harbour
Sept. 15th: Winds still high from the north. Good sea. Crew that came with me yesterday could not yet return. Said Mass this morning at Clark's where I am staying. A great congregation present. Collection fair considering the bad fishery. Am weather bound here at present.

I was home in Harbour Grace during the summers of 1892 and 1893 -JM

Labrador: July, Aug & Sept 1894

Left **Harbour Grace** July 17th. Arriving in **Battle Harbour** on July 23rd. Trip was very fine and agreeable. Fr. Browne separated at **Flowers Cove.** My intention was to proceed north at once and work south. But learning that the north was blocked with ice, I decided to stop at Indian Tickle and work south thus deferring my trip north until returning of Windsor Lake.

Indian Tickle
July 24th: Reached here-Indian Tickle today after a run of 24 hours from Battle Harbour. Reports of fish fair as we came north. No fish worth while here. Staying at Mr. Kavanagh's. All well. Heard report just now that Jas. Lunilan with two of his men has been drowned in Monday's Gail-no certainty as yet.

July 25th: Said Mass this morning at 8 o'clock after hearing the confessions of our five winter people of this place. A great many at Mass. Collection fair. Fish scarce. Report of the drowning of the three men at Cape Greene. Confirmed today. I reached **Griffin's Harbour** at 2 pm today. All well here.

Griffin's Harbour
July 26th: Said Mass this morning. Collection much the same as during past years but more uncertain owning to the scarcely of fish. Names of two men lost with Lunilan are George Furey and Jim Hannon. Collection left in charge of the heads of respective crews of P. Hickey, P. Ryan and Mr. Kennedy. Left Griffin's Harbour at 11am, reaching Domino at 1:30pm. Weather cool and wet. Fish here a shade better than at Griffin's Harbour.

Domino
July 27th: Said Mass this morning at Mr. Patrick Costigan's. Took collection as usual. Half the crew Protestant. Left collection in care of Mr. Costigan and Kent. Arrived at Mr. Kelly's-**Black Tickle** this evening. Fishery here about the same as at **Domino.** Windy today and cold.

July 28th: Said mass this morning . Keefe's went to Confession & Communion. Baptized child for Keefe and got one dollar-collection not so bad. All will depend on result of fishery. Wind very strong from North West. Cold but fine. Will leave this evening for **Batteau.** Arrived at Mr. J. Brien's at 4 pm. Called on Tom Brien on my way. He has very little fish so far. Mr. Jerry has done fair.

Batteau
July 30th: Said Mass here this morning. Small number of people and small collection. All promised to fish Lady Day.

July 31st: Wind high. No chance of going to **Punch Bowl.** Had sick call to **Webber's Cove** to Tom Farrell.

Punch Bowl
Aug. 1st: Came to Punch Bowl and said Mass this morning. Very few here as the greater of Brien's crew is with Tom. Took small collection and left same in care of Capt. Nick. Promised to fish Lady Day. Will know results only when I come back from the North. Left Punch Bowl 11:30 am and reached **Hiscock's Island** at 2:30 pm. Not as much sigh here as reported. Sent to **American Harbour** this evening for people of that place to attend Mass here tomorrow morning, thus saving me the trouble of going to see them.

American Harbour
Aug. 2nd: Said Mass here this morning. People came from American Harbour. Fish fair up to date. Will give Lady Day fish to Mr. Walsh-left after Mass for **Primum.** Long passage, cold and wet.

Primum
Aug. 3rd: Said Mass here this morning. All did well with fish and promised to exert themselves Lady Day. After Mass left for **Stylses**. Stayed short time here-saw all the people and passed on to V. Tickle. Steamer entered at 5pm going south.

V. Tickle
Aug. 4th: Said Mass at 5 o'clock. Men went fishing. People and family well here. Poor reports from down the shore. Left **V. Tickle** at 3pm and arrived at **Snug Harbour** two hours later. Splendid time. People did well here with the fish. No salmon except at Green Cove.

Snug Harbour
Aug. 5th: Said Mass this morning at 10 o'clock in Mr. Coady's store. It being Sunday there was an immense congregation. All attended except Fleming's crew from **Green Cove.** After dinner paid a visit to all the houses in the Harbour. All promised to fish Lady Day.

Aug 6th: Said Mass here again this morning. Have decided to rest here with the arrival of "Windsor Lake" from the South. Am more comfortable here than in any other place so far.

Aug. 7th: Said Mass this morning at 7 o'clock. Took steamer at noon for the north. Weather beautiful. Flies more plentiful than fish.

Aug. 8th: Passed Grady, Long Island & C. Very little fish. All discouraged.

Aug. 9th: Still going north. No fish.

Hopedale
Aug. 10th: Visited Hopedale today. Was treated kingly by the missionaries. Spent the night in Nain. "Hoskies" on board singing & C. Grand Time.

Aug. 11th: Came south today as far as Hope Dale. Met great number of crafts. Nearly all without fish.

Windsor's Harbour
Aug. 12th: Reached Windsor's Harbour this morning at 11 o'clock. Glad to find fishery has improved somewhat since we went north. The last two days have been very fair. Enjoyed pleasant day with Capt. John, Capt Connolly, and English Capt. People more cheerful and hopeful.

Aug. 13th: Said Mass this morning at 3 o'clock. All anxious to go fishing early. Prospects bright. Wind west-blowing nice breeze. SS Lady Glover called at W. Harbour at 10:00 am on her way to **Tournwick.** Reached Tournwick at 12 am. Having got passage from Capt. Norman. All well here. Fishery improved a little. Doing fair today.

Tournwick
Aug. 14th: Said Mass this morning at 4 o'clock. Lady Day promises well. Left Tournwick at 10 am. Called at **Barttette** on my way to Ilaac. No one being sick, I did not stay here. Reached Ilaac about 2 pm. Fishery poor here with traps. Getting little now.

Ilaac
Aug 15th: Said Mass this morning at 5am all went fishing after Mass and some did fair. Came to **Macovick** this evening. Dunn has done well this summer, still catching fish. Did fair today. Nearly all Protestants in this place.

Macovick
Aug. 16th: Said Mass this morning at 5 o'clock. Wet and disagreeable all day. Wind East. Stayed here all day. Very anxious to get along.

Aug. 17th: Started this morning at 10am and did not reach Roger's Harbour till 8pm. Very tired and cold. Only two crew here-Mr.. Patrick Convan and James Convan.

Roger's Harbour
Aug. 18th: Said Mass this morning. Wind strong from the south. Could not leave-very little fish in this place.

Aug. 19th: Today-Sunday said Mass and left for Ragged Islands at 10 am. Reached this place at dark-weather disagreeable and strong winds in the evening from NW.

Ragged Islands
Aug 20th: Stayed here all day with Dave Pumphrey. Not much fish. Saw all the people including Frost who invited me to his house.

Aug 21st: Said Mass at 5 this morning intending to go to Sloop Cove. Weather became very disagreeable-rain and wind and could not go. Took Lady Day catch, not bad. In the house all day.

Aug. 22nd: Strong winds again today and heavy sea. No chance of leaving. Will wait for steamer coming North.

Aug. 23rd: Today has been a fisherman's holiday-blowing a gale from the NE. Steamer expected.

Aug. 24th: Said Mass this morning. Wet and disagreeable. Here all day.

Aug. 25th: Steamer arrived this morning at 3 am. Letters from Bishop and friends. Fine day. Could not go to Sloop Cove. Men being out fishing all day.

Sloop Cove
Aug. 26th: Sunday-Mass at 10 o'clock. Rosary at 5 pm. All the people came to Mass. Wrote Bishop and Fr. Murphy.

Aug. 28th: Left Ragged Island this morning at 7:30. Called at **Cape Harrison** in Steamer. No Catholics here. Called at Sloop Cove. Fishery poor in this place; but improving. Went next to **Hollon.** All well here, but no fish. Passed Emily, White Bears, Smokey, and Indian Harbour.

Rigolette
Aug. 29th: Got to Rigolette this morning and reached Pack's Harbour at 7pm.

Pack's Harbour
Aug. 30th: Said Mass here this morning. No fish worth while. Lady Day a blank. After Mass, I started for **Long Island** calling on my way at Independent. Did a little better here. Reached Long Island at 3pm.

Long Island
Sept. 1st: Very disagreeable day. Wind strong from NNE-causing heavy sea.

Sept. 2nd: Today - Sunday-much worse than yesterday. Great sea.

Sept. 3rd: Wind still in the same point. Sea mountains higher. Mick Scanlon's stage went this morning. No chance of getting to Grady today.

Sept. 4th: Storm still continues to rage. Nothing better than yesterday. Cannot move today. Wind still from NNE.

Grady
Sept. 5th: More moderate today. Wind from the same point. but light. Came to Grady in trap skiff with seven men. Sea very high. Very near falling once. Weather something worse this evening.

Sept. 6th: Had Mass this morning for Grady people and Christening. Fishery poor here. Three men drove off from this place on Saturday last. They are in Mr. Morrison's men of Conception Harbour. No hearings of them since.

Sept 7th: Hills covered with snow this morning. Very cold: sea mountains high and strong winds from NNE. It froze last night. Too rough for steamer. No account of men yet.

Sept. 8th: Snow showers again this morning. Weather finer and less sea. Hopes of change soon. No news from men so far. Not very well today. Steamer came at 2 pm. Marriage of Hollett-Minister on board. Passed Long Island and stayed over night at **Pack's Harbour.**

Sept. 9th: Passed White Bears today-no wrecks so far. Reached **Emily** at noon. Went on board SS Leon with George Apsey & wife. Was Kindly entertained by Capt. of "Leon" wife and daughter. They are sweet, but speak English very well. In the evening I went to Mr. Martin's, slept and said Mass there. No Lady Day fish and no collection. Fishery very poor here. No crafter up yet.

Emily
Sept. 11th: Said Mass this morning. Lady Day catch almost nil. Wind-morning south blowing very strong with rain. Came to White Bear's this evening in a gale of wind. All well here.

White Bear
Sept. 12th: Said Mass here this morning. Lady Day catch small. Fishing fair. Steamer came from the north this evening and I passed on to Smokey, Indian Harbour, and Rigolette. Sea rough.

Long Harbour
Sept. 13th: Reached Long Island today. Wind N. Weather fine.

Snug Harbour
Sept. 14th: Came as far as Snug Harbour . Weather cold and disagreeable.

Battle Harbour
Sept. 15th: Reached Battle Harbour this evening and landed at Murphy's-steamer going to Sigh's Harbour.

Sept. 16th: Called on Mr. Wall-agent at Battle Harbour was treated very kindly. Went to Sigh's Harbour in steamer launch. Expecting SS Virginia Lake.

Sigh's Harbour
Sept. 18th: Still in same place-doing nothing.

Battle Harbour
Sept. 19th: Finished taking coal. Returned to Battle Harbour. No sign of steamer yet.

Sept. 20th: Said mass this morning at Murphy's. Steamer arrived at 9am. Got news of Fr. Forristal death R.I.P. Left for **Newfoundland** at 2 pm.

Conche
Sept 21st: Fr. Lynch came on board this morning at Conche. Saw Fr. Shean for a few moments. Had a little chat with Molly-Fr. Flynn being south.

Sept. 22nd: Saw Fr. R. Walsh for a few moments. Fr. Tarahan was absent on his rounds. Called at Tobin's at **Twillingate.** All are well.

Sept. 23rd: Arrived in **Harbour Grace** today at 10 am. All well-glad to meet old friends.

Harbour Grace Summer of 1895 - JM

Labrador: July and August 1896

On the 14th of July, I left **Harbour Grace** in the SS "Virginia Lake" to do missionary work, first in the Straits of Belle Isle and then on the whole Coast of **Labrador.**

The present day, the 15th, I was joined by Fr. Walker of **Bonavista** who intended talking a trip, for his health's sake, to the far north. Two days later Fr. Finn came on board at **Fogo** and proceeded as far as **Conche** to visit the place and pastor.

We saw Fr. Tarahan at **Twillingate** and Fr. O'Flynn at **Pilley's Island**. This meeting of old friend's rendered an otherwise very dull trip, quite pleasant and agreeable. The weather was beautiful from the time we left Harbour Grace till Sunday morning the 19th when I landed from the streamer at **Flower's Cove**. The fishery from Baccalieu to Cape John is almost a black. On the French Shore it is very good.

Flower's Cove
July 19th: About 100 souls in this place, with a nice little School-Chapel - P. Griffin teacher. Attendance at school: 30 winter. 8 summer. Had devotions this evening and heard forty confessions. No one sick at present. Not one died this winter.

July 20th: Mass this morning at 6 o'clock. Forty Communions. All the people on the other side fishing. No fish whatever here. People expected a hard winter. Intended leaving this place today but could not. Winds high, fog and sea. Had one baptism this morning and visited two old women in **Nameless Cove**.

Carroll's Cove
July 22nd: Came to Carroll's Cove this morning. Three Catholic families here. All doing well with the fish. Feel very tired.

July 23rd: Said Mass this morning a t 5 o'clock. Fourteen for Confession and as many for Communion. Some paid dues ($2.00); others promised wither to turn in their fish to Richard O'Dell or to send in the money by mail. Married one couple under very laughable circumstances in this place. Another in prospect but doubtful. Left here at 9 o'clock and came to **Piednow** and in the afternoon on to the Tickle. Fine weather and strong winds. Fish plentiful still along the coast, prospects splendid. As a fitting finale to this mornings transactions, Phil Tashey arrived here this afternoon to marry Maggie Pike. Phil stormed "the Point" against immense odds lose his way blushing and delighted bride. It was a real Labrador Wedding. Rain is falling in torrents. A wet evening crossing to the "main", there are nine Catholic families - over seventy souls. About 20 children attend school regularly during the winter months and in summer time about ten. Goff is said to be attentive.

Tickle
July 24th: Said Mass here in the "Tickle" this morning. Sixty for Confession and fifty-seven for Communion. Large congregation. This is a fisherman's holiday. Wind very strong. Impossible to venture out in a boat. Hard rain last night. Weather still wet and disagreeable. Obliged to stay here all night at Stephen MacDonald's.

July 25th: Said Mass here again this morning. Left about 11am and arrived at L'anse au Diable at 1pm. Five families here.

L'anse au Diable
July 26th: Said Mass here this morning-twenty Confessions and Communions. One Baptism. Doing well. All promised to send in their fish to Mr. Browne. After Mass, I left for **L'anse á Loup** where I arrived in time for dinner. In the evening I went to see the people in the **"Botton".**

L'anse a Loup
July 27th: Said Mass this morning at 5 o'clock in the "Bottom". Fifteen Confessions and Communions. All promised to turn in their fish to Mr. Browne. Paid a visit to the Light House this evening. People not to my liking.

July 28th: Mass this morning. Collection good-one Communion. Detained here today by wind, rain, fog, and tide. Heavy sea on. Very disagreeable. Went to Light House Forteau again this evening. Saw the whole place.

Forteau
July 29th: Said Mass and had three Communion here this morning. Returned to Mr. Browne's with Mr. Wyatt intending to Isle au Bois. No time. could not leave.

July 30th: Weather bound.

July 31st: Left **L'anse á Loup** this morning at 6 o'clock and arrived at Mr. Petherick's, **Isle au Bois,** at noon. Not feeling very well this evening. Only three Catholics on this room. Fishery good.

Isle au Bois
Aug. 1st: Came from Isle au Bois this morning at 6 o'clock & said Mass at **Barachois.** Four families in this place-all French. They speak a little English. John Baptiste le Templier is anxious to teach school in this place. All the Le Templier's maintain that Jean Baptist is the proper and the only person to keep it. There were six for Communion. Nearly all the people here go to their duty to the French priest at Long Point. With regard to the school, Jean Baptist is willing to hold it in his own house. This will save further trouble with the new-old school house which is past all hope and make it easy to procure fuel for the children.

Aug. 2nd: Went to **Bonne, Seperance & Salmon Bay** in the SS V Lake and reached Cape St. Charles tonight. Fishery good. Christian. Brothers (4) on board. Letters from home.

Battle Harbour
Aug. 3rd: Reached Battle Harbour 5 am. Steamer left again at 12:30 for the south. Lady Glover has not yet arrived.

Aug. 4th: Lady Glover got here at 4 o'clock. Fr. Walker came by here. She left again at 11am to take the mail south. Fr. Walker is gone home. Got letters from Fr. M. and Mrs. T. To late to reply.

Aug. 5th: Blowing strong today.

Aug. 6th: Wind still high-fisherman's holiday. Still here. No sign of steamer.

Aug. 7th: Mass again. Weary.

Aug. 8th: Mass. Invited to dinner by the Doctor of hospital-expecting steamer. Steamer arrived at 4pm. Left Battle Harbour an hour later and went to Francis Harbour.

Francis Harbour
Aug. 9th: Got as far as **Domino** today.

Aug. 10th: Reached **Smokey**. When at **Grady**, I learnt of the death a few days before of James Flynn of North River.

Aug. 11th: Steamer all day and all night. Saw Hayden & Pumphrey.

Windsor's Harbour
Aug. 12th: Got to Windsor's Harbour at 10 o'clock this morning. Steamer gone on to Nain. Dr. Granfield called here today. Not much fish here.

Aug. 13th: Said Mass here this morning. Am feeling well.

Aug. 14th: No improvement in fishery. SS "Lady Glover" reached here tonight.

Sloop Cove
Aug. 15th: Lady Day. Came as far as Sloop Cove. All well in Ports-Fishery improving just a little.

Rigolette
Aug. 16th: Got to Rigolette. Prepared man-Ryan by name-for death in Indian Harbour Hospital.

Domino
Aug. 17th: Reached Domino. All well. fishery poor.

Batteau
Aug. 18th: Prepared Richard Murphy for death at Batteau. Delaney of same place much improved in health.

Battle Harbour
Aug. 19th: Reached Battle Harbour at 4am. Virginia Lake came in at 6 o'clock. Left again at noon for home.

Harbour Grace
Aug. 22nd: Arrived in Harbour Grace this evening. All well.

Labrador: July, Aug & Sept 1899

Left **Harbour Grace** by "SS Labrador" July 29th. Touched at **Catalina** and then on to **Battle Harbour.** Reached Battle Harbour July 31st and then proceeded North to **Windsor's Harbour**. Fishery fair from **Grady South**; bad from **Grady North**.

Windsor's Harbour
Aug. 4th: Reached here this after noon. No fish. All well.

Aug. 5th: Said Mass this morning. A sign of fish. One boat had four quintals. Wrote Theresa, Fr. M. and the Bishop. Expecting Steamer. Left **Windsor's Harbour** 4 pm. Visited **Tournwick** and **Ilaac.** Still no fish at Tournwick. Capt. in low spirits. Little fish at Ilaac. Spent three hours at Keefe's and visited Pat who is not well.

Ilaac

Aug. 6th: Here at Ilaac all day. Wind south, blowing a gale. Capt. afraid to move.

Aug. 7th: Left Ilaac this morning at 11am. Visited **Mercuric.** Plenty of fish. All well. All night at Long Tickle.

Long Tickle

Aug. 8th: Left here this morning. Wind North East. Very foggy. Plenty of fish at **Ragger Island**, little at **Cape Harrison** and at **Sloop Cove.** Kennedy's doing fair and hoping to make a voyage. Stayed here all night.

Aug. 9th: Left at 8 am. Still foggy. No fish at **Holten** and none at **Emily.** Came to Emily at 8pm. Landed at Mr. Coady's. Jas Ryan of Spaniard's Bay called. Intend staying here a few days.

Emily

Aug. 10th: Wind still North East but not so foggy. Still no fish. Jas Ryan called again this morning. Intends sending his schooner North to **Ragged Islands** or some other place to get fish.

Aug. 11th: Fine day. Little fish. Doing fair at **Brig Harbour.**

Aug. 12th: Fine day. Visited Mr. Kennedy this morning and arranged for Mass in his store tomorrow. Called at Jim Ryan's and saw his vessel departs for the North. Ryan foreign vessel arrived this evening. Fish a little more plentiful today.

Aug. 13th: Mass in Kennedy's store this morning at 10 o'clock. Large congregation. Jim Deady and crew did not turn up. Took breakfast at Mr. Kennedy's.

Aug. 14th: Wind NE cold and wet. Little fish. Not well.

Aug. 15th: Mass at Mr. Coady's at 8 o'clock. All fishing. Catch fair for King's Cove and Avondale. Nothing for Harbour Grace. Wind NE still cold and wet. Dinner and tea at Jim Ryan's.

Aug. 16th: Still blowing from NE. Cold and raining much. Very little fish. Too rough to haul traps.

Aug. 17th: Wind NE cold and foggy. Heavy rain Very small catches of fish. Most traps taken in. Jim Ryan spent evening with us.

Aug. 18th: Calm today and great sea. Intended going to Brig Harbour but J Ryan who promised to take me there did not turn up.

Aug. 19th: Still cold and wet with winds. No change.

Aug. 20th: Mass at Kennedy's. Weather still bad.

Aug. 21st: Wet and cold. Health much better today. Jim Ryan called over this afternoon.

Aug. 22nd: Left this morning for **Bright Harbour.** Fine but cold. Before arriving saw mail boat in the distance and returned to get mail. Letters from Bishop, Fr. M., and account of Fr. O'Flynn's death. Mr. MacRoe went north. Steamer expected back next Sunday.

Aug. 23rd: Cold and very foggy. Steamer must be making very little progress. Wind east.

Aug. 24th: Fine today. Wind South but not clear. No fish this week.

Aug. 25th: Wind west. Finer than usual, but not fine enough to fish.

Aug. 26th: Wind E very stormy and wet no fishing.

Aug. 27th: Streamer arrived from the North at 7 am. Fine day. Doing well. No one sick. Visited Hospital at **Indian Harbour-** no Catholics here.

Aug. 28th: Called **Back's Harbour**. All well here. Fishery fair. No Lady Day catch. Weather too rough. Doing well at **Grady.** Reached **Indian Tickle** tonight and stayed at Mr. Windsor's.

Aug. 29th: Said no Mass this Morning. Fishery good here.

Black Tickle

Aug. 30th: Mass at Mr. Kavanagh's this morning. One Mr. Higgins died this spring. Came to Black Tickle today. Good time. Bad fishery here.

Aug. 31st: Said Mass this morning and all came. Ten for Communion. Came to Batteau after Mass. Fishery good here. Comfortable at Mr. Ryan's.

Batteau

Sept. 1st: Weather fine, all did well here.

Sept. 2nd: Still fine. One sick call.

Sept. 3rd: Mass this Morning in Mr. Ryan's store. Beautiful Altar. Congregation very large. Only few people here from Harbour Grace parish. Left after dinner and reached Corbett's Harbour about 6pm.

Corbett's Harbour

Sept. 4th: Weather very wet. Blowing gale of wind. Mass here this morning. Good crowd mostly from King's Cove parish.

Sept. 5th: Left today and called at Mr. Brien's. He is very sick but supposed to be better. Fishery good. Reached Hiscock's Island and had sick call to girl at **American Harbour.**

Hiscock's Island

Sept. 6th: Mass this morning. Weather miserable. No go.

Bolster's Rock

Sept. 7th: Came to Bolster's Rock today in a gale of wind. Stayed at Cullen's.

Sept. 8th: Mass here this morning. Wind strong. Sea mountains high. Came to Primum this evening.

Primum

Sept. 9th: Mass this morning and proceeded to Styles. Passed SS Leopard. Had to wait next morning for mail.

Styles
Sept. 11th: Mass at Mr. Doody's and then started for **Green Cove.** Got sick call to a vessel at Lord's Arm. People on board belong to Conception Harbour.

Lord's Arm
Sept. 12th: Mass here this morning. Fine day. Very comfortable here. All Carbonear people in this place. Went to Snug Harbour in the afternoon.

Snug Harbour
Sept. 13th: Mass at Mr. Finn's this morning. Good crowd. All came to **Dead Island** today and stayed at Mr. Gould's.

Visited Nolan's Harbour

Sept. 14th: Mass this morning and came on to Francis Harbour Bright.

Francis Harbour Bright
Sept. 15th: Mass here at Mr. Walsh's. Few people. Left for Murry's Harbour but had to return in storm of wind to Francis Harbour. Stormy and wet all day

Sept. 16th: Left again to **Murry's Harbour** and arrived at noon.

Murry's Harbour
Sept. 17th: Mass here today and good congregation. Two Confessions and Communions. Left for **Battle Harbour** in skiff and was forced to put back in gale of wind and sea. Very glad to get back safe.

Sept. 18th: Left again at 7am and arrived at Battle Harbour 12 pm. Visited people in **Mattes Cove** and prepared old Mr. Green for death. Visited also Mr. Croucher on the room and took tea with Mrs. & Dr. Aspell at the Hospital.

Sept. 20th: Reached **King's Cove** 6 pm. Chat with Fr. Lynch. Arrived at **Catalina** midnight.

Sept. 21st: Saw Fr. Tarahan. Visited friend's in **Bonavista.**

Sept. 22nd: Said Mass in Bonavista. Said good-bye to friend's and returned to Catalina.

Sept. 23rd: Left Catalina this morning at 5 o'clock & arrived in Old Pelican at 10am. Stayed here all day. Went to **Bay de Verde** in the Evening.

Sept. 24th: Mass here this morning. Pleasant day.

Sept. 25th: Came with James to **Northern Bay**. Saw Fr. Roe tonight. All well here.

Sept. 26th: Left with my own horse and carriage for **Harbour Grace.** Arriving here at 7 pm.

Thus ended my Sixth trip to the Labrador-1899

2nd Section of the Book:
Rt. Rev. John March's reign as See of Harbour Grace
1906

Oct 2nd, 1906: Received Bulls today appointing me Bishop of Hr. Grace. Wrote Rome within ten or twelve days, accepting.

Nov 4th, 1906: Consecrated today by his Grace Archbishop Howley. Assistants: Bishop McNeil and Bishop McDonald

1907

Jan 1st: Divided the Parish of Brigus and appointed Rev. S.J. Whelan D.D. first parish priest of the newly formed parish of North River.

May 7th: Laid Corner stone of St, Charles Church, North River. Private-Fr. Ashley present.

May 9th: Made place for nuns in sanctuary.

May 25th: Order Fr. Thibault from Bonavista to Conche.

May 26th: Told Fr. J. Lynch of my intention of sending him to Northern Bay. Made business statement to people in Cathedral and raised the dues to three dollars.

June 1st: Went to **Conception.**

June 2nd: Dedicated to St. Anne the new church at **Conception.**

June 9th: Took train at Avondale for **Rantem**

June 10th: Examined and confirmed of candidates-my first confirmation at Rantem. 2 adults.

June 11th: **Bellevue.** Examined and confirmed 24 candidates-4 of them being adults. Received address and pose. Consecrated chalice-first for Bellevue.

June 12th: Weather bound.

June 13th: **Chapel Arm.** Examined and Confirmed 18 candidates -6 being adults. Received address and pose.

June 14th: **S. Dildo**. Examined and confirmation 5 candidates-1 adult. Proceeded to **Hope All** and examined and confirmed there same morning. 5 candidates. Returned to Harbour Grace.

June 22nd: Visited **Northern Bay** parish for the first time as Bishop. Saw people of Western Bay this evening and received from them an address. Then proceeded to N. Bay. Gave benediction and received addresses from people, school children of N. Bay and Job's Cove.

June 23rd: Said Mass N. Bay - preached and made financial statement. Had meeting at Hall and named it St. John's Hall. Saw Theresa who came to N. Bay for the occasion.

June 24th: Visited **Small Point**. Saw people marked out spot for Church on west corner of Sharpe's lane, Mr. Sharpe and two sons consenting, Dr. Dunn, Fr. Nolan and others being present.

June 25th: Returned **Carbonear** by Ethie. Held visitation Carbonear convent. Returned to Harbour Grace late that evening.

June 27th: Went to **Conception** and appointed Rev. Sr. Cecilia Rev. Mother on place of Mother Bridget.

June 28th: Left for **St. John's.**

June 29th: Went to **Bell Island** with Archbishop McNeil, Dr. Whelan and Fr. Power. Visited mines.

June 30th: Archbishop blessed church, gave Confirmation.

July 1st: Returned to St. John's. Visited Littledale.

July 2nd: Consensus at **Little Dale**. Harbour Grace girls did well. Met for first time, Lady McGregor and Miss McGregor. Meeting at night with board of directors of St. Bonaventure's.

July 3rd: Called at **Gov. House** and at Sir. R.J. Reed. Went to Littledale. Meeting of Bishops. Started Sustentation fund for poor priests.

July 4th: Laying of corner stone. Conversational in the evening. Met many friends.

July 5th: Returned to **Harbour Grace**. Fr. Scully and Fr. Finn here.

July 17th: Left Harbour Grace for **Bay of Islands** with Fr. W.P. Finn.

July 17th: Spent afternoon with Mr. March. Took SS Home.

July 19th: Reached **Flower's Cove.**

July 20th: Confirmed 11. Two adults. 60 confessions.

July 21st: Left Flower's Cove and arrived at **Barachion** after two hours and half food said. Dinner " á la mode" at Madam Templieis. After dinner, confessions. Examined children for Confirmation, fourteen candidates-two adults.

July 22nd: Confirmation at 7am. Called on **Grant-Job's** agent-and all night-too windy to leave.

July 23rd: Mass at 8 o'clock still blowing hard.

July 24th: Came in "SS Dart" to **L'anse au Loup** and walked to Light House.

July 25th: Mass and confirmation at Light House. Mass at L'anse au Loup but no children for Confirmation. Came to **L'anse á Diable**.

July 26th: Mass here but no children for confirmation. Came to **West St. Modist.**

July 27th: Mass W. **St. Modist**. All children had gone to Predrion.

July 28th: Confirmed 14 children. **Predrion** today, three of them being adults, three converts and three marriages here. Received from Mark O'Dell $8.00-Lady Day money for 1906.

July 29th: Went to **Carroll's Cove.**

July 30th: Held Confirmation here and went to Red Bay.

July 31st: At **Red Bay**, guests of Joseph Penny.

Aug 1st: Still at Red Bay.

Aug 2nd: At Red Bay. Penny very kind. Took steamer for Battle Harbour.

Aug. 4th: Mass at **Battle Harbour.** Large Congregation. Asked for quota of fish from every man to help paint the Chapel.

Aug 5th: At Battle Harbour. Visited hospital.

Aug 6th: Went to **Chateau.**

Aug 7th: Mass Chateau. Proceed to Camps.

Aug 8th: Mass **Camps.** Came to Battle Harbour afternoon. After dinner left Battle Harbour for Murray's Harbour. Reached there before dark.

Aug. 9th: Mass at **Murray's Harbour**. Great congregation. All well.

Aug 10th: Reached **Francis Harbour Bight** yesterday morning. Said Mass here today and confirmed four. Left for Dead island and pressed on to Fury Harbour, calling at Green Cove.

Aug 11th: Mass at **Snug Harbour.** Proceeded to V. Tickle.

Aug 12th: Mass at **V. Tickle.** Confirmed two. Mother and daughter.

Aug 14th: Took "SS Virginia. Lake". Fr. McGrath and many tourists on board. Arrived at **Indian Tickle** this morning and landed, leaving Fr. Finn to visit the north.

Aug 15th: Said Mass here this morning. High wind blowing. Higgins could not get me from the island.

Aug. 16th: Higgins arrived today. Spent evening instructing them and preparing them for Communion and Confirmation.

Aug. 17th: Mass this morning. Five Confirmed-all adults. Left for Domino at 10am. Arrived 2pm. Sent messages to Fr. Finn and Mr. Lawton. Proceeded to **Black Tickle**. Put up at Mr. Burke's. Comfortable here.

Aug. 18th: Mass here. Large congregation. 13 Confirmed, 11 for Communion. After dinner went on to Batteau.

Aug. 19th: Mass this morning at 8:30. Large congregation. Collection. Intend to remain here till return of steamer. Visited Mrs. Burn of Cupids, who is sick.

Aug 20th: Mass this morning. Received ½ sov. from Mrs. Capt. Ellis for Miss Green.

Aug 21st: Still waiting for steamer.

Aug 22nd: "Virginia Lake" Arrived this morning. All well.

Aug 23rd: On steamer from **Battle Harbour**.

Aug 24th: Spent greater part of day in **Twillingate**-broke down.

Aug 25th: On our way south-called at **King's Cove**. Reached **Harbour Grace** at 10pm. Fr. McGrath landed here.

Aug 26th: Fr. McCarthy called. Dr. Whelan came down today.

Aug 27th: Correspondence all day.

Aug 28th: Children's picnic. Appointed Mr. R.K. Kennedy to Academy Harbour Grace and Mr. John Mackey to Academy Carbonear.

Aug 29th: Received "Silver Tea Set" from friends in Boston.

Sept 14th: Ordained Mr. Joseph Donnelly sub deacon in the Cathedral this morning-present Fr. Finn. Went to **Bay de Verde-** my first visit since consecration.

Sept 15th: Said Mass and preached in **Bay de Verde** today.
Sep 16th: Still here. Fr. J. Lynch came yesterday and is still here.

Sept 17th: Returned to **Harbour Grace** today. Fr. Donnelly went on to St. John's.

Sept 18th: Ordained Mr. Joseph Donnelly deacon at 8 o'clock this morning-present Fr. Finn.

Sept 21st: **ORDAINED** Mr. Donnelly to the priesthood this morning at 9 o'clock. Present: Msgr.'s Walsh and Veitch, Fr.'s Donnelly, Roe, Lynch, McCarthy, Whelan, and Finn. All left for home after dinner.

Sept 22nd: Fr. Joseph Donnelly said his first Mass at Carbonear this morning.

Oct 8th: Left for **Whitbourne** this morning. Confirmed 19 and proceeded to **Placentia Junction** and Confirmed 2. Selected site for school-chapel. Took train for Gambo.

Oct 9th: Confirmed 56 here. Visited **Mint Brook** and chapel.

Oct 10th: Arrived at **Glenwood** and Confirmed 13. This place almost deserted. No school.

Oct 11th: Visited **Botwood** Ville and Confirmed 3. Lunched with Mrs. Crow. Went to **Norris Arm.**

Oct 12th: Confirmed 17 at **Norris Arm**. Saw Mrs. Hut, whose husband was buried yesterday. Started for **Badger.**

Oct 13th: **Badger.** Confirmed 11 at small schoolhouse. Left for Grand Falls.

Oct 14th: Mass here. Raining all day.

Oct 15th: **Grand Falls**. Confirmed 16. Lunched with Mr. Beaton and obtained from him a piece of land to build a Church on. Consented to leave school matters as they are for the present. Took train for Bishop's Falls.

Oct 16th: **Bishop's Falls**. Confirmed 2. Lunched with Mr. Harris. Spent a short time with Mr. Sullivan.

Oct 17th: Reached home.

Oct 24th: Took train for Port Blanford on way to King's Cove. Capt. Blanford very kind.

Oct 25th: Reached **King's Cove** this evening at 5 o'clock. Received by Fr. Scully and people. Houses all illuminated.

Oct 26th: Visited **Open Hall**, called on Mrs. Ryan & Mrs. Doody.

Oct 27th: Said community Mass, preached, received address. Started for **Bonavista** and reached there at 5 o'clock. Received by Dr. Murphy. Dined and addressed the people at Benediction.

Oct 28th: Called on Mrs. Keough & Mrs. Devereux. Dined at Mrs. Ryan's. Reached **Catalina** at dark. Had supper at Mr. Murphy's. Met John White and talked matters over about the new school. Decided to consult Conroy.

Oct 30th: Turned the first Sod for the new Church-30 men working.

Oct 31st: 20 men at work today. Everything going well.

Nov 1st: Said Mass and preached and addressed he people about Church matters.

Nov 2nd: 50 men at work today. Will finish work Monday. Reached home this evening. All well.

Nov. 18th: Bazaar **Spaniard's Bay.**

Nov 19th: Went, with Fr. McCarthy, to **Heart's Desire.** Examined children.

Nov 20th: Said Mass, Confirmed 28. Moved on **to Turk's Cove.** Confirmed 11. Returned to Heart's Content.

Nov 21st: Said Mass & Confirmed 11. Received address. Returned to Harbour Grace.

Dec 1st: Said first_Mass and preached in new Church at **North River**.

1908

Jan 30th: Held visitation at Convent at **Brigus.**

Feb 8th: Paid my first official visit to **Harbour Main.** Received address at **Avondale.** Held visitation at Convent at Harbour Main.

Feb 9th: Said Parish Mass and preached. In the afternoon received Miss Hannon in religion Sr. M. Columba. Fr. Roe, Msgr. Veitch and Fr. Donnelly present. After dinner at convent went to **Conception Harbour.**

Feb 10th: Took train for **St. John's**.

Feb. 13th: Returned from St. John's.

Feb 15th: Went to **Brigus.** Msgr. Walsh unable to say Mass.

Feb 16th: Said Mass and preached.

Feb 17th: Returned home.

Feb. 18th: Transferred Mother Joseph Teresa from Brigus to Conception.

April 23rd: Professed Sr. Veronica lay Sister of Brigus.

June 14th: Laid Corner stone of New S. Heart church at Open Hall, **King's Cove** Parish.

June 8th: Laid Corner stone of the new "Holy Sacrament" church, **Northern Bay.**

June 30th: Started from Harbour Grace on confirmation tour through the parishes of **Conche** and **Coachman's Cove.**

Confirmations
July 5th: Landed at **Goose Cove.** Said Mass and Confirmed 8. Blessed cemetery and selected site for new school-house. Went to **Fishroad Island** and Confirmed 10 same evening.
July 6th: Went to **St. Julian's**, Confirmed 10, and proceeded by Munio Stream. Launch to **Croque.**
July 7th: Arrived in **Conche.**
July 8th: Resting in Conche today.
July 9th: Went to **Grais Islands.**
July 10th: Confirmed 17. People inclined to leave here and go to St. John's.
July 11th: Returned to Conche.
July 12th: Confirmed 60 at **Conche**; preached-large Congregation.
July 13th: Went to **Canada Harbour.**
July 14th: Confirmed 8. Returned to **Buttite** and Confirmed 6-all adults. Reached Conche same day.

Confirmations
July 21st: Came to **Coachman's Cove**.

July 22nd: Blessed cemetery at Coachman's Cove.
July 23rd: Went to **Fleur de Lys.**
July 24th: Confirmed 63. Blessed cemetery. Returned to **Coachman's Cove.**
July 25th: Examined children a Coachman's Cove.
July 26th: Gave Confirmation to 44. Left for **Brent's Cove** calling at **Hosndy Harbour**.
July 27th: Examined candidates.
July 28th: Confirmed 65 and went to **La Scie.**
July 29th: Confirmed 6 and went on to **Tilt Cove**.
July 30th: Examined children.
July 31st: Confirmed 25 and Blessed cemetery.

Aug 1st: Visited Mine. While in Tilt Cove, I was the guest of Mrs. J.M. Jackman, who with Mrs. J. Mary and Irene were very kind to me. Left by boat for Fortune Harbour.

Aug 2nd: Arrived at **Fortune Harbour** too late for mass, gave benediction and address congregation. Fr. Nugent here.

Aug 3rd: Said Mass this morning.

Aug 4th: Examined new Church.

Aug 5th: Left for **Lewisporte.**

Aug 6th: Reached **Harbour Grace.**

Aug 20th: Started with Fr. McCarthy for **St. George's.** Arrived next day.

Aug 23rd: Preached and dedicated Cathedral of St. Joseph at St. George's.

Aug 25th: Reached **Sydney.**

Aug 29th: Arrived home.

Sept 9th: Went to **Harbour Main**.

Sep 10th: Unveiled Cenotaph to Fr. P. O'Donnell. High Mass.

Sept 11th: Returned to **Harbour Grace.**

1909

Aug 5th: Blessed cemetery at **Norris Arm.**

Aug 8th: Blessed Chapel at **Grand Falls.**

Aug 10th: Blessed cemetery at **Gambo.**

Sept 25th: Blessed Chalice for **Northern Bay.**

Sep 30th: Appointed Fr. Dwyer to Grand Falls, Fr. J. Donnelly to Whitbourne and Fr. Battcock to Holyrood.

Oct 10th: Erected Stations of the Cross at **Colliers.**

Oct 27th: Notified Fr. Roe of my intention to divide Harbour Main parish.

Nov 10th: **Harbour Main** Parish divided today.

Nov 12th: opened church of S. Heart at Bay Robert's with Pontifical High Mass. Sermon by Fr. Finn.

1910

Jan 22nd: Held visitation at **Harbour Main** Convent.

Jan 23rd: Visitation at Conception Convent.

Jan 24th: Visitation at Brigus Convent.

Jan 27th: Funeral for Dr. A. Howley at St. John's Cathedral- Bishop McNeil appointed Archbishop of Vancouver on Jan 15th.

Feb 3rd: Visitation at **Carbonear** Convent.

Feb 5th: Visitation at **Harbour Grace** Convent.

March 16th: Fr. Joseph W. Donnelly left for New York sick.

April 26th: Sr. M. Columba Hannon professed today at Harbour Main in parish church. Present: Self, Msgr. Veitch, Fr.'s Battcock, and Shean. Fr. Roe very sick.

May 1st: Sr. M. Teresa McCarthy returned to Carbonear convent from Harbour Grace today.

May 23rd: Archbishop Howley with Fr. St. John left for Rome.

May 28th: Returned from Confirmation tour in the parishes **of Bonavista, King's Cove,** and **St. Brendan's**.

July 14th: Completed tour of Diocese with parishes of **Little Bay, Fortune Harbour,** and **Titling.** Fr. Roe returned to Harbour Main from hospital. Letter from his Grace.

Aug 15th: Archbishop Howley came today for Celebration.

Aug 16th: Archbishop and self met this afternoon and forwarded three names for Bishopric of St. George's. His Grace returned this afternoon.

Aug 22nd: Offered Fr. W.P. Finn Whitbourne as a Parish, gave him time to consider.

Sept: Fr. Battcock died suddenly.

Oct: Returned from trip.

Nov 14th: Fr W.P. Finn took charge of Whitbourne.

Dec: Rev. Mother Catherine died.

Dec 31st: Held visitation at **Harbour Grace** Convent. Appointed Sr. M. John -Rev. Mother.

1911

Jan 16th: Cecily entered Convent at Harbour Main today. (My Niece). Held visitation. Archbishop on visit-Fr. Roe went to Conception today.

Jan 17th: Held visitation at **Conception** today.

Jan 18th: Came to **Brigus.**

Jan 19th: Held visitation here today. Returned home.

June 16th: Fr. John Roe died today at Harbour Main.

June 18th: Church at Avondale destroyed by Lighting last night. No insurance.

June 19th: Funeral of Fr. Roe today.

June 25th: Said Mass at **Avondale** schoolhouse this morning. Resolved start new Church. Appointed Fr. Shean administrator of Harbour Main parish. Gave Benediction at Harbour Main and addressed the people.

1912

Feb 9th: Msgr. E.F. Walsh V.G. died today.

Feb 12th: Msgr. Walsh buried today.

Oct 25th: Left home for New York for medical treatment.

Dec 7th: Returned from New York today.

Dec 9th: Appointed Fr. McCarthy my new Vicar General.

1913

March 24th: MISSION commenced at **Conception.**

Sept 8th: Sr. Mary Angela professed at Harbour Main Convent. (My Niece).

Nov 5th: Blessed new Bell at **North River.**

1914

Feb 19th: Left for **Rome.**

June 14th: Returned from **Rome.**

Aug 20th: Pope Pius X died today.

Sept 3rd: Rev. John Kirwan **ORDAINED.**

Oct 15th: His Grace Archbishop Howley died today. Funeral on Oct 19th.

1915

Feb 22nd: Rev. Mother went to St. John's to consult with doctors.

Feb 23rd: Msgr. Roche appointed Archbishop of St. John's.

May 20th: Rev. Mother John of Harbour Grace died this evening.

May 22nd: Rev. Mother's funeral today.

May 24th: Bulls arrived to Msgr. Roche today.

June 3rd: Held visitation in **Harbour Grace** convent today and appointed St. M. Patrick-Rev. Mother.

June 15th: Nuns left today.

June 29th: Archbishop Roche consecrated today. Bishop Power preached.

Sept 8th: Sr. M. Columba Hipditch left Convent today.

Sept 21st: St. Joseph and Scholashca left Convent today.

1916

Feb 19th: MISSION Fathers-McNeil and McDonald arrived today.
Feb 20th: MISSION opened at **River Head**
Feb 27th: MISSION opened at **Sp. Bay**
March 5th: MISSION opened at **Harbour Main.**
March 12th: MISSION opened to **Avondale.**

May 18th: Rev. J. W. Donnelly died today.

May 20th: Fr. Donnelly's funeral took place in Carbonear today. Msgr. McCarthy preached.

1923

July 26th, 1923: Rev. S.J. Whelan D.D. died. Buried at North river.

1927

Feb 15th: Rev. R.M. Shean P.P. Harbour Main died and was buried at Brigus.

Aug: Rev. James Walker died and was buried at Brigus.

1931

July 5th: Rev. P. J. Hearn P.P. Coachman's Cove died at St. John's. Buried Conception Harbour.

1934

May 8th: Rev. G.A. Thibault P.P. North River died and was buried at North River.

1935

Aug 3rd: Rev. W.P. Finn P.P. Holyrood died and was buried at Holyrood.

1937

Aug 13th: Rev. F. J. Pumphrey P.P. St. Brendan's died at Montreal and was buried at Corner Brook.

Aug 24th: Rev. Nicholas Fitzgerald appointed P.P. of St. Brendan's.

Aug 23rd: Mother Angela appointed local superior of Harbour Main. Sr. Francis appointed local superior at Conception.

Aug 31st: Mother M. Laurels returned from St. John's much improved in health.

Sept 1st: Rev. Walter P. Walsh appointed Curate to Rev. John H. Scully at Conception.

May 30th: Laid Corner stone of New Church at Grand Falls Station.

Sept 18th: Mother Berchman died at Brigus today. Age 86.

Sept 20th: Mother Berchman's buried today.

Nov 4th: Anniversary of **my** consecration. His Grace Archbishop Roche and Bishop Renouf came to Harbour Grace and we had our meeting. Visitors returned to St. John's in the evening.

Nov 11th: Visit from Bishop Renouf and Father R. Green.

Nov 12th: Mother Joseph Noonan and another Sister came from St. John's today.

1938

March 17th: Rev. W.M. Tarahan P.P. died at Trinity and was buried at Trinity on March 19th. Fathers Murphy and Howard officiating.

March 23rd: Rev. J. Howard P.P. Bonavista gave charge of Trinity.

April 13th: Had slight heart attack. Forbidden by doctor to take any part in Holy Week ceremonies. Msgr. McCarthy officiated and Fr. O'Brien preached on Holy Thursday and Fr. Dwyer on Good Friday.

April 17th: Church and presbytery burnt to the ground at Coachman's Cove today. No insurance. Father Joseph P. Hogan in charge.

June 15th: Blessed and dedicated the new Church of Corpus Christi in Northern Bay, Fr. O'Brien P.P. and Msgr. McCarthy being present.

June 16th: Feast of Corpus Christi celebrated first Holy Mass in new Church, McCarthy and ten other priests being present, Rev. Dr. O'Neill preached.

Aug 18th: Appointed Rev. Michael J. Kinsella administrator of Trinity Parish with instructions to take charge Sept 1st.

Aug 26th: Rev. Walter P. Walsh appointed curate to Fr. Mackey at Bay de Verde.

Oct 20th: Gave Rev. J. Ronald Jones permission to absent himself form the Diocese for a year.

Oct 25th: Fr. Jones left the Diocese. Fr. McCarthy of St. John's appointed curate to Fr. Finn of Grand Falls.

Nov 14th: Received from Rome-Decree transferring Blanc Sablon from Harbour Grace to the Vicariate of the Gulf of St. Lawrence.

1939

Feb 10th: Pope Pius X died this morning R.I.P.

May 13th: Received from Del. Apparent request to sent Fr. Jones out of Canada.

May 15th: Ordered Fr. Jones to leave Canada.

June 13th: Msgr.'s McCarthy, Murphy, Father's Dwyer, Finn, and Dinn were appointed Consultors and sworn in at Harbour Grace.

3rd Section of the Book

Most Rev. Dr. John M. O'Neill D.D. reign as See of Harbour Grace-Grand Falls

1940

Jan 12th, 1940: Bishop March died. Funeral on the Sixteenth. Sermon by Archbishop Roche.

May 27th: Received first news of my appointment as Bishop.

June 12th: Appointment officially announced.

July 7th: Consecrated Bishop by the Apostolic Delegate Archbishop Antoniutti, Bishop H.T. Renouf, and Bishop J.A. Sullivan.

Confirmations

Aug 1st: Left for **Fogo.**
Aug 4th: First Confirmations at **Fogo**-51 confirmed.
Aug 5th- Confirmed 70 at **Tilting.**
Aug 5th- Confirmed 44 at **J. B. Arm**
Aug 6th- Confirmed 37 at **Is. Harbour**
Aug 6th- Confirmed 21 at **Boyd's Cove**
Aug 8th- Confirmed 49 at **Fortune Harbour**
Aug 9th- Confirmed 23 at **Little Bay**
Aug 10th-Confirmed 2 at **La Scie**
Aug 10th-Con*fir*med 40 at **Brent's Cove**
Aug 11th-Confirmed 45 at **Coachman's Cove**
Aug 11th-Confirmed 48 at **Fleur de Lys**
Aug 15th: Mass on board **N. Ranger**. Arrived at St. John's 8:30 pm.

Sept 30th: Following appointments sent out:
Rev. W. McC. Murphy P.P.-Holyrood
Rev W. H. Casey P.P.-Bay de Verde
Rev. J. A. Hinchey P.P. Fortune Harbour
Rev. J. P. Hogan P.P.-Bishop's Falls
Rev. W. P. Walsh P.P.-Coachman's Cove
Rev. W. Hennebury Admin.-King's Co

Oct 15th: Left for **Buchans** accompanied by Monsignor Dinn.

Oct 17th-Confirmed 35 at **Buchans**
Oct 17th-Confirmed 6 at **Millertown Jct.**
Oct 20th-Confirmed 175 at **Grand Falls**
Oct 20th-Confirmed 91 at **Windsor**
Oct 21st-Confirmed 27 at **Badger**
Oct 2nd-Confirmed 14 at **Botwood**
Oct 22nd-Confirmed 36 at **Norris Arm**
Oct 23rd-Confirmed 49 at **Bishop's Falls**

Went on to visit **Aguathuna** and **Corner Brook**. Arrived home on Oct 31st*Oct 15th:* Left for **Buchans** accompanied by Monsignor Dinn.

Oct 17th-Confirmed 35 at **Buchans**
Oct 17th-Confirmed 6 at **Millertown Jct.**
Oct 20th-Confirmed 175 at **Grand Falls**
Oct 20th-Confirmed 91 at **Windsor**
Oct 21st-Confirmed 27 at **Badger**
Oct 2nd-Confirmed 14 at **Botwood**
Oct 22nd-Confirmed 36 at **Norris Arm**
Oct 23rd-Confirmed 49 at **Bishop's Falls**

Went on to visit **Aguathuna** and **Corner Brook**. Arrived home on Oct 31st.

1941

March 2nd: Bishop Renouf died at St. Clare's hospital at 8:30pm.

March 6th: Bishop Renouf buried today at Belvedere-celebrant Rev. M. Brosnan. Sermon delivered by me.

March 19th-20th: Meeting with Archbishop Re: West coast-Episcopal Chair.

June 21st-Confirmed 28 at **Sp. Bay**
June 22nd-Confirmed 108 at **River Head**
June 22nd-Confirmed 59 at **Harbour Grace**

July 6th: Left by Kyle for **Conche**
July 8th- Confirmed 66 at **Conche**
July 8th- Confirmed 21 at **Gross Island**
July 9th- Confirmed 24 at **Canada Harbour**
July 10th-Confirmed 23 at **St. Julien's**
July 10th-Confirmed 10 at **Goose Cove**
July 12th: Left for **St. Anthony**-Confirmed 4.
July 13th: Arrived at **Black Tickle** and Confirmed 34.
July 15th: Left Black Tickle and arrived at **St. Francis Harbour Bight**-Confirmed 3.
July 16th: Arrived at P. **Hope Simpson** and Confirmed 7.

July 18th: Arrived at **Battle Harbour**-Confirmed 1.
July 19th: Arrived at **Pinware.**
July 20th: Confirmed 24 at Pinware.
July 21st: Confirmed 15 at **L'Anse au Loup.**
July 22nd: Arrived at **Point Amount.**

July 24th: Took Northern Ranger at **L'Anse au Loup.** Arrived home on the 28th.

Sept 9th: Most Rev. Michael O'Reilly D.D. consecrated Bishop of St. George's by Apostolic Delegate-Co-Consecrators were Most Rev. J. R. Sullivan D.D. and myself. Sermon by Archbishop Roche.

Sept 14th: Enthronement of Bishop O'Reilly at St.George's.

Oct 5th- Confirmed 116 at **Carbonear**
Oct 6th- Confirmed 92 at **Holyrood**
Oct 7th- Confirmed 85 at **Avondale**
Oct 9th- Confirmed 200 at **Conception**
Oct 10th-Confirmed 28 at **Heart's Content**
Oct 12th-Confirmed 88 at **North River**
Oct 16th-Confirmed 147 at **Northern Bay**
Oct 19th-Confirmed 142 at **Brigus**
Oct 26th & 27th-Confirmed 143 at **Bay de Verde**
Nov 2nd-Confirmed 90 at **Harbour Main**

1942

June 8th-Confirmed 11 at **Glenwood**
June 8th-Confirmed 8 at **Gander**
June 9th-Confirmed 56 at **Gambo**

June 17th: Attended Sacerdotal Silver Jubilee of Bishop O'Reilly at St. George's-arrived home on the 20th.

June 28th: Pontifical Mass in Cathedral at St. John's on the occasion of the o**ne hundredth anniversary o**f the arrival of the Sisters of Mercy.

June 30th: Confirmation at **Whitbourne** 30, **Chapel Arm** 17, and **Bellevue** 14.

1943

April 22nd: Nuns Confessors: Reappointed for Harbour Main, Conception, Brigus, Carbonear, Grand Falls.

Confirmations
June 24th: Took Kyle to **Trinity.** Arriving Friday morning.
June 26th: Confirmed 4 at **Trinity.** Proceeded to **Catalina** and confirmed 22.
June 27th: Sunday-confirmed 17 at **Bonavista.** Left for **King's Cove**. Confirmed 55 at K. Cove Sunday evening.
June 28th: Confirmed 47 at **Plate Cove**, 17 at **Summerville,** 34 at **Sweet Bay.**
June 29th: Returned to **Open Hall** and confirmed 11. On to King's Cove.
June 30th: Took boat at Open Hall for **St. Brendan's.** Arrived 6pm.
July 1st: Confirmed 52 at **St. Brendan's**. Took boat back to Open Halls. Very unpleasant trip. Crossed to **Trinity.** Lovely day. Arrived at 4pm. Held Confirmation-15. Left for **Heart's Content** and arrived home same evening.

Dec 8th: Consultors appointed and sworn in: Rt. Rev. McCarthy, Dinn, Murphy. Rev.'s Finn, Dwyer, & O'Brien.

1944

Feb 1st: **ORDAINED** Rev. Edward Shea to the Priesthood. Present were Msgr. McCarthy & Dinn, Rev.'s J. Peddle, F. Terry, ad L. Burke.

Confirmations
May 24th: Left for **Bishop's Falls**
May 25th-Confirmed 71 at **B. Falls**
May 26th-Confirmed 38 at **Norris Arm**
May 26th-Confirmed 6 at **Gander**
May 27th-Confirmed 24 at **Botwood**
May 28th-Confirmed 167 at **Grand Falls**
May 28th-Confirmed 107 at **Windsor**
May 29th-Confirmed 24 at **Badger**
May 30th-Confirmed 41 at **Buchans**
May 30th-Confirmed 6 at **Millertown**
May 30th-Confirmed 11 at **Buchans Junction**.

June 1st: Left by Pan American Clipper to attend th Consecration of Bishop Boyle of Charlottetown.

June 6th: Consecration of Bishop Boyle by Apostolic Delegate-Co-Consecrators were Archbishop Morrison and Bishop Bray. Sermon by Archbishop J.H. McDonald of Edmonton. Present also were Archbishop Robichand, Bishop LeBlanc, Bishop J.R. McDonald, and Archbishop McNally. Arrived home on June 10th.

June 20th: Rt. Rev. Monsignor Murphy died at St. Clare's Hospital after on illness of six months funeral at Brigus on June 22nd- large concave of priests.

June 25th: Rt. Rev. Monsignor McCarthy celebrated today the Sixtieth Anniversary of his ordination and was celebrant of Solemn High Mass.Carom Pontifice. Received the Pope's Blessing. He was the first priest in NFLD to celebrate his Diamond Jubilee-Rev. L. Burke preached.

June 30th: Shocked this morning by almost sudden passing of Monsignor McCarthy, who appeared so well on Sunday. Had attack of Cardiac Asthma at 7:00 am. Died at 9:00 am. Attended and anointed by Fr. Mackey-left estate valued at: Nil! "Theasauros ejus Auferanerunt Monus Pauperum." Hons Dei. R.I.P.

July 3rd: Monsignor McCarthy buried today-Solemn High Mass-Fr. Mackey celebrant, Fr. Joseph O'Brien deacon, Fr. Burke sub deacon, Fr. Shea M.C. Panegyric preached by Bishop.

Sept 1st: Following changes effective today:
Dr. Jones PP of Brigus
Rev. T. D. O'Neill PP of Carbonear
Rev. L.G. Fitzgerald PP of Buchans
Rev. M.. J. Kinsella PP of Tilting
Rev. L. Burke PP of Trinity
Rev. F.R. Terry PP of St. Brendan's

1945

Confirmations

Aug 6th: Took train to **Lewisporte** accompanied by Rev. Ronald Walsh newly **ordained** priest.
Aug 7th: Left Lewisporte for **Boyd's** Cove. Arrived moon-Confirmed 29-left for **Island Hr**-Confirmed 14 there and left for **Fogo**, arriving at dark. Strenuous day.
Aug 8th: Mass & Confirmation at **Fogo**-31 Confirmed-**Joe Batts Arm** 24 - **Tilting** 44 Another full day.
Aug 9th: Left Tilting-strong breeze W. West. Put in to Fogo and learned SS Ranger due there. Great piece of luck-took Ranger to **Coachman's Cove**. Arrived **Baie Verte** next evening-confirmed 14. Left next morning and arrived at Coachman's early. Visited **Fleur de Lys** in afternoon and confirmed 54. Back to C. Cove.
Aug 12th-Sunday: Confirmed 24 at **Coachman's.** Left on 13th for **Brent's Cove**-Confirmed 57. Left immediately for **Fortune Hr**. Arrived at 10:00pm-very tired.
Aug 14th: Confirmed 21 at **Fortune.**
Aug 15th: V.J. Day-Mass same place. Left after Mass for **Little Bay**. Confirmed 5 at Little Bay. Returned to **Springdale**. Thence to **South Brook** and by car to **Windsor** arriving midnight.
Aug 16th: Took train to **Whitbourne** hired taxi there and arrived home at 11:00am.

1946

Confirmations

June 9th: Confirmed 54 at **Hr. Grace**, 55 at **Riverhead**. 30 the next day at **Sp. Bay.**
June 14th: Confirmed 17 at **Norris Arm**. Blessed new Church.
June 15th: 26 at **Bishop's Falls.**
June 16th: 101 at **Grand Falls**-62 at **Windsor**. 29 at **Buchans** the next day. Appointed Fr. Meaney ordinary confessor.

July 7th: 6th Anniversary of Consecration. Confirmed in **Carbonear** that morning 104. **Hrts. Content** in afternoon 29.

Confirmations

July 31st: Left home for **Conche**. Took train to Grand Falls. Arrived there early morning.
Aug 1st: Said Mass. Fr. Meaney drove self and Fr. Peddle to **South Brook**. Boarded Wiseman's Boat at noon. Arrived at **Coachman's Cove** at 10:00pm. Good Run. Weather fine.
Aug 2nd: Left Coachman's and arrived at Conche at 4:30pm.
Aug 3rd: Visited **Grey Islands**-Confirmed 18. Returned to Conche.
Aug 4th: Sunday. Confirmed 50 at **Conche**. Left for **Grandsires** Confirmed 22 there and proceeded to **Goose Cove.**
Aug 5th: Confirmed 6 at **G. Cove** and proceeded to **Fortune Arm or Griquet.** Confirmed 10 and left for Conche arriving same night at 11:00pm. Stopped on way at **Fickot Island** and Confirmed 15.
Aug 6th: Proceeded to **Canada Hr**. Confirmed 24. Returned to Conche.
Aug 7th: Left Conche for home. Made it to **La Scie** that night.
Aug 8th: Arrived at South Brook at 3:00pm, arrived at Badger at 8:00pm, Grand Falls at 9:30pm. Took train at midnight and arrived at Hr. Grace following morning. Perfect weather whole trip!

Confirmations

Oct 6th: Confirmed 70 at **Bay de Verde & Grates Cove.**
Oct 13th: Confirmed 114 at **Northern Bay**.
Oct 20th: Confirmed 73 at **Holyrood** and 91 at **Hr. Main.**
Oct 21st: Confirmed 71 at **Avondale.**
Oct 27th: Confirmed 79 at **Brigus.**
Nov 3rd: Confirmed 102 at **Conception**, 63 at **Colliers.**
*Nov 10th:*Confirmed 53 at **N. River**, 30 at **Bay Roberts.**

1947

Feb 13th: My Brother Brendan died suddenly at Corner Brook hospital. Buried at Port au Port on Feb. 15th which is the anniversary of my Mother's death.

March 4th: Appointed Consultors "Ad Triennium": Msgr. Dinn and Finn, Fr. Scully, Dwyer, O'Brien, and Peddle.

March 11th: Nuns confessors reappointed:
--Msgr. Finn-ordinary for Grand Falls & extraordinary for Windsor and Bishop's Falls.
--Fr. Dwyer-ordinary for Hr. Main.
--Fr. Kavanagh-extraordinary for Hr. Main and Conception.
--Dr. Jones-ordinary for Brigus and extraordinary at Harbour Grace.
--Fr. Hogan-extraordinary for Grand Falls and ordinary at Bishop's Falls.
--Fr. Meaney-ordinary for Windsor.
--Fr. Scully-ordinary for Conception.
--Fr. O'Neill-ordinary for Carbonear.
--Fr. Peddle-ordinary for Hr. Grace, extraordinary for Brigus & Carbonear.

June 8th: Took train at **Whitbourne** for **Gambo**. Arrived at 6:00 pm. Confirmed 45 there the next day.
June 11th: Confirmed 63 at **St. Brendan's.**
June 12th: Left **St. Brendan's** for **Gambo.** Strong west winds-trip took over six hours. Arrived 5:00pm.
June 13th: Left Gambo by "Speeder"-confirmed 16 at **Glenwood** and returned to Gander. Left Gander by plane at 12:30 am. Arrived at St. John's at 1:15 and reached home Saturday the 14th.

June 24th: Archbishop of St. John's celebrated Golden Jubilee of ordination and 450th Anniversary of Cabot's Landing.

July 1st: Confirmation at **Whitbourne** 19, **Chapel Arm** 22, **Bellevue** 22.

Sept 8th: Rev. W.J. Hennebury PP of Conche died at St. Clare's Hospital after illness of several weeks.

Funeral at Hr. Grace Sept. 10th. Preacher Rt. Rev. Msgr. Dinn.

1948

Jan 30th: Fr. Scully died this morning at St. Clare's.

Feb 2nd - Funeral. Sermon by Fr. Dwyer.

June 11th: Confirmed 44 at **Gander.**

June 12th: **ORDAINED** Rev. Gregory Pumphrey at Grand Falls. Confirmed 129 at **G Falls** and 68 at **Windsor** the next day.

June 15th: Attended Silver Jubilee celebrations of Rev. L. G. Fitzgerald at Buchans.

July 18th: Left by car for **Bonavista**. Confirmed 15 there and 22 at **Catalina.**
July 19th: Confirmed 43 at **King's Cove**, 16 at **Open Hall** and 30 at **Plate Cove.**
July 21st: Left King's Cove for **Summerville.** Confirmed 17 there and proceeded to **Sweet Bay**. Confirmed 30 at Sweet Bay and left for home same day.

July 28th: Following Changes effective Aug 1st:
Rev. W. H. Casey PP-Conception
Rev. T. D. O'Neill PP-Colliers
Rev. M. J. Kinsella PP-Bay de Verde
Very Rev. J. W. Peddle PP-Carbonear
Rev. Jos. O'Brien PP-Tilting
Rev. E. A. Walsh PP-Conche
Rev. W. P. Walsh PP-Gambo
Rev. Ronald Walsh PP-Coachman's Cove
Rev. E. M. Shea Rector-Cathedral Hr. Grace
Rev. Wm. Hogan CC-Hr. Grace
Rev. Gregory B. Pumphrey CC-Grand Falls

Oct 28th: Father Cullen died at St. Clare's Hospital, following a long illness-a good priest and a loss to the diocese. About fifty six-R.I.P. Funeral at Carbonear.

1949

Confirmations
Oct 30th: Left by train for **Buchans**.
Nov 1st: Confirmation at **Buchans and Badger.**
Nov 2nd: Confirmation at **Windsor.**
Nov 3rd: Confirmation at **Bishop's Falls.**
Nov 4th: Confirmation at **Norris Arm & Botwood.**
Nov 6th: Confirmation at **Grand Falls**.
Nov 7th: Confirmation at **Gander.** Arrived home the next day.

1950

March 4th: Renewed faculties to Fr. Peddle for Nuns confessions: ordinary at Carbonear, extraordinary at Brigus. Msgr. Finn ordinary at Grand Falls, extraordinary at Windsor and Bishop's Falls. Fr. Shea ordinary at Harbour Grace. Fr. Casey ordinary at Conception. Fr. Meaney ordinary at Windsor and Fr. Hogan ordinary at Bishop's Falls, extraordinary at Grand Falls. Dr. Jones ordinary at Brigus and extraordinary at Harbour Grace. Fr. Kavanagh extraordinary at Conception. Fr. Dwyer ordinary at Harbour Main.

Appointed Consultors: Msgr. Finn, Very Rev. M.P. Dwyer, Very Rev. E. J. O'Brien, and Very Rev. Joseph W. Peddle.

June 11th: **ORDAINED** Rev. Frederick Terry to the priesthood at Harbour Main.

June 24th: Appointed Rev. G. M. Murphy CssR. Extraordinary Confessor to all convents in the diocese "Ad Triennium".

July 27th: Consultors sworn in at Littledale-"Ad Triennium".

Confirmations
Aug 1st: Left Carbonear by "Kyle" accompanied by Fr. Shea.
Aug 2nd: Landed at **Tilting** 11L30. Confirmed 25 at **Joe Batt's Arm**, 35 at **Fogo.**
Aug 3rd: Confirmed 8 at **Island Harbour** and 45 at **Tilting.**
Aug 4th: Left Fogo and arrived at **Boyd's Cove** at noon. Confirmed 11. Left 2:30 and arrived at **Fortune Harbour** at 9:30. Beautiful day and lovely trip.
Aug 5th: Confirmed 38 at **Fortune Harbour**. Left for **Little Bay**. Joined "Springdale" at **Leading Tickles**.
Aug 6th: Bad night. N.E. Wind and rain. Arrived at Little Bay 11:30am. No Chalice-so could not say Mass. Confirmed 19 at **Little Bay**. Left by car for **Springdale.** Took boat to **South Brook** and arrived at **Grand Falls** at 9 pm. Arrived home the next day.

Sept 23rd: His Grace, Archbishop Roche of St. John's died this afternoon at St. Clare's hospital. Age 76 and 7 months. R.I.P.

Sept 28th: Funeral of Archbishop. Present: Delegate, Bishop J. R. MacDonald, Bishop A. Leverman, Bishop M. O'Reilly, Bishop P. J. Skinner, and myself. Sermon by me.

Oct 25th: Left **Hr. Grace** for **Gander** accompanied by Dr. O'Kelly to **Avondale.**

Oct 26th: Left Gander for **Rome**, arriving next day.

Nov 1st: Was present at historic event of the Definition of the Dogma of the Assumption.

Nov 2nd: Left Rome and arrived home next day.

1951

Most Rev. P. J. Skinner c.j.m. D.D. appointed Archbishop of St. John's.

March 22nd: Received oath of allegiance to Holy See from Most Rev. P. J. Skinner c.j.m., D.D. at Palace, St. John's-Bulls Read. Official taking of possession of See. Historic occasion. Regnet Gloriose!!!

Confirmations-

June 3rd Confirmed 80 at **Holyrood.**
June 3rd Confirmed 81 at **Harbour Main,**
June 10th Confirmed 80 at **Avondale.**
June 11th Confirmed 45 at **Spaniard's Bay**.

July 29th: Left for **Grand Falls**. On the 30th -motored to **Springdale** and took boat for **Coachman's.** Arrived at **La Scie** that evening and confirmed 7 children.
July 31st: Proceeded to **Brent's Cove** and Confirmed 30, proceeded to **Baie Verte** and Confirmed 50. Arrived at Coachman's.
Aug 1st: Confirmed 43 at **Coachman's**-80 at **Fleur de Lys.**
Aug 2nd: Confirmed 27 at **Canada Hr.**

Nov 6th: Blessed new church at **Norris Arm**. Made first trip to **Corner Brook** and **Port au Port** over new highway. Road very rough and primitive in spots.

1952

July 1st: Celebrated Sacerdotal Silver Jubilee. Sermon by Archbishop Skinner. Present: Bishop O'Reilly and sixty priests. Marble Altar erected by priests and people.

July 6th: Confirmation administrated at **Whitbourne, Bellevue**, and **Chapel Arm**.
July 7th: Confirmation at **Heart's Desire**
Aug 7th: Confirmation at **Gambo.**
Aug 8th: Confirmation at **Glenwood.**
Aug 9th: Confirmation at **St. Brendan's.**

Sept 2nd: Father Frank Terry died at Brookfield hospital this morning. R.I.P.

Sept 25th: Appointed Rev. R. T. Woodford curate at Harbour Main and Rev. F. J. Terry administrator of Fortune Harbour, both effective Oct 15th.

Oct 1st: Appointed Rev. E. M. Shea parish priest of St.

Nov 16th: Rev. Michael Carey s.f.m. Came to the Diocese. Appointed assistant at Harbour Grace.

Nov 16th.Confirmed 84 at **Bishop's Falls.**
Nov 17th Confirmed 105 at **Grand Falls.**
Nov 18th Confirmed 146 at **Windsor.**
Nov 18th Confirmed 35 at **Badger.**
Nov 19th Confirmed 55 at **Buchans.**
Nov 21st Confirmed 38 at **Norris Arm.**

1953

Jan 31st: Rt. Rev. Msgr. William Finn, PP of Grand Falls for Forty years, died at St. Mary's Hospital, Montreal. Funeral at Grand Falls Feb 7th. Age 74.

Feb 18th: Reappointed nun's confessors "Ad Triennium"

March 25th: Rt. Rev. Monsignor Mark P. Dwyer P.P. of Hr. Main died suddenly after long illness. Aged 68 years. R.I.P. Funeral March 12th.

March 25th: Consecrated new marble Altar in the Cathedral at Harbour Grace. This Altar was presented by the priests and people of my Sacerdotal Silver Jubilee. Present for the Consecration were Rev. J.W. Peddle, Rev. W.P. Hogan, and Rev. M.P. Carey s.f.m.

April 2nd: Following Consultors appointed and sworn in: Rt. Rev. Monsignor M.F. Dinn, Very Rev. E.J. O'Brien; Very Rev. E.J. Jones, Very Rev. J.W. Peddle.

May 25th: Co-Cathedral erected in Grand Falls

June 1st: Reappointed Rev. G.M. Murphy CssR. extraordinary to all convents in diocese.

Confirmations
June 30th: Left by car for **Bonavista** peninsula-arrived **Plate Cove** 4:00pm. Confirmed children blessed new Church and Consecrated new bell. Left for Open Hall and Confirmed children, proceeded to King's Cove.
July 1st: Confirmation **King's Cove** and **Bonavista.**
July 2nd: Confirmation **Catalina**.
July 3rd: Confirmation **Summerville** and **Sweet Bay.**
July 4th: Confirmation **Gooseberry Cove**. Returned home.

<u>Appointments Effective Sept. 6th:</u>

Rev. Jeremiah Howard -P.P. of Harbour Main
Very. Rev. J.W. Peddle -Rector of Grand Falls
Rev. Leo Burke-Administrator of Carbonear
Rev. R.T. Woodford-P.P of Bonavista-Trinity
Rev. M.P. Carey-Administrator of Norris Arm-Fortune Hr.
Rev. G.B. Pumphrey-C.C. of Windsor
Rev. F.J. Terry-C.C. at Hr. Grace

Sept. 1st: Rev. J. Howard appointed ordinary Confessor of sisters at Hr. Main. Rev. Leo Burke ordinary confessor of sisters at Carbonear. Very Rev. Joseph W. Peddle ordinary confessor to Sisters at Grand Falls. Rev. L.G. Fitzgerald appointed ordinary confessor of nuns at Buchans. Rev. F.P. Meaney appointed ordinary confessor of nuns at Badge

1954

Confirmations

Sept 17th: Left St. John's by plane for **Gander**.
Sept 18th: Took private plane to **Gander Bay**, confirmed 7.
Sept 19th Confirmed 90 at **Gander.**
Sept 20th Confirmed 7 at **Black Island**.
Sept 21st Confirmed 35 at **Norris Arm.**
Sept 23rd Confirmed 30 at **Buchans.**
Sept 26th Confirmed 128 at **Grand Falls.**
Sept 26th Confirmed 53 at **Bishop's Falls.**
Sept 27th Confirmed 38 at **Windsor**.
Sept 28th Confirmed 30 at **Badger.**

**Moved Permanently to Grand Falls

1955

June 24th to 29th: Centenary celebrations of Consecration of Cathedral at St. John's.

*June:*_Bishop moved into new Residence at Grand Falls.

July 17th: Monsignor Dinn V.G. died shortly after midnight. July 19th -funeral at North River: Present: Archbishop of St. John's and nearly fifty priests. Mass and oration by me. I am now no. 10 in the Diocese; and have long passed the average age. How long more? God knows! May I make the most of the borrowed time!!

August: Mons. J.W. Peddle appointed Vicar General. Rev. Joseph P. Hogan appointed to North River. Rev. J.M. O'Brien appointed to Bishop's Falls, Rev. G.B. Pumphrey appointed to Tilting.

Confessors to sisters appointed as follows: Effective August 15th:

Msgr. Peddle to Bishop's Falls
Fr. Meaney to Grand Falls
Fr. O'Brien to Windsor
Fr. E.A. Walsh to Badger
Fr. Casey to Hr. Main
Fr. Howard to Conception
Fr. W. Hogan to Carbonear
Fr. Burke to Hr. Grace
Rev. P.A. McCormack appointed Parish Priest of Conche
Rev. E. A. Walsh appointed Parish Priest of Avondale, succeeding Rev. J.S. Kavanagh.
Rev. L. Kelly appointed curate at Badger
Rev. M.R. Hynes appointed curate at Grand Falls

Sept. 29th: Left for Boyd's Cove.

Sept 30th Confirmed 7 at **Boyd's Cove.**
Sept 30th Confirmed 14 at **Island Harbour.**
Sept 30th Confirmed 50 at **Fogo.**
Oct 1st Confirmed 50 at **Tilting.**
Oct 1st Confirmed 55 at **Joe Batts Arm**.
Oct 2nd Confirmed 23 at **Fortune Harbour.**
-Returned to Grand Falls

Nov. 11th: Confirmed 34 at **Little Bay**

1956

Feb. 29th: Today is the **One-Hundredth Anniversary** of the erection of the Diocese. Celebrations later in the year.

April 7th: Rev. T.D. O'Neill of Colliers died at St. Clare's hospital.

April 10th: Fr. O'Neill buried in Harbour Grace.

June 5th: Left Grand Falls for Harbour Grace.

Confirmations

Harbour Grace	92	**Carbonear**	156
Conception	93	**Riverhead**	114
Harbour Main	129	**Sp. Bay**	47
Holyrood	140	**Bay Roberts**	45
Northern Bay	120	**North River**	90
Grates Cove	12	**Brigus**	142
Bay de Verde	80	**Colliers**	90

Confirmations

July 1st Confirmed 10 at **La Scie.**
July 2nd Confirmed 52 at **Brent's Cove.**
July 2nd Confirmed 53 at **Coachman's Cove.**
July 2nd Confirmed 85 at **Baie Verte.**
July 3rd Confirmed 26 at **Canada Harbour.**
July 4th Confirmed 17 at **Grey Islands.**
July 4th Confirmed 50 at **Conche.**
July 5th Confirmed 30 at **Goose Cove.**
July 5th Confirmed 11 at **Fishnet Island.**
July 5th Confirmed 11 at **Grabbles Oies.**
July 6th Confirmed 58 at **Fleur de Lys.**

July 15th: Centenary Celebrations at Harbour Grace

Sept. 22nd: Reappointed Rev. L. G. Fitzgerald ordinary confessor of sisters at Buchans.

1957

Jan. 19th: My father died at St. Clare's Mercy hospital. Funeral Mass at Harbour Grace. *Jan. 21st:* Interment at Bay de Verde.

Feb. 11th: Rev. G. M. Murphy CssR. died at Charlottetown, PEI.

May 26th: Confirmed 184 at **Grand Falls,** 157 at **Windsor.**

June 9th: **ORDAINED** Rev. Linus Coady to priesthood at Harbour Grace.

June 10th: Confirmed 42 at **Whitbourne** and blessed new Church. Confirmed 22 at **Heart's Desire** and blessed new Church.

July 4th: Apostolic Delegate, Archbishop Giovanni Ponico visited Harbour Grace.

July 5th: Blessed corner stone of new convent at Gander and proceeded to Grand Falls.

July 10th: Confirmed 27 at **Glenwood**-86 at **Gambo.**
July 11th: Confirmed 11 at **Cull's Harbour** and 142 at **St. Brendan's.**

Sept. 6th: Appointed Rev. W.H. Casey ordinary confessor of sisters at Avondale.

Sept. 15th: Amid large gathering of priests, sisters, and people. Blessed and opened new school and convent at **Avondale.**

Sept. 19th: Appointed Rev. P.J. McCarthy ordinary confessor of sisters at Gander.

Sept 20th: Appointed following effective Oct 8th:

Rt. Rev. Joseph Peddle ordinary for sisters at Harbour Grace, Rev. J.M. O'Brien ordinary for sisters at Carbonear, Rev. L. Burke ordinary for sisters at Windsor, Rev. W.P. Hogan ordinary for sister at Bishop's Falls. Appointed Rev. F.P. Meaney confessor to Christian Brothers.

Sept: Appointed Monsignor Peddle Parish Priest of Carbonear, Rev. W.P. Hogan Rector of Co-Cathedral at Grand Falls, appointed Rev. J.M. O'Brien rector of Cathedral at Harbour Grace. Appointed Rev. Leo Burke Parish Priest of Bishop's Falls.

Sunday, Sept. 22nd: Confirmed 120 at **Bishop's Falls**-Confirmed 75 at **Buchans.**

Sat, Sept. 28th: Blessing and official opening of St. Michael's Regional High School.

Monday, Sept. 30th: Blessing and official opening of St. Joseph's school and convent at **Gander.**

Oct. 25th: Appointed Fr. Meaney ordinary confessor to Badger convent.

1958

July 7th & 8th: Confirmed 150 at **King's Cove** Parish.
July 8th & 9th: Confirmed 163 in **Bonavista** Parish.

Aug. 11th: Erected new parish at Badger and appointed Rev. R.J. Walsh first Parish Priest. Appointed Rev. L.J. Kelly Parish Priest of Baie Verte.

Sept. 8th: Fr. Walter Walsh died at St. Clare's.

Made third "Ad Limina" visit. Had private audience with Pope Pius XII on September 28th. He died on October 9th. October 28th-Cardinal Roncalli elected Pope, taking name of John XXIII. Returned via Boston.

1959

May 31st: Confirmed 139 at **Grand Falls**.

June 2nd: Fr. FP Meaney celebrated his Silver Jubilee-confirmed 118 at Windsor.

June 7th: **ORDAINED** Rev. R. Hawco and Rev. Ed. Hearn at Harbour Grace.

June 10th: Confirmed 105 children, 25 adults at **Gander.**
June 11th: Confirmed 106 at **Norris Arm.**

June 14th: **ORDAINED** Rev. Wm. Shallow to the Holy Priesthood. Present Frs. Meaney, Hogan, Burke, Carey, Coady, and McCarthy.

June 15th: Appointed Rev. M.R. Hynes parish priest of Gambo, Rev. L. Coady assistant at Baie Verte, Rev. R. Hawco assistant at Holyrood, Rev. Wm. Shallow assistant at Harbour Grace, Rev. Edward Hearn assistant at Grand Falls.

Confirmations

June 17th: Confirmed 28 at **Badger.**
June 21st: Confirmed 70 at **Bishop's** Falls, 48 at **Buchans.**
June 27th: Confirmed 22 at **Little Bay**.
June 28th: Confirmed 14 at **Grand Falls.**

Nov. 12th: Appointed Rev. M.J. Kinsella Parish Priest of Holyrood, Rev. E.M. Shea Parish Priest of Bay de Verde, Rev. J.R. Hawco administrator of St. Brendan's, and Rev. S. St. Croix Administrator of Colliers.

1960

Jan. 1st: Appointed Rev. R. J. Walsh ordinary confessor of sisters at Badger.

July 5th: Sailed for **Fogo**-confirmed 59 at **Fogo**, 61 at Joe **Batt's Arm**, 40 at **Island Harbour**, 71 at **Tilting**, 25 at **Boyd's Cove**, and 50 at **Fortune Harbour**.

1961

March 10th: Appointed Rev. Hawco Parish Priest of St. Brendan's.

June 11th: **ORDAINED** Rev. John Peddle to the Holy Priesthood for the Diocese of St. George's.

June 25th: **ORDAINED** Rev. Neil McDonald at Grand Falls.

Confirmations:

June 12th Confirmed 227 at **Carbonear**
June 13th Confirmed 165 at **Brigus**
June 13th Confirmed 158 at **North River**
June 14th Confirmed 125 at **Colliers**
June 14th Confirmed 143 at **Conception**
June 15th Confirmed 176 at **Harbour Main**
June 17th Confirmed 179 at **Avondale**
June 18th Confirmed 174 at **Holyrood**
June 18th Confirmed 84 at **Harbour Grace**
June 18th Confirmed 100 at **River Heard**
June 19th Confirmed 24 at **Grates Cove**
June 20th Confirmed 180 at **Northern Bay**

Effective August. 1st, 1961:

Rev. Ronald J. Walsh -Parish Priest of Conception
Rev. Edward Hearn-Administrator of Badger
Rev. Neil McDonald-Curate at Grand Falls

Confirmations

July 25th Confirmed 25 at **La Scie**.
July 25th Confirmed 70 at **Brent' Cove**.
July 26th Confirmed 38 at **Canada Harbour.**
July 26th Confirmed 98 at **Conche**.
July 27th Confirmed 43 at **Goose Cove.**
July 27th Confirmed 19 at **Fishhook Island**.

Sept. 26th: Red letter day at **Baie Verte**-blessed new eight -room school, new convent, and new Church-Bouquet, etc. Concluded festivities.

Sept. 27th: Arrived home, tired by happy-Father Kelly has done a tremendous job in three years. Father Coady doing remarkably well at **La Scie**. Divine Providence continue to bless our efforts.

Nov. 2nd: Rev. John Kavanagh died at St. Clare's-78 yrs. Buried in Belvedere.

1962

Feb. 2nd: Monsignor W.H. Casey died at St. Clare's.

Confirmations:

June 21st: Confirmed 57 at **Heart's Desire**.
And 60 at **Whitbourne.**
June 22nd: Confirmed 40 at **Chapel Arm**, 71 at **Bellevue.**
July 2nd: Confirmed 120 at **St. Brendan's**, 78 at **Gambo.**
July 3rd: Confirmed 40 at **Glenwood.**

1963

Confirmations:

June 10th Confirmed 30 at **Sweet Bay**
June 10th Confirmed 37 at **Summerville**
June 11th Confirmed 110 at **King's Cove**

June 11th Confirmed 73 at **Plate Cove**
June 11th Confirmed 35 at **Open Hall**
June 11th Confirmed 40 at **Bonavista**
June 11th Confirmed 89 at **Catalina**
June 16th Confirmed 290 at **Windsor**
June 16th Confirmed 270 at **Grand Falls**.
June 17th Confirmed 76 at **Buchans.**
June 18th Confirmed 157 at **Bishop's Falls**.
June 19th Confirmed 240 at **Gander.**

June 21st: Cardinal John Baptist Montini elected Pope. Took name of Paul VI.

1964

May 15th: Appointed Rev. G.B. Pumphrey P.P. of Brigus.

June 21st: **ORDAINED** Rev. J. Beresford, Rev. M. Walsh, and Rev. J. Crawford CssR. to the Holy Priesthood - 26 priests present.

First Mass said in New Co-Cathedral this day by Rt. Rev. W.P. Hogan.

June 22nd: Confirmed 80 at **Bishop's Falls**.

June 23rd: Appointed Rev. R.T. Woodford PP of Colliers, Rev. J. R. Hawco PP of Bonavista, Rev. W. Shallow PP of St. Brendan's, Rev. B.J. McCarthy PP of Tilting, Rev. J. Beresford curate at Harbour Grace, Rev. M. Walsh curate t Grand Falls.

Confirmations:

June 23rd Confirmed 94 at **Windsor**
June 24th Confirmed 101 at **Gander**
June 28th Confirmed 98 at **Grand Falls**

Name of Diocese was change to Grand Falls by decree fo S. Consistorial Congregation dated October 30th, 1964. Decree executed at Harbour Grace.

1965

Jan. 6th: Consultors present: Monsignor J.W. Peddle, E.J. O'Brien, & W.P. Hogan. Rev. P.J. McCarthy P.P. & Rev. J. P. Hogan P.P.

Feb. 17th: Appointed Rt. Rev. Monsignor O'Brien P.P. of Harbour Grace.

March 29th: Rev. Patrick McCormack died suddenly at Gander.

April 2nd: Royal assent given to bill changing name of Corporation to R.C. Episcopal Corporation of Grand Falls.

April 12th: Rev. Michael J. Kinsella died at St. Clare's after long illness. Appointed Rev. E. M. Shea Parish Priest of Holyrood, Rev. M.R. Hynes Parish Priest of Bay de Verde. Rev. Neil McDonald Administrator of Gambo.

Confirmations

*May 31st:*Confirmed 82 at **Windsor.**
June 3rd Confirmed 88 at **Gander.**
June 6th Confirmed 91 at **Grand Falls.**
June 7th Confirmed 80 at **Bishop's Falls**.
June 9th Confirmed 31 at **Boyd's Cove.**
June 9th Confirmed 135 at **Norris Arm.**

June 12th: **ORDAINED** Rev. Francis O'Brien to the Priesthood.

Confirmations:

June 15th: Confirmed 50 at **Tilting.** Opened and blessed new High School. First Pontifical Mass in Tilting.
June 15th Confirmed 50 at **Joe Batt's Arm.**
June 16th Confirmed 46 at **Island Harbour**.
June 16th Confirmed 71 at **Fogo.**
June 21st Confirmed 88 at **Badger.**
June 21st Confirmed 94 at **Buchans.**

June 26th: Ordained Rev. David Aylward and Rev. Kevin Barker Deacons.

August 12th: Appointed Rev. Linus Coady Parish Priest of Norris Arm to take effect September 5th. Appointed Rev. Ronald Bromley Parish Priest of La Scie to take effect September 5th.

August 26th: Confirmed 65 at **Little Bay.**

August 29th: Ordained Rev. William Matthew a deacon.

1966

Jan. 22nd: Reappointed Monsignor J.M. O'Brien confessor to sisters at North River.

May 29th: **ORDAINED** Rev. Aloysius Antle, Rev. William Matthews, and Rev. Kevin Barker tot he Priesthood.

Confirmation

June 7th Confirmed 181 **North River**
June 8th Confirmed 276 **Carbonear**
June 8th Confirmed 170 **Northern Bay**
June 9th Confirmed 103 **Bay de Verde**
June 9th Confirmed 63 **Spaniard's Bay**
June 10th Confirmed 157 **Conception Harbour**
June 10th Confirmed 138 **Colliers**
June 11th Confirmed 267 **Harbour Main**
June 11th Confirmed 202 **Holyrood**
June 12th Confirmed 103 **Harbour Grace**
June 12th Confirmed 103 **Riverhead**
June 13th Confirmed 258 **Brigus**

June 13th: Blessed two new schools at Brigus.

June 27th: Left for **Fleur de Lys**. Took boat to **Conche** on June 28th-confirmed 144 there. Proceeded to **Fishat Island** and Confirmed 42. Continued to **Goose Cove**.
June 29th: Confirmed 60 at **Goose Cove** and proceeded to **Canada Harbour**. Confirmed 32 at Canada Harbour. Left for **Fleur de Lys** and arrived Grand Falls 2:00 pm on June 30th:

July 2nd: **ORDAINED** Rev. John Mackey a deacon.

August 1st: Appointed Rev. M.R. Hynes Parish Priest of newly-erected Parish of Plate Cove, B.B. Appointed Rev. William Matthew curate at Northern Bay. Appointed Rev. Aloysius Antle curate at Harbour Grace. Appointed Rev. James Beresford administrator of King's Cove. Appointed Rev. Richard Woodford Parish Priest of Buchans. Appointed Rev. F.J. Terry Parish Priest of Colliers. Appointed Rev. M.J. Walsh administrator of Bay de Verde. Appointed Rev. Kevin Barker curate at Windsor.

Sept. 19th: Bishop O'Reilly celebrated Silver Jubilee of Episcopal Consecration.

Sept. 20th: New Cathedral consecrated at Corner Brook.

1967

Confirmations

Sept 21st Confirmed 125 **Brent's Cove**
Sept. 21st Confirmed 190 **Baie Verte**
Sept 22nd Confirmed 62 **Coachman's Cove**
Sept. 22nd Confirmed 104 **Fleur de Lys**
May 29th Confirmed 10 **Sweet Bay**
May 29th Confirmed 10 **Summerville**
May 29th Confirmed 28 **King's Cove**
May 30th Confirmed 11 **Plate Cove**
May 30th Confirmed 25 **Catalina**
May 31st Confirmed 88 **St. Brendan's**
June 3rd Confirmed 73 **Gambo**
June 4th Confirmed 20 **Glenwood**
June 11th Confirmed 40 **Bellevue**
June 12th Confirmed 30 **Chapel Arm**
June 14th Confirmed 28 **Whitbourne**

July 25th Appointed Rev. B.J. McCarthy Parish Priest of Gambo. Rev. Kevin Barker, Administrator of Tilting.

Dec. 1st: Appointed Rev. John Murphy curate at Northern Bay and Rev. William Matthews curate at Brigus.

Dec. 8th: Consecrated the Cathedral with Mass of Con-Celebration: Present were Monsignor Hogan, Fr. Stoeckel CssR., Fr. Burke, Fr. P.J. McCarthy, Fr. G. Pumphrey, Fr. L. Coady, Rev. L. Kelly, Fr. F. O'Brien, Fr. James Glavine CssR., Fr. John Mackey, Fr. B.J. McCarthy, Fr. R. Woodford, Fr. David Aylward.

1968

June 9th: **ORDAINED** Rev. Matthew Kane at Gander. First ordination there.

Nov. 18th: Rev. David Aylward left for Peru to join Halifax Mission band.

Nov. 19th: Appointed Rev. M. Kane curate at Gander.

Dec.: Appointed Rev. F.J. Terry director of the Propagation of the faith. Appointed Rev. William Houlahan director of the Holy Childhood.

1969

Confirmations

June 12th Confirmed 51 at **Bishop's falls**.
June 12th Confirmed 73 at **Gander.**
June 13th Confirmed 67 at **Windsor.**
June 13th Confirmed 53 at **Grand Falls.**
June 14th Confirmed 43 at **Buchans.**

June 15th: **ORDAINED** Rev. Ronald Cashin a Deacon.

June 15th Confirmed 9 at **Boyd's Cove.**
June 15th Confirmed 27 at **Norris Arm.**

June 22nd: **ORDAINED** my nephew Bernard to the Priesthood at Carbonear.

July 2nd: Appointed Rev. Linus Coady Parish Priest of Harbour Main. Appointed Rev. William Matthews Administrator of Norris Arm.

Aug. 22nd: Appointed Monsignor J.M. O'Brien a member of the Board of Consultors.

Aug 23rd: Ordained Martin Parsons and Aidan Beresford sub deacon.

Aug 24th: **ORDAINED** Martin Parsons and Aidan Beresford Deacons.

Dec 1st: Consultors appointed-Msgr. Peddle, J.M. O'Brien, W.P. Hogan, elected: Rev.'s F.J. Terry, P.J. McCarthy, and R. Woodford.

Dec. 21st: Blessed and opened new High School at Baie Verte. Present: Fr. Kelly, Parish Priest, Msgr. W.P. Hogan and Rev. Ronald Bromley, P.P. of Brent's Cove.

Dec. 22nd: **ORDAINED** Rev.David Heale to the Deaconate.

1970

Feb. 6th: Consultors sworn in at Grand Falls "Ad Triennium": Msgr. W.P. Hogan, Rev. P.J. McCarthy, Rev. R.T. Woodford.

Feb. 24th: Consultors sworn in at Carbonear "Ad Triennium": Msgr. J. W. Peddle and J. M. O'Brien, Rev. F.J. Terry.

July 22nd: Bishop McGrath ordained.

Sept 1st: Following appointments made:

Conche	Rev. John Murphy-P.P.
Baie Verte	Rev. G. B. Pumphrey-Admin.
" "	Rev. Matthew Kane-Asst.
Brent's Cove	Rev. William Houlahan-Admin.
Bonavista	Rev. Edward Brophy-P.P.
Buchans	Rev. J. R Hawco-P.P.
Grand Falls	Rev. David Aylward-Asst.
Windsor	Rev. Martin Parson-Asst.
Norris Arm	Rev. Aloysius Antle-P.P.
Gander	Rev. Ronald Cashin-Asst.
Brigus	Rev. R. T. Woodford-P.P.
Harbour Grace	Rev. M. Walsh-Asst.
Carbonear	Rev. Aidan Beresford-Asst.
Northern bay	Rev. Edward Hearn-P.P.
Bay de Verde	Rev. Wm Matthews-P.P.

1971

Jan. 31st: Confirmed 106 at **Grand Falls.**
March 8th: Confirmed 4 at **G. Falls** who were sick during previous ceremony.

April 15th: Rev. J.P. Hogan died.

Confirmations

March 21st Confirmed 31 at **Little Bay**
March 21st Confirmed 44 at **Badger**
March 28th Confirmed at **Gander** (Bishop McGrath)
April 4th Confirmed 150 at **Windsor**
May 26th Confirmed 13 at **Fortune Harbour**
June 6th Confirmed 54 at **Harbour Grace**
June 6th Confirmed 106 at **Carbonear**
June 7th Confirmed 55 at **Riverhead**
June 7th Confirmed 27 at **Spaniards Bay**
June 8th Confirmed 44 at **North River**
June 8th Confirmed 86 at **Brigus**
June 8th Confirmed 66 at **Northern Bay**
June 9th Confirmed 36 at **Colliers**
June 9th Confirmed 64 at **Conception Harbour**

Confirmations

June 10th Confirmed 64 at **Avondale.**
June 10th Confirmed 70 at **Harbour Main.**
June 10th Confirmed 52 at **Holyrood.**
June 13th Confirmed 115 at **Bishop's Falls.**
June 15th Confirmed 24 at **Island Harbour.**
June 15th Confirmed 20 at **Fogo.**
June 16th Confirmed 30 at **Joe Batts Arm**.
June 16th Confirmed 35 at **Tilting.**
June 16th Confirmed 83 at **Gambo.**
June 20th Confirmed 60 at **Buchans.**

June 30th: Appointed Monsignor Hogan P.P.

July 21st: Appointed Rev. Leonard J. Kelly Parish Priest of North River. Appointed Rev. Matthew Kane assistant at Windsor. Appointed Rev. Martin Parsons assistant at Gander. Rev. Ronald Cashin assistant at Baie Verte. Rev. William Houlahan Parish Priest of Brent's Cove.

1972

Confirmations

May 28th Confirmed 61 at **Heart's Desire.**
May 29th Confirmed 50 at **Whitbourne.**
May 29th Confirmed 41 at **Chapel Arm.**
May 30th Confirmed 57 at **Bellevue.**
May 30th Confirmed 8 at **Clarenville.**
June 3rd Confirmed 32 at **Sweet Bay**
June 3rd Confirmed 30 at **Summerville**
June 3rd Confirmed 67 at **Plate Cove**
June 4th Confirmed 115 at **Catalina**
June5th Confirmed 67 at **Brent's Cove**
June 6th Confirmed 31 at **Coachman's Cove**
June 6th Confirmed 54 at **Fleur de Lys**
June 6th Confirmed 102 at **Baie Verte**
June 16th Confirmed 96 at **St. Brendan's**

June 25th: **ORDAINED** Rev. Roy Walsh to Priesthood.

July 9th Confirmed 67 at **Conche**
July 10th Confirmed 55 at **Goose Bay**

Aug. 7th: Appointments to be effective September 1st:

Rev. Matthew Kane, Administrator of Baie Verte
Rev. Marin Parsons, Administrator of St. Brendan's
Rev. Ronald Cashin, Assistant of Windsor
Rev. Roy Walsh, Assistant of Gander

Last entry

Nov. 23rd: My resignation and appointed of Msgr. Alphonsus L. Penny as my successor announced today. Bishop of Diocese for 32 years, four months, and 17 days.

Last Section of the Book

The List Clergy that Served the Diocese in the Times of Bishop John March and Dr. O'Neill

Rt. Rev. Edward F. Walsh D.P.
Rt. Rev. Joseph V. Donnelly D.P.
Rt. Rev. William Veitch D.P
Rev. Richard F. Walsh
Very Rev. Richard M. Shean
Very Rev. John Roe
Very Rev. Walter M. Tarahan
Rt. Rev. Joseph Murphy D.P.
Rev. William F. Finn
Very Rev. John H. Scully
Rev. Stephen J. Whelan D.D
Rt. Rev. William P. Finn D.P.
Rev. John J. Nolan
Rev. John P. Mackey
Rev. George A. Thibault
Rev. John S. Kavanagh
Rt. Rev. Mark P. Dwyer
Rt. Rev. Edward J. O'Brien D.P., (hon.) O.M.I.
Rev. James J. Walker
Very Rev. Edward J. Jones D.D.
Rev. Patrick J. Hearn
Very Rev. Thomas D. O'Neill
Rt. Rev. Michael Dinn D.P.
Rt. Rev. William H. Casey D.P.
Rev. William McC. Murphy
Very Rev. William T. Cullen
Rev. James A. Hinchey
Rt. Rev. William J. Williams D.P.
Very Rev. Nicholas G. Fitzgerald
Rev. Jeremiah Howard
Rev. John M. O'Neill D.D.
Rev. Joseph P. Hogan
Rev. J. Ronald Jones
Rt. Rev. Joseph W. Peddle D.P.
Rev. Francis P. Meaney
Very Rev. Michael J. Kinsella
Rev. Philip J. McCarthy
Rev. Walter P. Walsh
Rev. Leo J. Burke
Rev. Francis R. Terry
Rev. William J. Hennebury
Rt. Rev. Joseph M. O'Brien D.P.

Rev. Edward M. Shea
Rev. Edward A. Walsh
Rev. Ronald J. Walsh
Rt. Rev. William P. Hogan D.P.
Rev. Gregory B. Pumphrey
Rt. Rev. Richard T. Woodford D.P.
Rev. Frederick J. Terry
Rev. Michael P. Carey s.f.m.
Rev. Michael R. Hynes
Rev. Leonard J. Kelly
Rev. Patrick A. McCormack
Rev. Linus J. Coady
Rev. J. Raymond Hawco
Rev. Edward F. Hearn
Rev. William Shallow
Rev. Brendan J. McCarthy
Rt. Rev. Edward T. Bromley P.H.
Rev. Ronald M. Bromley
Rev. James A. Beresford
Rev. Michael J. Walsh
Rev. Francis R. O'Brien
Rev. David L. Aylward
Rev. J. Kevin Barker
Rev. Aloysius Antle
Rev. William D. Matthews
Rev. John G. Mackey
Rev. William J. Houlahan
Rev. Edward R. Brophy
Rev. John Murphy
Rev. Matthew Kane
Rev. Ronald J. Cashin
Rev. Martin Parsons
Rev. Aidan Beresford
Rev. David W. Heale
Rev. Roy A. Walsh
Rev. A. Wayne Cummings
Rev. William E. Hearn
Rev. Francis J. Aylward

**Note: Rev.'s Aylward, Cummings, and W. Hearn were ecclesiastical students when Bishop O'Neill retired.

NOTE: Some of the original Diary entries have been highlighted and names of places have been added for emphasis.

HARBOUR GRACE

MARRIAGE RECORDS

1806-1845

APPENDIX C

HARBOUR GRACE MARRIAGE RECORDS 1806-1845

HARBOUR GRACE MARRIAGE RECORDS 1840-1845

The original 1806 book has a cover sheet with the following information. **+**

In the name of God Amen.

The Register of Marriages and Baptisms administered and contracted in the District of Harbor Grace from the 10 August A.D. 1806. to the February 1812 and from the month 1 May of the same year. and to be continued successively by every Mifsionary during the existence of the actual inhabitants of the District.

Da Domine xxxxxx hcat incepto.

Per Mr. Fitzsimmons

Taken from the register kept by Rev Mr. EWER

By Mr. Fitzsimons Esq..

God Save the King

The Harbour Grace RC Church marriage records for the period of 1806 to 1845 were all in one book even though the priests would go out to the neighboring Towns and missions to perform the marriage and come back to Harbour Grace to record the event in the one book. Both the births and marriages were entered together in the books from 1806 to 1817. After this period they are in separate books. The period from July to December 1811 were omitted in the register because Brother Fitzsimmons was attending to the duties of the Mission for Doctor Ewer during this period. Father Fitzsimmons marriages and baptisms were left with Doctor O'Connor in P. Grave in a trunk but expects it daily. The records start again in January 1812. Misspelling of the real early records could be as a result of: The priest or the person himself may not knowing how to spell the name. Some were written as they were heard pronounced, or how they remembered they were spelled back home. Misspelling could also be the result of the reader of the records:

They could not read the writing, poor copy of records, bad writing, or just bad interpretation by the compiler. Also the understanding of abbreviations in the early days; Jno for John, Richd for Richard, Mich' for Michael, Patk for Patrick, Nich' for Nicholas, Margt – for Margaret, Austy for Anastasia (I think). In the early times, the people wrote names as they sounded or how they were spoken. The spelling and writing of some of the entries were hard to read and had to be deciphered to the best spelling as possible. Some of the names are spelled differently from those of today but are probably pretty close to the following:

BARRETT – Barrit; BROWN – Bruen; BRYAN – Brien, O'Brien; CAHILL – Cahil,; COSTELLO – Costollo, ; COLBERT – Colbirt, ; COUGHAN – Coughen; CONNELL – Connol, Conol; CONNOLLY-Connelly, Conelly, Conly, Conolly, ; CONNORS – O'Connor's; CORBIN – Corben; CORMAKE, - Cormic; COSTELLO – Costolo; CROWLEY – Crowly; CUMMINS – Commins, Cummings; CULLIHAN – Culliall; CURRAN – Currin; CUSICK – Cisack; DAVIS – Davies DEAN – Deane; DEVINE – Divine; DIXON – Dickerson, Dickeson; DENNY – Dent, Dinney DELANEY – Delany; Dehani – Dinan, Deneen; DOHERTY – Doghert; DONAHUE – Donghue, Donaghoo;; DUNPHY – Dunfayl; DRISCOLL – Driscol,; EUSTACE – Huestice; EZEKIEL – Ezachiel, Ezichiel, Ezochiel ; FAHEY – Fahee; GANEY – Gany, ; GILLESPIE – Gelasby, Glasby; GILLARD –Jillard;; GLEESON – Gleason; HAMEN – Haman, Hamman; INNIS – Inis; KAVANAGH – Cavanagh, Cavanary, ; MALONEY – Malony; MAHONEY – Mahany, Mahaney; MEAGHER- Meigher, Meighers, Maugher, ;MULLOWNEY – Mullowny, Mollowny,; QUINN – Quin; MORRY – Mory; SMALLCOMB – Smalcome, Smoocumb, ; SMOKEHAM – Smoakum, Smoakham, smoocumb, smoakem.; SULLIVAN, Solevan, soolevan, soliva

MARRIAGES FROM HARBOUR GRACE RECORDS
1806-1845

DATEMARR	HISNAME	HERNAME	WITN1	WITN2	PRIEST
18060824	LEARY,TIM	JACOB,RUTH	HUNT,EDMUND	CAHILL,H.D.	
18061021	FOGERTY,BARTHOLEUM	REID,ELIZ	POWER,PAT	POWER,JAMES	
18061022	CONELLY,THOMAS	CLARKE,ANNE	MACKEY,MICHL	POWER,JOSEPH	
18061023	DRISCOL,MARTIN	LOW,MARGT	COMMINS,JOHN	ENGLISH,JAMES	
	FURLONG,JOHN	LOW,MARY	COMMINS,JOHN	ENGLISH,JAMES	
	KENNEDY,RICHARD	PRENDERGAST,ANN	BRODERICK,WILLIAM	MCCARTHY,DANL	
18061025	DELANY,JOHN	BYRNE,JOANNE	PHELAN,WILLIAM	PHELAN,THOMAS	
18061027	CONROY,JOHN	SLADE,SERA	DUREN,DENNIS	THISTLE,SEAN	
18061029	CULLINAN,JOHN	HOULET,SERA	MCCARTHY,CORNELIUS	MCCARTHY,JULIANNA	
18061118	NEWILL,LAWRENCE	CAVANAGH,MARY	LAWLESS,JOHN	GUILLY,J.	
	STRANGE,PAT	BUSSY,ANNE	BROWN,JOSEPH	RICHARDS,CHARLOTTE	
18061129	MEIGHER,THOMAS	MULLORY,ELEANOR	EZICHIEL,THOMAS	KENNEDY,JAMES	
18061202	HEATING,JOHN	MOORE,MARY	WOODFORD,JOHN	EZOCHIEL,THOMAS	
18061202?	KENNEDY,JAMES	MACKEY,MARY	CRAWLY,PAT	LUNDLAN,JOHN	
18061229	FARRIL,MICHAEL	WHELAN,MARGARET	BRENNEN,DENIS	DALTON,WILLM	
18061231	BARRON,JAMES	PEDDLE,GRACE	WELSH,JOHN	LAHY,MARY	
18070106	SMOAKUM,JOHN	HARRINGTON,MARY	BUTLER,WALTER	GRANT,JOHN	
18070110	DALTON,JAMES	SHEA,ELIZABETH	DUNN,DENNIS	MAGRATH,DENNIS	
18070112	BAGGS,WILLIAM	HEARN,JOANNE	HEARN,TIMOTHY	HEASE,LAWRENCE	
18070121	HIGGINS,PHILIP	WOODFORD,ELIZABETH	DUGGAN,WILLIAM	CORBAN,JOHN	
18070224	BARRETT,JOHN	HACO,SUSANNE	MULLOWNY,P.	MULLOWNY,ELIZABETH	
	CAHIL,PATRICK	MEANY,MARY	MEANY,WILLM	MACDONELL,PATRICK	
	HEATING,WILLIAM	O'CONNOR,MARY	KEATING,JOHN	O'CONNOR,DENNIS	
18070226	EZACHIEL,THOMAS	HICKEY,PATIENCE	O'NEAL,JOHN	KENNEDY,JOHN	
18070302	DRISCOL,BARTHOLEUM	DRISCOL,WINNY	COSTOLLO,THOMAS	COSTOLLO,JAMES	
18070328	DOOLING,TIMOTHY	LAVORY,CHARITY	NOONAN,DORIS	CONNELL,RICHD	
18070503	BARRY,JOHN	BUTT,CATH'	REILLY,PAT	CONNOR,MARNS	
18070519	MEIGHERS,THOMAS	WALL,ELEANOR	FLYNN,W.	O'LEARY,FANNY	
18070521	PHELAN,JAMES	MERRIGAN,MARY	PHELAN,DAVID	NOWLAN,ALICE	
18070605	WOOFORD,WILLIAM	O'NEAL,MARGT	CONDON,RICHD	CANE,BRIDGET	
18070614	MCCARTHY,FLORENCE	KENNEDY,JANE	MCCARTHY,CH.	MAHONY,PAT	
18070809	NOWLAN,RICHD	GREEN,BRIDGET	HURLEY,JOHN	GOOLY,ELLEN	
18071004	MAGEE,NICOLAS	MAHER,MARGARET	REGAN,RICHARD	MAHER,JOANNE	
18071018	NEARY,NICOLAS	JONES,ELIZA	COUGHLAN,MORRIS	COUGHLAN,JAMES	
18071101	HICKEY,PAT	KENNEDY,MARY	MOLLOWNY,JAMES	MOLLOWNY,WILLM	
18071115	REGAN,RICHD	DONOVAN,SUSAN	GREEN,WILLIAM	DONOVAN,DANIEL	
18071120	MOLLEA,WILLIAM	BUTT,DOROTHEA	DUNN,DENNIS	FORTUNE,MOSES	
18071121	MACDONALD,JAMES	WALL,SERA	NONAN,WILLM	FTIZGERALD,JAMES	
18071124	WHITE,RICHD	LAHER,ANNE	MACKEY,JAMES	CODY,RICHD	
18071228	MCCARTHY,CORNELIUS	SHEPARD,BRIDGET	NORCOTT,ABRAM	MCCARTHY,DENNIS	
18080108	DRISCOL,JOHN	COLLINS,MARY	HEARN,DANL	BROSNAN,HENRY	
18080118	BRIEN,JOHN	DOBBIN,MARY	CALL?,WILL	MASSEN,WSIL	
18080201	CORLIS,JOHN	COURAGE,MARY	CONROY,JOHN	DONAHY,JOHN	
18080205	HARBRY,JOHN	FAHEY,MARY	FAHEY,THOMAS	MCCARTHY,THOMAS	
18080206	BRODERICK,TERRY	WELLS,ANNE	CONNOR,GARRETT	DALY,THOMAS	
18080303	DOYLE,PATRICK	WALSH,MARY	DALTON,EDMUND	KENNEDY,JOHN	
18080506	DUNPHY,WILLIAM	KING,SERA	HEALE,MICHAEL	FLYNN,DAVID	
18080512	LANE,THOMAS	ALY?,ANNE	BRODERICK,WILLIAM	DONOVAN,DENIS	
18080606	PHELAN,MARTIN	MURPHY,ELLEN	MURPHY,PATRICK	CONNELL,RICHARD	

MARRIAGES FROM HARBOUR GRACE RECORDS
1806-1845

DATEMARR	HISNAME	HERNAME	WITN1	WITN2	PRIEST
18080610	REGAN, JOHN	BARRIY, ELIZA	BARRY, JOSEPH	BECKET, THOMAS	
18080928	COD, RICHARD	EDDY, ANNE	COTTEN, JAMES	CONNELL, RICHARD	
18081001	PORNL, JAMES	PORNL, ANNE	POWER, PATRICK	PORNL, THOMAS	
18081102	MAHONY, PHILIP	WALSH, MARY	MAHONY, JAMES	BARRY, MARY	
18081105	MAGRATH, JOH	MURPHY, HONORA	WRIGHT, LAWRENCE	HOGAN, JOHN	
18081121	LONNEGAN, WILLIAM	WALSH, WIDOW	MAHER, THOMAS	MACDONALD, JAMES	
18081126	SWEENEY, JOHN	GORG, ELIZABETH	PHELAN, STEHEN	PHELAN, THOMAS	
18080228	CORBIT, PATRICK	HACO, SERA	HACO, THOMAS	COSTELLO, MARTIN	
18090101	HEMP, JOSEPH	EARL, ABIGAIL	CONNOR, COATES	CONNOR, MARY	
18090110	GORMAN, JOHN	LECOUR, MARY	GORMAN, SIMON	KEATING, MICHAEL	
18090129	ELSON, JOHN	DALTON, ALICE	FOLEY, THOMAS	CONNELL, RICHARD	
	POWER, PATRICK	BARRETT, MARY	MAGER, DENIS	DENIHER, JOHN	
18090214	FLEMMING, JOSEPH	QUIRK, MARY	FOGARTY, DAVID	NONE LISTED	
	MORY, DANIEL	HEDOSTON, MARY	DALY, WILLIAM	HENN, PETER	
18090319	LOUIS, THOMAS	LEARY, CATHERINE	MULLOWNEY, WILLIAM	LEARY, DENIS	
18090528	GLEESON, THOMAS	GODFREY, MARY	FOGARTY, THOMAS	PONSIRE?, GEORGE	
18090601	BRODERICK, WILLIAM	MURPHY, HONORA	MURPHY, JOHN	LEOSE, JAMES	
18090606	CAROL, PHIL	DEIGOON, ELENOR	CLEARY, C OF N	CLEARY, WILLIAM	
18090612	KEEFE, JOHN	BUTLER, MARY	GLEASON, WILLIAM	BUTLER, JAMES	
18091003	DOODY, THOMAS	NOONAN, ELLENOR	CONNELL, RICHARD	DINEEN, JAMES	
18091005	BUTLER, JAMES	PESEY, KANE	MACNAMARA, FLORENCE	KEOUGH, WILLIAM	
18091008	COLE, DANNY	BUTLER, CATHERINE	WALSH, EDMUND	MERRIGAN, MORRIS	
	MERRIGAN, MORRIS	KING, OLIVE	MURPHY, JOHN	BARTY, CATHERINE	
18091106	DALTON, EDMUND	MURPHY, CATHERINE	KENNEDY, PAT	KENNEDY, JOHN	
	LEIVOR, WALTER	HACO, ELLEN	CAREY, WILLIAM	KENNEDY, ANTHONY	
18091108	MERRIGAN, EDMUND	CONWAY, MARY	BURK, WILLIAM	BURK, PAT	
	WALL, PATRICK	RYAN, ANASTASIA	REGAN, WILLIAM	MAHER, THOMAS	
18091109	MASON, JOSEPH	BAKER, ELIZA	MASON, GEORGE	MASON, THOMAS	
18091128	HOWARD, EDMUND	BRADBERRY, ANNE	CLARY, WILLIAM	FOGARTY, GRACE	
18100101	COUGLLAN, JAMES	FITZGERALD, MARY	FITZGERALD, JOHN	KENNEDY, FRANCES	
18100103	REDMOND, JOSEPH	RYAN, HONORA	WALSH, PAT	ROACH, ELLEN	
18100106	CORBIN, RICHARD	PHELAN, ELLEN	PHELAN, WILLIAM	BABCOCK, PAT	
	DONEVAN, KAND?	BOW, ELLEN	DONEVAN, DAN	BOW, XXX	
18100125	BRIEN, THOMAS	QUILTY, MARY	BYRNE, JAMES	QUILTY, J.	
18100206	HEALY, JOHN	MORRSY, JOANNA	CAHIL, PAT	KEOUGH, XX	
18100207	MARTIN, WILLIAM	SHEA, CATHERINE	DALTON, JAMES	GORMAN, MICHAEL	
18100219	FREENY, PETER	BRADBURY, PATIENCE	PHELAN, WILLIAM	CORBETT, ELLEN	
18100220	KENNEDY, WILLIAM	WADE, MARY	CONNELL, ROBERT	CONNELL, THOMAS	
18100301	LOUIS, ERIN	GOUDIN, ELIZA	KENNEDY, JOHN	KENNEDY, MARY	
18100303	MAHONY, MICHAEL	BARRY, MARY	COSTELLO, PAT	LOUIS, ELIZA	
18100313	PARNL, JOHN	CORBIN, PATIENCE	KEATING, REDMOND	CONNELL, CATHERINE	
18100402	DOYLE, JOHN	ENGLISH, ELLEN	ENGLISH, THOMAS	MURPHY, ELIZA	
18100407	PHELAN, MARTIN	POWELL, JANE	PHELAN, MARTIN	PHELAN, ELLEN	
18100410	WALSH, EDMUND	PIKE, CATHERINE	GODFREY, NICHAEL	REGAN, ELIZA	
18100423	BARRY, DAVID	REYNOLDS, NARY	CONNOR, DANIEL	DUNFAY, CATHERINE	
18100602	ROGERS, SAMUEL	GILFOY, ASASTASIA	DOBBIN, WILLIAM	BYRNE, MARY	
18100718	KEEFE, JAMES	DUORN, MARY	WALSH, MAURICE	MAY, ALICIA	
18100820	MACLANE, JOHN	HEFFERNON, CHARLOTTE	GLEESON, JAMES	BRADBURY, JANE	
18101006	NORTH, THOMAS	MANNING, LENA	NOONAN, JAMES	DENIN, T.	

MARRIAGES FROM HARBOUR GRACE RECORDS
1806-1845

DATEMARR	HISNAME	HERNAME	WITN1	WITN2	PRIEST
18101108	MASON,THOMAS	HICKS,ELIS	HICKS,THOMAS	KENNEDY,JOHN	
18101126	THISTLE,THOMAS	GOSS,CATHERINE	BARRETT,JOHN	TAYLOR,RICHARD	
18101217	WOODFORD,JAMES	EZECHIEL,FRANCES	CONWAY,PAT	HANE,MARY	
18101226	FITZGERALD,JOHN	KENNEDY,FRANCES	GEARY,THOMAS	HASTORY,MARY	
18101228	PHELAN,THOMAS	WHITE,RACHEL	PHELAN,DAVID	PHELAN,FRANCES	
18110131	GLAVIN,JAMES	BUTLER,ELIZA	PRILL,JAMES	PRILL,MRS	
	MORY,TIMOTHY	MARSHALL,ANN	MORY,PAT	MARSHALL,MARY	
18110205	POWERS,JAMES	LONNERGAN,MARY	HOLLAHAN,JAMES	WALSH,STEPHEN	
18110212	GOUSEN,CHARLES	COSTELLO,MARTHA	FOLEY,THOMAS	FOLEY,MARY	
18110303	MAHONY,THOMAS	ENGLISH,DIANA	BRODERICK,WILLIAM	ENGLISH,THOMAS	
18110331	HEALING,PAT	CONNOR,ELLEN	WOODFORD,WILLIAM	WOODFORD,WIFE	
	MURPHY,MICHAEL	HEALY,MARY	BUTLER,WILLIAM	BUTLER,WIFE	
18110403	HALY,EDMUND	MCCARTHY,MARY	MCCARTHY,WILLIAM	MAGRATH,MARY	
18110405	LAHOWNY,GEORGE	WOODFORD,MARTHA	WOODFORD,JOHN	VALLORY,KING	
18110508	FREEHAN,MICHAEL	HANLY,MARGARET	PORTER,LAWRENCE	REGAN,JUS	
18110517	HAYS,LUKE	KELLY,BRIDGET	KELLY,PDM	SMOAKHAM,MARY	
18111113	FAHEY,THOMAS	HARRINGTON,ELLEN	FAHEY,EDWARD	SMOAKHAM,MARY	HG
	FITZGERALD,WILLIAM	CONNELLY,MARY	FAHEY,EDWARD	KILAN?,ELIZABETH	HG
18120407	BARRY,N.	CONOLLY,MARY	BARRY,JOHN	ST.JOHN,ROBERT	HG
18120415	POWER,MAURICE	MAHER,SIBELLA	SULLIVAN,DANIEL	AND WIFE	HG
18120421	MACKEY,THOMAS	HICKEY,ELIZABETH	HICKEY,JOHN	MACKEY,MARGRIT	EWER,REV
18120531	CRANE,GEORGE	WHEELER,JANE	LANNY,WALTER	CONDON,ELLENOR	EWER,REV
	GREEN,DANIEL	GOSSE,RACHEL	FOLEY,THOMAS	CONDON,FANNY	EWER,REV
18120823	ALLEN,RICHARD	LATTIN,JUDITH	DELANEY,JAMES	MAGEE,MARY	HG
	COSTIGAN,VINCENT	KENNEDY,JOANNA	SHEA,RICHARD	MALONEY,ELIZABETH	HG
	MAGEE,PATRICK	CONNELL,MARY	ROACH,JOHN	MEANEY,MARY	HG
18120824	KEEFE,MICHAEL	HEFFERMAN,MARIA	MURPHY,MICHAEL	POWER,JOANNA	EWER,REEV
18121020	CUNNINGHAM,JOHN	DONNEVAN,MARY	DONNEVAN,PATRICK	--------	EWER,REV
	DUNN,THOMAS	MORRISSEY,MARY	PHELAN,WALTER	FARRELL,JAMES	EWER,REV
18121022	TROKE,JOHN?	BUTLER,MARY	POWER,THOMAS	POWER,MARY	EWER,REV
	WHITE,JOHN	BARRETT,JOANNA	MURPHY,RICHARD	BARRETT,ANN	EWER,REV
18121029	OLIVER,JOSEPH	ENGLISH,JANE	MCNAMARA,TERRY	OLIVER,ELIZABETH	EWER,REV
18121104	DOYLE,THOMAS	RYAN,HONOR	BROWN,JAMES	MAGHER,MARY	EWER,REV
18121105	HARTERY,JERRY	FRENCH,CATHERINE	NONE RECORDED	NONE RECORDED	EWER,REV
18121109	DONNOLLY,PATRICK	WOODFORD,SERA	KENNEDY,JAMES	COSTIGAN,JOANNA	EWER,REV
	PHELAN,EDWARD	COLE,ANN	KING,RICHARD	COLLAN,ANN	EWER,REV
18121113	MORRISSEY,PATRICK	MERRIN,SERA	FITZGERALD,WILLIAM	MORGAN,HANNA	EWER,REV
18121124	COMMINS,JOHN	BRIEN,CATHERINE	LANE,JAMES	FITZGERALD,MARY	EWER,REV
	KENNEDY,WILLIAM	KENT,ANN	KENNEDY,WILLIAM	OATES,ANN	EWER,REV
	MULEHARY,JOHN	BRIEN,MARY	MCGRATH,DENNIS	MCGRATH,MARY	EWER,REV
	TIELY,THOMAS?	CARTY,MARY	KAVANAGH,PATRICK	CONDON,JANY?	EWER,REV
18121125	GEER,PATRICK	MCNAMARA,MARY	SHEA,MARTIN	SULLIVAN,MARY?	EWER,REV
18121214	SULLIVAN,HUGEN	COOLUGEN,CATHERINE	HARRINGTON,JOHN	COOL,MARY	HG
18121215	FLOOD,THOMAS	PHELAN,MARY	PHELAN,RICHARD	WHITEWAY,ELIZABETH	EWER,REV
18121222	SHEAN,JOHN	GOSSE,MARGARET	GOSSE,JAMES	GREEN,ELIZABETH	EWER,REV
18121226	LECOURT,NICHOLAS	LEHUREY?,MARGARET	LEHURVE,JAMES	NOLAN,ANN?	EWER,REV
18121230	HEALY,THOMAS	HARRINGTON,CATHERINE	HICKEY,RICHARD	FAHEY,ELLEN	EWER,REV
18130110	TEARNEY,THOMAS	TERNEY,MARY	KENNEDY,JAMES	DUNPHY,BRIGIT	EWER,REV
18130121	MOXLEY,JOHN	ROACH,MARY	MEANEY,JOHN	KENNEDY,ELLEN	EWER,REV

MARRIAGES FROM HARBOUR GRACE RECORDS
1806-1845

DATEMARR	HISNAME	HERNAME	WITN1	WITN2	PRIEST
18130127	CONAWAY,PATRICK	DUNPHY,BRIGET	DUNPHY,JAMES	MAGHER,MARY	EWER,REV
18130210	CARROLL,THOMAS	COLLINS,CATHERINE	DONAHEY,JOHN	PALMER,ELIZABETH	EWER,REV
18130529	BRWN,LARRY	BURT,BRIDGET	CONNOL,ROBERT	CONNOL,JANE	EWER,REV
18130910	CAREY,PATRICK	WADE,ELIZABETH	WADE,EDMOND	BRIEN,BRIGIT	EWER,REV
18131010	COSTOLO,DAVID	BARRY,ELIZABETH	COSTELLO,MICHAEL	COSTELLO,ANN	EWER,REV
	COSTOLO,MICHAEL	WALSH,ANN	WADE,EDMOND	WADE,BRIDGET	EWER,REV
	WADE,EDMOND	KENNY,BRIGIT	FLANAGAN,JOHN	WALSH,ANN	EWER,REV
18131105	DUNN,JAMES	QUIN,MARY	QUIGLEY,PATRICK	PRENDERGAST,MARY	EWER,REV
18131112	HEALEY,JOHN	INIS,ANN	HEALY,JAMES	POWER,ANN	EWER,REV
18131117	SICILY,PATRICK	WHITEWAY,ELIZABETH	FITZGERALD,MORRIS	PHELAN,XXXXX	EWER,REV
18131118	MORY,WILLIAM	CONOL,MARG	MORY,DANIEL	HANRAHAN,ALICE	EWER,REV
18131122	CROAK,LAWRENCE	FLAHERTY,MARYANNE	TIERNEY,JAMES	NOWLAN,HONORA	HG
18131128	TARGOTA,JOHN	MULLOUWNEY,ANNE	WITCH,GEORGE	SULLIVAN,SERA	HG
18131201	BYRNE,JAMES	PLOUGHMAN,WIDOW	LEAN,CONSTANTINE	NONE RECORDED	HG
	WALSH,PHILIP	CORBIT,MARY	CORBIT,MICHAEL	WALSH,MARY	HG
18131203	WALSH,STEPHEN	MACKEY,MARGARET	WALSH,PATRICK	GUSHUE,MARY	HG
18131204	TRECHER,THOMAS	TOOLE,JOHANNA	TOOLE,PATRICK	GUSHUE,MARY(Finis1818)	HG
18131209	MULLALY,LAURENCE	HINGY,ANN	HERTING,WILLIAM	McNAMARA,SERA	EWER,REV
18131227	GEORGE,MARTIN	CLARK,PATIENCE	GEORGE,ROBERT	CLARK,GEORGE??	HG
18140111	DELANEY,PATRICK	PARSONS,JUDITH	DELANEY,JOHN	PARSONS,JULIAN	HG
	OWENS,PETER	POOR,MARY	SINNOTT,JAMES	DUGGAN,LAWRENCE	HG
18140116	ENNET,WILLIAM	HARTERY,MARIA	HARTERY,GEORGE	KENNEY,MATH	EWER,REV
18140123	DENEHEY,JOHN?	MAGRATH,ELLEN	GLAVINE,RICHARD	GLAVINE,JAMES??	EWER,REV
18140127	FOX,JAMES	MAGRATH,ALICE	KIRNEY,MATHEW	FOLEY,MARY	EWER,REV
18140130	COUGHLIN,JOHN	MCCARTHY,ELLEN	McCARTHY,JOHN	MCCARTHY,ELIZABETH	EWER,REV
18140131	PHELAN,JAMES	SULLIVAN,MARY	GOFF,JAMES	PHELAN,ELLEN	EWER,REV
18140204	COLBERT,MORRIS	COLLINS,CATHERINE	ERBONEEN,PHILIP	MULAHARY,MARY	EWER,REV
18140215	BARRETT,JOHN	POWER,BRIGET	MAGRATH,DENNIS	FOX ALICE	EWER,REV
18140222	BRADBURY,THOMAS	DOBBIN,HONOR	MORRISSEY,THOMAS	POWER,ANTHONY	EWER,REV
18140317	CONDON,PATRICK	PHELAN,BRIGET	COLLINS,JOHN	GELESBY,MARY	EWER,REV
18140331	BURKE,WILLIAM	LEWIS,ELIZ	WALL,GARRET	HICKS,ELIZ	HG
18140403	LEHURY,JAMES	LECOURT,ELIZ	GORMAN,JOHN	GORMAN,MRS	HG
18140410	BAKER,HENRY	SULLIVAN,ELIZ	KENNEDY,JOHN	KENNEDY,MARGT	HG
	HEARN,WILLIAM	MCNAMARA,JOANNA	HEARN,JOHN	HEARN,MARY	EWER,REV
18140426	MORRIS,PATRICK	FOLEY,MARY	MAGHER,THOMAS	CAWLEY,FANIFREDA	EWER,REV
18140430	MURPHY,MAURICE	COLBERT,MARY	DRISCOLL,MICHAEL	GUSHUE,MARY	HG
18140509	GEORGE,THOMAS	PALUM?,ELIZABETH	FLINN,JAMES	POWER,PATRICK	HG
18140518	DORAN,PETER	NOSIRY?,PATIENCE	GORDEN,MARK	NOSERY,SUSANNA	DEVEREAUX,REV
18140520	SHAYER,THOMAS	HOGAN,HANNA	LEGRCE,DANIEL	POWER,MARY	EWER,REV
18140616	HARRINGTON,DARBY	CULLEN,MARGARETH	DRISCOLL,JOHN	COLBERT,CATHERINE	EWER,REV
18140728	HARTERY,DENNIS	WALSH,WIDOW	CONNORS,DOCTOR	SHEEHAN,ELIZA	HG
	SHEEHAN,EDWARD	KAVANAGH,ANNE	CONNORS,DOCTOR	SHEEHAN,ELIZA	HG
18140903	WALSH,JOSEPH	COLE,MARY	MURPHY,MORRIS	GRIFFIN,ANN	EWER,REV
18140904	WALSH,EDWARD	WHITE,ANN	GOSSERT,CHARLES	COSTELLO,ANN	EWER,REV
18141018	HOLOHAN,EDMUND	BENNETT,ANN	NOONAN,THOMAS	NOONAN,MRS	HG
18141029	WOODFORD,MATTHEW	FAHEY,ELLEN	WOODFORD,JAMES	FAHEY,JOANNA	EWER,REV
18141110	WALL,NICHOLAS	WALSH,MARY	WALSH,MICHAEL	HICKEY,TIMOTHY	EWER,REV
18141111	POOR,JOHN??	GUHSUE,MARY	MURPHY,MAURICE	MURPHY,MARY	HG
18141114	KELLY,JOHN	BRIEN,MARY	POWER,DAVID	JONES,ALICE	EWER,REV

DATEMARR	HISNAME	HERNAME	WITN1	WITN2	PRIEST
18141116	KIRWICK,JOHN	HICKS,ELIZABETH	WALL,GARRET	HICKS,MARY	EWER,REV
18141117	HEALY,JAMES	HICKS,MARY	KIRWICK,JOHN	KIRWICK,ELIZABETH	EWER,REV
18141123	YOUNGS,JOHN	POWELL,ANNISTIS	YOUNGS,GEORGE	WHEELER,ELLEN	EWER,REV
18141130	KELLY,JOHN	TOOLE,CATHERINE	CONNELL,ROBERT	LEWIS,ELIZABETH	EWER,REV
18141201	SKANE,WILLIAM	COLE,MARY	SKANE,JOHN	WHELAN,ANNE	EWER,REV
18141203	KENDLER,DANIEL	MAGHER,MARY	TROY,PATRICK	HICKEY,MARGARET	EWER,REV
18150107	HEARN,JAMES	HEARN,MARY	CONWAY,PHILIP	CONWAY,BRIDGET	EWER,REV
18150118	CLEARY,EDMOND	GIBBS,JOHANNA	HICKEY,MICHAEL	HICKS,ELIZABETH	EWER,REV
18150119	BARRON,JAMES	WOODFORD,GRACE	WOODFORD,MICHAEL	HINES,ELIZABETH	EWER,REV
18150205	DAWLEY,JAMES	POOL,ANN	KENDLER,DANIEL	KENDLER,MARY	EWER,REV
18150206	FOGERTY,RICHARD	MACKEY,MARY	DOYLE,JAMES	SHEA,ELLEN	EWER,REV
18150207	HARRINGTON,PATRICK	BECKETT,ANN	WALSH,PATRICK	MADDOX,MARY	EWER,REV
18150302	LEARY,THOMAS	HOINES,MARY	HUHENGAME,THOMAS	POWER,ONOR?	EWER,REV
18150307	MURPHY,MARTIN	TOOMEY,MARY	BROADRICK,WILLIAM	BROADRICK,MRS	EWER,REV
18150310	MAGUIRE,PATRICK	PARSON,ELZABETH	MAGRATH,MATTHEW	MAGRATH,MRS	EWER,REV
18150404	RYAN,MARTIN	DUGGAN,SERA	BARRETT,JOHN	HARRIS?,MARGARET	EWER,REV
18150409	KEHOE,PATRICK	PHELAN,ELLEN	QUIGLEY,PATRICK	KENNEDY,ELLEN	EWER,REV
18150412	WOODFORD,WILLIAM	FARDY,CONSTANTIA	WHITNEY,THOMAS	PENNOL,ELLEN	EWER,REV
1815057	COLLINS,JOHN	GEARY,ELLEN	HEARN,MICHAEL	HAMILTON,JANE	EWER,REV
18150503	HEALY,MICHAEL	MURPHY,JOHANA	MACKEY,MR.	LOHEER,JANE	EWER,REV
18150511	THISTLE,JOHN	BALDEN,ONER?	ROACH,MR	ROACH,MRS	EWER,REV
18150528	FOLEY,LAURENCE	HACO,ANN	FEWER,WALTER	MEASON,CORA	EWER,REV
	KENNEDY,PATRICK	TERRY,CATHERINE	KENNEDY,WILLIAM J	TERRY,MRS	EWER,REV
18150603	CONAWAY,THOMAS	PRENDERGAST,CATHERINE	PRENDERGAST,M.	QUONEY,MARY	EWER,REV
18150617	MARA,THOMAS	NEVINS,BRIGET	POWER,DAVID	MANDOSEL,MARY	EWER,REV
18150628	KEHOE,JAMES	RYAN,JULIA	RYAN,MR	DEVEREX?,JOHN	EWER,REV
18150808	BOUGHEN,STEPHEN	BRYAN,CERA	BRYAN,MICHAEL	COOK,MARY	EWER,REV
18150902	DOYLE,PHILIP	KELLY,MARGARET	MAGRAPH,MICHAEL	NOWLIN,HANNAH	EWER,REV
18150904	PYBORN,THOMAS	DUGGAN,MARY	BRYAN,THOMAS	DALY,MARY	EWER,REV
18150930	WHITE,ROBERT	GRIFFEN,ANN	GUSHUE,GEORGE	LYONS,MICHAEL	EWER,REV
18151001	GRIFFIN,TIMOTHY	WHITE,MARY	MANGENT,WILLIAM	WHITE,ANN	EWER,REV
18151008	BRODERICK,MICHAEL	KENNEALY,MARY	WALSH,THOMAS	KENNEALY,MRS	
	MURREY,LAURENCE	CONNORS,MAGRET	FURLONG,PATRICK	RYAN,CATHERINE	EWER,REV
18151012	MCCARN,NEIL	OLIVER,ELIZABETH	FOWLOW,MR	FOWLOW,MRS	EWER,REV
18151028	MANDAVAL,THOMAS	SHEA,ELEANOR	HENNESSEY,MICHAEL	CONNORS,MRS	EWER,REV
18151030	KEHOE,JOHN	WOODFORD,UREOLA	WOODFORD,MICHAEL	KENNEDY,MRS	EWER,REV
18151101	HICKS,JOHN	WITCH,CATHERINE	WALL,GARRET	WITCH,MRS	EWER,REV
18151102	EAGAN,JOHN	HALLORAN,BRIDGET	FOLEY,CATHERINE	MANSFIELD,ROBERT	EWER,REV
	MAHONY,JAMES	FORAN,MARY	LYNES,BRIDGET	DAWLY,JAMES	EWER,REV
	TOOLE,PATRICK	WALL,MARY	CONNORS,DENNIS	WALL,MARY	EWER,REV
18151105	FITZGERALD,JAMES	MAHER,MARY	ST.JOHN,ROBERT	GRIFFIN,MRS	EWER,REV
18151107	RYAN,BRYAN	McDONALD,CATHERINE	MURPHY,LAURENCE	PHELAN,MRS	EWER,REV
18151114	KENNEDY,JOHN	GLASBY,MARY	KENNEDY,EDWARD	McCARTHY,ELIZABETH	EWER,REV
	SHEA,RICHARD	MCGRATH,MARY	CONNORS,DANIEL	KENNEDY,ELEANOR	EWER,REV
18151117	MULRONEY,PATRICK	MORAN,JUDE	MORAN,PATRICK	DUNN,MARY	EWER,REV
18151118	CUSTEEN,JOHN	CASHAN,JULIA	QUINLAN,MR	KEAN,MARIAN	EWER,REV
18151120	FAHEE,JAMES	FITZGERALD,MARY	FITZGERALD,MAURICE	FAHEE,MRS	EWER,REV
18151122	LAULEY,RICHARD	KING,MARGARET	KING,PATRICK	MURPHY,CATHERINE	EWER,REV
18151129	KALLINEN,RICHARD	PHELAN,FANNY	FARRELL,MR	FARRELL,MRS	EWER,REV

MARRIAGES FROM HARBOUR GRACE RECORDS
1806-1845

DATEMARR	HISNAME	HERNAME	WITN1	WITN2	PRIEST
18151129	POWER,JAMES	BURNS?,ANNE	BOHAN,MR	QUINLAN,MARY	EWER,REV
18151130	POOR,JAMES	BYRNE,NANCY	BYRNE,JOSEPH	BOHANS,MRS	EWER,REV
18151202	BRYAN,JAMES	MANDAVAL,MARY	MANDAVAL,THOMAS	KENNEDY,MRS	EWER,REV
18151210	ST.JOHN,JOHN	RYAN,CATHERINE	WALSH,THOMAS	BUTLER,MRS	EWER,REV
	WILLIAMS,JOHN	KELLY,BRIDGET	WALSH,PHILIP	WALSH,MRS	EWER,REV
18151219	CONNOLLY,PATRICK	RORKE,MARY	SHEA,MICHAEL	COOK,MARY	EWER,REV
18160101	THOMSON,JAMES	BYRNE,CATHERINE	MCGRATH,MR.	BUTLER,ELEANOR	EWER,REV
18160102	MORAY,DANIEL	GEORGE,JEAN	MORAY,MR	MORAY,MRS	EWER,REV
18160103	CODY,PIERCE	CODY,ANASTESIA	CODY,JOHN	MEHAN,MARY	EWER,REV
18160111	LAWLAR,JOHN	KING,MARY	FOX,WILLIAM	BARRY,MRS	EWER,REV
18160114	FITZGIBBONS,?	SULLIVAN,MARY	FENNELL,WM-MEEHAN,D	BINALEY,MARY-QUIN,M	EWER,REV
18160116	DALY,JOHN	NEIGLE,MARY	NEIGLE,MR-MRS	KENNEDY,ELINOR	EWER,REV
18160125	PUMPHREY,JEREMIAH	BARRY,BRIDGET	HEARN,JOHN	KENNEDY,ANASTASIA	EWER,REV
18160130	DUNPHY,PATRICK	CONNELL,HONORA	CONNELL,MAURICE	HANRAHAN,ELIZABETH	EWER,REV
	FURLONG,MICHAEL	WALSH,MARY	WALSH,JOHN	KENNEDY,MARY	EWER,REV
18160131	STAPLETON,BARTHOLEMEW	McCARTHY,ELIZABETH	McCARTHY,COLEMAN?	CANGATON?,MARY	EWER,REV
18160201	COSTELLO,JOHN	DOYLE,MARY	COSTELLO,DAVID	CONNELL,ELIZABETH	EWER,REV
	HYNES?,EDWARD	DELANEY,MARY	POWER,MARTIN	MOORE,MICHAEL	EWER,REV
18160204	SCULLY,JAMES	HICKEY,MARY	HICKEY,WILLIAM	LYONS,BRIDGET	EWER,REV
18160207	HARTERY,THOMAS	POWER,MARGERT	MAINERY?,MR	MAINERY?,MRS	EWER,REV
18160211	McGRATH,JOHN	BUTTON?,ALICE	McGRATH,MR	THOMPSON,CATHERINE	EWER,REV
18160218	WALSH,EDWARD	BROPHY,MARY	POWER,P-DOYLE,J	DENAHY?,ELINOR	EWER,REV
18160219	PENNEY,MATHEW	NOWLAN,HANAUGH	WOODFORD,MATTHEW	WOODFORD,MRS	EWER,REV
18160226	FLANIGAN,ROBERT	COOKE,MARY	COOKE,ROBERT	COOKE,MRS-WALSH,MRS	EWER,REV
	MEANEY,PATRICK	HANRAHAN,ALICE	MEANEY,PHILIP	HANRAHAN,MARY	EWER,REV
18160227	HOGAN,DANIEL	HAMILTON,JEAN	HOGAN,TIMOTHY?	HAMILTON,ELINOR	EWER,REV
	WALSH,WALTER	CAHILL,MARY	MEANEY,PAT-CAHILL,PAT	DUNPHY,MRS	EWER,REV
18160414	HARRIS,JOHN	GEARY,MARY	KELLY,JAMES	COTTER,ELLEN	EWER,REV
	LAHEE?,EDWARD	LACUIER,CATHERINE	COLEMAN,TIMOTHY?	CAREY,MARY	EWER,REV
18160416	WHELAN,WILLIAM	WHELAN,ELINOE	CORBAN-FARRELL,MR	CORBAN-FOSTER,MRS	EWER,REV
18160502	DOODY,PATRICK	GODFREY,HANAUGH?	GODFREY,MICHAEL	NORMAN,MRS	EWER,REV
	HEARNE,TIMOTHY	DWYER,CATHERINE	HICKEY,WILLIAM	REGGAN,MRS	EWER,REV
18160529	WALSH,JAMES	HARTERY,ELINOR	FOGARTY,JAMES	WALSH,JOHN?	EWER,REV
18160530	BUTLER,THOMAS	HENNESSEY,JUDITH	BUTLER,EDMUND	HENNESSEY,MARTIN?	EWER,REV
18160610	LANNAN?,THEARN?	WOODFORD,CHARLOTTE	WOODFORD,MICHAEL	WOODFORD,GRACE	EWER,REV
18160611	GRIFFIN,MICHAEL	CONEY?,MARY	BRODERICK,EDMOND	POWER,MARGARET	EWER,REV
18160701	THORN,WILLIAM	KANE,MARIAN?	KANE,THOMAS	QUINLAN,MRS	EWER,REV
18160725	DUNN,JOHN	COLLENS?,ALLY	CARROLL?,PETER	CAUL?,MARY	EWER,REV
18160812	FORRESTAL,JOHN	MULRONEY,ANN	DOOLEN,EDMOND?	MULRONEY,MRS	EWER,REV
	PHELAN,JOHN	CRIVTE?,HANAUGH?	DUGGAN,WILLIAM	PHELAN,CATHERINE	EWER,REV
18160825	FARRELL,THOMAS	LEARY,MARY	HIDEN?,RICHARD	BARREN,ANN	EWER,REV
18161014	RYAN,THOMAS	BRIEN,ELIZABETH	SHEA,HANRY	MURRAY?,MARY	EWER,REV
18161025	FARRELL?,THOMAS	GEARY,MARY	HEADEN?,RICHARD	BRENNAN,ANASTASIA	EWER,REV
18161102	MADDIGAN,TIMOTHY	SHEEHAY?,HONOR	CAREY,DANIEL	LEARY,CATHERINE	EWER,REV
18161103	MOORES,WILLIAM	MACKEY,BRIDGET	COLEMAN,PATRICK	BEESON,CORRA	EWER,REV
	SULLIVAN?,PETER	CHEEVEN?,MARY	FARRELL?,TIMOTHY	FARRELL?,CATHERINE	EWER,REV
18161107	BENNETT,JAMES	BEESON,JANE	BARRETT,ROGER	BEESON,CATHERINE	EWER,REV
	KELLY,JOHN	BARRETT,ELIZABETH	WALL,MR	WALL,CORA	EWER,REV
	POWER,RICHARD	BEESON,CORA	DUNN,PATRICK	KERIVECK?,MARGERET	EWER,REV

DATEMARR	HISNAME	HERNAME	WITN1	WITN2	PRIEST
18161109	ENGLISH,EDWARD	PRENDERGAST,MARGRET	ENGLISH,EDWARD	MURPHY,MARY	EWER,REV
	MANSFIELD,JOHN	BRYAN,ELLEN	GUSHUE,CHARLES	GUSHUE,MRS	EWER,REV
	WALL,PATRICK	MURPHY,JUDITH	PRENDERGAST,THOMAS	FRISBY?,DAVID	EWER,REV
18161110	GEARY,JAMES	MADDOCK,CATHERINE	DOOLEY,WILLIAM	NADDY?,CATHERINE	EWER,REV
	KING,PATRICK	MURRAY,CATHERINE	DELANEY,THOMAS	KING,DANIEL	EWER,REV
18161112	CARROLL,PATRICK	RYAN,MARY	CARROLL,ROBERT	RYAN,MARGARET	EWER,REV
18161114	RYAN,PATRICK	SHEHAN,HONOR	CURRIN?,DARBY?	OATES,CATHERINE	EWER,REV
18161119	HICHINGHAN?,THOMAS	POWER,JANE	MOORE,MORGAN	KEATING,CHARLOTTE	EWER,REV
18161127	PUMPHY,JOHN	MURRAY,ELLEN	McGRATH,JOHN	MURRAY?,JOHANA	EWER,REV
18161129	KENNY,LAWRENCE	MOREA,MARY	MOREA,WILLIAM	DUNPHY,HONOR	EWER,REV
	OATES,THOMAS	SHEA,CATHERINE	GOOBY,JEREMIAH	GOOBY,ELLEN	EWER,REV
18161131	WALL,JAMES	BRENNAN,MARY	WALSH,MARTIN	CANE,MARY	EWER,REV
18161204	SHEA,THOMAS	QUINTON?,MARY	DELANEY,THOMAS	GRANT,MARY	EWER,REV
18161210	O'DONNEL,JAMES	LYNCH,ANN	CHOVERS?,LAURENCE	CRAWLEY?,ELLEN	EWER,REV
18161225	KENT,JAMES	KELLY,JUDY	KENT,JOHN	POWXX,CATHERINE	EWER,REV
18170103	LINAHEN?,JOHN	MURPHY,CATHERINE	KANE,JAMES	GLAVINE,MARY	EWER,REV
18170104	BARRETT,ROGER	WITCH,JANE	WITCH,GEORGE	BARRETT,CHRISANNA?	EWER,REV
18170116	SHEA,MICHAEL	MULLOUWNEY,JOHANNA	MORRESSEY?,THOMAS	STRAP,CATHERINE	EWER,REV
18170121	MEANEY,JOHN	KENNEDY,MARY	KENNEDY,JAS-MARY	DINN,J-MAGEE,M	EWER,REV
18170126	INSIOL?,BARTHOLAMEW	MAHER,BRIDGET	VEALY?,MICHAEL	BXXX,MARGARET	EWER,REV
18170209	KAVANAGH,BRIAN	ASPEN?,MARY	KAVANAGH,JOHN	KAVANAGH,MARGARET	EWER,REV
18170211	DUNN,PATRICK	COULCHLOUGH,FRANCES	DUNN,JOHN	COULCHLOUGH,MARGARET	EWER,REV
18170213	FURLONG,NICHOLAS	RYAN,CATHERINE	GANTON?,JAMES	NOWLAN,ANNE	EWER,REV
	MURPHY,JOHN	SHEA,ELLEN	XXXX,JAMES	LYONS,BRIDGET	EWER,REV
181702XX	CASEY,MARTIN	BRIEN,BRIDGET	POWER,PATRICK	WALSH,MARY	EWER,REV
	HOGAN,MATTHEW	BRIEN,MARY	FOLEY,TIMOTHY?	FOLEY,CATHERINE	EWER,REV
	LAWLER,DAVID	DALTON,BRIDGET	CONAWAY?,PATRICK	DALTON,ELIZABETH	EWER,REV
18170304	HEAD,JAMES	SHEA,ALLEY	SULLIVAN?,GEORGE	CONNELL,ELIZABETH	HERRON,REV
18170426	HOGAN,RICHARD	HUSSEY?,CATHERINE	HOGAN,JAMES	HUSSEY,BRIDGET	HERRON,REV
18170504	COTTER,JOHN	QUIRK,MARY	COTTER,JAMES	KELLY,MARGARET	HERRON,REV
18170511	MURPHY,JOHN	HOWLETT,MARGARET	COTTER,JOHN	KELLY,MARGARET	HERRON,REV
18170526	KNOX,MICHAEL	GAIL,MARY	WALSH,JAMES	FULONG,MARY	HERRON,REV
18170610	DOYLE,MARTIN	McCARTHY,MARY	LAWLOR,DAVID	FLEMMING,MARY	HERRON,REV
18170615	DRYSDALE,ANDREW	PRENDERGAST,MARY	FOX,JAMES	LAMBERT,ELLEN	EWER,REV
18170619	BRYAN,PATRICK	COOKE,MARY	WALSH,MARTIN	SUTTON,CATHERINE	HERRON,REV
18170801	DOYLE,THOMAS	FEHZ??,MARGARET	FOGARTY,JAMES	QUINLAN,MARGARET	HERRON,REV
18170923	COLBERT,JAMES	MURPHY,MARGARET	MURPHY,JOSEPH	FOLEY,ELLEN	EWER,REV
18170927	WALSH,THOMAS	DOYLE,CATHERINE	MAGHER?,PATRICK	CROWLEY,ELLEN	EWER,REV
18171002	McCARTHY,DANIEL	KEHOE,ELLEN	SCANLAN,MARGARET?	DUNPHY,HONORA	EWER,REV
18171004	LEAMY,THOMAS	HICKEY,MARY	DELANEY,TIMOTHY	MALONE,MARY	HERRON,REV
18171010	WALSH,MICHAEL	WALL,SEARA?	XXXX,WILLIAM	WALL.ELLEN	EWER,REV
18171011	HACKETT,JAMES	KENNEDY,MARGARET	SHEA,DOCTOR	KENNEDY,MRS	HERRON,REV
18171013	STRAP,PATRICK	DEODY?,ALLEY	SHEA,HENRY	KENNEDY,MRS	HERRON,REV
18171016	BRANSFIELD,JOHN	ROSE,GRACE	MURPHY,TIMOTHY	SIMS?,MARY	HERRON,REV
18171020	MURPHY,WILLIAM	SHORTHILL?,MARY	MULLOUWNEY,PATRICK	PHELAN,MARY	HERRON,REV
18171022	CARROLL,DENNIS	BYRNE,CATHERINE	HINGEY,PATRICK	DUNN,MRS	EWER,REV
18171106	WALSH,MORRIS	DRISCOLL,MARGARET	CROWLY?,ELLEN?	SCANLAN?,MARGARET	EWER,REV
18171112	PENNELL,JOSEPH	KEHOE,MARGARET	KELLY,THOMAS	DOYLE,MARY	HERRON,REV
	QUILTY?,TIMOTHY?	POWER,CATHERINE	BRIEN,THOMAS	HUNT,BRIDGET	EWER,REV

MARRIAGES FROM HARBOUR GRACE RECORDS
1806-1845

DATEMARR	HISNAME	HERNAME	WITN1	WITN2	PRIEST
18171114	COLE,TIMOTHY	SHEAN,MARY	SHEAN,JAMES	BRIEN,ELLEN	HERRON,REV
	HAWCO,PHILIP	WALSH,JUDITH	CUNNINGHAM,JAMES	CRAWLEY,ELLEN	EWER,REV
18171117	SHEA,PATRICK	FOGARTY,ELLEN	FARRELL,MOVAN?	MURPHY,TIMOTHY	EWER,REV
18171119	HAWE,WILLIAM	DANTON,ANN	MURPHY,JOHN	PHELAN,MARGARET	EWER,REV
18171121	HURLEY,THOMAS	DRISCOLL,MARY	BENNETT,JAMES	MURPHY,MARY	EWER,REV
18171123	DOLLAN?,SAMUEL	MURRAY,MARY	DEMPSTER,JOHN	SHERSLAY?,JOANNA	EWER,REV
18171130	DOYLE,MICHAEL	DOOLEY,MARY	HARNETT,WILLIAM	FOWLER,MARY	HERRON,REV
18171204	WALSH,MARTIN	HUNT,BRIDGET	STONE,WILLIAM	BRIEN,MARY	EWER,REV
18171209	MEANEY,PHILIP	HEARLY?,MARGARET	HANLEY,JOHN	CAHILL,JOHANN	EWER,REV
18171227	GANEY,SAMUEL	BROPHY,MARY	MURPHY,WILLIAM	HERRON,ANN	EWER,REV
18180106	HAWCO,WILLIAM	SHORTELL,MARGARET	CRAWLY,HUMPHRY	HAWCO,MATTY	HG
18180109	KING,JOHN	MURRAY,ELLEN	NOT RECORDED	FITZGERALD,ANN	EWER,REV
18180111	HICKEY,JOHN	SULLIVAN,MARY	HICKEY,MICHAEL	WALSH,JUDITH	HG
18180125	FAHEY,PHILIP	DUNN,MARY	DUNN,JOHN	PHELAN,ANN	EWER,REV
18180129	BRITT,JAMES	BRIEN,CATHERINE	FLYNN,JAMES	CONDON,MARY	EWER,REV
18180130	MURPHY,JOHN	CHURLEY?,JOANNA	NO NAME GIVEN	NO NAME GIVEN	EWER,REV
18180131	FLAHERTY,PATRICK	SULLIVAN,NELLY	HARRINGTON,JOHN	SULLIVAN,SALLY	CRONIN,REV
	KENNY,FRERICK	XXXX,MARY	SHEA,MICHAEL	GRIFFIN,MARY	CRONIN,REV
181801XX	KENNEDY,EDWARD	GELESBY?,ANN	GELASBY?,WILLIAM	KENNEDY,JAMES	EWER,REV
	KENNEDY,TERRENCE	KENNY,JANE	McCARTHY,JOHN	SCHANE?,ANN	HG
18180210	BRENNAN,PATRICK	NORRIS,MARY	NORRIS,XXX	XXX,ANNE JANE	HG
18180212	McCARTHY,FELIX	COUGHLIN,MARGARET	McCARTHY,CALLAHAN	NAIL?,JANE	EWER,REV
18180217	KELLY,MICHAEL	HERRON,MARY	PRENDERGAST,JAMES	NAIL,ANN	EWER,REV
18180223	REDMOND,JAMES	HAMILTON,ELINOR	HAMILTON,JOHN	HAMILTON,MARGARET	HG
18180324	BABB,JOHN	GRANT,BRIDGET	XXX,ROBERT	WALSH,KITTY	CRONIN,REV
18180402	RYAN,THOMAS	TUBERET,ELIZABETH	TUBERET,THOMAS	RYAN,ELLEN	HERRON,REV
18180409	DOWER,PATRICK	MOORE,MARY	KENNEY,MARY	SCANLAN,MARGARET	EWER,REV
	KINSELLA,THOMAS	HEALY,CATHERINE	HEALY,TIMOTHY	MOORES,ELIZABETH	HERRON,REV
18180419	HEARNE,JAMES	KEASY?,MARY	BURTON,EDMOND	PLOWMAN,CATHERINE	HERRON,REV
18180420	DUNPHY,JOHN	HEARNE,ELIZABETH	ROGERS,JOHN	PHELAN?,CATHERINE	HERRON,REV
	FORD,JAMES	MCDONALD,ELIZABETH	PHELAN?,EDWARD	COLE,ELIZABETH	HERRON,REV
181804XX	FITZGERALD,MICHAEL	NADDY?,CATHERINE	GRACE,MICHAEL	DUGGAN,MARY	CRONIN,REV
	HARTERY,LAWRENCE	DENNING,LIVERETRA	BENNETT,JAMES	SCANLAN,XXXX	EWER,REV
18180502	DOOLEY,WILLIAM	MINAD?,ELIZABETH	MICHINAN?,NOLAN	ENGLISH,MARY	EWER,REV
18180504	CORBETT,BARTHOLEMEW	WELLS,ELIZABETH	BYRNE,PATRICK	CORBETT,MARY	HERRON,REV
	MASSENLY?,DENNIS	BUTTON,MARY	HOGAN,WILLIAM	OLIVER,MARY	HG
18180509	KENNEY,THOMAS	O'BRIEN,MARGARET	LANE,MICHAEL	CASEY,BRIDGET	EWER,REV
18180517	CODY,JAMES	LAWLESS,ANSTY	RYAN,JOSEPH	HEALY,PEGGY	CRONIN,REV
	XXX,MARTIN	MACKEY,ANNA	MAQUEU?,RXXXX	SMILLY,MARY	HG
18180523	HAGGERTY,WILLIAM	GAUL?,MARY	CUSTEAU,RICHARD	SCANLAN,PEGGY	CRONIN,REV
18180526	WALSH,WILLIAM	WILLIAMS,ELIZABETH	REARDON,CATHERINE	CONDON,REBECCA	CRONIN,REV
18180530	LAWLOR,RICHARD	FITZGERALD,ANN	PHELAN,TIMOTHY	DELANEY,BRIDGET	EWER,REV
181805XX	HAMILTON,JOHN	DONOVAN,ANN	HENNECY,M-COLLINS,J	HAMILTON,MARY	CRONIN,REV
18180605	BARRY,TIMOTHY	NOWLAN,ANN	DUNPHY,MATTHEW	CURRIN,MARY	EWER,REV
	CAVENOUGH?,JOHN	MURPHY,MARY	WALSH,JOHN	NARY?,CATHERINE	EWER,REV
18181015	COSTIGAN,WILLIAM	CONNELL,ELIZABETH	SHEA,HENRY	MAHONEY,CATHERINE	HERRON,REV
18181016	ENGLISH,THOMAS	PRENDERGRAST,ELIZABETH	ENGLISH,EDWARD	MURPHY,MRS	HERRON,REV
	HAFTON?,JOHN	ENGLISH,ELIZABETH	ENGLISH,JOHN	ENGLISH,MARY	HERRON,REV
18181018	LARMEY?,PATRICK	GRIFFIN,DRANIA	GRIFFIN,TIMOTHY	LYONS,CATHERINE	HERRON,REV

DATEMARR	HISNAME	HERNAME	WITN1	WITN2	PRIEST
18181019	FINIEKEN?,PATRICK	BRADBURY,MARY	WHELAN,JOHN	SHEA,MRS	CRONIN
18181021	DIVINE,JAMES	HACO,MARY	RYAN,PETER	DOYLE,MARY	HERRON,REV
18181026	TOOLE,ROGER	WALSH,JOHANNA	BARRY,JAMES	MAHONEY,XXXX	HERRON,REV
18181030	MCCARTHY,DANIEL	NOWLAN,BRIDGET	DEADY,TIMOTHY	HURLEY,MARY	EWER,REV
18181107	AIDE,MICHAEL	GORDON,ANNE	RICHARDSON,WILLIAM	FOGERTY?,JOHN	CRONIN,REV
18181111	CONNORS,MICHAEL	HARTERY,ELIZABETH	HARTERY,JEREMIAH	MURPHY,TIMOTHY	CRONIN
18181117	PURCELL,RICHARD	ROBERTS,MARY	LYNCH,JOHN	SULLIVAN,ELLINOR	CRONIN,REV
18181119	COSTELLO,JOHN	KERBY,MARGARET	MAHONEY,JAMES	COSTELLO,PATRICK	CRONIN,REV
18181124	MURPHY,THOMAS	MURPHY,ELLEN	MACCAN?,PATRICK	STRAP,CATHERINE	CRONIN,REV
18181126	ADAMS,THOMAS	DOYLE,ELLEN	BRIEN,PATRICK	BROWN,ELIZABETH	EWER,REV
18181204	FORRESTAL,MICHAEL	MURPHY,HONOR	MURPHY,ANTHONY	MULRONEY,JUDITH	EWER,REV
18181209	GAHEN,JOHN	CONAWAY,JUDITH	DUNN,PATRICK	HUNT,MARY	EWER,REV
18181212	QUONEY,JAMES	McCARTHY,HONOR	ENNETT,WILLIAM	LYONS,BRIDGET	EWER,REV
18190102	STACK,WILLIAM	MURRAY,CATHERINE	STACK,JOHN	CONNELL,ELIZABETH	HG
18190106	DWYER,EDMOND	McCARTHY,ELIZABETH	KEHOE,WILLIAM	KENNEDY,ELINOR	HG
18190603	LUE?,WILLIAM	SHERIDAN,ANN	DOYLE,JAMES	COLE,ANN	CRONIN,REV
18190621	MORAN,PATRICK	NOLAN,BETTY	KENNEDY,JOHN	WOODFORD,MARY	CRONIN,REV
18190629	MXXXX,JOHN	WALSH,HONORA	PHELAN,PIERCE	COKELY,MARGARET	HG
18190904	McDANIEL,MARK	CODY,MARY	CODY,JAMES	GORMAN,MARGARET	HG
18191003	ASPEL,MICHAEL	REARDON,MARY	WHELAN,WALTER	DOOLING,WINFORD	CRONIN,REV
18191004	HANLIN,TIMOTHY	RYAN,MARY	PRENDERGAST,EDWARD	MASON,MARY	HG
	NAL?,PATRICK	DELANEY,MARGARET	McGRATH,JOHN	DAULTON?,MARY	HG
18191005	GRIFFIN,JOHN	FOLEY,MARY	MADDOCK,JOHN	COTTER,MARY	HG
	MACKEY,MICHAEL	GINN?,MARY	KEHOE,MICHAEL	DUFF?,JOHN	HG
18191023	DUNN,JOHN	JANES,FANNE	DUNN,CATHERINE?	KING,CHARLOTE	HG
18191025	DELANEY,MICHAEL	DANIEL,BETTY	BECKETT,JAMES	BECKETT,JOHN?	HG
18191029	DOYLE,PATRICK	SCANLAN,MARY	RYAN,THOMAS	WALL,SERA	HG
	HARDEN,WILLIAM	MADDEN,MARY	FEWER,EDMOND	KENNEDY,MARY	HG
18191109	HURLEY,WILLIAM	SHEPPARD,JANE	HATCHER,JAMES	SULLIVAN,ANN	HG
	POWER,MICHAEL	PHELAN,ALICE	KEY,PATRICK	DRISCOLL,MARY	HG
18191117	BRITT,RICHARD	KELLY,MARY	BOWE,NICHOLAS	CONDON,ALICE	HG
18191120	HOWELL,NICHOLAS	FOWLER,JANE	NOWLAN,JOHN	HOLLEHAN?,HONOR	CRONIN,REV
	LANE,HENRY	FOWLER,MARY	HART,EDMOND	FOWLER,MARGARET	HG
18191123	FITZPATRICK,JOHN	LAHEY,BRIDGET	MULLONEY,THOMAS	HOGAN,MARY	HG
18191125	COTTER,WILLIAM	KENNEDY,BRIDGET	EDINGTON,FRANCIS	KENNEDY,MARY	HG
18191127	WALSH,PATRICK	MAHONEY,ELIZABETH	MALACKAY?,PHILIP	MAGRATH,CATHERINE	HG
18191130	HERRON,JAMES	JONES,ALICE	KEATON?,EDMOND	JONES,ELLEN	HG
	NOLAN,THOMAS	MULLOUWNEY,MARY	HUFF,NICHOLAS	PLEY?,CATHERINE	CRONIN,REV
	POWER,MICHAEL	CAHILL,MARGARET	HARDEN,RICHARD	CAHILL,MARY	HG
18191226	ENGLISH,RICHARD	BOLAN,MARY	ENGLISH,THOMAS	ENGLISH,MARY	HG
18200106	DELANEY,JAMES	CUMMINS,MARY	CALLAHAN,RICHARD	ENGLISH,FRANCES	HG
	LAYNIH?,FRANCIS	LYONS,BRIDGET	FOLEY,TIMOTHY	MACDONALD,MARY	HG
18200201	KEHOE,JOHN	TIERNEY?,MAGDALEN	DOYLE,JOHN	KEHOE,PHYLLIS	CRONIN,REV
18200215	TROY,PATRICK	DOYLE,CHRISTIANA	MURPHY,MICHAEL	CONDON,ALICE	HG
18200409	DUGGAN,WILLIAM	POWER,MARY	POWER,PATRICK	BROTHERS,JAMES	HG
18200506	BURKE,THOMAS	McNAMARA,BRIDGET	LYNCH,TIMOTHY?	DALTON,CATHERINE	HG
18200514	CALLAHAN,WILLIAM	WALSH,CATHERINE	DUGGAN,JOHN	KNOX,ELINOR	HG
18200531	WALSH,THOMAS	HAYES,MARGARET	CASEY,MARTIN	MARA,ANASTASIA	EWER,REV
18200603	JOY,MICHAEL	MAGEE,BRIDGET	POWER,JAMES	GUNNET?,TIMOTHY?	EWER,REV

MARRIAGES FROM HARBOUR GRACE RECORDS
1806-1845

DATEMARR	HISNAME	HERNAME	WITN1	WITN2	PRIEST
18200603	KEHOE,WILLIAM	CONNORS,MARY	McCARTHY,FELIX	KENNEDY,ELINOR	HG
18200627	MXXXAHAN,MICHAEL	HAWE,DORTHEA	MURPHY,TIMOTHY?	ENGLISH,CATHERINE	CRONIN,REV
182008XX	HALLON,DANIEL	RICHARD,MARY	RUSK,JOHN	MACDONALD,MARY	EWER,REV
18200917	KEHOE,JAMES	FLANNIGAN,MARY	NOONAN,DENNIS	COTTER,MARY	HG
	NEIL,THOMAS	JANES,MARY	TROY,MAURICE	COTTER,MARY	HG
18200918	FLEMING,MICHAEL	BLUNDEN,LETICA	MACKEY,RICHARD	DOODY,ELINOR	HG
18200919	KEYES,LAWRENCE	COLAN?,SUSANNA	MACKEY,RICHARD	DOODY,ELINOR	HG
18200921	MOORES,EDMOND	DUFFET?,ANN	NOONAN,THOMAS	DANTON,MARY	HG
18200923	MCCARTHY,JOHN	DANTON,MARY	MACKEY,RICHARD	DOODY,ELINOR	HG
18200926	KENNEFICK,MAURICE	NORRIS,MARY	COLLINS,JOHN	REGAN,ELINOR	HG
18200927	DONOVAN,CORNELIUS	HAYES,MARY	BXXX,LARRY	MAHONEY,MARY	EWER,REV
	POWER,MICHAEL	SULLIVAN,SERA	McCARTHY,THOMAS	MAHONEY,MARY	HG
18200928	MURPHY,DAVID	GLANIEN?,ELINOR	BRANDRCK?,WILLIAM	MURPHY,HONOR	HG
18201002	MORRISSEY,MORGAN	DELAHANTY,MARY	FONNEY?,EDMOND	KINSELLA,MARY	HG
18201007	WOODFORD,JAMES	FAHEY,MARY	WOODFORD,MATTHEW	WOODFORD,ANN	CRONIN,REV
18201011	POWER,PATRICK	LYNCH,MARY	MIESON?,JAMES	JONES,ELLEN	CRONIN,REV
18201012	DOYLE,JAMES	POWER,ELINOR	DALTON,WILLIAM	KENNEDY,ELINOR	HG
18201017	MURPHY,PATRICK	REDMOND,ELINOR	POWER,JOHN	SCANLAN,MARGARET	HG
18201029	McCARTHY,FELIX	CANDLER,ELINOR	McCARTHY,JOHN	SHEAN,ANN	DEVEREAUX,REV
182010XX	HENRICKS,PATRICK	BUTTER?,JANE	KEEFE,JOHN	BUTTER?,MARY	HG
18201102	HOGAN,JAMES	FOLEY,MARGARET	DUGGAN,WILLIAM	ENGLISH,CATHERINE	HG
18201105	MULCAHY,WILLIAM	JANES,MARY	MURPHY,PHILIP	CONDON,MARY	CRONIN,REV
18201106	FLYNN,MICHAEL	FLAHERTY,PEGGY	ROCKETT?,ROBERT	MURPHY,MARGARET	CRONIN,REV
18201110	DEATO?,WILLIAM	DANIEL,ANN	PENNY,WILLIAM	COLE,ANN	HG
18201111	KEEFE,DAVID	CXXXEY?MARY	JOY,JAMES	KNOX,NELLY	CRONIN,REV
18201112	SHERIDON?,JOHN	POWER,NANCY	POWER,JAMES	McGRATH,ANNE	CRONIN,REV
18201120	DELANEY,THOMAS	KING,MARY	WHELAN,WALTER	DUNN,PEGGY	CRONIN,REV
18201122	MORGAN,DENNIS	CXXXXHY,MARY	MILLANE?,NED	CLARY,ELLEN	CRONIN,REV
18201123	WHELAN,MICHAEL	BUTT,CHARLOT	GEARE?,MARK	KENNEDY,ELINOR	CRONIN,REV
18201124	HARVEY,PETER	HANLON?,MARGARET	HANLON?,JOSEPH	CRAWLEY,ELLEN	CRONIN,REV
18201125	GARE?,MICK	AUSTIN,MARY	BORDON,WILLIAM	KELLOWAY,ELIZABETH	CRONIN,REV
18201126	FLAHERTY,GEORGE	FLEMING,CATHERINE	FLEMING,MARTIN	GODFREY?,JANE	DEVEREAUX,REV
18201127	CALOCHAN?,JAMES	FALKERTY?,BRIDGET	POWER,EDMOND	FITZGERALD,ELLEN	CRONIN,REV
	GILLESBY,WILLIAM	KING,MARY	McCARTHY,FELIX	McCARTHY,ELINOR	CRONIN,REV
18201130	DOANA?,JOHN	CURRIN,PEGGY	FOX,JAMES	SCANLON,PEGGY	CRONIN,REV
18201228	KENNEDY,WILLIAM	KENNEDY,ELLEN	CLARKE,JOHN	KENNEDY,XXXHAN	HG
	WALSH,RICHARD	WALSH,ELIZABETH	DOYER?,JAMES	WALSH,MARY	DEVEREAUX,REV
18210105	DELANG?,WILLIAM	SNOW,ELIZABETH	TROY,RICHARD	SNOW,REBECCA	HG
18210107	HART,EDMOND	LANE,JANE	BRINE,DANIEL	HALLAHAN,HONOR	DEVEREAUX,REV
	KELLY,THOMAS	RONAN?,MARY	CODY,THOMAS	MADDOCK,MARY	HG
	WELLS,JOSEPH	FLYNN,ELLEN	FLYNN,WILLIAM	FLYNN,MARY	HG
18210109	POWER,EDWARD	JANES,CATHERINE	QUILTY?,JOHN	JANES,ELIZABETH	CRONIN,REV
18210114	FINN,PATRICK	FITZGERALD,ELINOR	BUTLER,THOMAS	BUTLER,MARY	HG
18210117	SHEA,MICHAEL	SNOW,ROOCHELL?	POWER,PERCE	HIVELY?,JULIA	CRONIN,REV
18210123	FITZGERALD,MAURICE	DALTON,ELIZABETH	FAHEY,JAMES	WHITEWAY,JANE	HG
18210127	SKANE,JAMES	LYONS,ALICE	SKANE,JOHN	SKANE,NARY	DEVEREAUX,REV
182101XX	GRACE,OLIVER	MASON,MARY	KENNEDY,JEREMIAH	SCIVIER?,MARY	DEVEREAUX,REV
	MURPHY,JOHURE?	PHELAN,BRIDGET	BUTLER,PATRICK	PHELAN,NANCY	CRONIN,REV
18210201	FITZPATRICK,THOMAS	CAHILL,ELIZABETH	DUGGAN,WILLIAM	ENGLISH,CHRISTIAN	HG

DATEMARR	HISNAME	HERNAME	WITN1	WITN2	PRIEST
18210213	SHEEHAN?,LAWERENCE	HOLLARON?,JULIA	MAHONEY,JAMES	HOLLARAN,BRIDGET	CRONIN,REV
18210221	DOYLE,JAMES	KELLY,ELIZABETH	PHELAN,WALTER	DUNN,PEGGY	CRONIN,REV
18210222	HANRAHAN,PATRICK	CAHILL,JOAN	CAHILL,PATRICK	KEEFE,MARY	HG
	LEARY,PATRICK	POWER,PEGGY	SHEA,RICHARD	KENNEDY,BRIDGET	CRONIN,REV
18210226	FANNY,JOHN	CONDON,ELLEN	BYRNE,PATRICK	CONDON,MARY	EWER,REV
18210304	SHEA,JOHN	XXXWIN,ELLEN	HANNAHAN,JOHN	CANTY?,MARY	HG
18210305	FOGARTY,CORNELIUS	FOLEY,CATHERINE	MARCH,JAMES	DALTON,MARY	HG
18210306	BRENNAN,JOHN	SULLIVAN,ELINOR	SULLIVAN,JAMES	LYNCH,ELINOR	CRONIN,REV
	FLYNN,MICHAEL	ROWE,PEGGY	DONEVAN,DANIEL	JONES,ELLEN	CRONIN,REV
	HALEY,JOHN	KELLY,MARIA	BREEN,PATRICK	FLAHERTY,BRIDGET	CRONIN,REV
	WALSH,PEIRRE	KENNEDY,MARY	CODY,THOMAS	DOYLE,MARY	HG
18210510	MULCAHEY?,TIMOTHY?	RICHARD,MARY	MOOR?,ANTHONY	HURLEY,JULIAN	EWER,REV
	ROARK,PATRICK	MADDOCK,MARY	NAIL?,JAMES	POWER,BRIDGET	EWER,REV
18210511	MURPHY,BRINE	HEARN,CATHERINE	KEARY?,GEORGE	PHELAN,JOANNAH	DEVEREAUX,REV
18210512	RYAN,JOHN	WALL,MARY	SULLIVAN,TIMOTHY?	KEATING,CATHERINE	DEVEREAUX,REV
18210513	BURN,JOHN	WALL,ELINOR	BURN,PETER	WALL,ANN	DEVEREAUX,REV
	HARNETT?,WILLIAM	HAMILTON,PEGGY	LEE,THOMAS	HEALY,MARGARET	CRONIN,REV
	RYAN,THOMAS	PHELAN,JOANNA	SHEAN,JAMES	SHEAN,ANN	EWER,REV
18210516	DWYER,EDWARD	SWEENEY,MARY	LALLAHAN?,PATRICK	MURPHY,CATHERINE	EWER,REV
18210521	CONNORS,MICHAEL	ASPELL?,ANASTASIA	PHELAN,WALTER	PHELAN,MARGARET	DEVEREAUX,REV
18210529	LEE,THOMAS	DRISCOLL,MARY	CONNORS,DANIEL	McKEE,MARY	DEVEREAUX,REV
18210530	SHERIN?,MICHAEL	HURLEY,JULIA	HURLEY,MATTHEW	ENGLISH,CATHERINE	CRONIN,REV
18210531	DOOLING?,MATTHEW	FOSTER,SERAH	FITZGIBBON,JAMES	FITZGIBBON,ANN	CRONIN,REV
18210614	KING,HENRY	COTTER,JULIA	KING,SAMUEL	GEARY,ELINOR	DEVERAUX,REV
18210722	RYLEY,EDWARD	FINN,ANASTASIA	WHITE,THOMAS	FOWLER,SUSANNA	HG
18210817	RUSSELL,PATRICK	BURN,SUSAN	MELONE,THOMAS	GOLAHOE?,JANE	HG
18210823	MORRICY,RICHARD	MORRICY,ELLEN	CRAWLEY,ELLEN	FITZGERLAD,RICHARD	HG
18210829	QUILTY?,JOHN	GOLAHAR?,JANE	POWER,EDMOND	GOLLIHAR?,ELIZABETH	HG
18210908	KEHOE,MICHAEL	HENNEBURY,ELINOR	SINNOTT,MICHAEL	KINSELLA,MARY	HG
18211117	CZEKIEL?,PETER	WOODFORD,CATHERINE	CZEKIEL?,THOMAS	GORMIN,MARY	DEVEREAUX,REV
18211118	LEARY,JOHN	HEDDERSON,MARGARET	LEARY,JAMES	BARTLETT,JOANNA	DEVEREAUX,REV
	McCUE?,JOHN	BARTLET,JOANNA	LEARY,JAMES	HEDDERSON,MARGARET	DEVEREAUX,REV
	QUNLEY?,DANIEL	MURPHY,JUDY	CONLY,THOMAS	MOORES,ELIZABETH	DEVEREAUX,REV
18211119	BRODERICK,MICHAEL	HOGAN,BRIDGET	TOOL,TIMOTHY	KIDNEY?,ELIZABETH	HG
	GORMAN,THOMAS	GORMAN,MARGARET	GORMAN,JOHN	GORMAN,MARY	DEVEREAUX,REV
	MURPHY,JOHN	GORMIN,JOANNA	GORMIN,JOHN	GORMIN,MARY	DEVEREAUX,REV
	WALL,THOMAS	FURY,JOANNNA	GORMIN,JOHN	GORMIN,MARY	DEVEREAUX,REV
18211121	MURPHY,EDWARD	DOBBINS,MARY	WALL,THOMAS	MURPHY,ELIZABETH	HG
18211125	HAMILTON,OWEN	HEALY,MARGARET	HAMILTON,JOHN	HAMILTON,MARGARET	HG
18211127	TOBIN,THOMAS	DANNELL?,ELIZABETH	TINAN?,PATRICK	GORMAN,CATHERINE	HG
18211129	MACRUNTY?,BARTTE?	COSH,ANN	BOWLIN,JOHN	BUTTEN?,MARY	HG
18211221	COSTELLO,JOSEPH	DOODY,MARY	GUSHUE,CHARLES	WALSH,ELIZABETH	CRONIN,REV
18211227	POWER,JOSEPH	DALTON,MARY	WARDE,JAMES	MACKEY,MARY	CRONIN,REV
18220108	DONAGHUE?,JEREMY	FOGARTY,MARY	HOGAN,THOMAS	HOGAN,MARY	CRONIN,REV
18220210	FAHEY,PATRICK	MOLLOY,SERA	STERLING,WILLIAM	STERLING,MRS	EWER,REV
18220510	LAVERS?,EDMOND	DRISCOLL,ELIZABETH	ROCHE,JOHN	ROCHE,MARGARET	CRONIN,REV
18220512	JOY,JOHN	PENNY,JANE	KENNEDY,JOHN	PENNY,ELINOR	DEVEREAUX,REV
18220515	TOBIN,PATRICK	FOLEY,ANN	HEALY,ANDREW	GRANT?,ANN	EWER,REV
18220516	SYMMES?,GEORGE	ODLE,PEGGY	ROCHE,JOHN	KENNEDY,CATEHERINE	CRONIN,REV

MARRIAGES FROM HARBOUR GRACE RECORDS
1806-1845

DATEMARR	HISNAME	HERNAME	WITN1	WITN2	PRIEST
18220520	NUGENT,MICHAEL	CARBORY?,JOHANNA	MORREY,MICHAEL	MURPHY,CATHERINE	EWER,REV
18220525	CUNNINGHAM,JAMES	HINES,CATHERINE	BECKER,THOMAS	CUNNINGHAM,MARGARET	HG
18220526	MURPHY,MICHAEL	PIKE,CARROLIN	KELLY,PATRICK	CONDON,ELLEN	EWER,REV
18220527	MILLEO?,WILLIAM	SULLIVAN,JOANNE	FAHEY,PHILIP	CONNELL,MARY	CRONIN,REV
	ROACH,LAWRENCE	COULCHLOUGH,MARGARET	PHELAN,EDWARD	CRAWLEY,ELLEN	EWER,REV
18220530	MARKS,THOMAS	KENNEDY,ELLEN	FITZGERALD,JOHN-MULLOY,E	TAYLOR,JULIA	EWER,REV
18220605	MANUOY?,JAMES	DELANEY,MARY	SHEA,RICHARD	SHEA,BRIDGET	CRONIN,REV
18220615	DUNN,JOHN	INONEY?,MARTHA	DUGGAN,WILLIAM	MOORE,MARY	HG
18220623	HAWCO,THOMAS	CORBETT,MARY	CORBETT,PATRICK	BARRETT,SARAH	HG
18220628	ROW,RICHARD	COUGHLIN?,MARY	PHELAN,RICHARD	HEALY,MARIA	CRONIN,REV
18220630	WALSH,RICHARD	DUNFORD?,ALICE	CLANCY,JAMES	GRANT,ELLEN	CRONIN,REV
182206XX	ROE?,JOHN	BLACK,MARTHA	BLACK,JAMES	BUTLER,JANE	HG
18220913	DRISCOLL,MICHAEL	CHAMPION,ANN	McCARTHY,TIMOTHY?	MASKY?,ANN	DEVEREAUX,F
18220915	BUTLER,THOMAS	CURTIS,MARY	HOGAN,WILLIAM	TOBIN,MARGARET	DEVEREAUX,F
18221005	HENNECY?,JOHN	CLONEY?,ELINOR	HENNEY?,JAMES	XXX,XXX	DEVEREAUX,F
	SIMMONS,LAURENCE	BXXXX,FRANCES	KELLY,JAMES	WALL,ANN	HG
18221027	BOW,NICHOLAS	HENNACY,MARY	CONDON,RICHARD	JONES,ELLEN	EWER,REV
18221102	SKEANS,JAMES	BRINE,ELINOR	COLE,MICHAEL	SKANE,MARY	DEVEREAUX,F
18221103	HALL,EDMOND	FOGERTY,MARY	BRINE,WILLIAM	MAHAR,MARY	DEVEREAUX,F
18221104	SKEANS,JOHN	CAHILL,MARGARET	FLOOD,RICHARD	WALSH,CATHERINE	DEVEREAUX,F
18221107	KEEFE,JOHN	CONDON,MARY	KENNEDY,TIMOTHY?	JONES,ELLEN	EWER,REV
18221109	HOGAN,THOMAS	CRAWLY,PATIENCE	POWER,MICHAEL	MURPHY,JUDITH	DEVEREAUX,F
18221110	BYRNE,RICHARD	POWER,ANASTASIA	DUNN,EDMOND	CONNOLLY,JANE	MACKIN,REV
18221112	DOOLY,WILLIAM	MADDOCK,BRIDGET	CODY,THOMAS	POWER,BRIDGET	DEVEREAUX,F
	FURLONG,MICHAEL	O'BRIEN,MARY	FLEMING,PATRICK	COLBERT,RACHAEL	MACKIN,REV
	POWER,JAMES	SCANLON,MARGARET	POWER,MICHAEL	FINN,ELIZABETH	DEVEREAUX,F
	TALBOTT,THOMAS	BUTLER,MARY	KNOX,MICHAEL	WALSH,JOANNAH	DEVEREAUX,F
	WILLIAMS,JOHN	STICKLER,MARY	WALSH,MICHAEL	BARRETT,SARAH	DEVEREAUX,F
18221114	KAVANAGH,MORGAN	HURLEY,SUSANNA	KAVANAGH,JAMES	CONNEY,ANNE	MACKIN,REV
18221117	SHEA,MARTIN	WILLIAMS,XXX	MARCH,GEORGE	McGRATH,MARY	DEVEREAUX,F
18221121	FINN,JAMES	CLEARY,CATHERINE	KENNA?,RICHARD	KNOX,ELINOR	DEVEREAUX,F
18221122	COLBERT,JOHN	COLBERT,ANNE	GALL,EDMOND	DELANEY,BRIDGET	MACKIN,REV
	HURLEY,JOHN	CUMMINS,JANE	KASHESY?,DENNIS	CUMMINS,MARGARET	MACKIN,REV
	ROSE,JOSEPH	CORBETT,MARY	CODY,EDMUND	CORBITT,JOANNA	MACKIN,REV
18221123	BUTLER,THOMAS	ELMS,SUSANNAH	DELANEY,RICHARD	ELMS,MAC	DEVEREAUX,F
18221124	BRIAN,JOHN	CONNOR,MARY	JOY,JAMES	POWER,BRIDGET	DEVEREAUX,F
	KEANE,DAVID	FINN,ELIZABETH	HEALY,ANDREW	WILLY,ELINOR	MACKIN,REV
18221125	KENT,WILLIAM	KENNEDY,MARY	KENT,JOHN	KENT,MARY	DEVEREAUX,F
	TEWRY?,NICHOLAS	LEARY,ANNE	KEYS,MICHAEL	LEARY,CATHERINE	MACKIN,REV
18221127	KAVANAGH,MICHAEL	MEKIFFE?,SUSANNA	WALSH,PATRICK	WALSH,ANNE	MACKIN,REV
18221128	DWYER,EDMOND	MORRY?,ELIZABETH	KEYS,PATRICK	MARSHALL,ELIZABETH	MACKIN,REV
18221130	GUSHUE,JAMES	CROKE,CATHERINE	DXXX,JOHN	XXXX,ANASTASHIA	HG
18221210	HUNT,PATRICK	BRINE,JUDITH	BRINE,JAMES	HUNT,MARY	HG
18221221	MURPHY,MICHAEL	CONDON,JANE	ROCHE,PATRICK	SULLIVAN,JOHANNA	MACKIN,REV
18221224	POWER,PATRICK	GLAVEEN,ELINOR	MOORE,PATRICK	GLAVEEN,ELIZABETH	MACKIN,REV
18221226	DUNPHY,PATRICK	PENNY,MARGARET	FOLEY,JAMES	PENNY,ELINOR	DEVEREAUX,F
18221227	GRENEY?,JOHN	EGAN?,MARY	SCALLAN,THOMAS	XXXX,MARY	MACKIN,REV
18230107	SOOLEVAN,JOHN	NOWLAN,ALICE	NOWLAN,WILLIAM	SOOLEVAN,MARY	DEVEREAUX,F
18230115	LONG,JOHN	BURN,BRIDGET	HACHETT,JAMES	DENNING,CHARLOTT	DEVEREAUX,F

DATEMARR	HISNAME	HERNAME	WITN1	WITN2	PRIEST
18230127	POWER,JAMES	SOLEVAN,JOANNA	REARDEN,MAURICE	MORRACY,ANN	HG
18230129	BYRNE,JAMES	DENING,MARY	DENING,CHARLES	DENING,CHARLOTTE	HG
18230130	HUNT,JAMES	CORBETT,JANE	CORBETT,GEORGE	MALONE,MARY	DEVEREAUX,REV
182301XX	HICKEY,MICHAEL	MURPHY,ELINA	SULLIVAN,JOHN	KEATING,MARGARET	HG
18230202	MULLOY,PATRICK	PIKE,CATHERINE	QUIGLY?,PATRICK	CULLIN,CATHERINE	HG
18230206	ROCHFORD,JOHN	KEANE,ELIZABETH	THORNE,WILLIAM	THORNE,MARY ANN	HG
18230304	CONNELL,MICHAEL	FURLONG,MARY	GUFSN?,CHARLES	COSTELLO,MARY	HG
18230413	WALSH,PATRICK	NADDY,BRIDGET	MURPHY,JAMES	MURPHY,CATHERINE	HG
18230425	HOGAN,JAMES	FLEMING,MARGARET	FLAHERTY,GEORGE	TOXXX,CATHERINE	DEVEREAUX,REV
18230506	WALSH,JAMES	WELLS,ELLEN	FINN,THOMAS	KENNEDY,MARGARET	EWER,REV
18230512	GRAY,MICHAEL	CULLEN,MARY	CONNER,JOHN	HEALEY,MARY	HG
	LOTHER?,JAMES	MURRY,ELLEN	SHARLY,PAUL	MURPHY,JUDITH	HG
18230515	WHITE,THOMAS	NOX?,ELLEN	SHEA,MICHAEL	WALSH,JANNA	HG
18230518	MAHON,PATRICK	WXXXX,MARY OF SYLVESTER MALONE	HUNT,JAMES	KING,CATHERINE	MACKIN,REV
18230521	DOYLE,EDMOND	DOYLE,MARY	ROURKE,JOHN	DONAVAN,CATHERINE	MACKIN,REV
18230525	McCARTHY,JOHN	CONDLER,MARY	McCARTHY,CALLAGHAN	McCARTHY,DOROTHY	MACKIN,REV
18230601	RYAN,MICHAEL	KEHOE,ALICIA	NAGLE?,JOHN	CONNELL,CATHERINE	MACKIN,REV
18230606	BIRK,PATRICK	MAHONEY,ANNA	KENNEDY,MARTIN	CONNOLL,ELLEN	HG
18231001	PHELAN,JOHN	POWER,MARY	DONERVAN,PATRICK	PHELAN,ALICA	HG
18231016	BUDGEN,JAMES	MURPHY,CATHERINE	GOOLEY,JERRY	MANOUGHON,MARY	HG
18231020	HANLON,JAMES	KING,ELINOR	POWER,PATRICK	DELANEY,BRIDGET	MACKIN,REV
18231105	WALSH,RICHARD	KELLY,MARY	MORGAN,RICHARD	DAWE,GRACE	MACKIN,REV
18231113	MAHER,JAMES	KINCHELA?,MARY	DWYER,JAMES	McDONNELL,MARY	MACKIN,REV
18231116	WALSH,WILLIAM	FLOEY,MARGARET	MOORE,THOMAS	CONLY,JANE	DEVEREAUX,REV
18231120	DEOLY?,THOMAS	HICKEY,CATHERINE	NORRIS,RICHARD	HICKEY,ANASTASIA	DEVEREAUX,REV
18231123	AUSTIN,JOHN	CORBITT,JOHANNA	SLINEY?,PATRICK	WALSH,ANNE	MACKIN,REV
	GEORGE,EDWARD	CLARK,MARY	CLARK,STEPHEN	FLYNN,MARY	HG
	KELLY,JAMES	GRIFFIN,ELINOR	LARRIFSEY?,PATRICK	LECRY?,CATHERINE	MACKIN,REV
	MAGRATH,JOHN	GARDNER,ELLEN	FOLEY,JOHN	MINIGAN,MARY	HG
18231124	MURPHY,PATRICK	FARRELL,MARY	XXANVILL,PATRICK	DUNN,MARGARET	DEVEREAUX,REV
	POWER,WALTER	TERRY,MARY	WALSH,JAMES	KENNEDY,ELIZABETH	MACKIN,REV
18231126	CLANCY?,JOHN	QUINLAN,MARGARET	KEIFE?,THOMAS	SULLIVAN,MARY	MACKIN,REV
	KIELY,JAMES	BEESON,SUSANNAH	DOYLE,JAMES	DOYLE,MARY	MACKIN,REV
18231127	KEEFE,THOMAS	KENNEDY,MARY	SHEA,HENRY	FURLONG,ELINOR	MACKIN,REV
	WALSH,MAURICE	KIDNY?,ELIZABETH	SOOLEVAN?,PATRICK	RICHARDS,MARY	DEVEREAUX,REV
18231129	HAMILTON,PATRICK	MURRAY,MARY	WHITTY,WILLIAM	RICHARDS,MARY	DEVEREAUX,REV
18231203	MULLONEY,PATRICK	DWYER,MARGARET	BRGAN?,PATRICK	LEDROWE?,MARRIA	MACKIN,REV
18231204	ENGLISH,JAMES	FOGARTY,MARY	COLFORD?,PATRICK	ENGLISH,JANE	DEVEREAUX,REV
	HAWSEY,DENNIS	RIORDAN?,CATHERINE	MACKEY,PATRICK	RAFER?,MARGARET	MACKIN,REV
18231207	BURROW,ROBERT	MACCARTHY,ELLEN	MACCARTHY,JOHN	BAP?,BRIDGET	EWER,REV
18231211	DANLY,PATRICK	McNAMARA?,ANN	HURLY,MICHAEL	CODY,MARY	DEVEREAUX,REV
	KING,THOMAS	NOSIRY?,PATIENCE	KING,JOHN	WALKER,ANN	DEVEREAUX,REV
	PURRELL?,JAMES	COLBERT,RACHAEL	POWER,THOMAS	WHELAN,MARGARET	MACKIN,REV
18231212	COLFORD,PATRICK	ENGLISH,JANE	ENGLISH,JOHN	FOGARTY,MARY	DEVEREAUX,REV
18231213	COAL,MICHAEL	COAL,ANN	POOR,THOMAS	POWER,ELINOR	DEVEREAUX,REV
18231217	DOOLING,JOHN	TOBIN,MARGARET	RAWLEY,RICHARD	RYAN,ELINOR	MACKIN,REV
18231221	AUSTIN,THOMAS	CORBIT,MARGARET	MURRY,JOHN	AUSTIN,JOANNAH	DEVEREAUX,REV
18231223	FINN,MICHAEL	FOWLER,MARY	POWER,NICHOLAS	FOWLER,NICHOLAS	MACKIN,REV

DATEMARR	HISNAME	HERNAME	WITN1	WITN2	PRIEST
18231229	BROWNE,WILLIAM	MONAHAN,MARY	GOOLEY,JEREMIAH	WALSH,MARY	MACKIN,REV
18231230	CRAWLEY,JOHN	WALL,ANN	CRAWLEY,JAMES	WALL,SARAH	DEVEREAUX,REV
	DELANEY,MATTHEW	TIPPETT,SUSANNA	BRADBURY,JAMES	GEARLY?,ALICIA	MACKIN,REV
	HENNIFIN,CORNELIUS	NOWLAN,HANNAH	DUNCHINGH?,BARTHOLEMEW	SULLIVAN,MARY	DEVEREAUX,REV
18240101	HANNEN?,EDMOND	GORMAN,MARY	CARROLL,JOSEPH	KEATING,CATHERINE	DEVEREAUX,REV
18240102	KEYES?,MICHAEL	MURRY,MARY	KENNEDY,JEREMIAH	PENNELL,ELIZABETH	DEVEREAUX,REV
18240103	WHITE,THOMAS	FITZGERALD,ELINOR	WALSH,MAURICE	MURPHY,ELINOR	MACKIN,REV
18240104	GRACE,EDWARD	MULLOWNEY,ELINOR	DUNFORD,THOMAS	GRANT,ELINOR	MACKIN
18240108	O'DAUNELL?,JOHN	CASEY,BRIDGET	CALAHAN,PATRICK	NORRIS,MARY	MACKIN,REV
18240111	GEORGE,RICHARD	FARRELL,HONORA	PHELAN,JOHN	GEORGE,MARGARET	DEVEREAUX,REV
18240113	CODDLE,RICHARD	SAVANEY,CHARLOTTE	HALY,JOHN	KELLY,MARIA	MACKIN,REV
18240118	BOUZAN,THOMAS	WALSH,ELINOR	SULLIVAN,JEREMIAH	EGENTOU?,MARGARET	MACKIN
18240120	BABBE?,RICHARD	KENNEDY,BRIDGET	BABBE,WILLIAM	KENNEDY,CATHERINE	MACKIN,REV
18240129	KELLY,PATRICK	CONDON,ALICIA	CONDON,GARRETT	CONDON,REBECCA	MACKIN,REV
	MOORE,PATRICK	WISEMAN,ELINOR	RYAN,JOHN	RICHARDS,JANE	DEVEREAUX,REV
18240201	MURPHY,ANTHONY	NORRIS,MARY	CRANE,DANIEL	NOWLAN,ANN	DEVEREAUX,REV
18240204	FAHEY,MICHAEL	LYNCH,ELLEN	FAHEY,WILLIAM	FAHEY,ELIZABETH	EWER,REV
18240208	SHEA,MICHAEL	WALSH,JOANNAH	HARDING,WILLIAM	HOLLY,ANN	DEVEREAUX,REV
18240219	FARRELL,MAURICE	CARBURY,MARY	PURCELL,RICHARD	ROBERTS,MARGARET	MACKIN,REV
18240220	BRENNAN,PETER	MARSHALL,ELIZABETH	MARSHALL,WILLIAM	BARRETT,EDMOND	EWER,REV
	McCARTHY,DENNIS	DOOLING,MARGARET	XXXX,JOHN	RYAN,JOHN????	EWER,REV
18240226	BOLEN,JOHN	BARREN,MARY	RYAN,JAMES	QUINLIN,ELIZABETH	DEVEREAUX,REV
18240229	JOY,MICHAEL	MARSHALL,ANN	NOX?,MICHAEL	KENNY,MARGARET	EWER,REV
18240301	RICHARDS,GEORGE	DWER?,MARY	RONAN,FRANCIS	RONAN,MARY	EWER,REV
18240317	GEAR,THOMAS	MAGRATH,MARY	MAGRATH,JOHN	CONNELL,MARY	EWER,REV
18240320	McCAB,JAMES	DRISCOLL,BRIDGET	DOOLING,THOMAS	GUSS,JOANNAH	DEVEREAUX,REV
18240423	HICKEY,PATRICK	GILVAY,MARY	BOLEN,DENNIS	KELLY,BRIDGET	DEVEREAUX,REV
18240502	PEARSON,ROBERT	BARNES,MARY	MURPHY,EDMOND	ENGLISH,ELIZABETH	MACKIN,REV
18240513	WALSH,JAMES	DELANEY,ANN	RYAN,PETER	WALSH,ANN	DEVEREAUX,REV
18240516	KAVANAGH,JAMES	TILLEY,ELIZABETH	WALSH,JOHN	NOONAN,JOHANNA	MACKIN,REV
18240519	HEARN,WILLIAM	BOLAND,SARAH	FAHEY,JOHN	FITZGERALD,JOHANNA	MACKIN,REV
18240520	PHELAN,EDMOND	MULLONY,CATHERINE	RACH?,LUKE	PHELAN,CATHERINE	DEVEREAUX,REV
18240602	FREANY?,RICHARD	BIGGS,SARAH	DONNELLY,WILLIAM	FOSTER,FRANCES	DEVEREAUX,REV
18240609	PAUL,PATRICK	DRISCOLL,CATHERINE	HARRINGTON,TIMOTHY?	ENGLISH,CATHERINE	MACKIN,REV
18240610	BRAZIL,JOHN	FOSTER,FRANCIS?	FREANY,JAMES	BIGGS,SARAH	DEVEREAUX,REV
	BRAZIL,WILLIAM	BARRETT,SRAH	FREANY,JAMES	FOSTER,FRANCES	DEVEREAUX,REV
18240910	FITZGERALD,MICHAEL	PEARLE,,MARY	BRENNAN,PATRICK	WALSH,JOHANNA	MACKIN,REV
18240914	BRODERICK,JOSEPH	KEEFE,MARY	BURKE,JOHN	MULLONEY,ANN	MACKIN,REV
18241014	GRACE,EDMOND	WALL,ELINOR	HEARN,JAMES	SCANLAN,JOANNA	DEVEREAUX,REV
	McGAHEY,FRANCIS	GUFSN?,JOANNA	FARLEY,OWN	GUFSN,ANN	DEVEREAUX,REV
18241015	NOWLAN,JOHN	HAYSE,ELISA	COB?,JAMES	HAYSE,ANN	DEVEREAUX,REV
18241018	WALSH,EDMOND	HOGAN,MARGARET	WALSH,PATRICK	HOGAN,JULIAN	DEVEREAUX,REV
18241101	KEHOE,MICHAEL	LEARY,CATHERINE	GRIFFIN,RICHARD	COLE,ELIZA	DEVEREAUX,REV
18241104	COLLINS,THOMAS	HOULAHAN,HONOR	WALSH,PATRICK	CONOLLY,JANE	MACKIN,REV
	DIERNEY,PHILIP	SKEHAN,ELIZABETH	CALUHAN,PATRICK	DELANEY,AMELIA	MACKIN,REV
	DROHAN,JOHN	HALLEHAN,ELINOR	CEARY,GEORGE	WALSH,MARY	DEVEREAUX,REV
18241108	DELANEY,JOHN	MIFSN?,FRANCES	DELANEY,MATTHEW	CUMMINS,MARY	DEVEREAUX,REV
18241110	GULLIVANTA?,THOMAS	KEET?,MARGARET	CARYE?,GEORGE	WITCH,JOHANA	HG
18241111	COSCORAS?,MICHAEL	HYNES,MARY	HYNES,RICHARD	HARRINGTON,MARY	MACKIN,REV

DATEMARR	HISNAME	HERNAME	WITN1	WITN2	PRIEST
18241116	FOGARTY,THOMAS	BIGGS,ANN	FOGARTY,PHILIP	HOGAN,MARY	DEVEREAUX,REV
	TOBIN,RICHARD	HOGAN,MARGARET	TOBIN,JAMES	RIGS,ANN	DEVEREAUX,REV
18241117	CONLY,JAMES	RICHARDS,CATHERINE	MACKEY,JOHN	BURN,JUDITH	DEVEREAUX,REV
18241119	DOYLE,MICHAEL	ENGLISH,ELIZABETH	FARRELL,MORGAN	ENGLISG,SARAH	DEVEREAUX,REV
18241123	HARTY,PHILIP	CARBERRY,HANNAH	EGENTON?,FRANCIS	EGENTON?,MARY	MACKIN,REV
	MOORE,PHILIP	GORDON,CATHERINE	DALTON,THOMAS	FOX,JOHANNA	MACKIN,REV
	SEWARD,JAMES	FARDY,MALY?	HOLLOHAN,JOHN	EGENTON,ELINOR	MACKIN,REV
18241125	CONNELL,JOHN	BRAWTHER,SARAH	CURRAN,RICHARD	McCARTHY,ELINOR	MACKIN,REV
	TOBIN,THOMAS	RICHARDSON,MARY	MULCAHY,TIMOTHY?	KELLY,MARY	MACKIN,REV
18241127	CONNERY,JAMES	MURPHY,JOHANNA	DUNN,PATRICK	CANTY,MARGARET	MACKIN,REV
	MEANY,PHILIP	CONNELL,JOANNA	MEANY,JOHN	McGEE,MARY	DEVEREAUX,REV
18241130	BRODERICK,JOHN	KELLY,MARY	FENNELL?,SLYVESTER	GRACE,SARAH	MACKIN,REV
1824117	HARDEN,WILLIAM	HALLY?,ANN	MACKEY,JOHN	McKEE,MARY	DEVEREAUX,REV
18241207	SULLIVAN,CORNELUS	WOODFORD,MARY	REGAN,DENNIS	KEATING,CATHERINE	DEVEREAUX,REV
	WHELAN,MICHAEL	HEARN,ELINOR	MADDIN,NICHOLAS	HAYES,MARY?	MACKIN,REV
18241210	RYAN,PETER	ROACHFORD,MARGARET	GRACE,EDMOND	KETAING,CATHERINE	DEVEREAUX,REV
	TIMOTHY,ROURK	BISON,RACHAEL	WETCH?,JOHN	BARRETT,ANN	DEVEREAUX,REV
18241214	WETCH,JOHN	LUIS?,ELIZA	LUIS,MOSES	WALSH,BRIDGET	DEVEREAUX,REV
18241220	FLYNN,WILLIAM	KENNEDY,ANNIE	CLARKE,STEPHEN	FLYNN,MARY	MACKIN,REV
	LYNCH,PATRICK	BRITT,MARGARET	GUSHUE,DENNIS	BRITT,MARY	MACKIN,REV
18241230	KEET?,DAVID	MURPHY,CATHERINE	WALSH,PATRICK	WALSH,MARY	MACKIN,REV
18250108	KEEFE,JOHN	WALSH,ELIZA	WALSH,THOMAS	MAHONEY,MARY	DEVEREAUX,REV
18250111	HAWCO,THOMAS	BARRETT,SARAH	HAWCO,JOHN	KENNEDY,BRIDGET	DEVEREAUX,REV
	POWER,JOSEPH	MERRIGAN,MARY	BYRNE,JAMES	ST.JOHN,CATHERINE	MACKIN,REV
	POWER,WILLIAM	McDONNELL,MARY	MALONE,THOMAS	MAHER,MARY	MACKIN,REV
18250112	TUOMEY,(KENNEDY)?	GORDON,JANE	HANRAHAN,ROGER	DALY,CATHERINE	MACKIN,REV
18250113	LEE,WILLIAM	WELLS,FRANCES	HEFFERNAN,RICHARD	McCARTHY,ELINOR	MACKIN,REV
18250115	BARTLER,PIERCE	GEORGE,MARGARET	WHELAN,JOHN	WHELAN,ELISA	DEVEREAUX,REV
18250125	FLYNN,WILLIAM	WALSH,MARY	KENNEDY,TIMOTHY?	PRENDERGAST	DEVEREAUX,REV
18250127	BEACON?,THOMAS	LEARY,MARY	LEARY,PETER	CUDAGH?,MARY	DEVEREAUX,REV
	CODY,JOHN	WALSH,HONORA	MALONE,THOMAS	ENGLISH,CATHERINE	DEVEREAUX,REV
18250201	GRIFFIN,WALTER	LYNCH,EMILIA	MADDEN,JAMES	RYAN,ELINOR	DEVEREAUX,REV
	PENDERGAST,JAMES L	BRANSFIELD,MARGARET	FITZGERALD,JOHN	McCARTHY,ELISA	MACKIN
18250211	CORBIN,RICHARD	McGUIRE,ELIZABETH	DONNELY,JOHN	HUNT,JOHN	DEVEREAUX,REV
18250215	MORRISSEY,THOMAS	FARRELL,JOHANNA	CALLAGHAN,PATRICK	TOBIN,MARY	MACKIN,REV
18250307	LEARY,JAMES	WALL,SARAH	WHELAN,EDMUND	FINLEY?,MARGARET	MACKIN,REV
18250426	MACKEY,JOHN	McCARTHY,ELIZABETH	McCARTHY,JOHN	McCARTHY,MARY	DEVEREAUX,REV
18250513	WHELAN,THOMAS	WALKER,SUSANNAH	WALKER,WILLIAM	WHELAN,ALICIA	MACKIN,REV
18250523	BURN?,JOHN	DELANEY,EMILIA	GORDON,MARK	DOYLE,MARY	DEVEREAUX,REV
18250605	McCARTHY,FELIX	PIKE,JULIA	HAMILTON,CHARLES	MORRY?,ELIZABETH	MACKIN,REV
18250620	MURPHY,THOMAS	GEARY,JOANNAH	MURPHY,THOMAS	GEARY,ELINOR	DEVEREAUX,REV
18250918	DWYER,JAMES	ENGLISH,SARAH	ENGLISH,WILLIAM	BOLAN?,ELINOR	DEVEREAUX,REV
18250925	NOWLAN,WILLIAM	QUINLAN,BRIDGET	SHEA,RICHARD	PENNELL?,MARGARET	MACKIN,REV
18250929	POWER,JOHN	CARRELL,ANN	NEIL,THOMAS	KEHOE,JOHN????	DEVEREAUX,REV
18251013	BENNETT,JAMES	BARRETT,FRANCES	BROWN,NICHOLAS	KENNEDY,MARY	MACKIN,REV
18251111	LYNCH,JOHN	PENNELL,ANN	LAMB,MICHAEL	MARSHALL,ELISA	DEVEREAUX,REV
18251113	KAVANAGH,MORGAN	WALSH,SARAH	RYAN,THOMAS	WALSH,MARY	MACKIN,REV
18251117	MURPHY,PETER	MCDONALD,MARY	FITZGERALD,JOHN	FOGARTY,BRIDGET	DEVEREAUX,REV
18251122	BARRETT,EDMOND	DALTON,MARY	BRAND,PATRICK	GORMAN,ELIZABETH	DEVEREAUX,REV

MARRIAGES FROM HARBOUR GRACE RECORDS
1806-1845

DATEMARR	HISNAME	HERNAME	WITN1	WITN2	PRIEST
18251124	POWER,WILLIAM	WALSH,MARY	HITCHENHAM,THOMAS	CONNOLLY,JANE	MACKIN,REV
18251126	KEYES,PATRICK	ROACH,MARGARET	MACKEY,JOHN	ROACH,ELINOR	DEVEREAUX,REV
18251127	WALSH,WILLIAM	FLYNN,CATHERINE	WALL,JOHN	MYERS,MARY	MACKIN,REV
18251128	HUNT,JAMES	KEANE,MARY	SHEEHAN,EDMUND	LANDERS,MARY	MACKIN,REV
18251201	CORBETT,BARTHOLMEW	CHATMAN,ANN	DEE,PATRICK	MORACY?,ELINOR	DEVEREAUX,REV
18251217	WALSH,MICHAEL	McGRATHY,MARY	HOLLOHAN,JOHN	EHGLISH,CATHERINE	MACKIN,REV
18260105	JONES,JAMES	FITZGERALD,MARY	HARNEY,JOHN	JONES,MARGARET	MACKIN,REV
	NORCOTT,WILLIAM	WISEMAN,REBECCA	RICHARDS,WILLIAM	RICHARDS,ISABELLA	MACKIN,REV
	SCANLON,JEREMIAH	RONAN,REBECCA	BAYLEY,JOHN	FOWLER,SUSANNAH	MACKIN,REV
18260109	HEARN,TIMOTHY?	JONES,JOHANNA	WHELAN,MICHAEL	HEARN,CATHERINE	MACKIN,REV
18260116	HARRINGTON?,DANIEL	KELLY,CATHERINE	MEANY,PATRICK	MACHLER?,MARGARET	MACKIN,REV
18260202	POWER,JOHN	DONEVAN,MARAGRET	CEARY?,PATRICK	WALSH,MARY	DEVEREAUX,REV
18260206	MOLLEY,RICHARD	CAHILL,ELINOR	ALWARD?,NICHLOAS	PYNNE,PATIENCE	MACKIN,REV
18260207	BUTLER,PATRICK	THOMEY,ELIZABETH	HUNT,EDMOND	HOWES,PATRICK	DEVEREAUX,REV
18260317	LONG,PATRICK	DOBBIN,HONORA	MANSFIELD,ROBERT	SMART,MARY	MACKIN,REV
18260411	POWER,JAMES	McCARTHY,DOROTHY	McCARTHY,CHARLES	McCARTHY,MARY	DEVEREAUX,REV
18260412	PARSONS,EDWARD	NORCOTT,ALICIA	BOLAND,DENNIS	DUGGAN,ANASTASIA	MACKIN,REV
18260413	LEONARD,JEREMIAH	MURPHY,ANN	BOLAND,DENNIS	ENGLISH,CATHERINE	MACKIN,REV
18260512	BRINE,THOMAS	KEHOE,ALICE	MOLLEY,RICHARD	WALSH,MARY	DEVEREAUX,REV
18260520	HULAND?,JAMES	PEDDLE,PATIENCE	ST.JOHN,EDMOND	CODY,ELINOR	DEVEREAUX,REV
	SOOLEVAN,THOMAS	CONNELL,MARY	LONRIGAN?,RICHARD	MURPHY,JAMES?	DEVEREAUX,REV
18260521	DEALNEY,RICHARD	COMMINS,ELIZABETH	DELANEY,JAMES	CUMMINS,MARY	DEVEREAUX,REV
	FAHEY,JOHN	NOSEWORTHY,ELIZABETH	KAVANAGH,PATRICK	NOSEWORTHY,SUSANNA	MACKIN,REV
	HAYES,JOHN	McCARTHY,MARY	CAREY,GEORGE	JAMES,MARY	MACKIN,REV
18260523	DOOLING,JOHN	MULCAHY,MARY	RYAN,JERRY	RYAN,ANNE	DEVEREAUX,REV
18260524	WALSH,JAMES	HICKEY,ANASTASIA	TALLENT,TOBIAS	CALLEHAN,PATRICK	DEVEREAUX,REV
18260525	CLANCEY,THOMAS	DEALY,ANN	KEAN,DAVID	CRAWLY,ELINOR	DEVEREAUX,REV
18260528	BRAHAN,JAMES	MURPHY,ANNE	WRIGHT,JOHN	LYNG?,WILLIAM???	DEVEREAUX,REV
18260605	McGRATH,THOMAS	PENNELL?,ELIZABETH	GRACE,EDMOND	KEATINS?,CATHERINE	DEVEREAUX,REV
18260608	POWER,JOHN	ROSE,MARY	HEARN,WILLIAM	HAYDEN,ELIZABETH	MACKIN,REV
18260611	BAYLY,JOHN	CAHILL,CATHERINE	CAHILL,JOHN	CONNORS,JOHANNA	MACKIN,REV
18260612	BRINE,PATRICK	PLOWMAN?,CATHERINE	DOYLE,JAMES	KELLY,ELIZABETH	DEVEREAUX,REV
18260614	COLE,JAMES	KEATING,MARGARET	GORMAN,JOHN	GORMAN,MARTHA	MACKIN,REV
18260615	DAWSON,JAMES	RUFSELL,MABILLA	WHELAN,PIERCE	RUFSELL,ANNE	MACKIN,REV
18260617	MORAN,NICHOLAS	McCARTHY,ANNE	MACKEY,JOHN	MORAR?,MARY	MACKIN,REV
18260621	GORMAN,THOMAS	GEARY,BRIDGET	DOYLE,MORGAN	SULLIVAN,CORNELIUS	DEVEREAUX,REV
18260622	KING,JAMES	DELANEY,BRIDGET	MOLLOY,NICHOLAS	BYRNE,JAMES???	DEVEREAUX,REV
18260623	LEARY,WILLIAM	CONWAY,CATHERINE	LLOYD,THOMAS	HOGAN,EDWARD	DEVEREAUX,REV
18260624	CONNORS,PATRICK	COLBIRT?,ELIZABETH	BYRNE,JAMES	MAHAR,BRIDGET	DEVEREAUX,REV
18260904	CULLEN,MICHAEL	WALSH,MARGARET	POWER,THOMAS	DUNN,JAMES	DEVEREAUX,REV
18260910	ENGLISH,WILLIAM	DELANEY,CATHERINE	DWYER,JAMES	HICKS,RICHARD	DEVEREAUX,REV
18261008	JAMES,JOHN	WALSH,ELIZABETH	TAYLOR,EDMUND	DOYLE,ELIZABETH	MACKIN,REV
18261010	KELLY,JOHN	JAMES,HENNIETTA	MOLLOY,NICHOLAS	BURKE,MARY	MACKIN,REV
	SLINEY?,PATRICK	HAWCO,MARTHA	DUFF,ARTHUR	MYERS,MARY	MACKIN,REV
18261014	CORBETT,PATRICK	MURPHY,JOHANNA	WALSH,JAMES	HACKETT,JAMES??	MACKIN,REV
18261028	CURRIN,JAMES	WITCH,SOFIA	WITCH,JOHN	WITCH,ELIZABETH	DEVEREAUX,REV
	MURPHY,PATRICK	POWER,MARY	BUNSELL,PATRICK	KELLY,PATRICK??	DEVEREAUX,REV
18261102	COLE,WILLIAM	MOORES,ELIZABETH	BRYAN,JOHN	COLE,CHARLOTTE	MACKIN,REV
	GRIFFIN,RICHARD	COLE,ELIZABETH	GUSHUE,JOHN	GUSHUE,MARGARET	MACKIN,REV

DATEMARR	HISNAME	HERNAME	WITN1	WITN2	PRIEST
18261104	KELLY,EDMOND	DEE,MARGARET	DEE,MICHAEL	ENGLISH,MARY	HG
18261107	KEHOE,CAROLAN?MAN	BRYAN,BRIDGET	EARLE,THOMAS	SCANLAN,REBECCA	MACKIN,REV
18261112	CROKE,RICHARD	POWER,BRIDGET	CASEY,JOHN	CALLAHAN,XXXX	DEVEREAUX,REV
18261113	FORD,THOMAS	DOBBIN,MARY	BYRNE,JOHN	GALWAY,ELIZABETH	MACKIN,REV
	NORCOTT,JOSEPH	BYRNE,MARY	DOBBIN,NICHOLAS	KILFOYLE?,ELIZABETH	MACKIN,REV
18261116	GOODSVILLE?,JOHN	WHELAN,ALICE	WALSH,JAMES	BUGS?,SARAH	DEVEREAUX,REV
	MEANY,PATRICK	DRICOLL,MARIA	MACKEY,JOHN	KENNEDY,MARGARET	MACKIN,REV
18261117	KINSELLA,JAMES	BOWE,CATHERINE	BAYLEY,JAMES	DONOVAN,CATHERINE	MACKIN,REV
18261118	WHELAN,MARTIN	BRINE,MARGARET	MANIVELL,TOBIAS	CASHMAN?,JOHN	DEVEREAUX,REV
18261120	MURPHY,JOHN	BRITT,MARY	HEARN,TIMOTHY	GLAVEEN?,RICHARD	DEVEREAUX,REV
18261125	BRINE,BARTHOLEMEW	WITCH,ELIZABETH	KIELY,JOHN	WITCH,JOHN	DEVEREAUX,REV
	HEARN,JOHN	DALTON,MARY	KIDNY?,PATRICK	FITZGERALD,ELIZABETH	DEVEREAUX,REV
18261127	HINCHY?,WILLIAM	FITZGERALD,ELINOR	DUNN,JOHN	POWER,NICHOLAS	DEVEREAUX,REV
18261128	GAMBON?,JOHN	NUGENT,MARY	MEANY,PATRICK	NUGENT,WILLIAM	DEVEREAUX,REV
	MORAN,JOHN	McCARTHY,MARIA	McCARTHY,JOHN	McCARTHY,MARY	MACKIN,REV
18261130	CONDON,GARRETT	CASEY,MARY	POWER,JAMES	BAYLEY,FRANCES	DEVEREAUX,REV
	HEARN,WILLIAM	FITZGERALD,JANE	FAHEY,JOHN	FITZGERALD,JOHN	DEVEREAUX,REV
	HOWES,PATRICK	CONNOR,CATHERINE	HUNT,EDMOND	BUTLER,PATRICK	DEVEREAUX,REV
	McCARTHY,CHARLES	CANTY,NARGARET	HOWARD,DAVID	RICHARDS,ISUBELLA?	MACKIN,REV
18261204	WHELAN,JAMES	OSBURN,MARY	FORD,THOMAS	FORD,MARY	DEVEREAUX,REV
18261210	BROPHY,MICHAEL	KELLY,MARGARET	BYRNE,JOHN	MYERS,MARY	MACKIN,REV
18261219	RICHARS,WILLIAM	MACKEY,ANNE	PHELAN,WALTER	GRUBERT?,ARTHUR	DEVEREAUX,REV
182612XX	FITZGERALD,PATRICK	DOOLIND?,ANASTASIA	HIANE?,MICHAEL	SOUGHLIN?,MARGARET	MACKIN,REV
18270102	DUGGAN,JOHN	CRONAN,BRIDGET	HEARN,WILLIAM	FINN,PATRICK??	DEVEREAUX,REV
18270104	TOBIN,PATRICK	FITZGERALD,ANN	KEATING,MICHAEL	TRAPNELL,ELIZABETH	DEVEREAUX,REV
18270107	BECKETT,WILLIAM	WHELAN,ELIZABETH	BECKETT,JOHN	KENNEDY,THOMAS??	DEVEREAUX,REV
	MURPHY,DENNIS	MAGHER?,CICCLIA?	BONAN?,PATRICK	FLEMING,CATHERINE	DEVEREAUX,REV
18270108	BRITT,PIERCE	HUNT,MARY	FLYNN,EDMOND	ROCHE?,MARGARET	MACKIN,REV
	MURPHY,DAVID	WALSH,JOHANNA	KENNY,DAVID	CONNELL,ELINOR	MACKIN,REV
18270109	GUSHUE,NICHOLAS	SKEHAN?,ANNE	SHEHAN?,JOHN	GUSHUE,MARGARET	MACKIN,REV
18270110	PURCELL,WILLIAM	MACKEY,BRIDGET	COONEY,PATRICK	BEESON,MARY	MACKIN,REV
18270111	KENNEDY,ROGER	WALSH,BRIDGET	LEWIS,MOSES	KENNEDY,MARY	MACKIN,REV
18270112	DUFF,ARTHUR	MYERS,MARY	BROWN,NICHOLAS	KEATING,CATHERINE	MACKIN,REV
18270113	CRAWLEY,JAMES	MULLONEY,MARY	SULLIVAN,TIMOTHY?	MULLONEY,ELIZABETH	MACKIN,REV
18270114	BUTLER,PATRICK	DUNEVAN,CATHERINE	QUIGLEY,PATRICK	BUCKLY,JOHN	DEVEREAUX,REV
18270116	McCARTHY,DANIEL	McCARTHY,MARGARET	FARRELL,DANIEL	McCARTHY,WILLIAM	DEVEREAUX,REV
	SULLIVAN,JOHN	FARRELL,ELINOR	KEEFE,THOMAS	FOSTER,ELIZABETH	MACKIN,REV
18270123	DUHIGG?,MICHAEL	DONOVAN,ELINOR	WALSH,JAMES	LEARY,EDMOND	MACKIN,REV
18270128	McDERMOTT,PATRICK	GOLD,ELIZABETH	GOLD,JAMES	HEARN,JOHN???	DEVEREAUX,REV
	PHELAN,EDMOND	BRINE,MARY	BRINE,MICHAEL	WRIGHT,JOHN???	DEVEREAUX,REV
18270130	HURLY,JOHN	McGUIRE,FRANCES	CONNELL,JOHN	HURLY,MAURICE	DEVEREAUX,REV
18270210	WALSH,JAMES	KELLY,SARAH	KELLY,JAMES	TOBIN,MICHAEL	DEVEREAUX,REV
18270322	CULLEN,MICHAEL	KENNY,MARY	CONNELL,RICHARD	GUSHUE,MARGARET	MACKIN,REV
18270501	PHELAN,JOHN	BAGGS,JANE	GUSELE?,JOHN	FINGRACE?,RICHARD	EWER,REV
18270503	NONNAN,THOMAS	CULLINAN,MARY	MOLLEY,EDMOND	HELY,MARY	MACKIN,REV
18270513	BRODERS,JOHN	DUFFETT,CATHERINE	BRADY,JOHN	COTTER,EDMOND	DEVEREAUX,REV
18270514	DREADY,MAURICE	CODY,ELINOR	MORRIARTY,RICHARD	MORAHEM?,MARGARET	MACKIN,REV
18270516	DRISCOLL,WILLIAM	FLYNN,MARY	SEE?,WILLIAM	HURLEY,MARY	MACKIN,REV
18270521	CULLEN,EDMOND	PRENDERGAST,MARY	POWER,DAVID	MEEGHER?,MARY	MACKIN,REV

MARRIAGES FROM HARBOUR GRACE RECORDS
1806-1845

DATEMARR	HISNAME	HERNAME	WITN1	WITN2	PRIEST
18270521	PHELAN,JOHN	BAGGS,JANE	COSTELLO,JOHN	COSTELLO,ANESTIC?	HG
18270522	DOBBIN,NICHOLAS	GALWAY,ELIZABETH	DOBBIN,GEORGE	FAD,MARY	MACKIN,REV
	SLATTEY,MICHAEL	FLEMING,MARGARET	KINCHELA?,JOHN	FLEMING,ELINOR	MACKIN,REV
18270523	BRITT,JAMES	WALSH,JOHANNA	INNOTT?,JOSEPH	CONDON,REBECCA	MACKIN,REV
	SHEA,THOMAS	FOWLER,SUSANNAH	FRISBY,JOHN	CASEY,MARGARET	MACKIN,REV
18270527	JONSON,WILLIAM	MURPHY,ANN	COLBERT,JAMES	MURPHY,MARY	DEVEREAUX,REV
18270529	MURPHY,JAMES	ROSE,ELIZABETH	LONREGAN?,RICHARD	POWER,JOHN	DEVEREAUX,REV
18270603	BRENNAN,RICHARD	BRENNAN,CATHERINE	DOWLING,JOHN	MADDOCKS,MARGARET	MACKIN,REV
18270605	MARSHALL,WILLIAM	CROKE,MARGARET	CUDDIHY,JAMES	LANIGAN?,ELINOR	MACKIN,REV
18270606	MADDON,NICHOLAS	HEARN,CATHERINE	HEARN,JOHN	HICKEY,MARY	MACKIN,REV
18270609	SCANLAN,PATRICK	DOOLY,CATHERINE	CONNELL,JOHN	BOE,THOMAS	DEVEREAUX,REV
18270610	DOOLY,DANIEL	BURKE,MARY	MARSHALL,ROBERT	SCANDLAN?,JERRY?	DEVEREAUX,REV
	POWER,RICHARD	NOSEWORTHY,JANE	FLYNN,DAVID	CONNELLY,JANE	MACKIN,REV
18270611	SWORDS,JAMES	SKENHAN,MARY	SEXTON?,LAWRENCE	RICHARDS,MARTHA	MACKIN,REV
18270612	FANTON,THOMAS	POWER,BRIDGET	HOGAN,DANIEL	ENGLISH,CATHERINE	DEVEREAUX,REV
18270624	KENNA,PATRICK	WHELAN,ELIZABETH	HARDING,ROBERT	CASEY,MARGARET	MACKIN,REV
18270712	WALLACE,PATRICK	FARRELL,MARY	GRENNE?,DANIEL	RICHARDS,MARY	MACKIN,REV
182707XX	BEALY,JAMES	CROAK? OF MUSKECTY?	ROURK,PATRICK	HEADEN,MARY	EWER,REV
18270914	ENGLISH,THOMAS	NEIL,ANASTAIA	BROWNE,HENRY	SLOGAN,JANE	MACKIN,REV
18270918	BURKE,WILLIAM	HEALY,MARY	CULLIN,NICHOLAS	McGEE,MARY	DEVEREAUX,REV
18270923	MOUIPEY?,LAWRENCE	BAGGES,SARAH	MURPHY,PATRICK	DUNN,MARY	MACKIN,REV
18271008	WHELAN,JOHN	WHITE,ANASTASIA	WHELAN,PATRICK	BUTLER,MARGARET	MACKIN,REV
18271009	GEARY,WILLIAM	FARRELL,MARY	BRAHAN,EDMOND	GRIFFIN,MARGARET	MACKIN,REV
18271011	LYNCH,JOHN	DERMODY?,DOROTHY	BRENNAN,JOHN	FAHEY,ELINOR	MACKIN,REV
18271016	WALSH,RICHARD	FARY,MARGARET	ROURK?,MICHAEL	LUIS?,ANN	DEVEREAUX,REV
18271028	ROACH,STEPHAN	HOWLAN,CATHERINE	WALSH,MAURICE	HABERLIN?,MARY-ANN	DEVEREAUX,REV
18271101	SMITH,MICHAEL	CAVANARY,SUSANNA	RYAN,JAMES	FREEMAN,MICHAEL	DEVEREAUX,REV
18271103	CEAREA,JOHN	POWER,MARY	SHOW?,WILLIAM	HEALY,CATHERINE	DEVEREAUX,REV
18271104	HENNESSEY,JOHN	DORAN,ANASTAIA	HURLEY,MICHAEL	DORAN,CATHERINE	MACKIN,REV
18271105	POWER,NICHOLAS	WALSH,BRIDGET	FRYNN?,PATRICK	CAREY,MARY	EWER,REV
18271111	CONNORS,DAVID	PRENDERGAST,ELIZABETH	FANNING,PATRICK	DUNN,MARGARET	MACKIN,REV
18271118	DAWLEY,WILLIAM	KENNY,MARY	CASHMAN?,PATRICK	CUSICK?,JOHN	DEVEREAUX,REV
18271119	HICKS,RICHARD	MURPHY,HONORA	MURPHY,JOHN	MURPHY,MARY	DEVEREAUX,REV
18271120	HIGGINS,PATRICK	WHELAN,MARY	DUHY?,MICHAEL	MULCAHY,MARY	DEVEREAUX,REV
	TROL?,JOHN	BRINE,SUSANNA	HAYSE,THOMAS	McCARTHY,MICHAEL	DEVEREAUX,REV
18271121	BOMAN?,WILLIAM	SCULLY,JUDITH	FITZPATRICK,EDMOND	CEACY,MARGARET	DEVEREAUX,REV
18271129	CRAWLEY,JOHN	RIARDEN?,HONORA	KENT,JOHN	LONG,JOHN	DEVEREAUX,REV
18271201	FLYNN,THOMAS	RYAN,BRIDGET	BROWN,JOHN	CAREY,MARGARET	EWER,REV
	KANE,JOHN	COSSLY?,JANE	CONLY?,JEFFERY	CONLY,MARGARET	DEVEREAUX,REV
18271203	KING,MICHAEL	SPARK,MARY	FLYNN,PATRICK	WHELAN,THOMAS	DEVEREAUX,REV
18271204	BRINE,DANIEL	QUINLIN,ELIZABETH	GALL,PATRICK	QUINLIN,BRIDGET	DEVEREAUX,REV
	HAYES,JOHN	WALKER,MARY	NOWLAN,JOHN	WALKER,WILLIAM	DEVEREAUX,REV
18271206	ETCHINGHAM?,THOMAS	McGUIRE,ELIZABETH	WILLIAMS,THOMAS	MARTIN,ELINOR	DEVEREAUX,REV
18271207	GORDON,MARK	RYAN,MARY	HENNECY?,JAMES	HEALY,CATHERINE	DEVEREAUX,REV
18271210	LUIS?,JOHN	MULLOWNY?,ELIZABETH	KENNEDY,ROGER	WOODFORD,ANN	DEVEREAUX,REV
18271214	WALSH,PATRICK	SHAUCHENRY?,MARY	PHELAN,RICHARD	DALTON,BARBARA	EWER,REV
18271215	WOODFORD,WILLIAM	WOODFORD,ANN	JOY,JAMES	GORMAN,JOHN	DEVEREAUX,REV
18271216	KENNY,DAVID	WALSH,MARGARET	WADE,JAMES	COSMELL?,ELINOR	DEVEREAUX,REV
	WALSH,JOHN	SULLIVAN,MARY	TERRY,WILLIAM	MOORES,CATHERINE	DEVEREAUX,REV

DATEMARR	HISNAME	HERNAME	WITN1	WITN2	PRIEST
18271217	SOLIVAN,JERRY	TXXXX,ELLEN	COLLINS,JOHN	MAGHER,MARY	EWER,REV
18271218	GRACE,EDMOND	PENNELL?,MARGARET	KIEFFE?,THOMAS	KEATING,CATHERINE	DEVEREAUX,REV
18271219	XXX,DANIEL	HOW,NORRY?	GLASTER,PATRICK	MORREY,CATHERINE	EWER,REV
18271222	LOID?,CHARLES	QUINLIN,BRIDGET	GALL,PATRICK	WHELAN,CATHERINE	DEVEREAUX,REV
	PENNELL?,WILLIAM	KEATING,CATHERINE	JOY,JAMES	GORMAN,MARTHA	DEVEREAUX,REV
18271223	NOWLAN,JERRY	MAHONY,MARY	FLINN?,WILLIAM	CONNELL,ELINOR	DEVEREAUX,REV
	SWEETMAN?,NICHOLAS	JOY,JANE	SHEA,JOHN	KEATING,CATHERINE	DEVEREAUX,REV
18280101	DORAN,PETER	MADDICK,CATHERINE	BRENAN,WILLIAM	DOYLE,ANNE	DEVEREAUX,REV
18280103	BUTLER,THOMAS	DORAN,CATHERINE	DUNN,JOHN	HINBERT?,MARGARET	EWER,REV
	KINT?,JOHN	DOBBIN,ANN	CRAWLY,JOHN	LONG,JOHN	DEVEREAUX,REV
18280106	BROWN,MICHAEL	CLARKE,CATHERINE	FLYNN,PATRICK	CLARKE,ELLEN	EWER,REV
18280108	GRIFFIN,THOMAS	MUGHER?,MARY	PHELAN,RICHARD	CROWLEY,ELLEN	EWER,REV
	McCARTHY,CHARLES	BRANSFIELD	McCARTHY,JOHN	McCARTHY,MARY	EWER,REV
	SHEEHAN,EDWARD	RICHARDS,MARTHA	DUFFIT,PHILIP	WHELAN,WLATER	DEVEREAUX,REV
18280113	MOORE,LORENSA	KINNDY,CATHERINE	MEANY,JOHN	CULLIN,CATHERINE	DEVEREAUX,REV
18280117	HAMILTON,CHARLES	CAFS?,MAURICE	REDMOND,JAMES	CAHILL,JOHN	DEVEREAUX,REV
18280120	BRANSCOMBE,WILLIAM	KENNEDY,MARGARET	MOORE,LORENSO	MARKS,THOMAS	DEVEREAUX,REV
18280122	RYAN,JOHN	BUTT,JANE	COCRANE,JOHN	BUTT,SAMUEL	DEVEREAUX,REV
18280202	McCARTHY,COLEMAN	KIMBEL,JUDITH	COTTER,JAMES	GORMAN,ELIZABETH	DEVEREAUX,REV
18280204	ANDERSON,RICHARD	MOKILER,MARGARIT	POWER,MICHAEL	HICKEY,JOHN	DEVEREAUX,REV
18280225	HAWE,JAMES	RYAN,MARGARET	DUFFE?,PHILIP	McGEE,MARY	MACKIN,REV
18280226	BRIAN,MATTHEW	WHELAN,ELINOR	MACKEY,RICHARD	NICCO,MARY	DEVEREAUX,REV
18280414	COSTELLO,JOHN	CAREY,ALICIA	WADE,JAMES	COSTELLO,PATRICK	MACKIN,REV
18280503	BRIAN,MICHAEL	REDMOND,MARY	WHELAN,PATRICK	WHITE,ANASTASIA	DEVEREAUX,REV
	DWYER,THOMAS	DIMMOY?,ELINOR	MULCAHY,PATRICK	SHEA,ELINOR	DEVEREAUX,REV
18280504	LEWIS,ELIAS	KENNEDY,MARY	MULLONEY,WILLIAM	LEWIS,ELIZABETH	MACKIN,REV
	SHELLY,EDMOND	MORRASY,BRIDGET	POWER,MAURICE	MOREHAN?,MARGARET	DEVEAUX,REV
18280511	QUINLIN,JEREMIAH	MOORES,MARY	CONNORS,JOHN	KEYS,MARY	MACKIN,REV
18280524	HEFFERNAN,RICHARD	RIDDY,MARY	MAHON,JAMES	GUEFE?,FRANCES	MACKIN,REV
	LYNCH,JOHN	KEETTE?,SARAH	DENNUN?,THOMAS	NORTH,BRIDGET	DEVEREAUX,REV
18280525	WALLIS,EDMOND	LONEY?,ELINOR	HURLEY,MICHAEL	LAKUR?,SUSANNA	DEVEREAUX,REV
18280607	COLE,JOHN	GORMAN,MARTHA	BRYAN,JOHN	COLE,CHAROLOTTE	MACKIN,REV
	DOYLE,THOMAS	CONNORS,ANASTASIA	HICKEY,JOHN	CROWLEY,ELINOR	MACKIN,REV
18280628	CEACY?,JOHN	RICHARDS,ISABELLA	BROWN,PETER	DWYER,JUSTIN??	DEVEREAUX,REV
18280901	McAULIFFE?,JOHN	BYRNE,MARY	HURLEY,MICHAEL	NOWLAN,BRIDGET	MACKIN,REV
18280902	FITZPATRICK,THOMAS	CONWAY,CATHERINE	McAULIFFE?,JOHN	MURPHY,MARY	MACKIN,REV
	KENNEDY,THOMAS	COLLINS,MARY	CAMPEN?,FRANCIS	FITZPATRICK,XXXXXX	EWER,REV
	WHELAN,THOMAS	WHELAN,ANNNE	POWER,MARTIN	RIGGES,MARY	MACKIN,REV
18280906	RICE,PATRICK	DOYLE,MARY	KILFOYLE,JAMES	MARTIN,ANNA	MACKIN,REV
	WHITE,RICHARD	EVOY,MARY	BRODERICK,WILLIAM	BRODERICK,HONORA	MACKIN,REV
18280907	MURPHY,THOMAS	WHITNEY,MARY	HICKS,RICHARD	NOWLAN,MARGARET	MACKIN,REV
18280910	ENGLISH,WILLIAM	KINSELLA,ANASTASIA	STAFFORD,JOHN	ENGLISH,MARY	MACKIN,REV
	KELLY,PATRICK	ENGLISH,MARY	BROWNE,HENRY	JOHNSON,ANNE	MACKIN,REV
18280920	HAYES,JOHN	DILLEHUNTY?,ANASTASIA	RYAN,JOHN	WHELAN,ANASTASIA	DEVEREAUX,REV
18280925	DUGGAN,JAMES	KILFOYLE,CATHERINE	DUGGAN,JOHN	NORCOTT,MARY	MACKIN,REV
18280930	BYRAN,WILLIAM	MAGRATH,ELIZABETH	POWER,NORRIS	ENVIL?,ELIZABETH	EWER,REV
18281001	MAGRATH,JOSEPH	MELREIN,LUCINDA	POWER,MAURICE	DYER?,ELIZABETH	MACKIN,REV
18281002	KEEFE,MICHAEL	CORBETT,CATHERINE	KEEFE,PATRICK	DUNN,MARGARET	MACKIN,REV
18281012	WALSH,ROBERT	ROHAN,CATHERINE	WADE,JAMES	COSTELLO,ANNE	DEVEREAUX,REV

DATEMARR	HISNAME	HERNAME	WITN1	WITN2	PRIEST
18281021	RYAN,PATRICK	MARTIN,ELINOR	WALSH,PATRICK	NEAGLE,THOMAS	DEVEREAUX,REV
18281024	DUGGAN,RICHARD	MACKEY,MARY	GEORGE,THOMAS	SULLIVAN,MARY	MACKIN,REV
18281030	SNOW,WILLIAM	MANDEVIL?,CATHERINE	SNOW,EDWARD	SNOW,RUTH	DEVEREAUX,REV
18281109	KEEFE,LAURENCE	CONDON,REBECCA	POWER,JAMES	CONDON,RICHARD	DEVEREAUX,REV
18281114	CAWFIELDS,PETER	REARDEN,MARY	RYAN,PATRICK	CAIN?,THOMAS??	DEVEREAUX,REV
18281116	CONNORS,MICHAEL	QUINN,MARY	KEEVIN?,JOHN	KEEFE,MARY	MACKIN,REV
	MORRACY,JOHN	WALSH,HONORA	JOY,MICHAEL	DELANEY,EDWARD	DEVEREAUX,REV
18281117	MORRIS,THOMAS	FORD,CORNILIA	MACLANE,JOHN	FORD,ANNE	DEVEREAUX,REV
	NEAGLE?,THOMAS	WHELAN,ALICE	RYAN,PATRICK	WALSH,PATRICK	DEVEREAUX,REV
	SULLIVAN,TIMOTHY	MOORE,CATHERINE	POWER,WALTER	MYRES,CATHERINE	DEVEREAUX,REV
	SUMMERS,EDWARD	LAMB,MARGARET	LAMB,WILLIAM	DELANEY,CORNILIUS???	DEVEREAUX,REV
18281119	DUNFORD,THOMAS	LUMBURT,ELLEN	DWYER,JUSTIN	PENDERGAST,LUCY	EWER,REV
18281120	FAHEY,JOHN	FOGARTY,ELLEN	HOGAN,JOSEPH	HOGAN,JANE	EWER,REV
18281121	MULLOY?,EDWARD	BYRON?,CATHERINE	DEMPSEY,GARRET	DWNEY?,MARY	EWER,REV
18281124	FARY?,CHARLES	MEASON,ANN	MEASON,JAMES	MEGER?,MARY	DEVEREAUX,REV
18281125	DOBBIN,JOHN	BRADBURY,SUSANNA	DOBBIN,GEORGE	BYREN,MARY	EWER,REV
18281126	LEWIS,MOSES	WOODFORD,ANASTASIA	CONNELL,RICHARD	JOY,ELIZABETH	DEVEREAUX,REV
	POWER,RICHARD	MACDONOL?,JANE	FITZGERALD,JOHN	KING,ANN	EWER,REV
18281127	BEESON,MICHAEL	WALL,SARAH	CONNELL,RICHARD	ROURK?,TIMOTHY?	DEVEREAUX,REV
	FARRELL,MORGAN	MEANEY,JOANNA	HEADEN,WILLIAM	BRITTEN,ELLEN	EWER,REV
	FLYNN,WILLIAM	SULLIVAN,ANNE	CONNELL,RICHARD	SHEA,JOHN	DEVEREAUX,REV
	MURPHY,DENNIS	CONNORS,ANN	POWER,NICHOLAS	POWER,MARY	EWER,REV
18281129	COLLINS,JOHN	BRIDE,ELLEN	KELLY,JOHN	BRIDE,JOANNA	EWER,REV
	JOY,PATRICK	BUTLER,ELLEN	DAYLY,MICHAEL	PHELAN,ELLEN	EWER,REV
	KENNEDY,JOHN	KENNEDY,MARY	KENNEDY,NICHOLAS	SCOTT,SOPHIA	EWER,REV
18281130	GRIFFIN,JOHN	COLE,MARGARET	GRIFFIN,RICHARD	GRIFFIN,JUDITH	DEVEREAUX,REV
18281217	SQUIRES,WILLIAM	HOGAN,JULIA	ANTHONY,JOSEPH	DOYLE,ANNE	DEVEREAUX,REV
18290103	KEEFE,EDMUND	DALY,MARY	CONDON,GARRETT	KEEFE,MARY	MACKIN,REV
18290106	DUNN,JOHN	PURCELL,MARGARET	SCALLAN,STEPHEN	DOYLE,JUDITH	MACKIN,REV
18290108	HANNAN,JOHN	KEEFE,MARY	THOMEY,DENNIS	LAWLESS,JOSEPH	DEVEREAUX,REV
18290110	HICKEY,JOHN	GELASPY?,JULIA	MARTIN,PETER	HICKEY,CATHERINE	DEVEREAUX,REV
18290112	MULLOWNY?,MICHAEL	POWER,ELINOR	MAHER,THOMAS	BRIEN,ELINOR	DEVEREAUX,REV
18290115	GOULD,JAMES	LYONS,MARY	GOULD,MICHAEL	LYONS,WILLIAM	DEVEREAUX,REV
	MALONE,EDMOND	BRYAN,ANASTASIA	KEEFE,RICHARD	KEEFE,CATHERINE	MACKIN,REV
	MULCAHY,PHILIP	JONES,ELEANOR	JONES,THOMAS	JONES,MARY	MACKIN,REV
18290120	FARRELL,EDMOUND	HONAHAN?,MARGARET	WALSH,ROBERT	BROWN,WILLIAM	DEVEREAUX,REV
18290128	POWER,PATRICK	KING,CATHERINE	LAWLEFS,MAURICE	NEVILLE,BRIDGET	MACKIN,REV
18290201	TALBOT,WILLIAM	MURPHY,MARY(ALIES BUCKLEY)	FOLEY,THOMAS	ENGLISH,CATHERINE	MACKIN,REV
18290217	FITZPATRICK,JAMES	KEARLEY,LUCINDA	NEIL,RICHARD	RUPELL,ELINOR	MACKIN,REV
18290221	MAGRATH,JOHN	SMART,MARY	HICKEY,JOHN	HICKEY,JULIA	MACKIN,REV
18290223	KING,JOHN	McCARTHY,ANASTASIA	NOFTER?,JACOB	HURLEY,CATHERINE	MACKIN,REV
18290226	LOFTELL?,JACOB	HURLEY,CATHERINE	HURLEY,MAURICE	LOFTELL,ELIZABETH	DEVEREAUX,REV
18290301	BUTLER,JOHN	DEMPSEY,MARY	HARDING,ROBERT	BROWN,JOHN???	EWER,REV
18290302	DUNN,EDMOND	POWER,BRIDGET	NAGLE,THOMAS	SWEENEY,MARY	MACKIN,REV
	GALL,PATRICK	WHELAN,CATHERINE	FLANAGAN,WILLIAM	WHELAN,MARY-ANN	MACKIN,REV
18290303	HANRAHAN,JOHN	KINSELLA,MARGARET	MOORES,PATRICK	DAWNEY?,TIMOTHY?	HG
18290317	HICKEY,JOHN	MURPHY,MARGARET	CONNELL,RICHARD	MYERS,CATHERINE	MACKIN,REV
18290512	DRISCOLL,CORNELIUS	DUGGAN,ELINOR	CULLINAN,EDMOND	ROHAN,ELINOR	MACKIN,REV

DATEMARR	HISNAME	HERNAME	WITN1	WITN2	PRIEST
18290514	HOWARD,DAVID	TANKARD?,MARGARET	CASHIN,PATRICK	KENNY,MARY	MACKIN,REV
18290517	ENGLISH,WILLIAM	WHITE,ANNE	ENGLISH,JOHN	ENGLISH,MARY	DEVEREAUX,REV
18290518	GILL,JOHN	HART,MARY	BOLAN,JOHN	BOLAN,SARAH	DEVEREAUX,REV
18290521	COSTIGAN?,MICHAEL	BYRNE,JUDITH	MURPHY,MICHAEL	CASCY?,MARGARET	MACKIN,REV
	DALTON,JAMES	SHENAHAN,ANASTASIA	MACKEY,JOHN	DALTON,CATHERINE	MACKIN,REV
18290522	DOOLEY,PATRICK	KEET?,BRIDGET	DOOLEY,JOHN	WALSH,MARY-ANN	EWER,REV
18290524	FINN,THOMAS	HOWELL,FRANCES	BAYLEY,JAMES	BAYLEY,ELINOR	MACKIN,REV
18290526	MURPHY,LAWRENCE	DOYLE,BRIDGET	DOYLE,PHILIP	DOYLE,MARY	MACKIN,REV
18290528	HARTY,BARTEL	RICHARDS,ELIZABETH	RICHARDS,JOHN	GELASBY?,JUDITH	EWER,REV
18290530	KELLY,MARTIN	SLANTRY?,JULIA	POWER,JAMES	MURPHY,JUDITH	MACKIN,REV
18290531	REDMONDS,RICHARD	HARTLEY,CATHERINE	FLYNN,MICHAEL	FLEMING,CATHERINE	MACKIN,REV
18290601	BRIADY?,JOHN	BLUNDELL,ANNE	HURLEY,MICHAEL	BRIAN,OWEN	DEVEREAUX,REV
	HARLY,MICHAEL	DUFFETT,JOHANNA	MANNING,JOHN	BRIADY?,JOHN	DEVEREAUX,REV
18290605	BARANS,ISAC	KENNEDY,MARGARET	KENNEDY,JAMES	KENNEDY,BRIDGET	EWER,REV
	CONNELL,JOHN	CANTY,ELLEN	KELLY,JOHN	BURT,JULIA	EWER,REV
	KEHOE,JOHN	POWER,MARY	HAYES,JOHN	KEAFY?,CATHERINE	MACKIN,REV
	RYAN,JOHN	SHEAN,MARY	DWYER,WILLIAM	SHEAN,ALICE	EWER,REV
18290607	CALLAHAN,PATRICK	RYAN,ANASTASIA	DWYER,EDMOND	HICKEY,MARY	MACKIN,REV
18290609	CAHILL,JOHN	BROWN,HONORA	DOOLY,DANIEL	ENGLISH,CATHERINE	DEVEREAUX,REV
18290627	FLYNN,MICHAEL	FLEMING,CATHERINE	MIRIGAN?,THOMAS	REDMOND,RICHARD	DEVEREAUX,REV
18290701	BUTLER,THOMAS	BREEN?,ELINOR	BOWE,JOHN	DUMPHY,MARTIN??	DEVEREAUX,REV
18290816	ENGLISH,EDWARD	KINSELLA,ELINOR	RYAN,JOHN	ENGLISH,MARY	DEVEREAUX,REV
18290905	SEARY?,JOHN	DERMODY?,MARY	HEARN,WILLIAM	LYNCH,DOROTHY	MACKIN,REV
18290907	ENGLISH,JOHN	PARSONS,JANE	KELLY,PATRICK	JOHNSON,ANNE	MACKIN,REV
18290915	KEHOE,JAMES	NOONAN,JOHANNA	WELLS,THOMAS	FITZPATRICK,CATHERINE	MACKIN,REV
18291004	FUREY,WILLIAM	CORBETT,MARGARET	CORBETT,THOMAS	KELLY,MARY	DEVEREAUX,REV
18291006	HOGAN,JOSEPH	JOHNSON,MARY	McNAMARA,WILLIAM	NORMAN,MARGARET	MACKIN,REV
18291023	THOMEY,DENNIS	CORYEAR?,ELINOR	THOMEY,WILLIAM	THOMAEY,MARY	MACKIN,REV
18291027	POWER,JOHN	PEARLE,ANASTAIA	FITZGERLAD,JAMES	FITZGERLAD,MARY	MACKIN,REV
18291028	DOBBIN,GEORGE	GALWAY,CATHERINE	GALWAY,JOHN	BYRNE,MARGARET	MACKIN,REV
18291101	HAYDEN,WILLIAM	RYAN,DIANA	WRIGHT,JOHN	KAVANAGH,ANASTASIA	MACKIN,REV
18291103	DALY?,MICHAEL	MURPHY,JUDITH	KEATING,MICHAEL	HENDERSON,JOANNA	MACKIN,REV
18291104	BUTLER,WILLIAM	WATERS,CATHERINE	BROWN,JOHN	REDMONDS,MARY	MACKIN,REV
	POWER,DAVID	LAMBERT,JOHANNA	KENNY,LUKE	CAHILL,HONORA	MACKIN,REV
18291107	COSTELLO,JOHN	POWER,BRIDGET	CROAK,WLATER	COSTELLO,ANNE	DEVEREAUX,REV
18291109	HEALY,DENNIS	MURPHY,ELIZABETH	TOBIN,MICHAEL	RYAN,MARY	MACKIN,REV
	SHEA,EDWARD	HOWLEY,MARGARET	QUONEY,PATRICK	COMMINS,MARGARET	EWER,REV
18291111	BRINE,JAMES	SIMS,DIANA	BRINE,JOHN	GORMAN,JANE	DEVEREAUX,REV
	DEVOREUX,PATRICK	MAGHER,ELIZABETH	BECKETT,JOHN	GRIFFON?,MARY	EWER,REV
	DOYLE,WILLIAM	SNELGROVE,SARAH	DOYLE,JAMES	MEANY,JAMES	DEVEREAUX,REV
	GOOLEY,LAWRENCE	SHEA,ELIZABETH	GOLMAN,LAWRENCE	McCARTHY,MARGARET	MACKIN,REV
	GRIFFIN,JOHN	HEALY,MARY	RYAN,DENNIS	MURPHY,ELIZABETH	MACKIN,REV
	SHEEHAN,JOHN	DRISCOLL,ANNE	KENNY,LUKE	DRICOLL,MARY	MACKIN,REV
18291112	CAIN,THOMAS	WALL,MARY	WHELAN,EDWARD	DUNN,LUKE	DEVEREAUX,REV
18291113	CURRIN,JOHN	CONNELL,ELEANOR	CONNELL,ROBERT	MAHONEY,MICHAEL	DEVEREAUX,REV
	RONDALLS,RICHARD	RYAN,MARY	GRIFFIN,JOHN	GRIFFIN,MARY	MACKIN,REV
18291114	LYNCH,ANDREW	SUHWE?,JOHANNA	SUGHWE?,DANIEL	BUTT,JULIA	MACKIN,REV
18291115	KEEFE,MICHAEL	CULLAQHAN?,JOHANNA	FITZGERALD,MAURICE	DRISCOLL,JOHANNA	MACKIN,REV
18291116	SULLIVAN,WILLIAM	DAWLEY,MARY	DUGGAN,DANIEL	HOWARD,MARGARET	MACKIN,REV

DATEMARR	HISNAME	HERNAME	WITN1	WITN2	PRIEST
18391129	REED,JAMES	MCHASTY,MARGARET	MACMARA,MOSES	ENGLISH,ANNE	WALSH,REV
18391130	PHELAN,THOMAS	BRINE,MARY	BRINE,WILLIAM	BRINE,ELLIN	DALTON,REV
18400102	FITZGERALD,THOMAS	POWER,ELLIN	KEEFE,WILLIAM	POURS?,MARY	CUMMINS,REV
18400126	WALSH,JAMES	SHANEHAN,BRIDGET	KELLY,EDMOND	SHEA,ELLEN	CUMMINS,REV
18400226	DUNPHY,JOHN	GORDON,LUISA	CAHIL,JOHN	CAHIL,MARY	DALTON,REV
18400503	BRADBURY,CHARLES	McLEAN,CHARLET	KEEFE,JAMES	McLANE,MARIA	DALTON,REV
18400504	CUMMINS,NICHOLAS	WELLS,ANN	LONSTON,EDWARD	KINSELA,JOHANNA	WALSH,REV
	KEEFE,PETER	KENIHAN?,MARY	RYAN,DENNIS	COSTIGAN,CATHERINE	WALSH,REV
18400506	CORNISH,JOHN	GRACE,BRIDGET	MURPHY,PATT	MOLLOY,MARY	DALTON,REV
18400508	GAFS?,ALFRED	FLINN,ANN	FLINN,JOHN	FLINN,CATHERINE	DALTON,REV
18400514	McCARTHY,OWN	BATTEN,ELIZABETH	HARTY,PHILIP	CARBARY?,BRIDGET	WALSH,REV
18400515	MULLONE,THOMAS	BROWN,MARY	BROWN,JOHN	BROWN,ABBY	DALTON,REV
18400518	ROGERS,MICHAEL	BRITT,MARY	BRITT,JAMES	BRITT,JOHANNA	DALTON,REV
18400524	KENNELLY?,JAMES	GALD?,JOHANA	CALLAHAN,JOHN	WATERS,ELIZABETH	WALSH,REV
18400526	FOLEY,EDMOND	KEEFE,MARY	SHELLY,EDMOND	KEEFE,ELLEN	DALTON,REV
18400527	NEIL,CORNELIUS	MOCLES,BRIDGET	HOWLETT,WILLIAM	McDONALD,MARY-ANN	CUMMINS,REV
18400606	BYRNE,PATT	NICIAL?,JULIA	POWER,MAURICE	DALTON,BARBARA	DALTON,REV
18401107	NORCOTT,WILLIAM	LIAERA,MARY	NORCOTT,JAMES	NORCOTT,CATHERINE	DALTON,REV
18401113	GAFS?,DAVID	HUNT,ELLEN	KELLY,JOHN	CALDING?,MARY	DALTON,REV
18401117	BOWLER,WILLIAM	CONNERS,BETTY	GRANTFIELD?,ROBERT	GARBLY,MARY	O'CONNOR,REV
18401120	SHELY,JAMES	WALSH,MARY	MOGHER,MICHAEL	QUIN,MARY	O'CONNOR,REV
18401126	ROLAN,JOHN	BARRON,JOHANA	ROLAN,THOMAS	BARRON,BETTY	O'CONNOR,REV
18401128	CODY,MATTHEW	BUTLER,CATHERINE	DUGGIN,JOHN	McGRATH,CATHERINE	CUMMINS,REV
	HARPER,PATRICK	CODY,ELLEN	WRIGHT,EDWARD	CODY,ELLEN	CUMMINS,REV
	MORRISSSEY,PATRICK	DERMIDY,MARGARET	DARMODY,JOHN	MORRISSEY,SUSANNA	O'CONNOR,REV
18401230	SMOOKER,STEPHEN	SHERN,MARY	SMOOKER,MICHAEL	SMOOKER,MARY	O'CONNOR,REV
18410109	BINGHAN,JAMES J	CARROLL,BRIDGET	BRIEN,JAMES	CARROLL,MARY	CUMMINS,REV
	POWER,JAMES	BURKE,MARGARET	POURS,MATTHEW	MEANY,ANASTASIA	CUMMINS,REV
18410112	BRYAN,WILLIAM	THOMAS,MARGARET	McCARTHY,MICHAEL	BRYNING?,XXX	O'CONNOR,REV
18410119	FLEMING,RICHARD	CODY,MARGARET	RYAN,JOHN	FLEMING,JANE	O'CONNOR,REV
18410121	KEEFE,TIMOTHY	WHITE,CATHERINE	GORMAN,MICHAEL	WHITE,MARY	CUMMINS,REV
18410204	FITZGERALD,MICHAEL	GREEN,REACHES?	GREEN, [illegible]HN	GREEN,BRIDGET	O'CONNOR,REV
18410322	HEORD?,JAMES	FLING?,CATHERINE	FLING,JOHN	HEADENS,MARY	O'CONNOR,REV
18410424	SKEEHAN?,JOHN	KENNEDY,MARY	RYAN,JOHN	MURPHY,ELLEN	CUMMINS,REV
18410429	COOMD?,JOHN	McCARTHY,ANN	XXXX,CATHERINE	COOMD,MARY	CUMMINS,REV
18410430	WHELAN,PATRICK	MEANY,JANE	SCANLIN,THOMAS	LANNERS,MARY	CUMMINS,REV
18410515	SMOOCUMB,CORNELIOUS	GARDNER,HESTER	SHEA,RICHARD	SHEA,ANN	O'CONNOR,REV
18410516	CASHMAN,JOHN	AYLWARD,MARY	XXXX,MICHAEL	AYLWARD,JOANNA	CUMMINS,REV
18410530	MURPHY,JOHN	WEBB,ELLEN	TOBIN,THOMAS	JORDIN,ANN	CUMMINS,REV
18410602	WALSH,DAVID	DUFFY,ELIZABETH	WALSH,EDMOND	HARDING,MARY	CUMMINS,REV
18410902	MAHONEY,JAMES	HINGY?,MARY	DUHOW,THOMAS	DUNFORD,MARY	O'CONNOR,REV
18411023	SULLIVAN,JOHN	BUTTLER,ANTY	KENNEDY,HARRIS	GRACE,ANTY	CUMMINS,REV
18411107	COLFORD,GEORGE	LEE,ELLEN	DOYLE,MAURICE	BENSON,MARY	CUMMINS,REV
18411108	RYAN,JOSEPH	COWNY,REBECCA	RYAN,DAVID	POURS,ALAS	CUMMINS,REV
18411109	WALSH,MAURICE	LANDY?,JUDITH	DONIHOO?,MICHAEL	HAYSE,MARGARET	CUMMINS,REV
18411112	BURN,WILLIAM	HEFFERD?,ELIZABETH	BURN,JAMES	BURN,MARY	CUMMINS,REV
18411114	MADDOCK,ROBIRST	KINSELLA,JOUNNA	KEEFE,PETER	RONAN,CATHERINE	CUMMINS,REV
18411116	FORRESTAL,GREGORY	WHELAN,MARTHA	MURPHY,GERRET	CARTRY,ELLEN	CUMMINS,REV
	MURPHY,SIMON	REDMOND,CATHERINE	HEARN,THOMAS	REDMOND,MARY	CUMMINS,REV

DATEMARR	HISNAME	HERNAME	WITN1	WITN2	PRIEST
18411118	MEANY,DANIEL	FLEMING,MARY	DOYLE,MAURICE	FLEMING,MARGARET	CUMMINS,REV
18411119	HARTY,MICHAEL	MARTIN,ELIZABETH	MARTIN,JAMES	DALTON,CATHERINE	O'CONNOR,REV
	WOLFORD,WILLIAM	BUYRE,MARGARET	CANDLER,THOMAS	SHEA,ELIN	O'CONNOR,REV
18411121	FURLONG,PETER	JORDAN,ANN	FLINN,EDMOND	BARRY,ANN	CUMMINS,REV
18411122	TOMMY,WILLIAM	HARTY,DIANA	HARTY,WILLIAM	MULOY,ELIZABETH	O'CONNOR,REV
18411124	GOOLIN?,CHARLES	COGHLIN,ANN	HXXX,WILLIAM	COGHLIN,JANE	DALTON,REV
18411125	McCARTHY,JOHN	KENNEDY,CATHERINE	KENNEDY,TIMOTHY	McCARTHY,ELIZABETH	O'CONNOR,REV
18411126	COOING,EDMOND	KEEFE,ELOM	TROBY,MILES	KEEFE,ALICE	O'CONNOR,REV
	FLINN,WILLIAM	QUN?,MARY	CUDDAHY,PATT	CANTRY?,JOHANA	DALTON,REV
	MORRIS,EDMOND	LEE,CATHERINE	SWEENEY,EDMOND	PUMPHREY,MARY	CUMMINS,REV
	SMART,MICHAEL	BUTLER,CATHERINE	SMART,THOMAS	KELEY,ELIZABETH	O'CONNOR,REV
	SULLIVAN,JOHN	MORRESSEY,CATHERINE	COUSHAN,WILLIAM	MAROSEY,MARY	O'CONNOR,REV
18411127	DONAHAN,TIMOTHY	MORIARTY,NELLY	CONNOERS,MICHAEL	SHEDHAN,ELLEN	DALTON,REV
18411128	DUNN,WILLIAM	CONNELL,ALAS	DUNN,ROBIRTH	CONNELL,BRIDGET	CUMMINS,REV
18420113	DROVER,NICHOLAS	BYRN?,BRIDGET	BRADBERRY,THOMAS	BYRN,MARIA	DALTON,REV
18420115	QUINLON,THOMAS	GLAVEEN,JOHANA	BYRN,JAMES	GLAVEEN,ELLEN	DALTON,REV
18420118	SWEENY,JAMES	MORY,MARGARET	CLULAN,EDMOND	GEARY,BRIDGET	CUMMINS,REV
18420121	MULLINS,GEORGE	WHITE,MARGARET	KEEFE,TIMOTHY	WHITE,CATHERINE	CUMMINS,REV
18420126	McCARTHY,FLORRNCE	KENNEDY,SERAH	KENNEDY,WILLIAM	FLINN,MARGARET	CUMMINS,REV
18420131	FURLONG,THOMAS	HAIL?,MARY	BROWN,JAMES	HAYES,CATHERINE	CUMMINS,REV
	LONG,PATRICK	KAIN,MARY	KEEFE,JAMES	REDMOND,ELIZABETH	CUMMINS,REV
18420202	BRANSFIELD,JOHN	MEANY,ANASTASIA	McCARTHY,FELIX	McKEE,ELIZABETH	CUMMINS,REV
18420207	MURPHY,EDMOND	MURPHY,CATHERINE	DALTON,RICHARD	CARBERY,ELLEN	CUMMINS,REV
18420406	CANDLER,THOMAS	TOOMEY,ELLEN	FOX,JAMES	GREEN,BRIDGET	CUMMINS,REV
18420508	KELLY,CORELIOUS	MALUD?,MARY	NEIL,MATTHEW	RONAN,CATHERINE	CUMMINS,REV
18420509	COSTELLO,MARTIN	FOSTER,ALICE	CULLON,JAMES	CALLAN,CATHERINE	DALTON,REV
18420516	KEHOE,JAMES	McCARTHY,ELLEN	MOKISTY?,THOMAS	MOKISTY?,MARGARET	CUMMINS,REV
18420519	SULLIVAN,WILLIAM	CRAIN,CATHERINE	CRAIN,DANIEL	BROWN,ABBY	DALTON,REV
18420521	RYAN,XXX	CONNELLY,ELIZABETH	HIGGINS,JAMES	CONNELLY,MARIA	DALTON,REV
18420525	GLAVEEN,RICHARD	HAGERTY,CATHERINE	GLAVEEN,JAMES	HAGERTY,MARY	DALTON,REV
18420602	HAMON?,JAMES	CAVANAGH?,HONORA	CLIFFORD,PATRICK	WALSH,ANASTASIA	DALTON,REV
	HENNESSEY,MICHAEL	DALTON,BARBARA	FOX,JAMES	WALSH,ANASTASIA	DALTON,REV
18420710	BIGGS,JOHN W.	HENNEBURY,MARY	HUNT,PHILIP	HASEY,ELLEN	GLEESON,REV
18420717	KEHOE,THOMAS	CODY,ELLENER	DIVORIN?,PATK	CASEY,MARY	DALTON,REV
18420801	REDMOND,MICHAEL	BURN,MARGARET	GLEESON,JAMES	MURPHY,MARY	CUMMINS,REV
18420824	GRIFFIN,THOMAS	KENNA,ELLEN	FOLEY,JOHN	GRANVILLE,MARGARET	DALTON,REV
18420911	WHITE,JOHN	CONNELL,BRIDGET	HYDIN,TIMOTHY	WHITE,ELIZABETH	DALTON,REV
18421009	NEIL,MICHAEL	GREEN,MARGARET	MAHER,PIERCE	MURPHY,ANN	CUMMINS,REV
18421023	MEANY,PATRICK	BRIEN,MARY	CORMICK,LAWRENCE	COLBERT,ANASTASIA	GLEESON,REV
18421030	QUISTIC?,JAMES	KELLY,ANN	BYRNE,RICHARD	KELLY,CATHERINE	DALTON,REV
18421102	LEAHY,MICHAEL	YOUNG,CATHERINE	LEAHY,PATRICK	HSO---,BETSY	GLEESON,REV
18421113	SAUNDERS,WALTER	COSTIGAN,CATHERINE	CIRBAN,THOMAS	XXXX,SARAH	GLEESON,REV
18421115	WISEMAN,WILIAM	TOBIN,ELIZABETH	MAHER,PIERCE	XXX,ISABELLA	CUMMINS,REV
18421125	FOLEY,JAMES	BRADBURY,ANN	HIGGINS,THOMAS	BRADBURY,CATHERINE	DALTON,REV
18421126	MANGAN?,JOHN	CALLAHAN,PATIENCE	CALLAHAN,DANIEL	SHEA,CATHERINE	GLEESON,REV
	PUMPHERY,JOHN	BENSON,MARY	HOGAN,WILLIAM	PUMPHREY,MARY	GLEESON,REV
18421129	NEUGB?,HUGH	FITZGERLAD,ELLEN	KEEFE,WILLIAM	DUFFY,SERA	HG
184211XX	MCCARTHY,WILLIAM	XXX,BRIDGET	BYRNE,RICHARD	MERCER,FRANCES	DALTON,REV
18430101	HICKEY,PATRICK	COONEY,ELLEN	STAPLETON,MICHAEL	COONEY,MARGARET	CUMMINS,REV

MARRIAGES FROM HARBOUR GRACE RECORDS

1806-1845

DATEMARR	HISNAME	HERNAME	WITN1	WITN2	PRIEST
18430101	SMALCOME,PETER	GIED,MARY	GILESBY,SAMUEL	SMALCOMBE,MARY	CUMMINS,REV
18430104	HURLEY,MORRICE	LOFTY,CHARLOTTE	FORRESTOR,JOHN	XXXX,MARY	HG
18430114	KENNEDY,RICHARD	HANRAHAN,ELIZABETH	McCARTHY,JOHN	DWYER,XXX	CUMMINS,REV
18430115	FITZGERALD,MICHAEL	GUHAN,JOANNA	KENNEDY,MAURICE	WALSH,MARY	CUMMINS,REV
18430126	WALSH,WILLIAM	WALSH,CATHERINE	KEEFE,JOHN	CAREW,MARGARET	CUMMINS,REV
18430129	KEARNY,WILLIAM	LINGNAUE?,MARY	FITZGERALD,THOMAS	LYNCH,JOHANNA	GLEESON,REV
18430208	CONNOLLY,WILLIAM	ADDOMS,JANE	ADDOMS,JAMES	CAVEL?,SOPHY	DALTON,REV
18430507	HIRLY?,WILLIAM	KING,JULIA	KING,EDWARD	XXX,SUZANNA	DALTON,REV
18430508	BAGS,JERIMIAH	BYRNE,MARY	KIDNY,JOHN	BYRNE,MARIA	DALTON,REV
18430512	DOYLE,MAURICE	SCANLAN,BRIDGET	FITZGERALD,JOHN	HANRAHAN,MARY	DALTON,REV
18430514	NEIL,MATT	DONEVAN,MARGARET	HOWLET,WILLIAM	DONEVAN,ELLEN	DALTON,REV
18430527	GILLESPY,SAM	AHEARN,CATHERINE	AHEARN,MICHAEL	SMAL___?,MARY	DALTON,REV
18430606	LEYDEA?,MARTIN	MORRISSEY,SUSANNAH	FITZGERALD,EDWARD	CIRSEARTY?,ELLEN	GLEESON,REV
	SINGLETON,RICHARD	MULLALBY,BRIDGET	BAGS,TONY	MURPHY,MARGARET	DALTON,REV
18430726	MULLOWAY?,MICHAEL	ZECAREY?,ELLIZA	GEORGE,ARTHUR J	REDMOND,MARGARET	DALTON,REV
18430801	RYAN,JOHN	SAMPSON,MARY	HATSH,JOHN	CULN,FRANCIS	DALTON,REV
18430819	STAPLETON,JAMES	LEGGE,EMMA	McCARTHY,RICHARD	LEGGE,CATHERINE	GLEESON,REV
18430820	KIDNEY,TIMOTHY	XXX,JULIA	BAGGS,TIM	KIDNEY,ELLEN	DALTON,REV
18431102	McGULLTEN?,JAMES	QUINN,ANNE	McCARTHY,PATRICK	MURPHY,MARY	DALTON,REV
18431108	NEPTUNE,SIBS	HARRINGTON,MARY	SHEA,PHILIP	CURRY,JULIANNA	CUMMINS,REV
18431116	BRADBURY,THOMAS	MYSOR?,MARY	KELLY,DAVID	BRADBURY,CATHERINE	CUMMINS,REV
18431126	AYLWARD,EDWARD	BYRNE,SUSAN	McDONALD,JAMES	FLEMING,ELLEN	CUMMINS,REV
18431128	REDMOND,JOHN	MARSHALL,MARY	REDMOND,JAMES	MARSHALL,BRIDGET	CUMMINS,REV
	SHERBRAY,BARTHOLEMU	CUMMINS,ELLEN	BRITT,RICHARD	SHARBRAY,JOHANNA	CUMMINS,REV
18431130	BYRNE,WILLIAM	COLBERT,ANASTASIA	BYRNE,JOHN	KEHOE,MARGARET	CUMMINS,REV
	CODY,WILLIAM	WALSH,ELIZABETH	McGRATH,PATRICK	CAVANAGH,BRIDGET	CUMMINS,REV
	CURRY,MICHAEL	LAWBYS,ANASTASIA	LANIGAN,EDMOND	HUNT,MARY	CUMMINS,REV
	DUGGAN,MICHAEL	DOYLE,ANASTASIA	SHUHAN,THOMAS	DUGGAN,ELLEN	CUMMINS,REV
	MERRIGAN,PATRICK	BUCKLEY,JANE	FINERTY,PATRICK	LEE,ELLEN	CUMMINS,REV
	MURPHY,THOMAS	GARY,ELIZABETH	CONDON,JAMES	JOY,MARY-ANN	CUMMINS,REV
18431201	CORBIN,PHILIP	FLEMING,JANE	SCHEHAN,PHILIP	FLEMING,MARY	DALTON,REV
18431202	DUNN,JOHN	RICARDAN,MARY	RICARDAN,JOHN	KING,REBECCA	DALTON,REV
	HOGAN,WILLIAM	PUMPHREY,MARY	PUMPHREY,JOHN	[illegible]NSON,MARY	DALTON,REV
	RINALDS,PATRICK	HURLEY,MARY	McCARTHY,WILLIAM	HIANS,MARY	DALTON,REV
18431224	FARRELL,PATRICK	SHOUGHROE,JOHANA	SCANLAN,THOMAS	CANTY,CATHERINE	DALTON,REV
1843XX08	GOFF,DAVID	HUNT,CATHERINE	HACKETT,PATRICK	KELLY,MARY	DALTON,REV
18440128	McGUINES,HUGH	HIER?,RIDGET	BRUNE,JAMES	DWYER,MARY	DALTON,REV
18440220	GRANVILLE,ARTHUR	HARDEN,MARY	FITZGERALD,THOMAS	LYNCH,MARY	DALTON,REV
18440508	DIERA?,JOHN	FINNAL,CATHERINE	DANSIE?,FREDERICK JAMES	MIAN,WMILY	DALTON,REV
18440513	McDONNEL,JOHN	SHUGHRUE,JOLIANA	SHUGHRUE,BARTHOLOMEW	DOYLE,BRIDGET	DALTON,REV
18440514	ANDERSON,WILLIAM	BRINE,ELLEN	FINNAL,JOHN	WALSH,MARY	DALTON,REV
18440516	HADE?,THOMAS	DWYER,ANNE	GEAR,THOMAS	DWYER,MARY	GLEESON,REV
	MIREA,RICHARD	GRIFFIN,ANNE	MOREA,JOHN	MADDOCK,BRIDGET	GLEESON,REV
18440526	DONNOLLY,JOHN	SCANLAN,CATHERINE	POWER,MATTHEW	DOYLE,CATHERINE	GLEESON,REV
18440917	NOONAN,JOHN	FOGARTY,LEALY	OATES,EDWARD	CRONEY,MARY-ANNE	GLEESON,REV
18441009	DWYER,EDMOND	PHELAN,MARY	HICKS,RICHARD	PHELAN,MARGARET	GLEESON,REV
18441027	LEARY,PATRICK	MURPHY,ELIZABETH	FITZGERALD,PATRICK	FITZGERALD,ANASTASIA	CUMMINS,REV
18441029	DONAGHUE,MICHAEL	SHEEHAN,ELLEN	MURPHY,PATRICK	CODY,MARY-ANN	CUMMINS,REV
18441031	CLARKE,ABSALOM	MOREY,JANE	SWEENEY,EDWARD	GEARY,CATHERINE	GLEESON,REV

DATEMARR	HISNAME	HERNAME	WITN1	WITN2	PRIEST
18441031	KEEFE,JOHN	WALSH,MARY	CONDON,JAMES	KEHOE,MARGARET	GLEESON,REV
	REDMOND,LAURINCE	HENNESSEY,MARGARET	MORIS,THOMAS	BURKE,MARGARET	GLEESON,REV
	WELLS,JOHN	McCARTHY,MARGARET	KNOX,JAMES	HOGAN,ELLEN	GLEESON,REV
18441102	FITZGERALD,MICHAEL	HADDOCK,BRIDGET	KENNEDY,MAURICE	WALSH,ANASTASIA	GLEESON,REV
18441103	CALLAHAN,JOHN	BRIDE,CATHERINE	HIARN,DARRIC	POWER,ELLEN	CUMMINS,REV
18441105	BYRNE,WILLIAM	ZEATMAN,FRANEY	BYRN,EDWARD	BYRN,MARIA	CUMMINS,REV
18441106	McCARTHY,OWEN	PORTER,JULIA	WASNER?,BCSG?	CONALY?,ELLEN	GLEESON,REV
18441107	WARFORD,HENRY	DRISCAL,JOHANNA	KEEFE,MICHAEL	DRISCOL,ELLEN	CUMMINS,REV
18441108	KEHOE,JAMES	TONES?,ANNE	CONDON,JOHN	SHEA,MARY	GLEESON,REV
18441110	STAPLEON,JAMES	FLEMING,MARGARET	HICKEY,RICHARD	POWER,MARY	CUMMINS,REV
18441114	DRAKE,THOMAS	FARRELL,MARY	MACKEY,JOHN	FARRELL,CATHERINE	GLEESON,REV
	FINERTY,PATRICK	LARYER?,SARA	KING,PATRICK	MARSHALL,CAROLINE	GLEESON,REV
	WHELAN,EDWARD	MORRISSEY,MARY	SWEENY,EDWARD	MORRISSEY,HONORA	GLEESON,REV
18441116	BUTT,LEIR	DUGGAN,ELLEN	DOYLE,JOHN	DUGGAN,ALLAS	CUMMINS,REV
	FARRELL,JOHN	BRENNAN,JOHANNA	BRENNAN,THOMAS	PURCELL,MARY	CUMMINS,REV
18441117	FITZGERALD,JOHN	BURKE,ELLEN	FITZGERALD,WILLIAM	CULLAHAN,CATHERINE	CUMMINS,REV
	HICKEY,JAMES	COONY?,MARGARET	CODY,JOHN	CODY,CATHERINE	CUMMINS,REV
18441121	MAGUIRE,THOMAS	BYRNE,MARGARET	WHELAN,JOHN	WHELAN,ELLEN	GLEESON,REV
18441123	MURPHY,JOHN	CARROLL,MARY	HYNES,PATRICK	RULY?,MARY	CUMMINS,REV
18441124	SMALLCOMBE,MICHAEL	HEARN,MARY	HEARN,SIMON	SHEA,ANN	CUMMINS,REV
	WALSH,FRANCIS	SMALLCOMBE,MARY	HEARN,MICHAEL	FAHEY,ELLEN	CUMMINS,REV
18441125	KEEFE,JOHN	WALSH,MARY	CONDON,JOHN	KEHOE,MARGARET	GLEESON,REV
	KELLY,EDMOND	KELLY,ELLEN	BOHAN,JOHN	TONES?,MARGARET	GLEESON,REV
18441130	HARPER,MATTHEW	DALTON,ANN	KEEFE,PETER	POWER,MARY	CUMMINS,REV
18441202	KEHOE,FRANCIS	FINN,CATHERINE	CONNELL,WILLIAM	McCARTHY,ELLEN	DALTON,REV
18450101	BYAN,MICHAEL	DOOLING,ELLEN	PARSONS,MICHAEL	BUTLER,MARGARET	GLEESON,REV
	CALLAHAN,DANIEL	DOHERTY,ANN	PRXXX,MICHAEL	SHEA,MARY	GLEESON,REV
18450102	DALTON,PATRICK	BRINE,ELLEN	SHEA,DENNIS	CAHILL,MARGARET	CUMMINS,REV
	LACEY,JOHN	LOG?,MARY-ANNE	BREEN,JAMES	POWER,MARY	GLEESON,REV
18450109	CONNORY,THOMAS	HASSAJUN?,MARY	BUTLER,JAMES	CONNORY,CATHERINE	GLEESON,REV
	RYAN,JAMES	MURPHY,ANN	CLIFFORD,PATRICK	INNOTT,HARRIOTT	CUMMINS,REV
18450126	MORRISSEY,PATRICK	CALLIHAN,CATHERINE	KEEFE,PETER	BURKE,MARY	CUMMINS,REV
18450129	McGRATH,PATRICK	COPPI?,PATIENCE	CARROLL,THOMAS	GARDNER,ANN	CUMMINS,REV
18450202	SMYTH,ANTHONY	POWER,ELLEN	MILLICAN,MARTIN	McDONALD,BRIDGET	CUMMINS,REV
18450204	FITZGERALD,EDWARD	MAXWELL,BRIDGET	SHEA,PHILIP	YOCELLA?,MARY	CUMMINS,REV
18450509	MALONE,JOHN	KEEFE,ALICE	GRIFFIN,JOHN	DEVEREAUX,ELIZABETH	GLEESON,REV
18450516	KIRBY,THOMAS	KENNY,MARGARET	MARTIN,JOHN	FINN,CATHERINE	CUMMINS,REV
18450525	LEARY,JOHN	DALTON,CATHERINE	MARTIN,WILLIAM	HARPER,JOHN	CUMMINS,REV
18450527	HALL,JAMES	GALIAN?,MAY	KIRAN,PHILIP	FLEMING,ELLEN	CUMMINS,REV
18450529	DEMORDY,JOSEPH	DWYER,MARY	DEVEREAUX,JOHN	WHELAN,ELLEN	GLEESON,REV
18450601	KEEFE,WILLIAM	DEALY,SUSANNA	CONDON,GARRET	LMOTT?,SUSANNA	CUMMINS,REV
18450604	FAHEY,PATRICK	FOGARTY,CATHERINE	FAHEY,THOMAS	SHEA,MARY	GLEESON,REV
18450605	MARTIN,WILLIAM	CONNELL,MAY	LEARY,JAMES	CONNELL,ANN	CUMMINS,REV
18450622	BUTT,ALEXANDER	KENNEDY,AMELIA	KENNEDY,EDMOND	KENNEDY,MARY	GLEESON,REV
	BUTT,AMBROSE	SHEAHAN,ANASTASIA	KENNEDY,MICHAEL	SHEAHAN,ANN	GLEESON,REV
18451021	REDMOND,JOHN	HEARN,ELLEN	HAERN,JAMES	REDMOND,MARY	GLEESON,REV
	STAPLETON,RICHARD	FLYNN,MARY	McCARTHY,RICHARD	McCARTHY,ANNE	GLEESON,REV
18451026	LAHEY,MAURICE	LYONS,JOHANNA	SCANLAN,THOMAS	ROWS?,BRIDGET	CUMMINS,REV
18451106	GRAHAM,JOSEPH	KELLY,CATHERINE	RONAN,FRANCIS	RIDLEY,MRS THOMAS	DALTON,REV

MARRIAGES FROM HARBOUR GRACE RECORDS
1806-1845

DATEMARR	HISNAME	HERNAME	WITN1	WITN2	PRIEST
18451123	HADEN?,WILLIAM	GLAVINE,ELLEN	BROADERS,EDWARD	RONAN,JOHANNA	CUMMINS,REV
	PURAL,MICHAEL	HAYSE,HONORA	PERCIL,JOSEPH	RONAN,CATHERINE	CUMMINS,REV
18451125	CODY,PATRICK	POWER,ELLEN	SHEA,STEPHEN	RIGLY,MARY	CUMMINS,REV
	HEARN,MICHAEL	POWER,CATHERINE	HYNES,THOMAS	CODY,CATHERINE	CUMMINS,REV
18451126	DOYLE,JAMES	DUGGAN,ANASTASIA	RIGSIL?,JOSEPH	DOYLE,MAY	CUMMINS,REV
1845XX03	HICKEY,RICHARD	CODY,JULIA	WALSH,JAMES	CODY,ELIZABETH	DALTON,REV
	XXXFILL,JAMES	DOYLE,MARY	HEALY,PATRICK	XXXXFILL,MARY	DALTON,REV
1845XX29	GLENDON,WILLIAM	SEAN,JANE	WALSH,DAVID	HARDING,MARY	GLEESON,REV
1845XXXX	CLARKE,SAMUEL	THISTLE,MARIA	THISTLE,FRANCIS	RYAN,MARY	GLEESON,REV
XXXXXXXX	MACKEY,JOHN	GRIFFIN,MARY	DRAKE,JOHN	FARRELL,MARY	GLEESON,REV

BIBLIOGRAPHY

Adelphian Magazines, St. Bon's, St. John's, Various Issues.
All Hallow College Annuals, various Issues.
Alyward, Rev Edward, Parish Priest of Harbour Grace.
Archdiocese, Roman Catholic, SJ. *"Centenary of Cathedral 1855-1955".*
Benevolent Irish Society (BIS), *"Centenary Volume, 1806-1906"*. 1906.
Beresford, Rev. James, Parish Priest of Harbour Grace, Information and papers.
Bolatets, Rev Ramon, Parish Priest of Harbour Grace, Info and Assistance.
Bowman, Bill, Editor of Compass Newspaper, Carbonear Office.
Bradbury, Mrs. Paula, Info on Mackenzie Jesuits Priests Twins.
Brazil, Gerald, Research assistance on Harbour Grace and Spaniard's Bay.
Butt, W. John, Gracious help with many old Newfoundland Books.
Byrne, Cyril, J., *"Gentlemen-Bishops and Faction Fighters."*
Carroll, Mary, Carbonear, Personal Interviews & Info. over 15 years.
Census, 1921, Carbonear, Harbour Grace and St. John's.
Coady, Linus, Rev. Interviews and Research information.
Collins, (Hoskins) Angela, Carbonear, Personal Interviews & Info.
Compass Newspaper, Carbonear, Various Issues. (Original.)
Connolly, R. J. *"1856 Centenary of the Diocese of Harbor Grace 1956"*
Connolly, R. J. *"History of Roman Catholic Church in Harbor Grace."*
Connolly, R. J. *"Compendium of History,"* Unpublished. HG Library.
Connolly, R. J. Personal Interviews & Info over Ten years.
Coombs, Reg and Dorothy, Harbour Grace Information and records.
Crosbie, Gert, Booklets, Maritime History Archive, MUN, 1825-1890.
Currie, Bishop, Martin, Bishop of Grand Falls, support and encouragement.
Darcy, J. B. Brother, Personal interviews and his publications.
Darcy, J. B. Brother, *"Fair or Foul the Weather",* St. Bon's, 1999.
Darcy, J. B. Brother, *"Fire on Earth",* Bishop Fleming, 2003.
Decks Awash, Extension Dept., MUN. Various Issues.
Directories (Almanacs): 1849, 1862, 1864-5, 1885-6, 1894-5, 1898, 1928 & 1936.
Devine & O'Mara, "Notable Events in the History of Newfoundland"., 1900.
Dohey, Larry, Archivist at RC Archdiocese, St. John's.
Evening Telegram, The, Various Issues.
Fahey, Michael, Sharon and Sharleen, School records and pictures.
Fitzgerald, Dr John, Memorial University History Professor, St. John's.
Fleming, James M. Sr. *"Three Generations of Mackey's"*, Manuscript, MUN.
Fleming, James M. Sr. *"Alexander O'Donovan",* Manuscript, MUN.
Fleming, James M. Sr. *"St. Patrick's RC Parish of Carbonear.*" 2002.
Fleming, James M. Jr. Setup website, www.newfoundlandcatholic.com
Gaye, Jonathan, Archives at Grand Falls. Outstanding research assistance.
Grand Falls Archives. Great deal of research and information.
Grand Falls Diocesan Records. Parish and Cemetery Information.
Grand Falls, Knights of Columbus *"Notre Dame Council, # 2053."*

Grand Falls, "Our Diocese" Papers, Various Issues.
Harbour Grace Standard, Newspaper, Various Issues, 1800s.
Harbour Grace, Knight of Columbus *"Dalton Council # 1448."*
Harbour Grace, Roman Church Records and Cemetery Records.
Harrington, Michael, Dec, Offbeat History, Evening telegram, Var. issues.
Harrington, Michael, Dec, Personal Interviews & Info over ten years.
Harvey, Rev M. *"Newfoundland in 1897"*. Queen Victoria Diamond Jubilee Year.
Hatton, Joseph & Harvey, Rev M., *"Newfoundland"*, 1883.
Howley, Very Rev, M. F., *"Ecclesiastical History of Newfoundland"*, 1888.
Internos Magazines, St. Bride's College of Our Lady of Mercy, Var. Issues.
Kennedy, Sister, Perpetua. Archivist of Presentation Sisters, St. John's.
Mackenzie, Sister, Angela, Interviews and information.
Mackey, John & Marie. Grand Falls, Interview and books.
Mackey, Leo, Carbonear, Research Papers.
Maddox, Bride, Housekeeper of Msgr J. M. O'Brien, Interviews-Papers, HG.
Maryknoll Missions, Archives, New York.
Matthews, Rev. William, Retired, Interviews and Information.
McCarthy, Michael, Mt. Pearl, NF, Consultation, Research & Information.
McCarthy, Michael, *"Irish in Newfoundland"*.
McCarthy, Michael & Frank Galgay, *"Olde St. John's"*, 2001.
Mercer, Daphne, Town of HG Tourism Department. Pictures & Info
Monitor, The, RC Archdiocese of St. John's, Various Issues.
Newfoundland and Labrador Encyclopedia's, Volume 1-5.
Newfoundland Quarterly, Various Issues.
Neary, Peter and O'Flaherty, Patrick, *"Part of the Main,* 1983.
O'Brien, Msgr. Joseph, Dec., Interviews and important papers.
O'Brien, Sister Magdalene, Archivist at RC Grand Falls Diocese.
O'Neill, Paul, *"The Oldest City" & "A Seaport Legacy"*, 2 Volumes. 1975-76.
Parmenter, Brenda, Province Library Office. Assistance.
Parsons, Bert, Carbonear, Personal Interviews and Information.
Pedley, Rev Charles, *"The History of Newfoundland"*, 1863.
Penney, Sister Paula, Archivist Mercy Nuns.
Prendergast, Jim and Patricia. Corner Brook, Assistance & Information.
Prowse, D.W., *"A History of Newfoundland,"* 1896.
Redemporists Order, Archives, Ontario, Canada.
Reports of Public Schools under RC Board: 1885, 1901-1917; 1921-22; 1922-23.
Pike, Gordon, Harbour Grace Historical Society.
Riggs, Bert, Archivist as Memorial University, Writings and Papers.
Rollmann, Dr., Hans, Memorial University, Research Papers and Internet.
Roman Catholic Board of Education Minutes, Carbonear, 1843-1852 (Original)
Ryan, Lillian, Riverhead, Harbour Grace. Papers and Pictures.
Scarboro Missions, Archives, Ontario, Canada.
Skanes, Joyce, Rectory, Immaculate Conception Parish, Info and papers.
Smallwood, Premier, Joseph Jr, *"The Books of Newfoundland"*, Volumes I-V.
St. George's, Diocese Papers, Various Issues.
St. John, Wm Charles, *"Catechism of the History of Newfoundland"*, 1855.

St. Vincent de Paul, Carbonear, 1874. (Original).
Tocque, Rev Phillip, Newfoundland, *"As it was and as it is in 1877"*, 1878.
Town of Harbour Grace, Daphne Mercer, Tourism Section. 2003
Waterford Parish, Ireland, Church records.
Whalen, Edward, Historical Information.
Whalen, (Fahey) Peggy, Extraordinary Research and Information.
Withers, Peter. *"In '97 Come to Heaven"*, Little Paradise Reunion. 1997.

CATHOLIC & NFLD WEBSITES OF INTEREST

Knights of Columbus – http://www.kofc.nf.ca
*Grand Falls Diocese – http://home.thezone.net/-rcecgf/
St. John's Archdiocese – http://www.stjohnsarchdiocese.nf.ca/
St. George's Diocese – **http://members.aol.com/diosg/**
Archdiocese of Toronto – http://www.ca-catholics.net
James M. Fleming Sr – **www.newfoundlandcatholic.com**
Obituaries – Holyrood – http:/www.geocities.com/holyrood_genealogy/obits.htm
Photo of gravestone (Archdeacon Thomas O'Connor) –
Website - http://ngb.chebucto.org/Cemetery/oconnor-thomas.shtml
Rollmann, MUN Religions – www.ucs.mun.ca/-hrollman/
Dr Rollmann, MUN History of RC Church
Memorial Univ. (religion) - www.mun.ca/rels/rc/texts/rchistory/htm
Cardinals – (Bio Falconio) – http://www.fiu.edu/-mirandas/bios-f.htm#Falconio
LDS – Church of Later Day Saints =http://www.familysearch.org/Engt/Library/

*Grand Falls have links to: Vatican, St. John's, St. George's, Knights of Columbus, Canadian Conference of Catholic Bishops, Catholic Canada Directory.